JONATHAN AGNEW'S
Cricket Year

WITH CONTRIBUTIONS BY

Mark Baldwin • Tony Cozier • Gulu Ezekiel
Vic Marks • Christopher Martin-Jenkins • Jim Maxwell

28TH EDITION

September 2008 to September 2009

A & C Black • London

Edited by Mark Baldwin
with contributions by
Paul Bolton
Tony Cozier
Gulu Ezekiel
Simon Hughes
Martin Johnson
Richard Latham
Vic Marks
Christopher Martin-Jenkins
Jim Maxwell
Mark Pennell
Vikram Solanki
Bruce Talbot
Tim Wellock
Andy Wilson

With special thanks to the England & Wales Cricket Board.

First published in 2009 by
A & C Black Ltd
36 Soho Square
London W1D 3QY

www.acblack.com

A copy of the CIP entry for this book is available from the British Library.

ISBN: 978-14081-1332-5

10 9 8 7 6 5 4 3 2 1

This book is produced using paper that is made from wood grown in managed,
sustainable forests. It is natural, renewable and recyclable. The logging and
manufacturing processes conform to the environmental regulations of the country
of origin.

Project editor: Julian Flanders
Design: Kathie Wilson
Statistics and county information: Press Association
Pictures © PA Photos, except pages 50, 52 © Getty Images

Printed and bound by Scotprint, Haddington

CONTENTS

IN MY VIEW

by Jonathan Agnew

Even by its own traditionally hectic and unpredictable standards, English cricket has experienced quite a year. From the triumph in the Ashes – for both men and women – to what amounted to a vote of no confidence in the administration by the country's professional cricketers, with terrorist attacks and the sudden and unexpected removal of Kevin Pietersen and Peter Moores as captain and coach in the New Year, cricket has seldom been off the back pages for good reason or bad.

As we reflected last year, international cricket is currently heading into unchartered waters on two fronts. The potentially damaging 'referral system' which was considered by all of us who witnessed its dress rehearsal in the Caribbean to be a disaster, is now enshrined in our game. How the ICC could push this through into all Test cricket so soon after it was shown to be a laughing stock is a matter of grave concern. I can say with absolute certainty that Test cricket will never be the same again as a consequence.

Andrew Flintoff, meanwhile, became the first big name player to reject the offer of an ECB contract and go freelance. His case was largely brought about by his chronic knee problem, but others more fit and able than he are sure to follow suit.

Why, after all, would someone prefer to earn less while touring overseas for months for his board rather than make maybe ten times as much in a quick-fire Twenty20 tournament? The answer, of course, is the prestige and honour of playing for your country, but then again look at the truly appalling situation in the Caribbean where, thanks to a dispute between, admittedly, a chaotic board and a clearly militant players union, the region's top cricketers have spent much of the past few months on strike. Hence a severely weakened team lost its Test series to Bangladesh and the once proud but seriously threatened Caribbean plumbed new and embarrassing depths.

We should not have been surprised by the attitude in the West Indies dressing room, however. Chris Gayle, the captain, virtually admitted that Twenty20 cricket was the way forward during the early summer tour of England, which he and his players showed no respect for from the very start. Compare that approach to those teams from the West Indies who toured before them, and observe how much attitudes have changed.

However, from previously only being able to grumble about the frankly tiresome schedule the administrators are now preparing, but being able to do nothing, the modern, one-day cricketer can vote with his feet – and others will do so too as more seven-match series are crammed into a schedule that already reeks of overkill.

It is purely financial interest that produces the scenario in which, following an Ashes contest that more

It's the Ashes! Graeme Swann has just had Australia's Mike Hussey caught by Alastair Cook at short leg, to confirm England's victory in the deciding final Test at The Oval. The celebrations are, literally, just about to start.

than lived up to its billing, seven one-day matches were then thrust upon a tiring public, and played by tired players. Paul Collingwood, Stuart Broad and James Anderson were all rested from the England team before the outcome of the series had been decided – a damning indictment on how the cricketers and the coaching staff viewed its importance.

The paying public will not stand for much more of this – but England and Australia are scheduled to play each other in 24 one-day internationals between 2009 and 2013 – and that does not include the tour England will make to Australia in the meantime. It is nothing but sad that a once special, and much anticipated encounter between the sport's oldest rivals has now been reduced to this – a one-day series every year for five years.

The England and Wales Cricket Board has explained it as 'taking cricket around the country'. We will see how the nation's appetite for the 50-overs formula, which now definitely appears to be failing, holds up.

It does not help a regular pundit's possibly weary view that England's record at 50-over cricket is nothing short of wretched. Until the Champions Trophy, they had won six of their 19 matches in 2009 – and one of those was gifted by a mistake by John Dyson, now the former West Indies coach.

It was during one of those series – the truncated contest in India – that the first of two terrorist atrocities rocked the game of cricket. The attack on the Taj Mahal hotel in Mumbai hit England's tourists particularly hard – the players had recently stayed there and had left their Test match uniforms there to await their return a few weeks' later.

With morale so low among the England players anyway (India were deservedly 5-0 up when the one-day series was abandoned) and with Christmas just around the corner, no one gave much of a price on England's Test squad returning after a short break at home. But return they did – a triumph for good sense, and a great

Even his disastrous spell as England captain has not affected the iconic status in which Andrew Flintoff is held by English cricket followers, especially after his all-round heroics in the 2005 Ashes. Here, he leads England off the field during the 2006-07 Ashes series, which Australia won 5-0.

example of how life must continue if possible in the face of such horrors.

However, the deliberate attack three months later on the Sri Lankan team in Lahore, and the international officials who were in the motorised convoy with them, moved the goalposts still further. It has ensured that no one will tour Pakistan for a very long time, thereby seriously threatening the future of cricket there but, crucially, no longer can anyone claim that cricketers are not terrorist targets.

Stifling security helped to ensure that England's tour of India was able to resume, but is that really the future of cricket tours? For a start, the cost makes it prohibitive for many. And would Londoners, say, really stand for the street closures and sweeping cavalcades that are now the norm on the subcontinent in order to get two cricket teams to Lord's?

The attack in Lahore also now means the players have much more of a say about their safety – and please let's not forget the travelling supporters and press corps, too.

Kevin Pietersen was the captain in India, and played a significant role in gently cajoling his team to return. That said, his appointment following Michael Vaughan's resignation, was a truly desperate shot in the dark. Pietersen is a fine batsman, but is a singular individual. The only reason for choosing him above Andrew Strauss was to unify the captaincy and, at the time, it seemed that Strauss's one-day international career was over. There was a brief honeymoon period with wins over a South African team that had clearly had enough, following a long Test tour here, but it was not long before Pietersen's demand that Moores should go were made public.

No one is absolutely sure who was responsible for that, but Vaughan, before Pietersen, also had his issues

Above left Amid tight security, England captain Kevin Pietersen and his team prepare to leave the eastern seaboard city of Bhubaneswar following news of the Mumbai terrorist attacks.

Above right England captain Andrew Strauss and team director Andy Flower, here pictured during the Champions Trophy tournament in South Africa, proved an excellent management partnership after being thrown together at the start of 2009.

with Moores's style and approach while he was in charge. Once in the open, the ECB had little option but to get shot of both. It was clearly an intolerable position for the captain to demand the sacking of the coach, while it was also obvious that Moores's popularity in the dressing room was not high – although apparently not as low as Pietersen believed. And so it was that Strauss and Andy Flower found themselves thrust together in the Caribbean, where they forged a partnership that, one could tell, could take England forward.

Looking back now, in the afterglow of the Ashes success which from England's perspective did so much to light up the summer of 2009, it was undoubtedly a good thing that the watershed occurred when it did, when there was still time to repair broken trust and

damaged relationships before the summer began in earnest. Meanwhile, the captaincy has made Strauss flourish both as a batsman and as a man, and that turbulent January is now a distant memory.

The celebrations following the Ashes triumph were more subdued than four years' previously, but that was a fair reflection of the series itself – it had its moments, but not the fireworks of its unforgettable predecessor.

It also endorses my prediction that unlike the disappointing aftermath of 2005, Strauss and Flower will be utterly determined that their Ashes victory is not the climax, but merely the beginning.

Jonathan Agnew
Leicestershire, October 2009

STUART BROAD

JONATHAN AGNEW, Editor of *Cricket Year* and BBC Cricket Correspondent, recalls the moment when England fast bowler STUART BROAD added his name to the elite list of Ashes legends…

Pundits and players alike might continue to pore over the bare statistics of the 2009 Ashes series, and wonder how England emerged triumphant. For those of us lucky to be at The Oval on the Saturday of the deciding Test, however, it was clear that one devastating spell of controlled pace bowling made all the difference.

Prior to that remarkable afternoon, though, in which Stuart Broad's 5 for 19 routed Australia, who collapsed from 73 for no wicket to 160 all out, there was a feeling that the youngster had not enjoyed the best of series. Indeed, despite Broad having taken 6 for 91 in the previous game at Headingley, there was more than just one voice in the commentary boxes suggesting that he should not play in the final Test at all.

There was an element of consolation about those figures at Headingley because, in terms of accuracy, Broad was equally as wayward as his colleagues, and this contributed in no small part to Australia's overwhelming victory there. But the fact that he was singled out, despite taking a Test-best haul, illustrated the view that there was an element of uncertainty about the effectiveness of his bowling.

This was felt close to home. I encountered a furious Chris Broad in the lift of the media centre at Lord's, who was as dismayed as I at the way Broad junior had clearly been instructed to bowl by the England hierarchy. Bear in mind, too, that Stuart took the new ball ahead of Andrew Flintoff in the first Ashes Test at Cardiff, and it is clear how muddled the England strategy was.

He was instructed to bowl a hostile, short-pitched length, based on one brief spell at Chester-le-Street earlier in the

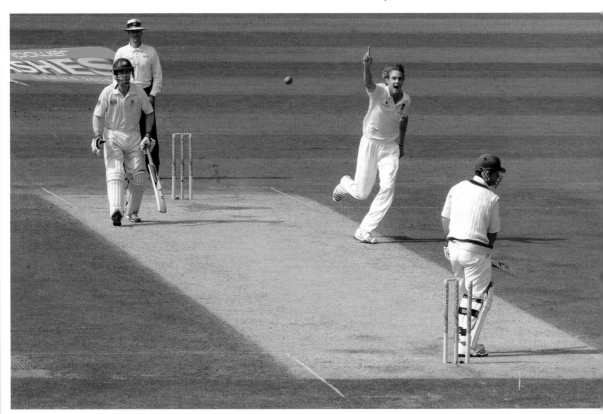

Ricky Ponting, the Australia captain, plays on to Stuart Broad at The Oval during the England bowler's Ashes-deciding spell.

season in which he spectacularly roughed up Ramnaresh Sarwan on a slow pitch. The result of this policy in the first two Tests put Broad senior on the verge of spontaneous combustion. What a marked difference we saw at The Oval, however, where Broad bowled a fuller, probing length and, vitally, swung the ball.

Being very tall, this gives him a huge advantage with batsmen reluctant to come forward, therefore allowing him an extra foot to pitch the ball up and swing it some more. It is not difficult to fathom, and one wonders what on earth the England think-tank was up to in identifying Broad as their new 'beat-up' bowler.

This is not new, though. I remember my frustration at Lord's in 2008 when Broad started a spell against South Africa from the Nursery End and immediately bowled a string of outswingers. But this

The natural talent that Stuart Broad also possesses with the bat has led many observers to predict that he could become England's leading Test match all-rounder in succession to Andrew Flintoff.

failed to impress a captain as astute, even, as Michael Vaughan who took him off and brought him back from the Pavilion End. No swing there, but England wanted aggression from Broad, not fine skill.

It is tempting to go for pace, especially on the bland pitches we see too often in Test cricket these days. Some extra bounce, or a yard of pace can make all the difference, and the ball does not swing every day. But Broad showed us in the West Indies that he is capable of learning new tricks, like cutters and slower balls, and although he had a moan about the surfaces there, it was obvious that his experience on the flat tracks would make him a better bowler.

Now, following his success at The Oval, not only will the coaching staff realise precisely what his role should be – metronomic and probing accuracy with Glenn McGrath-like

bounce – but Broad will also have the confidence to plough his own furrow and do what he now knows is best for him.

With Flintoff retiring from Test cricket, Broad's development could not be better timed. Let's not forget that he originally made his way as a batsman and simply because he has been listed to bat at No. 8 or 9 for England, while sometimes opening the bowling, does not necessarily mean that he is a better bowler than batsman. Increasingly, he has played important innings low down the order, and in Flintoff's absence, he should now be given the responsibility of moving up to No. 7, a key all-rounder's position, and take the opportunity that comes with it. Broad will have to show the discipline to bat alongside top-order batsmen, rather than tail-enders, which in turn, should improve what is already a pretty decent technique.

The iconic Oval gasholder provides the backdrop as Stuart Broad walks from the field and into Ashes legend at tea, following his magnificent bowling spell on the second afternoon of the fifth Test.

In Stuart Broad, England clearly have unearthed a gem. He is the best all-round cricketer of his age in the world and is fiercely competitive. Just occasionally, that aggression threatens to boil over – reminding us that Broad, after all, is just 23 years old and has had responsibility beyond his years thrust upon him.

Dad, a former Test cricketer and Ashes hero himself and now a respected ICC match referee, will quietly but firmly remind him that questioning the umpire is not a sensible policy and, having now unquestionably found himself, Broad has the talent – and the time – to rewrite the history books.

ENGLAND

THE ASHES: ENGLAND v. AUSTRALIA
by Jonathan Agnew

The 2009 Ashes did not threaten the dizzy heights of 2005, largely because there were not the same agonisingly close matches but also, possibly, because the series was not accessible on terrestrial television.

In some ways, it is a good thing that 2005 clearly stood unchallenged because I will not see the like of it again in my lifetime. However, this series, anticipated to be a closely fought contest between two evenly matched teams, lived up to its billing.

Looking back at the five matches now, even with the benefit of hindsight and a great deal of consideration, the statistics and the outcome struggle to add up. Australia's batsmen notched up eight centuries between them, with six of their top seven scoring more than 250 runs in the series. Only two Englishmen scored hundreds – one being Jonathan Trott in his first appearance in the final match – and only Andrew Strauss passed the 350-run mark. It was equally unbalanced in the bowling department, too, with three Australians taking 20 wickets or more, while Stuart Broad topped England's averages with 18 victims at 30 runs each.

But statistics only tell part of the story and crucial passages of play were dominated by England. Ricky Ponting must still have nightmares about the last 11 overs at Cardiff where England's tenth wicket pair,

The crowd at Cardiff's Swalec Stadium, formerly Sophia Gardens, is expectant as the two teams line up at the start of the 2009 Ashes series.

FIRST TEST – ENGLAND v. AUSTRALIA
8-12 July 2009 at Cardiff

ENGLAND

	First Innings		Second Innings	
AJ Strauss (capt)	c Clarke b Johnson	30	c Haddin b Hauritz	17
AN Cook	c Hussey b Hilfenhaus	10	lbw b Johnson	6
RS Bopara	c Hughes b Johnson	35	lbw b Hilfenhaus	1
KP Pietersen	c Katich b Hauritz	69	b Hilfenhaus	8
PD Collingwood	c Haddin b Hilfenhaus	64	c Hussey b Siddle	74
*MJ Prior	b Siddle	56	c Clarke b Hauritz	14
A Flintoff	b Siddle	37	c Ponting b Johnson	26
JM Anderson	c Hussey b Hauritz	26	(10) not out	21
SCJ Broad	b Johnson	19	(8) lbw b Hauritz	14
GP Swann	not out	47	(9) lbw b Hilfenhaus	31
MS Panesar	c Ponting b Hauritz	4	not out	7
Extras	b 13, lb 11, w 2, nb 12	38	b 9, lb 9, w 4, nb 11	33
	(all out 106.5 overs)	435	(9 wkts 105 overs)	252

	First Innings				Second Innings			
	O	M	R	W	O	M	R	W
Johnson	22	2	87	3	22	4	44	2
Hilfenhaus	27	5	77	2	15	3	47	3
Siddle	27	3	121	2	18	2	51	1
Hauritz	23.5	1	95	3	37	12	63	3
Clarke	5	0	20	0	3	0	8	0
Katich	2	0	11	0	3	0	7	0
North	-	-	-	-	7	4	14	0

Fall of Wickets
1-21, 2-67, 3-90, 4-228, 5-241, 6-327, 7-329, 8-355, 9-423
1-13, 2-17, 3-31, 4-46, 5-70, 6-127, 7-159, 8-221, 9-233

AUSTRALIA

	First Innings	
PJ Hughes	c Prior b Flintoff	36
SM Katich	lbw b Anderson	122
RT Ponting (capt)	b Panesar	150
MEK Hussey	c Prior b Anderson	3
MJ Clarke	c Prior b Broad	83
MJ North	not out	125
*BJ Haddin	c Bopara b Collingwood	121
MG Johnson		
PM Siddle		
BW Hilfenhaus		
NM Hauritz		
Extras	b 9, lb 14, w 4, nb 7	34
	(6 wkts dec 181 overs)	674

	First Innings			
	O	M	R	W
Anderson	32	6	110	2
Broad	32	6	129	1
Swann	38	8	131	0
Flintoff	35	3	128	1
Panesar	35	4	115	1
Collingwood	9	0	38	1

Fall of Wickets
1-60, 2-299, 3-325, 4-331, 5-474, 6-674

Umpires: Aleem Dar (Pakistan) & BR Doctrove (West Indies)
Toss: England
Man of the Match: RT Ponting

Match drawn

Monty Panesar and James Anderson, withstood everything Australia could throw at them to save the game. The fact that this included Marcus North's gentle off breaks, not a single over of Simon Katich's potentially confusing wrist spin and a lack of hostility from the pacemen, greatly assisted England's cause. As we have seen before, it was the team that escaped almost certain defeat that took the psychological benefit into the next match, where Andrew Flintoff's inspired spell finished off an insipid batting performance by the visitors.

At Edgbaston, Australia's first innings was inadequate, meaning that they needed the weather to help them save the Test, and at The Oval – after thrashing England at Headingley – Australia's batting let them down again as Broad destroyed their first innings on the Friday afternoon. Those moments accounted for England's 2-1 victory and Strauss summed it up perfectly, reflecting, 'When we were bad we were very bad and when we were good, we managed to be good enough'.

The choice of the Swalec Stadium (formerly Sophia Gardens) in Cardiff to host the opening match of the series was laced with controversy. The purpose-refurbished ground had never staged a Test before, and both the chief executive and the head groundsman had lost their jobs after a fiasco of a one-day international the previous summer.

AGGERS' VIEW

'For 11.3 overs, Monty Panesar and Jimmy Anderson kept out the increasingly desperate Australians and provided the Cardiff crowd, at the end of their inaugural Test match, with some of the most gripping and dramatic cricket that only the five-day game is capable of delivering. At the time we thought it would be a defining moment in the series, preventing Australia going 1-0 up and seizing control, but subsequent events only magnified the vital nature of the Panesar/Anderson resistance. It is a stand that now takes its place in Ashes legend. Both Jimmy and Monty are better batsmen than they are often given credit for, but it was still an astonishing escape and a remarkable passage of play. It was sad, though, for Panesar that his poor form of last summer meant that he did not also play a part in the series with the ball. If he had been on song, he would certainly have played at The Oval too, alongside Graeme Swann.'

James Anderson drives powerfully to the boundary during his match-saving innings of 21 not out in the final, tense overs of the First Test.

This, surely, was proof that money talks louder than anything when it comes to bidding for the privilege of staging a Test match, and Cardiff, which can count on the financial muscle of the Welsh Assembly, appears to have a massive advantage over other, established venues. Certainly, Chester-le-Street and Trent Bridge could be forgiven for feeling let down after substantial and very expensive ground improvements while those who hold tradition dear found the fact that there was no Test at Old Trafford – the scene of so much Ashes history – a situation that was hard to bear.

In fact, Cardiff's first experience went smoothly and they were rewarded with the most exciting climax of the series when Panesar and Anderson prevented Australia, who had dominated the match, from taking an early lead.

England squandered a promising foundation in their first innings in which almost every batsman made double figures, slipping from 228 for 3 to 329 for 7. Kevin Pietersen's bizarre dismissal on 69, top edging a sweep so wide of his off stump he could barely reach it, again stirred his critics into action, but the lower order resisted and, on the second morning, Anderson,

Broad and Graeme Swann put the bowling to the sword, adding 99 in fewer than 17 overs to post a respectable 435.

This though was spectacularly put into perspective by the Australians who, led by Ponting, amassed 674 for 6. Ponting made 150, Katich 122 and North an unbeaten 125 as England's spinners, in particular, were wholly inadequate. Even the normally belligerent and confident Swann bowled full tosses and long hops, bowling 28 wicketless overs for 131. Panesar managed one wicket in 35 overs. But, after only three days of the series, England's Plan A – beat the Aussies with spin – had been torn up.

There was nothing left for England other than to stave off what appeared to be certain defeat and, when Pietersen was bowled playing no stroke to Hilfenhaus and Strauss edged a wide delivery from Nathan Hauritz, England were 46 for 4, and at lunch on the final day were apparently hopelessly placed on 102 for 5, still 137 runs behind.

Only two wickets fell in the afternoon, however, with Flintoff and Matt Prior and, crucially, Collingwood resisting with their usual tenacity. Broad made 14 from

CARDIFF PASSES FIRST TEST

VIC MARKS, Cricket Correspondent of the *Observer* and popular member of the *Test Match Special* commentary team, looks back on the dramatic opening skirmish of the 2009 Ashes...

At Cardiff we got more than we could possibly have bargained for. The Good Lord smiled upon Bill Morris, Paul Russell, the ECB and England.

It might have been a disaster; it ended as something of a surreal triumph as every forward defensive stroke from Jimmy Anderson or Monty Panesar against the self-effacing off spin of Marcus North (what was he doing bowling the penultimate over?) triggered the sort of rapturous adulation that is usually reserved for a mazy Shane Williams try in those parts.

They were lucky at Cardiff: that the sun shone – except when England were really struggling; that such a dead pitch, unsuitable for Test cricket, could produce such a compelling climax; that England escaped with the draw that proved the catalyst for another mesmerising Ashes series.

For much of the time the cricket lacked the vibrant quality sustained throughout the 2005 series but in the last hour no one cared about that.

But the success of Cardiff's Test was not just down to luck. Forget the nature of the pitch, which at least soothed any fears that we might be popping back over the bridge after three days. Everything else worked like clockwork. And there were more smiles than you could experience in a day at Disneyland.

One morning when mounting the four flights of stairs to the media centre, I counted 25 cheery 'good mornings' from the array of good-natured stewards. I was exhausted and practically hoarse from replying to everyone by the time I eventually got to the top. There a welcome cup of hot coffee was immediately offered by yet another beaming face. Headingley it was not.

The most cynical critic of Cardiff's heist of Test cricket was bound to mellow a bit after such a bombardment of smiles, though actually they also smile quite a lot nowadays at Lord's.

We hoped for a different type of surface there, which would bring the slip cordon into play against the faster bowlers. At Cardiff they were almost redundant. Only Andrew Flintoff – on the last day – was caught off a genuine edge in the slips against the pacemen and then the ball only just carried.

That was one of the most uplifting moments of the Test, which was my vote for the Champagne Moment in the *TMS* box (I was outvoted as usual) since this was a rare passage of play in the 21st century.

Flintoff, understandably, hesitated after edging the ball but he did not plead with the umpires to refer the catch upstairs, which is the modern way. Instead he looked to Ricky Ponting, who had taken the catch, for confirmation that it had carried. Ponting indicated that it had and Flintoff departed.

However, any notion that England were playing undiluted Corinthian cricket was swept away by the emergence of the physio and a rather bewildered Bilal Shafayat, carrying unnecessary gloves, just before the close. To be fair, Anderson did not seem to want to have anything to do with the two intruders, and nor did Panesar, and I got the distinct impression that Ponting did not welcome their presence out in the middle either.

Such an unjustified intrusion did not alter the result but it stained England's achievement of scrambling to a draw. And it stirred the pot nicely. It would not have been the Ashes without a few spats: Kevin Pietersen getting in Mitchell Johnson's 'space' at practice on the last day might have led to some interesting battles as the series progressed, though, of course, injury prevented that particular duel from developing.

This article first appeared on the TestMatchExtra.com cricket website.

Left Andrew Strauss and Ricky Ponting, the two captains, walk out for the toss before the start of the opening Ashes Test at Cardiff.

Right Monty Panesar and James Anderson march from the field after securing England's unlikely and thrilling draw in the First Test.

Australia's Mike Hussey hardly has time to flinch as another Andrew Flintoff thunderbolt flashes past.

47 balls and Swann faced a fiery burst from the second new ball, which was taken with 25 overs to go and England having only three wickets in hand.

After 63 balls, Swann fell for the double bluff, with the field set for another short ball, and was lbw to Hilfenhaus for 31, and seven overs later, with England still six runs behind, Collingwood was taken in the gully at the second attempt by Mike Hussey for a courageous 74 which had taken him an astonishing 83 overs.

Anderson managed to take England into the lead with a jab for four, but the drama had not finished as they then employed some distinctly naive and deliberate time-wasting tactics – including an unscheduled and spectacular pitch invasion by their temporary (and sizeable) physiotherapist, who was seen off by the umpires.

As time ticked away, and England's lead slowly grew, Ponting knew the game was up. A full house roared its approval – largely in Welsh – when he shook hands with the defiant last wicket pair who had survived for 69 balls. Ponting's tactics were roundly criticised for lacking imagination and nous, and we wondered how significant England's great escape might prove to be.

The Lord's Test followed hard on Cardiff's heels and insomuch as England again failed to capitalise on a fine

SECOND TEST – ENGLAND v. AUSTRALIA
16-20 July 2009 at Lord's

ENGLAND

	First Innings			Second Innings		
AJ Strauss (capt)	b Hilfenhaus		161	c Clarke b Hauritz		32
AN Cook	lbw b Johnson		95	lbw b Hauritz		32
RS Bopara	lbw b Hilfenhaus		18	c Katich b Hauritz		27
KP Pietersen	c Haddin b Siddle		32	c Haddin b Siddle		44
PD Collingwood	c Siddle b Clarke		16	c Haddin b Siddle		54
*MJ Prior	b Johnson		8	run out		61
A Flintoff	c Ponting b Hilfenhaus		4	not out		30
SCJ Broad	b Hilfenhaus		16	not out		0
GP Swann	c Ponting b Siddle		4			
JM Anderson	c Hussey b Johnson		29			
G Onions	not out		17			
Extras	b 15, lb 2, nb 8		25	b 16, lb 9, w 1, nb 5		31
	(all out 101.4 overs)		425	(6 wkts dec 71.2 overs)		311

	First Innings				Second Innings			
	O	M	R	W	O	M	R	W
Hilfenhaus	31	12	103	4	19	5	59	0
Johnson	21.4	2	132	3	17	2	68	0
Siddle	20	1	76	2	15.2	4	64	2
Hauritz	8.3	1	26	0	16	1	80	3
North	16.3	2	59	0	-	-	-	-
Clarke	4	1	12	1	4	0	15	0

Fall of Wickets
1-196, 2-222, 3-267, 4-302, 5-317, 6-333, 7-364, 8-370, 9-378
1-61, 2-74, 3-147, 4-174, 5-260, 6-311

AUSTRALIA

	First Innings			Second Innings		
PJ Hughes	c Prior b Anderson		4	c Strauss b Flintoff		17
SM Katich	c Broad b Onions		48	c Pietersen b Flintoff		6
RT Ponting (capt)	c Strauss b Anderson		2	b Broad		38
MEK Hussey	b Flintoff		51	c Collingwood b Swann		27
MJ Clarke	c Cook b Anderson		1	b Swann		136
MJ North	b Anderson		0	b Swann		6
*BJ Haddin	c Cook b Broad		28	c Collingwood b Flintoff		80
MG Johnson	c Cook b Broad		4	b Swann		63
NM Hauritz	c Collingwood b Onions		24	b Flintoff		1
PM Siddle	c Strauss b Onions		35	b Flintoff		7
BW Hilfenhaus	not out		6	not out		4
Extras	b 4, lb 6, nb 2		12	b 5, lb 8, nb 8		21
	(all out 63 overs)		215	(all out 107 overs)		406

	First Innings				Second Innings			
	O	M	R	W	O	M	R	W
Anderson	21	5	55	4	21	4	86	0
Flintoff	12	4	27	1	27	4	92	5
Broad	18	1	78	2	16	3	49	1
Onions	11	1	41	3	9	0	50	0
Swann	1	0	4	0	28	3	87	4
Collingwood	-	-	-	-	6	1	29	0

Fall of Wickets
1-4, 2-10, 3-103, 4-111, 5-111, 6-139, 7-148, 8-152, 9-196
1-17, 2-34, 3-78, 4-120, 5-128, 6-313, 7-356, 8-363, 9-388

Umpires: BR Doctrove (West Indies) & RE Koertzen (South Africa)
Toss: England
Man of the Match: A Flintoff

England won by 115 runs

start, it followed a similar pattern. Strauss and Alastair Cook set things up with an opening stand of 196, with Cook desperately disappointed to fall lbw to a still erratic Mitchell Johnson for 95.

Pietersen scored 32 but by the close of the first day, England's platform had disintegrated to 364 for 6, with Strauss unbeaten on 161 from 266 balls. He survived only one more, offering no shot to the second ball of the second day and lost his off stump to Hilfenhaus, leaving England dependent once again on lower-order runs. These came in the form of a riotous last wicket partnership of 47 between an unusually liberated Anderson and Graham Onions, which hoisted the total from 378 for 9 to 425 all out.

This appeared to knock the stuffing out of the Australians who were quickly 10 for 2 and 111 for 5. Ponting was adjudged to have been caught at slip off Anderson when, in fact, the ball hit his boot and he might have been given out lbw. His failure precipitated the collapse that would cost Australia the match – and their first defeat at Lord's since 1934.

Anderson claimed 4 for 55 and Onions 3 for 41 as Australia conceded a lead of 210, and England consolidated their position through the third day before Strauss declared on the fourth morning, leaving Australia 522 to win in 191 overs. It was unthinkable, of course, that Australia might blow the record books apart at the seams, but Michael Clarke's 136 took them to within 209 of England with five wickets in hand with a day to go.

AGGERS' VIEW

‘ Andrew Flintoff's spell on the final morning at Lord's, clinching for England the win that put them 1-0 up in the Ashes series, was completely awesome. There is still no finer sight in cricket than a truly fast bowler running in and giving the batsmen an unnerving examination of their physical and mental abilities. What was especially magnificent, in his own farewell series, was that Freddie was on this occasion able to rise above his chronic knee injury problems and bowl flat out for a lengthy spell, and to get the reward for his accuracy and hostility that was so often not the case during his Test career. He reminded me of some of the great West Indies fast bowlers of the 1980s in that spell, so bruising and intimidating was he; batsmen were being hurt as well as being roughed up, and every good Test team needs someone who is capable of doing that. ’

THIRD TEST – ENGLAND v. AUSTRALIA
30 July–3 August 2009 at Edgbaston

AUSTRALIA

	First Innings		Second Innings	
SR Watson	lbw b Onions	62	c Prior b Anderson	53
SM Katich	lbw b Swann	46	c Prior b Onions	26
RT Ponting (capt)	c Prior b Onions	38	b Swann	5
MEK Hussey	b Onions	0	c Prior b Broad	64
MJ Clarke	lbw b Anderson	29	not out	103
MJ North	c Prior b Anderson	12	c Anderson b Broad	96
*GA Manou	b Anderson	8	not out	13
MG Johnson	lbw b Anderson	0		
NM Hauritz	not out	20		
PM Siddle	c Prior b Anderson	13		
BW Hilfenhaus	c Swann b Onions	20		
Extras	b 5, lb 7, w 2, nb 1	15	b 4, lb 6, w 2, nb 3	15
	(all out 70.4 overs)	263	(5 wkts 112.2 overs)	375

	First Innings				Second Innings			
	O	M	R	W	O	M	R	W
Anderson	24	7	80	5	21	8	47	1
Flintoff	15	2	58	0	15	0	35	0
Onions	16.4	2	58	4	19	3	74	1
Broad	13	2	51	0	16	2	38	2
Swann	2	0	4	1	31	4	119	1
Bopara	–	–	–	–	8.2	1	44	0
Collingwood	–	–	–	–	2	0	8	0

Fall of Wickets
1-85, 2-126, 3-126, 4-163, 5-193, 6-202, 7-202, 8-203, 9-229
1-47, 2-52, 3-137, 4-161, 5-346

ENGLAND

	First Innings	
AJ Strauss (capt)	c Manou b Hilfenhaus	69
AN Cook	c Manou b Siddle	0
RS Bopara	b Hilfenhaus	23
IR Bell	lbw b Johnson	53
PD Collingwood	c Ponting b Hilfenhaus	13
*MJ Prior	c sub b Siddle	41
A Flintoff	c Clarke b Hauritz	74
SCJ Broad	c & b Siddle	55
GP Swann	c North b Johnson	24
JM Anderson	c Manou b Hilfenhaus	1
G Onions	not out	2
Extras	b 2, lb 4, w 6, nb 9	21
	(all out 93.3 overs)	376

	First Innings			
	O	M	R	W
Hilfenhaus	30	7	109	4
Siddle	21.3	3	89	3
Hauritz	18	2	57	1
Johnson	21	1	92	2
Watson	3	0	23	0

Fall of Wickets
1-2, 2-60, 3-141, 4-159, 5-168, 6-257, 7-309, 8-348, 9-355

Umpires: Aleem Dar (Pakistan) & RE Koertzen (South Africa)
Toss: Australia
Test debut: GA Manou
Man of the Match: MJ Clarke

Match drawn

One or two Australians dared to dream, but their hopes were shattered by an explosive spell from Flintoff who thundered in like a man possessed from the Pavilion End and, within 21 overs, the job was finished. Flintoff took 5 for 92 – only his third five-wicket haul in Tests but none was so valuable. England one up? We could hardly believe it.

Poor weather, and another century from Clarke, conspired to deny England a second victory at Edgbaston. The Australian selectors had shown their first sign of panic by replacing Hughes with Shane Watson – a decision that both stunned and dismayed many of Australia's pundits.

In fact Watson – better known as a one-day cricketer, and certainly not as a Test opener – scored 62 and enjoyed a reasonable series, but Australia's batting again fell short in its first innings, scoring just 263 as Anderson took 5 for 80.

England had also made a significant change, with Pietersen missing the rest of the series following an operation on an Achilles heel injury, and Ian Bell, his replacement, scored a half-century while Flintoff made a belligerent 74 from 79 balls to give England a not insignificant lead of 113. Meanwhile, another casual stroke from Bopara turned up the heat on his position.

With the elements frustrating England, Australia needed to bat until tea on the final day to be safe. But they lost Ponting cheaply, bowled Swann, before the close of play on the fourth day to give England hope. But Clarke's undefeated 103 and a fine 96 from North steered Australia to a lead of 262 and a comfortable draw.

The Headingley Test, in which England were thrashed despite appearing to have all the momentum going into the game, proved that cricket is entirely unpredictable. England did not help themselves, first by dithering over Flintoff's fitness – he was left out on the morning of the game, much to his apparent disappointment – and then by suffering another injury due to their mindless determination to play football in the warm-ups. Prior was the victim this time, suffering a back spasm and inflicting a crazy hour on England, and on Strauss in particular.

The toss was delayed but Strauss gave his customary round of interviews before dashing to the dressing room to get padded up. Moments later he was taking guard in the middle and were it not for an aberration by umpire Bowden, Strauss would have been lbw first ball. He scored only three, and England just 102 as Siddle and Stuart Clark enjoyed the conditions.

It was England's lowest first innings score at Headingley and their sixth lowest against Australia, and if the batsmen had underperformed, the bowlers went from bad to worse. What drivel they served up, long-hop after long-hop on a pitch crying out for a full, disciplined

MATT PRIOR

SIMON HUGHES, television's 'The Analyst' and *Daily Telegraph* columnist, studies the progress made in 2009 by England wicketkeeper Matt Prior...

Have a guess who was England's second highest run-scorer in the Ashes after Andrew Strauss. Alastair Cook? Paul Collingwood? Stuart Broad? Actually, it was Matt Prior with 261 runs at 32.62.

That may have been only fractionally more than half Strauss's total, but it still represents more consistency than anyone else in the top six. And it wasn't only the runs he scored but the way he scored them, always positive, always forthright, never cowed by a situation or persuaded into a backward step... that was impressive.

His first innings of the series, after England's scratchy beginnings in Cardiff, set the right tone. As with his very first Test innings – at Lord's in 2007, he seemed galvanised by the situation and took the bowlers on. He had contributed a stylish fifty and looked poised for more when a slight loss of concentration caused him to drive over-ambitiously and ultimately one-handedly at Peter Siddle and he was bowled.

Disappointingly, despite other excellent contributions including a notably defiant 37 not out in England's abysmal collapse at Headingley, that 61 was his highest score of the series. And that is the challenge he faces now.

He has got the attributes (and the Test average – 44) to bat No. 6 in a Test match side. He has a very solid, sometimes intimidating defence, he is quick on his feet and his driving and cutting have a kick like a mule. His running between the wickets, too, is ultra-committed. He gets as low as a sprinter in his turn for two, using his left hand on the ground for leverage. But he must ward against being too excited once he gets to fifty and convert that into something more substantial. Hundreds are expected from a No. 6 (Ian Bell has made a few there, for instance), not feisty sixties.

Most encouragingly, Prior's wicketkeeping in the series was outstanding. He rarely let a bye through, and was a model of tidiness, clearing up loose throws and double-bouncing deliveries. Vitally, he never dropped a catch, and in fact England's fielding generally was, apart from an attack of the collywobbles on the last day, very sound.

Prior's error-prone ways have been forgotten by all but Ryan Sidebottom, off whom he dropped half a dozen chances in the summer of 2007. He took a couple of blinders too, notably the horizontal one-hander at Edgbaston off Jimmy Anderson.

There is some criticism of the number of England support staff (criticism, funnily enough, that has suddenly quietened down!) but former Nottinghamshire and England keeper Bruce French's work with Prior has clearly been invaluable. French upped the intensity of his training sessions and worked hard on Prior's mobility, getting his weight a bit more forward and agile in the crouch. It has clearly worked.

Prior also spent time working with Andy Flower on taking off spin during The Oval Test. That paid dividends too, with the stunning catch of Mitchell Johnson in the first innings and the stumping of Marcus North in the second.

Stuart Broad got the all-round plaudits at The Oval, augmented by Graeme Swann's 8 for 158 and half-century, but, in one-day cricket as well as five, Matt Prior has now become the lead machinist in England's engine room.

This article first appeared on the TestMatchExtra.com cricket website.

Matt Prior, England's wicketkeeper-batsman, sweeps during the 2009 Ashes series.

FOURTH TEST – ENGLAND v. AUSTRALIA
7-11 August 2009 at Headingley

ENGLAND

	First Innings		Second Innings	
AJ Strauss (capt)	c North b Siddle	3	lbw b Hilfenhaus	32
AN Cook	c Clarke b Clark	30	c Haddin b Johnson	30
RS Bopara	c Hussey b Hilfenhaus	1	lbw b Hilfenhaus	0
IR Bell	c Haddin b Johnson	8	c Ponting b Johnson	3
PD Collingwood	c Ponting b Clark	0	lbw b Johnson	4
*MJ Prior	not out	37	(7) c Haddin b Hilfenhaus	22
SCJ Broad	c Katich b Clark	3	(8) c Watson b Siddle	61
GP Swann	c Clarke b Siddle	0	(9) c Haddin b Johnson	62
SJ Harmison	c Haddin b Siddle	0	(10) not out	19
JM Anderson	c Haddin b Siddle	3	(6) c Ponting b Hilfenhaus	4
G Onions	c Katich b Siddle	0	b Johnson	0
Extras	b 5, lb 8, w 1, nb 3	17	b 5, lb 5, w 5, nb 11	26
	(all out 33.5 overs)	102	(all out 61.3 overs)	263

	First Innings				Second Innings			
	O	M	R	W	O	M	R	W
Hilfenhaus	7	0	20	1	19	2	60	4
Siddle	9.5	0	21	5	12	2	50	1
Johnson	7	0	30	1	19.3	3	69	5
Clark	10	4	18	3	11	1	74	0

Fall of Wickets
1-11, 2-16, 3-39, 4-42, 5-63, 6-72, 7-92, 8-98, 9-102
1-58, 2-58, 3-67, 4-74, 5-78, 6-86, 7-120, 8-228, 9-259

AUSTRALIA

	First Innings	
SR Watson	lbw b Onions	51
SM Katich	c Bopara b Harmison	0
RT Ponting (capt)	lbw b Broad	78
MEK Hussey	lbw b Broad	10
MJ Clarke	lbw b Onions	93
MJ North	c Anderson b Broad	110
*BJ Haddin	c Bell b Harmison	14
MG Johnson	c Bopara b Broad	27
PM Siddle	b Broad	0
SR Clark	b Broad	32
BW Hilfenhaus	not out	0
Extras	b 9, lb 14, w 4, nb 3	30
	(all out 104.1 overs)	445

	First Innings			
	O	M	R	W
Anderson	18	3	89	0
Harmison	23	4	98	2
Onions	22	5	80	2
Broad	25.1	6	91	6
Swann	16	4	64	0

Fall of Wickets
1-14, 2-133, 3-140, 4-151, 5-303, 6-323, 7-393, 8-394, 9-440

Umpires: Asad Rauf (Pakistan) & BF Bowden (New Zealand)
Toss: England
Man of the Match: MJ North

Australia won by an innings and 80 runs

FIFTH TEST – ENGLAND v. AUSTRALIA
20-24 August 2009 at The Oval

ENGLAND

	First Innings		Second Innings	
AJ Strauss (capt)	c Haddin b Hilfenhaus	55	c Clarke b North	75
AN Cook	c Ponting b Siddle	10	c Clarke b North	9
IR Bell	b Siddle	72	c Katich b Johnson	4
PD Collingwood	c Hussey b Siddle	24	c Katich b Johnson	1
IJL Trott	run out	41	c North b Clark	119
*MJ Prior	c Watson b Johnson	18	run out	4
A Flintoff	c Haddin b Johnson	7	c Siddle b North	22
SCJ Broad	c Ponting b Hilfenhaus	37	c Ponting b North	29
GP Swann	c Haddin b Siddle	18	c Haddin b Hilfenhaus	63
JM Anderson	lbw b Hilfenhaus	0	not out	15
SJ Harmison	not out	12		
Extras	b 12, lb 5, w 3, nb 18	38	b 1, lb 15, w 7, nb 9	32
	(all out 90.5 overs)	332	(9 wkts dec 95 overs)	373

	First Innings				Second Innings			
	O	M	R	W	O	M	R	W
Hilfenhaus	21.5	5	71	3	11	1	58	1
Siddle	21	6	75	4	17	3	69	0
Clark	14	5	41	0	12	2	43	1
Johnson	15	0	69	2	17	1	60	2
North	14	3	33	0	30	4	98	4
Watson	5	0	26	0	-	-	-	-
Katich	-	-	-	-	5	2	9	0
Clarke	-	-	-	-	3	0	20	0

Fall of Wickets
1-12, 2-114, 3-176, 4-181, 5-229, 6-247, 7-268, 8-307, 9-308
1-27, 2-34, 3-39, 4-157, 5-168, 6-200, 7-243, 8-333, 9-373

AUSTRALIA

	First Innings		Second Innings	
SR Watson	lbw b Broad	34	lbw b Broad	40
SM Katich	c Cook b Swann	50	lbw b Swann	43
RT Ponting (capt)	b Broad	8	run out	66
MEK Hussey	lbw b Broad	0	c Cook b Swann	121
MJ Clarke	c Trott b Broad	3	run out	0
MJ North	lbw b Swann	8	st Prior b Swann	10
*BJ Haddin	b Broad	1	c Strauss b Swann	34
MG Johnson	c Prior b Swann	11	c Collingwood b Harmison	0
PM Siddle	not out	26	c Flintoff b Harmison	10
SR Clark	c Cook b Swann	6	c Cook b Harmison	0
BW Hilfenhaus	b Flintoff	6	not out	4
Extras	b 1, lb 5, nb 1	7	b 7, lb 7, nb 6	20
	(all out 52.5 overs)	160	(all out 102.2 overs)	348

	First Innings				Second Innings			
	O	M	R	W	O	M	R	W
Anderson	9	3	29	0	12	2	46	0
Flintoff	13.5	4	35	1	11	1	42	0
Swann	14	3	38	4	40.2	8	120	4
Harmison	4	1	15	0	16	5	54	3
Broad	12	1	37	5	22	4	71	1
Collingwood	-	-	-	-	1	0	1	0

Fall of Wickets
1-73, 2-85, 3-89, 4-93, 5-108, 6-109, 7-111, 8-131, 9-143
1-86, 2-90, 3-217, 4-220, 5-236, 6-327, 7-327, 8-343, 9-343

Umpires: Asad Rauf (Pakistan) & BF Bowden (New Zealand)
Toss: England
Test debut: IJL Trott
Man of the Match: SCJ Broad
Men of the Series: MJ Clarke and AJ Strauss

England won by 197 runs

England won series 2-1

length. Australia racked up 445, North scoring 110 and Clarke 93 and while Broad claimed 6 for 91, it was more with an air of consolation than penetration.

England batted again on the second day – and were 82 for 5 at the close. Broad (61) and Swann (62) added 108 from only 78 balls and savaged Australia's willing bowlers, but it did nothing to distract one from what had been a simply dreadful team performance. It was so bad as to be inexplicable, and with the series now level at one Test each, it was Australia who had grasped the initiative.

The focus of attention in the few days that followed fell on Bill Gordon, the long-serving groundsman at The Oval, the venue for the decider. Could the tradition of preparing featherbeds be set aside just once, and a pitch that could produce a result be preferred? Bill rose to the occasion splendidly, and although there was much muttering from the Australian camp, they had misread the conditions so spectacularly as to leave out a spinner.

This was Flintoff's farewell to Test cricket, which had now become simply too stressful for his chronic knee injury to bear and, in terms of figures, he made little impact on the game. But, with him in the dressing room, England managed to shrug off the hangover of their Headingley thrashing, and they posted 332 on a quickly wearing pitch.

The following day we witnessed a spell of bowling that both secured the Ashes and minimised the loss felt by Flintoff's departure. Broad claimed 5 for 19 in 46 balls after lunch, ripping the heart out of Australia's batting through clever and controlled swing bowling. This had nothing whatsoever to do with the pitch.

Australia lost ten wickets for 87 as they succumbed for just 160, and although England were 58 for 3 at the end of a second day that had seen 15 wickets fall for 243, the platform was there for Trott, in his first Test match, to score his maiden hundred. Trott represented South Africa Under-19s and, with times now very different to those in which the Smith brothers and Allan Lamb qualified for England in the 1980s, there is an argument to deny Trott that clinical career decision, but this remained a supremely confident innings of 119.

Strauss declared on 373 for 9, a lead of 545 with 20 overs remaining on the third day and, again to entice the optimists, the openers Watson and Katich added 80 before stumps. Both were dismissed within the first five overs of the fourth day, but Ponting and Hussey added 127 determinedly before Hussey called Ponting for a sharp run to mid on. Flintoff moved briskly to his left and threw flat and hard at the striker's wicket. With

Andrew Strauss holds the replica Ashes urn aloft as England's players celebrate a stunning series win at the presentation ceremony.

SERIES AVERAGES
England v. Australia

ENGLAND

Batting	M	Inns	NO	Runs	HS	Av	100	50	c/st
IJL Trott	1	2	0	160	119	80.00	1	–	1/–
AJ Strauss	5	9	0	474	161	52.66	1	3	4/–
KP Pietersen	2	4	0	153	69	38.25	–	1	1/–
GP Swann	5	8	1	249	63	35.57	–	2	1/–
A Flintoff	4	7	1	200	74	33.33	–	1	1/–
MJ Prior	5	9	1	261	61	32.62	–	2	11/1
SJ Harmison	2	3	2	31	19*	31.00	–	–	–/–
SCJ Broad	5	9	1	234	61	29.25	–	2	1/–
IR Bell	3	5	0	140	72	28.00	–	2	1/–
PD Collingwood	5	9	0	250	74	27.77	–	3	4/–
AN Cook	5	9	0	222	95	24.66	–	1	7/–
JM Anderson	5	8	2	99	29	16.50	–	–	2/–
RS Bopara	4	7	0	105	35	15.00	–	–	3/–
MS Panesar	1	2	1	11	7*	11.00	–	–	–/–
G Onions	3	4	2	19	17*	9.50	–	–	–/–

Bowling	Overs	Mds	Runs	Wkts	Av	Best	5/inn	10m
SCJ Broad	154.1	25	544	18	30.22	6-91	2	–
G Onions	77.4	11	303	10	30.30	4-58	–	–
SJ Harmison	43	10	167	5	33.40	3-54	–	–
GP Swann	170.2	30	567	14	40.50	4-38	–	–
JM Anderson	158	38	542	12	45.16	5-80	1	–
A Flintoff	128.5	18	417	8	52.12	5-92	1	–
PD Collingwood	18	1	76	1	76.00	1-38	–	–
MS Panesar	35	4	115	1	115.00	1-115	–	–

Also bowled: RS Bopara 8.2-1-44-0.

AUSTRALIA

Batting	M	Inns	NO	Runs	HS	Av	100	50	c/st
MJ Clarke	5	8	1	448	136	64.00	2	2	8/–
MJ North	5	8	1	367	125*	52.42	2	1	3/–
RT Ponting	5	8	0	385	150	48.12	1	2	11/–
SR Watson	3	5	0	240	62	48.00	–	3	2/–
BJ Haddin	4	6	0	278	121	46.33	1	1	15/–
SM Katich	5	8	0	341	122	42.62	1	1	6/–
MEK Hussey	5	8	0	276	121	34.50	1	2	6/–
NM Hauritz	3	3	1	45	24	22.50	–	–	–/–
GA Manou	1	2	1	21	13*	21.00	–	–	3/–
BW Hilfenhaus	5	6	4	40	20	20.00	–	–	–/–
PJ Hughes	2	3	0	57	36	19.00	–	–	1/–
PM Siddle	5	6	1	91	35	18.20	–	–	3/–
MG Johnson	5	6	0	105	63	17.50	–	1	–/–
SR Clark	2	3	0	38	32	12.66	–	–	–/–

Bowling	Overs	Mds	Runs	Wkts	Av	Best	5/inn	10m
BW Hilfenhaus	180.5	40	604	22	27.45	4-60	–	–
PM Siddle	161.4	24	616	20	30.80	5-21	1	–
NM Hauritz	103.2	17	321	10	32.10	3-63	–	–
MG Johnson	162.1	15	651	20	32.55	5-69	1	–
SR Clark	47	12	176	4	44.00	3-18	–	–
MJ North	67.3	13	204	4	51.00	4-98	–	–
MJ Clarke	19	1	75	1	75.00	1-12	–	–

Also bowled: SM Katich 10-2-27-0, SR Watson 8-0-49-0.

Ponting straining every sinew, the ball struck the stumps and the first replay showed that Ponting was just short.

It was a brilliant, speculative piece of fielding that left Flintoff's spectacular mark on his final Test. Hussey continued to make 121, but the Australian spirit was broken leaving Swann to capture the final wicket – his fourth – when Hussey was taken by Cook at short leg.

If the celebrations were low-key it was because of the (retrospective) criticism following the open-top bus trip in 2005 and also because both teams, the press and the public had still to brace themselves for no fewer than nine one-day games. Nine! Has there ever been a more shamelessly avaricious programme in world cricket?

After the two Twenty20 games at Old Trafford were wrecked by the weather, the only remotely exciting 50-over match in the NatWest Series – the opening game at The Oval – was won by Australia by four runs.

Although nothing thereafter should detract from a fine Australian effort, the rest were dreary, drab and irrelevant with England choosing to rest Anderson, Broad and Collingwood before the series had even been decided – a damning indictment from the dressing room of the absurd schedule.

Australia led 6-0 going into the final game, with the only shred of interest left lying in the ghoulish fact that no team had ever lost a one-day series 7-0 before. Swann took 5 for 28 to bowl Australia out for 176 and although England faltered on their way, losing five wickets for 35, they finally managed to break their duck with five wickets in hand. So ended the first seven of the absurd 24 ODIs to be played in England between the two teams before the end of 2013.

Opposite Jonathan Trott acknowledges The Oval crowd after completing his magnificent debut hundred in the deciding Ashes Test.

TWENTY20 INTERNATIONALS

Match One
30 August 2009 at Old Trafford
Australia 145 for 4 (20 overs) (CL White 55)
England 4 for 2 (1.1 overs)
Match abandoned - no result

Match Two
1 September 2009 at Old Trafford
Australia v. **England**
Match abandoned - no result
Series drawn

ONE-DAY INTERNATIONALS

Match One
4 September 2009 at The Oval
Australia 260 for 5 (50 overs) (CJ Ferguson 71*, CL White 53)
England 256 for 8 (50 overs) (MG Johnson 3 for 24)
Australia won by 4 runs

Match Two
6 September 2009 at Lord's
Australia 249 for 8 (50 overs) (CJ Ferguson 55)
England 210 all out (46.1 overs) (PD Collingwood 56)
Australia won by 39 runs

Match Three
9 September 2009 at the Rose Bowl
England 228 for 9 (50 overs) (AJ Strauss 63, SR Watson 3 for 36)
Australia 230 for 4 (48.3 overs) (CL White 105, MJ Clarke 52)
Australia won by 6 wickets

Match Four
12 September 2009 at Lord's
England 220 all out (46.3 overs) (AJ Strauss 63, B Lee 5 for 49)
Australia 221 for 3 (43.4 overs) (MJ Clarke 62*, TD Paine 51)
Australia won by 7 wickets

Match Five
15 September 2009 at Trent Bridge
England 299 all out (50 overs) (EJG Morgan 58)
Australia 302 for 6 (48.2 overs) (RT Ponting 126, MJ Clarke 52)
Australia won by 4 wickets

Match Six
17 September 2009 at Trent Bridge
Australia 296 for 8 (50 overs) (TD Paine 111, MEK Hussey 65, JM Anderson 4 for 55)
England 185 all out (41 overs) (JR Hopes 3 for 32)
Australia won by 111 runs

Match Seven
20 September 2009 at the Riverside
Australia 176 all out (45.5 overs) (RT Ponting 53, GP Swann 5 for 28)
England 177 for 6 (40 overs) (JL Denly 53)
England won by 4 wickets
Australia won the series 6–1

AUSTRALIA'S OTHER TOUR MATCHES

24–27 June 2009 at Hove
Australians 349 for 7 dec (90 overs) (BJ Haddin 69, NM Hauritz 65*, PSE Sandri 3 for 73)
& 379 for 7 dec (95.1 overs) (PJ Hughes 78, RT Ponting 71, MJ Clarke 75*)
Sussex 311 all out (80.2 overs) (B Lee 3 for 53)
& 373 for 7 (89 overs) (MH Yardy 67, CD Hopkinson 115)
Match drawn

1–4 July 2009 at New Road
Australians 358 all out (96.4 overs) (SM Katich 95, MEK Hussey 150, G Onions 3 for 70, TT Bresnan for 46, SJ Harmison 4 for 80)
& 438 for 4 dec (103 overs) (MJ North 191, MJ Clarke 80, MEK Hussey 62rh)
England Lions 352 all out (96 overs) (JL Denly 66, SC Moore 120, SM Davies 53, AU Rashid 66, B Lee 6 for 76)
& 162 for 4 (47.2 overs)
Match drawn

24–26 July 2009 at Northampton
Australians 308 for 8 dec (79 overs) (SR Watson 84, MEK Hussey 75 ro)
& 270 for 3 dec (53 overs) (PJ Hughes 68, AB McDonald 75, SR Watson 50, GA Manou 59*)
Northamptonshire 226 for 7 dec (49.3 overs) (AG Wakely 62, MH Wessels 50, PM Siddle 3 for 53)
& 217 all out (64.1 overs) (NJ O'Brien, AB McDonald 4 for 15)
Australians won by 135 runs

15–16 August 2009 at Canterbury
Australians 340 for 9 dec (81 overs) (SR Watson 95, MEK Hussey 65, G Keedy 3 for 70)
England Lions 237 all out (80.4 overs) (JWM Dalrymple 58, B Lee 3 for 37)
Australians won by 103 runs

BAGGY GREEN AURA OVER

MARTIN JOHNSON, of the *Sunday Times*, turns his playful attentions
to Australia and the sudden loss of their 'aura'...

They think it's all aura. It is now. When Andrew Strauss suggested that the Australian team that came to England in 2009 didn't quite have the intimidation factor of the three previous dynasties, he was merely stating what we already knew.

And also, the fact that England were saved at the start by some unlikely batting heroics from Monty Panesar, and assisted at the end by an Oval pitch with the kind of topping you'd normally sprinkle on some rhubarb before putting it in the oven, should serve as some kind of reality check. If victory in 2005 represented a notable scalp, then 2009 was the equivalent of slicing off a bald man's wig.

Just at this moment, it appears that the Australian Cricket Factory is no longer belching smoke from all chimneys, and a far better barometer of England's standing in Test cricket is just around the corner in South Africa. Mind you, it will help that we're playing them at home, what with Jonathan Trott representing one of more than 50 Yarpies currently playing in county cricket.

Trott may well turn out to be a bit of a find, which is much needed with all the question marks elsewhere in England's top order, but we'll see how he goes on in the country of his birth this winter before deciding whether we've snaffled another Pietersen from the Veldt. And we should also be wary of anointing Stuart Broad as the new Ian Botham. We've lost count of the number of all-rounders hailed as being ready to step into Superman's tights, but not one of them, not even Andrew Flintoff, has seriously threatened to earn the right to wear his underpants outside his trousers.

Broad batting at No. 7 is an interesting one, as this is a high enough spot for him to be expected to make runs, rather than, as has previously been the case, treating England all-rounders as something of a luxury item. Mind you, he's got a batsman's pedigree in his genes, and there were also signs in this Ashes series that he has more than

Ricky Ponting leaves the field after being run out by Andrew Flintoff's direct hit from mid on. Flintoff's brilliant throw left the tourists on 217 for 3 but more importantly their spirit was broken and wickets began to tumble.

a drop of his father Chris's competitive blood in his veins. And Chris was so competitive in his playing days that his elevation to an ICC match referee was the rough equivalent of appointing Ronnie Biggs chairman of Railtrack.

Stuart, like Chris, is not short on confidence, although it would have been interesting to see whether what was a game-turning spell at The Oval would even have taken place had England, as many thought they should have done, picked two spinners. Careers can sometimes turn on such decisions, and Broad went from being under pressure for his place to national hero in the space of around an hour.

Full marks, though, to the selectors for not going in for wholesale chopping and changing post-Headingley, something they've been as hooked on as 40-a-day smokers down the years. And full marks too to The Oval groundsman and that coin in Strauss's pocket with a tail on both sides. Bill Gordon, we are asked to believe, received no input into preparing a pitch that had apparently not been close to a watering can since 2005, in which case I must remember, when Christmas Eve comes around, to leave a mince pie and a glass of sherry out for Santa.

Would the pitch have been the same if Shane Warne had still been playing? Do me a favour. Nathan Hauritz is no Warne, but someone on the Australian team must have glanced at the playing surface before announcing their final XI, which, as we all know, is a job not entrusted to the captain. Australia had two selectors back at home, with two on the ground, and between them they managed to pick a side that was the equivalent of taking the ladder off a fire engine.

The groundsman would have been a strong contender for England's man of the series, had there not been so much competition from the umpires, and Ricky Ponting, having already received two fat lips during a fielding mishap, did well not to draw more blood from biting through his tongue when stoically declining to point the finger at the officials.

There is now a case for teams preparing a Justin Langer style dossier before a Test series. 'Billy Bowden: Don't bother appealing to the first ball of a game, as he'll still be fast asleep. Or gazing at himself in a vanity mirror.' 'Rudi Koertzen: Don't just appeal for lbw if you hit the pad, ask for bowled, stumped, caught, hit wicket, handled ball, and obstructing the field as well. He'll definitely give it out, but not for the right reason.'

The referral system will be back with us soon, and you'd have to wonder whether England would have won the Ashes

The unmistakeable figure of Billy Bowden, the New Zealand umpire who has rarely endeared himself to Australians.

had it been in operation this summer. But for pity's sake let's not include that ridiculous gadget Hawkeye in the decision-making process. Every pitch, according to Hawkeye, has identically uniform bounce, and as for its angles, well, suffice to say that when the TV technicians tried it out for a bit of fun in its early days, employing it for a ball that had actually hit the stumps, Hawkeye had it missing. You can also include, to my mind anyway, Hotspot and Snicko in the chocolate teapot variety of useless articles.

The one thing, though, that has to come soon, is some kind of automated beeping device to detect a no-ball – a bit like that service machine at Wimbledon. Umpiring is hard enough without, given the front foot rule, having to look down and then suddenly look up again, and this is one technical leg-up they should have without delay. One day, of course, all an umpire will be required to do is count up to six, although on the evidence of this series Bowden can't even manage that.

This article first appeared on the TestMatchExtra.com cricket website.

ENGLAND v. WEST INDIES
by Jonathan Agnew

A decade or two ago, the prospect of back-to-back series against West Indies would have filled any English cricketer with dread. Times have changed, though, and while at first glance the schedulers appeared to have had another brainstorm in planning two series within a couple of months of each other, the visit by West Indies to England was as a chosen replacement for Zimbabwe.

It would have provided a break for the players had the two Tests not gone ahead at all and, as it turned out, so embarrassingly demotivated were West Indies on that short trip – despite being very generously remunerated – it might have been better for all had the tour not taken place. The attitude of Chris Gayle's squad betrayed the unhappiness in the background, the influence of WIPA, the players' union, and the general malaise within West Indian cricket.

This was a great shame because, although much of the cricket in the previous series was rather dull, owing to desperately slow and flat pitches, West Indies secured a morale-boosting win to regain the Wisden Trophy. The feel-good factor should have acted as a spur to regenerate interest in the region but it was quickly lost on their return to England.

It was also a series that was marred by the final dress rehearsal of the umpires' referral system. This was such a disaster that David Richards, the man responsible for its introduction at the ICC, had to fly out for the final Test to ensure the procedures were correctly followed. From what we witnessed on this tour, it beggars belief that the ICC voted only three months later to roll it out throughout Test cricket.

England lost the series in the Caribbean because of a crazy session in the opening Test in Jamaica in which they were blown away for just 51 in their second innings. Jerome Taylor was the bowler responsible, taking 5 for 11 as England collapsed to an unbelievable 26 for 7, and they lost by an innings and 23 runs before tea on the fourth day.

Questions were again raised about the quality of England's early tour preparation, and it seems

Jerome Taylor, the West Indies fast bowler, acknowledges the applause of the crowd after England had been humbled at Sabina Park thanks mainly to his 5 for 11.

inevitable that unhappiness following the departures of Kevin Pietersen and Peter Moores as captain and coach rumbled on in the background (Pietersen made an excellent 97 in the first innings before, not for the first time, perishing while trying to hit a six for his hundred).

The Antigua Test, scheduled to take place at the Sir Vivian Richards Stadium, proved to be a dreadful embarrassment for the local board when the game had to be abandoned after only ten balls because the outfield was almost entirely a sandpit.

FIRST TEST – WEST INDIES v. ENGLAND
4–7 February 2009 at Kingston

ENGLAND

	First Innings		Second Innings	
AJ Strauss (capt)	c Ramdin b Taylor	7	c Ramdin b Taylor	9
AN Cook	c Sarwan b Powell	4	c Smith b Taylor	0
IR Bell	c Smith b Gayle	28	c Ramdin b Benn	4
KP Pietersen	c Ramdin b Benn	97	b Taylor	1
PD Collingwood	lbw b Benn	16	b Taylor	1
A Flintoff	c Nash b Powell	43	b Edwards	24
*MJ Prior	c & b Benn	64	b Taylor	0
SCJ Broad	c Benn b Taylor	4	c Marshall b Benn	0
RJ Sidebottom	not out	26	lbw b Benn	6
SJ Harmison	lbw b Taylor	7	b Benn	0
MS Panesar	lbw b Benn	0	not out	0
Extras	b 7, lb 8, nb 7	22	b 2, nb 4	6
	(all out 122.2 overs)	**318**	(all out 33.2 overs)	**51**

	First Innings				Second Innings			
	O	M	R	W	O	M	R	W
Taylor	20	4	74	3	9	4	11	5
Edwards	14	1	58	0	1	0	1	1
Powell	20	5	54	2	7	3	5	0
Benn	44.2	13	77	4	14.2	2	31	4
Gayle	24	9	40	1	2	1	1	0

Fall of Wickets
1-8, 2-31, 3-71, 4-94, 5-180, 6-241, 7-256, 8-288, 9-313
1-1, 2-11, 3-12, 4-20, 5-23, 6-23, 7-26, 8-50, 9-51

WEST INDIES

	First Innings	
CH Gayle (capt)	b Broad	104
DS Smith	lbw b Flintoff	6
RR Sarwan	b Flintoff	107
XM Marshall	lbw b Broad	0
S Chanderpaul	lbw b Broad	20
BP Nash	c Prior b Broad	55
*D Ramdin	c Collingwood b Panesar	35
JE Taylor	lbw b Harmison	8
SJ Benn	c Cook b Broad	23
DB Powell	c Prior b Harmison	9
FH Edwards	not out	10
Extras	b 6, lb 8, w 1	15
	(all out 157.4 overs)	**392**

	First Innings			
	O	M	R	W
Sidebottom	24	5	35	0
Flintoff	33	11	72	2
Harmison	20.4	4	49	2
Broad	29	7	85	5
Panesar	47	14	122	1
Pietersen	4	1	15	0

Fall of Wickets
1-18, 2-220, 3-220, 4-235, 5-254, 6-320, 7-341, 8-371, 9-376

Umpires: AL Hill (New Zealand) & RE Koertzen (South Africa)
Toss: England
Man of the Match: JE Taylor

THIRD TEST – WEST INDIES v. ENGLAND
15–19 February 2009 at St John's

ENGLAND

	First Innings		Second Innings	
AJ Strauss (capt)	c & b Edwards	169	c Smith b Edwards	14
AN Cook	c Smith b Gayle	52	c Smith b Hinds	58
OA Shah	run out	57	(4) b Powell	14
KP Pietersen	b Taylor	51	(5) c Ramdin b Benn	32
JM Anderson	c Ramdin b Edwards	4	(3) c Ramdin b Powell	20
PD Collingwood	c Smith b Hinds	113	b Hinds	34
A Flintoff	b Taylor	0	(9) c Hinds b Benn	0
*MJ Prior	c Chanderpaul b Nash	39	(7) not out	15
SCJ Broad	c Ramdin b Hinds	44	(8) run out	1
GP Swann	not out	20	(10) not out	7
SJ Harmison				
Extras	b 10, lb 1, w 1, nb 5	17	b 12, lb 3, w 5, nb 6	26
	(9 wkts dec 165.2 overs)	**566**	(8 wkts dec 50 overs)	**221**

	First Innings				Second Innings			
	O	M	R	W	O	M	R	W
Taylor	28	7	73	2	9	2	34	0
Edwards	26	2	75	2	9	1	36	1
Powell	26	3	103	0	7	0	33	2
Gayle	13	1	41	1	–	–	–	–
Benn	39	5	143	0	14	1	58	2
Hinds	22.2	4	86	2	11	1	45	2
Nash	11	3	34	1	–	–	–	–

Fall of Wickets
1-123, 2-276, 3-295, 4-311, 5-405, 6-405, 7-467, 8-529, 9-566
1-23, 2-69, 3-97, 4-145, 5-189, 6-195, 7-201, 8-206

WEST INDIES

	First Innings		Second Innings	
CH Gayle (capt)	c Anderson b Harmison	30	lbw b Swann	46
DS Smith	b Swann	38	lbw b Harmison	21
DB Powell	c Collingwood b Swann	22	(10) not out	22
RR Sarwan	c Flintoff b Swann	94	(3) b Broad	106
RO Hinds	c Prior b Flintoff	27	(4) c Shah b Broad	6
S Chanderpaul	c Prior b Broad	1	(5) c Prior b Broad	55
BP Nash	c Collingwood b Flintoff	18	(6) lbw b Swann	23
*D Ramdin	c & b Swann	0	(7) b Anderson	21
JE Taylor	c & b Flintoff	19	(8) c sub b Anderson	11
SJ Benn	lbw b Swann	0	(9) lbw b Swann	21
FH Edwards	not out	1	not out	5
Extras	b 17, lb 5, w 2, nb 11	35	b 21, lb 7, w 1, nb 4	33
	(all out 89.2 overs)	**285**	(9 wkts 128 overs)	**370**

	First Innings				Second Innings			
	O	M	R	W	O	M	R	W
Anderson	19	1	55	0	25	6	68	2
Flintoff	14.2	3	47	3	17	5	32	0
Harmison	12	3	44	1	22	3	54	1
Broad	14	4	24	1	21	3	69	3
Swann	24	7	57	5	37	12	92	3
Pietersen	2	0	14	0	3	0	15	0
Collingwood	4	0	22	0	–	–	–	–
Shah	–	–	–	–	3	0	12	0

Fall of Wickets
1-45, 2-109, 3-130, 4-200, 5-201, 6-251, 7-251, 8-278, 9-279
1-59, 2-81, 3-96, 4-244, 5-261, 6-287, 7-313, 8-322, 9-353

Umpires: DJ Harper (Australia) & RE Koertzen (South Africa)
Toss: West Indies
Man of the Match: RR Sarwan

West Indies won by an innings and 23 runs

Second Test abandoned

Match drawn

Thousands of English supporters had made the trip and, hastily, the old Recreation Ground in St John's was spruced up and, miraculously, successfully brought out of retirement only two days later. It was a great game of cricket too, with the West Indies' last pair surviving in failing light for ten overs to save the Test and protect their lead.

In all, 1,442 runs were scored in a game many feared would last only two or three days with Strauss scoring 169 and Paul Collingwood 113 in England's first innings while Ramnaresh Sarwan countered with 94. But West Indies were set 503 to win, and had already lost three wickets before the start of the final day.

Sarwan batted for 254 minutes for his match-saving 106 and Chanderpaul's 55 was eked out in four hours. Broad, Anderson and Swann kept England in the hunt, but Powell and Edwards, the two fast bowlers, urged on

Graeme Swann, the England off spinner, has a spring in his step as he bowls during the St John's Test.

FOURTH TEST – WEST INDIES v. ENGLAND
26 February–2 March 2009 at Bridgetown

ENGLAND

	First Innings				Second Innings			
AJ Strauss (capt)	b Powell			142	b Gayle			38
AN Cook	c Hinds b Taylor			94	not out			139
OA Shah	c Smith b Benn			7	lbw b Benn			21
KP Pietersen	lbw b Edwards			41	not out			72
PD Collingwood	c Nash b Edwards			96				
RS Bopara	c Taylor b Edwards			104				
*TR Ambrose	not out			76				
SCJ Broad	not out			13				
GP Swann								
RJ Sidebottom								
JM Anderson								
Extras	b 5, lb 3, w 11, nb 8			27	b 6, nb 3			9
	(6 wkts dec 153.2 overs)			**600**	(2 wkts dec 81 overs)			**279**

	First Innings				Second Innings			
	O	M	R	W	O	M	R	W
Taylor	29.2	7	107	1	4	0	15	0
Edwards	30	0	151	3	10	1	41	0
Powell	24	3	107	1	12	0	35	0
Benn	30	7	106	1	21	1	64	1
Gayle	15	4	28	0	17	5	46	1
Hinds	14	2	62	0	14	1	56	0
Nash	9	1	20	0	-	-	-	-
Sarwan	2	0	11	0	3	0	16	0

Fall of Wickets
1-229, 2-241, 3-259, 4-318, 5-467, 6-580
1-88, 2-129

WEST INDIES

	First Innings			
DS Smith	lbw b Swann			55
CH Gayle (capt)	lbw b Anderson			6
RR Sarwan	b Sidebottom			291
RO Hinds	lbw b Swann			15
S Chanderpaul	lbw b Anderson			70
BP Nash	lbw b Swann			33
*D Ramdin	b Swann			166
JE Taylor	b Swann			53
SJ Benn	c Ambrose b Anderson			14
DB Powell	not out			13
FH Edwards				
Extras	b 15, lb 11, w 1, nb 6			33
	(9 wkts dec 194.4 overs)			**749**

	First Innings			
	O	M	R	W
Anderson	37	9	125	3
Sidebottom	35	4	146	1
Broad	32	4	113	0
Swann	50.4	8	165	5
Pietersen	9	1	38	0
Bopara	13	0	66	0
Collingwood	16	1	51	0
Shah	2	0	19	0

Fall of Wickets
1-13, 2-121, 3-159, 4-281, 5-334, 6-595, 7-672, 8-701, 9-749

Umpires: Aleem Dar (Pakistan) & RB Tiffin (Zimbabwe)
Toss: England
Man of the Match: RR Sarwan

Match drawn

Andrew Strauss led from the front in the Caribbean, scoring three hundreds and topping 500 runs in the Test series against West Indies.

by a rapidly growing and enthusiastic crowd, managed to cling on in the gloom.

The Barbados Test was played to a full house, but on a featherbed which produced only 17 wickets throughout. England's 600 for 6 declared was dwarfed by West Indies' 749 for 9 and a draw (which by now West Indies were happy with) was a nailed-on certainty.

Ravi Bopara scored 104 on his return to the Test team and Strauss scored another hundred, but Edwards apart, no bowler on either side could make an impression. Sarwan compiled a brilliant 291 from 452 balls, but this was overshadowed by a number of inconsistencies in the use of the referral system that by now had lost credibility with all but the ICC.

It was clear that West Indies were determined to do no more than play for a draw in the final Test in Port of Spain when they left out their spinner, Sulieman Benn, for Lendl Simmons, a batsman: England would have to do all the chasing to salvage the series, and they got within two wickets of doing so. Again Strauss led the way with 142; Collingwood scored 161 and Prior 131 not out, enabling a declaration 19 overs before the close of the second day on 546 for 6. Even Gayle was painstaking in reply, making 102 in 170 balls and Chanderpaul 147 as West Indies came within two runs on first innings.

England had to bat swiftly to set up a declaration and Pietersen stepped in with his first hundred of the tour. West Indies were set 240 to win from 66 overs – generous, and it preyed on their defensive mindset to the extent that they inexplicably slipped to 90 for 6. A hamstring injury prevented Gayle from batting until No. 8, and he was swiftly lbw to Panesar, but Nash and Edwards stood firm for eight overs to secure the Wisden Trophy for the West Indies after nine years in English hands.

England won the one-day series 3-2, not least because of a mental block in the opening game by West Indies' coach John Dyson. He miscalculated the Duckworth-Lewis par score, and ordered his batsmen from the crease one run too soon, to much amusement all round.

In no time, it seemed, the teams were facing each other again in conditions that were simply too cold to give Test cricketers a fair chance. This might also have affected the

AGGERS' VIEW

'Assuming the England captaincy has had a dramatic effect on Strauss the batsman, which has been very good news indeed for the whole team. There were signs of his batting form going up a level or two in India before Christmas, but in the Caribbean against the West Indies he really flourished and his authority at the top of the order was one of the main reasons for England's Ashes success. There are areas of his captaincy that can still be improved – he was far too cautious in his approach in the West Indies, for example – but he is very bright, very personable and his players will be very loyal to him. Winning the Ashes will develop him hugely as a captain, of course, and what is also important to him now is that his development into an outstanding batsman has meant that there is no argument about his place in England's ODI side either. That's a big plus for Strauss, going forward.'

FIFTH TEST – WEST INDIES v. ENGLAND
6–10 March 2009 at Port of Spain

SERIES AVERAGES
West Indies v. England

ENGLAND

	First Innings		Second Innings	
AJ Strauss (capt)	b Edwards	142	c & b Gayle	14
AN Cook	c Ramdin b Powell	12	c Ramdin b Hinds	24
OA Shah	run out	33	c Ramdin b Baker	1
KP Pietersen	b Hinds	10	c sub b Edwards	102
PD Collingwood	lbw b Baker	161	c & b Hinds	9
*MJ Prior	not out	131	b Baker	61
SCJ Broad	c Simmons b Baker	19	not out	13
GP Swann	not out	11		
A Khan				
JM Anderson				
MS Panesar				
Extras	b 8, lb 7, w 1, nb 11	27	b 5, lb 3, w 1, nb 4	13
	(6 wkts dec 158.5 overs)	546	(6 wkts dec 38.4 overs)	237

	First Innings				Second Innings			
	O	M	R	W	O	M	R	W
Edwards	24	5	63	1	11.4	1	67	1
Powell	16	1	79	1	-	-	-	-
Baker	23	4	77	2	8	1	39	2
Nash	23	3	77	0	3	0	21	0
Gayle	26	1	80	0	3	0	16	1
Hinds	39.5	2	126	1	8	0	57	2
Smith	1	0	3	0	-	-	-	-
Simmons	6	0	26	0	5	0	29	0

Fall of Wickets
1-26, 2-156, 3-263, 4-268, 5-486, 6-530
1-26, 2-27, 3-72, 4-101, 5-207, 6-237

WEST INDIES

	First Innings		Second Innings	
CH Gayle (capt)	c Strauss b Swann	102	(8) lbw b Panesar	4
DS Smith	b Panesar	28	(1) lbw b Swann	17
DB Powell	c Pietersen b Broad	0	(9) b Anderson	0
RR Sarwan	lbw b Khan	14	(3) c Collingwood b Swann	14
LMP Simmons	b Panesar	24	(2) c Collingwood b Anderson	8
S Chanderpaul	not out	147	(5) lbw b Swann	6
BP Nash	c Collingwood b Broad	109	(6) lbw b Anderson	1
RO Hinds	st Prior b Swann	23	(4) c Collingwood b Panesar	20
*D Ramdin	lbw b Anderson	15	(7) not out	17
FH Edwards	c Prior b Broad	8	not out	1
LS Baker	lbw b Swann	0		
Extras	b 35, lb 12, w 11, nb 16	74	b 17, lb 6, w 1, nb 2	26
	(all out 178.4 overs)	544	(8 wkts 65.5 overs)	114

	First Innings				Second Innings			
	O	M	R	W	O	M	R	W
Anderson	32	7	70	1	16	7	24	3
Broad	30	11	67	3	5	3	9	0
Khan	25	1	111	1	4	0	11	0
Swann	45.4	12	130	3	21	13	13	3
Panesar	43	6	114	2	19.5	9	34	2
Pietersen	3	0	5	0	-	-	-	-

Fall of Wickets
1-90, 2-96, 3-118, 4-203, 5-437, 6-482, 7-519, 8-526, 9-543
1-25, 2-31, 3-58, 4-80, 5-85, 6-90, 7-107, 8-109

Umpires: DJ Harper (Australia) & RB Tiffin (Zimbabwe)
Toss: England
Test debuts: A Khan, LMP Simmons
Man of the Match: MJ Prior
Man of the Series: RR Sarwan

Match drawn

West Indies won series 1–0

WEST INDIES

Batting	M	Inns	NO	Runs	HS	Av	100	50	c/st
RR Sarwan	5	6	0	626	291	104.33	3	1	1/-
S Chanderpaul	5	6	1	299	147*	59.80	1	2	1/-
D Ramdin	5	6	1	254	166	50.80	1	-	11/-
CH Gayle	5	6	0	292	104	48.66	2	-	1/-
BP Nash	5	6	0	239	109	39.83	1	1	2/-
DS Smith	5	6	0	165	55	27.50	-	1	7/-
FH Edwards	5	5	4	25	10*	25.00	-	-	1/-
JE Taylor	4	4	0	91	53	22.75	-	1	1/-
RO Hinds	4	5	0	91	27	18.20	-	-	3/-
DB Powell	5	6	2	66	22*	16.50	-	-	-/-
LMP Simmons	1	2	0	32	24	16.00	-	-	1/-
SJ Benn	4	4	0	58	23	14.50	-	-	2/-
XM Marshall	1	1	0	0	0	0.00	-	-	1/-
LS Baker	1	1	0	0	0	0.00	-	-	-/-

Bowling	Overs	Mds	Runs	Wkts	Av	Best	5/inn	10m
JE Taylor	100.2	24	319	11	29.00	5-11	1	-
LS Baker	31	5	116	4	29.00	2-39	-	-
SJ Benn	162.4	29	479	12	39.91	4-31	-	-
FH Edwards	126.2	11	494	9	54.88	3-151	-	-
RO Hinds	109.1	10	432	7	61.71	2-45	-	-
CH Gayle	100	21	252	4	63.00	1-16	-	-
DB Powell	112	15	416	6	69.33	2-33	-	-
BP Nash	46	6	152	1	152.00	1-34	-	-

Also bowled: DS Smith 1-0-3-0, RR Sarwan 5-0-27-0, LMP Simmons 11-0-55-0.

ENGLAND

Batting	M	Inns	NO	Runs	HS	Av	100	50	c/st
RS Bopara	1	1	0	104	104	104.00	1	-	-/-
MJ Prior	4	6	2	310	131*	77.50	1	2	6/1
AJ Strauss	5	9	1	541	169	67.62	3	-	1/-
PD Collingwood	5	7	0	430	161	61.42	2	1	7/-
KP Pietersen	5	8	1	406	102	58.00	1	3	1/-
AN Cook	5	9	2	384	139*	54.85	1	3	1/-
RJ Sidebottom	3	2	1	32	26*	32.00	-	-	-/-
OA Shah	4	6	0	133	57	22.16	-	1	1/-
SCJ Broad	5	7	2	94	44	18.80	-	-	-/-
A Flintoff	3	4	0	67	43	16.75	-	-	2/-
IR Bell	1	2	0	32	28	16.00	-	-	-/-
JM Anderson	4	2	0	24	20	12.00	-	-	1/-
SJ Harmison	2	3	1	14	7*	7.00	-	-	-/-
MS Panesar	3	2	1	0	0*	0.00	-	-	-/-
TR Ambrose	1	1	1	76	76*	-	-	1	1/-
GP Swann	3	2	2	31	20*	-	-	-	1/-
A Khan	1	0	0	0	0	-	-	-	-/-

Bowling	Overs	Mds	Runs	Wkts	Av	Best	5/inn	10m
GP Swann	178.2	52	457	19	24.05	5-57	2	-
A Flintoff	64.2	19	151	5	30.20	3-47	-	-
SCJ Broad	131	32	367	12	30.58	5-85	1	-
SJ Harmison	54.4	10	147	4	36.75	2-49	-	-
JM Anderson	129	30	342	9	38.00	3-24	-	-
MS Panesar	109.5	29	270	5	54.00	2-34	-	-
A Khan	29	1	122	1	122.00	1-111	-	-
RJ Sidebottom	59	9	181	1	181.00	1-146	-	-

Also bowled: OA Shah 5-0-31-0, RS Bopara 13-0-66-0, PD Collingwood 20-1-73-0.

diffident approach of the West Indies tourists who succumbed meekly in both Tests and also lost an utterly forgettable rain-affected one-day series 2-0.

The one success story was Bopara, who gave chances along the way but, nevertheless, scored centuries at No. 3 in each Test. At Lord's he made 143 in England's 377 and Graham Onions took 5 for 38 and 2 for 64 as West Indies scored only 152 and 256 to give England a ten-wicket victory.

At Chester-le-Street (of all venues in mid-May) Bopara scored 108 and Cook 160 as England racked up 569 for 6. Anderson's 5 for 87 condemned the distracted tourists to the follow-on, and they fell in a heap on the final day to lose by an innings and 83 runs.

After initially launching a staunch defence of the timing of this series, the ECB later announced that it would not happen again. We shall see.

ONE-DAY INTERNATIONALS

Match One
20 March 2009 at Guyana
England 270 for 7 (50 overs) (PD Collingwood 69, OA Shah 62)
West Indies 244 for 7 (46.2 overs) (LMP Simmons 62, RR Sarwan 57, SCJ Broad 3 for 41)
England won by 1 run – DL Method: target 246 from 46.2 overs

Match Two
22 March 2009 at Guyana
West Indies 264 for 8 (50 overs) (S Chanderpaul 112*, RR Sarwan 74, JM Anderson 3 for 38, PD Collingwood 3 for 49)
England 243 all out (48.2 overs) (AJ Strauss 105)
West Indies won by 21 runs

Match Three
27 March 2009 at Bridgetown
England 117 all out (41.3 overs)
(DJ Bravo 4 for 19, FH Edwards 3 for 28)
West Indies 117 for 2 (14.4 overs) (CH Gayle 80)
West Indies won by 8 wickets – DL Method: target 117 from 44 overs

Match Four
29 March 2009 at Bridgetown
West Indies 239 for 9 (50 overs) (DJ Bravo 69, AD Mascarenhas 3 for 26, SCJ Broad 3 for 62)
England 136 for 1 (18.3 overs) (AJ Strauss 79*)
England won by 9 wickets – DL Method: target 135 from 20 overs

Match Five
3 April 2009 at Gros Islet
England 172 for 5 (29 overs)
West Indies 146 all out (28 overs)
(A Flintoff 5 for 19)
England won by 26 runs
England won the series 3–2

Ravi Bopara enjoyed a golden run of form for England against West Indies: in three Tests, first in the Caribbean and then in the return series at home, he scored 104, 143 and 108 in consecutive innings.

FIRST TEST – ENGLAND v. WEST INDIES
6–8 May 2009 at Lord's

ENGLAND

	First Innings		Second Innings	
AJ Strauss (capt)	c Ramdin b Taylor	16	not out	14
AN Cook	b Edwards	35	not out	14
RS Bopara	c Nash b Taylor	143		
KP Pietersen	c Ramdin b Edwards	0		
PD Collingwood	c Smith b Edwards	8		
*MJ Prior	c Simmons b Edwards	42		
SCJ Broad	c Taylor b Benn	38		
G Onions	lbw b Benn	9		
GP Swann	not out	63		
JM Anderson	c Ramdin b Edwards	1		
TT Bresnan	b Edwards	0		
Extras	b 1, lb 5, w 7, nb 9	22	nb 4	4
	(all out 111.3 overs)	377	(0 wkts 6.1 overs)	32

	First Innings				Second Innings			
	O	M	R	W	O	M	R	W
Taylor	24	2	83	2	3	0	20	0
Edwards	26.3	4	92	6	3.1	0	12	0
Baker	24	5	75	0	-	-	-	-
Benn	27	4	84	2	-	-	-	-
Nash	2	1	2	0	-	-	-	-
Simmons	5	1	24	0	-	-	-	-
Gayle	3	0	11	0	-	-	-	-

Fall of Wickets
1-28, 2-92, 3-92, 4-109, 5-193, 6-262, 7-275, 8-368, 9-377

WEST INDIES

	First Innings		Second Innings (following on)	
CH Gayle (capt)	b Broad	28	c Swann b Anderson	0
DS Smith	b Swann	46	b Onions	41
RR Sarwan	c Prior b Broad	13	b Anderson	1
LMP Simmons	c Strauss b Onions	16	c Cook b Onions	21
S Chanderpaul	c Collingwood b Swann	0	c Bopara b Swann	4
BP Nash	c Collingwood b Swann	4	c Cook b Broad	81
*D Ramdin	lbw b Onions	5	b Broad	61
JE Taylor	c Prior b Onions	0	lbw b Swann	15
SJ Benn	c Swann b Onions	2	b Swann	0
FH Edwards	not out	10	c Onions b Broad	2
LS Baker	lbw b Onions	17	not out	2
Extras	lb 10, w 1	11	b 8, lb 18, w 2	28
	(all out 32.3 overs)	152	(all out 72.2 overs)	256

	First Innings				Second Innings			
	O	M	R	W	O	M	R	W
Broad	11	0	56	2	19.2	2	64	3
Swann	5	2	16	3	17	4	39	3
Anderson	7	0	32	0	15	6	38	2
Onions	9.3	1	38	5	12	2	64	2
Bresnan	-	-	-	-	7	3	17	0
Bopara	-	-	-	-	2	0	8	0

Fall of Wickets
1-46, 2-70, 3-99, 4-99, 5-117, 6-117, 7-117, 8-119, 9-128
1-14, 2-22, 3-70, 4-75, 5-79, 6-222, 7-243, 8-246, 9-249

Umpires: SJ Davis (Australia) & EAR de Silva (Sri Lanka)
Toss: West Indies
Test debuts: TT Bresnan & G Onions
Man of the Match: GP Swann

England won by 10 wickets

SECOND TEST – ENGLAND v. WEST INDIES
14–18 May 2009 at the Riverside

ENGLAND

	First Innings	
AJ Strauss (capt)	c Ramdin b Gayle	26
AN Cook	c Gayle b Benn	160
RS Bopara	b Baker	108
JM Anderson	b Edwards	14
KP Pietersen	c Simmons b Benn	49
PD Collingwood	not out	60
*MJ Prior	c Benn b Simmons	63
SCJ Broad	not out	28
TT Bresnan		
GP Swann		
G Onions		
Extras	b 20, lb 5, w 8, nb 28	61
	(6 wkts dec 147 overs)	569

	First Innings			
	O	M	R	W
Taylor	20	2	68	0
Edwards	25	1	113	1
Baker	30	3	119	1
Gayle	14	2	31	1
Benn	43	8	146	2
Simmons	14	0	60	1
Sarwan	1	0	7	0

Fall of Wickets
1-69, 2-282, 3-326, 4-410, 5-419, 6-513

WEST INDIES

	First Innings		Second Innings (following on)	
DS Smith	b Anderson	7	lbw b Swann	11
CH Gayle (capt)	lbw b Anderson	19	c Strauss b Onions	54
RR Sarwan	c Bresnan b Broad	100	lbw b Onions	22
LMP Simmons	c Strauss b Anderson	8	c sub b Anderson	10
S Chanderpaul	c Prior b Broad	23	c Collingwood b Anderson	47
BP Nash	c Swann b Anderson	10	c sub b Bresnan	1
*D Ramdin	c Swann b Anderson	55	c Anderson b Bresnan	0
JE Taylor	lbw b Onions	10	b Anderson	5
SJ Benn	run out	35	b Anderson	0
FH Edwards	c Strauss b Broad	11	c sub b Bresnan	4
LS Baker	not out	0	not out	4
Extras	b 2, lb 21, w 2, nb 7	32	b 8, lb 5, w 5	18
	(all out 84.3 overs)	310	(all out 44 overs)	176

	First Innings				Second Innings			
	O	M	R	W	O	M	R	W
Anderson	26.3	5	87	5	16	5	38	4
Broad	16	2	62	3	5	1	21	0
Onions	18	6	52	1	6	0	46	2
Bresnan	10	2	35	0	14	2	45	3
Swann	14	4	51	0	3	0	13	1

Fall of Wickets
1-18, 2-38, 3-68, 4-167, 5-188, 6-205, 7-216, 8-286, 9-310
1-53, 2-88, 3-89, 4-141, 5-142, 6-146, 7-163, 8-167, 9-168

Umpires: SJ Davis (Australia) & EAR de Silva (Sri Lanka)
Toss: England
Man of the Match: JM Anderson
Men of the Series: RS Bopara & FH Edwards

England won by an innings and 83 runs

England won series 2–0

SERIES AVERAGES
England v. West Indies

ENGLAND

Batting	M	Inns	NO	Runs	HS	Av	100	50	c/st
RS Bopara	2	2	0	251	143	125.50	2	–	1/–
AN Cook	2	3	1	209	160	104.50	1	–	2/–
PD Collingwood	2	2	1	68	60*	68.00	–	1	3/–
SCJ Broad	2	2	1	66	38	66.00	–	–	–/–
MJ Prior	2	2	0	105	63	52.50	–	1	3/–
AJ Strauss	2	3	1	56	26	28.00	–	–	4/–
KP Pietersen	2	2	0	49	49	24.50	–	–	–/–
G Onions	2	1	0	9	9	9.00	–	–	1/–
JM Anderson	2	2	0	15	14	7.50	–	–	1/–
TT Bresnan	2	1	0	0	0	0.00	–	–	1/–
GP Swann	2	1	1	63	63*	–	–	1	3/–

Bowling	Overs	Mds	Runs	Wkts	Av	Best	5/inn	10m
GP Swann	39	10	119	7	17.00	3-16	–	–
JM Anderson	64.3	16	195	11	17.72	5-87	1	–
G Onions	45.3	7	182	10	18.20	5-38	1	–
SCJ Broad	51.2	5	203	8	25.37	3-62	–	–
TT Bresnan	31	9	115	3	38.33	2-46	–	–

Also bowled: RS Bopara 2-0-8-0.

WEST INDIES

Batting	M	Inns	NO	Runs	HS	Av	100	50	c/st
RR Sarwan	2	4	0	136	100	34.00	1	–	–/–
D Ramdin	2	4	0	121	61	30.25	–	2	4/–
DS Smith	2	4	0	105	46	26.25	–	–	1/–
CH Gayle	2	4	0	101	54	25.25	–	1	1/–
BP Nash	2	4	0	96	81	24.00	–	1	1/–
LS Baker	2	4	3	23	17	23.00	–	–	–/–
S Chanderpaul	2	4	0	74	47	18.50	–	–	1/–
LMP Simmons	2	4	0	55	21	13.75	–	–	2/–
SJ Benn	2	4	0	37	35	9.25	–	–	1/–
FH Edwards	2	4	1	27	11	9.00	–	–	–/–
JE Taylor	2	4	0	30	15	7.50	–	–	1/–

Bowling	Overs	Mds	Runs	Wkts	Av	Best	5/inn	10m
FH Edwards	54.4	5	217	7	31.00	6-92	1	–
CH Gayle	17	2	42	1	42.00	1-31	–	–
SJ Benn	70	12	230	4	57.50	2-84	–	–
LMP Simmons	19	1	84	1	84.00	1-60	–	–
JE Taylor	47	4	171	2	85.50	2-83	–	–
LS Baker	54	8	194	1	194.00	1-119	–	–

Also bowled: BP Nash 2-1-2-0, RR Sarwan 1-0-7-0.

ONE-DAY INTERNATIONALS

Match One
24 May 2009 at Bristol
West Indies 160 all out (38.3 overs) (DJ Bravo 50, SCJ Broad 4 for 46, PD Collingwood 3 for 16)
England 161 for 4 (36 overs)
England won by 6 wickets

Match Two
21 May 2009 at Headingley
England v. **West Indies**
Match abandoned

Match Three
26 May 2009 at Edgbaston
England 328 for 7 (50 overs) (MJ Prior 87, OA Shah 75, AJ Strauss 52, JE Taylor 3 for 59)
West Indies 270 all out (49.4 overs) (S Chanderpaul 68, JM Anderson 3 for 58)
England won by 58 runs
England won the series 2–0

OTHER WEST INDIES TOUR MATCHES

20–22 April 2009 at Grace Road
Leicestershire 182 all out (62.3 overs) (AP Richardson 3 for 46, SJ Benn 4 for 31)
& 238 for 6 (91 overs) (MAG Boyce 55, JJ Cobb 53)
West Indians 320 for 6 dec (99.5 overs) (LMP Simmons 102rh, BP Nash 78rh, ACF Wyatt 3 for 42)
Match drawn

25–27 April 2009 at Chelmsford
Essex 263 all out (80.2 overs) (V Chopra 50, JC Mickleburgh 58, N Deonarine 3 for 32)
& 175 for 3 (47 overs) (AN Cook 74*)
West Indians 146 all out (44.1 overs) (S Chanderpaul 66*, MS Westfield 3 for 25, MA Chambers 4 for 62)
Match drawn

30 April–2 May 2009 at Derby
West Indians 203 all out (64 overs) (DE Bernard 58, CR Woakes 6 for 43)
& 179 all out (45.1 overs) (LMP Simmons 63, S Chanderpaul 50, AU Rashid 3 for 66, LE Plunkett 4 for 30)
England Lions 311 all out (72.5 overs) (TR Ambrose 117, AU Rashid 72, JE Taylor 3 for 54, NT Pascal 4 for 68)
& 72 for 0 (9.5 overs)
England Lions won by 10 wickets

ENGLAND IN INDIA
by Jonathan Agnew

England's visit to India before Christmas was interrupted in the most dramatic and appalling circumstances by the terrorist attacks on Mumbai (Bombay) and the Taj Mahal hotel, in particular. This was England's traditional base in the city, which they had visited only a couple of weeks previously and where they were due to stay again later on the tour. Their Test match outfits – whites and blazers – were being stored in the hotel at the time.

The graphic images shown repeatedly on the increasingly hysterical and confusing television news channels shocked the team and the travelling media to the core. Although the tourists were on the other side

of India at the time of the attack, there was no sensible alternative but for the players to return home.

Given everything, it seemed most unlikely that they would return. This was now just weeks before Christmas, the one-day series had been little short of humiliating (India led 5-0 at the time) and there would be no time to prepare properly for Test cricket. I don't think anyone seriously believed that the team was a target (the attack on the Sri Lankan team in Lahore had not yet taken place) but security was an issue, and something that had to be sorted out if there was to be any chance of England returning.

After much discussion, cajoling and reassuring, it was agreed to a man that England would return to play two rescheduled Tests at Chennai (Madras) and Mohali. There was little time to practice, although they had a few days in Abu Dhabi while the final preparations were made, and the decision was widely and sincerely applauded and admired.

Two weeks after the attack, England captain Kevin Pietersen won the toss in the centre of a stadium swamped by machine-gun toting Special Forces and surrounded by armoured vehicles. Blue anti-riot nets

Paul Collingwood square cuts on his way to a fine hundred against India on the fourth day of the Chennai Test.

Monty Panesar, the England left-arm spinner, had a tough time of it on his second tour of India.

were hanging between the spectators and the field of play, seriously obscuring the view. It was enough to get the game on, but is this really the way Test cricket might be played from now on?

Undeterred, Andrew Strauss compiled a patient 123 as England scored 316 while an understandably distracted Indian team managed only 241 in reply. The question of whether they should be playing cricket at such a time, meanwhile, was being widely played out in the media. England's spirited effort continued as Strauss hit his second hundred of the match, and Paul Collingwood 108, to leave India 387 to win in four sessions – no team had ever scored 300 in the final innings to win a Test in India.

But Virender Sehwag continued his outstanding form from the one-day internationals to hit a breathtaking 50 from only 32 balls. By the close, India were 131 for 1 and needed only 256 more to win – Sehwag's 83 came from 68 balls, including four sixes and eleven fours.

The key battle on the last day was between Monty Panesar and Sachin Tendulkar on a pitch giving some assistance to the spinner, but the combination of poor fields, metronomic and predictable bowling and Tendulkar's brilliance and motivation, led to India achieving the unthinkable and securing the fourth highest fourth innings run chase in the history of Test cricket.

It had been a wonderful match, which more than succeeded in giving the grieving Indian nation something else to think about. That a Mumbaiker – indeed, Bombay's favourite son, Tendulkar – scored a hundred to win the game was entirely fitting and more than anyone could possibly have asked for.

Little surprise, then, that the Second Test in Mohali was an anticlimax. To play a Test so far north in winter was due entirely to the circumstances and, every morning, a choking thick fog meant lengthy delays. India had no interest in winning the game either, which had they batted with greater intent in their second innings, they might well have done.

Gautam Gambhir and Rahul Dravid both hit hundreds as India scored 453 in their first innings, which spanned two days, and England replied with 302, with Pietersen hitting an outstanding 144. But he and Andrew Flintoff (62) both fell in the dying moments of the third day to set up the opportunity for India to press on which, sadly, they chose to ignore. Indeed, to set England 403 to win from 43 overs, having taken 73 overs to reach their total of 251 for 7, was absurd, and entirely failed to appreciate the sprit in which this tour had been undertaken.

In the background, meanwhile, Pietersen was already calling meetings with the ECB to discuss what he perceived England's way forward to be – a future without Peter Moores, the coach, and Andy Flower, the batting coach. Just a fortnight later, Pietersen was to discover that, in fact, England's future did not include him continuing as captain, and his reign of just three Tests was brought abruptly to a halt.

ONE-DAY INTERNATIONALS

Match One
14 November 2008 at Rajkot
India 387 for 5 (50 overs) (Yuvraj Singh 138*, V Sehwag 85, G Gambhir 51)
England 229 all out (37.4 overs) (KP Pietersen 63, RS Bopara 54*, Zaheer Khan 3 for 26)
India won by 158 runs

Match Two
17 November 2008 at Indore
India 292 for 9 (50 overs) (Yuvraj Singh 118, G Gambhir 70, YK Pathan 50*, SCJ Broad 4 for 55)
England 238 all out (47 overs) (OA Shah 58, Yuvraj Singh 4 for 28, V Sehwag 3 for 28)
India won by 54 runs

Match Three

20 November 2008 at Kanpur
England 240 all out (48.4 overs) (RS Bopara 60,
Harbhajan Singh 3 for 31)
India 198 for 5 (40 overs) (V Sehwag 68, A Flintoff 3 for 31)
India won by 16 runs – DL Method: target 183 from 40 overs

Match Four

23 November 2008 Day/Night at Bangalore
India 166 for 4 (22 overs) (V Sehwag 69)
England 178 for 8 (22 overs) (OA Shah 72)
India won by 19 runs – DL Method: target 198 from 22 overs

Match Five

26 November 2008 Day/Night at Cuttack
England 270 for 4 (50 overs) (KP Pietersen 111*, OA Shah 66*)
India 273 for 4 (43.4 overs) (V Sehwag 91, SK Raina 53*,
SR Tendulkar 50, MS Dhoni 50)
India won by 6 wickets
India won the series 5–0

Kevin Pietersen's 111 not out in the fifth one-day international at Cuttack was not enough to prevent England from going 5-0 down in the series.

FIRST TEST – INDIA v. ENGLAND
11–15 December 2008 at Chennai

ENGLAND

	First Innings		Second Innings	
AJ Strauss	c & b Mishra	123	c Laxman b Harbhajan Singh	108
AN Cook	c Zaheer Khan b Harbhajan Singh	52	c Dhoni b Sharma	9
IR Bell	lbw b Zaheer Khan	17	c Gambhir b Mishra	7
KP Pietersen (capt)	c & b Zaheer Khan	4	lbw b Yuvraj Singh	1
PD Collingwood	c Gambhir b Harbhajan Singh	9	lbw b Zaheer Khan	108
A Flintoff	c Gambhir b Mishra	18	c Dhoni b Sharma	4
JM Anderson	c Yuvraj Singh b Mishra	19	(10) not out	1
*MJ Prior	not out	53	(7) c Sehwag b Sharma	33
GP Swann	c Dravid b Harbhajan Singh	1	(8) b Zaheer Khan	7
SJ Harmison	c Dhoni b Yuvraj Singh	6	(9) b Zaheer Khan	1
MS Panesar	lbw b Sharma	6		
Extras	lb 7, nb 1	8	b 10, lb 13, w 2, nb 7	32
	(all out 128.4 overs)	316	(9 wkts dec 105.5 overs)	311

	First Innings				Second Innings			
	O	M	R	W	O	M	R	W
Zaheer Khan	21	9	41	2	27	7	40	3
Sharma	19.4	4	32	1	22.5	1	57	3
Harbhajan Singh	38	2	96	3	30	3	91	1
Mishra	34	6	99	3	17	1	66	1
Yuvraj Singh	15	2	33	1	3	1	12	1
Sehwag	1	0	8	0	6	0	22	0

Fall of Wickets
1-118, 2-164, 3-180, 4-195, 5-221, 6-229, 7-271, 8-277, 9-304
1-28, 2-42, 3-43, 4-257, 5-262, 6-277, 7-297, 8-301, 9-311

INDIA

	First Innings		Second Innings	
G Gambhir	lbw b Swann	19	c Collingwood b Anderson	66
V Sehwag	b Anderson	9	lbw b Swann	83
R Dravid	lbw b Swann	3	c Prior b Flintoff	4
SR Tendulkar	c & b Flintoff	37	not out	103
VVS Laxman	c & b Panesar	24	c Bell b Swann	26
Yuvraj Singh	c Flintoff b Harmison	14	not out	85
*MS Dhoni (capt)	c Pietersen b Panesar	53		
Harbhajan Singh	c Bell b Panesar	40		
Zaheer Khan	lbw b Flintoff	1		
A Mishra	b Flintoff	12		
I Sharma	not out	8		
Extras	b 4, lb 11, nb 6	21	b 4, lb 12, nb 4	20
	(all out 69.4 overs)	241	(4 wkts 98.3 overs)	387

	First Innings				Second Innings			
	O	M	R	W	O	M	R	W
Harmison	11	1	42	1	10	0	48	0
Anderson	11	3	28	1	11	1	51	1
Flintoff	18.4	2	49	3	22	1	64	1
Swann	10	0	42	2	28.3	2	103	2
Panesar	19	4	65	3	27	4	105	0

Fall of Wickets
1-16, 2-34, 3-37, 4-98, 5-102, 6-137, 7-212, 8-217, 9-219
1-117, 2-141, 3-183, 4-224

Umpires: BF Bowden (New Zealand) & DJ Harper (Australia)
Toss: England
Test debut: GP Swann
Man of the Match: V Sehwag

India won by 6 wickets

SECOND TEST – INDIA v. ENGLAND
19–23 December 2008 at Mohali

SERIES AVERAGES
India v. England

INDIA

	First Innings			Second Innings	
G Gambhir	c Cook b Swann	179	c Bell b Swann	97
V Sehwag	c Prior b Broad	0	run out	17
R Dravid	c Panesar b Swann	136	b Broad	0
SR Tendulkar	lbw b Swann	11	c Swann b Anderson	5
VVS Laxman	lbw b Flintoff	0	run out	15
Yuvraj Singh	c Prior b Panesar	27	run out	86
*MS Dhoni (capt)	c sub b Anderson	29	c & b Panesar	0
Harbhajan Singh	c Swann b Panesar	24	not out	5
Zaheer Khan	b Flintoff	7		
A Mishra	b Flintoff	23		
I Sharma	not out	1		
Extras	b 5, lb 5, nb 6	16	b 10, lb 8, w 5, nb 3	26
	(all out 158.2 overs)	453	(7 wkts dec 73 overs)	251

	First Innings				Second Innings			
	O	M	R	W	O	M	R	W
Anderson	32	5	84	1	19	8	51	1
Broad	26	9	84	1	14	2	50	1
Flintoff	30.2	10	54	3	13	1	39	0
Panesar	23	2	89	2	10	0	44	1
Swann	45	11	122	3	17	3	49	1
Collingwood	2	0	10	0	–	–	–	–

Fall of Wickets
1-6, 2-320, 3-329, 4-337, 5-339, 6-379, 7-418, 8-418, 9-446
1-30, 2-36, 3-44, 4-80, 5-233, 6-241, 7-251

ENGLAND

	First Innings			Second Innings	
AJ Strauss	lbw b Zaheer Khan	0	not out	21
AN Cook	lbw b Zaheer Khan	50	c Laxman b Sharma	10
IR Bell	b Sharma	1	not out	24
KP Pietersen (capt)	lbw b Harbhajan Singh	144		
PD Collingwood	c Dhoni b Mishra	11		
A Flintoff	c Gambhir b Mishra	62		
JM Anderson	not out	8		
*MJ Prior	c Dhoni b Harbhajan Singh	2		
SCJ Broad	b Harbhajan Singh	1		
GP Swann	b Zaheer Khan	3		
MS Panesar	c Gambhir b Harbhajan Singh	5		
Extras	b 1, lb 7, w 1, nb 6	15	b 4, w 1, nb 4	9
	(all out 83.5 overs)	302	(1 wkt 28 overs)	64

	First Innings				Second Innings			
	O	M	R	W	O	M	R	W
Zaheer Khan	21	3	76	3	3	0	11	0
Sharma	12	0	55	1	5	1	7	1
Yuvraj Singh	6	1	20	0	–	–	–	–
Harbhajan Singh	20.5	2	68	4	11	3	25	0
Mishra	24	0	75	2	8	1	16	0
Dhoni	–	–	–	–	1	0	1	0

Fall of Wickets
1-0, 2-1, 3-104, 4-131, 5-280, 6-282, 7-285, 8-290, 9-293
1-18

Umpires: Asad Rauf (Pakistan) & DJ Harper (Australia)
Toss: India
Man of the Match: G Gambhir
Man of the Series: Zaheer Khan

Match drawn

India won series 1–0

INDIA

Batting	M	Inns	NO	Runs	HS	Av	100	50	c/st
G Gambhir	2	4	0	361	179	90.25	1	2	5/-
Yuvraj Singh	2	4	1	212	86	70.66	-	2	1/-
SR Tendulkar	2	4	1	156	103*	52.00	1	-	-/-
R Dravid	2	4	0	143	136	35.75	1	-	1/-
Harbhajan Singh	2	3	1	69	40	34.50	-	-	-/-
MS Dhoni	2	3	0	82	53	27.33	-	1	5/-
V Sehwag	2	4	0	109	83	27.25	-	1	1/-
A Mishra	2	2	0	35	23	17.50	-	-	1/-
VVS Laxman	2	4	0	65	26	16.25	-	-	2/-
Zaheer Khan	2	2	0	8	7	4.00	-	-	2/-
I Sharma	2	2	2	9	8*	-	-	-	-/-

Bowling	Overs	Mds	Runs	Wkts	Av	Best	5/inn	10m
Zaheer Khan	72	19	168	8	21.00	3-40	-	-
I Sharma	59.3	6	151	6	25.16	3-57	-	-
Yuvraj Singh	24	4	65	2	32.50	1-12	-	-
Harbhajan Singh	99.5	10	280	8	35.00	4-68	-	-
A Mishra	83	8	256	6	42.66	3-99	-	-

Also bowled: MS Dhoni 1-0-1-0, V Sehwag 7-0-30-0.

ENGLAND

Batting	M	Inns	NO	Runs	HS	Av	100	50	c/st
AJ Strauss	2	4	1	252	123	84.00	2	-	-/-
KP Pietersen	2	3	0	149	144	49.66	1	-	1/-
MJ Prior	2	3	1	88	53*	44.00	-	1	3/-
PD Collingwood	2	3	0	128	108	42.66	1	-	1/-
AN Cook	2	4	0	121	52	30.25	-	2	1/-
A Flintoff	2	3	0	84	62	28.00	-	1	2/-
JM Anderson	2	3	2	28	19	28.00	-	-	-/-
IR Bell	2	4	1	49	24*	16.33	-	-	3/-
MS Panesar	2	2	0	11	6	5.50	-	-	3/-
GP Swann	2	3	0	11	7	3.66	-	-	2/-
SJ Harrison	1	2	0	7	6	3.50	-	-	-/-
SCJ Broad	1	1	0	1	1	1.00	-	-	-/-

Bowling	Overs	Mds	Runs	Wkts	Av	Best	5/inn	10m
A Flintoff	84	14	206	7	29.42	3-49	-	-
GP Swann	100.3	16	316	8	39.50	3-122	-	-
MS Panesar	79	10	303	6	50.50	3-65	-	-
JM Anderson	73	17	214	4	53.50	1-28	-	-
SCJ Broad	40	11	134	2	67.00	1-50	-	-
SJ Harrison	21	1	90	1	90.00	1-42	-	-

Also bowled: PD Collingwood 2-0-10-0.

SACHIN TENDULKAR

One of India's leading cricket writers, GULU EZEKIEL, profiles India's
batting genius Sachin Tendulkar, cricket's 'Little Master'…

India was a very different place from what it is today when Sachin Tendulkar stepped into the cauldron of international cricket in Pakistan 20 years ago. Events rapidly followed that debut in November 1989, in all of which Tendulkar was not a direct catalyst. But his presence at the centre of these massive changes in both India and the game of cricket was like the planets lining up in the rare celestial occurrence called planetary alignment.

India's was a closed economy two decades back. But then in 1991, current Prime Minister and then Finance Minister Manmohan Singh ushered in the opening of India's markets to the world. That same year Rupert Murdoch planted his electronic footprint in India with the arrival of the STAR TV satellite channels. Today every conceivable luxury brand has a presence in India. And the Indian viewer has a choice of well over 200 channels, including dozens of 24/7 news channels in dozens of languages including English.

After making an immediate impression as a baby-faced 16-year-old in Pakistan, Tendulkar then captured the hearts of the cricket world in 1990 when he became the youngest player to score a Test century on English soil. A year later he repeated the feat at Sydney and Perth, leading Australian captain Allan Border to exclaim, 'If he can play like this at 18, I shudder to think what he will be like at 25'.

The seemingly endless saga of centuries had begun and, 20 years later, it shows no signs of abating. Indeed, he currently holds the records for the most Test runs and centuries, plus the most ODI runs and centuries.

When in 1995 Tendulkar signed a multi-million dollar endorsement deal with the late Mark Mascarenhas, he led another revolution, that of the super-rich cricketer. The ripple effect of that deal can be seen today in the vast sums of money being splurged on the Indian Premier League. If the Indian market drives the cricket world's economy, a major reason for that is Tendulkar's phenomenal success.

Tendulkar is arguably cricket's first $100 million man and no doubt the first of many. Yet, after hundreds of matches and enough money to last his family for generations, he still retains the enthusiasm of a teenager when he steps onto the field. 'Every morning I just can't wait to get out on the park,' he said in a recent interview marking his 20th anniversary as a Test match cricketer and icon of the game.

When I got down to writing the first major biography of Tendulkar in late 2001, I was struck by the fact that over and above his major batting feats, there was not a speck of dirt on his image. Indians like their sporting heroes to be squeaky clean, family-orientated and upholding traditional middle-class values. Tendulkar ticks all these boxes, even though his marriage at the age of 22 raised some eyebrows – it was after all a 'love marriage' to an older career woman who was half-English to boot. As for his upbringing, the Tendulkar family was solidly middle-class, though the fact that his professor father allowed him to discontinue his education before graduation was considered rather radical for the time.

When Tendulkar was chosen for that maiden tour of Pakistan, one of the selectors asked, 'What if he fails?' Chief selector Naren Tamhane's response – 'Gentlemen, Sachin Tendulkar never fails' – has become part of Indian cricket folklore. But if there has been one area where he has indeed failed it is with the national captaincy. Two stints – 1996 to

Sachin Tendulkar was only 17 when he toured England with India in 1990.

Tendulkar turns to leg during his match-winning century in the first Test against England at Chennai in December 2008.

1998 and 1999 to 2000 – both ended in failure, bitter recriminations and even tears, and two years as captain of the richest franchise in the IPL, Mumbai Indians, has been a major disappointment.

Though much of the cricket world and all of India had proclaimed him to be the best batsman in the world, it took the ringing endorsement of the greatest of them all, Sir Don Bradman, to place the final seal of approval on the batting maestro. In 1996 Sir Don anointed him as his spiritual heir and when 'Bradman's Best' was released posthumously in 2001, Tendulkar was the only contemporary player in his all-time XII.

All those runs, all that wealth, all those awards and all that fame... and yet, it took a tragedy of staggering proportions to bring out the best in Tendulkar. When the English team returned to India just weeks after the horror of the terrorist attack on Mumbai in November last year, Tendulkar's match-winning century in the Chennai Test made it more than just a game. It was a moment of national joy and vindication. It was as if the Indian spirit had proven its resilience.

It brought to mind what poet and columnist C.P. Surendran had written so poignantly of the 'Little Master' some years back. Every time he walks to the wicket, he wrote, 'a whole nation, tatters and all, marches with him to the battle arena. A pauper people pleading for relief, remission from the lifelong anxiety of being Indian... seeking a moment's liberation from their India-bondage through the exhilarating grace of one accidental bat.'

It is doubtful if cricket will ever see his like again.

SACHIN RAMESH TENDULKAR

Born 24 April 1973, Bombay

Aged 15, he became the youngest Indian to score a first-class century on debut, when representing Bombay at the Wankhede Stadium.

FIRST-CLASS DEBUT 11 December 1988 v Gujarat (Bombay)

TEST DEBUT 15 November 1989 v Pakistan (Karachi)

First-class record:

M	Inns	NO	Runs	HS	Ave	100s
261	412	43	21,662	248*	58.70	69

List A one-day record:

M	Inns	NO	Runs	HS	Ave	100s
517	504	53	20,455	186*	45.35	55

Tests: 159, scoring 12,773 runs at 54.58, with 42 hundreds
ODIs: 430, scoring 16,903 runs at 44.48, with 44 hundreds
As at 24 October 2009

ICC CHAMPIONS TROPHY

by Jonathan Agnew

England's Champions Trophy adventure, which began almost in fairytale fashion with unexpected wins against both Sri Lanka and South Africa, two of the competition favourites, ended at the semi-final stage when they ran into Ricky Ponting's unyielding Australians.

Shane Watson, the tournament's outstanding individual performer, and Ponting himself both made brilliant unbeaten hundreds after Tim Paine had fallen early on to Graham Onions. Australia's nine-wicket victory was a thumping statement of their utter superiority over an England team they had thrashed 6-1 during the previous month's NatWest Series on English soil.

Ponting's 111 not out, from 115 balls, was his 28th one-day international century and took him past 12,000 ODI runs. He was out cheaply in the final, against an injury-ravaged New Zealand, but Watson again shone with 105 not out – going to three figures and completing the six-wicket triumph with his fourth six, off Jeetan Patel.

As he held the Champions Trophy aloft at Centurion, however, after a victory that underlined Australia's modern-day dominance of 50-overs cricket, I wonder whether Ponting was still thinking about the little Ashes urn that got away?

Few, meanwhile, gave England any hope of competing with the best in the world after the beating they had been given by Australia in the NatWest Series. But victory in the final match of that series, at Durham, not only prevented a shameful 7-0 hammering – which would have been the first of its kind in ODI history – but gave Andrew Strauss's side at least something to build on when they landed in South Africa less than 48 hours later.

Five days after the Durham win, moreover, England found themselves walking out at the Wanderers Stadium in Johannesburg to take on the highly talented and much-fancied Sri Lankans. Fortune was on their side,

Australia's Shane Watson hits out against New Zealand fast bowler Ian Butler during the Champions Trophy final at Centurion.

AB de Villiers, who had emerged as a runner for South Africa's stricken captain Graeme Smith, is sent away again by England captain Andrew Strauss.

though, as Strauss won the toss and inserted Sri Lanka on a green-tinged surface.

Soon, England's opponents were reeling at 17 for 4. Onions sent back Sanath Jayasuriya and Kumar Sangakkara, and the outstanding Jimmy Anderson removed Tillakeratne Dilshan and Mahela Jayawardene. Perhaps the most dangerous top four in the competition had been cut down in half-an-hour of mayhem, and England had got the flying start they could only have dreamed about.

Half-centuries from Thilina Kandamby and Angelo Mathews did help to haul Sri Lanka up just beyond 200, but Strauss could even afford to recall Mathews when he was run out after the batsman protested that he had been blocked by bowler Onions when turning for an optimistic second run.

Strauss and Denly fell cheaply to the new ball, but England's previously flaky middle-order was now solidity itself as Owais Shah, Paul Collingwood, Eoin Morgan and Matt Prior eased them home by six wickets with five overs still unbowled.

Two days later, at Centurion, those same batsmen surpassed themselves and shocked hosts South Africa by knocking them out of the competition. This time Shah swung six sixes in a cavalier 89-ball 98, Collingwood displayed all his nous with 82 from 94 balls and Morgan made even the most cynical of England-watchers sit up and take notice of a major new talent when he scored a thrilling 67 from only 34 balls.

There were five sixes and four fours in Morgan's calculated assault, but what caught the eye as much as his rate of scoring was the purity of his strokeplay. This was not slogging, and the 23-year-old Irishman from Middlesex could be a feature of England's limited-overs middle-order for a decade on the evidence of this virtuoso performance against high-class opponents.

After England's total had been propelled to 323 for 8, not even a quite superb 141 from 134 balls from Graeme Smith could save South Africa from defeat, and

elimination at the group stage. Strauss also displayed the ruthlessness that lies behind his affable exterior by quite correctly refusing Smith a runner late in his career-best ODI innings when the South African captain began to suffer badly from cramp.

Anderson was again the pick of England's attack, going past 150 ODI wickets, although Stuart Broad also held his nerve well under pressure to take three wickets of his own and Graeme Swann clean bowled the dangerous JP Duminy during a skilful over of off spin variations.

England's management will rightly take great heart from the performances against Sri Lanka and South Africa, as they seek between now and the 2011 World Cup to make England truly competitive again in 50-over cricket for the first time in almost 20 years.

Yet the flaky batting collapse to 146 all out against New Zealand, in the meaningless final group match, and the slide to 101 for 6 in the semi-final against Australia, before Tim Bresnan and Luke Wright salvaged the innings with a brave 107-run stand, showed that there is still much work to be done in this regard – even with the returns of Kevin Pietersen and, hopefully, Andrew Flintoff to come.

Shah and Ravi Bopara, indeed, were the main casualties when the one-day squad for this winter's tour of South Africa was announced soon after the end of the Champions Trophy trip. There may well be more, too, before England can finally settle on the group of players to take them into the next World Cup.

England's James Anderson celebrates taking the wicket of Sri Lanka opener Tillakeratne Dilshan at Johannesburg.

30 September 2009 at Centurion
Pakistan 205 for 6 (50 overs)
Australia 206 for 8 (50 overs) (MEK Hussey 64)
Australia won by 2 wickets

30 September 2009 Day/Night at Johannesburg
West Indies 129 (36 overs) (P Kumar 3 for 22,
A Nehra 3 for 31)
India 130 for 3 (32.1 overs) (V Kohli 79*)
India won by 7 wickets

	P	W	L	T	NR	RR	Pts
Australia	3	2	0	0	1	+0.51	5
Pakistan	3	2	1	0	0	+0.99	4
India	3	1	1	0	1	+0.29	3
West Indies	3	0	3	0	0	-1.53	0

Group B

22 September 2009 Day/Night at Centurion
Sri Lanka 319 for 8 (50 overs) (TM Dilshan 106,
DPMD Jayawardene 77, KC Sangakkara 54, DW Steyn 3 for 47,
WD Parnell 3 for 79)
South Africa 206 for 7 (37.4 overs) (GC Smith 58,
BAW Mendis 3 for 30)
*Sri Lanka won by 55 runs – DL Method: target 262 from
37.4 overs*

24 September 2009 at Centurion
New Zealand 214 all out (47.5 overs) (LRPL Taylor 72,
WD Parnell 5 for 57)
South Africa 217 for 5 (41.1 overs) (AB de Villiers 70*)
South Africa won by 5 wickets

25 September 2009 Day/Night at Johannesburg
Sri Lanka 212 all out (47.3 overs) (SHT Kandamby 53,
AD Mathews 52, JM Anderson 3 for 20, SCJ Broad 3 for 49)
England 213 for 4 (45 overs) (EJG Morgan 62*)
England won by 6 wickets

27 September 2009 at Johannesburg
New Zealand 315 for 7 (50 overs) (JD Ryder 74, MJ Guptill 66,
ST Jayasuriya 3 for 39)
Sri Lanka 277 all out (46.4 overs) (DPMD Jayawardene 77,
KMDN Kulasekara 57*, KD Mills 3 for 69)
New Zealand won by 38 runs

27 September 2009 Day/Night at Centurion
England 323 for 8 (50 overs) (OA Shah 98, PD Collingwood 82,
EJG Morgan 67, WD Parnell 3 for 60)

Group A

23 September 2009 Day/Night at Johannesburg
West Indies 133 all out (34.3 overs) (NO Miller 51,
Mohammad Aamer 3 for 24, Umar Gul 3 for 28)
Pakistan 134 for 5 (30.3 overs) (GC Tonge 4 for 25)
Pakistan won by 5 wickets

26 September 2009 at Johannesburg
Australia 275 for 8 (50 overs) (RT Ponting 79, MG Johnson 73*)
West Indies 225 all out (46.5 overs) (TM Dowlin 55,
ADS Fletcher 54)
Australia won by 50 runs

26 September 2009 Day/Night at Centurion
Pakistan 302 for 9 (50 overs) (Shoaib Malik 128,
Mohammad Yousuf 87, A Nehra 4 for 55)
India 248 (44.5 overs) (R Dravid 76, G Gambhir 57)
Pakistan won by 54 runs

28 September 2009 Day/Night at Centurion
Australia 234 for 4 (42.3 overs) (MEK Hussey 67,
RT Ponting 65, TD Paine 56)
India
No result

South Africa 301 for 9 (50 overs) (GC Smith 141, JM Anderson 3 for 42, SCJ Broad 3 for 67)
England won by 22 runs

29 September 2009 Day/Night at Johannesburg
England 146 all out (43.1 overs) (GD Elliott 4 for 31, SE Bond 3 for 21)
New Zealand 147 for 6 (27.1 overs) (MJ Guptill 53, SCJ Broad 4 for 39)
New Zealand won by 4 wickets

	P	W	L	T	NR	RR	Pts
New Zealand	3	2	1	0	0	+0.78	4
England	3	2	1	0	0	-0.48	4
Sri Lanka	3	1	2	0	0	-0.08	2
South Africa	3	1	2	0	0	-0.17	2

Semi-finals

2 October 2009 Day/Night at Centurion
England 257 all out (47.4 overs) (TT Bresnan 80, PM Siddle 3 for 55)
Australia 258 for 1 (41.5 overs) (SR Watson 136*, RT Ponting 111*)
Australia won by 9 wickets

3 October 2009 Day/Night at Johannesburg
Pakistan 233 for 9 (50 overs) (Umar Akmal 55, IG Butler 4 for 44, DL Vettori 3 for 43)
New Zealand 234 for 5 (47.5 overs) (GD Elliott 75*)
New Zealand won by 5 wickets

NEW ZEALAND

*BB McCullum (capt)	c Paine b Siddle	0
AJ Redmond	st Paine b Hauritz	26
MJ Guptill	c & b Hauritz	40
LRPL Taylor	c Hussey b Johnson	6
GD Elliott	lbw b Lee	9
NT Broom	run out	37
JEC Franklin	b Lee	33
KD Mills	run out	12
IG Butler	lbw b Hauritz	6
JS Patel	not out	16
SE Bond	not out	3
Extras	b 1, lb 2, w 9	12
	(9 wkts 50 overs)	**200**

	O	M	R	W
Lee	10	1	45	2
Siddle	10	1	30	1
Johnson	10	1	35	1
Watson	10	0	50	0
Hauritz	10	0	37	3

Fall of Wickets
1-5, 2-66, 3-77, 4-81, 5-94, 6-159, 7-166, 8-174, 9-187

AUSTRALIA

SR Watson	not out	105
*TD Paine	c Taylor b Bond	1
RT Ponting (capt)	lbw b Mills	1
CL White	b Mills	62
MEK Hussey	c Patel b Mills	11
JR Hopes	not out	22
CJ Ferguson		
MG Johnson		
B Lee		
NM Hauritz		
PM Siddle		
Extras	lb 3, w 1	4
	(4 wkts 45.2 overs)	**206**

	O	M	R	W
Mills	10	2	27	3
Bond	10	2	34	1
Butler	9	0	50	0
Franklin	9	0	42	0
Patel	6.2	0	44	0
Elliott	1	0	6	0

Fall of Wickets
1-2, 2-6, 3-134, 4-156

Umpires: Aleem Dar (Pakistan) & IJ Gould (England)
Toss: New Zealand
Man of the Match: SR Watson
Man of the Tournament: RT Ponting

Australia won by 6 wickets

The boys are all white: Ricky Ponting and Australia celebrate Champions Trophy success in the specially tailored jackets presented to the winning team.

GOOD CRICKET or BIG PROFITS?

CHRISTOPHER MARTIN-JENKINS, long-serving *Test Match Special* commentator, despairs at the lack of balance in England's cricket playing structure...

Why can the ECB never quite bring itself to do what is truly in the best interests of England cricket? We all know the answer. Because they look at income to the game first, cricketing requirements second.

The structure for 2010, bearing little relation to the one announced with more of a fanfare almost exactly a year before, looks on the surface to be an improvement on the jumbled, overcrowded fixture list that only the players, and the loyal, surprisingly large core of diehard supporters, can fully understand.

However, the new structure – an unchanged Championship, an extended Twenty20 and a 40-over tournament involving 21 teams playing initially in pools of seven, mainly on Sundays, has been arrived at only because the England and Wales Commercial Board, as it should properly be called, failed to get its half-cock, blinkered attempt at a second Twenty20 tournament off the drawing board.

Hinting in its latest statement that it is all the fault of the counties, who voted for 40 overs rather than 50, ECB chairman Giles Clarke sheltered behind the hope that the ICC might ditch 50-over internationals after the 2011 World Cup. But he must know that even if that is the eventual outcome, it will take years before it happens. Meanwhile, there is little excuse for a decision to play a format that differs from what the England team will be asked to play, and has generally played rather badly.

Greed and ambition, stirred by agents, are also alive and thriving in the county game. What went on at Worcester in the last few weeks of the season might be described as rape, except that those who are being plundered by richer counties are complicit. Steven Davies and Gareth Batty are off to Surrey. Stephen Moore, widely expected to move to Warwickshire, has joined Lancashire.

Worcestershire were delighted to announce that they had held on to Moore last season on a three-year contract but it transpired that he had a clause allowing him to move if the club should be relegated. Three times Worcestershire have reached the first division of the LV County Championship; three times they have gone straight back down to the second.

Stephen Moore, the England Lions batsman, was at the centre of the significant transfer activity that accompanied Worcestershire's relegation from the County Championship's first division.

What matters most in the modern game: cricket and cricketers or filling empty seats? Despite the ECB's claims that the ODIs against Australia last summer were all sell outs, poor weather, weakened teams and a lack of competitiveness ensured a significant number of empty seats.

Moore cannot honestly claim that a move would further his ambitions to play for England when he has twice represented the England Lions against Australia this season and is already close to following Jonathan Trott into the Test team.

Transfers were bound to increase once the decision was taken to divide the County Championship. In one way, it is working. In another, more insidious one, it is probably having the effect that many whose agenda was to reduce the overall number of professional clubs had hoped for. Worcestershire may have been a first division club this season, unlike Surrey, but they are as Tranmere Rovers to Surrey's Liverpool.

Balance is what we are looking for from the ECB – but it seems unlikely that we will get it. Look at next year's international programme and ask yourself if the good ship ECB does not deserve to sink with all hands. England will play two Tests against Bangladesh and three one-day internationals in the period from 27 May to 17 June. A further five one-day internationals will be played against Australia from 22 June to 3 July. Australia will play Pakistan in two Twenty20 internationals and two Test matches from 5 to 25 July. England will then play a four-match Test series with Pakistan from 29 July to 30 August and five ODIs and two international Twenty20s from 5 to 21 September. The England Lions team will also compete in a series of one-day internationals against New Zealand A and India A in July.

The ECB is doing great things, I believe, below the surface of professional cricket. Despite any unfortunate effects of limiting the live television audience to satellite subscribers, both the official figures and anecdotal evidence suggests that participation amongst the young – perhaps the Board's second most important objective after a successful England team – is healthy and rising.

Hurrah for that, but the overloaded international programme next season invites further subordination of county cricket in the newspapers. Imagine how much space the domestic game will receive during the football World Cup in South Africa in June, let alone more ODIs against Australia.

This article first appeared on the TestMatchExtra.com cricket website.

ICC WORLD TWENTY20

by Jonathan Agnew

No one could claim that the ICC World Twenty20, hosted by England in 2009, was anything other than a great success. Bringing together the men's and women's game for the first time also brought women's cricket more sharply into the public's awareness, drawing decent crowds as the tournament progressed.

And with Pakistan's cricket urgently needing a boost, no one would argue that the outcome of the men's final was just what that beleaguered nation of enthusiastic cricket lovers needed. Indeed, their captain Younis Khan made this very point on the winner's podium.

Far from being a slogathon, or a run-fest, the bowlers had a say thanks to wonderfully honed yorkers and subtle variations on the familiar slower ball theme. Tillakeratne Dilshan led the way when it came to batting improvisation with an extraordinary scooped

sweep stroke that sent the ball from a good length flying straight over his helmet.

The tournament began with a real jolt when England contrived to lose their opening match to the Netherlands at Lord's. It degenerated into a comedy of errors as the Netherlands embarked on their chase for 163 with run out chances going begging, including off the very last ball which gifted the winning run through overthrows. But, fortunately for the hosts, they caught Pakistan before they gained any momentum and beat them by 48 runs to stay in the competition.

Australia, however, went crashing out at the early stage after they were roasted by Chris Gayle at The Oval and then lost to Sri Lanka. Meanwhile Ireland created another upset – they are becoming used to the role of giant killer – when they bumped out Bangladesh.

South Africa had been the popular favourites to win the tournament, and they scarcely put a foot wrong as they progressed into the semi-finals. They beat all in their path – England, India and West Indies – with the pace bowling of youngster Wayne Parnell catching the eye in particular. The question was, without Australia, who might stop them?

Sri Lanka's Tillakeratne Dilshan demonstrates how to play his famous 'Dilscoop' stroke over the wicketkeeper's head.

A key battle in that group proved to be between England and India – surely the most likely challenger to South Africa – but who came unstuck by just three runs as they failed to chase 154 at Lord's. There was a curious change to the batting order with Ravi Jadeja appearing at No. 4 and facing 35 balls for his 25.

It left the others too much to do, but England still had to defeat West Indies at The Oval to reach the semis. Rain reduced West Indies's target to 80 from nine overs and, for once, the accuracy of Anderson, Sidebottom and Broad deserted them. Yorkers became full tosses and West Indies got home with four balls left.

In the other pool, Sri Lanka looked strong with Dilshan in outrageous form. Malinga, Muralitharan and Mendis were all hard to hit, while their fielding had also gained in athleticism – best displayed by an extraordinary catch taken over the boundary edge by Angelo Mathews at Trent Bridge and declared legal because at no stage were his feet touching the ground as he threw up the ball and completed the catch on the field of play. Pakistan, meanwhile, were starting to warm up by now and saw off New Zealand, who were bowled out for only 99, with Umar Gul taking 5 for 6, and they duly progressed to the semis when they disposed of Ireland.

Pakistan faced South Africa in the first semi-final and the form book went out of the window as South Africa fielded poorly and then faltered after Jacques Kallis's 64 seemed to put them well on course for their target of 150. Afridi's darting leg breaks dispatched Gibbs and de Villiers as he took 2 for 16 and the favourites fell eight runs short of victory.

The second semi-final delighted the traditionalists in that it showed that even Twenty20 matches can be dull if one team starts its innings badly. After Sri Lanka rattled up a challenging 158 for 5, thanks to another brilliant innings from Player of the Tournament, Dilshan, West Indies found themselves 1 for 3 at the end of the first over of their reply! Game over, although a bemused Gayle did hit an unbeaten 63 and carried his bat.

The men's final at Lord's was preceded by the women's play-off between England – who had seen off Australia in the semi-final – and New Zealand, the other strong team in their tournament. Emily Brunt, the Yorkshire pace bowler, took 3 for 7 as New Zealand disintegrated to just 85 all out and although England lost Charlotte Edwards and Sarah Taylor early, Claire Taylor – dropped on 0 – played some glorious strokes in her unbeaten 39 to see England home with three overs and six wickets in hand.

It was a good appetiser for the main event, which pitted Sri Lanka against Pakistan in front of an expectant – and largely Pakistani – full house at Lord's.

Sri Lanka chose to bat first and posted 138 for 6 – a score perhaps 15 runs light but not helped by Dilshan

bagging a duck in the first over of the match. Sangakkara made 62 and Mathews chimed in with 35 not out from 24 balls at the end, but Pakistan were now favourites. Akmal and Shahzaib put on 48, and then Afridi concluded a fine personal fortnight by plundering 54 from 40 balls, giving Pakistan victory by eight wickets with eight balls to spare.

The tournament was a roaring success, confirming the attraction of Twenty20 cricket, and reigniting the debate about the future of 50-over one-day internationals.

Group A

6 June 2009 Day/Night at Trent Bridge
India 180 for 5 (20 overs) (G Gambhir 50)
Bangladesh 155 for 8 (20 overs) (PP Ojha 4 for 21)
India won by 25 runs

8 June 2009 at Trent Bridge
Bangladesh 137 for 8 (20 overs) (DT Johnston 3 for 20)
Ireland 138 for 4 (18.2 overs)
Ireland won by 6 wickets

10 June 2009 Day/Night at Trent Bridge
Ireland 112 for 8 (18 overs) (Zaheer Khan 4 for 19)
India 113 for 2 (15.3 overs) (RG Sharma 52*)
India won by 8 wickets

	P	W	L	T/NR	RR	Pts
India	2	2	0	0/0	+1.23	4
Ireland	2	1	1	0/0	-0.16	2
Bangladesh	2	0	2	0/0	-1.00	0

Group B

5 June 2009 Day/Night at Lord's
England 162 for 5 (20 overs) (LJ Wright 71)
Netherlands 163 for 6 (20 overs) (JM Anderson 3 for 23)
Netherlands won by 4 wickets

7 June 2009 Day/Night at The Oval
England 185 for 5 (20 overs) (KP Pietersen 58)
Pakistan 137 for 7 (20 overs) (SCJ Broad 3 for 17)
England won by 48 runs

9 June 2009 at Lord's
Pakistan 175 for 5 (20 overs)
Netherlands 93 all out (17.3 overs) (Shahid Afridi 4 for 11, Saeed Ajmal 3 for 20)
Pakistan won by 82 runs

	P	W	L	T/NR	RR	Pts
England	2	1	1	0/0	+1.18	2
Pakistan	2	1	1	0/0	+0.85	2
Netherlands	2	1	1	0/0	-2.03	2

Group C

6 June 2009 at The Oval
Australia 169 for 7 (20 overs) (DA Warner 63)
West Indies 172 for 3 (15.5 overs) (CH Gayle 88,
ADS Fletcher 53)
West Indies won by 7 wickets

8 June 2009 Day/Night at Trent Bridge
Australia 159 for 9 (20 overs) (BAW Mendis 3 for 20,
SL Malinga 3 for 36)
Sri Lanka 160 for 4 (19 overs) (KC Sangakkara 55*, TM Dilshan 53)
Sri Lanka won by 6 wickets

10 June 2009 at Trent Bridge
Sri Lanka 192 for 5 (20 overs) (ST Jayasuriya 81,
TM Dilshan 74, LMP Simmons 4 for 19)
West Indies 177 for 5 (20 overs) (DJ Bravo 51)
Sri Lanka won by 15 runs

	P	W	L	T/NR	RR	Pts
Sri Lanka	2	2	0	0/0	+0.63	4
West Indies	2	1	1	0/0	+0.72	2
Australia	2	0	2	0/0	-1.33	0

Group D

6 June 2009 at The Oval
Scotland 89 for 4 (7 overs) (IG Butler 3 for 19)
New Zealand 90 for 3 (6 overs)
New Zealand won by 7 wickets

7 June 2009 at The Oval
South Africa 211 for 5 (20 overs) (AB de Villiers 79*)
Scotland 81 all out (15.4 overs)
South Africa won by 130 runs

9 June 2009 Day/Night at Lord's
South Africa 128 for 7 (20 overs)
New Zealand 127 for 5 (20 overs) (BB McCullum 57)
South Africa won by 1 run

	P	W	L	T/NR	RR	Pts
South Africa	2	2	0	0/0	+3.28	4
New Zealand	2	1	1	0/0	+0.31	2
Scotland	2	0	2	0/0	-5.28	0

Super Eight Stage

Group E

11 June 2009 Day/Night at Trent Bridge
England 111 all out (19.5 overs) (WD Parnell 3 for 14)

South Africa 114 for 3 (18.2 overs) (JH Kallis 57*)
South Africa won by 7 wickets

12 June 2009 Day/Night at Lord's
India 153 for 7 (20 overs) (Yuvraj Singh 67, DJ Bravo 4 for 38,
FH Edwards 3 for 24)
West Indies 156 for 3 (18.4 overs) (DJ Bravo 66*)
West Indies won by 7 wickets

13 June 2009 at The Oval
South Africa 183 for 7 (20 overs) (HH Gibbs 55,
JE Taylor 3 for 30)
West Indies 163 for 9 (20 overs) (LMP Simmons 77,
WD Parnell 4 for 13)
South Africa won by 20 runs

14 June 2009 Day/Night at Lord's
England 153 for 7 (20 overs) (Harbhajan Singh 3 for 30)
India 150 for 5 (20 overs)
England won by 3 runs

15 June 2009 Day/Night at The Oval
England 161 for 6 (20 overs) (RS Bopara 55)
West Indies 82 for 5 (8.2 overs)
West Indies won by 5 wickets – DL Method: target 80 from 9 overs

16 June 2009 Day/Night at Trent Bridge
South Africa 130 for 5 (20 overs) (AB de Villiers 63)
India 118 for 8 (20 overs) (J Botha 3 for 16)
South Africa won by 12 runs

	P	W	L	T/NR	RR	Pts
South Africa	3	3	0	0/0	+0.79	6
West Indies	3	2	1	0/0	+0.06	4
England	3	1	2	0/0	-0.41	2
India	3	0	3	0/0	-0.47	0

Group F

11 June 2009 at Trent Bridge
New Zealand 198 for 5 (20 overs) (AJ Redmond 63)
Ireland 115 (16.4 overs) (NL McCullum 3 for 15)
New Zealand won by 83 runs

12 June 2009 at Lord's
Sri Lanka 150 for 7 (20 overs)
Pakistan 131 for 9 (20 overs) (Younis Khan 50, SL Malinga 3 for 17)
Sri Lanka won by 19 runs

13 June 2009 Day/Night at The Oval
New Zealand 99 all out (18.3 overs) (Umar Gul 5 for 6)
Pakistan 100 for 4 (13.1 overs)
Pakistan won by 6 wickets

14 June 2009 at Lord's
Sri Lanka 144 for 9 (20 overs) (DPMD Jayawardene 78, AR Cusack 4 for 18)
Ireland 135 for 7 (20 overs)
Sri Lanka won by 9 runs

15 June 2009 at The Oval
Pakistan 159 for 5 (20 overs) (Kamran Akmal 57)
Ireland 120 for 9 (20 overs) (Saeed Ajmal 4 for 19)
Pakistan won by 39 runs

16 June 2009 at Trent Bridge
Sri Lanka 158 for 5 (20 overs)
New Zealand 110 all out (17 overs) (BAW Mendis 3 for 9)
Sri Lanka won by 48 runs

	P	W	L	T/NR	RR	Pts
Sri Lanka	3	3	0	0/0	+1.27	6
Pakistan	3	2	1	0/0	+1.19	4
New Zealand	3	1	2	0/0	-0.23	2
Ireland	3	0	3	0/0	-2.18	0

Semi-finals

18 June 2009 Day/Night at Trent Bridge
Pakistan 149 for 4 (20 overs) (Shahid Afridi 51)
South Africa 142 for 5 (20 overs) (JH Kallis 64)
Pakistan won by 7 runs

19 June 2009 Day/Night at The Oval
Sri Lanka 158 for 5 (20 overs) (TM Dilshan 96*)
West Indies 101 all out (17.4 overs) (CH Gayle 63*, AD Mathews 3 for 16, M Muralitharan 3 for 29)
Sri Lanka won by 57 runs

FINAL – PAKISTAN v. SRI LANKA
21 June 2009 at Lord's

SRI LANKA

TM Dilshan	c Hasan b Aamer	0
ST Jayasuriya	b Abdul Razzaq	17
J Mubarak	c Hasan b Abdul Razzaq	0
*KC Sangakkara (capt)	not out	64
DPMD Jayawardene	c Misbah-ul-Haq b Abdul Razzaq	1
LPC Silva	c Ajmal b Umar Gul	14
I Udana	b Shahid Afridi	1
AD Mathews	not out	35
SL Malinga		
M Muralitharan		
BAW Mendis		
Extras	lb 3, w 2, nb 1	6
	(6 wkts 20 overs)	**138**

	O	M	R	W
Mohammad Aamer	4	1	30	1
Abdul Razzaq	3	0	20	3
Shahid Afridi	4	0	20	1
Saeed Ajmal	4	0	28	0
Shoaib Malik	1	0	8	0
Umar Gul	4	0	29	1

Fall of Wickets: 1-0, 2-2, 3-26, 4-32, 5-67, 6-70

PAKISTAN

*Kamran Akmal	st Sangakkara b Jayasuriya	37
Shahzaib Hasan	c Jayasuriya b Muralitharan	19
Shahid Afridi	not out	54
Shoaib Malik	not out	24
Younis Khan (capt)		
Misbah-ul-Haq		
Fawad Alam		
Abdul Razzaq		
Umar Gul		
Saeed Ajmal		
Mohammad Aamer		
Extras	lb 2, w 2, nb 1	5
	(2 wkts 18.4 overs)	**139**

	O	M	R	W
Mathews	2	0	17	0
Udana	4	0	44	0
Malinga	3.4	0	14	0
Muralitharan	3	0	20	1
Mendis	4	0	34	0
Jayasuriya	2	0	8	1

Fall of Wickets: 1-48, 2-63

Umpires: DJ Harper (Australia) & SJA Taufel (Australia)
Toss: Sri Lanka
Man of the Match: Shahid Afridi
Man of the Tournament: TM Dilshan

Pakistan won by 8 wickets

Pakistan's players celebrate their uplifting victory in the ICC World Twenty20 final at Lord's.

CHAMPIONS LEAGUE

by Bruce Talbot

It was typical of the apathy in England surrounding the inaugural Champions League tournament that the story that attracted most of the column inches at home concerned something which did not happen on the pitch.

Marcus Trescothick had bravely decided to confront his demons and undertake his first overseas trip for three years as part of Somerset's challenge. But after failing with the bat in the Sabres' two opening round games the 33-year-old succumbed to the same stresses from playing abroad which had prematurely ended his England career and he flew home while his team-mates were preparing for their second-round matches.

Trescothick had been joined by wife Hayley and Somerset had looked into several options to safeguard his well-being. One was to stay in an Indian holiday resort and another involved basing himself in Dubai. Neither proved practical, however, and even being in the cocoon of his team-mates was not enough to stave off what Trescothick has described as his 'black wings' and what his psychologists have referred to as 'separation anxiety'.

Somerset, even without their star opener, at least flew the English flag in the second phase. They recovered from 99 for 7 to silence the home crowd in Hyderabad and beat Deccan Chargers by one wicket, and although they were well beaten by Trinidad & Tobago, their superior run rate was enough to secure qualification.

But if they had not already realised, the standard in the second round was a step up and defeats against Diamond Eagles and Royal Challengers Bangalore brought their campaign and the Justin Langer era at the club to an end, the former Australian batsman having confirmed his retirement as captain at the end of the domestic season. However, like English champions Sussex Sharks, the Sabres will have gained a lot from their experience.

If the tournament failed to fire the imagination back home that was not the case in India. Lalit Modi, the head of the BCCI, hinted at expanding the tournament to 16 teams in the future. This would ensure that all of the groups contained an IPL team and avoid the embarrassing scenes in Delhi when the only first-round

Somerset wicketkeeper Craig Kieswetter leaps for joy as another Deccan Chargers wicket falls in Hyderabad. Sadly for the English county team, however, victory in that game was as good as it got.

double-header not involving an Indian side started with barely 500 spectators inside a 44,000 capacity stadium.

By the time Sussex and Diamond Eagles got underway four hours later, however, the crowd had swelled to 10,000 as the presence of Indian leg spinner Piyush Chawla in the Sussex side clearly helped to spark local interest.

Expanding the event would also safeguard the participation of both of England's domestic Twenty20 Cup finalists. The BCCI ran the event in conjunction with Australia and South Africa and England were the only other country with two participants who were not involved in its organisation.

For Somerset and Sussex, who lost both of their first-round games, the competition represented a huge learning curve. Sussex coach Mark Robinson said, 'It was a fantastic event to be involved in and the best thing I have experienced as a coach but it also showed up how much we can improve.

'We played New South Wales and Eagles, from South Africa, and both teams contained 11 proper athletes and they both out-fielded us. Our domestic schedule has a lot to do with it. We do not have the time to devote to practice that other sides have. Some of the other coaches couldn't believe the amount of cricket we play in England but it's going to get even worse in 2010, even though we are playing one less competition.

'Like Somerset, we would love to come back in 2010 because we have learned so much, not least in what we have to do in terms of our approach if we are to compete with the best Twenty20 teams in the world.'

New South Wales ran out winners of a fascinating and highly entertaining tournament that Modi said would quickly 'become the premier cricketing tournament in the world and will be for cricket what the Champions League has become in club football'. The Aussies, captained by Simon Katich and with Brett Lee in irresistible form with both bat and ball, overpowered an exciting and previously unbeaten Trinidad & Tobago team in the final at Hyderabad to win by 41 runs.

Bruce Talbot of the Brighton Evening Argus, *travelled to India to report on the inaugural Champions League tournament*

Group A
(Deccan Chargers, Somerset Sabres, Trinidad & Tobago)

10 October 2009 Day/Night at Hyderabad
Deccan Chargers 153 for 9 (20 overs) (BJ Phillips 3 for 31)
Somerset Sabres 157 for 9 (20 overs) (RP Singh 3 for 23)
Somerset Sabres won by 1 wicket

12 October 2009 Day/Night at Bangalore
Trinidad & Tobago 150 for 9 (20 overs) (CM Willoughby 3 for 35)
Somerset Sabres 106 all out (20 overs) (DJ Bravo 4 for 23)
Trinidad & Tobago won by 44 runs

14 October 2009 Day/Night at Hyderabad
Trinidad & Tobago 149 for 7 (20 overs) (FH Edwards 3 for 32)
Deccan Chargers 146 for 9 (20 overs) (AC Gilchrist 51, DJ Bravo 3 for 24)
Trinidad & Tobago won by 3 runs

	P	W	L	T	NR	RR	Pts
Trinidad & Tobago	2	2	0	0	0	+1.17	4
Somerset Sabres	2	1	1	0	0	-1.00	2
Deccan Chargers	2	0	2	0	0	-0.17	0

Group B
(Diamond Eagles, New South Wales Blues, Sussex Sharks)

9 October 2009 Day/Night at Delhi
NSW Blues 144 for 6 (20 overs) (SM Katich 53)
Diamond Eagles 91 for 9 (20 overs) (SR Clark 3 for 12)
New South Wales won by 53 runs

11 October 2009 Day/Night at Delhi
NSW Blues 130 for 2 (20 overs) (PJ Hughes 62*, MC Henriques 51*)
Sussex Sharks 95 for 8 (20 overs) (MC Henriques 3 for 23)
New South Wales won by 35 runs

13 October 2009 Day/Night at Delhi
Sussex Sharks 119 for 7 (20 overs)
Diamond Eagles 119 for 4 (20 overs) (RR Rossouw 65)
Eagles won in a Super-over

	P	W	L	T	NR	RR	Pts
NSW Blues	2	2	0	0	0	+2.20	4
Diamond Eagles	2	1	1	0	0	-1.32	2
Sussex Sharks	2	0	2	0	0	-0.87	0

Group C
(Cape Cobras, Royal Challengers Bangalore, Otago Volts)

8 October 2009 Day/Night at Bangalore
Bangalore 180 for 4 (20 overs) (LRPL Taylor 53*, RV Uthappa 51)
Cape Cobras 184 for 5 (19.4 overs) (JP Duminy 99*, PS Kumar 3 for 32)
Cape Cobras won by 5 wickets

10 October 2009 Day/Night at Hyderabad
Cape Cobras 193 for 4 (20 overs) (AG Puttick 104*)
Otago Volts 139 all out (17.1 overs) (RK Kleinveldt 3 for 24)
Cape Cobras won by 54 runs

12 October 2009 Day/Night at Bangalore
Bangalore 188 for 2 (20 overs) (JH Kallis 73*)
Otago Volts 108 all out (17.5 overs) (JH Kallis 3 for 18)
Royal Challengers Bangalore won by 80 runs

	P	W	L	T	NR	RR	Pts
Cape Cobras	2	2	0	0	0	+1.52	4
Bangalore	2	1	1	0	0	+1.83	2
Otago Volts	2	0	2	0	0	-3.35	0

Group D

(Delhi Daredevils, Victoria Bushrangers, Wayamba Elevens)

9 October 2009 Day/Night at Delhi
Delhi Daredevils 98 for 8 (20 overs) (CJ McKay 3 for 17)
Victoria 100 for 3 (16.4 overs)
Victoria won by 7 wickets

11 October 2009 Day/Night at Delhi
Delhi Daredevils 170 for 5 (20 overs) (V Sehwag 66,
KD Karthik 61)
Wayamba 120 for 7 (20 overs) (DPMD Jayawardene 53,
DP Nannes 4 for 24)
Delhi Daredevils won by 50 runs

13 October 2009 Day/Night at Delhi
Wayamba 118 for 9 (20 overs) (SM Harwood 3 for 14)
Victoria 103 for 4 (20 overs)
Wayamba won by 15 runs

	P	W	L	T	NR	RR	Pts
Delhi Daredevils	2	1	1	0	0	+0.70	2
Victoria	2	1	1	0	0	+0.13	2
Wayamba	2	1	1	0	0	-0.87	2

League A

16 October 2009 Day/Night at Hyderabad
Somerset Sabres 132 for 8 (20 overs) (WJ Durston 57,
CJD de Villiers 4 for 17)
Diamond Eagles 133 for 5 (18.4 overs)
Eagles won by 5 wickets

16 October 2009 Day/Night at Hyderabad
NSW Blues 170 for 4 (20 overs) (PJ Hughes 83,
DA Warner 63, DJ Bravo 3 for 31)
Trinidad & Tobago 171 for 6 (18.3 overs)
(KA Pollard 54*)
Trinidad & Tobago won by 4 wickets

Not even the big hitting of West Indian all-rounder Dwayne Smith could prevent Sussex from suffering two deflating defeats in their Champions League group... the second following a Super-over 'shoot-out'.

18 October 2009 Day/Night at Hyderabad
Somerset Sabres 111 for 7 (20 overs) (SR Clark 3 for 15)
NSW Blues 112 for 4 (11.5 overs)
New South Wales won by 6 wickets

18 October 2009 Day/Night at Hyderabad
Trinidad & Tobago 213 for 4 (20 overs) (A Barath 63)
Diamond Eagles 189 for 5 (20 overs)
Trinidad & Tobago won by 24 runs

	P	W	L	T	NR	RR	Pts
Trinidad & Tobago	3	3	0	0	0	1.38	6
NSW Blues	3	2	1	0	0	1.84	4
Diamond Eagles	3	1	2	0	0	-1.11	2
Somerset Sabres	3	0	3	0	0	-2.01	0

League B

15 October 2009 Day/Night at Bangalore
Bangalore 127 for 6 (20 overs) (AB McDonald 4 for 21)
Victoria 133 for 3 (15.5 overs)
Victoria won by 7 wickets

17 October 2009 Day/Night at Bangalore
Victoria 125 for 5 (17 overs)
Cape Cobras 129 for 2 (16 overs) (H Davids 69*)
Cape Cobras won by 8 wickets

17 October 2009 Day/Night at Bangalore
Delhi Daredevils 138 for 6 (20 overs) (A Kumble 3 for 20)
Bangalore 139 for 2 (15.1 overs) (LRPL Taylor 65)
Royal Challengers Bangalore won by 8 wickets

19 October 2009 Day/Night at Delhi
Delhi Daredevils 114 for 6 (20 overs)
Cape Cobras 84 all out (18.3 overs) (DP Nannes 3 for 19)
Delhi Daredevils won by 30 runs

	P	W	L	T	NR	RR	Pts
Victoria	3	2	1	0	0	0.91	4
Cape Cobras	3	2	1	0	0	-0.22	4
Bangalore	3	1	2	0	0	-0.11	2
Delhi Daredevils	3	1	2	0	0	-0.58	2

Semi-finals

21 October 2009 Day/Night at Delhi
NSW Blues 169 for 7 (20 overs) (CJ McKay 3 for 27)
Victoria 90 for 9 (20 overs) (MC Henriques 3 for 11)
New South Wales won by 79 runs

22 October 2009 Day/Night at Hyderabad
Cape Cobras 175 for 5 (20 overs) (JP Duminy 61*)
Trinidad & Tobago 178 for 3 (19.2 overs) (DJ Bravo 58*)
Trinidad & Tobago won by 7 wickets

FINAL – NSW BLUES v. TRINIDAD & TOBAGO
23 October 2009 at Hyderabad

NEW SOUTH WALES BLUES

DA Warner	c Mohammed b Bravo	19
PJ Hughes	b Rampaul	3
SM Katich (capt)	c Barath b Bravo	16
MC Henriques	c S Ganga b Pollard	4
BJ Rohrer	c S Ganga b Mohammed	16
SPD Smith	c Simmons b S Ganga	33
*DLR Smith	b Rampaul	3
B Lee	c Perkins b Rampaul	48
NM Hauritz	run out	10
SR Clark	not out	0
DE Bollinger		
Extras	lb 5, w 2	7
	(9 wkts 20 overs)	159

	O	M	R	W
S Ganga	4	0	29	1
Rampaul	4	0	20	3
Bravo	3	0	27	2
Pollard	3	0	27	1
Mohammed	3	0	19	1
Simmons	2	0	23	0
Stewart	1	0	9	0

Fall of Wickets
1-24, 2-32, 3-45, 4-47, 5-75, 6-83, 7-132, 8-159, 9-159

TRINIDAD & TOBAGO

WKD Perkins	b Lee	0
A Barath	c DLR Smith b SPD Smith	14
LMP Simmons	c & b Lee	4
*D Ganga	c Warner b SPD Smith	19
DJ Bravo	b Bollinger	17
D Ramdin (capt)	c SPD Smith b Clark	16
KA Pollard	c Lee b Hauritz	26
S Ganga	c Henriques b Hauritz	5
ND Stewart	c Henriques b Clark	4
D Mohammed	c Hughes b Clark	1
R Rampaul	not out	0
Extras	lb 5, nb 3, w 4	12
	(all out 15.5 overs)	118

	O	M	R	W
Lee	2	0	10	2
SPD Smith	4	0	32	2
Bollinger	4	0	27	1
Clark	3.5	0	21	3
Hauritz	2	0	23	2

Fall of Wickets
1-1, 2-21, 3-21, 4-45, 5-68, 6-93, 7-107, 8-113, 9-118

Umpires: DJ Harper (Australia) & RE Koertzen (South Africa)
Toss: Trinidad & Tobago
Man of the Match: B Lee

NSW Blues won by 41 runs

COUNTY REVIEW *North East*

TIM WELLOCK, who has covered Durham's cricket fortunes since 1992, tips neighbours Yorkshire as the team to challenge their dominance of the LV County Championship...

Durham were so dominant in the 2009 County Championship they must be short odds to become the first team since Yorkshire in 1966–68 to do the hat-trick. But if a strong challenger is to emerge in the next few seasons Yorkshire look as good a bet as any.

Nowhere else among the county clubs is there such a crop of young talent as that provided at Yorkshire by Joe Sayers, Andrew Gale, Jonny Bairstow, Adam Lyth and Joe Root in the batting; Adil Rashid, Azeem Rafiq and David Wainwright as spin-bowling all-rounders, and Tim Bresnan (still only 24), Ajmal Shahzad and James Lee among the seamers.

While Sayers enjoyed a hugely successful rehabilitation after his disastrous 2008 season, Player of the Year Gale confirmed his adaptability between the four-day and one-day game, and Bairstow looked a class act in the second half of the season. Lyth's opportunities were restricted

initially by the presence of Michael Vaughan, which had a detrimental effect when the opposite was expected. Although unable to contribute heavily with the bat, Vaughan's retirement still had an unsettling effect, perhaps because there was a greater onus on skipper Anthony McGrath to provide the middle-order experience. His loss of form put pressure on Nos. 7–9 to bale out the team, which Rashid, Shahzad and Wainwright did very successfully.

The seam bowling, however, never had the potency that might have been expected. The retention of Rana Naved-ul-Hasan as the overseas player proved misguided – and the selection of his successor will be crucial – while Bresnan appeared to suffer from his flirtations with England, and Matthew Hoggard shone only in taking the hat-trick at Hove that helped to stave off relegation. Shahzad had his moments and looks an excellent all-round prospect if he keeps his feet on the ground.

Joe Sayers, one of a clutch of promising young Yorkshire cricketers, sweeps the ball away to leg.

Graham Onions (centre, facing) is joined by his delighted Durham team-mates after dismissing Somerset's Craig Kieswetter.

Yorkshire and Somerset were the only teams to avoid defeat by unbeaten Durham, with the weather helping Somerset to hang on home and away. Durham conceded a first innings deficit only once, at Headingley, where they trailed by 135 runs yet came back with 421 for 9 declared. This epitomised Yorkshire's season. Bland pitches didn't help, but an inability to turn the screw probably stemmed largely from the fact that they couldn't match Durham's seam attack. But, there again, no county came close to that.

After six games, one of which he missed because of England Lions duty, Graham Onions had 40 wickets. His nearest rival nationally at the time was Steve Harmison with 28. Onions played only two more games because of Test calls, but that in turn allowed Liam Plunkett to come to the fore. He continued to blow hot and cold, but his consistency steadily improved and by the end of the season he looked worthy of a return to the England squad. He also averaged 44.4 with the bat, while Mark Davies, Callum Thorp and Mitch Claydon also played a part with the ball.

Six of Durham's eight wins came at the Riverside, but to suggest they played on 'result' pitches there would be unfair. They made their own record total of 645 for 5 at home to second-placed Nottinghamshire, who were beaten by an innings home and away. That was a measure of the gulf between Durham and the rest. They were greatly strengthened by Ian Blackwell, who showed that the Riverside is no longer a desert for spinners by taking 5 for 7 against his former Somerset colleagues. He finished the season with 43 Championship wickets; ten more than David Graveney's record haul for a Durham spinner, in 1993.

Against Nottinghamshire there were four century-makers in a Durham innings for the first time in Michael Di Venuto, Kyle Coetzer, Dale Benkenstein and Shivnarine Chanderpaul; Benkenstein's century was his 15th for Durham, taking him

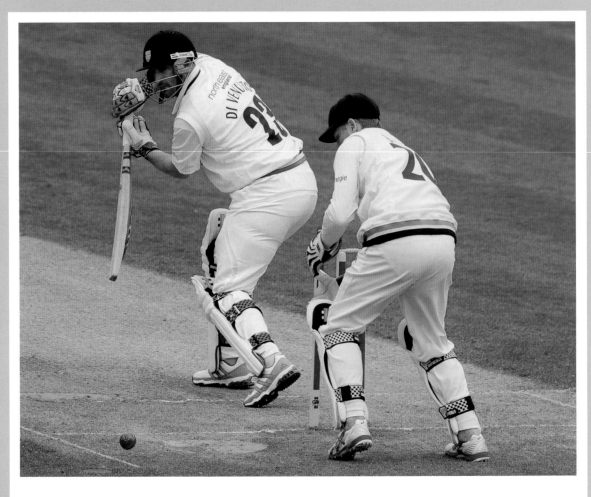

Durham opener Michael Di Venuto guides the ball away on the offside during their match against Yorkshire at the Riverside.

to the top of their list after sharing the lead with John Morris and Paul Collingwood. Di Venuto equalled Collingwood's 2005 Durham record of six Championship centuries in a season and raised the county's record run tally to 1,601.

The only disappointment for Durham was the lack of progress by home-grown batsmen. After playing no Championship cricket in 2008, Gordon Muchall was given the chance to re-establish himself but was unable to build on an early season century at Hove. Mark Stoneman opened the innings for most of the season but made only one half-century. He remains highly rated and at 22 still has time

on his side, while leg-spinning all-rounder Scott Borthwick is also an outstanding prospect.

But the Riverside cupboard does not look as well stocked with talent as Headingley's. Durham will, however, have the same squad available for the next two years, having fostered a family atmosphere that should be the envy of all. That and the seam attack set them apart from the rest, plus perhaps the refusal to be seduced by Twenty20 riches. Neither Durham nor Yorkshire created any waves in one-day cricket. They prefer to leave such superficial fripperies to the soft southerners, who can't produce a pace bowler worth a light.

LV COUNTY CHAMPIONSHIP

by Mark Baldwin

Round One: 15–18 April

Defending champions Durham sat out a low-key start to the County Championship season in which all three second division matches were drawn and there was just one positive result in the two first division fixtures.

Hampshire got off to a flier in the top tier, beating Worcestershire by seven wickets at the Rose Bowl with a relative ease that was a harbinger of future harsh struggles for Vikram Solanki's team, promoted in 2008.

The absence of Graeme Hick from the Worcestershire middle-order left one gaping hole – Hick, after all, had spent 25 prolific seasons at New Road before his

retirement the previous September – but another former England cricketer, fast bowler Simon Jones, was also injured again after spearheading the promotion-winning attack for much of 2008 with 42 Championship wickets at a cost of just 18 runs apiece.

Dominic Cork, Hampshire's shrewd winter signing from Lancashire, snapped up 4 for 10 on debut for his third county as Worcestershire subsided for 132 in their first innings and only Solanki, with 73, offered much resistance as the home seamers dismissed their visitors for 189 second time around.

Hampshire's batsmen had also found run-scoring hard work in the mid-April conditions, but Liam Dawson's 66 had ensured a handy enough lead and Michael Carberry's 58 made sure the modest victory

James Hildreth, of Somerset, began the new season in magnificent fashion with a triple-century against Warwickshire at Taunton.

Round One: 15–18 April Division One

MCC v. DURHAM 9–12 April at Lord's

Bad weather ruined the traditional season's opener between MCC and the champion county at Lord's, although there was still time for a former England player to remind the watching national selectors of his ability and for three pretenders to England's Test No. 3 position to fall cheaply at the start of an Ashes summer... to two Australians.

Michael Vaughan, Rob Key and Ian Bell made just 29 runs between them as Callum Thorp, a West Australian, and his fellow paceman Mitchell Claydon, from New South Wales, got in among the MCC batsmen. Both Aussies play county cricket under British passports. Only Worcestershire and England Lions opener Stephen Moore, with 45, looked comfortable as Thorp took 4 for 15 and MCC declined to 126 for 7 in reply to Durham's 311 for 4 declared following a third day washout.

Durham had reached 244 for 4 in the 72 overs of play possible on day one, and only 17 overs were played on the second day as the weather closed in. But Ian Blackwell, signed from Somerset in the winter and who played the last of his 34 one-day internationals for England in 2005–06, was able to complete a brilliant hundred on that truncated second day.

Blackwell's 102 not out took him only 109 balls, with 16 fours, and he dominated an unbroken fifth wicket stand of 179 with his young captain Will Smith, who was delighted to score 71 not out himself in his first innings after taking over from Dale Benkenstein.

Earlier, Michael Di Venuto had hit 53 from 79 balls in an opening partnership of 104 with Mark Stoneman, who was bowled by Tim Bresnan one short of his own fifty.

Durham 311 for 4 dec (89 overs) (ID Blackwell 102*, WR Smith 71*, MJ Di Venuto 53)
MCC 126 for 7 (47 overs) (CD Thorp 4 for 15)
Match drawn

HAMPSHIRE v. WORCESTERSHIRE – at the Rose Bowl

WORCS	First Innings		Second Innings	
DKH Mitchell	c Lumb b Tremlett	31	c Lumb b Cork	4
SC Moore	c Cork b Balcombe	25	b Tremlett	1
VS Solanki (capt)	c Pothas b Balcombe	6	c Carberry b Tomlinson	73
BF Smith	c Pothas b Dawson	21	c Carberry b Balcombe	19
MM Ali	c Dawson b Tomlinson	12	c Ervine b Tomlinson	3
*SM Davies	c Cork b Ervine	4	c Cork b Ervine	8
GJ Batty	lbw b Cork	5	c Adams b Balcombe	0
Kabir Ali	lbw b Cork	1	lbw b Tomlinson	1
CD Whelan	lbw b Cork	0	c Pothas b Tremlett	47
MS Mason	c Pothas b Cork	7	b Cork	25
Imran Arif	not out	0	not out	4
Extras	b 2, lb 10, w 3, nb 6	21	b 1, lb 1, w 2	4
	(all out 52.1 overs)	132	(all out 68 overs)	189

Bowling
Tremlett 13-4-18-1. Tomlinson 13.1-2-47-1. Balcombe 8-3-21-2. Cork 8-2-10-4. Ervine 8-4-13-1. Dawson 2-0-11-1.
Tremlett 16-8-24-2. Cork 14-6-27-2. Balcombe 14-3-56-2. Tomlinson 15-5-53-3. Ervine 3-1-9-1. Dawson 4-0-18-0.
Fall of Wickets: 1-41, 2-50, 3-91, 4-101, 5-112, 6-120, 7-124, 8-124, 9-132 1-5, 2-9, 3-34, 4-39, 5-48, 6-52, 7-53, 8-150, 9-163

HAMPSHIRE	First Innings		Second Innings	
MA Carberry	c Davies b Kabir Ali	4	b Mitchell	58
JHK Adams	lbw b Arif	49	lbw b Batty	8
JP Crawley	c Solanki b Mason	2	not out	31
MJ Lumb	c Davies b Kabir Ali	0	c Kabir Ali b Mitchell	0
SM Ervine	c Mason b Whelan	28	not out	8
DJ Balcombe	b Kabir Ali	0		
*N Pothas (capt)	c Davies b Arif	13		
LA Dawson	c Kabir Ali b Mason	66		
DG Cork	c Moore b Arif	25		
CT Tremlett	lbw b Arif	0		
JA Tomlinson	not out	0		
Extras	lb 2, w 9, nb 8	19	nb 2	2
	(all out 63.4 overs)	216	(3 wkts 33 overs)	107

Bowling
Kabir Ali 18-3-74-3. Mason 17.4-6-47-2. Batty 7-1-17-0. Arif 11-1-42-4. Whelan 10-2-34-1.
Kabir Ali 5-0-23-0. Mason 5-1-13-0. Arif 5-0-18-0. Batty 10-3-23-1. Whelan 7-1-30-0. Mitchell 1-1-0-2.
Fall of Wickets: 1-4, 2-7, 3-10, 4-73, 5-91, 6-111, 7-116, 8-207, 9-214 1-38, 2-99, 3-99

*Hampshire won by 7 wickets –
Hampshire (18pts), Worcestershire (3pts)*

SOMERSET v. WARWICKSHIRE – at Taunton

WARWICKSHIRE	First Innings		Second Innings	
DL Maddy	b Phillips	17	c Turner b Suppiah	36
T Frost	c Kieswetter b Phillips	7	not out	46
IR Bell	c Kieswetter b Phillips	172	not out	13
UL Trott	lbw b Phillips	0		
JO Troughton	c Phillips b Willoughby	77		
*TR Ambrose (capt)	b Banks	57		
R Clarke	c Kieswetter b Turner	0		
NM Carter	lbw b Willoughby	21		
CR Woakes	c Langer b Willoughby	63		
AG Botha	c de Bruyn b Turner	15		
JE Anyon	not out	15		
Extras	b 24, lb 19, w 11, nb 2	56	b 1, lb 4, w 2, nb 6	13
	(all out 129.4 overs)	500	(1 wkt 38 overs)	108

Bowling
Willoughby 31.4-7-87-3. Phillips 28-9-100-4. Turner 21-3-82-2. Trego 12-2-56-0. de Bruyn 16-3-44-0. Banks 20-2-88-1.
Willoughby 5-2-10-0. Phillips 4-1-6-0. Turner 9-1-29-0. Banks 6-3-9-0. Suppiah 6-1-34-1. Trescothick 5-2-10-0. Trego 3-1-5-0.
Fall of Wickets: 1-12, 2-66, 3-66, 4-220, 5-361, 6-362, 7-385, 8-399, 9-433 1-71

SOMERSET	First Innings	
ME Trescothick	c Maddy b Woakes	52
AV Suppiah	c Frost b Anyon	38
JL Langer (capt)	b Woakes	76
JC Hildreth	not out	303
Z de Bruyn	c Clarke b Woakes	4
*C Kieswetter	not out	150
PD Trego		
BJ Phillips		
OAC Banks		
ML Turner		
CM Willoughby		
Extras	b 17, lb 8, w 4, nb 20	49
	(4 wkts dec 154.1 overs)	672

Bowling
Carter 11-1-44-0. Woakes 27-4-107-3. Anyon 33-6-124-1. Botha 41-6-178-0. Maddy 7.1-0-31-0. Clarke 22-0-99-0. Trott 13-1-64-0.
Fall of Wickets: 1-104, 2-118, 3-343, 4-354

*Match drawn – Somerset (12pts),
Warwickshire (10pts)*

Round One: 15–18 April Division Two

LEICESTERSHIRE v. NORTHAMPTONSHIRE – at Grace Road

NORTHANTS	First Innings	
SD Peters	lbw b White	31
BH Howgego	lbw b Harris	24
RA White	b Allenby	7
N Boje (capt)	lbw b Harris	9
*MH Wessels	b Cliff	21
AJ Hall	not out	124
DJ Willey	c White b Harris	60
JJ van der Wath	c Nixon b Harris	24
DS Lucas	c Nixon b Cliff	15
MS Panesar	c Nixon b White	24
DH Wigley	lbw b Henderson	0
Extras	b 18, lb 10, w 6, nb 14	48
	(all out 115.5 overs)	387

Bowling
Harris 29-6-106-4. Cliff 23-2-92-2. Allenby 20-6-47-1. White 17-5-54-2. Henderson 22.5-5-49-1. New 3-1-10-0. Cobb 1-0-1-0.
Fall of Wickets: 1-66, 2-73, 3-75, 4-95, 5-111, 6-274, 7-322, 8-354, 9-384

LEICESTERSHIRE	First Innings		Second Innings (following on)	
TJ New	lbw b van der Wath	0	(2) b van der Wath	11
MAG Boyce	c Wessels b van der Wath	4	(1) c Hall b Wigley	25
HH Dippenaar	c Wessels b Lucas	12	not out	68
HD Ackerman	lbw b van der Wath	0	c Howgego b Hall	20
JJ Cobb	lbw b Lucas	1	lbw b Hall	4
*PA Nixon (capt)	b Hall	31	not out	39
J Allenby	not out	62		
WA White	c Wessels b Lucas	6		
CW Henderson	c Boje b Lucas	10		
SJ Cliff	b van der Wath	26		
AJ Harris	lbw b Wigley	17		
Extras	lb 2, w 2	14	b 1, lb 3, w 1, nb 2	7
	(all out 71.1 overs)	183	(4 wkts 63 overs)	174

Bowling
van der Wath 14-3-40-4. Lucas 19-5-46-4. Wigley 14.1-5-32-1. Panesar 16-6-30-0. Hall 6-1-20-1. Boje 2-0-3-0.
van der Wath 10-3-19-1. Lucas 10-1-26-0. Panesar 18-3-57-0. Wigley 10-3-35-1. Willey 5-0-22-0. Hall 7-5-5-2. Boje 3-1-6-0.
Fall of Wickets: 1-0, 2-13, 3-13, 4-18, 5-19, 6-72, 7-102, 8-118, 9-151 1-16, 2-53, 3-94, 4-104

*Match drawn – Leicestershire (7pts),
Northamptonshire (11pts)*

SURREY v. GLOUCESTERSHIRE – at The Oval

GLOS	First Innings	
CM Spearman	lbw b Nel	0
Kadeer Ali	lbw b Benning	90
HJH Marshall	lbw b Nel	76
APR Gidman (capt)	c Batty b Benning	69
CG Taylor	lbw b Nel	9
JEC Franklin	c Spiegel b Dernbach	11
*SD Snell	b Dernbach	4
ID Saxelby	b Dernbach	0
J Lewis	not out	39
V Banerjee	c Jordan b Nel	16
SP Kirby	b Dernbach	0
Extras	lb 9, w 3, nb 7	19
	(all out 101.3 overs)	333

Bowling
Nel 22-6-52-4. Dernbach 18.3-1-79-4. Jordan 12-3-46-0. Benning 7-1-25-2. Hussain 23-7-61-0. Schofield 18-1-60-0. Spiegel 1-0-1-0.
Fall of Wickets: 1-0, 2-126, 3-247, 4-250, 5-265, 6-276, 7-276, 8-283, 9-326

SURREY	First Innings		Second Innings (following on)	
MJ Brown (capt)	b Franklin	8	(2) not out	35
LJ Evans	b Franklin	1	(1) c Snell b Lewis	9
MNW Spiegel	lbw b Lewis	0	c Spearman b Taylor	10
U Afzaal	c Franklin b Saxelby	65	not out	10
*JN Batty	b Kirby	11		
JGE Benning	lbw b Kirby	0		
CJ Jordan	c Spearman b Franklin	7		
CP Schofield	b Banerjee	29		
Murtaza Hussain	c Kadeer Ali b Saxelby	8		
A Nel	b Banerjee	9		
JW Dernbach	not out	9		
Extras	b 2, lb 4, w 1, nb 6	13	lb 4, nb 2	6
	(all out 61.5 overs)	160	(2 wkts 30 overs)	64

Bowling
Lewis 12-2-28-1. Franklin 12-3-23-3. Kirby 14-5-44-2. Saxelby 10.5-2-33-2. Banerjee 13-4-26-2.
Lewis 4-0-13-1. Franklin 3-0-7-0. Banerjee 12-4-29-0. Taylor 11-5-11-1.
Fall of Wickets: 1-10, 2-11, 3-11, 4-35, 5-35, 6-46, 7-91, 8-108, 9-133 1-20, 2-24

*Match drawn – Surrey (7pts),
Gloucestershire (10pts)*

ESSEX v. DERBYSHIRE – at Chelmsford

DERBYSHIRE	First Innings		Second Innings	
SD Stubbings	c Foster b ten Doeschate	28	c Gallian b Masters	0
GT Park	b Wright	41	c Foster b Chambers	7
SG Law	c Foster b Wright	29	c Foster b Wright	3
DJ Redfern	c Foster b Masters	50	c Foster b Masters	26
WW Hinds	c Masters b ten Doeschate	24	(7) c Foster b Middlebrook	8
GM Smith	lbw b Middlebrook	36	(5) c ten Doeschate b Middlebrook	0
*DJ Pipe (capt)	c Mickleburgh b Chambers	39	(6) not out	64
GG Wagg	not out	24		
JL Clare	c Foster b Masters	2		
T Lungley	b Wright	2		
ID Hunter	b Wright	2		
Extras	b 1, lb 18, w 2, nb 30	51	lb 3, w 1, nb 8	12
	(all out 105.4 overs)	326	(6 wkts dec 55 overs)	179

Bowling
Masters 28-11-40-2. Wright 29.4-7-86-4. Chambers 17-3-63-1. ten Doeschate 19-1-95-2. Middlebrook 12-5-23-1.
Masters 9-5-6-1. Wright 10-2-17-1. Chambers 10-0-53-1. ten Doeschate 11-1-57-1. Middlebrook 15-3-43-2.
Fall of Wickets: 1-75, 2-101, 3-132, 4-166, 5-235, 6-260, 7-295, 8-307, 9-318 1-0, 2-9, 3-19, 4-64, 5-153, 6-179

ESSEX	First Innings		Second Innings	
V Chopra	c Pipe b Lungley	39	c Park b Hunter	56
JER Gallian	c Stubbings b Hunter	11	not out	44
JC Mickleburgh	c Pipe b Hunter	5	lbw b Hunter	1
MJ Walker	c Park b Smith	17	c Pipe b Clare	7
ML Pettini (capt)	c Pipe b Hunter	28	not out	1
*JS Foster	c Lungley b Hunter	40		
RN ten Doeschate	c Pipe b Clare	1		
JD Middlebrook	lbw b Hunter	0		
CJC Wright	c sub b Clare	8		
DD Masters	c Redfern b Smith	20		
MA Chambers	not out	2		
Extras	b 2, lb 6, w 7, nb 8	23	lb 1, w 6, nb 4	11
	(all out 69 overs)	194	(3 wkts 29 overs)	120

Bowling
Lungley 12-2-60-1. Hunter 23-4-46-5. Clare 18-7-44-2. Park 5-0-12-0. Smith 11-4-24-2.
Lungley 11-62-0. Hunter 10-2-42-2. Smith 2-0-7-0. Park 1-1-0-0. Clare 3-2-1-1. Redfern 2-0-7-0.
Fall of Wickets: 1-50, 2-56, 3-87, 4-93, 5-140, 6-141, 7-142, 8-151, 9-188 1-88, 2-100, 3-114

*Match drawn – Essex (7pts),
Derbyshire (10pts)*

target was comfortably reached. Nic Pothas, the acting Hampshire captain, said, 'This was a clinical performance and I am delighted'.

Taunton's pitch, even in April, proved the winner in the other Division One game as Somerset and Warwickshire batted out a high-scoring draw. James Hildreth, with an unbeaten 303 including four sixes and 35 fours, compiled the earliest triple-century ever scored in an English season.

Hildreth added an unbroken stand of 318 with Craig Kieswetter, whose 150 not out with six sixes and ten fours was a maiden first-class hundred, until Justin

Langer, the Somerset captain, unwittingly declared with the pair only two runs short of the county's fifth-wicket record. Ian Bell didn't mind the early-season shirtfront either, as he batted more than seven hours for 172 in Warwickshire's own big first innings total.

No play on the second day at Grace Road denied Northamptonshire a likely win against Leicestershire, while Gloucestershire might have forced a victory at The Oval, where Surrey were made to follow on. All out for 160 in reply to the visitors 333, Surrey were 64 for 2 in the second innings when rain arrived to wash away the third day.

Dominic Cork, Hampshire's new signing from Lancashire, celebrates taking the wicket of Warwickshire's Darren Maddy at Edgbaston.

Round Two: 21–25 April

There were victories for Nottinghamshire and
Lancashire, both boosted by the presence of high-profile
England players, while Durham and Warwickshire had
to be content with draws as Yorkshire and Hampshire,
respectively, managed to bat out time.

James Anderson's career-best match figures of 11 for
109 was the reward for a magnificent and sustained
display of fast swing bowling at Hove, where Sussex
were well beaten by eight wickets. Ed Joyce was the
only batsman to flourish against Anderson, who was
superbly supported by Glen Chapple in the first innings
and Gary Keedy, the experienced left-arm spinner, in
Sussex's second innings slide to 167 all out.

England's James Anderson took eleven wickets in the match to
spearhead Lancashire's victory against Sussex at Hove in April.

Round Two: 21–25 April Division One

NOTTINGHAMSHIRE v. WORCESTERSHIRE – at Trent Bridge

NOTTS	First Innings	
MA Wagh	c Davies b Mason	19
BM Shafayat	c Mitchell b Arif	14
SR Patel	run out	95
AC Voges	c Davies b Mason	99
AD Brown	lbw b Whelan	4
*CMW Read (capt)	c Mason b Whelan	125
GP Swann	c Davies b Mason	26
SCJ Broad	b Whelan	60
MA Ealham	not out	21
AR Adams	st Davies b Batty	4
DJ Pattinson	run out	19
Extras	b 5, lb 8, w 2, nb 4	19
	(all out 138.2 overs)	505

Bowling
Noffke 25-8-73-0. Mason 26-9-83-3. Arif 26-4-120-1. Whelan 27-1-116-3.
Batty 33.2-6-90-1. Ali 1-0-10-0.
Fall of Wickets: 1-23, 2-46, 3-186, 4-199, 5-313, 6-352, 7-456, 8-461, 9-469

WORCS	First Innings		Second Innings (following on)	
DKH Mitchell	c Brown b Swann	80	c Read b Ealham	9
SC Moore	lbw b Broad	8	lbw b Adams	4
VS Solanki (capt)	c Brown b Broad	50	(4) c Broad b Swann	64
BF Smith	c Adams b Broad	0	(5) b Adams	24
MM Ali	c & b Broad	3	(6) c Read b Ealham	8
*SM Davies	c Adams b Patel	126	(7) c Read b Broad	11
GJ Batty	c Read b Broad	22	(8) lbw b Broad	3
AA Noffke	c Shafayat b Swann	39	(9) lbw b Patel	13
CD Whelan	lbw b Patel	2	(3) lbw b Adams	0
MS Mason	c & b Swann	4	not out	1
Imran Arif	not out	1	c Patel b Swann	3
Extras	b 5, w 2, nb 12	19	b 3, lb 1, nb 2	6
	(all out 134.4 overs)	354	(all out 67.2 overs)	146

Bowling
Broad 31-5-79-5. Pattinson 12-0-45-0. Ealham 22-5-63-0. Adams 27-9-71-0.
Swann 22.4-5-52-3. Patel 20-6-39-2.
Broad 17-7-27-2. Adams 21-6-59-3. Ealham 10-4-19-2. Patel 9-3-18-1.
Swann 10.2-5-19-2.
Fall of Wickets: 1-11, 2-111, 3-111, 4-115, 5-209, 6-257, 7-330, 8-344, 9-344
1-8, 2-8, 3-16, 4-49, 5-64, 6-83, 7-89, 8-120, 9-142

*Nottinghamshire won by
an innings and 5 runs – Nottinghamshire (21pts),
Worcestershire (5pts)*

Round Two: 21–25 April Division Two

GLOUCESTERSHIRE v. ESSEX – at Bristol

GLOS	First Innings		Second Innings	
Kadeer Ali	c Foster b Masters	6	(2) c Foster b ten Doeschate	27
CM Spearman	c Foster b Masters	11	(1) lbw b Chambers	28
HJH Marshall	lbw b ten Doeschate	64	c Foster b ten Doeschate	3
APR Gidman (capt)	c Foster b Wright	1	lbw b Chambers	5
CG Taylor	c Chopra b ten Doeschate	10	c Foster b Chambers	16
JEC Franklin	c Foster b Masters	21	(7) c Gallian b Masters	13
*SD Snell	c Foster b ten Doeschate	18	(6) b Masters	7
ID Saxelby	lbw b Wright	10	lbw b Masters	0
J Lewis	c Pettini b ten Doeschate	2	b Wright	1
V Banerjee	b ten Doeschate	0	c Foster b ten Doeschate	11
SP Kirby	not out	6	not out	2
Extras	lb 4, nb 2	6	lb 2, w 4	6
	(all out 64.3 overs)	155	(all out 49.1 overs)	119

Bowling
Masters 16-8-16-3. Wright 15.3-5-38-2. ten Doeschate 18-1-62-5.
Chambers 12-2-25-0. Middlebrook 1-0-6-0. Chopra 2-0-4-0.
Masters 12-5-12-3. Wright 13-3-40-1. Chambers 13-1-30-3.
ten Doeschate 11.1-0-35-3.
Fall of Wickets: 1-10, 2-21, 3-22, 4-38, 5-93, 6-128, 7-141, 8-149, 9-149
1-51, 2-59, 3-61, 4-75, 5-86, 6-87, 7-87, 8-88, 9-110

ESSEX	First Innings		Second Innings	
V Chopra	lbw b Franklin	15	c Spearman b Kirby	1
JER Gallian	lbw b Franklin	8	c Spearman b Saxelby	11
JC Mickleburgh	c Snell b Gidman	32	lbw b Lewis	0
MJ Walker	lbw b Lewis	9	not out	48
CJC Wright	c sub b Saxelby	21		
ML Pettini (capt)	run out	8	(5) not out	28
*JS Foster	c Marshall b Lewis	0		
RN ten Doeschate	c Saxelby b Gidman	42		
JD Middlebrook	c Snell b Gidman	17		
DD Masters	c sub b Marshall	0		
MA Chambers	not out	0		
Extras	b 6, lb 11, w 2, nb 6	25	b 5, lb 7, w 1	13
	(all out 77.1 overs)	177	(3 wkts 27 overs)	101

Bowling
Lewis 23-7-39-2. Kirby 18-4-49-0. Saxelby 12-2-34-1. Franklin 6-3-7-2.
Gidman 15-1-6-23-3. Banerjee 1-0-7-0. Marshall 2-1-1-1.
Lewis 10-1-34-1. Kirby 7-2-14-1. Saxelby 5-3-16-1. Marshall 4-0-24-0.
Taylor 1-0-1-0.
Fall of Wickets: 1-24, 2-27, 3-48, 4-79, 5-105, 6-107, 7-109, 8-175, 9-177
1-1, 2-6, 3-46

*Essex won by 7 wickets – Gloucestershire (3pts),
Essex (17pts)*

Round Two: 21–25 April Division One

SUSSEX v. LANCASHIRE – at Hove

SUSSEX	First Innings		Second Innings	
MH Yardy (capt)	lbw b Anderson	35	b Anderson	22
CD Nash	c Sutton b Anderson	22	c Sutton b Anderson	13
EC Joyce	b Anderson	90	lbw b Keedy	55
MW Goodwin	c Prince b Chapple	11	st Sutton b Keedy	20
*MJ Prior	c Horton b Chapple	4	lbw b Keedy	0
LJ Wright	c & b Anderson	6	c Sutton b Anderson	35
RSC Martin-Jenkins	b Anderson	67	c Sutton b Anderson	13
TMJ Smith	lbw b Anderson	10	c Horton b Anderson	1
DG Wright	lbw b Chapple	4	c Chilton b Keedy	1
RG Aga	not out	1	c Chilton b Keedy	2
CD Collymore	lbw b Chapple	0	not out	1
Extras	b 19, lb 14, w 4, nb 2	39	lb 4	4
	(all out 120 overs)	**289**	(all out 61.5 overs)	**167**

Bowling
Anderson 32-11-56-6. Chapple 31-6-69-4. Mahmood 19-6-48-0. Smith 28-10-58-0. Keedy 5-0-15-0. Croft 3-2-6-0. du Plessis 2-0-4-0.
Anderson 19-4-53-5. Chapple 11-2-24-0. Mahmood 6-2-18-0. Smith 3-0-16-0. Keedy 20.5-4-45-5. du Plessis 2-0-7-0.
Fall of Wickets: 1-43, 2-116, 3-132, 4-142, 5-160, 6-250, 7-271, 8-276, 9-284
1-24, 2-45, 3-95, 4-95, 5-148, 6-150, 7-156, 8-163, 9-166

LANCASHIRE	First Innings		Second Innings	
PJ Horton	lbw b Collymore	1	(2) c Goodwin b Collymore	4
TC Smith	c Prior b Collymore	0	(1) c Nash b Collymore	5
AG Prince	b Wright LJ	56	not out	91
F du Plessis	c Prior b Martin-Jenkins	6	not out	58
MJ Chilton	lbw b Martin-Jenkins	89		
SJ Croft	c Joyce b Wright LJ	59		
*LD Sutton	c Prior b Wright LJ	20		
G Chapple (capt)	c Prior b Martin-Jenkins	4		
SI Mahmood	lbw b Wright LJ	26		
G Keedy	c Prior b Wright LJ	7		
JM Anderson	not out	9		
Extras	b 4, lb 9, w 1, nb 8	22	lb 2	2
	(all out 113.5 overs)	**299**	(2 wkts 41.4 overs)	**160**

Bowling
Collymore 27-7-73-2. Wright DG 21-10-43-0. Martin-Jenkins 25-10-50-3. Aga 7-0-28-0. Wright LJ 27.5-8-80-5. Smith 4-1-11-0. Nash 2-1-1-0.
Collymore 7-3-11-2. Wright DG 9-3-19-0. Martin-Jenkins 8-4-23-0. Wright LJ 5-0-27-0. Smith 8.4-0-59-0. Nash 4-0-19-0.
Fall of Wickets: 1-1, 2-2, 3-31, 4-102, 5-209, 6-253, 7-257, 8-273, 9-284
1-7, 2-12

Lancashire won by 8 wickets – Sussex (5pts), Lancashire (19pts)

DURHAM v. YORKSHIRE – at the Riverside

DURHAM	First Innings		Second Innings	
MJ Di Venuto	c Hoggard b Bresnan	36	(2) c Bresnan b Rashid	143
MD Stoneman	c Brophy b Bresnan	2	(1) lbw b Hoggard	0
WR Smith (capt)	c Brophy b Hoggard	21	c & b Rashid	67
GJ Muchall	c Brophy b Patterson	13	not out	51
DM Benkenstein	c Brophy b Kruis	17	(6) c Rashid b Hoggard	22
ID Blackwell	c Brophy b Hoggard	95	(5) c Rudolph b Rashid	6
*P Mustard	not out	94	not out	1
LE Plunkett	c sub b Bresnan	10		
CD Thorp	c & b Hoggard	42		
G Onions	c Brophy b Hoggard	4		
SJ Harmison	lbw b Rashid	3		
Extras	b 10, lb 10, w 5	25	b 4, lb 6, w 3	13
	(all out 112.3 overs)	**362**	(5 wkts dec 79 overs)	**303**

Bowling
Hoggard 24-5-82-4. Bresnan 27-7-63-3. Kruis 22-2-80-1. Patterson 22-6-61-1. McGrath 9-5-19-0. Rashid 8.3-0-37-1.
Hoggard 15-1-57-2. Bresnan 9-2-40-0. Kruis 9-1-31-0. Patterson 17-2-62-0. Rashid 26-1-88-3. McGrath 3-0-15-0.
Fall of Wickets: 1-20, 2-41, 3-69, 4-82, 5-129, 6-236, 7-257, 8-343, 9-353
1-0, 2-204, 3-233, 4-239, 5-295

YORKSHIRE	First Innings		Second Innings	
AW Gale	b Onions	11	(5) c Muchall b Plunkett	27
JA Rudolph	c Mustard b Harmison	51	(1) b Onions	16
MP Vaughan	c Mustard b Harmison	24	c Mustard b Onions	20
A McGrath (capt)	c Stoneman b Thorp	27	c Di Venuto b Onions	26
*GL Brophy	st Mustard b Blackwell	75	(6) c Onions b Harmison	27
TT Bresnan	b Plunkett	40	(7) c Mustard b Onions	20
AU Rashid	c Benkenstein b Harmison	11	(8) not out	6
JJ Sayers	c Plunkett b Harmison	5	(2) c Mustard b Onions	30
SA Patterson	c Mustard b Onions	3	not out	4
MJ Hoggard	lbw b Onions	1		
GJ Kruis	not out	0		
Extras	b 10, lb 8, nb 6	24	b 4, lb 7, w 2, nb 4	17
	(all out 85.1 overs)	**272**	(7 wkts 90.4 overs)	**193**

Bowling
Harmison 23.1-3-76-4. Thorp 18-2-57-1. Onions 19-4-49-3. Plunkett 13-3-38-1. Benkenstein 2-0-15-0. Blackwell 10-5-19-1.
Harmison 23-8-32-1. Onions 28-9-56-5. Thorp 11.4-5-18-0. Blackwell 11-2-21-0. Plunkett 17-3-55-1.
Fall of Wickets: 1-40, 2-83, 3-96, 4-142, 5-247, 6-247, 7-267, 8-270, 9-272
1-29, 2-71, 3-72, 4-116, 5-150, 6-174, 7-186

Match drawn – Durham (11pts), Yorkshire (9pts)

WARWICKSHIRE v. HAMPSHIRE – at Edgbaston

HAMPSHIRE	First Innings		Second Innings	
MA Carberry	c Ambrose b Miller	77	c Clarke b Botha	65
JHK Adams	c Clarke b Rankin	1	c Rankin b Botha	39
JP Crawley	c Clarke b Miller	30	c Clarke b Botha	6
†MJ North	c Ambrose b Maddy	15		
SM Ervine	lbw b Rankin	30	c Clarke b Rankin	21
*N Pothas (capt)	not out	122	not out	65
LA Dawson	c Troughton b Clarke	22	lbw b Botha	2
DG Cork	c Bell b Miller	5	not out	7
CT Tremlett	b Woakes	36		
DJ Balcombe	lbw b Rankin	0		
JA Tomlinson	c Maddy b Clarke	8		
MJ Lumb			(4) b Rankin	84
Extras	b 4, lb 8, w 5, nb 16	33	b 5, lb 4, w 1, nb 2	12
	(all out 123.5 overs)	**379**	(6 wkts 103 overs)	**301**

Bowling
Woakes 33-8-93-1. Rankin 25-7-64-3. Miller 27-5-79-3. Clarke 11.5-0-63-2. Maddy 19-7-48-1. Bell 3-0-7-0. Botha 5-0-13-0.
Woakes 18-4-49-0. Rankin 24-5-76-2. Botha 42-7-103-4. Miller 9-0-29-0. Clarke 5-1-14-0. Maddy 5-1-21-0.
Fall of Wickets: 1-24, 2-115, 3-121, 4-167, 5-183, 6-239, 7-271, 8-341, 9-344
1-95, 2-103, 3-140, 4-177, 5-264, 6-279
† Replaced by MJ Lumb

WARWICKSHIRE	First Innings	
DL Maddy	c Ervine b Cork	8
T Frost	run out	4
IJL Trott	c Cork b Tomlinson	22
JO Troughton	c Cork b Carberry	223
IR Bell	c Cork b Tremlett	29
*TR Ambrose (capt)	b Adams	153
R Clarke	c Ervine b Dawson	112
AG Botha	c Carberry b Dawson	51
CR Woakes	not out	8
AS Miller		
WB Rankin		
Extras	b 1, lb 7, nb 12	20
	(8 wkts dec 148.5 overs)	**630**

Bowling
Cork 19-4-55-1. Tremlett 24-5-87-1. Balcombe 22-1-97-0. Tomlinson 29-3-104-1. Ervine 17-3-50-0. Dawson 8.5-0-75-2. Carberry 17-1-105-1. Adams 12-0-49-1.
Fall of Wickets: 1-12, 2-12, 3-54, 4-120, 5-455, 6-476, 7-614, 8-630

Match drawn – Warwickshire (12pts), Hampshire (9pts)

Round Two: 21–25 April Division Two

DERBYSHIRE v. SURREY – at Derby

SURREY	First Innings		Second Innings	
SA Newman	c Lawson b Wagg	12	c Pipe b Park	124
MJ Brown (capt)	c Stubbings b Wagg	1	c Law b Hunter	28
LJ Evans	c Law b Wagg	6	b Clare	7
U Afzaal	b Wagg	3	c & b Clare	59
*JN Batty	lbw b Wagg	36	(6) c Pipe b Hunter	9
JGE Benning	c Park b Smith	5	(7) c Hunter b Smith	36
CJ Jordan	lbw b Wagg	6	(8) b Wagg	3
CP Schofield	lbw b Clare	10	(9) not out	31
A Nel	b Smith	12	(10) b Park	15
JW Dernbach	not out	4	(5) c Smith b Hunter	6
PT Collins	c Pipe b Smith	1	b Park	8
Extras	b 13, lb 7, w 1, nb 14	35	b 10, lb 16, w 2, nb 6	34
	(all out 53 overs)	**131**	(all out 107.3 overs)	**360**

Bowling
Wagg 15.4-5-35-6. Hunter 12-3-27-0. Clare 14-5-31-1. Smith 11.2-7-18-3.
Wagg 29-6-94-1. Hunter 26-2-88-3. Smith 14-5-35-1. Clare 17-3-53-2. Lawson 12-1-39-0. Park 9.3-1-25-3.
Fall of Wickets: 1-5, 2-19, 3-31, 4-32, 5-43, 6-58, 7-124, 8-125, 9-126
1-83, 2-129, 3-204, 4-217, 5-255, 6-259, 7-276, 8-314, 9-342

DERBYSHIRE	First Innings		Second Innings	
SD Stubbings	c Batty b Collins	7	b Schofield	83
GT Park	c Jordan b Dernbach	4	lbw b Collins	50
SG Law	c Batty b Nel	0	c Schofield b Nel	7
DJ Redfern	c Batty b Collins	28	c Nel b Jordan	17
WW Hinds	lbw b Jordan	26	c Batty b Schofield	9
GM Smith	not out	94	not out	27
*DJ Pipe (capt)	lbw b Collins	6	not out	8
JL Clare	b Collins	0		
GG Wagg	lbw b Schofield	35		
MAK Lawson	c Batty b Jordan	0		
ID Hunter	b Collins	47		
Extras	b 5, lb 6, nb 16	27	lb 4, w 7, nb 8	19
	(all out 71.4 overs)	**274**	(5 wkts 75.5 overs)	**220**

Bowling
Nel 7.4-1-26-1. Dernbach 18.2-3-64-1. Collins 19.4-5-75-5. Benning 3-0-5-0. Jordan 14-0-59-2. Afzaal 2-1-1-0. Schofield 7-1-33-1.
Dernbach 16-6-38-0. Collins 15-3-47-1. Nel 14-6-23-1. Schofield 13.5-4-42-2. Jordan 11-2-44-1. Benning 5-1-22-0. Afzaal 1-1-0-0.
Fall of Wickets: 1-6, 2-7, 3-21, 4-68, 5-76, 6-88, 7-88, 8-190, 9-191
1-89, 2-116, 3-166, 4-183, 5-192

Derbyshire won by 5 wickets – Derbyshire (19pts), Surrey (3pts)

KENT v. NORTHAMPTONSHIRE – at Canterbury

NORTHANTS	First Innings		Second Innings	
SD Peters	c Jones GO b Jones PS	32	c Key b Tredwell	107
BH Howgego	c Tredwell b Azhar Mahmood	18	run out	5
RA White	lbw b Azhar Mahmood	41	c van Jaarsveld b Tredwell	70
N Boje (capt)	c Jones GO b Tredwell	98	(5) not out	70
*MH Wessels	c Jones GO b Saggers	27	(6) c van Jaarsveld b Tredwell	8
AJ Hall	lbw b Stevens	38	(7) b Saggers	3
DJ Willey	c Jones GO b Saggers	31	(8) b Key	47
JJ van der Wath	c Edwards b Azhar Mahmood	12		
DS Lucas	b Azhar Mahmood	9	(4) c Jones GO b Saggers	13
MS Panesar	c Stevens b Tredwell	15	(9) not out	2
DH Wigley	not out	10		
Extras	lb 4, w 2, nb 18	24	b 7, lb 6, w 2, nb 8	23
	(all out 128.2 overs)	**355**	(7 wkts 135 overs)	**348**

Bowling
Jones PS 25-8-68-1. Saggers 23-8-48-2. Azhar Mahmood 23-6-73-4. Stevens 12-2-42-1. Edwards 14-1-31-0. Tredwell 30.2-9-84-2. van Jaarsveld 1-0-5-0.
Jones PS 20-2-64-0. Azhar Mahmood 10-3-39-0. Edwards 16-2-54-0. Saggers 20-7-42-2. Tredwell 37-16-67-3. Denly 21-7-51-0. Stevens 2-1-4-0. Key 9-3-14-1.
Fall of Wickets: 1-32, 2-98, 3-100, 4-161, 5-233, 6-300, 7-310, 8-322, 9-333
1-8, 2-142, 3-181, 4-235, 5-249, 6-259, 7-346

KENT	First Innings	
JL Denly	c Peters b Hall	27
RWT Key (capt)	lbw b Lucas	2
*GO Jones	c & b Wigley	103
M van Jaarsveld	c Hall b Panesar	107
DI Stevens	c Wessels b Hall	73
JB Hockley	b Lucas	27
Azhar Mahmood	c Wigley b Hall	35
JC Tredwell	not out	15
PS Jones	c Peters b Panesar	10
P Edwards	lbw b Willey	0
MJ Saggers	b Willey	0
Extras	lb 7, w 1, nb 10	18
	(all out 107.4 overs)	**417**

Bowling
van der Wath 6-0-26-0. Lucas 26-6-68-2. Wigley 19-0-96-1. Hall 20-2-89-3. Panesar 22-2-75-2. Boje 8-2-35-0. Willey 6.4-1-21-2.
Fall of Wickets: 1-18, 2-87, 3-179, 4-306, 5-324, 6-361, 7-393, 8-412, 9-413

Match drawn – Kent (11pts), Northamptonshire (10pts)

MIDDLESEX v. GLAMORGAN – at Lord's

GLAMORGAN	First Innings		Second Innings	
GP Rees	c Scott b Murtagh	6	lbw b Murtagh	9
MJ Cosgrove	lbw b Dexter	120	c Berg b Murtagh	8
BJ Wright	c Murtagh b Udal	38	b Berg	28
MJ Powell	lbw b Malan	51	lbw b Richardson	24
JWM Dalrymple (capt)	c Morgan b Evans	28	not out	112
TL Maynard	c Scott b Dexter	16	(7) lbw b Evans	0
*MA Wallace	c Dexter b Udal	128	(8) b Evans	17
RDB Croft	b Murtagh	42	(9) c Richardson b Dexter	52
DS Harrison	c Udal b Berg	51		
AJ Shantry	c Richardson b Udal	1	(6) c Malan b Udal	20
GJP Kruger	not out	4		
Extras	b 5, lb 14, w 1	20	b 2, nb 6	8
	(all out 140.3 overs)	**505**	(8 wkts dec 89.5 overs)	**278**

Bowling
Murtagh 30-3-103-2. Richardson 30-8-54-0. Evans 22-1-121-1. Berg 20-3-65-1. Udal 22.3-0-87-3. Malan 5-0-19-1. Dexter 11-4-37-2.
Murtagh 12-2-38-2. Richardson 24-5-72-1. Berg 15-4-46-1. Evans 20-2-69-2. Udal 14-2-28-1. Dexter 4.5-0-23-1.
Fall of Wickets: 1-10, 2-86, 3-185, 4-250, 5-260, 6-281, 7-381, 8-498, 9-500
1-17, 2-17, 3-65, 4-82, 5-127, 6-128, 7-154, 8-278

MIDDLESEX	First Innings		Second Innings	
BA Godleman	c & b Harrison	23	c Wallace b Harrison	3
PJ Hughes	b Kruger	118	not out	65
NJ Dexter	c Powell b Kruger	72	c Maynard b Harrison	0
EJG Morgan	lbw b Harrison	26	b Shantry	8
DJ Malan	c Cosgrove b Harrison	88	not out	13
*BJM Scott	lbw b Kruger	14		
GK Berg	c Powell b Kruger	3		
SD Udal (capt)	lbw b Dalrymple	20		
TJ Murtagh	not out	23		
A Richardson	not out	3		
D Evans				
Extras	b 8, lb 9, w 5, nb 2	24	lb 2, w 1, nb 2	5
	(8 wkts dec 105 overs)	**414**	(3 wkts 28 overs)	**94**

Bowling
Shantry 22-3-69-0. Kruger 20-3-85-4. Harrison 25-3-117-3. Croft 28-6-79-0. Cosgrove 4-1-12-0. Dalrymple 6-0-35-1.
Kruger 7-0-42-0. Harrison 10-1-26-2. Croft 5-1-7-0. Shantry 4-1-8-1. Cosgrove 2-0-9-0.
Fall of Wickets: 1-67, 2-221, 3-226, 4-261, 5-293, 6-311, 7-349, 8-404
1-22, 2-22, 3-31

Match drawn – Middlesex (11pts), Glamorgan (11pts)

Phillip Hughes narrowly avoids a collision with a Glamorgan fielder at Lord's, but overall the 20-year-old Australian prodigy had few alarms during his prolific early-season spell with Middlesex.

Luke Wright, a putative England all-rounder, impressed with 5 for 80 as Lancashire won a narrow first innings lead chiefly through the efforts of Mark Chilton's 89, but the home side had nothing in their bowling attack to match the penetrative class of Anderson, and Ashwell Prince's unbeaten 91 meant Lancashire cantered to their fourth innings target.

Chris Read's 125, plus 99 from Adam Voges and 95 from Samit Patel, set up Notts at Trent Bridge but then it was Stuart Broad, following up his 62-ball 60 with 5 for 79, and his England team-mate Graeme Swann who ensured Worcestershire could not wriggle off the hook in reply to the home team's 505.

Swann's off breaks brought him five wickets in the match as Worcestershire were bowled out for 354 and 146, while Broad collected seven scalps as only Steven Davies, with a first innings 126, and Vikram Solanki, who scored 64 in a losing cause after the follow-on had been enforced, flourished against the Notts attack.

Durham initially struggled to 129 for 5 on the opening day against Yorkshire at the Riverside, but Ian Blackwell and Phil Mustard led the recovery and they were in charge from then on – with Michael Di Venuto hitting a second innings 143 – although not even Graham Onions's 5 for 56 on the last afternoon could force the win.

Warwickshire's 630 for 8 declared at Edgbaston was the ninth highest total in the county's history, with Jim Troughton batting 443 minutes for his 223 and adding a county fifth wicket record of 335 with Tim Ambrose, who finished on 153. Rikki Clarke also contributed 112

from just 86 balls but Nic Pothas, with unbeaten innings of 122 and 65, led the Hampshire resistance. Michael Carberry also batted well in the game and Dominic Cork occupied the crease for an hour at the end to ensure the draw.

A seaming pitch at Bristol saw Essex beat Gloucestershire well inside three days, with Ryan ten Doeschate making much of the difference with his all-round contribution, while Graham Wagg's destructive first day 6 for 35 and significant efforts with both bat and ball from Greg Smith helped Derbyshire to a five-wicket victory against Surrey.

Dull draws at both Canterbury and Lord's were enlivened only by the batting, respectively, of Northants' Nicky Boje and Stephen Peters, and the home team's Martin van Jaarsveld and Geraint Jones, scoring 103 in his first outing at No. 3, and by the unique slashing strokeplay of Middlesex's 20-year-old Australian prodigy, Phillip Hughes, who hit 118 and 65 not out in a match which also featured hundreds from Glamorgan's Mark Cosgrove, Mark Wallace and Jamie Dalrymple, against his former county.

Round Three: 28 April–2 May

Four weather-affected draws in Division One nevertheless produced some memorable individual performances, and none more so that at Taunton where Somerset escaped against Durham despite being skittled for just 69 in their first innings in reply to the visitors' imposing 543, based upon Dale Benkenstein's 181.

Graham Onions, who earlier that morning had learned of his England Test call-up, scythed through the Somerset batting with 6 for 31 as, from 39 for 1, only Justin Langer resisted. And the veteran Australian was at the heart of the great escape, too, again remaining unbeaten on 122 and adding 197 with Craig Kieswetter, who made 106 from 113 balls, after a second wicket partnership of 151 between Marcus Trescothick and James Hildreth.

Trescothick fought through more than five and a half hours for his 105, while Hildreth's 71 took him almost as long. Only 24 overs had been possible on day three, however, and the Somerset top order were determined to bat out time, which they did successfully at 485 for 5.

At Headingley there were fine centuries for Jacques Rudolph, who batted ten hours for his 198, Anthony McGrath, Moeen Ali and Vikram Solanki, who went on to reach an unbeaten 206 as Worcestershire batted out time, while the draws at the Rose Bowl and Old Trafford at least featured further fine hundreds from Sean Ervine, Matt Prior and Ashwell Prince.

In Division Two, there was a remarkable win for Kent after being asked to follow on by Essex at Chelmsford. Wayne Parnell, with bat and ball, was initially Kent's only real challenge as Essex – for whom Matt Walker scored 98 against his former county and

Round Three: 28 April–2 May Division One

Round Three:
28 April–2 May Division Two

ESSEX v. KENT – at Chelmsford

ESSEX	First Innings		Second Innings	
V Chopra	b Parnell	12	c Jones GO b Parnell	10
AN Cook	c Hockley b Saggers	4	c Tredwell b Parnell	4
JC Mickleburgh	c van Jaarsveld b Parnell	7	lbw b Joseph	15
MJ Walker	lbw b Joseph	98	b Joseph	16
ML Pettini (capt)	b Saggers	27	lbw b Joseph	0
*JS Foster	c Jones GO b Saggers	99	c Kemp b Joseph	13
DD Masters	c van Jaarsveld b Joseph	0	(9) c Denly b Tredwell	20
RN ten Doeschate	c Jones GO b Jones PS	3	(7) c van Jaarsveld b Parnell	36
CJC Wright	c Kemp b Parnell	6	(8) b Joseph	0
Danish Kaneria	c Denly b Parnell	4	c Stevens b Joseph	4
MA Chambers	not out	4	not out	0
Extras	b 6, lb 13, w 1, nb 30	50	b 4, lb 5, nb 28	37
	(all out 104.5 overs)	370	(all out 57.2 overs)	155

Bowling
Joseph 20-2-104-2. Parnell 27.5-7-78-4. Saggers 22-8-45-3. Jones 17-3-61-1. Stevens 7-1-15-0. Kemp 9-2-35-0. Tredwell 2-0-13-0.
Parnell 19-3-56-3. Saggers 8-3-17-0. Joseph 13.2-0-55-6. Jones PS 9-5-9-0. Tredwell 8-5-9-1.
Fall of Wickets: 1-31, 2-69, 3-72, 4-115, 5-309, 6-313, 7-320, 8-338, 9-366 1-11, 2-22, 3-34, 4-34, 5-74, 6-79, 7-79, 8-151, 9-153

KENT	First Innings		Second Innings (following on)	
JL Denly	c Foster b Masters	0	c sub b Wright	19
JC Tredwell	c Foster b ten Doeschate	10	c Cook b Danish Kaneria	79
*GO Jones	c Foster b Wright	1	b Chambers	45
M van Jaarsveld (capt)	run out	35	c Foster b Masters	102
DI Stevens	lbw b Chambers	15	not out	136
JM Kemp	c Foster b Masters	3	c Cook b Danish Kaneria	22
JB Hockley	b Danish Kaneria	46	c Pettini b Wright	72
WD Parnell	c Masters b Wright	69	c Chopra b Danish Kaneria	3
PS Jones	lbw b Danish Kaneria	0	c Cook b Chambers	16
RH Joseph	c sub b Chambers	1	lbw b Danish Kaneria	0
MJ Saggers	not out	5	not out	
Extras	b 4, lb 1, w 1, nb 14	20	lb 6, w 2, nb 10	18
	(all out 62 overs)	205	(9 wkts dec 149.4 overs)	512

Bowling
Masters 14-6-18-2. Wright 13-2-49-2. ten Doeschate 11-2-40-1. Chambers 11-1-45-2. Danish Kaneria 13-2-48-2.
Masters 31-9-82-1. Wright 32-5-98-2. Danish Kaneria 46-7-172-4. ten Doeschate 16-3-51-0. Chambers 12.4-1-58-2. Chopra 4.1-1-17-0. Mickleburgh 7.5-1-28-0.
Fall of Wickets: 1-4, 2-13, 3-19, 4-54, 5-57, 6-96, 7-134, 8-134, 9-159 1-35, 2-113, 3-237, 4-272, 5-312, 6-478, 7-481, 8-509, 9-510

Kent won by 192 runs –
Essex (7pts), Kent (18pts)

James Foster 99 in a fifth wicket partnership worth 194 – took control at the halfway stage.

But, having been bowled out for 205 and facing a first innings deficit of 165, Kent hit back with centuries from both Martin van Jaarsveld and Darren Stevens, plus excellent 70s from James Tredwell and James Hockley, and in the end were able to declare at 512 for 9. A deflated Essex were then shot out for 155 by Robbie Joseph's 6 for 55 and three more wickets by Parnell, and Kent's victory by 192 runs was the largest winning margin in cricket history for a side that had followed on.

There was another excellent game of cricket at Northampton, too, where Gloucestershire defied injuries to three of their six front-line bowlers to emerge winners by 44 runs against a Northamptonshire side who, when Andrew Hall was making 91 and Steven Crook a powerful 55, looked capable of chasing down a stiff fourth innings target on a pitch which provided the almost-perfect balance between bat and ball.

The other two second division fixtures produced draws, with James Taylor's superb maiden first-class hundred saving Leicestershire after they had followed on against a Middlesex team kick-started by Andrew Strauss's sublime 150 and further centuries from Phillip Hughes and Eoin Morgan. At Cardiff, the loss to rain of all but 38 overs on the first day and then the whole of the third day meant that Derbyshire avoided almost certain defeat against Glamorgan, for whom Mike Powell and Jamie Dalrymple both hit first innings hundreds.

NORTHANTS v. GLOUCESTERSHIRE – at Northampton

GLOS	First Innings		Second Innings	
Kadeer Ali	b Lucas	9	(2) c White b Wigley	45
WTS Porterfield	c O'Brien b Wigley	25	(1) c O'Brien b Lucas	0
HJH Marshall	c Wessels b Hall	12	b Boje	69
APR Gidman (capt)	c Hall b Wigley	39	(8) c O'Brien b Lucas	11
CG Taylor	c Wakely b Wigley	32	(4) c O'Brien b Wigley	55
JEC Franklin	b Boje	38	c O'Brien b Hall	11
*SD Snell	c Wessels b Wigley	47	(5) c Crook b Wigley	11
J Lewis	lbw b Boje	0	(7) c Hall b Panesar	9
ID Saxelby	not out	60	(11) not out	5
V Banerjee	c Wakely b Wigley	4	(9) c O'Brien b Lucas	16
SP Kirby	b Wigley	0	(10) lbw b Lucas	3
Extras	b 5, lb 14, w 1, nb 6	26	b 2, lb 8, w 11	21
	(all out 101 overs)	294	(all out 67.4 overs)	237

Bowling
Crook 15-2-62-0. Lucas 17-3-32-1. Wigley 25-5-72-6. Hall 15-5-22-1. Panesar 13-2-49-0. Willey 5-0-19-0. Boje 11-4-19-2.
Lucas 12.4-3-39-4. Wigley 20-3-80-3. Panesar 17-2-49-1. Crook 6-1-23-0. Boje 7-3-23-1. Hall 5-0-13-1.
Fall of Wickets: 1-17, 2-37, 3-57, 4-135, 5-136, 6-213, 7-213, 8-262, 9-294 1-0, 2-107, 3-140, 4-152, 5-192, 6-193, 7-207, 8-207, 9-222

NORTHANTS	First Innings		Second Innings	
RA White	b Kirby	26	c Snell b Marshall	23
*NJ O'Brien	lbw b Lewis	13	lbw b Lewis	9
AG Wakely	c sub b Kirby	4	b Lewis	1
N Boje (capt)	c sub b Banerjee	58	(5) c Taylor b Banerjee	17
MH Wessels	lbw b Banerjee	23	(4) c Snell b Kirby	50
AJ Hall	c Snell b Lewis	5	lbw b Gidman	91
DJ Willey	c sub b Banerjee	3	c Porterfield b Banerjee	47
SP Crook	b Kirby	9	b Lewis	55
DS Lucas	c Kadeer Ali b Banerjee	2	c sub b Kirby	13
MS Panesar	lbw b Kirby	0	not out	5
DH Wigley	not out	0	c Porterfield b Kirby	0
Extras	lb 3, nb 8	11	b 1, lb 8, nb 6	15
	(all out 60.1 overs)	161	(all out 89.5 overs)	326

Bowling
Franklin 8-2-23-0. Kirby 14.1-2-41-4. Lewis 12-5-24-2. Banerjee 21-5-62-4. Taylor 5-2-8-0.
Lewis 23-5-85-3. Kirby 20.5-3-76-3. Marshall 22-0-19-1. Banerjee 32-6-90-2. Kadeer Ali 4-0-15-0. Franklin 2-0-14-0. Taylor 2-0-7-0. Gidman 4-0-11-1.
Fall of Wickets: 1-48, 2-48, 3-74, 4-117, 5-128, 6-142, 7-151, 8-161, 9-161 1-17, 2-25, 3-60, 4-98, 5-102, 6-218, 7-283, 8-321, 9-321

Gloucestershire won by 44 runs –
Northamptonshire (3pts), Gloucestershire (19pts)

MIDDLESEX v. LEICESTERSHIRE – at Southgate

MIDDLESEX	First Innings			
AJ Strauss	c Nixon b White	150		
BA Godleman	lbw b Harris	1		
PJ Hughes	c Nixon b Harris	139		
NJ Dexter	c Nixon b O'Brien	27		
EJG Morgan	not out	114		
DJ Malan	b Harris	0		
*BJM Scott	c Nixon b White	3		
SD Udal (capt)	b White	0		
TJ Murtagh	not out	51		
ST Finn				
A Richardson				
Extras	b 5, lb 1, nb 2	8		
	(7 wkts dec 113 overs)	493		

Bowling
O'Brien 24-2-116-1. Harris 23-4-105-3. White 20-1-94-3. Crowe 42-6-158-0. Taylor 1-0-5-0. New 3-0-9-0.
Fall of Wickets: 1-2, 2-246, 3-294, 4-354, 5-354, 6-383, 7-383

LEICESTERSHIRE	First Innings		Second Innings (following on)	
MAG Boyce	c Scott b Finn	27	lbw b Murtagh	1
TJ New	c Dexter b Udal	66	c Malan b Udal	43
HH Dippenaar	lbw b Finn	0	lbw b Murtagh	93
HD Ackerman	lbw b Richardson	29	b Murtagh	60
JJ Cobb	c Finn b Richardson	60	lbw b Murtagh	0
*PA Nixon (capt)	c Richardson b Finn	8	c sub b Malan	31
JWA Taylor	c sub b Dexter	9	not out	122
WA White	b Murtagh	32	c sub b Murtagh	19
CD Crowe	lbw b Malan	10	not out	25
IE O'Brien	c & b Malan	2		
AJ Harris	not out	0		
Extras	lb 4, w 1, nb 10	15	b 3, lb 3	6
	(all out 84.1 overs)	258	(7 wkts 135 overs)	400

Bowling
Richardson 22-11-42-2. Murtagh 15.1-4-60-1. Udal 20-4-54-1. Malan 7-2-21-2. Finn 14-1-56-3. Dexter 6-1-21-1.
Murtagh 32-8-83-5. Richardson 22-5-58-0. Finn 21-1-107-0. Udal 34-6-91-1. Dexter 8-1-14-0. Malan 14-2-28-1. Strauss 2-1-10-0. Hughes 2-0-3-0.
Fall of Wickets: 1-49, 2-55, 3-125, 4-125, 5-151, 6-206, 7-212, 8-241, 9-243 1-2, 2-81, 3-196, 4-196, 5-205, 6-313, 7-355

Match drawn – Middlesex (12pts),
Leicestershire (8pts)

GLAMORGAN v. DERBYSHIRE – at Cardiff

GLAMORGAN	First Innings			
GP Rees	c Redfern b Wagg	11		
MJ Cosgrove	b Hunter	50		
BJ Wright	c Lawson b Wagg	6		
MJ Powell	b Wagg	108		
JWM Dalrymple (capt)	b Park	102		
TL Maynard	not out	51		
*MA Wallace	lbw b Park	40		
JAR Harris	not out	17		
RDB Croft				
DS Harrison				
GJP Kruger				
Extras	b 5, lb 3, nb 10	18		
	(6 wkts dec 116 overs)	403		

Bowling
Wagg 21-5-50-3. Hunter 22-6-46-1. Park 16-5-51-2. Clare 14-1-72-0. Lawson 23-1-77-0. Needham 11-0-60-0. Smith 9-1-39-0.
Fall of Wickets: 1-26, 2-38, 3-100, 4-280, 5-303, 6-371

DERBYSHIRE	First Innings		Second Innings (following on)	
SD Stubbings	lbw b Harris	4	not out	15
GT Park	c Wright b Harrison	64	c Dalrymple b Croft	6
WW Hinds	lbw b Harris	12	st Wallace b Croft	1
DJ Redfern	c Harrison b Harris	13	b Croft	3
GM Smith	c & b Croft	19	not out	0
*DJ Pipe (capt)	c Wright b Harrison	44		
GG Wagg	b Harrison	1		
JL Clare	lbw b Harrison	4		
J Needham	c Dalrymple b Croft	4		
MAK Lawson	not out	24		
ID Hunter	c Maynard b Croft	8		
Extras	b 6, lb 2, nb 4	12	lb 3, w 1, nb 2	6
	(all out 64.5 overs)	210	(3 wkts 21 overs)	34

Bowling
Harrison 18-3-60-4. Harris 14-2-54-3. Croft 21.5-5-45-3. Kruger 7-0-28-0. Dalrymple 4-0-15-0.
Harris 3-0-7-0. Kruger 3-0-8-0. Croft 8-5-6-3. Dalrymple 7-1-10-0.
Fall of Wickets: 1-17, 2-37, 3-63, 4-90, 5-150, 6-169, 7-169, 8-178, 9-184 1-16, 2-18, 3-28

Match drawn – Glamorgan (12pts),
Derbyshire (7pts)

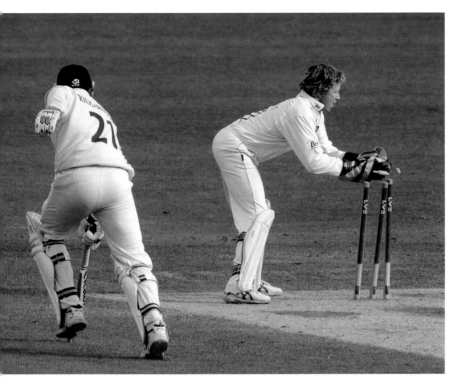

Surrey wicketkeeper Jon Batty completes the run out of Middlesex's Alan Richardson and a remarkable match at The Oval ends in a draw.

fine unbeaten 94 by Liam Plunkett, while Chris Nash's composed 85 not out made sure of the draw on the last afternoon.

Warwickshire's draw with Yorkshire, meanwhile, was a turgid affair with interest only surrounding the continued travails of Michael Vaughan, out for 16 in the first innings and suffering a hamstring injury which prevented him from batting later in the game, and two new county partnership records. First, there was the 346 which Joe Sayers and Anthony McGrath put on for Yorkshire's third wicket and then, far more unexpectedly, came the 233 for the Warwickshire ninth wicket between Jonathan Trott and Jeetan Patel.

Joining Trott with Warwickshire in some distress at 241 for 8 in reply to Yorkshire's massive 600 for 8 declared, New Zealand off spinner Patel scored 120 with two sixes and 16 fours. It was his maiden first-class hundred and, with Trott remaining unbeaten on 161, the pair shattered the county's previous ninth wicket record of 154, which had stood since 1925.

In Division Two there were victories for a resurgent Gloucestershire, who had finished winless and bottom in 2008, Kent and Northamptonshire and a remarkable draw at The Oval where Middlesex somehow failed to beat Surrey and, in the process, almost handed their London rivals a win of their own.

Anthony Ireland's first innings burst of 6 for 31, which saw Leicestershire tumbling to 133 all out, plus a determined 159 from captain Alex Gidman, was the basis of Gloucestershire's second successive victory and their proud confirmation as early second division leaders, while Andrew Hall's all-round excellence and two fine knocks from Rob White was at the heart of Northants' eight-wicket win against Essex.

Round Four: 6–9 May

Nottinghamshire's potent seam attack, in which 20-year-old local boy Luke Fletcher stood out, plus the batting of Adam Voges and Alistair Brown, combined to consign Somerset to a six-wicket defeat at Trent Bridge, despite their second innings resistance of Marcus Trescothick, while the first division's other winners were Lancashire, who overwhelmed Worcestershire at New Road.

There was no recovery for the home side after Glen Chapple, with 6 for 34, and Sajid Mahmood, who took 4 for 65, had dismissed them for 167 on the opening day. There was a chink of light for Worcestershire when their opponents slid to 181 for 7 in reply but then Chapple joined Kyle Hogg in an eighth wicket stand of 123 which took the game away from them.

Chapple's 89 included a six and 13 fours, with Hogg reaching 60, and then it was the turn of Mahmood again with the ball to finish off the struggling hosts. Moeen Ali did resist with 80, but the pacy Mahmood's second innings 6 for 75 gave him the first ten-wicket match-haul of his career.

Bat ruled ball at both Hove and Edgbaston, although Sussex had slipped to 109 for 5 in reply to Durham's 380 before Andrew Hodd's 101 from No. 7 rallied them. There were three Durham hundreds too, plus a

Round Four: 6–9 May Division One

NOTTINGHAMSHIRE v. SOMERSET – at Trent Bridge

SOMERSET	First Innings		Second Innings	
ME Trescothick	c Adams b Fletcher	13	c Shafayat b Fletcher	98
AV Suppiah	c Read b Fletcher	0	c Read b Adams	14
JL Langer (capt)	c Ealham b Adams	11	(5) c Read b Ealham	35
JC Hildreth	b Fletcher	2	b Ealham	18
Z de Bruyn	c Read b Sidebottom	64	(6) b Fletcher	54
*C Kieswetter	lbw b Adams	5	(7) c Read b Ealham	52
PD Trego	c Read b Adams	4	(8) b Fletcher	23
OAC Banks	b Sidebottom	28	(3) lbw b Sidebottom	4
BJ Phillips	lbw b Sidebottom	0	c Shafayat b Adams	39
DA Stiff	c Adams b Fletcher	9	st Read b Patel	21
CM Willoughby	not out	0	not out	0
Extras	lb 2	2	lb 23, w 2	25
	(all out 59.4 overs)	**138**	(all out 99 overs)	**383**

Bowling
Sidebottom 19-7-32-3. Fletcher 16.4-8-38-4. Ealham 13-4-36-0. Adams 11-3-30-3.
Sidebottom 21-3-86-1. Fletcher 22-3-71-3. Adams 23-3-70-2. Ealham 21-4-74-3. Patel 12-1-59-1.
Fall of Wickets: 1-0, 2-13, 3-17, 4-43, 5-53, 6-61, 7-129, 8-129, 9-130
1-50, 2-59, 3-92, 4-153, 5-193, 6-287, 7-304, 8-325, 9-373

NOTTS	First Innings		Second Innings	
BM Shafayat	c Kieswetter b Willoughby	19	c Kieswetter b Stiff	32
AD Hales	lbw b Willoughby	0	c Langer b Stiff	28
MA Wagh	c Hildreth b Phillips	10	lbw b Willoughby	14
SR Patel	lbw b Willoughby	11	lbw b Willoughby	35
AC Voges	lbw b Willoughby	63	not out	73
AD Brown	c Hildreth b Trego	63	not out	63
*CMW Read (capt)	c Phillips b Willoughby	41		
MA Ealham	c Langer b Trego	5		
AR Adams	b Trego	24		
RJ Sidebottom	c Hildreth b Stiff	13		
LJ Fletcher	not out	0		
Extras	lb 2, w 8, nb 2	12	b 6, lb 4, w 6	16
	(all out 82.5 overs)	**261**	(4 wkts 71.1 overs)	**261**

Bowling
Willoughby 28.5-7-81-5. Phillips 15-6-30-1. Stiff 20-3-63-1. Trego 12-3-53-3. de Bruyn 2-0-13-0. Banks 3-0-13-0. Suppiah 2-0-6-0.
Willoughby 24-5-89-2. Stiff 19-7-57-2. Phillips 10-1-40-0. Banks 6.1-1-22-0. Trego 4-0-21-0. de Bruyn 8-3-22-0.
Fall of Wickets: 1-1, 2-20, 3-37, 4-56, 5-175, 6-183, 7-189, 8-231, 9-261
1-51, 2-78, 3-79, 4-137

Nottinghamshire won by 6 wickets – Nottinghamshire (19pts), Somerset (3pts)

WORCESTERSHIRE v. LANCASHIRE – at New Road

WORCS	First Innings		Second Innings	
DKH Mitchell	lbw b Chapple	9	c Smith b Hogg	20
SC Moore	c Chilton b Chapple	0	b Hogg	53
VS Solanki (capt)	c Sutton b Mahmood	22	b Mahmood	35
BF Smith	c Prince b Chapple	1	lbw b Smith	43
MM Ali	c Sutton b Chapple	35	c Chapple b Mahmood	80
*SM Davies	lbw b Chapple	48	c Prince b Mahmood	9
GJ Batty	b Chapple	0	lbw b Mahmood	0
GM Andrew	c & b Mahmood	14	b Keedy	30
CD Whelan	c Prince b Mahmood	7	c Sutton b Mahmood	7
MS Mason	c Sutton b Mahmood	9	c Croft b Mahmood	14
Imran Arif	not out	4	not out	0
Extras	b 8, lb 9, w 1	18	b 1, lb 7, nb 2	10
	(all out 47.3 overs)	**167**	(all out 103.1 overs)	**301**

Bowling
Chapple 17-9-34-6. Mahmood 17.3-5-65-4. Hogg 7-0-23-0. Smith 5-0-28-0. Croft 1-1-0-0.
Chapple 23-6-54-0. Mahmood 28.1-7-75-6. Hogg 20-3-77-2. Keedy 17-5-44-1. Smith 15-2-43-1.
Fall of Wickets: 1-1, 2-26, 3-28, 4-36, 5-124, 6-124, 7-133, 8-142, 9-156
1-42, 2-81, 3-121, 4-223, 5-236, 6-236, 7-259, 8-267, 9-301

LANCASHIRE	First Innings		Second Innings	
PJ Horton	lbw b Whelan	5	(2) c Smith b Arif	24
TC Smith	lbw b Whelan	22	(1) b Whelan	18
AG Prince	c Davies b Whelan	18	c Mitchell b Batty	21
F du Plessis	c Davies b Arif	10	c Davies b Andrew	34
MJ Chilton	c Mitchell b Mason	55	not out	11
SJ Croft	lbw b Mason	43	not out	9
*LD Sutton	b Mason	9		
KW Hogg	b Whelan	60		
G Chapple (capt)	c Mason b Arif	89		
SI Mahmood	c Moore b Whelan	0		
G Keedy	not out	1		
Extras	b 6, lb 9, w 4, nb 16	35	b 2, lb 3	5
	(all out 90 overs)	**347**	(4 wkts 33.5 overs)	**122**

Bowling
Mason 24-8-76-3. Whelan 25-2-95-5. Arif 10-0-65-2. Andrew 5-0-32-0. Batty 20-3-49-0. Mitchell 6-1-15-0.
Mason 6-3-16-0. Whelan 6-2-11-1. Arif 8-0-40-1. Andrew 8-1-35-1. Batty 5.5-1-15-1.
Fall of Wickets: 1-18, 2-44, 3-59, 4-73, 5-141, 6-178, 7-181, 8-304, 9-340
1-27, 2-47, 3-91, 4-107

Lancashire won by 6 wickets – Worcestershire (3pts), Lancashire (20pts)

SUSSEX v. DURHAM – at Hove

DURHAM	First Innings		Second Innings	
MJ Di Venuto	c Hodd b Wright DG	20	(2) c Hodd b Martin-Jenkins	103
MD Stoneman	b Wright DG	2	(1) c Hodd b Rayner	24
WR Smith (capt)	lbw b Martin-Jenkins	12	run out	7
GJ Muchall	c Hodd b Wright LJ	24	not out	106
DM Benkenstein	c Nash b Wright DG	136	c sub b Wright LJ	7
ID Blackwell	lbw b Collymore	2	not out	39
*P Mustard	lbw b Martin-Jenkins	32		
LE Plunkett	not out	94		
CD Thorp	c Yardy b Rayner	29		
ME Claydon	b Wright LJ	6		
SJ Harmison	c Hodd b Rayner	0		
Extras	b 5, lb 10, w 2, nb 6	23	b 3, lb 4, w 4, nb 2	13
	(all out 115.5 overs)	**380**	(4 wkts dec 95 overs)	**299**

Bowling
Collymore 18-4-74-1. Wright DG 26.5-10-64-3. Martin-Jenkins 18.1-5-65-2. Rayner 18.5-1-51-2. Wright LJ 26-3-82-2. Hamilton-Brown 2-1-2-0. Nash 6-0-27-0.
Collymore 16-4-52-0. Martin-Jenkins 22-7-52-1. Wright LJ 14-4-38-1. Rayner 27-2-83-1. Hamilton-Brown 6-1-28-0. Yardy 2-0-8-0. Nash 8-1-31-0.
Fall of Wickets: 1-10, 2-37, 3-41, 4-101, 5-104, 6-162, 7-310, 8-369, 9-377
1-39, 2-67, 3-196, 4-211

SUSSEX	First Innings		Second Innings	
MH Yardy (capt)	b Claydon	51	c Plunkett b Harmison	12
CD Nash	b Plunkett	40	not out	85
EC Joyce	c Mustard b Claydon	0	b Thorp	3
MW Goodwin	c Mustard b Plunkett	0	lbw b Claydon	21
RJ Hamilton-Brown	c Mustard b Plunkett	0	c Benkenstein b Plunkett	12
LJ Wright	c Muchall b Blackwell	67	c Muchall b Plunkett	4
*AJ Hodd	lbw b Plunkett	101	not out	21
RSC Martin-Jenkins	c Mustard b Claydon	3		
OP Rayner	c Mustard b Harmison	25		
DG Wright	not out	41		
CD Collymore	lbw b Claydon	4		
Extras	b 1, lb 13, w 3, nb 14	31	lb 7, w 2, nb 2	11
	(all out 98 overs)	**363**	(5 wkts 50 overs)	**169**

Bowling
Harmison 23-2-59-1. Thorp 14-5-48-0. Plunkett 24-1-105-4. Claydon 20-1-90-4. Blackwell 13-3-30-1. Benkenstein 4-0-17-0.
Harmison 13-3-41-1. Thorp 10-3-29-1. Plunkett 13-2-36-2. Claydon 6-0-29-1. Blackwell 7-0-16-0. Smith 1-0-11-0.
Fall of Wickets: 1-81, 2-90, 3-95, 4-97, 5-109, 6-259, 7-282, 8-310, 9-332
1-13, 2-16, 3-71, 4-92, 5-105

Match drawn – Sussex (11pts), Durham (11pts)

Round Four: 6–9 May Division Two

GLOUCESTERSHIRE v. LEICESTERSHIRE – at Bristol

LEICESTERSHIRE	First Innings		Second Innings	
MAG Boyce	b Ireland	23	c Snell b Lewis	85
TJ New	c Snell b Stayt	54	c Snell b Kirby	41
HH Dippenaar	b Ireland	0	c Snell b Stayt	52
HD Ackerman	lbw b Ireland	2	st Snell b Taylor	10
JWA Taylor	c Lewis b Ireland	8	c Snell b Ireland	35
*PA Nixon (capt)	c Porterfield b Ireland	0	lbw b Lewis	8
WA White	c Taylor b Lewis	14	c Porterfield b Lewis	0
CD Crowe	c Kadeer Ali b Woodman	0	not out	41
AJ Harris	b Ireland	0	c & b Ireland	9
IE O'Brien	c Kadeer Ali b Kirby	23	c Porterfield b Lewis	31
ACF Wyatt	not out	1	b Kirby	0
Extras	b 4, w 2, nb 2	8	b 4, lb 13, nb 2	19
	(all out 65 overs)	**133**	(all out 112 overs)	**331**

Bowling
Lewis 17-7-22-1. Kirby 13-3-39-1. Ireland 14-4-31-6. Stayt 12-4-19-1. Gidman 7-1-14-0. Woodman 2-1-4-1.
Ireland 21-3-78-2. Lewis 23-8-39-4. Kirby 23-5-70-2. Stayt 22-3-58-1. Taylor 12-4-44-1. Gidman 8-2-21-0. Woodman 3-2-4-0.
Fall of Wickets: 1-83, 2-83, 3-86, 4-89, 5-89, 6-95, 7-95, 8-96, 9-128
1-127, 2-146, 3-165, 4-212, 5-237, 6-243, 7-257, 8-275, 9-330

GLOS	First Innings		Second Innings	
Kadeer Ali	c Taylor b Harris	3	(2) not out	38
WTS Porterfield	c Boyce b Wyatt	12	(1) not out	32
HJH Marshall	c Taylor b O'Brien	0		
APR Gidman (capt)	c Ackerman b Crowe	159		
CG Taylor	c Taylor b Wyatt	18		
SP Kirby	c Ackerman b Crowe	27		
RJ Woodman	lbw b Crowe	6		
*SD Snell	c O'Brien b Harris	85		
TP Stayt	c New b O'Brien	36		
J Lewis	c Taylor b Harris	3		
AJ Ireland	not out	0		
Extras	b 20, lb 14, w 8, nb 2	44	b 2	2
	(all out 123.3 overs)	**393**	(0 wkts 15.1 overs)	**72**

Bowling
O'Brien 32-8-78-2. Harris 30.3-8-85-3. Wyatt 20-6-44-2. White 10-2-31-0. Crowe 22-5-84-3. Taylor 7-1-20-0. New 2-0-17-0.
Harris 5-1-15-0. Wyatt 7-0-39-0. Crowe 2-0-7-0. Nixon 1.1-0-9-0.
Fall of Wickets: 1-7, 2-8, 3-20, 4-70, 5-152, 6-166, 7-294, 8-383, 9-393

Gloucestershire won by 10 wickets – Gloucestershire (21pts), Leicestershire (2pts)

KENT v. GLAMORGAN – at Canterbury

KENT	First Innings		Second Innings	
SA Northeast	c Wallace b Kruger	87	st Wallace b Croft	15
RWT Key (capt)	lbw b Shantry	25	c Wallace b Shantry	13
*GO Jones	lbw b Shantry	0	c Dalrymple b Harrison	133
M van Jaarsveld	lbw b Shantry	0	lbw b Harrison	182
DI Stevens	run out	3		
JB Hockley	b Kruger	4	(5) not out	19
JC Tredwell	lbw b Dalrymple	59	not out	2
WD Parnell	c & b Croft	90	(6) c Wright b Shantry	18
PS Jones	c Rees b Croft	0		
RH Joseph	not out	0		
MJ Saggers	run out	0		
Extras	b 4, lb 7, w 3	14	b 9, lb 14, w 4	27
	(all out 79.3 overs)	**282**	(5 wkts dec 91 overs)	**409**

Bowling
Harrison 15-0-66-0. Shantry 20-3-54-3. Kruger 15-4-42-2. Croft 17-2-66-2. Dalrymple 10.3-1-35-1. Wright 2-0-8-0.
Kruger 15-1-66-0. Shantry 21-2-68-2. Harrison 18-0-100-2. Croft 26-2-96-1. Dalrymple 9-0-41-0. Wright 2-0-15-0.
Fall of Wickets: 1-63, 2-63, 3-65, 4-76, 5-84, 6-131, 7-282, 8-282, 9-282
1-31, 2-41, 3-350, 4-372, 5-400

GLAMORGAN	First Innings		Second Innings	
GP Rees	c Hockley b Parnell	5	c van Jaarsveld b Tredwell	25
MP O'Shea	c Hockley b Joseph	50	lbw b Tredwell	25
BJ Wright	c sub b Jones PS	41	b Tredwell	81
MJ Powell	b Saggers	65	c & b Tredwell	1
JWM Dalrymple (capt)	c Northeast b Tredwell	79	c Jones PS b Tredwell	10
TL Maynard	c Northeast b Tredwell	4	c Key b Jones PS	4
*MA Wallace	b Tredwell	1	c sub b Tredwell	0
RDB Croft	c Hockley b Saggers	17	c Jones GO b Parnell	7
DS Harrison	b Saggers	0	b Tredwell	1
AJ Shantry	b Parnell	14	c van Jaarsveld b Tredwell	0
GJP Kruger	not out	11	not out	5
Extras	b 1, lb 7, nb 12	20	b 3, lb 11, w 1, nb 6	21
	(all out 95.4 overs)	**307**	(all out 69 overs)	**180**

Bowling
Parnell 25.4-6-97-2. Saggers 20-5-59-3. Joseph 15-3-50-1. Jones PS 6-0-30-1. Tredwell 24-8-54-3. van Jaarsveld 5-1-9-0.
Joseph 10-0-32-0. Parnell 17-5-29-1. Tredwell 28-7-66-8. van Jaarsveld 11-0-31-0. Jones PS 3-1-8-1.
Fall of Wickets: 1-8, 2-94, 3-100, 4-239, 5-243, 6-251, 7-279, 8-279, 9-290
1-39, 2-99, 3-101, 4-139, 5-144, 6-145, 7-154, 8-163, 9-167

Kent won by 204 runs – Kent (19pts), Glamorgan (6pts)

NORTHAMPTONSHIRE v. ESSEX – at Northampton

ESSEX	First Innings		Second Innings	
V Chopra	c Crook b Hall	42	c O'Brien b Crook	0
JC Mickleburgh	c Boje b Hall	62	b Lucas	16
MJ Walker	c White b Wigley	16	b Panesar	35
ML Pettini (capt)	c White b Wigley	3	lbw b Wigley	29
*JS Foster	c Hall b Boje	38	c White b Crook	84
RN ten Doeschate	c O'Brien b Crook	10	c Nelson b Boje	45
JD Middlebrook	c O'Brien b Hall	18	c O'Brien b Crook	19
GR Napier	c Willey b Boje	7	lbw b Crook	16
CJC Wright	c Wigley b Hall	2	not out	16
Danish Kaneria	lbw b Hall	0	c Wigley b Crook	17
MA Chambers	not out	0	lbw b Hall	5
Extras	lb 13, w 2, nb 8	23	b 6, lb 11, w 1, nb 8	26
	(all out 76.1 overs)	**221**	(all out 108.4 overs)	**308**

Bowling
Crook 12-2-37-1. Lucas 13-4-27-0. Daggett 8-1-31-0. Wigley 17-4-61-2. Hall 13.1-4-29-5. Panesar 4-0-9-0. Boje 9-2-14-2.
Crook 15-3-71-5. Lucas 21-8-59-1. Wigley 22-7-66-1. Panesar 27-11-33-1. Hall 15.4-4-42-1. Boje 8-2-20-1.
Fall of Wickets: 1-94, 2-138, 3-138, 4-153, 5-182, 6-199, 7-211, 8-221, 9-221
1-2, 2-30, 3-78, 4-102, 5-177, 6-227, 7-264, 8-275, 9-301

NORTHANTS	First Innings		Second Innings	
RA White	c Foster b Wright	70	not out	76
*NJ O'Brien	c Wright b Napier	23	c Mickleburgh b Middlebrook	29
MH Wessels	b Danish Kaneria	84	c ten Doeschate b Danish Kaneria	24
N Boje (capt)	c Middlebrook b Wright	0	not out	34
MAG Nelson	c Chopra b Napier	27		
AJ Hall	c ten Doeschate b Middlebrook	58		
DJ Willey	c Foster b Napier	30		
SP Crook	c Pettini b Wright	13		
DS Lucas	lbw b Danish Kaneria	13		
†MS Panesar	b Napier	4		
DH Wigley	not out	4		
LM Daggett				
Extras	b 5, lb 6, nb 17	28	b 4, lb 2, w 1, nb 6	13
	(all out 91.5 overs)	**354**	(2 wkts 39.2 overs)	**176**

Bowling
Napier 23.5-5-107-4. Wright 22-2-77-3. Chambers 15-4-59-0. Danish Kaneria 18-5-46-2. ten Doeschate 9-1-49-0. Middlebrook 4-2-5-1.
Napier 7-0-37-0. Wright 8-1-37-0. Danish Kaneria 15-3-44-1. Chambers 2-0-20-0. Middlebrook 6-1-21-1. Walker 1.2-0-11-0.
Fall of Wickets: 1-63, 2-122, 3-122, 4-195, 5-245, 6-311, 7-326, 8-340, 9-350
1-81, 2-113
† Replaced by LM Daggett

Northamptonshire won by 8 wickets – Northamptonshire (21pts), Essex (4pts)

WARWICKSHIRE v. YORKSHIRE – at Edgbaston

YORKSHIRE	First Innings		Second Innings	
JA Rudolph	c Ambrose b Clarke	62	c Frost b Clarke	30
JJ Sayers	c Clarke b Patel	173	c Ambrose b Woakes	14
MP Vaughan	c Troughton b Woakes	16		
A McGrath (capt)	b Carter	211	(3) not out	53
AW Gale	c Patel b Carter	12		
*GL Brophy	not out	40	(4) lbw b Clarke	0
AU Rashid	c Trott b Carter	0	(5) not out	58
Naved-ul-Hasan	c Ambrose b Carter	32		
A Shahzad	c Ambrose b Trott	5		
GJ Kruis	not out	1		
MJ Hoggard				
Extras	b 5, lb 10, w 1, nb 32	48	b 1, lb 5, w 1	7
	(8 wkts dec 167.4 overs)	600	(3 wkts dec 42 overs)	162

Bowling
Woakes 28-10-68-1. Rankin 27-6-85-0. Carter 30.4-4-129-4. Patel 36-1-150-1. Clarke 25-8-64-1. Trott 16-2-62-1. Bell 5-0-27-0.
Woakes 10-2-29-1. Rankin 9-1-48-0. Carter 2-0-5-0. Clarke 8-2-38-2. Patel 11-1-40-0. Trott 2-0-6-0.
Fall of Wickets: 1-93, 2-124, 3-470, 4-505, 5-514, 6-514, 7-578, 8-597
1-49, 2-63, 3-63

WARWICKSHIRE	First Innings		Second Innings	
IJ Westwood (capt)	lbw b Naved-ul-Hasan	41	not out	19
T Frost	c Rudolph b Kruis	8	c Brophy b Kruis	5
IR Bell	c Shahzad b Kruis	37	not out	30
IJL Trott	not out	161		
JO Troughton	lbw b Naved-ul-Hasan	0		
*TR Ambrose	c Brophy b Naved-ul-Hasan	0		
R Clarke	b Shahzad	9		
NM Carter	b Rashid	32		
CR Woakes	b Rashid	30		
JS Patel	c McGrath b Shahzad	120		
WB Rankin	lbw b Hoggard	0		
Extras	b 16, lb 16, nb 12	44	b 2, lb 1, w 1, nb 2	6
	(all out 122.1 overs)	482	(1 wkt 16 overs)	60

Bowling
Hoggard 16.1-2-67-1. Kruis 22-3-89-2. Rashid 26-6-89-2. Naved-ul-Hasan 27-5-102-3. Shahzad 21-2-72-2. McGrath 14-4-31-0.
Hoggard 3-1-5-0. Kruis 6-1-25-1. Rashid 5-0-19-0. Shahzad 2-0-8-0.
Fall of Wickets: 1-12, 2-90, 3-119, 4-119, 5-121, 6-138, 7-193, 8-241, 9-474
1-11

*Match drawn – Warwickshire (9pts),
Yorkshire (11pts)*

SURREY v. MIDDLESEX – at The Oval

SURREY	First Innings		Second Innings	
SA Newman	c Malan b Finn	22	c Hughes b Murtagh	2
MJ Brown (capt)	c Scott b Murtagh	7	c Hughes b Udal	73
MR Ramprakash	c Richardson b Finn	133	c Hughes b Murtagh	37
U Afzaal	b Udal	82	c Dexter b Udal	6
*JN Batty	lbw b Murtagh	29	c Dexter b Udal	30
GD Elliott	c Dexter b Richardson	1	c Morgan b Finn	22
CP Schofield	c Godleman b Finn	47	c Hughes b Udal	20
Murtaza Hussain	c Scott b Murtagh	0	not out	26
A Nel	c Dexter b Udal	32	b Udal	2
JW Dernbach	not out	16	c Dexter b Finn	4
SC Meaker	b Richardson	3	c Godleman b Udal	15
Extras	lb 12, nb 4	16	lb 1, nb 4	5
	(all out 131.2 overs)	388	(all out 86.1 overs)	242

Bowling
Murtagh 31-5-97-3. Richardson 25.2-6-64-2. Finn 26-2-111-3. Dexter 15-6-26-0. Udal 22-8-47-2. Malan 9-0-20-0. Compton 2-0-5-0. Hughes 1-0-6-0.
Murtagh 10-0-45-2. Richardson 6-2-20-0. Udal 33.1-12-74-6. Malan 10-5-24-0. Finn 22-4-58-2. Dexter 5-1-20-0.
Fall of Wickets: 1-25, 2-31, 3-174, 4-254, 5-263, 6-318, 7-319, 8-355, 9-373
1-2, 2-82, 3-90, 4-136, 5-159, 6-193, 7-197, 8-200, 9-209

MIDDLESEX	First Innings		Second Innings	
BA Godleman	c Elliott b Nel	37	(6) st Batty b Schofield	1
PJ Hughes	c Batty b Dernbach	195	c Batty b Schofield	57
NJ Dexter	c Batty b Hussain	8	(5) b Schofield	28
EJG Morgan	c Batty b Dernbach	13	(3) c Ramprakash b Hussain	41
DJ Malan	c Brown b Nel	86	(4) b Schofield	1
NRD Compton	lbw b Hussain	23	(1) b Hussain	28
*BJM Scott	c Newman b Hussain	0	not out	1
SD Udal (capt)	b Meaker	36	b Hussain	6
TJ Murtagh	c Batty b Meaker	5		
ST Finn	c Elliott b Hussain	0	(9) lbw b Hussain	0
A Richardson	not out	0	(10) run out	1
Extras	b 5, lb 15, w 6, nb 15	41	b 5, lb 4, w 1, nb 10	20
	(all out 124.1 overs)	445	(9 wkts 25 overs)	184

Bowling
Nel 20-3-78-2. Dernbach 17-2-52-2. Hussain 44-11-101-4. Meaker 20.1-1-86-2. Elliott 2-0-15-0. Schofield 19-0-85-0. Afzaal 2-0-8-0.
Hussain 13-0-70-4. Nel 4-0-45-0. Schofield 6-0-49-4. Meaker 2-0-11-0.
Fall of Wickets: 1-165, 2-178, 3-223, 4-317, 5-377, 6-377, 7-415, 8-433, 9-439
1-93, 2-99, 3-107, 4-169, 5-175, 6-176, 7-183, 8-183, 9-184

*Match drawn – Surrey (10pts),
Middlesex (11pts)*

Kent, meanwhile, were indebted to two 19-year-olds – opener Sam Northeast, who scored 87 as a late replacement for the ill Joe Denly, and Wayne Parnell, with an aggressive late-order 90 – for a position of halfway parity against Glamorgan at Canterbury. Then, after Geraint Jones and Martin van Jaarsveld had turned on the power in their second innings, James Tredwell produced career-best figures of 8 for 66 to send the Welsh county spinning from 99 for 1 to 180 all out and defeat by 204 runs on the final afternoon.

The opening exchanges of the Surrey-Middlesex match were dominated by Mark Ramprakash and Phillip Hughes. Ramprakash, who had missed the first two Championship fixtures as a result of his suspension following the fracas with Sussex's Murray Goodwin the previous August, showed with a blissful 133 that at 39 he had lost none of his ability or run-making desire.

But Hughes replied with a coruscating 195, with 28 fours, to give Middlesex a handy lead. Shaun Udal's 6 for 74 then gave his side an unexpected chance of victory, with 186 required from the last 25 overs of the match, and Hughes's 46-ball 57 soon had Surrey looking flustered.

Eoin Morgan, too, batted with great skill to score 41 from 34 balls but it was the left-hander's dismissal, to a wild swipe when all he had to do was keep his head, which began a crazy Middlesex collapse from 169 for 3. Udal entered in the final over to hit his first ball far over long on for six, and leave Middlesex needing only three more runs from four balls, but then he fell lbw to Murtaza Hussain, swinging unnecessarily. Steve Finn missed his first ball and was lbw to his second, and when Alan Richardson was run out, trying to complete a second run to deep square leg, Middlesex had failed by one run even to level the scores and Surrey were left just one wicket away from victory themselves.

Round Five: 6–9 June

Graham Onions and Steve Harmison combined to brush Hampshire aside with almost contemptuous ease at the Riverside, as Durham stepped up the defence of their title with a victory by an innings and 110 runs.

Hampshire were dismissed for just 105 and 96 as Harmison, with a first innings 4 for 43, and Onions, who took 6 for 58 in the second innings and nine in the match, proved far too potent for the visiting batsmen. When Durham batted, however, Will Smith's 80 and 68 from 85 balls by Ian Blackwell showed there was nothing too alarming about the conditions as the home side reached 311.

Rain ruined the games at Old Trafford and Edgbaston, where no play was possible at all on both days one and two, but Yorkshire and Sussex fought out a fascinating battle at Headingley which ended with the visitors shutting up shop at 257 for 8 after a brave effort at chasing down a target of 281 from 71 overs.

Gerard Brophy's 75 not out and Ed Joyce's skilful unbeaten 100 had kept Yorkshire and Sussex, respectively, afloat in their first innings but as batting conditions eased a superb tussle developed. Mike Yardy's 110 gave his Sussex side hope of reaching their target, despite wickets falling at regular intervals, but in the end it was the brilliant run out by Rana Naved of Matt Prior, who made 46 from 52 balls, which proved conclusive.

The bad weather also hit the second division in this round of matches, with all four games ending in draws as a result of long rain interruptions. There was no play at all on days one and two at Leicester, and it was all but the same story at both Chesterfield and Cardiff, where Mark Ramprakash hit his 105th first-class hundred and Jade Dernbach took 6 for 82 as Surrey had the better of exchanges with Glamorgan.

England's two Test openers were on opposite sides at Chelmsford, meanwhile, with Andrew Strauss stroking 14 fours in a classy 97 for Middlesex, after Gareth Berg and Murali Kartik's eighth wicket stand of 99 had rallied them from 139 for 7 in their first innings. Berg and the impressive Steven Finn, who bowled with real pace and bounce to take 5 for 57, had put Middlesex in charge as Essex tumbled to 157 all out but only 30.1 overs were possible on the final day and Alastair Cook's 84 not out saw the home side to safety.

Round Five:
6–9 June Division One

DURHAM v. HAMPSHIRE – at the Riverside

HAMPSHIRE	First Innings		Second Innings	
MA Carberry	c Muchall b Onions	0	lbw b Onions	0
JHK Adams	c Harmison b Thorp	8	b Onions	11
JP Crawley	c Di Venuto b Onions	10	c Smith b Harmison	5
MJ Lumb	lbw b Claydon	20	c Mustard b Harmison	32
SM Ervine	c Mustard b Onions	2	(7) c Claydon b Thorp	22
*N Pothas (capt)	c Muchall b Harmison	35	(8) lbw b Onions	8
LA Dawson	b Claydon	0	(9) not out	6
DG Cork	c Di Venuto b Harmison	13	(10) c Mustard b Onions	6
Imran Tahir	b Harmison	0	(11) c Mustard b Onions	0
DA Griffiths	c Thorp b Harmison	2	(6) b Onions	2
JA Tomlinson	not out	6	(5) b Thorp	1
Extras	lb 4, w 1, nb 6	11	lb 2, w 1	3
	(all out 50.4 overs)	105	(all out 34.2 overs)	96

Bowling
Onions 19-7-22-3. Harmison 17.4-5-43-4. Thorp 9-4-16-1. Claydon 5-0-20-2.
Onions 12-2-58-6. Harmison 8-4-15-2. Thorp 12-4-21-2.
Fall of Wickets: 1-0, 2-20, 3-20, 4-26, 5-59, 6-59, 7-88, 8-88, 9-92
1-0, 2-13, 3-49, 4-50, 5-53, 6-66, 7-76, 8-86, 9-96

DURHAM	First Innings	
MJ Di Venuto	c Crawley b Tomlinson	7
MD Stoneman	c Cork b Imran Tahir	44
WR Smith (capt)	lbw b Griffiths	80
GJ Muchall	c Dawson b Cork	28
DM Benkenstein	c Dawson b Imran Tahir	22
ID Blackwell	c Pothas b Imran Tahir	68
*P Mustard	b Ervine	32
CD Thorp	b Tomlinson	0
ME Claydon	b Imran Tahir	10
G Onions	not out	1
SJ Harmison	b Imran Tahir	0
Extras	b 4, lb 3, w 2, nb 10	19
	(all out 103 overs)	311

Bowling
Cork 20-5-45-1. Tomlinson 23-7-72-2. Griffiths 20-6-73-1. Imran Tahir 27-7-85-5.
Ervine 13-5-29-1.
Fall of Wickets: 1-7, 2-75, 3-140, 4-191, 5-208, 6-280, 7-281, 8-308, 9-311

*Durham won by an innings and 110 runs –
Durham (20pts), Hampshire (3pts)*

LANCASHIRE v. SOMERSET – at Old Trafford

LANCASHIRE	First Innings		Second Innings	
PJ Horton	c Kieswetter b Thomas	69	(2) c Suppiah b Willoughby	68
TC Smith	c Willoughby b Stiff	12	(1) c Phillips b Stiff	0
MB Loye	c Trego b Stiff	31	lbw b de Bruyn	39
AG Prince	c Suppiah b Trego	48	c Trego b de Bruyn	34
MJ Chilton	c Langer b Trego	2	c Langer b de Bruyn	15
F du Plessis	c Langer b Thomas	4	c Langer b Suppiah	4
*LD Sutton	c Kieswetter b Suppiah	20	not out	6
G Chapple (capt)	b Suppiah	55	not out	4
SI Mahmood	b Stiff	1		
OJ Newby	c Kieswetter b Stiff	15		
G Keedy	not out	2		
Extras	b 4, lb 7, w 1, nb 19	31	lb 6, w 5, nb 10	21
	(all out 82 overs)	286	(6 wkts 61 overs)	191

Bowling
Willoughby 11-3-30-0. Phillips 11-2-34-0. Thomas 17-4-80-2. Stiff 20-4-72-4.
Trego 14-3-34-2. Suppiah 9-2-25-2.
Stiff 6-2-21-1. Willoughby 13-4-38-1. Phillips 7-3-11-0. Thomas 7-1-11-0.
Suppiah 13-3-45-1. Trego 6-2-12-0. de Bruyn 9-1-47-3.
Fall of Wickets: 1-35, 2-75, 3-162, 4-166, 5-171, 6-178, 7-206, 8-217, 9-281
1-0, 2-106, 3-122, 4-159, 5-172, 6-176

SOMERSET	First Innings	
ME Trescothick	st Sutton b Keedy	95
AV Suppiah	b Newby	47
JL Langer (capt)	c Sutton b Newby	2
JC Hildreth	b du Plessis	60
*C Kieswetter	c Sutton b Chapple	45
PD Trego	b du Plessis	0
Z de Bruyn	c & b Chapple	7
BJ Phillips	not out	41
AC Thomas	c Prince b Keedy	17
DA Stiff	c Prince b Keedy	7
CM Willoughby	c Chapple b Keedy	5
Extras	b 4, lb 5, nb 8	17
	(103.5 overs)	343

Bowling
Mahmood 19-2-82-0. Chapple 24-7-45-2. Newby 16-4-58-2. Smith 15-3-49-0.
Keedy 25.5-5-86-4. du Plessis 4-0-14-2.
Fall of Wickets: 1-131, 2-135, 3-179, 4-250, 5-262, 6-273, 7-274, 8-317, 9-330

*Match drawn – Lancashire (9pts),
Somerset (10pts)*

WARWICKSHIRE v. NOTTINGHAMSHIRE – at Edgbaston

WARWICKSHIRE	First Innings	
IJ Westwood (capt)	c Jefferson b Fletcher	73
T Frost	c Read b Ealham	37
IR Bell	c Wagh b Patel	60
IJL Trott	c Read b Fletcher	37
JO Troughton	b Shreck	73
*TR Ambrose	c Voges b Patel	0
KHD Barker	b Fletcher	0
NM Carter	c Shreck b Pattinson	47
CR Woakes	c Brown b Fletcher	33
JS Patel	not out	3
JE Anyon	not out	14
Extras	b 5, lb 8, nb 12	25
	(9 wkts dec 104.2 overs)	402

Bowling
Shreck 26-5-95-1. Pattinson 19-4-84-1. Fletcher 24.2-4-115-4. Ealham 18-5-46-1.
Patel 17-3-49-2.
Fall of Wickets: 1-87, 2-143, 3-220, 4-224, 5-239, 6-242, 7-313, 8-382, 9-384

NOTTS	First Innings	
WI Jefferson	c Frost b Patel	21
BM Shafayat	c Ambrose b Anyon	20
MA Wagh	c Ambrose b Carter	147
SR Patel	c Ambrose b Woakes	4
AC Voges	c Ambrose b Patel	76
AD Brown	run out	64
*CMW Read (capt)	not out	15
MA Ealham	not out	14
LJ Fletcher		
CE Shreck		
DJ Pattinson		
Extras	b 8, lb 3, nb 4	15
	(6 wkts 77.2 overs)	376

Bowling
Woakes 17-0-68-1. Carter 16-3-51-1. Anyon 11.2-1-75-1. Barker 14-1-54-0.
Patel 14-0-97-2. Trott 5-0-20-0.
Fall of Wickets: 1-36, 2-64, 3-68, 4-216, 5-340, 6-353

*Match drawn – Warwickshire (11pts),
Nottinghamshire (11pts)*

YORKSHIRE v. SUSSEX – at Headingley

YORKSHIRE	First Innings		Second Innings	
JA Rudolph	c Rayner b Collymore	15	b Collymore	89
JJ Sayers	b Martin-Jenkins	29	lbw b Collymore	15
MP Vaughan	c Rayner b Collymore	0	c Prior b Smith	39
A McGrath (capt)	c Rayner b Collymore	24	c Goodwin b Yardy	58
AW Gale	c Martin-Jenkins b Lewry	11	c Smith b Lewry	25
*GL Brophy	not out	75	(7) not out	7
TT Bresnan	c Hodd b Martin-Jenkins	7	(8) c Thornley b Yardy	6
Naved-ul-Hasan	c Martin-Jenkins b Lewry	7	(6) c Rayner b Yardy	5
DJ Wainwright	c Martin-Jenkins b Collymore	36	not out	1
Azeem Rafiq	c Rayner b Smith	13		
GJ Kruis	c Joyce b Smith	0		
Extras	b 1, lb 11, w 2	14	b 7, lb 11, w 1, nb 6	25
	(all out 94.5 overs)	225	(7 wkts dec 67 overs)	272

Bowling
Lewry 27-8-66-1. Collymore 27-9-68-4. Martin-Jenkins 18-5-38-3. Smith 9.5-4-22-2.
Rayner 13-4-19-0.
Lewry 17-4-67-1. Collymore 18-2-54-2. Rayner 14-4-56-0. Smith 14-2-62-1.
Yardy 2-0-15-3.
Fall of Wickets: 1-19, 2-19, 3-58, 4-75, 5-95, 6-108, 7-110, 8-206, 9-225
1-67, 2-150, 3-162, 4-223, 5-250, 6-254, 7-265

SUSSEX	First Innings		Second Innings	
MH Yardy (capt)	lbw b Kruis	8	c Sayers b Wainwright	110
MA Thornley	lbw b Naved-ul-Hasan	8	b Naved-ul-Hasan	19
EC Joyce	not out	100	lbw b Rafiq	24
MW Goodwin	c Sayers b McGrath	0	c Bresnan b Rafiq	19
MJ Prior	c Sayers b Kruis	20	run out	46
*AJ Hodd	lbw b Bresnan	1	b Wainwright	7
DR Smith	c Kruis b Bresnan	0	b Naved-ul-Hasan	14
RSC Martin-Jenkins	b Rafiq	33	b Wainwright	3
OP Rayner	c Gale b Rafiq	4	not out	2
CD Collymore	c Gale b Rafiq	11	not out	2
JD Lewry	b Naved-ul-Hasan	12		
Extras	b 1, lb 13, w 2, nb 4	20	b 5, lb 3, w 1, nb 2	11
	(all out 82.3 overs)	217	(8 wkts 70.5 overs)	257

Bowling
Bresnan 24-9-44-2. Kruis 17-7-36-2. Naved-ul-Hasan 19.3-3-59-2.
McGrath 9-3-26-1. Rafiq 11-0-34-3. Wainwright 2-0-4-0.
Bresnan 18-4-44-0. Kruis 12-2-40-0. Naved-ul-Hasan 9.5-1-45-2.
McGrath 5-0-19-0. Wainwright 16-4-45-3. Rafiq 16-2-35-2.
Fall of Wickets: 1-9, 2-34, 3-43, 4-89, 5-90, 6-94, 7-150, 8-162, 9-192
1-69, 2-114, 3-170, 4-203, 5-211, 6-241, 7-252, 8-252

*Match drawn – Yorkshire (8pts),
Sussex (8pts)*

Graham Onions bowled himself into England's Test squad in the summer of 2009 with a string of superb County Championship performances for Durham.

Round Five:
6-9 June Division Two

LEICESTERSHIRE v. KENT – at Grace Road

LEICESTERSHIRE First Innings

MAG Boyce	b McLaren	38
JJ Cobb	c Jones b Kemp	46
HH Dippenaar	c Denly b Cook	89
HD Ackerman	c Stevens b Cook	67
JWA Taylor	c Jones b Cook	0
TJ New	not out	85
*PA Nixon (capt)	lbw b McLaren	14
WA White	c Kemp b Cook	11
CW Henderson	b Cook	0
AJ Harris	lbw b Joseph	0
HF Gurney	not out	0
Extras	b 11, lb 6, w 8, nb 28	53
	(9 wkts dec 110.3 overs)	**403**

Bowling
Joseph 25.3-2-89-1. Saggers 15.5-3-53-0. Cook 26-8-78-5. McLaren 16-3-62-2. Tredwell 2-0-20-0. Kemp 13.1-3-49-1. Stevens 12-0-35-0.
Fall of Wickets: 1-80, 2-116, 3-247, 4-247, 5-304, 6-349, 7-382, 8-386, 9-387

KENT First Innings

JL Denly	not out	116
SA Northeast	c Nixon b Gurney	26
*GO Jones (capt)	run out	87
M van Jaarsveld (capt)	not out	13
DI Stevens		
JM Kemp		
R McLaren		
JC Tredwell		
SJ Cook		
MJ Saggers		
RH Joseph		
Extras	b 4, lb 8, w 3, nb 8	23
	(2 wkts 63.5 overs)	**265**

Bowling
Harris 12-4-37-0. Gurney 17.5-6-55-1. Henderson 24-3-99-0. Taylor 3-0-10-0. White 7-0-52-0.
Fall of Wickets: 1-57, 2-238

*Match drawn – Leicestershire (9pts),
Kent (9pts)*

DERBYSHIRE v. GLOUCESTERSHIRE – at Chesterfield

GLOS First Innings

Kadeer Ali	c Lawson b Hunter	0
GP Hodnett	c Park b Wagg	31
HJH Marshall	c Pipe b Hunter	158
APR Gidman (capt)	b Hinds	135
CG Taylor	not out	38
CM Spearman	b Lungley	16
*SD Snell	not out	4
J Lewis		
AJ Ireland		
SP Kirby		
RKJ Dawson		
Extras	b 3, lb 8, w 10	21
	(5 wkts dec 107.5 overs)	**403**

Bowling
Wagg 24-5-71-1. Hunter 15-3-65-2. Lungley 20.5-0-88-1. Smith 17-2-64-0. Lawson 10-0-46-0. Hinds 11-1-28-1. Park 10-0-30-0.
Fall of Wickets: 1-1, 2-73, 3-306, 4-361, 5-390

DERBYSHIRE First Innings

SD Stubbings	b Ireland	6
CJL Rogers (capt)	lbw b Lewis	104
GT Park	c Snell b Hodnett	62
DJ Redfern	st Snell b Taylor	74
WW Hinds	c Snell b Ireland	30
GM Smith	c Taylor b Kirby	24
*DJ Pipe	c & b Dawson	0
GG Wagg	c Spearman b Lewis	28
T Lungley	not out	29
ID Hunter	not out	29
MAK Lawson		
Extras	lb 10, w 6	16
	(8 wkts 95 overs)	**402**

Bowling
Kirby 22-8-51-1. Ireland 14-2-77-2. Lewis 17-3-71-2. Dawson 25-3-118-1. Gidman 5-1-23-0. Marshall 1-0-4-0. Hodnett 6-0-41-1. Taylor 5-3-7-1.
Fall of Wickets: 1-31, 2-177, 3-201, 4-262, 5-293, 6-298, 7-334, 8-345

*Match drawn – Derbyshire (10pts),
Gloucestershire (11pts)*

GLAMORGAN v. SURREY – at Cardiff

SURREY First Innings / Second Innings

	First Innings			Second Innings	
SA Newman	lbw b Kruger	0	b Kruger		7
MJ Brown	lbw b Kruger	40	b Shantry		6
MR Ramprakash	c Harris b Shantry	138	c & b Croft		35
MA Butcher (capt)	lbw b Shantry	65	not out		27
Murtaza Hussain	lbw b Kruger	5			
U Afzaal	c Powell b Shantry	13	(5) not out		1
SJ Walters	lbw b Harris	2			
*JN Batty	lbw b Shantry	42			
RJ Harris	c Croft b Kruger	4			
A Nel	not out	31			
JW Dernbach	b Kruger	10			
Extras	all out b 7, lb 8, w 3	18	b 2, lb 4		6
	(all out 99.3 overs)	**368**	(3 wkts 30 overs)		**82**

Bowling
Harris 28-2-113-2. Shantry 25-7-73-4. Kruger 16.3-2-77-4. Cosgrove 9-1-36-0. Croft 18-4-41-0. Dalrymple 3-0-13-0.
Harris 7-2-19-0. Kruger 4-2-3-1. Shantry 7-1-16-1. Croft 8-1-23-1. Dalrymple 4-0-15-0.
Fall of Wickets: 1-0, 2-58, 3-156, 4-163, 5-195, 6-198, 7-314, 8-314, 9-336 1-7, 2-24, 3-80

GLAMORGAN First Innings

GP Rees	c Ramprakash b Nel	1
MJ Cosgrove	c Brown b Dernbach	59
WD Bragg	c Batty b Dernbach	12
MJ Powell	b Dernbach	10
JWM Dalrymple (capt)	c Nel b Dernbach	72
BJ Wright	c Batty b Harris	27
*MA Wallace	c Batty b Dernbach	13
JAR Harris	c Butcher b Hussain	9
RDB Croft	c Butcher b Dernbach	2
AJ Shantry	not out	23
GJP Kruger	c Butcher b Harris	15
Extras	b 3, lb 9, nb 16	28
	(all out 85 overs)	**271**

Bowling
Nel 17-5-50-1. Harris 17.5-5-66-2. Hussain 26-10-56-1. Dernbach 23-4-82-6. Afzaal 1-0-1-0. Walters 1-0-4-0.
Fall of Wickets: 1-28, 2-62, 3-88, 4-115, 5-177, 6-215, 7-224, 8-229, 9-238

*Match drawn – Glamorgan (9pts),
Surrey (11pts)*

ESSEX v. MIDDLESEX – at Chelmsford

MIDDLESEX First Innings / Second Innings

	First Innings			Second Innings	
AJ Strauss	c Wheater b Wright	16	b Chambers		97
NRD Compton	b Wright	24	lbw b Masters		44
SD Robson	c Wheater b Masters	43	lbw b Danish Kaneria		23
NJ Dexter	c Wheater b Masters	29	lbw b Danish Kaneria		42
DJ Malan	b Wright	1	c Cook b Danish Kaneria		3
*DC Nash	c & b Wright	3	c Wheater b Masters		26
GK Berg	b Masters	56	c & b Danish Kaneria		9
SD Udal (capt)	lbw b Danish Kaneria	7	not out		36
M Kartik	not out	62			
CEW Silverwood	c Cook b Masters	9			
ST Finn	c Cook b Masters	12			
Extras	lb 8, nb 4	12	b 11, lb 4, nb 2		17
	(all out 72.4 overs)	**274**	(7 wkts dec 88.1 overs)		**297**

Bowling
Masters 20.4-4-65-5. Wright 21-5-71-4. Chambers 14-0-50-0.
Danish Kaneria 4-0-21-0. Walker 1-0-7-0.
Masters 20.1-3-39-2. Wright 16-1-60-0. Chambers 11-1-35-1.
Danish Kaneria 28-6-85-4. Middlebrook 13-1-63-0.
Fall of Wickets: 1-23, 2-60, 3-117, 4-120, 5-124, 6-124, 7-139, 8-238, 9-248 1-146, 2-152, 3-201, 4-213, 5-232, 6-242, 7-297

ESSEX First Innings / Second Innings

	First Innings			Second Innings	
AN Cook	c Strauss b Kartik	31	not out		84
JER Gallian	c Kartik b Finn	10	b Finn		12
V Chopra	c Dexter b Finn	0	b Finn		0
MJ Walker	c Nash b Finn	5	c Nash b Finn		19
DD Masters	lbw b Berg	22			
ML Pettini (capt)	b Berg	10	(5) lbw b Kartik		21
JD Middlebrook	c Nash b Berg	2	(6) not out		9
*AJ Wheater	c Kartik b Berg	0			
CJC Wright	c Nash b Finn	19			
Danish Kaneria	c Dexter b Finn	37			
MA Chambers	not out	8			
Extras	b 4, lb 8, w 1	13	b 8, lb 2, nb 4		14
	(all out 55.3 overs)	**157**	(4 wkts 62.1 overs)		**159**

Bowling
Silverwood 15-5-40-0. Finn 21.3-8-57-5. Kartik 2-1-1-1. Berg 13-2-35-4.
Dexter 4-2-12-0.
Silverwood 12-2-34-0. Finn 17-1-67-3. Berg 8-3-14-0. Kartik 15.1-7-19-1.
Udal 10-3-15-0.
Fall of Wickets: 1-34, 2-34, 3-48, 4-48, 5-86, 6-87, 7-87, 8-98, 9-120 1-34, 2-40, 3-90, 4-145

*Match drawn – Essex (7pts),
Middlesex (9pts)*

Round Six: 11–14 June

Division One began to take shape after this round of games, with all four fixtures producing results. Durham, Nottinghamshire and Somerset all won, as did Sussex against bottom team Worcestershire, but it was hard to look beyond Durham as potential champions again after their 138-run demolition of Lancashire at the Riverside.

Even with Andrew Flintoff in their side, Lancashire were twice bundled out on a pitch of some variable bounce. Durham did not have everything their own way, with Flintoff taking 4 for 47 in their first innings of 244 and then Sajid Mahmood picking up a second innings 6 for 30 as only the impressive Ian Blackwell carried the fight back to the Lancashire attack.

Yet, in Steve Harmison and Graham Onions, Durham had even more firepower. The pace duo shared eight wickets in each Lancashire innings, with Flintoff falling for 3 and 0 and his great friend Harmison wrapping up the match for Durham with 5 for 46 on the third, and what proved to be the last, day.

Nottinghamshire, however, deserved great credit for the way they fought hard to overwhelm Hampshire at the Rose Bowl, winning in the end by 191 runs despite being 147 for 7 in their first innings and then 47 for 4 second time around.

An eighth wicket stand of 152 between the veteran Mark Ealham, who finished unbeaten on 70, and the young fast bowler Luke Fletcher, who hit out with unexpected élan to make 92 with three sixes and nine fours, rallied Notts to a first innings 326. And, despite Jimmy Adams's 112, Hampshire conceded a narrow halfway deficit as Samit Patel took 5 for 81 with his developing left-arm spin.

Hampshire's last chance disappeared when they could not take advantage of Notts's second innings wobble

Round Six: 11–14 June Division One

DURHAM v. LANCASHIRE – at the Riverside

DURHAM	First Innings		Second Innings	
MJ Di Venuto	c Sutton b Flintoff	16	(2) c Newby b Mahmood	0
MD Stoneman	c Flintoff b Mahmood	45	(1) c Flintoff b Mahmood	2
WR Smith (capt)	c Sutton b Newby	11	c Sutton b Mahmood	1
GJ Muchall	c du Plessis b Mahmood	18	lbw b Newby	18
DM Benkenstein	c Flintoff b Chapple	26	c Prince b Chapple	1
ID Blackwell	b Chapple	20	c & b Mahmood	74
*P Mustard	c du Plessis b Flintoff	51	c Sutton b Flintoff	7
CD Thorp	c Horton b Chapple	4	c Horton b Mahmood	24
ME Claydon	c Sutton b Flintoff	0	c Prince b Mahmood	0
G Onions	not out	12	not out	7
SJ Harmison	c Loye b Flintoff	35	c du Plessis b Flintoff	0
Extras	b 2, lb 10, w 9, nb 14	35	lb 6, w 1, nb 4	11
	(all out 69.5 overs)	244	(all out 50.4 overs)	145

Bowling
Chapple 25-5-58-3. Mahmood 14-4-62-2. Flintoff 15.5-3-47-4. Newby 15-2-65-1.
Flintoff 15.4-9-30-2. Mahmood 14-7-30-6. Chapple 9-2-33-1. Newby 6-0-26-1.
Keedy 5-0-19-0. du Plessis 1-0-1-0.
Fall of Wickets: 1-42, 2-84, 3-84, 4-117, 5-143, 6-196, 7-172, 8-203, 9-244
1-0, 2-2, 3-3, 4-10, 5-40, 6-57, 7-138, 8-138, 9-138

LANCASHIRE	First Innings		Second Innings	
PJ Horton	c Mustard b Onions	0	(2) c Mustard b Harmison	11
MB Loye	lbw b Onions	14	(1) c Muchall b Harmison	30
AG Prince	lbw b Onions	17	lbw b Harmison	3
F du Plessis	c Mustard b Harmison	41	c Mustard b Harmison	5
MJ Chilton	c Stoneman b Harmison	2	c Mustard b Claydon	22
A Flintoff	b Harmison	3	c Claydon b Onions	0
*LD Sutton	c Thorp b Claydon	21	not out	19
G Chapple (capt)	c Mustard b Claydon	5	c Di Venuto b Harmison	21
SI Mahmood	c Mustard b Harmison	7	c Mustard b Onions	16
OJ Newby	c Blackwell b Onions	1	b Blackwell	0
G Keedy	not out	0	b Onions	0
Extras	b 4, lb 4, nb 2	10	b 1, lb 2, w 1, nb 4	8
	(all out 43.1 overs)	116	(all out 52 overs)	135

Bowling
Onions 13-4-40-4. Harmison 14.1-5-28-4. Claydon 7-4-19-2. Thorp 7-2-21-0.
Onions 14-4-28-3. Harmison 17-7-46-5. Claydon 9-1-29-1. Thorp 10-4-19-0.
Blackwell 2-0-10-1.
Fall of Wickets: 1-4, 2-34, 3-37, 4-48, 5-56, 6-83, 7-83, 8-115, 9-116
1-18, 2-36, 3-50, 4-63, 5-64, 6-78, 7-113, 8-133, 9-134

Durham won by 138 runs – Durham (18pts), Lancashire (3pts)

HAMPSHIRE v. NOTTINGHAMSHIRE – at the Rose Bowl

NOTTS	First Innings		Second Innings	
WI Jefferson	c Pothas b Ervine	12	c Pothas b Tomlinson	2
BM Shafayat	c Benham b Griffiths	20	c Pothas b Tomlinson	11
MA Wagh	c Ervine b Griffiths	21	lbw b Imran Tahir	20
SR Patel	c Pothas b Tomlinson	41	c Vince b Tomlinson	0
AC Voges	lbw b Imran Tahir	25	lbw b Imran Tahir	82
AD Brown	c Cork b Ervine	5	c sub b Carberry	148
*CMW Read (capt)	c Pothas b Ervine	16	not out	116
MA Ealham	not out	70	not out	10
LJ Fletcher	b Imran Tahir	92		
DJ Pattinson	c Cork b Griffiths	12		
CE Shreck	b Griffiths	5		
Extras	lb 3, nb 4	7	b 3, lb 9, nb 12	24
	(all out 103.2 overs)	326	(6 wkts dec 86 overs)	380

Bowling
Cork 15-5-36-0. Tomlinson 21.1-6-73-1. Ervine 13.5-7-22-3. Griffiths 16.2-4-48-4.
Imran Tahir 34-5-130-2. Carberry 2-0-7-0. Adams 1-0-7-0.
Cork 14-1-56-0. Tomlinson 15-4-60-3. Imran Tahir 29-8-103-1. Griffiths 15-2-67-1.
Carberry 10-0-64-1. Adams 1-0-5-0. Vince 2-0-13-0.
Fall of Wickets: 1-32, 2-34, 3-60, 4-123, 5-125, 6-146, 7-147, 8-299, 9-320
1-5, 2-16, 3-26, 4-47, 5-157, 6-343

HAMPSHIRE	First Innings		Second Innings	
MA Carberry	c Jefferson b Fletcher	27	c Jefferson b Fletcher	5
JHK Adams	c Shafayat b Patel	112	c Read b Pattinson	6
MJ Lumb	st Read b Patel	43	(4) c b Patel	26
JM Vince	c Jefferson b Ealham	13	(5) c Voges b Fletcher	75
AC Benham	c Jefferson b Fletcher	13	(6) b Read b Fletcher	7
*N Pothas (capt)	c Shafayat b Patel	36	(7) not out	63
SM Ervine	c Read b Fletcher	1	(8) c Jefferson b Voges	21
DG Cork	lbw b Ealham	26	(9) c Read b Ealham	4
Imran Tahir	c Ealham b Patel	0	(11) c Voges b Pattinson	0
DA Griffiths	c Brown b Patel	1	b Pattinson	5
JA Tomlinson	not out	3	(3) c Shafayat b Pattinson	2
Extras	b 1, lb 2, w 3, nb 14	20	b 4, lb 3, w 1	8
	(all out 90.4 overs)	295	(all out 81.5 overs)	220

Bowling
Pattinson 16-3-62-0. Shreck 14-1-59-0. Fletcher 16-3-56-3. Patel 28-10-81-5.
Ealham 16.4-4-52-2.
Fletcher 11-4-24-2. Pattinson 15.5-4-53-4. Patel 29-3-79-1. Shreck 11-4-22-1.
Ealham 11-4-32-1. Voges 4-1-31-1.
Fall of Wickets: 1-57, 2-166, 3-185, 4-211, 5-238, 6-254, 7-266, 8-266, 9-287
1-8, 2-14, 3-14, 4-96, 5-115, 6-138, 7-181, 8-202, 9-220

Nottinghamshire won by 191 runs – Hampshire (5pts), Nottinghamshire (20pts)

YORKSHIRE v. SOMERSET – at Headingley

YORKSHIRE	First Innings		Second Innings	
JA Rudolph	b Thomas	14	c Trego b Willoughby	22
JJ Sayers	c Langer b Willoughby	60	c Langer b Trego	18
A McGrath (capt)	c Kieswetter b Stiff	16	(4) b Thomas	9
AW Gale	lbw b Trego	35	(5) c Trego b Munday	30
JM Bairstow	b Munday	28	(6) not out	82
*GL Brophy	c & b Thomas	33	(7) lbw b Stiff	14
TT Bresnan	c Willoughby b Munday	48	(8) c Trescothick b Stiff	7
Naved-ul-Hasan	b Willoughby	10	(3) c Langer b Willoughby	22
A Shahzad	not out	8	(10) c Trego b Willoughby	4
DJ Wainwright	c Trescothick b Thomas	1	(11) c Trescothick b Munday	23
MJ Hoggard	c Kieswetter b Willoughby	1	(3) c Kieswetter b Thomas	4
Extras	b 5, lb 12, w 2, nb 4	23	b 4, lb 1, w 6, nb 2	13
	(all out 99.3 overs)	277	(all out 78.1 overs)	248

Bowling
Stiff 17-2-47-1. Willoughby 23.3-11-30-3. Thomas 20-1-48-3. Suppiah 3-1-9-0.
Trego 13-4-31-1. Munday 16-0-68-2. de Bruyn 7-2-27-0.
Willoughby 24-9-46-3. Stiff 12-1-49-2. Thomas 21-4-78-2. Munday 9.1-0-46-2.
Trego 2-1-24-0.
Fall of Wickets: 1-35, 2-72, 3-111, 4-166, 5-166, 6-248, 7-261, 8-269, 9-274
1-26, 2-33, 3-49, 4-87, 5-92, 6-111, 7-133, 8-181, 9-193

SOMERSET	First Innings		Second Innings	
ME Trescothick	c Brophy b Hoggard	0	c Bairstow b Wainwright	78
AV Suppiah	lbw b Wainwright	20	b Shahzad	15
JL Langer (capt)	c Brophy b Hoggard	21	c Bairstow b Naved-ul-Hasan	46
JC Hildreth	c McGrath b Hoggard	20	c Rudolph b Wainwright	5
Z de Bruyn	lbw b Hoggard	1	not out	70
*C Kieswetter	c Brophy b Shahzad	83	c Bairstow b Bresnan	25
PD Trego	c Gale b Hoggard	3	c Bairstow b Shahzad	23
AC Thomas	not out	64	not out	12
DA Stiff	c McGrath b Wainwright	28		
MK Munday	c McGrath b Wainwright	1		
CM Willoughby	b Shahzad	0		
Extras	b 2, lb 9	11	b 5, lb 15, nb 2	22
	(all out 74.5 overs)	230	(6 wkts dec 85.3 overs)	296

Bowling
Hoggard 16-3-56-5. Naved-ul-Hasan 15-1-47-0. Bresnan 12-3-26-0.
Shahzad 14.5-3-41-2. Wainwright 17-4-49-3.
Hoggard 14-1-52-0. Naved-ul-Hasan 17-3-57-1. Shahzad 15.3-3-45-2.
Bresnan 20-4-55-1. Rudolph 1-0-1-0. Wainwright 18-0-66-2.
Fall of Wickets: 1-0, 2-0, 3-26, 4-30, 5-84, 6-97, 7-149, 8-215, 9-219
1-36, 2-131, 3-139, 4-179, 5-221, 6-274

Somerset won by 4 wickets – Yorkshire (5pts), Somerset (18pts)

WORCESTERSHIRE v. SUSSEX – at New Road

WORCS	First Innings		Second Innings	
DKH Mitchell	b Collymore	19	c Joyce b Chawla	99
SC Moore	lbw b Kirtley	0	b Kirtley	6
VS Solanki (capt)	b Collymore	5	b Chawla	33
BF Smith	run out	80	lbw b Chawla	1
MM Ali	c Hodd b Martin-Jenkins	4	c Hodd b Kirtley	124
*SM Davies	c Joyce b Chawla	15	b Nash	35
AA Noffke	st Hodd b Chawla	89	lbw b Chawla	3
GJ Batty	c Hodd b Smith	17	c Kirtley b Chawla	3
CD Nelson	c Chawla b Collymore	5	b Smith	9
MS Mason	not out	7	not out	24
P Chawla			not out	22
Extras	b 5, lb 2, w 1, nb 4	12	b 10, lb 14, w 8, nb 4	36
	(all out 89.3 overs)	288	(all out 130.1 overs)	392

Bowling
Collymore 17-5-42-3. Kirtley 17-2-57-1. Martin-Jenkins 13-2-41-1. Smith 20-8-44-2.
Chawla 21.3-2-89-2. Yardy 2-0-8-0.
Collymore 12-2-37-0. Kirtley 13.5-1-61-2. Smith 18.2-6-46-1. Chawla 51-11-152-6.
Martin-Jenkins 8-1-18-0. Yardy 9-1-19-0. Nash 18-7-35-1.
Fall of Wickets: 1-0, 2-23, 3-64, 4-91, 5-118, 6-176, 7-216, 8-234, 9-262
1-6, 2-59, 3-73, 4-285, 5-297, 6-297, 7-305, 8-344, 9-346

SUSSEX	First Innings		Second Innings	
MH Yardy (capt)	c Davies b Whelan	152	not out	34
CD Nash	c Hodd b Smith	52	not out	25
EC Joyce	c Ali b Kabir Ali	21		
MW Goodwin	c Davies b Whelan	16		
MJ Prior	c Solanki b Whelan	82		
*AJ Hodd	lbw b Noffke	43		
DR Smith	c Batty b Noffke	77		
RSC Martin-Jenkins	c Moore b Noffke	20		
P Chawla	not out	102		
RJ Kirtley	c Davies b Noffke	33		
CD Collymore	not out	5		
Extras	b 3, lb 11, w 1, nb 6	21	b 1, lb 1	2
	(9 wkts dec 130.1 overs)	620	(0 wkts 10 overs)	61

Bowling
Kabir Ali 22-1-79-1. Mason 27-2-112-0. Noffke 27-3-92-4. Batty 29-5-123-0.
Whelan 26-1-151-3. Mitchell 7-0-19-0. Ali 3-0-30-0.
Kabir Ali 3-0-22-0. Mason 2-0-14-0. Whelan 2-0-10-0. Batty 2-0-9-0.
Mitchell 1-0-4-0.
Fall of Wickets: 1-93, 2-144, 3-196, 4-315, 5-343, 6-458, 7-467, 8-492, 9-597

Sussex won by 10 wickets – Worcestershire (4pts), Sussex (22pts)

Piyush Chawla, the Indian leg spinner, made a spectacular Championship debut with bat and ball for Sussex at New Road.

against the new ball, and a swashbuckling 148 from 175 balls by Alistair Brown, and a further 116 not out by Chris Read, enabled the visitors to declare and go on to complete victory in some comfort.

Yorkshire's below-par batting let in Somerset at Headingley, with Marcus Trescothick and Zander de Bruyn's fourth innings strokeplay proving ultimately decisive, but Somerset also needed Craig Kieswetter's battling first innings 83 to keep them in the match as Matthew Hoggard took 5 for 56. On his first-class debut, meanwhile, there was an exciting unbeaten 82 from 19-year-old Jonny Bairstow, son of former Yorkshire and England wicketkeeper David Bairstow.

Piyush Chawla, the young Indian leg-spinning all-rounder, enjoyed a memorable Sussex debut as Worcestershire were trounced at New Road. Mike Yardy's five-hour 152 was another big factor in Sussex's success, but the game belonged to Chawla, who struck a dashing maiden first-class century from just 86 balls, with six sixes, and then took 6 for 152 from 51 overs to chip away at some spirited home resistance led by Moeen Ali and Daryl Mitchell.

In Division Two, Andre Nel's first innings 6 for 36 and a magnificent, ten-hour innings of 204 not out from Usman Afzaal set up Surrey's first Championship victory in 21 matches, sealed as Northamptonshire were bowled out a second time by Chris Schofield's 5 for 40.

But Ryan Harris, the Australian all-rounder, also played a major role by hitting a 94-ball 94 to dominate a match-deciding seventh wicket stand of 149 with Afzaal after Surrey had stuttered somewhat to 244 for 6. That they eventually reached 530 was down to Afzaal's determination and stamina, and further lower-order support from Murtaza Hussain and Jade Dernbach.

In the only other second division game, honours finished even in the drawn encounter between Derbyshire and Glamorgan at Derby. Jamie Dalrymple's fine form continued for Glamorgan, with 128, while Wavell Hinds completed his first first-class hundred for two and a half years and Robert Croft impressed with eight wickets in the game.

Round Six: 11–14 June Division Two

NORTHAMPTONSHIRE v. SURREY – at Northampton

NORTHANTS	First Innings		Second Innings	
SD Peters	c Ramprakash b Dernbach	59	c Butcher b Schofield	78
RA White	c Batty b Nel	6	c Batty b Nel	8
MAG Nelson	c Batty b Nel	12	lbw b Dernbach	1
N Boje (capt)	c Batty b Dernbach	4	c Brown b Schofield	15
DJ Willey	c Harris b Nel	4	lbw b Schofield	1
AJ Hall	b Harris	23	c Newman b Hussain	45
*D Murphy	c Batty b Nel	14	b Dernbach	14
JJ van der Wath	c sub b Nel	28	c Afzaal b Schofield	35
DS Lucas	b Nel	0	lbw b Schofield	4
MS Panesar	c Batty b Dernbach	38	not out	6
DH Wigley	not out	2	c Nel b Hussain	1
Extras	b 4, lb 10, w 1, nb 4	19	b 7, lb 6, w 1, nb 4	18
	(all out 59.2 overs)	209	(all out 76.4 overs)	226

Bowling
Nel 19-3-36-6. Harris 16.5-1-69-1. Dernbach 16.3-3-74-3. Hussain 7-2-16-0.
Nel 14-3-37-1. Dernbach 12-2-56-2. Schofield 21-5-40-5. Hussain 27.4-3-72-2.
Afzaal 2-1-8-0.
Fall of Wickets: 1-31, 2-55, 3-66, 4-97, 5-107, 6-123, 7-145, 8-147, 9-205
1-28, 2-33, 3-57, 4-65, 5-141, 6-162, 7-184, 8-194, 9-223

SURREY	First Innings	
SA Newman	c Murphy b van der Wath	10
MJ Brown	b Lucas	12
MR Ramprakash	b Wigley	17
MA Butcher (capt)	c van der Wath b Wigley	32
U Afzaal	not out	204
*JN Batty	c Murphy b Lucas	48
CP Schofield	c Peters b Lucas	15
RJ Harris	lbw b Wigley	94
Murtaza Hussain	c Murphy b Boje	34
A Nel	b Wigley	6
JW Dernbach	c White b van der Wath	19
Extras	b 8, lb 15, w 5, nb 6, p 5	39
	(all out 164 overs)	530

Bowling
van der Wath 22-5-76-2. Lucas 26-5-83-3. Wigley 35-4-134-4. Hall 22-6-55-0.
Panesar 28-9-69-0. Boje 26-8-66-1. Willey 5-2-19-0.
Fall of Wickets: 1-21, 2-24, 3-73, 4-94, 5-224, 6-244, 7-393, 8-462, 9-471

Surrey won by an innings and 95 runs –
Northamptonshire (3pts), Surrey (21pts)

DERBYSHIRE v. GLAMORGAN – at Derby

DERBYSHIRE	First Innings		Second Innings	
CJL Rogers (capt)	c Wallace b Cosgrove	27	(2) c Cosker b Shantry	21
SD Stubbings	lbw b Croft	43	(1) lbw b Croft	49
GT Park	c Kruger b Cosker	76	b Dalrymple	10
DJ Redfern	c Powell b Shantry	11	c Powell b Dalrymple	1
WW Hinds	lbw b Cosgrove	30	not out	119
GM Smith	b Cosgrove	12	run out	0
*DJ Pipe	b Kruger	22	c Rees b Croft	10
GG Wagg	st Wallace b Croft	0	c Dalrymple b Croft	4
T Lungley	lbw b Croft	0	lbw b Croft	33
TD Groenewald	c Powell b Croft	24	not out	27
ID Hunter	not out	33		
Extras	b 9, lb 16, nb 4	29	b 9, lb 7, w 1, nb 6	20
	(all out 120.4 overs)	307	(8 wkts dec 107 overs)	294

Bowling
Harris 20-4-59-0. Kruger 20-4-46-1. Shantry 18-2-44-1. Cosgrove 8-1-30-3.
Cosker 17-5-29-1. Croft 37.4-14-74-4.
Kruger 6-0-56-0. Harris 5-0-16-0. Shantry 4-1-15-1. Dalrymple 23-4-73-2.
Croft 42-13-62-4. Cosker 27-5-59-0.
Fall of Wickets: 1-56, 2-129, 3-150, 4-191, 5-215, 6-222, 7-227, 8-227, 9-245
1-44, 2-55, 3-59, 4-118, 5-118, 6-139, 7-149, 8-213

GLAMORGAN	First Innings		Second Innings	
GP Rees	lbw b Smith	42	c Redfern b Wagg	0
MJ Cosgrove	lbw b Wagg	0	not out	74
BJ Wright	lbw b Lungley	14	b Wagg	4
MJ Powell	c Park b Lungley	0	not out	42
JWM Dalrymple (capt)	c Park b Hunter	128		
*MA Wallace	c Pipe b Wagg	0		
JAR Harris	c Pipe b Smith	20		
RDB Croft	c & b Groenewald	28		
DA Cosker	not out	46		
AJ Shantry	lbw b Smith	13		
GJP Kruger	c Lungley b Wagg	0		
Extras	b 7, lb 9, w 4, nb 6	26	b 8, lb 2, nb 6	16
	(all out 111 overs)	317	(2 wkts 38 overs)	136

Bowling
Wagg 36-5-87-3. Hunter 12-0-39-1. Lungley 18-2-67-2. Groenewald 18-3-45-1.
Hinds 4-0-10-0. Smith 21-7-41-3. Park 3-0-12-0.
Wagg 13-1-46-2. Smith 5-1-13-0. Lungley 3-1-4-0. Hunter 7-2-17-0.
Redfern 5-0-23-0. Groenewald 4-1-18-0. Park 1-0-5-0.
Fall of Wickets: 1-1, 2-31, 3-35, 4-117, 5-118, 6-166, 7-236, 8-273, 9-316
1-2, 2-10

Match drawn – Derbyshire (10pts), Glamorgan (10pts)

Round Seven: 16–21 June Division One

SUSSEX v. SOMERSET – at Hove

SOMERSET	First Innings		Second Innings	
ME Trescothick	run out	109	c Martin-Jenkins b Wright	11
AV Suppiah	lbw b Chawla	49	c Prior b Chawla	50
JC Hildreth	b Chawla	2	b Smith	23
Z de Bruyn	c Hodd b Chawla	50	c Yardy b Chawla	5
JL Langer (capt)	lbw b Chawla	4	c Joyce b Smith	33
*C Kieswetter	c Prior b Chawla	1	c Yardy b Smith	7
PD Trego	not out	92	lbw b Chawla	5
AC Thomas	b Nash	4	b Chawla	22
MTC Waller	b Lewry	15	b Chawla	2
DA Stiff	b Lewry	4	not out	14
CM Willoughby	run out	23	b Chawla	0
Extras	b 5, lb 8, w 1	14	lb 5, w 1	6
	(all out 106.2 overs)	**367**	(all out 59.3 overs)	**178**

Bowling
Lewry 20-7-82-2. Martin-Jenkins 9-2-30-0. Smith 13-1-31-0. Wright 15.2-2-54-0. Chawla 35-7-118-5. Nash 14-5-39-1.
Lewry 7-0-33-0. Wright 8-1-24-1. Smith 23-4-64-3. Chawla 21.3-4-52-6.
Fall of Wickets: 1-138, 2-140, 3-191, 4-202, 5-212, 6-235, 7-240, 8-284, 9-298
1-21, 2-82, 3-88, 4-97, 5-112, 6-127, 7-140, 8-153, 9-170

SUSSEX	First Innings		Second Innings	
MH Yardy (capt)	c Langer b Thomas	5	lbw b Willoughby	6
CD Nash	lbw b Thomas	4	c Kieswetter b Thomas	134
EC Joyce	c Trescothick b Willoughby	45	(4) b Trego	30
MW Goodwin	lbw b Thomas	0	(3) lbw b Thomas	5
*MJ Prior	c Hildreth b Thomas	59	c Suppiah b Waller	11
LJ Wright	c Suppiah b Thomas	10	(7) c Suppiah b Willoughby	11
AJ Hodd	c Kieswetter b Stiff	11	(8) lbw b Thomas	2
DR Smith	lbw b Waller	30	(9) lbw b Willoughby	24
RSC Martin-Jenkins	not out	17	(10) c Trescothick b Willoughby	27
P Chawla	lbw b Stiff	0	(11) not out	27
JD Lewry	b Waller	0	(6) b Stiff	25
Extras	b 2, lb 2, w 8, nb 4	16	lb 8, w 1, nb 2	11
	(all out 65.4 overs)	**197**	(all out 88.5 overs)	**313**

Bowling
Willoughby 20-9-43-1. Thomas 18-6-53-5. Trego 2-0-8-0. de Bruyn 4-0-19-0. Stiff 11-1-43-2. Waller 10.4-2-27-2.
Willoughby 24.5-6-80-4. Thomas 25-3-99-3. Stiff 15-0-49-1. Waller 9-2-30-1. Trego 7-1-25-1. de Bruyn 8-2-22-0.
Fall of Wickets: 1-4, 2-9, 3-9, 4-104, 5-130, 6-130, 7-175, 8-196, 9-196
1-28, 2-40, 3-134, 4-158, 5-218, 6-222, 7-227, 8-247, 9-270

Somerset won by 35 runs – Sussex (3pts), Somerset (21pts)

WARWICKSHIRE v. DURHAM – at Edgbaston

DURHAM	First Innings		Second Innings	
MJ Di Venuto	lbw b Woakes	40	(2) not out	13
MD Stoneman	c Rankin b Woakes	64		
WR Smith (capt)	lbw b Woakes	1	(1) not out	9
GJ Muchall	lbw b Woakes	39		
DM Benkenstein	c Troughton b Carter	14		
ID Blackwell	b Rankin	158		
*P Mustard	c Bell b Patel	24		
GR Breese	c Troughton b Carter	48		
CD Thorp	st Ambrose b Patel	7		
G Onions	not out	1		
SJ Harmison	c Bell b Patel	1		
Extras	b 13, lb 11, w 8, nb 4	36		0
	(all out 125 overs)	**433**	(0 wkts 4 overs)	**22**

Bowling
Woakes 32-7-105-4. Rankin 24-5-68-1. Carter 23-5-90-2. Patel 33-2-112-3. Trott 1-1-0-0. Botha 12-2-34-0.
Woakes 2-0-6-0. Rankin 2-0-16-0.
Fall of Wickets: 1-31, 2-97, 3-114, 4-120, 5-206, 6-304, 7-397, 8-420, 9-430

WARWICKSHIRE	First Innings		Second Innings (following on)	
IJ Westwood (capt)	b Onions	8	c sub b Blackwell	8
T Frost	c Breese b Benkenstein	56	c Mustard b Onions	3
IR Bell	c Di Venuto b Blackwell	79	b Onions	57
IJL Trott	b Harmison	25	c Thorp b Onions	32
JO Troughton	c Muchall b Harmison	16	lbw b Onions	5
*TR Ambrose	c Mustard b Harmison	10	c Benkenstein b Harmison	9
AG Botha	not out	29	not out	34
NM Carter	lbw b Blackwell	0	c Benkenstein b Harmison	23
CR Woakes	c Thorp b Harmison	24	c Mustard b Onions	1
JS Patel	c Breese b Harmison	6	b Onions	2
WB Rankin	b Onions	7	c Thorp b Onions	2
Extras	b 1, lb 10, w 5	16	lb 1	1
	(all out 92.1 overs)	**276**	(all out 78 overs)	**177**

Bowling
Onions 22.1-2-89-2. Harmison 20-6-44-5. Thorp 11-2-25-0. Blackwell 25-7-47-2. Breese 9-2-43-0. Benkenstein 5-1-17-1.
Onions 22-9-38-7. Harmison 17-5-59-2. Thorp 6-1-19-0. Blackwell 25-4-53-1. Breese 8-4-7-0.
Fall of Wickets: 1-17, 2-146, 3-168, 4-197, 5-200, 6-211, 7-212, 8-253, 9-259
1-3, 2-28, 3-100, 4-101, 5-106, 6-119, 7-153, 8-157, 9-163

Durham won by 10 wickets – Warwickshire (4pts), Durham (22pts)

LANCASHIRE v. HAMPSHIRE – at Liverpool

LANCASHIRE	First Innings		Second Innings	
PJ Horton	lbw b Mascarenhas	37	(2) lbw b Tremlett	39
MB Loye	lbw b Cork	18	(1) lbw b Imran Tahir	55
A Flintoff	c Benham b Mascarenhas	12	c Lumb b Mascarenhas	54
VVS Laxman	c Pothas b Tremlett	21	(5) run out	1
F du Plessis	c Benham b Tremlett	6	(6) c Adams b Imran Tahir	15
SJ Croft	c Pothas b Tremlett	7	(7) c Adams b Imran Tahir	0
*LD Sutton	lbw b Cork	25	(8) c Benham b Tremlett	17
KW Hogg	lbw b Tremlett	9	(4) c Cork b Imran Tahir	16
G Chapple (capt)	lbw b Cork	27	not out	34
SI Mahmood	not out	30	c Pothas b Imran Tahir	0
G Keedy	lbw b Tomlinson	2	c Cork b Imran Tahir	0
Extras	lb 2, w 2, nb 10	14	b 8, lb 1, nb 14	23
	(all out 60.5 overs)	**208**	(all out 79.5 overs)	**254**

Bowling
Tremlett 13-3-49-4. Tomlinson 9.5-0-54-1. Cork 16-4-43-3. Mascarenhas 15-4-46-2. Imran Tahir 7-2-14-0.
Tremlett 11-3-35-2. Mascarenhas 16-2-43-1. Cork 8-1-17-0. Imran Tahir 32.5-4-108-6. Tomlinson 9-2-32-0. Carberry 3-1-10-0.
Fall of Wickets: 1-47, 2-70, 3-75, 4-101, 5-101, 6-113, 7-127, 8-168, 9-181
1-83, 2-128, 3-176, 4-177, 5-181, 6-187, 7-204, 8-237, 9-238

HAMPSHIRE	First Innings		Second Innings	
MA Carberry	c Croft b Keedy	25	not out	62
JHK Adams	c Sutton b Chapple	9	not out	46
MJ Lumb	lbw b Hogg	16		
JM Vince	c Sutton b Chapple	46		
CC Benham	c Sutton b Keedy	1		
*N Pothas	b Hogg	86		
AD Mascarenhas (capt)	c Sutton b Mahmood	108		
DG Cork	c Horton b Flintoff	5		
CT Tremlett	c Croft b Flintoff	0		
JA Tomlinson	c Sutton b Chapple	6		
Imran Tahir	not out	24		
Extras	b 1, lb 2, w 2, nb 14	19	b 10	10
	(all out 86.1 overs)	**345**	(0 wkts 23.1 overs)	**118**

Bowling
Chapple 23-6-77-3. Mahmood 18.1-0-98-1. Hogg 9-0-48-2. Flintoff 17-2-60-2. Keedy 19-5-59-2.
Chapple 5-1-19-0. Flintoff 3-1-12-0. Keedy 10-1-52-0. Mahmood 1-0-7-0. du Plessis 4.1-0-18-0.
Fall of Wickets: 1-13, 2-50, 3-65, 4-71, 5-157, 6-212, 7-235, 8-235, 9-313

Hampshire won by 10 wickets – Lancashire (4pts), Hampshire (20pts)

Round Seven: 16–21 June Division Two

GLOUCESTERSHIRE v. MIDDLESEX – at Bristol

MIDDLESEX	First Innings		Second Innings	
AJ Strauss	c Banerjee b Franklin	32	b Lewis	0
NRD Compton	c Snell b Lewis	7	b Lewis	17
OA Shah	c Kadeer Ali b Kirby	25	c Spearman b Banerjee	57
EJG Morgan	b Kirby	6	lbw b Kirby	10
NJ Dexter	c Marshall b Lewis	6	b Kirby	43
*DC Nash	b Lewis	10	(7) run out	38
GK Berg	c Spearman b Ireland	29	(8) c Snell b Lewis	8
SD Udal (capt)	c Taylor b Banerjee	8	(9) c Snell b Ireland	27
CEW Silverwood	c Porterfield b Ireland	1	(10) not out	26
ST Finn	not out	24	(6) b Kirby	1
DA Burton	c Snell b Banerjee	1	lbw b Banerjee	0
Extras	lb 2, nb 2	4	lb 5, w 1	6
	(all out 50.5 overs)	**153**	(all out 66.2 overs)	**233**

Bowling
Lewis 13-2-34-3. Kirby 9-3-16-2. Franklin 10-2-33-1. Ireland 11-2-42-2. Banerjee 7.5-2-26-2.
Lewis 14-3-54-3. Franklin 13-2-50-0. Kirby 14-5-30-3. Ireland 9-2-28-1. Banerjee 16.2-3-66-2.
Fall of Wickets: 1-21, 2-49, 3-69, 4-72, 5-80, 6-99, 7-123, 8-125, 9-130
1-0, 2-45, 3-65, 4-111, 5-124, 6-147, 7-170, 8-180, 9-232

GLOS	First Innings		Second Innings	
Kadeer Ali	lbw b Dexter	21	(2) not out	8
WTS Porterfield	c Nash b Finn	53	(1) c Strauss b Berg	4
HJH Marshall	c Nash b Berg	18	not out	28
CM Spearman (capt)	c Nash b Burton	57		
CG Taylor	lbw b Burton	40		
JEC Franklin	lbw b Burton	67		
*SD Snell	c Berg b Udal	15		
J Lewis	c Dexter b Burton	54		
V Banerjee	c Nash b Udal	2		
SP Kirby	not out	2		
AJ Ireland	c Morgan b Burton	1		
Extras	lb 7, w 1, nb 4	12	lb 5	5
	(all out 100.2 overs)	**342**	(1 wkt 9.5 overs)	**45**

Bowling
Silverwood 20-3-68-0. Finn 21-2-69-1. Berg 17-3-65-1. Burton 18.2-2-68-5. Dexter 14-5-39-1. Udal 10-4-26-2.
Finn 4-1-16-0. Shah 1-0-1-0. Berg 3.5-2-20-1. Silverwood 1-0-3-0.
Fall of Wickets: 1-62, 2-88, 3-104, 4-193, 5-200, 6-225, 7-328, 8-339, 9-339
1-11

Gloucestershire won by 9 wickets – Gloucestershire (20pts), Middlesex (3pts)

KENT v. ESSEX – at Tunbridge Wells

ESSEX	First Innings		Second Innings	
AN Cook	lbw b Joseph	8	c Jones b Cook	30
JER Gallian	b Khan	1	b Khan	14
V Chopra	b Joseph	3	c van Jaarsveld b McLaren	63
MJ Walker	lbw b Cook	41	c Jones b Cook	5
ML Pettini (capt)	c Tredwell b Kemp	55	not out	101
*JS Foster	lbw b Tredwell	36	c Kemp b McLaren	37
RN ten Doeschate	c Jones b McLaren	40	c van Jaarsveld b McLaren	0
GR Napier	not out	64	not out	48
CJC Wright	c Kemp b McLaren	0		
DD Masters	b McLaren	2		
Danish Kaneria	b McLaren	12		
Extras	b 1, lb 4, w 5, nb 8	18	b 6, lb 5, w 1, nb 10	22
	(all out 90.5 overs)	**280**	(6 wkts dec 99.4 overs)	**320**

Bowling
Joseph 13.3-2-43-2. Khan 17-3-46-1. Cook 14-5-27-1. Tredwell 17-4-40-1. McLaren 17.2-2-80-4. Kemp 10-3-27-1. Stevens 2-0-12-0.
Khan 22-5-58-1. Cook 22-6-56-2. McLaren 20-9-72-3. Tredwell 11-4-23-0. Kemp 14.4-3-58-0. Stevens 9-1-40-0. Denly 1-0-2-0.
Fall of Wickets: 1-4, 2-12, 3-18, 4-90, 5-133, 6-173, 7-230, 8-236, 9-244
1-47, 2-47, 3-57, 4-152, 5-230, 6-230

KENT	First Innings		Second Innings	
JL Denly	lbw b Masters	0	c Masters b Cook	123
RWT Key (capt)	lbw b Napier	0	b Masters	21
A Khan	c Foster b Masters	18	(10) b Danish Kaneria	16
*GO Jones	c Foster b Masters	9	b Danish Kaneria	28
M van Jaarsveld	c Foster b Napier	13	lbw b Masters	73
DI Stevens	c Chopra b Masters	6	c Masters b Danish Kaneria	43
JM Kemp	lbw b Napier	36	lbw b Danish Kaneria	6
JC Tredwell	b Napier	28	(3) c Cook b Danish Kaneria	8
R McLaren	c Foster b ten Doeschate	1	(8) b Danish Kaneria	2
SJ Cook	lbw b ten Doeschate	1	(9) not out	8
RH Joseph	not out	9	c & b Napier	1
Extras	nb 2	2	b 11, lb 13, nb 2	26
	(all out 50.3 overs)	**123**	(all out 120.2 overs)	**355**

Bowling
Masters 19-8-34-4. Napier 15-4-32-4. Wright 10-2-34-0. Danish Kaneria 4-0-19-0. ten Doeschate 2.3-0-4-2.
Masters 34-14-78-2. Napier 15.2-4-54-1. Wright 11-2-36-0. ten Doeschate 16-2-62-0. Danish Kaneria 42-8-92-6. Walker 1-0-4-0. Cook 1-0-5-1.
Fall of Wickets: 1-0, 2-0, 3-15, 4-36, 5-46, 6-50, 7-106, 8-113, 9-113
1-84, 2-117, 3-186, 4-206, 5-312, 6-321, 7-323, 8-328, 9-352

Essex won by 122 runs – Kent (3pts), Essex (19pts)

LEICESTERSHIRE v. SURREY – at Grace Road

LEICESTERSHIRE	First Innings		Second Innings	
MAG Boyce	b Dernbach	5	lbw b Hussain	29
JJ Cobb	c Schofield b Dernbach	1	c Butcher b Hussain	40
HH Dippenaar (capt)	c Butcher b Hussain	39	c sub b Afzaal	143
HD Ackerman	c Batty b Jordan	21	b Afzaal	180
J Allenby	c Schofield b Jordan	0	c Batty b Afzaal	11
JWA Taylor	lbw b Jordan	16	not out	23
*TJ New	c Batty b Dernbach	44	not out	27
CW Henderson	c Batty b Dernbach	12		
JHK Naik	lbw b Dernbach	7		
AJ Harris	c Butcher b Dernbach	13		
HF Gurney	not out	0		
Extras	lb 6, w 1	7	b 8, lb 10, w 10, nb 6	34
	(all out 44.1 overs)	**165**	(5 wkts 146 overs)	**487**

Bowling
Dernbach 14.1-3-47-6. Jordan 16-3-54-3. Meaker 7-0-32-0. Schofield 5-1-25-0. Hussain 2-1-1-1.
Dernbach 19-1-83-0. Jordan 22-5-80-0. Meaker 18-0-71-0. Hussain 34-6-96-2. Schofield 31-5-66-0. Afzaal 18-1-51-3. Newman 2-0-10-0. Brown 2-0-12-0.
Fall of Wickets: 1-7, 2-16, 3-43, 4-49, 5-87, 6-87, 7-110, 8-122, 9-154
1-67, 2-90, 3-404, 4-412, 5-421

SURREY	First Innings	
SA Newman	c Cobb b Henderson	40
MJ Brown	c Henderson b Gurney	101
MR Ramprakash	c New b Gurney	85
MA Butcher (capt)	c Cobb b Harris	7
U Afzaal	lbw b Allenby	29
*JN Batty	lbw b Allenby	0
CP Schofield	c New b Harris	16
CJ Jordan	c New b Gurney	18
Murtaza Hussain	b Gurney	1
JW Dernbach	not out	1
SC Meaker	c New b Gurney	9
Extras	b 6, lb 14, nb 2	22
	(all out 115 overs)	**329**

Bowling
Harris 27-5-81-2. Gurney 31-8-82-5. Allenby 30-7-73-2. Henderson 26-2-71-1. Taylor 1-0-2-0.
Fall of Wickets: 1-58, 2-216, 3-231, 4-282, 5-282, 6-282, 7-311, 8-317, 9-317

Match drawn – Leicestershire (7pts), Surrey (10pts)

WORCESTERSHIRE v. YORKSHIRE - at New Road

WORCS	First Innings		Second Innings	
DKH Mitchell	b Rafiq	68	lbw b Rafiq	32
SC Moore	lbw b Hoggard	60	b Kruis	52
VS Solanki (capt)	c Bairstow b Shahzad	1	c Rudolph b Rafiq	48
BF Smith	c Rudolph b Kruis	15	not out	48
MM Ali	b Kruis	55	not out	14
*SM Davies	c Bairstow b Kruis	112		
AA Noffke	lbw b Shahzad	35		
GJ Batty	c Rudolph b Bresnan	25		
Kabir Ali	c Rafiq b Hoggard	3		
CD Whelan	c Sayers b Bresnan	5		
MS Mason	not out	11		
Extras	b 8, lb 14, w 1, nb 2	25	lb 6, w 1, nb 2	9
	(all out 121.3 overs)	415	(3 wkts 57 overs)	203

Bowling
Hoggard 29-3-88-2. Bresnan 23.3-8-58-2. Shahzad 25-3-93-2. Kruis 20-5-65-3.
Rafiq 19-5-62-1. Rudolph 5-0-27-0.
Bresnan 4-0-19-0. Shahzad 13-2-43-0. Rafiq 20-0-82-2. Kruis 7-1-15-1.
Rudolph 8-0-24-0. Sayers 2-0-3-0. Gale 1-0-11-0.
Fall of Wickets: 1-104, 2-105, 3-147, 4-173, 5-265, 6-346, 7-375, 8-389, 9-400
1-67, 2-95, 3-176

YORKSHIRE	First Innings	
JA Rudolph	c Davies b Mason	9
JJ Sayers	c Batty b Noffke	44
MP Vaughan	c Batty b Whelan	43
A McGrath (capt)	c Davies b Whelan	6
AW Gale	c Mason b Batty	101
*JM Bairstow	c Mitchell b Whelan	0
TT Bresnan	c Mitchell b Kabir Ali	97
A Shahzad	lbw b Whelan	19
Azeem Rafiq	c Mason b Batty	100
MJ Hoggard	not out	56
GJ Kruis	b Ali	16
Extras	lb 16, w 1, nb 8	25
	(all out 131 overs)	516

Bowling
Kabir Ali 25-2-127-1. Mason 22-8-67-1. Noffke 28-8-77-1. Whelan 25-4-130-4.
Batty 25-5-79-2. Mitchell 4-1-11-0. Ali 2-0-9-1.
Fall of Wickets: 1-15, 2-97, 3-107, 4-107, 5-108, 6-278, 7-328, 8-334, 9-484

Match drawn – Worcestershire (11pts), Yorkshire (12pts)

GLAMORGAN v. NORTHAMPTONSHIRE - at Cardiff

GLAMORGAN	First Innings		Second Innings	
GP Rees	c Murphy b Wigley	4	not out	116
MJ Cosgrove	not out	102	b Panesar	22
BJ Wright	b Wigley	6	lbw b Boje	15
MJ Powell	c Willey b Hall	88	lbw b Boje	2
JWM Dalrymple (capt)	c Murphy b Wigley	1	not out	70
*MA Wallace	b Panesar	32		
JAR Harris	c Murphy b Willey	17		
RDB Croft	c Hall b Wigley	43		
DA Cosker	c Murphy b Hall	10		
AJ Shantry	lbw b Wigley	1		
DS Harrison	c Nelson b Hall	1		
Extras	w 1, nb 2	3	lb 1, nb 6	7
	(all out 92.1 overs)	308	(3 wkts dec 59 overs)	232

Bowling
van der Wath 16-2-64-0. Wigley 20-3-78-5. Hall 12.1-3-37-3. Willey 11-1-37-1.
Panesar 28-4-81-1. Boje 5-2-11-0.
van der Wath 6-1-32-0. Wigley 10-3-42-0. Panesar 20-6-68-1. Boje 20-6-62-2.
Hall 2-0-14-0. Wakely 1-0-13-0.
Fall of Wickets: 1-19, 2-29, 3-144, 4-202, 5-233, 6-291, 7-306, 8-307, 9-307
1-42, 2-79, 3-83

NORTHANTS	First Innings		Second Innings	
*D Murphy	lbw b Harris	2		
SD Peters	c Dalrymple b Harrison	6	(1) c Wallace b Harris	7
RA White	lbw b Harris	2	(2) lbw b Croft	12
AG Wakely	not out	113	(3) b Harris	0
N Boje (capt)	lbw b Harrison	10	(4) b Shantry	52
MAG Nelson	b Shantry	10	(5) c Wallace b Shantry	38
AJ Hall	c & b Cosker	44	(6) not out	17
DJ Willey	lbw b Croft	0	not out	4
JJ van der Wath	b Harrison	26	(7) c Wallace b Cosker	5
MS Panesar	not out	0		
DH Wigley				
Extras	lb 2	2	b 1, lb 4	5
	(8 wkts dec 91.1 overs)	215	(6 wkts 66.5 overs)	140

Bowling
Harris 24-7-59-2. Harrison 23.1-6-71-3. Shantry 11-4-25-1. Croft 24-5-43-1.
Cosker 9-2-15-1.
Harris 9-3-37-2. Harrison 3-0-9-0. Croft 22-14-16-1. Cosker 23-10-46-1.
Dalrymple 2.5-0-5-0. Shantry 7-2-22-2.
Fall of Wickets: 1-4, 2-10, 3-10, 4-37, 5-80, 6-164, 7-165, 8-215
1-10, 2-10, 3-48, 4-105, 5-116, 6-123

Match drawn – Glamorgan (9pts), Northamptonshire (8pts)

Round Seven: 16–21 June

A fascinating and closely fought contest at Hove finally went Somerset's way, by just 35 runs, after Sussex had been inspired by Chris Nash's excellent 134 from 259 balls as they attempted to chase down 349 in the fourth innings.

Nash struck 22 fours and was sixth out at 222, but the Sussex lower order continued to chip away at the required runs and Somerset were much relieved when Robin Martin-Jenkins was finally dismissed after a 43-run stand for the last wicket with Piyush Chawla. The Indian leg-spinner had earlier claimed 11 wickets in the match, bowling Sussex back into the game with a second innings haul of 6 for 52.

But even with such a hard-won victory Somerset, who had initially taken charge through Marcus Trescothick's 109, Pete Trego's rumbustious unbeaten 92 from 107 balls with four sixes and Alfonso Thomas's first innings 5 for 53, could make no impression on champions Durham, who thrashed Warwickshire by ten wickets at Edgbaston.

Geoff Cook, the Durham head coach, called it 'one of our very best wins' after seeing Graham Onions and Steve Harmison wreak havoc on a slow, low pitch especially prepared by the home club to neuter Durham's fast bowling spearhead. Harmison's 5 for 44 forced Warwickshire to follow on, after Ian Blackwell's 158 had ensured maximum batting points, and Onions administered the stunning coup de grace with his pace and accuracy bringing him second innings figures of 7 for 38.

Lancashire's hopes of joining in the title race were badly hit by a ten-wicket defeat at Liverpool, where Hampshire outplayed them with bat and ball. Tim Tremlett's 4 for 49, plus three wickets for a determined Dominic Cork against the county which had released him the previous winter, gave Hampshire the early advantage and Nic Pothas, with 86, and Dimitri Mascarenhas, who included two sixes and 14 fours in an equally combative 108, further strengthened their position.

Mal Loye and Andrew Flintoff, whose 54 showed a welcome return to some sort of batting form ahead of the Ashes, did their best to lead a fightback but Imran Tahir's leg spin – which earned him 6 for 108 – was too potent for the Lancashire middle and later order and soon Michael Carberry, with a 73-ball 62 not out, and Jimmy Adams were sprinting to the finish line.

Yorkshire, in some bother at 108 for 5 in reply to Worcestershire's 415 at New Road, rallied impressively to reach 516 with Andrew Gale (101) and Tim Bresnan (97) leading the recovery and Azeem Rafiq, becoming at 18 one of the county's youngest century-makers with a superb 100 off 95 balls with three sixes and 13 fours, being joined by Matthew Hoggard in a ninth wicket partnership worth 150. The game ended in a draw, though.

Gloucestershire remained on top of the second division with an efficient nine-wicket victory at Bristol against Middlesex. Andrew Strauss was bowled for a third ball second innings duck by Jon Lewis as the Gloucestershire seamers held sway, and a solid first innings progress to 342 – featuring four half-centuries – did the rest.

David Masters and Graham Napier made the decisive thrusts at Tunbridge Wells, where they each took four first innings wickets as Kent slid to 123 all out and, in the end, not even an excellent second innings 123 by Joe Denly, and 73 from Martin van Jaarsveld could prevent Essex from wrapping up victory as Danish Kaneria finished with 6 for 92.

Both remaining Division Two matches were drawn, with Boeta Dippenaar and HD Ackerman hitting big hundreds to deny Surrey at Grace Road after Jade Dernbach, with 6 for 47, and runs from Michael Brown (101) and Mark Ramprakash (85) had put Leicestershire firmly on the back foot. At Cardiff, meanwhile, Northamptonshire were perhaps fortunate to escape with a draw against Glamorgan after all but 15.2 overs of the second day had been washed out.

Round Eight: 30 June–3 July

Durham and Somerset were again the first division winners of this round of games, while a frustrated Nottinghamshire were denied the chance of beating Lancashire at Trent Bridge when only 27 overs of play were possible on the final day. The batting of David Hussey and Mark Wagh, plus 5 for 31 from the evergreen Mark Ealham, had made Notts heavy favourites to complete a victory that would have stepped up their own title challenge.

Liam Plunkett was at the heart of Durham's five-wicket win against Worcestershire at the Riverside, collecting career-best match figures of 11 for 119 as the visitors were dismissed for 193 and 179. But Worcestershire did not give up without a fight, with Durham badly needing Phil Mustard's unbeaten 63 as Kabir Ali took 6 for 68 to keep his side very much in the game at the halfway stage, before Michael Di Venuto's unbeaten 100 from 123 balls swept them to victory.

But it was Somerset's win against Yorkshire at Taunton which was the performance of the season, as they chased down a target of 476 in 90 overs to complete a remarkable four-wicket triumph with 4.3 overs to spare and rain beginning to fall.

Even accounting for the trueness of the pitch, it was a magnificent achievement to maintain an asking rate of more than five runs an over. Until Yorkshire's second innings declaration, it was a game dominated by successive major innings from left-handers Jacques

Marcus Trescothick was in powerful and prolific form for Somerset throughout the 2009 season.

Rudolph, Joe Sayers and Marcus Trescothick, although Matthew Hoggard had taken 5 for 82 to give Yorkshire a 112-run first innings advantage.

But then Trescothick, with 96, and Arul Suppiah, with a career-best 131, added 187 for the first wicket to set up Somerset's astounding chase, and Pete Trego came in to thump 103 not out from a mere 54 balls – with nine sixes and six fours – to complete the job. It was the second highest successful Championship chase and the eighth highest in all first-class cricket.

In Division Two Kent hit back from their defeat by Essex in the previous round to move themselves into promotion contention by beating leaders Gloucestershire at Beckenham. Two half-centuries by Martin van Jaarsveld anchored the home batting and Simon Cook's first innings 5 for 22 was the decisive bowling performance of the match. Azhar Mahmood and James Tredwell then shared nine Gloucestershire second innings wickets.

Round Eight: 30 June–3 July Division One

DURHAM v. WORCESTERSHIRE – at the Riverside

WORCS	First Innings		Second Innings	
DKH Mitchell	c Mustard b Plunkett	13	c Di Venuto b Davies	15
AN Kervezee	c Di Venuto b Davies	6	c Mustard b Plunkett	66
MM Ali	c Plunkett b Benkenstein	9	c Coetzer b Plunkett	10
BF Smith	b Claydon	33	c Coetzer b Thorp	3
DA Wheeldon	c Di Venuto b Thorp	7	c Di Venuto b Claydon	0
AA Noffke	c Mustard b Plunkett	50	lbw b Blackwell	11
GJ Batty (capt)	b Plunkett	19	b Plunkett	4
Kabir Ali	c Thorp b Plunkett	28	not out	30
*JP Knappett	not out	4	c Mustard b Blackwell	1
CD Whelan	b Plunkett	0	b Plunkett	21
MS Mason	c Thorp b Plunkett	2	c Thorp b Plunkett	5
Extras	b 9, lb 5, w 2, nb 6	22	lb 5, nb 8	13
	(all out 79.1 overs)	**193**	(all out 74 overs)	**179**

Bowling
Thorp 16-8-34-1. Claydon 17-4-32-1. Davies 13-5-29-1. Plunkett 23.1-3-63-6. Benkenstein 2-1-11-1. Blackwell 8-5-10-0.
Claydon 11-0-50-1. Thorp 13-6-27-1. Davies 10-2-19-1. Plunkett 24-6-56-5. Blackwell 16-7-22-2.
Fall of Wickets: 1-18, 2-26, 3-56, 4-80, 5-80, 6-137, 7-187, 8-187, 9-191
1-36, 2-57, 3-66, 4-71, 5-108, 6-116, 7-117, 8-124, 9-169

DURHAM	First Innings		Second Innings	
MJ Di Venuto	b Kabir Ali	0	not out	100
KJ Coetzer	b Kabir Ali	30	c Knappett b Noffke	15
WR Smith (capt)	b Kabir Ali	0	c Smith b Whelan	16
GJ Muchall	c Knappett b Mason	0	c Mitchell b Mason	14
DM Benkenstein	c Knappett b Kabir Ali	25	c Knappett b Mason	17
ID Blackwell	b Mason	1	c Wheeldon b Mason	3
*P Mustard	not out	63	not out	2
LE Plunkett	c Batty b Mason	29		
CD Thorp	lbw b Kabir Ali	17		
ME Claydon	c Knappett b Kabir Ali	6		
M Davies	b Whelan	6		
Extras	b 4, lb 5, w 2, nb 6	17	b 2, lb 6, nb 4	12
	(all out 55.5 overs)	**194**	(5 wkts 41 overs)	**179**

Bowling
Kabir Ali 18-4-68-6. Mason 21-8-55-3. Noffke 10-4-28-0. Whelan 6.5-1-34-1.
Kabir Ali 6-0-23-0. Mason 11-2-35-3. Noffke 7-2-11-1. Batty 10-1-48-0.
Whelan 5-0-37-1. Ali 2-0-17-0.
Fall of Wickets: 1-0, 2-0, 3-1, 4-56, 5-59, 6-59, 7-105, 8-140, 9-171
1-47, 2-90, 3-115, 4-137, 5-155

Durham won by 5 wickets – Durham (17pts), Worcestershire (3pts)

SOMERSET v. YORKSHIRE – at Taunton

YORKSHIRE	First Innings		Second Innings	
JA Rudolph	b Stiff	191	c Trescothick b Willoughby	0
JJ Sayers	b Thomas	8	b de Bruyn	152
A McGrath (capt)	c Kieswetter b Trego	40	b Willoughby	25
A Lyth	c Hildreth b de Bruyn	36	c Kieswetter b Stiff	71
AW Gale	c Trescothick b Willoughby	17	c Trescothick b Thomas	16
*JM Bairstow	c Kieswetter b Thomas	39	not out	66
Azeem Rafiq	c Kieswetter b Thomas	4		
A Shahzad	not out	27	(7) not out	16
MJ Hoggard	c Thomas b Stiff	26		
SA Patterson	c Kieswetter b Stiff	8		
JE Lee	c Trescothick b Stiff	2		
Extras	b 13, lb 11, w 8, nb 8	40	b 1, lb 3, w 3, nb 10	17
	(all out 112 overs)	**438**	(5 wkts dec 96.5 overs)	**363**

Bowling
Willoughby 23-3-78-1. Thomas 24-3-65-3. Caddick 20-2-94-0. Stiff 19-2-92-4. Trego 13-4-30-1. Suppiah 8-4-28-0. de Bruyn 5-1-27-1.
Willoughby 19-6-39-2. Thomas 13-1-63-1. Caddick 15-4-45-0. Suppiah 27.5-4-99-0. Trego 6-0-34-0. Stiff 11-0-52-1. de Bruyn 5-0-27-1.
Fall of Wickets: 1-24, 2-104, 3-222, 4-267, 5-338, 6-370, 7-375, 8-409, 9-436
1-0, 2-58, 3-181, 4-221, 5-329

SOMERSET	First Innings		Second Innings	
ME Trescothick	c & b Lee	146	b Hoggard	96
AV Suppiah	c Sayers b Hoggard	17	c McGrath b Rafiq	131
JL Langer (capt)	lbw b Patterson	4	(5) c Bairstow b Patterson	24
JC Hildreth	b Shahzad	51	(3) b Hoggard	18
Z de Bruyn	c Gale b Lee	31	(8) not out	27
*C Kieswetter	b Shahzad	28	b Rafiq	17
PD Trego	lbw b Hoggard	7	not out	103
AC Thomas	c Bairstow b Hoggard	13		
DA Stiff	not out	6	(4) c Bairstow b Hoggard	49
AR Caddick	b Hoggard	1		
CM Willoughby	c Bairstow b Hoggard	6		
Extras	lb 15, w 1	16	b 1, lb 7, w 2, nb 4	14
	(all out 79.4 overs)	**326**	(6 wkts 85.3 overs)	**479**

Bowling
Hoggard 19.4-2-82-5. Shahzad 20-3-57-2. Patterson 14-2-55-1. Lee 13-1-63-2. Rafiq 13-0-54-0.
Hoggard 24-0-118-3. Shahzad 19-1-119-0. Patterson 21-2-98-1. Lee 6-0-50-0. Rafiq 14.3-0-72-2. Rudolph 1-0-14-0.
Fall of Wickets: 1-51, 2-64, 3-144, 4-215, 5-277, 6-287, 7-313, 8-315, 9-316
1-187, 2-246, 3-292, 4-307, 5-338, 6-414

Somerset won by 4 wickets – Somerset (20pts), Yorkshire (8pts)

NOTTINGHAMSHIRE v. LANCASHIRE – at Trent Bridge

NOTTS	First Innings		Second Innings	
WI Jefferson	c Sutton b Newby	11	b Newby	2
BM Shafayat	lbw b Newby	14	c sub b Keedy	30
MA Wagh	c Laxman b Croft	40	c Chilton b Hogg	131
SR Patel	c Sutton b Croft	25	lbw b Hogg	1
DJ Hussey	c Hogg b Brown	126	b Chapple	74
AD Brown	c Sutton b Brown	54	c Sutton b Chapple	7
*CMW Read (capt)	lbw b Keedy	1	not out	21
MA Ealham	c Sutton b Chapple	18	c Sutton b Keedy	5
RJ Sidebottom	b Newby	46	not out	0
DJ Pattinson	lbw b Chapple	4		
CE Shreck	not out	12		
Extras	b 9, lb 13, w 5, nb 10	37	b 8, lb 5, w 1, nb 4	18
	(all out 101.3 overs)	**388**	(7 wkts dec 67 overs)	**289**

Bowling
Chapple 28-6-82-2. Newby 22.3-5-68-3. Hogg 15-1-58-0. Croft 6-0-42-2. Keedy 23-4-76-1. Horton 1-0-10-0. Brown 6-0-30-2.
Chapple 16-2-69-2. Newby 6-0-32-1. Keedy 27-1-98-2. Hogg 13-1-49-2. Croft 3-0-21-0. Brown 2-0-7-0.
Fall of Wickets: 1-12, 2-41, 3-94, 4-116, 5-286, 6-295, 7-305, 8-340, 9-354
1-11, 2-72, 3-79, 4-220, 5-230, 6-275, 7-280

LANCASHIRE	First Innings		Second Innings	
PJ Horton	c Brown b Pattinson	9	(2) run out	0
KR Brown	lbw b Ealham	3	(1) c Hussey b Sidebottom	19
MB Loye	b Patel	84	(4) not out	31
VVS Laxman	c Shafayat b Ealham	30		
MJ Chilton	lbw b Ealham	5	not out	7
SJ Croft	lbw b Shreck	25		
*LD Sutton	c Read b Sidebottom	34		
G Chapple (capt)	b Sidebottom	55		
KW Hogg	not out	17	(3) b Pattinson	34
OJ Newby	b Ealham	4		
G Keedy	c & b Ealham	0		
Extras	b 1, lb 6, w 2, nb 10	19	b 4, nb 2	6
	(all out 107 overs)	**285**	(3 wkts 33 overs)	**97**

Bowling
Sidebottom 26-8-59-2. Pattinson 18-7-55-1. Shreck 27-5-87-1. Ealham 18-6-31-5. Patel 18-4-46-1.
Sidebottom 8-1-23-1. Pattinson 8-1-25-1. Shreck 9-0-32-0. Ealham 3-2-10-0. Patel 3-0-3-0. Hussey 2-2-0-0.
Fall of Wickets: 1-9, 2-31, 3-112, 4-126, 5-158, 6-186, 7-261, 8-274, 9-283
1-1, 2-45, 3-68

Match drawn – Nottinghamshire (11pts), Lancashire (9pts)

Round Eight: 30 June–3 July Division Two

KENT v. GLOUCESTERSHIRE – at Beckenham

KENT	First Innings		Second Innings	
SA Northeast	c Snell b Franklin	10	lbw b Kirby	30
RWT Key (capt)	c Spearman b Lewis	33	lbw b Kirby	12
*GO Jones	b Kirby	46	c Marshall b Kirby	4
M van Jaarsveld	c Franklin b Kirby	53	c Snell b Kirby	62
DI Stevens	c Snell b Franklin	31	c Snell b Banerjee	3
JM Kemp	c Lewis b Banerjee	40	c Gidman b Banerjee	41
Azhar Mahmood	c & b Banerjee	10	c Gidman b Banerjee	4
JC Tredwell	c Porterfield b Banerjee	3	(9) c Hussain b Lewis	6
R McLaren	b Hussain	0	(10) c Porterfield b Banerjee	42
SJ Cook	c Porterfield b Hussain	0	(11) not out	40
A Khan	not out	0	(8) lbw b Kirby	5
Extras	lb 5	5	lb 16, w 1	17
	(all out 74.2 overs)	**231**	(all out 96 overs)	**266**

Bowling
Lewis 13-2-27-1. Franklin 14-2-38-2. Hussain 14-1-73-2. Kirby 13-2-25-2. Banerjee 19.2-4-58-3. Marshall 1-0-5-0.
Lewis 20-6-57-1. Franklin 17-4-57-0. Kirby 26-9-44-5. Banerjee 25-4-58-4. Hussain 8-0-34-0.
Fall of Wickets: 1-21, 2-75, 3-115, 4-157, 5-189, 6-210, 7-222, 8-225, 9-225
1-25, 2-37, 3-72, 4-82, 5-137, 6-145, 7-163, 8-177, 9-179

GLOS	First Innings		Second Innings	
Kadeer Ali	c van Jaarsveld b Tredwell	27	(2) c Kemp b Tredwell	38
WTS Porterfield	c Kemp b Tredwell	19	(1) c Key b Azhar Mahmood	11
HJH Marshall	c Kemp b Azhar Mahmood	4	c van Jaarsveld b A Mahmood	45
APR Gidman (capt)	c Stevens b Tredwell	28	lbw b Tredwell	12
CM Spearman	c van Jaarsveld b Cook	47	lbw b Azhar Mahmood	13
JEC Franklin	c Kemp b Cook	7	(7) c Jones b Tredwell	41
*SD Snell	lbw b Cook	0	(8) lbw b Azhar Mahmood	8
GM Hussain	c Jones b Cook	8	(9) c van Jaarsveld b Cook	8
J Lewis	c Kemp b Cook	7	(10) not out	61
V Banerjee	c van Jaarsveld b A Mahmood	0	(6) c Key b Tredwell	1
SP Kirby	not out	0	c van Jaarsveld b A Mahmood	0
Extras	b 6, lb 10, w 3	19	b 6, lb 5, w 6	17
	(all out 56.1 overs)	**166**	(all out 82.3 overs)	**255**

Bowling
Khan 12-6-23-0. McLaren 5-1-18-0. Tredwell 16-4-52-3. Azhar Mahmood 12-3-35-2. Cook 11.1-3-22-5.
Azhar Mahmood 16.3-5-39-5. Khan 5-1-29-0. Tredwell 34-9-84-4. Cook 16-3-45-1. McLaren 8-2-29-0. van Jaarsveld 3-0-18-0.
Fall of Wickets: 1-43, 2-48, 3-92, 4-101, 5-134, 6-136, 7-151, 8-164, 9-166
1-20, 2-79, 3-107, 4-123, 5-128, 6-150, 7-161, 8-179, 9-236

Kent won by 76 runs - Kent (18pts), Gloucestershire (3pts)

DERBYSHIRE v. LEICESTERSHIRE – at Derby

LEICESTERSHIRE	First Innings		Second Innings	
MAG Boyce	b Hunter	9	c Hunter b Hayward	7
JJ Cobb	lbw b Wagg	8	c Pipe b Wagg	4
HH Dippenaar (capt)	b Hunter	38	run out	1
HD Ackerman	c Pipe b Hunter	49	c Wagg b Needham	31
J Allenby	run out	96	c Pipe b Hunter	52
JWA Taylor	lbw b Hunter	89	lbw b Wagg	4
*TJ New	c Stubbings b Smith	66	not out	63
GW Walker	lbw b Hunter	3	c sub b Wagg	13
IE O'Brien	c Pipe b Hayward	5	not out	0
AJ Harris	b Wagg	4		
HF Gurney	not out	1		
Extras	b 16, lb 17, w 7, nb 4	44	b 6, lb 10, w 2, nb 16	34
	(all out 118.1 overs)	**412**	(7 wkts 51 overs)	**209**

Bowling
Wagg 22.1-6-72-2. Hayward 25-6-68-1. Hunter 26-6-82-5. Smith 19-5-64-1. Needham 12-0-51-0. Hinds 7-1-24-0. Park 7-0-18-0.
Wagg 15-3-70-3. Hunter 7-2-34-1. Hinds 5-0-15-0. Hayward 10-0-36-1. Needham 11-3-29-1. Smith 3-0-9-0.
Fall of Wickets: 1-21, 2-25, 3-115, 4-116, 5-293, 6-349, 7-375, 8-386, 9-402
1-7, 2-19, 3-47, 4-73, 5-92, 6-143, 7-208

DERBYSHIRE	First Innings	
CJL Rogers (capt)	c New b Gurney	47
SD Stubbings	lbw b Gurney	19
GT Park	c Dippenaar b Walker	72
DJ Redfern	c New b Allenby	50
WW Hinds	c New b O'Brien	40
GM Smith	c Allenby b O'Brien	40
*DJ Pipe	c New b O'Brien	49
GG Wagg	c Ackerman b O'Brien	16
J Needham	c New b O'Brien	6
ID Hunter	not out	3
M Hayward	c New b O'Brien	0
Extras	b 8, lb 5, nb 10	23
	(all out 113.3 overs)	**365**

Bowling
O'Brien 29.3-3-87-6. Harris 20-4-92-0. Allenby 18-4-30-1. Gurney 20-4-68-2. Walker 26-7-75-1.
Fall of Wickets: 1-60, 2-103, 3-207, 4-213, 5-279, 6-336, 7-345, 8-356, 9-365

Match drawn – Derbyshire (11pts), Leicestershire (12pts)

MIDDLESEX v. SURREY – at Lord's

MIDDLESEX	First Innings		Second Innings	
BA Godleman	run out	48	c Jordan b Tudor	21
NRD Compton	lbw b Nel	2	not out	100
OA Shah	c Walters b Nel	159	c sub b Hussain	61
NJ Dexter	c Tudor b Hussain	14	(7) not out	8
DJ Malan	c Batty b Nel	54	(6) c Walters b Afzaal	30
ST Finn	lbw b Jordan	5		
*DC Nash	c Brown b King	43		
GK Berg	c Jordan b Nel	0		
SD Udal (capt)	c Butcher b King	33	(4) c Butcher b Hussain	2
M Kartik	not out	8	(5) st Batty b Afzaal	4
CEW Silverwood	c Butcher b King	7		
Extras	b 4, lb 3, w 1, nb 4	12	b 2, lb 5, w 3, nb 10	20
	(all out 130.3 overs)	**385**	(5 wkts dec 67.5 overs)	**246**

Bowling
Nel 27-9-59-4. Jordan 29-9-81-1. Tudor 23-3-76-0. Walters 5-1-14-0. King 16.3-0-61-3. Hussain 25-2-75-1. Afzaal 5-1-12-0.
Nel 11-6-15-0. Jordan 11-5-24-0. King 6-0-34-0. Tudor 11-6-37-1. Afzaal 13.5-0-60-2. Hussain 15-1-69-2.
Fall of Wickets: 1-3, 2-160, 3-186, 4-259, 5-269, 6-304, 7-304, 8-360, 9-371
1-50, 2-170, 3-173, 4-178, 5-233

SURREY	First Innings		Second Innings	
*JN Batty	c Malan b Berg	24	c Kartik b Finn	0
MJ Brown	c Nash b Dexter	44	lbw b Finn	13
MR Ramprakash	lbw b Kartik	136	not out	49
MA Butcher (capt)	c Udal b Silverwood	49	(6) lbw b Udal	2
U Afzaal	c Berg b Finn	58	c Malan b Kartik	1
SJ Walters	lbw b Kartik	6	(4) lbw b Kartik	3
CJ Jordan	not out	34	not out	30
AJ Tudor	c Berg b Kartik	0		
Murtaza Hussain	c Udal b Kartik	13		
A Nel	c Compton b Finn	9		
SJ King	c Nash b Kartik	0		
Extras	b 8, lb 4, w 3, nb 4	19	lb 1	1
	(all out 134.2 overs)	**392**	(5 wkts 40 overs)	**99**

Bowling
Finn 26-5-120-2. Silverwood 22-6-61-1. Berg 15-0-42-1. Dexter 4-2-10-1. Kartik 39.2-12-65-5. Udal 26-1-72-0. Malan 2-0-10-0.
Finn 12-5-29-2. Silverwood 5-1-15-0. Kartik 14-5-26-2. Udal 7-0-24-1. Malan 2-0-4-0.
Fall of Wickets: 1-62, 2-87, 3-188, 4-297, 5-326, 6-349, 7-349, 8-378, 9-391
1-0, 2-23, 3-34, 4-40, 5-55

Match drawn – Middlesex (10pts), Surrey (10pts)

No play on day four at Derby cruelly ruled out an intriguing finish to the match between Derbyshire and Leicestershire, for whom Tom New batted with great maturity and Iain O'Brien impressed with the ball. At Lord's, meanwhile, Mark Ramprakash continued his great record against former club Middlesex by ensuring Surrey escaped with a draw in the London derby.

Owais Shah batted brilliantly for Middlesex, hitting 23 fours in a first innings 159 and then adding 61 to help Nick Compton (100 not out) to set up a last day declaration, but the home side must have regretted not being a little bit more ambitious as Surrey folded to 55 for 5 with 19 overs still to be bowled. Ramprakash, however, following his first innings 136, remained immoveable as he reached 49 not out.

Mark Wallace, the Glamorgan wicketkeeper-batsman, has both feet off the ground as he pulls a ball to leg.

Round Nine: 7–10 July Division One

WARWICKSHIRE v. SUSSEX – at Edgbaston

WARWICKSHIRE First Innings / Second Innings

Batsman	First Innings		Second Innings	
IJ Westwood (capt)	c Rayner b Collymore	5	c Yardy b Collymore	4
T Frost	lbw b Yasir Arafat	0	c Rayner b Smith	17
IR Bell	c Hodd b Collymore	2	not out	55
IJL Trott	c Hodd b Wright	166	not out	9
JO Troughton	st Hodd b Rayner	18		
*TR Ambrose	c Rayner b Yasir Arafat	28		
R Clarke	c Joyce b Wright	36		
AG Botha	b Yasir Arafat	46		
NM Carter	c Hopkinson b Wright	17		
CR Woakes	not out	49		
N Tahir	c & b Rayner	22		
Extras	lb 5, w 1, nb 12	18	b 5, lb 1, nb 6	12
	(all out 115.1 overs)	407	(2 wkts 33.4 overs)	97

Bowling
Yasir Arafat 28-7-106-3. Collymore 20-6-54-2. Smith 9-1-45-0. Wright 26-2-94-3. Rayner 29.1-6-82-2. Nash 3-0-21-0.
Yasir Arafat 6-0-19-0. Collymore 6-1-9-1. Nash 8-0-34-0. Smith 9-1-15-1. Rayner 3-1-7-0. Hodd 1.4-0-7-0.
Fall of Wickets: 1-5, 2-7, 3-16, 4-71, 5-140, 6-212, 7-308, 8-329, 9-342 1-11, 2-70

SUSSEX First Innings

Batsman	First Innings	
MH Yardy (capt)	c Ambrose b Hodd	57
CD Nash	c Botha b Tahir	31
EC Joyce	c Trott b Botha	29
MW Goodwin	c Woakes b Tahir	22
CD Hopkinson	c Botha b Trott	119
LJ Wright	c Frost b Tahir	71
*AJ Hodd	not out	59
DR Smith	c Clarke b Trott	0
Yasir Arafat	lbw b Carter	11
OP Rayner		
CD Collymore		
Extras	b 3, lb 12, w 1, nb 14	30
	(8 wkts dec 117.2 overs)	429

Bowling
Woakes 14-1-67-0. Carter 22.2-1-96-1. Tahir 28-7-83-4. Botha 29-5-84-1. Clarke 10-1-54-0. Trott 12-2-26-2. Westwood 2-0-4-0.
Fall of Wickets: 1-55, 2-99, 3-148, 4-151, 5-303, 6-390, 7-390, 8-429

Match drawn – Warwickshire (11pts), Sussex (12pts)

Round Nine: 7–10 July Division Two

ESSEX v. GLAMORGAN – at Chelmsford

GLAMORGAN First Innings

Batsman	First Innings	
GP Rees	c Foster b Masters	59
HH Gibbs	b ten Doeschate	53
BJ Wright	lbw b Napier	1
MJ Powell	c Maunders b Napier	102
AJ Shantry	b Middlebrook	38
JWM Dalrymple (capt)	c Maunders b Wright	50
*MA Wallace	c Amla b Napier	37
JAR Harris	not out	76
RDB Croft	c Maunders b Middlebrook	30
DS Harrison	c Amla b Middlebrook	13
GJP Kruger	not out	28
Extras	b 1, lb 7, nb 20	28
	(9 wkts dec 132 overs)	515

Bowling
Masters 34-7-79-1. Wright 26-2-119-1. Napier 27-5-112-3. ten Doeschate 24-0-110-1. Middlebrook 21-3-87-3.
Fall of Wickets: 1-115, 2-118, 3-138, 4-210, 5-299, 6-350, 7-365, 8-410, 9-452

ESSEX First Innings / Second Innings (following on)

Batsman	First Innings		Second Innings (following on)	
V Chopra	b Shantry	31	lbw b Harrison	8
JK Maunders	lbw b Harris	35	c Gibbs b Harrison	8
HM Amla	b Harris	4	lbw b Croft	181
MJ Walker	c Wallace b Shantry	4	c Wallace b Harris	15
ML Pettini (capt)	c Wallace b Shantry	10	c Dalrymple b Croft	21
*JS Foster	c Dalrymple b Shantry	0	b Dalrymple	64
RN ten Doeschate	c Wallace b Harris	26	not out	88
GR Napier	c Gibbs b Shantry	13	not out	10
JD Middlebrook	not out	15		
DD Masters	c Dalrymple b Kruger	33		
CJC Wright	c Rees b Croft	1		
Extras	b 12, lb 11, w 1, nb 4	28	b 4, lb 6, nb 6	16
	(all out 57.5 overs)	200	(6 wkts 127 overs)	411

Bowling
Harrison 12-2-39-0. Harris 15-3-37-3. Kruger 13-4-34-1. Shantry 15-0-62-5. Croft 2.5-0-5-1.
Harris 23-8-58-1. Harrison 19-2-64-2. Shantry 17-6-56-0. Croft 41-4-107-2. Kruger 14-2-64-0. Dalrymple 13-0-52-1.
Fall of Wickets: 1-53, 2-76, 3-83, 4-93, 5-93, 6-93, 7-118, 8-145, 9-199 1-16, 2-17, 3-56, 4-85, 5-227, 6-379

Match drawn – Essex (7pts), Glamorgan (12pts)

NORTHAMPTONSHIRE v. DERBYSHIRE – at Northampton

NORTHANTS First Innings / Second Innings

Batsman	First Innings		Second Innings	
SD Peters	c Rogers b Hayward	175	not out	64
BH Howgego	c Rogers b Hayward	0	lbw b Smith	36
RA White	lbw b Hayward	18	not out	1
AG Wakely	c Stubbings b Hayward	4		
*MH Wessels	lbw b Smith	27		
N Boje (capt)	c & b Needham	30		
AJ Hall	st Pipe b Needham	52		
DJ Willey	st Pipe b Needham	5		
JJ van der Wath	c Hayward b Hunter	82		
DS Lucas	not out	12		
DH Wigley				
Extras	b 1, lb 7, nb 20	28	w 1, nb 2	3
	(9 wkts dec 96.4 overs)	433	(1 wkt 41 overs)	104

Bowling
Hayward 22-2-99-4. Hunter 15.4-2-90-1. Clare 18-3-92-0. Smith 20-3-81-1. Needham 16-2-47-3. Hinds 2-1-4-0. Park 3-0-12-0.
Clare 6-2-15-0. Hunter 6-1-17-0. Smith 9-1-32-1. Needham 14-2-25-0. Redfern 6-0-15-0.
Fall of Wickets: 1-1, 2-38, 3-54, 4-89, 5-143, 6-250, 7-292, 8-369, 9-433 1-98

DERBYSHIRE First Innings

Batsman	First Innings	
CJL Rogers (capt)	lbw b Hall	49
SD Stubbings	lbw b van der Wath	42
GT Park	c Wessels b van der Wath	33
DJ Redfern	b Boje	95
WW Hinds	lbw b van der Wath	148
GM Smith	b Wigley	22
*DJ Pipe	c Howgego b Lucas	63
JL Clare	c Hall b Wigley	6
J Needham	not out	17
ID Hunter	b Lucas	7
M Hayward		
Extras	b 3, lb 5, w 6, nb 6	20
	(9 wkts dec 135.5 overs)	502

Bowling
van der Wath 26-3-97-3. Lucas 19.5-5-64-2. Wigley 25-7-96-2. Hall 20-8-52-1. Boje 32-8-111-1. Wakely 9-0-45-0. Willey 4-0-29-0.
Fall of Wickets: 1-82, 2-132, 3-133, 4-370, 5-400, 6-433, 7-451, 8-492, 9-502

Match drawn – Northamptonshire (11pts), Derbyshire (12pts)

Round Nine: 7–10 July

Both second division and the single Division One game in this round ended in draws, with rain interruptions especially hitting Warwickshire's match against Sussex at Edgbaston. But the bat was well on top there anyway, with Jonathan Trott's 247-ball 166 the pick.

There was some heavy scoring in the second tier too, with Hashim Amla taking the main honours for leading Essex to safety against Glamorgan at Chelmsford. The home team had been forced to follow on with Adam Shantry taking 5 for 62 as they were tumbled out for just 200 in reply to a big Welsh total centred upon Mike Powell's 102 and a promising 84-ball 76 not out from young James Harris.

Amla, the South African Test batsman acting as a short-term replacement for Danish Kaneria, batted just short of seven hours for his 181, while both James Foster (64) and Ryan ten Doeschate, with an unbeaten 88 also frustrated the Glamorgan bowlers.

Stephen Peters had a prolific match at Wantage Road, scoring 175 in ten hours in the first innings and then an unbeaten 64 as Northamptonshire's fixture with Derbyshire drifted to a draw. Wavell Hinds also impressed with 148, as did the 19-year-old Dan Redfern with 95, while Johan van der Wath offered the most violent batting of the match with six sixes and seven fours in his 82 from 71 balls.

Round Ten: 10–15 July

There was a three-day finish at Old Trafford, where Lancashire beat Worcestershire by seven wickets but only after Mike Denness, the former England captain and ECB pitch officer, had been required to inspect the surface after 18 wickets fell on the opening day.

Denness was happy with the pitch, despite Lancashire disintegrating to 119 for 8 by stumps in reply to Worcestershire's 172 as seam and swing ruled day one. And Denness's verdict was upheld as Stephen Moore hit a second innings 107 to seemingly give Worcestershire the chance of a first win of the season after Matt Mason's 7 for 39 had confirmed Lancashire's first innings decline to 145.

The pitch, though, was now becoming easier and easier to bat on and VVS Laxman's unbeaten 64, following an excellent 77 by Paul Horton, enabled Lancashire to emerge with the win instead.

Hampshire followed on at Taunton, despite Michael Carberry's 123 and after James Hildreth with 155 in 446 minutes and 5 for 91 from a fiery David Stiff had put Somerset in charge. Carberry, however, then led some superb second innings resistance in which John Crawley, Liam Dawson, Sean Ervine and Nic Pothas also distinguished themselves, and Hampshire came away with a well-earned draw.

Round Ten: 10–15 July Division One

LANCASHIRE v. WORCESTERSHIRE – at Old Trafford

WORCS	First Innings		Second Innings	
DKH Mitchell	c Laxman b Mahmood	0	c Sutton b Mahmood	12
SC Moore	b Newby	23	b Hogg	107
VS Solanki (capt)	c Sutton b Chapple	35	lbw b Hogg	9
BF Smith	lbw b Hogg	16	c Croft b Keedy	28
MM Ali	lbw b Hogg	8	c Laxman b Keedy	3
*SM Davies	c Sutton b Mahmood	39	run out	25
AA Noffke	lbw b Chapple	5	c Laxman b Mahmood	16
GJ Batty	c Sutton b Hogg	1	c Sutton b Hogg	4
GM Andrew	run out	9	not out	19
CD Whelan	not out	13	c Horton b Keedy	3
MS Mason	c & b Mahmood	15	b Keedy	2
Extras	lb 7, w 1	8	lb 3, w 1, nb 4	8
	(all out 57.3 overs)	172	(all out 72.1 overs)	236

Bowling
Chapple 16-4-36-2. Mahmood 15.3-3-51-3. Newby 13-1-47-1. Hogg 12-6-26-3. Keedy 1-0-5-0.
Chapple 9-2-29-0. Mahmood 16-3-42-2. Hogg 19-6-53-3. Newby 11-0-49-0. Keedy 17.1-2-60-4.
Fall of Wickets: 1-9, 2-35, 3-71, 4-81, 5-86, 6-101, 7-104, 8-136, 9-148 1-33, 2-54, 3-133, 4-143, 5-188, 6-192, 7-196, 8-219, 9-230

LANCASHIRE	First Innings		Second Innings	
PJ Horton	c Solanki b Noffke	4	(2) c Mitchell b Batty	77
MB Loye	lbw b Mason	24	(1) lbw b Mason	17
MJ Chilton	c Solanki b Noffke	13	c Smith b Batty	45
VVS Laxman	lbw b Mason	19	not out	64
SJ Croft	c Smith b Mason	9	not out	40
KW Hogg	lbw b Mason	12		
*LD Sutton	c Batty b Mason	0		
G Chapple (capt)	c Whelan b Mason	44		
SI Mahmood	b Noffke	3		
OJ Newby	c Davies b Mason	14		
G Keedy	not out	1		
Extras	lb 6, w 5, nb 2	13	b 8, lb 7, nb 6	21
	(all out 44 overs)	145	(3 wkts 88.1 overs)	264

Bowling
Noffke 16-3-48-3. Mason 17-11-39-7. Whelan 6-1-31-0. Andrew 5-0-21-0.
Noffke 16-4-46-0. Mason 32-13-77-1. Batty 21-1-71-2. Andrew 11-0-26-0. Whelan 4.1-1-17-0. Ali 4-1-12-0.
Fall of Wickets: 1-18, 2-38, 3-54, 4-71, 5-72, 6-72, 7-77, 8-82, 9-124 1-42, 2-151, 3-173

Lancashire won by 7 wickets –
Lancashire (17pts), Worcestershire (3pts)

SOMERSET v. HAMPSHIRE – at Taunton

SOMERSET	First Innings		
ME Trescothick	c Crawley b Mascarenhas	22	
AV Suppiah	c Crawley b Tremlett	52	
JL Langer (capt)	lbw b Tomlinson	30	
JC Hildreth	c Mascarenhas b Tomlinson	155	
Z de Bruyn	c Crawley b Tomlinson	24	
*C Kieswetter	c Crawley b Imran Tahir	43	
PD Trego	c sub b Tremlett	50	
AC Thomas	c Tomlinson b Ervine	70	
DA Stiff	st sub b Dawson	25	
AR Caddick	b Ervine	3	
CM Willoughby	not out	0	
Extras	b 4, lb 2, nb 30	36	
	(all out 127.4 overs)	510	

Bowling
Mascarenhas 33-9-87-1. Tremlett 25-11-111-2. Tomlinson 27-1-119-3. Imran Tahir 30-0-141-1. Ervine 7.4-1-39-2. Dawson 5-1-7-1.
Fall of Wickets: 1-38, 2-81, 3-147, 4-182, 5-282, 6-358, 7-445, 8-498, 9-505

HAMPSHIRE	First Innings		Second Innings (following on)	
MA Carberry	c Willoughby b Stiff	123	c & b Suppiah	52
JHK Adams	c Trescothick b Willoughby	33	lbw b Caddick	29
MJ Lumb	c Suppiah b Thomas	11	lbw b Suppiah	3
JP Crawley	c Trescothick b Stiff	2	not out	81
LA Dawson	c de Bruyn b Stiff	0	lbw b Trego	69
SM Ervine	c Hildreth b Suppiah	10	lbw b Suppiah	58
AD Mascarenhas (capt)	c Trescothick b Stiff	0		
*N Pothas	c Hildreth b Stiff	15	(7) not out	49
CT Tremlett	c Trescothick b Suppiah	7		
JA Tomlinson	not out	14		
Imran Tahir	c Kieswetter b Thomas	33		
Extras	lb 4, w 2, nb 10	16	lb 1, nb 15	16
	(all out 61.3 overs)	264	(5 wkts 121 overs)	357

Bowling
Willoughby 14-5-48-1. Caddick 11-1-60-0. Stiff 15-1-91-5. Trego 1-0-12-0. Thomas 10.3-4-22-2. Suppiah 10-5-27-2.
Willoughby 25-6-86-0. Thomas 22-8-59-0. Suppiah 24-7-58-3. Caddick 22-6-68-1. Stiff 13-3-46-0. Trego 11-2-33-1. de Bruyn 4-1-6-0.
Fall of Wickets: 1-89, 2-126, 3-157, 4-157, 5-185, 6-186, 7-204, 8-208, 9-216 1-51, 2-68, 3-87, 4-185, 5-273

Match drawn – Somerset (12pts),
Hampshire (8pts)

YORKSHIRE v. DURHAM – at Headingley

DURHAM	First Innings		Second Innings	
MJ Di Venuto	b Rashid	29	(2) b Bresnan	84
MD Stoneman	run out	22	(1) b Rashid	12
KJ Coetzer	c Bairstow b Shahzad	0	(4) b Hoggard	38
GJ Muchall	b Rashid	8	(5) lbw b Rashid	15
DM B'enstein (capt)	c Bairstow b Hoggard	62	(6) lbw b Rashid	36
ID Blackwell	b Rashid	12	(7) c Bairstow b Shahzad	32
*P Mustard	c Rudolph b Naved-ul-Hasan	7	(8) c & b Bresnan	85
LE Plunkett	lbw b Shahzad	5	(9) c Hoggard b Naved-ul-Hasan	65
ME Claydon	c Bairstow b Hoggard	20	(10) not out	1
SJ Harmison	lbw b Rashid	0		
M Davies	not out	0	(3) c Bairstow b Hoggard	6
Extras	b 5, lb 4, nb 14	23	b 20, lb 14, w 1, nb 12	47
	(all out 70.2 overs)	178	(9 wkts dec 147.4 overs)	421

Bowling
Hoggard 17.2-6-36-2. Bresnan 13-3-24-0. Shahzad 12-3-39-3.
Bresnan 29-1-69-2. Hoggard 29-9-67-3. Rashid 43-7-124-2. Shahzad 18-3-55-1. Naved-ul-Hasan 25.4-9-64-1. Rudolph 3-0-8-0.
Fall of Wickets: 1-47, 2-53, 3-55, 4-62, 5-82, 6-101, 7-128, 8-171, 9-176 1-20, 2-39, 3-148, 4-158, 5-178, 6-231, 7-268, 8-415, 9-421

YORKSHIRE	First Innings		Second Innings	
JA Rudolph	c Mustard b Claydon	5	c Plunkett b Blackwell	39
JJ Sayers	c Stoneman b Harmison	37	c Stoneman b Plunkett	14
A McGrath (capt)	c Coetzer b Harmison	19	lbw b Plunkett	0
A Lyth	c Mustard b Harmison	4	c Muchall b Blackwell	5
AW Gale	b Blackwell	84	not out	24
*JM Bairstow	c Plunkett b Davies	8	not out	9
TT Bresnan	c Coetzer b Harmison	14		
AU Rashid	lbw b Blackwell	32		
Naved-ul-Hasan	c Stoneman b Harmison	22		
A Shahzad	not out	41		
MJ Hoggard	c Di Venuto b Blackwell	0		
Extras	b 1, lb 9, w 1, nb 14	25	b 8, lb 2	10
	(all out 104 overs)	313	(4 wkts 50.3 overs)	98

Bowling
Harmison 25-6-60-5. Claydon 21-4-76-1. Plunkett 19-4-68-0. Davies 13-6-33-1. Blackwell 16-4-66-3.
Harmison 11-3-22-0. Claydon 3-0-17-0. Blackwell 21-10-23-2. Plunkett 11-4-22-2. Davies 3.3-2-4-0. Benkenstein 1-1-0-0.
Fall of Wickets: 1-9, 2-71, 3-74, 4-77, 5-93, 6-147, 7-198, 8-229, 9-313 1-47, 2-51, 3-63, 4-68

Match drawn – Yorkshire (10pts), Durham (7pts)

There was a similar story at Headingley where Durham faced a first innings deficit of 135, despite Steve Harmison's 5 for 60, before countering with a second innings 421 for 9 declared, in which Phil Mustard and Liam Plunkett added an eighth wicket 147. Set 287 in what proved to be 51 overs, Yorkshire had to be content with securing the draw.

Leicestershire's first victory of the season hauled them off the bottom of Division Two and pushed a dispirited Middlesex, whom they beat by eight wickets, into last place. The win at Grace Road owed much to the seam and swing bowling of AJ Harris and Iain O'Brien, the New Zealander who took 6 for 39 in Middlesex's first innings, and to the batting of Josh Cobb (95) and Tom New, after the home side had slipped to 53 for 5.

Derbyshire had to work hard for their 185-run win at Cheltenham over Gloucestershire, who looked to be losing momentum after their fine start to the season. A career-best 126 from Greg Smith, initial runs at the top of the order by Chris Rogers and a brilliant second innings 170 not out from Wayne Madsen tamed the Gloucestershire bowling, and on-loan Steffan Jones undermined the home side's first innings with 4 for 44.

Leicestershire fast bowler Andrew Harris, who turned 36 in midsummer, proved a shrewd signing from Nottinghamshire and was re-engaged for 2010.

Round Ten: 10–15 July Division Two

LEICESTERSHIRE v. MIDDLESEX – at Grace Road

MIDDLESEX	First Innings		Second Innings	
BA Godleman	lbw b Allenby	12	lbw b Harris	14
NRD Compton	lbw b O'Brien	4	b O'Brien	0
OA Shah	b O'Brien	12	c New b Gurney	18
EJG Morgan	c Allenby b O'Brien	30	c Boyce b Harris	1
DJ Malan	not out	67	lbw b Allenby	13
*DC Nash	c Allenby b Harris	9	c Dippenaar b Harris	14
GK Berg	lbw b O'Brien	0	c New b O'Brien	10
SD Udal (capt)	b O'Brien	0	c New b Harris	5
M Kartik	b Gurney	11	not out	2
TJ Murtagh	c & b Gurney	1	c Dippenaar b Harris	4
ST Finn	lbw b O'Brien	5	lbw b O'Brien	1
Extras	lb 8	8	b 4, lb 3, w 2	9
	(all out 52.3 overs)	159	(all out 40.2 overs)	91

Bowling
O'Brien 15.3-6-39-6. Harris 15-5-49-1. Allenby 10-4-17-1. Gurney 11-0-46-2. Walker 1-1-0-0.
O'Brien 15.2-5-29-3. Harris 13-6-24-4. Gurney 9-2-30-1. Allenby 3-2-1-2.
Fall of Wickets: 1-15, 2-27, 3-37, 4-75, 5-84, 6-101, 7-101, 8-131, 9-141
1-5, 2-24, 3-32, 4-50, 5-64, 6-76, 7-84, 8-84, 9-90

LEICESTERSHIRE	First Innings		Second Innings	
JJ Cobb	c Godleman b Murtagh	95	c Nash b Finn	2
MAG Boyce	lbw b Finn	0	b Murtagh	4
HH Dippenaar (capt)	b Finn	4	not out	4
HD Ackerman	c Berg b Finn	8	not out	0
J Allenby	b Murtagh	2		
JWA Taylor	c Nash b Finn	5		
*TJ New	c Berg b Udal	42		
GW Walker	c Morgan b Murtagh	5		
IE O'Brien	lbw b Murtagh	20		
AJ Harris	b Berg	13		
HF Gurney	not out	24		
Extras	b 14, lb 10, nb 2	26		0
	(all out 70.2 overs)	244	(2 wkts 4.1 overs)	10

Bowling
Finn 24-5-76-4. Murtagh 17-1-70-4. Kartik 12-2-29-0. Berg 7.2-1-25-1. Udal 10-4-20-1.
Finn 2.1-1-6-1. Murtagh 2-1-4-1.
Fall of Wickets: 1-1, 2-11, 3-21, 4-89, 5-53, 6-126, 7-138, 8-188, 9-195 1-2, 2-6

*Leicestershire won by 8 wickets –
Leicestershire (18pts), Middlesex (3pts)*

GLOUCESTERSHIRE v. DERBYSHIRE – at Cheltenham

DERBYSHIRE	First Innings		Second Innings	
CJL Rogers (capt)	b Lewis	81	c Snell b Franklin	3
WL Madsen	c Snell b Lewis	7	not out	170
GT Park	c Snell b Lewis	25	c Snell b Lewis	9
DJ Redfern	c Marshall b Kirby	4	lbw b Marshall	31
WW Hinds	c Marshall b Kirby	0	(6) b Kirby	54
GM Smith	c Snell b Franklin	126	(7) c Lewis b Ireland	34
*DJ Pipe	b Banerjee	22	(8) not out	0
GG Wagg	c Snell b Ireland	31		
TD Groenewald	c Marshall b Franklin	26		
J Needham	not out	1	(5) c Spearman b Kirby	5
PS Jones	c Marshall b Franklin	0		
Extras	lb 3	3	b 8, lb 7, w 2	17
	(all out 88.4 overs)	326	(6 wkts dec 89 overs)	323

Bowling
Franklin 18.4-3-59-3. Kirby 14-3-50-2. Lewis 17-4-40-3. Ireland 14-2-79-1.
Banerjee 19-0-84-1. Taylor 6-1-11-0.
Lewis 11-3-24-1. Franklin 14-4-28-1. Kirby 19-5-58-2. Ireland 16-3-51-1.
Banerjee 18-3-95-0. Taylor 2-0-9-0. Marshall 2-0-11-1. Gidman 7-2-32-0.
Fall of Wickets: 1-34, 2-112, 3-117, 4-117, 5-119, 6-183, 7-231, 8-321, 9-326 1-3, 2-28, 3-117, 4-126, 5-243, 6-321

GLOS	First Innings		Second Innings	
Kadeer Ali	b Wagg	25	(2) b Jones	44
CM Spearman	c Pipe b Jones	7	(1) c Pipe b Jones	27
HJH Marshall	run out	7	b Groenewald	0
APR Gidman (capt)	lbw b Jones	55	b Groenewald	60
CG Taylor	c Pipe b Groenewald	6	c Pipe b Groenewald	9
JEC Franklin	b Smith	14	b Needham	109
*SD Snell	b Jones	2	c Rogers b Needham	13
J Lewis	c Needham b Jones	6	c Rogers b Needham	0
SP Kirby	c Hinds b Smith	9	c Rogers b Wagg	16
V Banerjee	not out	16	c Needham b Wagg	8
AJ Ireland	b Groenewald	0	not out	2
Extras	lb 5, w 1, nb 6	12	lb 9, w 1, nb 2	12
	(all out 56.2 overs)	164	(all out 95.4 overs)	300

Bowling
Jones 18.2-6-44-4. Wagg 15.4-3-49-1. Groenewald 13.2-1-48-2. Smith 7-3-12-2.
Needham 2-0-6-0.
Jones 27-7-64-2. Wagg 33-4-96-2. Groenewald 20-4-64-3. Needham 14.4-3-51-3.
Smith 1-0-16-0.
Fall of Wickets: 1-21, 2-34, 3-74, 4-89, 5-121, 6-121, 7-127, 8-138, 9-138 1-71, 2-76, 3-76, 4-91, 5-185, 6-213, 7-213, 8-261, 9-276

*Derbyshire won by 185 runs –
Gloucestershire (3pts), Derbyshire (20pts)*

SURREY v. KENT – at The Oval

SURREY	First Innings		Second Innings	
*JN Batty	c Kemp b Tredwell	44	b McLaren	48
MJ Brown	run out	55	c Key b Tredwell	25
MR Ramprakash	c van Jaarsveld b Kemp	86	c Key b Tredwell	5
MA Butcher (capt)	c Key b McLaren	9	not out	60
U Afzaal	c van Jaarsveld b Khan	46	not out	24
SJ Walters	b Parnell	12		
CJ Jordan	c Jones b Tredwell	28		
CP Schofield	c McLaren b Khan	54		
AJ Tudor	c Kemp b Tredwell	0		
Murtaza Hussain	c Jones b Khan	24		
PT Collins	not out	1		
Extras	b 5, lb 12, nb 10	27	b 1, lb 3, nb 4	8
	(all out 115 overs)	386	(3 wkts 62 overs)	170

Bowling
Parnell 16-3-59-1. Khan 18-5-56-3. Stevens 2-1-1-0. McLaren 24-3-87-1.
Cook 21-5-66-0. Tredwell 25-4-76-3. van Jaarsveld 6-2-10-0. Kemp 3-1-14-1.
Khan 7-3-14-0. McLaren 6-1-26-1. Tredwell 23-7-42-2. Cook 7-1-12-0. van Jaarsveld 12-3-52-0. Denly 3-0-7-0. Key 4-1-13-0.
Fall of Wickets: 1-105, 2-114, 3-137, 4-255, 5-271, 6-275, 7-329, 8-329, 9-385 1-40, 2-48, 3-104

KENT	First Innings	
JL Denly	run out	123
RWT Key (capt)	run out	123
*GO Jones	c Batty b Collins	0
M van Jaarsveld	lbw b Tudor	110
DI Stevens	c Batty b Collins	0
JM Kemp	c Walters b Hussain	183
JC Tredwell	c Walters b Hussain	60
R McLaren	not out	4
WD Parnell		
A Khan		
SJ Cook		
Extras	b 10, lb 4, w 1, nb 2	17
	(7 wkts dec 154.2 overs)	620

Bowling
Jordan 22-2-93-0. Collins 32-7-107-2. Walters 2-1-5-0. Tudor 27-5-110-1.
Hussain 54.2-4-208-2. Schofield 4-0-18-0. Afzaal 13-0-65-0.
Fall of Wickets: 1-247, 2-252, 3-265, 4-269, 5-483, 6-606, 7-620

*Match drawn – Surrey (9pts),
Kent (12pts)*

Alex Gidman, the Gloucestershire captain, did his best to resist in both innings, while James Franklin hit a second innings 109, but the Derbyshire bowlers chipped away with Tim Groenewald and off spinner Jake Needham picking up three wickets apiece.

Kent's first innings scorecard at The Oval, meanwhile, had a bizarre look with four of their top six scoring hundreds – for the first time in the county's history – but the other two batsmen, Geraint Jones and Darren Stevens, recording ducks! But despite the run-making exploits of Joe Denly, Rob Key, Martin van Jaarsveld and Justin Kemp, who top-scored with 183, the match against Surrey was long destined for a dull draw.

Round Eleven: 15–18 July

The destination of the 2009 County Championship looked clear after table toppers Durham crushed Nottinghamshire, one of their closest challengers, by an innings and 102 runs at a stunned Trent Bridge.

Nottinghamshire started the game well enough, but after losing three wickets to the new ball, Durham pulled away to reach 356 as Will Smith, the young captain, was joined by his predecessor Dale Benkenstein in a fourth wicket partnership worth 193. Smith was finally dismissed for 87 but Benkenstein went on to reach 105.

Soon Notts were 54 for 5 in reply and although they did recover slightly to total 171 they lost three cheap

wickets to Ian Blackwell and Liam Plunkett finished with 4 for 56. It was Steve Harmison, though who delivered the blows that really floored Notts and left them so dispirited. Following on, they were hustled out for a mere 83 with a rampant Harmison taking 6 for 20. Put simply, Notts could not handle his pace.

Elsewhere in Division One there were draws at Arundel and Edgbaston, in part due to frequent weather interruptions. But batsmen were also on top in the play that was possible, with hundreds for Luke Wright of Sussex, Michael Carberry of Hampshire and an important one for Warwickshire's Ian Bell, with an England recall on the cards.

Rob Key's career-best 270 not out spearheaded the innings and 45-run win over Glamorgan at Cardiff that took Kent to the top of the second division table. Key batted in all for 339 balls, hitting four sixes and 24 fours.

Glamorgan reached 317 in their first innings, with Gareth Rees scoring 80, before it all began to go wrong. Key, on 23 not out at the end of day two, was still there unbeaten on 202 twenty-four hours later – and, on the final morning, he led another blitz on the bowling, in the company of Justin Kemp, before declaring at 557 for 5. Rees then fell to the first ball of the Glamorgan second innings and James Tredwell, with four wickets, spun his way through the middle-order after Wayne Parnell and Amjad Khan had reduced the Welsh county to 21 for 3 with the new ball.

Round Eleven: 15–18 July Division One

NOTTINGHAMSHIRE v. DURHAM – at Trent Bridge

DURHAM First Innings

MJ Di Venuto	lbw b Sidebottom	22
MD Stoneman	c & b Adams	24
WR Smith (capt)	c Read b Ealham	87
GJ Muchall	c Read b Adams	10
DM Benkenstein	b Ealham	105
†ME Claydon	c Hussey b Adams	3
ID Blackwell	c Adams b Sidebottom	38
*P Mustard	c Read b Sidebottom	40
LE Plunkett	c Wagh b Ealham	9
CD Thorp	lbw b Sidebottom	5
M Davies	not out	1
SJ Harmison		
Extras	b 1, lb 9, nb 2	12
	(all out 122.5 overs)	356

Bowling
Sidebottom 27.5-5-65-4. Shreck 31-6-112-0. Ealham 22-5-40-3. Adams 26-4-80-3. Patel 15-3-39-0. Hussey 1-0-10-0.
Fall of Wickets: 1-44, 2-51, 3-63, 4-256, 5-257, 6-269, 7-316, 8-349, 9-351
† Replaced by SJ Harmison

NOTTS First Innings / Second Innings (following on)

	First Innings		Second Innings (following on)	
MJ Wood	c Stoneman b Harmison	12	c Mustard b Davies	9
BM Shafayat	lbw b Thorp	16	c Mustard b Harmison	12
MA Wagh	c Di Venuto b Thorp	1	c Benkenstein b Davies	4
SR Patel	c Thorp b Plunkett	7	c Smith b Harmison	14
DJ Hussey	c Mustard b Plunkett	9	lbw b Thorp	5
AD Brown	b Blackwell	36	c Davies b Harmison	5
*CMW Read (capt)	lbw b Blackwell	48	c Mustard b Harmison	4
MA Ealham	c Blackwell b Plunkett	24	not out	17
AR Adams	c Benkenstein b Blackwell	6	c Plunkett b Harmison	2
RJ Sidebottom	c Mustard b Plunkett	3	c Stoneman b Harmison	0
CE Shreck	not out	1	c Thorp b Blackwell	6
Extras	lb 3, w 3, nb 2	8	lb 1	1
	(all out 62.2 overs)	171	(all out 32.4 overs)	83

Bowling
Claydon 2-0-0-0. Davies 12-5-31-0. Harmison 16-7-45-1. Thorp 11-4-30-2. Plunkett 13.2-1-56-4. Blackwell 8-3-6-3.
Harmison 13-5-20-6. Davies 7-2-13-2. Thorp 9-2-33-1. Blackwell 3.4-0-16-1.
Fall of Wickets: 1-14, 2-17, 3-33, 4-47, 5-54, 6-135, 7-158, 8-166, 9-168
1-9, 2-19, 3-38, 4-51, 5-55, 6-60, 7-66, 8-68, 9-76

Durham won by an innings and 102 runs –
Nottinghamshire (2pts), Durham (20pts)

SUSSEX v. HAMPSHIRE – at Arundel Castle

SUSSEX First Innings / Second Innings

	First Innings		Second Innings	
MH Yardy (capt)	lbw b Tomlinson	5	not out	47
CD Nash	c Carberry b Imran Tahir	57	c Cork b Tomlinson	37
EC Joyce	lbw b Tomlinson	2	c Burrows b Imran Tahir	43
MW Goodwin	c Dawson b Mascarenhas	65	not out	3
CD Hopkinson	c Burrows b Imran Tahir	49		
LJ Wright	c Carberry b Imran Tahir	104		
*AJ Hodd	c Burrows b Imran Tahir	11		
Yasir Arafat	lbw b Tomlinson	37		
OP Rayner	c Imran Tahir b Mascarenhas	60		
CD Collymore	lbw b Imran Tahir	0		
JD Lewry	not out	9		
Extras	b 4, lb 2, w 2, nb 34	42	b 4, lb 4	8
	(all out 117.2 overs)	441	(2 wkts 32.1 overs)	138

Bowling
Tomlinson 27-6-108-3. Cork 21-6-54-0. Ervine 12-1-68-0. Mascarenhas 20-6-57-2.
Imran Tahir 36.2-4-140-5. Dawson 1-0-8-0.
Tomlinson 6-0-27-1. Cork 3-0-15-0. Imran Tahir 6-0-29-1. Ervine 7-2-22-0.
Dawson 9-0-41-0. Carberry 1-0-14-0. Mascarenhas 0.1-0-0-0.
Fall of Wickets: 1-20, 2-26, 3-96, 4-187, 5-205, 6-253, 7-312, 8-397, 9-404
1-49, 2-135

HAMPSHIRE First Innings

MA Carberry	c Joyce b Rayner	112
JHK Adams	c & b Rayner	33
MJ Lumb	c Yardy b Collymore	46
JP Crawley	lbw b Collymore	26
LA Dawson	c Rayner b Lewry	5
SM Ervine	b Collymore	17
AD Mascarenhas (capt)	lbw b Collymore	22
*TG Burrows	lbw b Wright	2
DG Cork	c Nash b Yasir Arafat	36
Imran Tahir	not out	25
JA Tomlinson	c Goodwin b Rayner	0
Extras	b 2, lb 7, w 1, nb 12	22
	(all out 119.1 overs)	346

Bowling
Yasir Arafat 22-2-89-1. Lewry 14-0-60-1. Collymore 29-10-66-4. Rayner 31.1-9-61-3.
Wright 17-3-41-1. Yardy 5-0-19-0. Nash 3-2-1-0.
Fall of Wickets: 1-107, 2-183, 3-228, 4-237, 5-239, 6-278, 7-279, 8-297, 9-325

Match drawn – Sussex (12pts),
Hampshire (10pts)

WARWICKSHIRE v. LANCASHIRE – at Edgbaston

WARWICKSHIRE First Innings

IJ Westwood (capt)	c Smith b Hogg	60
T Frost	lbw b Hogg	5
IR Bell	c Sutton b Newby	106
IJL Trott	b Mahmood	79
JO Troughton	b Loye b Keedy	2
*TR Ambrose	c Chilton b Newby	28
R Clarke	c du Plessis b Newby	54
AG Botha	c Sutton b Hogg	37
CR Woakes	not out	0
N Tahir	not out	18
WB Rankin		
Extras	lb 3, w 2, nb 6	11
	(8 wkts dec 117.1 overs)	403

Bowling
Mahmood 26.1-4-100-1. Hogg 27-4-80-3. Smith 10-1-45-0. Newby 17-4-62-3.
Keedy 36-6-104-1. du Plessis 1-0-5-0.
Fall of Wickets: 1-2, 2-132, 3-210, 4-227, 5-274, 6-281, 7-317, 8-365

LANCASHIRE First Innings

PJ Horton	c Troughton b Woakes	43
TC Smith	lbw b Tahir	5
MB Loye	c Ambrose b Rankin	29
VVS Laxman	c Trott b Tahir	9
MJ Chilton	c Westwood b Botha	85
F du Plessis	c Tahir b Botha	79
*LD Sutton (capt)	c Trott b Botha	26
KW Hogg	c Clarke b Botha	1
SI Mahmood	b Tahir	7
OJ Newby	b Tahir	6
G Keedy	not out	1
Extras	lb 19, w 5, nb 2	26
	(all out 81 overs)	317

Bowling
Tahir 17-5-55-4. Rankin 13-4-33-1. Clarke 10-1-36-0. Woakes 15-3-51-1.
Botha 17-2-86-4. Trott 9-1-37-0.
Fall of Wickets: 1-16, 2-81, 3-93, 4-101, 5-244, 6-298, 7-299, 8-302, 9-310

Match drawn – Warwickshire (12pts),
Lancashire (9pts)

Round Eleven:
15–18 July Division Two

GLAMORGAN v. KENT – at Cardiff

GLAMORGAN	First Innings		Second Innings	
GP Rees	c van Jaarsveld b McLaren	80	c Kemp b Parnell	0
HH Gibbs	lbw b Cook	36	lbw b Khan	4
BJ Wright	c Kemp b Cook	0	c Tredwell b Parnell	10
MJ Powell	c Kemp b Parnell	30	c Key b Tredwell	60
JWM Dalrymple (capt)	lbw b McLaren	35	c van Jaarsveld b Khan	24
*MA Wallace	c Kemp b Khan	23	c Key b Tredwell	4
JAR Harris	lbw b McLaren	4	c Stevens b Tredwell	28
RDB Croft	c Jones b Cook	36	lbw b McLaren	28
DA Cosker	lbw b McLaren	25	lbw b McLaren	0
AJ Shantry	c Jones b Parnell	17	c Key b Tredwell	6
GJP Kruger	not out	4	not out	4
Extras	b 1, lb 12, nb 14	27	b 1, lb 12, w 4, nb 10	27
	(all out 99.3 overs)	317	(all out 61.5 overs)	195

Bowling
Parnell 20-6-61-2. Khan 15-1-62-1. McLaren 18.3-6-51-4. Cook 15-5-35-3. Stevens 3-1-14-0. Tredwell 27-8-71-0. Kemp 1-0-10-0.
Parnell 12-3-44-2. Khan 11-3-33-2. Tredwell 20.5-7-48-4. Cook 10-5-10-0. McLaren 8-1-47-2.
Fall of Wickets: 1-51, 2-51, 3-123, 4-192, 5-201, 6-209, 7-257, 8-277, 9-303 1-0, 2-21, 3-21, 4-103, 5-116, 6-135, 7-172, 8-172, 9-184

KENT	First Innings	
JL Denly	lbw b Harris	1
RWT Key (capt)	not out	270
*GO Jones	c Wallace b Kruger	68
M van Jaarsveld	c Wallace b Croft	96
DI Stevens	c Cosker b Harris	12
JM Kemp	c Rees b Harris	90
JC Tredwell		
R McLaren		
WD Parnell		
SJ Cook		
A Khan		
Extras	b 1, lb 7, w 10, nb 2	20
	(5 wkts dec 123.4 overs)	557

Bowling
Harris 29.4-5-118-3. Kruger 21-0-107-1. Shantry 18-2-74-0. Cosker 28-4-122-0. Croft 22-1-99-1. Wright 4-0-18-0. Dalrymple 1-0-11-0.
Fall of Wickets: 1-10, 2-125, 3-305, 4-342, 5-557

Kent won by an innings and 45 runs –
Glamorgan (4pts), Kent (22pts)

SURREY v. ESSEX – at Guildford

ESSEX	First Innings		Second Innings	
V Chopra	lbw b Dernbach	2	c & b Schofield	85
JK Maunders	c Batty b Jordan	31	lbw b Dernbach	0
HM Amla	c Batty b Jordan	26	not out	81
MJ Walker	c Batty b Linley	27	c Walters b Linley	21
ML Pettini (capt)	c Batty b Jordan	10	not out	9
*JS Foster	c Murtagh b Nel	48		
RN ten Doeschate	not out	159		
GR Napier	c Murtagh b Linley	43		
JD Middlebrook	c Ramprakash b Jordan	16		
DD Masters	c Batty b Linley	9		
AP Palladino	c Dernbach b Linley	5		
Extras	b 1, lb 7, w 9, nb 8	25	b 2, w 1, nb 2	5
	(all out 123.5 overs)	401	(3 wkts 54.1 overs)	201

Bowling
Nel 31-6-87-1. Dernbach 25-3-74-1. Linley 22.5-1-77-4. Jordan 26-3-84-4. Schofield 19-1-71-0.
Nel 7-2-22-0. Dernbach 8-1-25-1. Jordan 3-1-10-0. Schofield 19-0-78-1. Afzaal 13-1-54-0. Linley 4.1-1-10-1.
Fall of Wickets: 1-10, 2-61, 3-66, 4-88, 5-116, 6-214, 7-297, 8-358, 9-383 1-9, 2-150, 3-187

SURREY	First Innings	
*JN Batty	c Maunders b Napier	30
MJ Brown	c Walker b Palladino	17
MR Ramprakash	c Foster b Masters	0
SJ Walters (capt)	c Walker b Masters	142
U Afzaal	c Chopra b Masters	116
CP Murtagh	c Maunders b Masters	15
CJ Jordan	b Napier	8
CP Schofield	not out	7
A Nel	c Chopra b Middlebrook	0
JW Dernbach	not out	0
TE Linley		
Extras	b 8, lb 7, w 2	17
	(8 wkts dec 118.3 overs)	352

Bowling
Masters 39-16-86-4. Palladino 31-8-72-1. ten Doeschate 11-4-44-0. Napier 14.3-2-59-2. Middlebrook 23-1-76-1.
Fall of Wickets: 1-28, 2-29, 3-66, 4-288, 5-328, 6-335, 7-350, 8-351

Match drawn – Surrey (11pts), Essex (10pts)

Usman Afzaal (left) and Stewart Walters take to the field during their double-century partnership for Surrey against Essex at Guildford.

Rain delays, and a turgid pitch, combined to condemn Surrey's fixture with Essex at Guildford to a tedious draw. Surrey did have an early chance to inconvenience their visitors, when they slipped initially to 116 for 5, but Ryan ten Doeschate led such a successful counter-attack, with the support of both James Foster and Graham Napier, that he finished unbeaten on 159 and shepherded Essex to maximum batting points.

Even with Mark Ramprakash falling for a rare duck, Surrey replied strongly with the bat with Stewart Walters marking his first match as captain with 142 and being joined in a fourth wicket stand of 222 by Usman Afzaal, who made 116.

Round Twelve: 20–24 July

No play on day one effectively cost Somerset a golden opportunity to put some pressure back on Durham, the leaders, as they ran out of time after forcing bottom club Worcestershire to follow on at New Road. The resultant draw there was also matched by events at Scarborough, where Nottinghamshire had Yorkshire in trouble but, again, were denied by bad weather.

Round Twelve: 20–24 July Division One

WORCESTERSHIRE v. SOMERSET – at New Road

SOMERSET	First Innings	
ME Trescothick	c Davies b Mason	142
AV Suppiah	lbw b Mason	47
JL Langer (capt)	c Smith b Mason	107
PD Trego	c Batty b Mitchell	1
*C Kieswetter	not out	59
JC Hildreth	b Andrew	16
Z de Bruyn	c Batty b Mitchell	9
DA Stiff	not out	0
AC Thomas		
AR Caddick		
CM Willoughby		
Extras	b 8, lb 21, w 12, nb 6	47
	(6 wkts dec 87.3 overs)	**428**

Bowling
Mason 28-6-111-3. Whelan 10-0-67-0. Andrew 26-2-111-1. Jones 4.3-0-29-0.
Batty 12-1-56-0. Mitchell 7-0-25-2.
Fall of Wickets: 1-140, 2-309, 3-312, 4-363, 5-391, 6-425

WORCS	First Innings		Second Innings (following on)	
DKH Mitchell	b Caddick	20	c Kieswetter b Willoughby	4
SC Moore	lbw b Willoughby	7	c Kieswetter b Thomas	17
VS Solanki (capt)	c Hildreth b Stiff	12	b de Bruyn	93
BF Smith	c Suppiah b Trego	38	not out	80
MM Ali	c Langer b Willoughby	0	c & b Caddick	16
*SM Davies	c Langer b Suppiah	44	not out	7
GJ Batty	c Kieswetter b Thomas	4		
GM Andrew	not out	43		
RA Jones	lbw b Suppiah	0		
CD Whelan	c Kieswetter b Caddick	12		
MS Mason	c Kieswetter b Caddick	4		
Extras	b 1, lb 1, w 7, nb 32	41	lb 4, nb 4	8
	(all out 62.1 overs)	**225**	(4 wkts 56 overs)	**225**

Bowling
Willoughby 16-5-45-2. Thomas 11-3-34-1. Stiff 5-0-38-1. Caddick 14.1-3-53-3.
Trego 5-0-25-1. Suppiah 11-3-28-2.
Willoughby 14-6-40-1. Caddick 11-2-42-1. Thomas 6-0-31-1. Stiff 10-0-47-0.
Trego 4-1-29-0. de Bruyn 6-1-31-1. Suppiah 5-4-1-0.
Fall of Wickets: 1-7, 2-49, 3-60, 4-73, 5-109, 6-131, 7-180, 8-180, 9-217
1-4, 2-40, 3-176, 4-209

Match drawn – Worcestershire (7pts), Somerset (12pts)

YORKSHIRE v. NOTTINGHAMSHIRE – at Scarborough

NOTTS	First Innings	
MJ Wood	c Rashid b Bresnan	4
BM Shafayat	lbw b Hoggard	7
MA Wagh	c Brophy b Bresnan	6
DJ Hussey	c Sayers b Rashid	189
SR Patel	c Sayers b Bresnan	8
AD Brown	c Rashid b Bresnan	5
*CMW Read (capt)	b Hoggard	20
PJ Franks	b Rashid	48
LJ Fletcher	lbw b Kruis	0
AR Adams	c Brophy b Kruis	84
RJ Sidebottom	not out	10
Extras	lb 4, w 10	14
	(all out 96.1 overs)	**395**

Bowling
Hoggard 21-5-57-2. Bresnan 30-5-116-4. Kruis 19.1-3-79-2. Rashid 14-0-97-2.
Wainwright 12-3-42-0.
Fall of Wickets: 1-11, 2-15, 3-33, 4-43, 5-84, 6-125, 7-272, 8-273, 9-302

YORKSHIRE	First Innings		Second Innings (following on)	
JA Rudolph	lbw b Sidebottom	0	c Hussey b Sidebottom	12
JJ Sayers	c Read b Adams	17	c Adams b Sidebottom	36
A McGrath (capt)	b Adams	15	lbw b Adams	9
DJ Wainwright	c Hussey b Adams	29		
AW Gale	c Hussey b Adams	6	(4) c Sidebottom b Franks	99
JM Bairstow	not out	84	(5) c Adams b Sidebottom	4
*GL Brophy	c Patel b Sidebottom	5	(6) not out	51
TT Bresnan	c Brown b Sidebottom	7	(7) not out	16
AU Rashid	c Brown b Sidebottom	4		
MJ Hoggard	c Wagh b Franks	11		
GJ Kruis	c Adams b Sidebottom	37		
Extras	lb 4, nb 12	16	b 1, nb 4	5
	(all out 80.5 overs)	**231**	(5 wkts 75 overs)	**232**

Bowling
Sidebottom 21.5-7-59-5. Fletcher 19-8-44-0. Adams 20-9-39-4. Franks 11-1-50-1.
Patel 7-0-27-0. Hussey 2-0-8-0.
Sidebottom 18-4-66-3. Adams 21-7-58-1. Fletcher 9-3-20-0. Patel 13-1-46-0.
Franks 13-2-35-1. Brown 1-0-6-0.
Fall of Wickets: 1-0, 2-25, 3-61, 4-72, 5-73, 6-81, 7-97, 8-105, 9-149
1-14, 2-31, 3-117, 4-131, 5-182

Match drawn – Yorkshire (8pts), Nottinghamshire (11pts)

HAMPSHIRE v. WARWICKSHIRE – at the Rose Bowl

WARWICKSHIRE	First Innings		Second Innings	
IJ Westwood (capt)	c Tremlett b Tomlinson	13	not out	14
T Frost	c Burrows b Tomlinson	15	c Tremlett b Imran Tahir	3
IR Bell	c Burrows b Tomlinson	7	b Imran Tahir	0
IJL Trott	not out	184	not out	0
JO Troughton	c Burrows b Ervine	12		
*TR Ambrose	c Burrows b Mascarenhas	4		
R Clarke	lbw b Mascarenhas	46		
AG Botha	st Burrows b Dawson	40		
CR Woakes	not out	131		
N Tahir				
WB Rankin				
Extras	b 10, lb 7, w 1, nb 14	32	b 4, nb 2	6
	(7 wkts dec 129 overs)	**484**	(2 wkts 13.1 overs)	**23**

Bowling
Tremlett 30-5-101-0. Tomlinson 27-5-102-3. Ervine 20-2-97-1.
Mascarenhas 18-2-63-2. Imran Tahir 28-0-91-0. Dawson 6-2-13-1.
Imran Tahir 7-5-2-2. Dawson 6-3-7-0. Carberry 0.1-0-10-0.
Fall of Wickets: 1-30, 2-35, 3-52, 4-85, 5-90, 6-156, 7-262
1-13, 2-13

HAMPSHIRE	First Innings	
MA Carberry	c Clarke b Tahir	204
JHK Adams	c Trott b Westwood	90
MJ Lumb	c Trott b Rankin	20
JP Crawley	c Clarke b Rankin	14
LA Dawson	c Troughton b Rankin	18
SM Ervine	c Westwood b Frost	82
AD Mascarenhas (capt)	retired hurt	0
*TG Burrows	lbw b Woakes	0
CT Tremlett	b Botha	28
Imran Tahir	c Botha b Westwood	8
JA Tomlinson	not out	7
Extras	b 7, lb 11, w 2, nb 14	34
	(all out 135.1 overs)	**505**

Bowling
Rankin 27-1-117-3. Tahir 17-1-71-1. Woakes 17-1-67-1. Botha 35-4-111-1.
Clarke 15-1-59-0. Westwood 15-2-39-2. Trott 4-0-11-0. Frost 5.1-1-12-1.
Fall of Wickets: 1-261, 2-333, 3-351, 4-359, 5-376, 6-387, 7-461, 8-470, 9-505

Match drawn – Hampshire (11pts), Warwickshire (11pts)

Round Twelve: 20–24 July Division Two

GLOUCESTERSHIRE v. NORTHAMPTONSHIRE – at Cheltenham

GLOS	First Innings		Second Innings	
Kadeer Ali	c Boje b Lucas	0	(2) b Lucas	6
WTS Porterfield	b Lucas	0	(1) c Peters b Lucas	4
HJH Marshall	lbw b Lucas	6	lbw b Lucas	0
APR Gidman (capt)	lbw b Lucas	8	lbw b Lucas	7
CG Taylor	c Wessels b Lucas	51	lbw b Lucas	0
JEC Franklin	c Lucas b Hall	24	c Wakely b Wigley	26
*SD Snell	c Wessels b Hall	0	lbw b Hall	1
RKJ Dawson	c Wessels b van der Wath	21	b van der Wath	44
J Lewis	not out	13	not out	29
SP Kirby	b van der Wath	0	b Lucas	4
AJ Ireland	c Wakely b van der Wath	2	lbw b Lucas	0
Extras	b 4, lb 4, nb 14	22	b 2, lb 5, w 4, nb 10	21
	(all out 42.4 overs)	**147**	(all out 33.3 overs)	**142**

Bowling
van der Wath 14.4-4-47-3. Lucas 15-4-49-5. Hall 5-1-20-2. Wigley 5-1-16-0.
Boje 1-0-2-0. Panesar 2-0-5-0.
van der Wath 11-4-27-1. Lucas 10.3-1-24-7. Hall 6-0-45-1. Wigley 6-0-39-1.
Fall of Wickets: 1-2, 2-10, 3-17, 4-66, 5-68, 6-126, 7-132, 8-132, 9-139
1-13, 2-13, 3-22, 4-22, 5-31, 6-34, 7-88, 8-122, 9-138

NORTHANTS	First Innings		Second Innings	
SD Peters	c sub b Franklin	1	c Snell b Taylor	25
BH Howgego	lbw b Kirby	0	not out	28
RA White	lbw b Franklin	0	not out	5
AG Wakely	lbw b Lewis	30		
*MH Wessels	lbw b Lewis	23		
N Boje (capt)	not out	87		
AJ Hall	c Lewis b Kirby	41		
JJ van der Wath	lbw b Franklin	16		
MS Panesar	c Dawson b Kirby	0		
DS Lucas	lbw b Kirby	0		
DH Wigley	c Porterfield b Lewis	9		
Extras	b 4, lb 10, w 2, nb 9	25		0
	(all out 68.4 overs)	**232**	(1 wkt 17.2 overs)	**58**

Bowling
Kirby 21-3-75-4. Franklin 20-3-60-3. Lewis 9.4-1-39-3. Ireland 10-3-30-0.
Dawson 8-3-14-0.
Kirby 2-0-10-0. Franklin 1-0-1-0. Ireland 3-0-21-0. Dawson 7-0-20-0.
Taylor 4.2-1-6-1.
Fall of Wickets: 1-1, 2-1, 3-8, 4-39, 5-91, 6-162, 7-199, 8-208, 9-208
1-49

Northamptonshire won by 9 wickets – Gloucestershire (3pts), Northamptonshire (18pts)

DERBYSHIRE v. MIDDLESEX – at Derby

DERBYSHIRE	First Innings		Second Innings	
CJL Rogers (capt)	lbw b Murtagh	0	c Robson b Malan	76
WL Madsen	c Morgan b Finn	43	c Shah b Udal	71
GT Park	c Richardson b Finn	32	c Finn b Udal	16
DJ Redfern	lbw b Murtagh	13	c Malan b Udal	43
WW Hinds	lbw b Murtagh	7	not out	25
GM Smith	c Nash b Murtagh	6	(7) c Robson b Finn	4
*DJ Pipe	c Nash b Murtagh	7		
GG Wagg	c Nash b Murtagh	14	(6) c Malan b Finn	5
TD Groenewald	c Morgan b Murtagh	48	(8) c Nash b Finn	7
PS Jones	not out	54		
M Hayward	b Finn	6		
Extras	b 4, lb 5, nb 8	17	lb 3, w 2, nb 6	11
	(all out 75.4 overs)	**247**	(7 wkts dec 61.1 overs)	**258**

Bowling
Murtagh 22-5-82-7. Finn 18.4-0-59-3. Richardson 15-6-32-0. Berg 15-5-45-0.
Udal 5-1-20-0.
Murtagh 11-1-52-0. Finn 10.1-0-49-3. Richardson 12-0-53-0. Berg 4-0-19-0.
Udal 16-3-53-3. Malan 8-1-29-1.
Fall of Wickets: 1-6, 2-83, 3-92, 4-106, 5-109, 6-120, 7-139, 8-230, 9-230
1-97, 2-130, 3-199, 4-220, 5-231, 6-241, 7-258

MIDDLESEX	First Innings		Second Innings	
SD Robson	c Rogers b Wagg	1	run out	29
NRD Compton	b Hayward	6	not out	62
OA Shah	not out	129	not out	23
EJG Morgan	c sub b Wagg	7		
DJ Malan	lbw b Jones	11		
*DC Nash	c Redfern b Wagg	9		
GK Berg	b Wagg	12		
SD Udal (capt)	b Groenewald	0		
TJ Murtagh	c sub b Groenewald	5		
ST Finn	b Wagg	8		
A Richardson	not out	18		
Extras	b 7, w 1, nb 12	20	b 1, lb 3, w 3	7
	(9 wkts dec 68.4 overs)	**226**	(1 wkt 24 overs)	**121**

Bowling
Jones 12.4-3-30-1. Wagg 30-4-88-5. Hayward 11-3-43-1. Groenewald 13-2-41-2.
Smith 2-0-17-0.
Hayward 4-1-13-0. Wagg 12-0-56-0. Jones 3-1-12-0. Smith 3-0-19-0.
Groenewald 2-0-17-0.
Fall of Wickets: 1-1, 2-39, 3-62, 4-107, 5-141, 6-157, 7-158, 8-168, 9-195
1-86

Match drawn – Derbyshire (8pts), Middlesex (8pts)

LEICESTERSHIRE v. ESSEX – at Grace Road

ESSEX	First Innings	
V Chopra	lbw b O'Brien	5
JK Maunders	c New b Gurney	56
HM Amla	c New b Allenby	118
MJ Walker	not out	116
ML Pettini (capt)	b Walker	24
*JS Foster	c New b Allenby	85
RN ten Doeschate	c Dippenaar b Allenby	0
GR Napier		
DD Masters		
CJC Wright		
AP Palladino		
Extras	lb 19, w 2, nb 2	23
	(6 wkts dec 115.3 overs)	**427**

Bowling
O'Brien 24-6-82-1. Harris 25-6-75-0. Gurney 22-1-96-1. Allenby 20.3-6-70-3.
Walker 23-0-84-1. Cobb 1-0-1-0.
Fall of Wickets: 1-10, 2-143, 3-212, 4-269, 5-427, 6-427

LEICESTERSHIRE	First Innings		Second Innings (following on)	
JJ Cobb	c Walker b Palladino	14	lbw b Masters	6
MAG Boyce	lbw b Palladino	4	not out	45
HH Dippenaar (capt)	c Foster b Masters	7	lbw b Palladino	9
HD Ackerman	b Wright	15	b Wright	19
J Allenby	c Foster b Masters	71	not out	34
JWA Taylor	c Masters b ten Doeschate	88		
*TJ New	c Foster b Palladino	9		
GW Walker	lbw b Palladino	0		
IE O'Brien	c Foster b Wright	1		
AJ Harris	b Wright	0		
HF Gurney	not out	8		
Extras	b 2, lb 10, w 1, nb 8	21	w 6, nb 4	10
	(all out 62.2 overs)	**238**	(3 wkts 26 overs)	**123**

Bowling
Masters 18-6-49-2. Palladino 18-3-68-4. Wright 16-3-52-3. Napier 9-1-53-0.
ten Doeschate 1.2-0-4-1.
Masters 5-2-13-1. Palladino 7-3-26-1. Wright 7-1-38-1. ten Doeschate 4-0-33-0.
Napier 3-1-13-0.
Fall of Wickets: 1-8, 2-25, 3-27, 4-81, 5-135, 6-162, 7-162, 8-173, 9-173
1-16, 2-30, 3-62

Match drawn – Leicestershire (7pts), Essex (12pts)

Hampshire's Michael Carberry continued his fine mid-season form with a double century against Warwickshire.

Somerset's 428 for 6 declared was based, as so often in recent seasons, on significant contributions from Marcus Trescothick and Justin Langer. They added 169 for the second wicket, with Trescothick reaching 142 and Langer 107, and the Somerset bowlers shared the wickets around as Worcestershire slumped to 225 all out in reply. Vikram Solanki's 89-ball 93, with 19 fours, rallied his struggling side, however, and an unbeaten 80 from Ben Smith further frustrated the visitors.

At North Marine Road, meanwhile, Yorkshire supporters had to watch despairingly as David Hussey put the home bowlers to the sword in an innings of 189 from 205 balls which contained seven sixes and 26 fours.

He was joined in his merriment by Andre Adams, who appeared at No. 10 to thrash 84 and take Notts to 395.

Soon, in reply, Yorkshire were 149 for 9, with Ryan Sidebottom on his way to figures of 5 for 59 against his former county and Adams weighing in with four wickets of his own, and it took a characterful 84 not out from young Jonny Bairstow – plus 37 from last man Deon Kruis – to haul Yorkshire up to 231 all out. They still followed on, however, giving Notts a chance of completing a badly needed victory on the final day.

Sidebottom took another three wickets, but then tired, and with rain lopping off the best part of 30 overs from the day's allocation – in addition to the 62 lost on day one – Andrew Gale, out a single short of a deserved century, and Gerard Brophy were able to lead Yorkshire to the sanctuary of the draw.

A rain-ruined match at the Rose Bowl, where only 13.4 overs were possible on the opening day, at least featured some high-quality batting from Warwickshire's Jonathan Trott, who hit 22 fours in his unbeaten 184, and Hampshire opener Michael Carberry, who continued his run of fine form with 204 and was joined in a first wicket stand of 261 by Jimmy Adams (90).

Yet perhaps the best news for English cricket was the batting performance of Warwickshire's highly-rated 20-year-old fast bowler Chris Woakes, who came in at No. 9 to hit a superb unbeaten 131, from 183 balls and including a six and 16 fours, which more than hinted at a future as a genuine all-rounder.

In Division Two there was a thumping win for Northamptonshire at Cheltenham, where no play was possible at all on day two but the match still finished on the third day with Gloucestershire beaten by nine wickets.

Sixteen wickets fell on the opening day, with David Lucas taking 5 for 49 and being well supported by Johan van der Wath and Andrew Hall as Gloucestershire were bundled out for 147. Northants, in reply, were struggling at 91 for 5 before Nicky Boje played a captain's innings of 87 not out to earn his side a valuable 85-run lead.

Left-arm paceman Lucas then destroyed the Gloucestershire second innings to finish with career-best figures of 7 for 24 and a career-best match analysis of 12 for 73. The home side scraped their way to 142, but it was not enough to prevent an easy Northants victory chase.

Draws at Derby and Leicester were largely predictable once the first day's play was washed away at both venues, although Essex were particularly unlucky not to have more time to finish off Leicestershire at Grace Road after Hashim Amla and Matt Walker had scored centuries and the home side had been asked to follow on. Owais Shah's brilliant unbeaten 129 held Middlesex together at Derby, where there would have been an interesting finish had the game been allowed to run its natural course.

Round Thirteen: 31 July–3 August

Durham beat Sussex by nine wickets at the Riverside, thanks in large part to Michael Di Venuto's superb 254 not out, while Somerset and Nottinghamshire, their nearest challengers for the title, fought out a weather-interrupted draw at Taunton.

Di Venuto batted for eight and a half hours in all, hitting a six and 35 fours, to anchor Durham's drive to 473 for 4 declared. He was joined in a second wicket stand of 231 by Will Smith, who made 101, and Callum Thorp's 5 for 86 then helped to give the champions the opportunity to enforce the follow-on as Sussex were dismissed for 245.

Mike Yardy was run out for 97 in the Sussex first innings, while the only sustained resistance second time around was from Luke Wright, who remained 118 not out from 128 balls in a total of 304. Steve Harmison and Mark Davies took three wickets apiece and Di Venuto was at the crease again when Durham completed victory.

Ryan Sidebottom's 5 for 106, meanwhile, could not prevent Somerset from reaching 401 for 8 declared in their first innings, with five individual half-centuries, and Notts needed a spirited eighth wicket partnership of 116 between Chris Read and Mark Ealham to get close following the on-loan Scott Newman's early sprint to 87.

There was only time left, however, for Somerset to bat it out for the draw with Marcus Trescothick dismissed one short of his hundred after adding 229 for the first wicket with Arul Suppiah, who went on to a career-best 151. Andrew Caddick, Somerset's former England fast bowler, chose this game to announce that he would be retiring at the end of the season.

Round Thirteen: 31 July–3 August Division One

DURHAM v. SUSSEX – at the Riverside

DURHAM	First Innings		Second Innings	
MJ Di Venuto	not out	254	(2) not out	39
MD Stoneman	c Yardy b Yasir Arafat	5	(1) c Yardy b Rayner	18
WR Smith (capt)	b Collymore	101	not out	21
GJ Muchall	c Hodd b Yasir Arafat	14		
DM Benkenstein	c Joyce b Nash	69		
ID Blackwell	not out	2		
*P Mustard				
LE Plunkett				
CD Thorp				
SJ Harmison				
M Davies				
Extras	b 2, lb 11, w 1, nb 14	28	nb 2	2
	(4 wkts dec 137 overs)	473	(1 wkt 18.4 overs)	80

Bowling
Lewry 21-8-56-0. Yasir Arafat 30-6-96-2. Wright 19-1-75-0. Collymore 24-6-61-1. Rayner 29-2-107-0. Yardy 10-1-56-0. Nash 4-1-9-1.
Yasir Arafat 4-0-32-0. Collymore 1-0-5-0. Rayner 8-3-16-1. Nash 5.4-1-27-0.
Fall of Wickets: 1-16, 2-247, 3-280, 4-453
1-49

SUSSEX	First Innings		Second Innings (following on)	
MH Yardy (capt)	run out	97	c Muchall b Davies	20
CD Nash	lbw b Thorp	19	c Mustard b Thorp	55
EC Joyce	c Mustard b Davies	36	b Blackwell	14
MW Goodwin	b Thorp	6	c Mustard b Thorp	13
CD Hopkinson	b Thorp	14	lbw b Davies	7
LJ Wright	c Stoneman b Thorp	0	not out	118
*AJ Hodd	c Smith b Plunkett	4	c Plunkett b Davies	33
Yasir Arafat	c Di Venuto b Plunkett	10	c Di Venuto b Blackwell	18
OP Rayner	c Muchall b Harmison	24	lbw b Harmison	1
CD Collymore	c Muchall b Thorp	11	b Harmison	10
JD Lewry	not out	4	b Harmison	0
Extras	lb 11, w 1, nb 8	20	b 4, lb 7, nb 4	15
	(all out 76.2 overs)	245	(all out 79.3 overs)	304

Bowling
Harmison 20.2-5-58-1. Davies 16-4-41-1. Thorp 25-5-86-5. Plunkett 11-2-34-2. Blackwell 4-0-15-0.
Davies 18-5-44-3. Harmison 12.3-1-68-3. Plunkett 8-2-50-0. Thorp 16-0-79-2. Blackwell 25-10-52-2.
Fall of Wickets: 1-38, 2-131, 3-155, 4-166, 5-167, 6-181, 7-205, 8-205, 9-241
1-34, 2-71, 3-97, 4-104, 5-115, 6-227, 7-257, 8-258, 9-304

Durham won by 9 wickets – Durham (21pts), Sussex (2pts)

SOMERSET v. NOTTINGHAMSHIRE – at Taunton

SOMERSET	First Innings		Second Innings	
ME Trescothick	c Brown b Adams	37	c Pattinson b Patel	99
AV Suppiah	c Read b Sidebottom	51	b Voges	151
JL Langer (capt)	lbw b Sidebottom	79		
Z de Bruyn	c Voges b Sidebottom	74	not out	28
WJ Durston	c Read b Sidebottom	0	(3) not out	54
*C Kieswetter	c Read b Ealham	67		
PD Trego	not out	66		
AC Thomas	c Read b Ealham	6		
MTC Waller	lbw b Sidebottom	1		
AR Caddick	not out	11		
CM Willoughby				
Extras	b 2, lb 3, nb 4	9	b 4, lb 2, nb 6	12
	(8 wkts dec 100.4 overs)	401	(2 wkts 97.3 overs)	344

Bowling
Sidebottom 26.4-6-106-5. Pattinson 11-0-82-0. Adams 21-3-86-1. Ealham 23-5-62-2. Patel 15-3-52-0. Franks 3-0-7-0. Voges 3-0-1-1. Trego 1-1-0-0.
Sidebottom 8-2-28-0. Adams 11-2-22-0. Pattinson 16-1-73-0. Franks 15-5-37-0. Ealham 7-0-12-0. Patel 27-1-113-1. Voges 11.3-0-41-1. Brown 2-0-12-0.
Fall of Wickets: 1-45, 2-167, 3-172, 4-172, 5-280, 6-361, 7-382, 8-389
1-229, 2-276

NOTTS	First Innings	
SA Newman	lbw b Suppiah	87
MJ Wood	c Suppiah b Caddick	9
PJ Franks	c Kieswetter b Willoughby	4
AC Voges	c Suppiah b Caddick	10
RJ Sidebottom	lbw b Willoughby	5
SR Patel	c Kieswetter b Caddick	19
AD Brown	c Kieswetter b Waller	28
*CMW Read (capt)	c Waller b Willoughby	98
MA Ealham	not out	64
AR Adams	c Suppiah b Thomas	6
DJ Pattinson	b Willoughby	1
Extras	b 4, lb 6, w 1, nb 14	25
	(all out 92.3 overs)	356

Bowling
Willoughby 22.3-6-71-4. Caddick 20-2-96-3. Thomas 23-3-83-1. Suppiah 7-1-12-1. Waller 11-2-37-1. Trego 7-0-34-0. Durston 2-0-13-0.
Fall of Wickets: 1-24, 2-37, 3-73, 4-97, 5-147, 6-147, 7-222, 8-338, 9-345

Match drawn – Somerset (12pts), Nottinghamshire (10pts)

WORCESTERSHIRE v. WARWICKSHIRE – at New Road

WARWICKS	First Innings		Second Innings	
U Westwood (capt)	c Solanki b Andrew	22	not out	18
NM Carter	b Arif	13	c Arif b Mason	4
UL Trott	c Davies b Jones	67	not out	16
JO Troughton	c Mitchell b Woakes	6		
T Frost	c Davies b Mason	37		
*TR Ambrose	c Mitchell b Mason	63		
R Clarke	b Jones	50		
AG Botha	c Davies b Andrew	18		
CR Woakes	c Mitchell b Andrew	2		
N Tahir	lbw b Jones	5		
WB Rankin	b Jones	1		
Extras	lb 11, w 2, nb 12	25	lb 1, nb 8	9
	(all out 79.1 overs)	309	(1 wkt 8.5 overs)	47

Bowling
Mason 21-4-51-2. Arif 15-1-78-1. Andrew 14-2-57-3. Jones 20.1-4-66-4. Mitchell 6-0-19-0. Ali 2-0-4-0. Solanki 1-0-3-0.
Mason 4-0-13-1. Arif 4-1-28-0. Jones 0.5-0-5-0.
Fall of Wickets: 1-22, 2-56, 3-79, 4-154, 5-160, 6-276, 7-292, 8-295, 9-298
1-9

WORCS	First Innings		Second Innings (following on)	
DKH Mitchell	c Ambrose b Rankin	6	c Clarke b Tahir	20
SC Moore	c Clarke b Woakes	28	c Brophy b Woakes	88
VS Solanki (capt)	c Ambrose b Woakes	27	c Troughton b Rankin	46
BF Smith	lbw b Carter	1	b Rankin	2
MM Ali	b Carter	4	c Ambrose b Tahir	41
*SM Davies	c Ambrose b Carter	19	c Ambrose b Rankin	0
AN Kervezee	lbw b Carter	0	c Ambrose b Carter	26
GM Andrew	lbw b Woakes	1	c Ambrose b Tahir	14
RA Jones	lbw b Carter	4	lbw b Tahir	3
MS Mason	c Ambrose b Woakes	2	c Botha b Rankin	0
Imran Arif	not out	0	not out	0
Extras	lb 7, nb 12	19	b 2, lb 4, nb 12	18
	(all out 37.5 overs)	111	(all out 73.5 overs)	244

Bowling
Rankin 7-0-31-1. Tahir 5-3-6-0. Woakes 13.5-4-30-4. Carter 12-2-37-5.
Rankin 20-7-56-4. Tahir 19.5-5-67-5. Woakes 10-1-35-0. Carter 14-5-46-1. Trott 5-0-25-0. Clarke 5-3-9-0.
Fall of Wickets: 1-8, 2-69, 3-70, 4-70, 5-76, 6-76, 7-77, 8-88, 9-105
1-19, 2-140, 3-144, 4-152, 5-152, 6-198, 7-229, 8-233, 9-234

Warwickshire won by 9 wickets – Worcestershire (3pts), Warwickshire (20pts)

LANCASHIRE v. YORKSHIRE – at Old Trafford

YORKSHIRE	First Innings		Second Innings	
JA Rudolph	b Mahmood	14	c Horton b Keedy	127
JJ Sayers	c Laxman b Smith	34	c Laxman b Mahmood	1
A McGrath	c Sutton b Smith	9	lbw b Smith	14
AW Gale	c Loye b Mahmood	54	lbw b Smith	121
JM Bairstow	c Chilton b Smith	5	not out	52
*GL Brophy	c Mahmood b Smith	15	not out	21
TT Bresnan	c Sutton b Smith	0		
AU Rashid	c Sutton b Hogg	2		
RM Pyrah	c Sutton b Smith	0		
A Shahzad	not out	26		
MJ Hoggard	c Sutton b Mahmood	1		
Extras	b 9, lb 2, w 2, nb 8	21	b 8, lb 2, w 2, nb 6	18
	(all out 52.3 overs)	181	(4 wkts 104.4 overs)	354

Bowling
Mahmood 14.3-3-57-3. Hogg 14-7-23-1. Smith 13-3-46-6. Newby 11-1-44-0.
Mahmood 17-1-71-1. Hogg 13.5-15-0. Keedy 40-5-132-1. Smith 18-3-62-2. du Plessis 4-0-7-0. Newby 11.4-0-57-0. Horton 1-1-0-0.
Fall of Wickets: 1-39, 2-56, 3-77, 4-91, 5-115, 6-115, 7-121, 8-122, 9-158
1-9, 2-39, 3-257, 4-299

LANCASHIRE	First Innings	
PJ Horton	c Brophy b Bresnan	84
TC Smith	c Brophy b Hoggard	40
MB Loye	b Rashid	146
VVS Laxman	c Rudolph b Rashid	109
F du Plessis	c Sayers b Shahzad	18
MJ Chilton	not out	38
*LD Sutton (capt)	not out	30
KW Hogg		
SI Mahmood		
OJ Newby		
G Keedy		
Extras	b 5, lb 12, w 5, nb 2	24
	(5 wkts dec 138 overs)	489

Bowling
Hoggard 29-7-86-1. Bresnan 34-11-90-1. Shahzad 30-6-107-1. Pyrah 17-1-58-0. Rashid 27-0-126-2. Sayers 1-0-5-0.
Fall of Wickets: 1-107, 2-156, 3-381, 4-402, 5-426

Match drawn – Lancashire (12pts), Yorkshire (5pts)

Another mighty innings from the prolific Mark Ramprakash saw him hit 274 for Surrey against Leicestershire in a match long destined as a draw.

Worcestershire's woes continued when they were trounced by nine wickets by West Midlands rivals Warwickshire at New Road, even after the loss of day two to rain, with Neil Carter and Chris Woakes combining to shatter the home first innings and Naqqash Tahir and Boyd Rankin doing

KENT v. DERBYSHIRE – at Canterbury

DERBYSHIRE	First Innings		Second Innings	
CJL Rogers (capt)	c Denly b McLaren	53	st Jones b Tredwell	107
WL Madsen	lbw b Cook	3	run out	19
GT Park	c Kemp b Tredwell	11	lbw b Tredwell	53
DJ Redfern	c van Jaarsveld b Cook	29	c Kemp b Cook	13
WW Hinds	c Kemp b Tredwell	74	b Kemp	16
GM Smith	c Key b Tredwell	0	c Jones b Parnell	44
*FA Klokker	c Jones b Khan	13	c Jones b Kemp	6
GG Wagg	c Kemp b Tredwell	21	c sub b Tredwell	23
TD Groenewald	c Jones b Parnell	7	c Jones b Kemp	3
J Needham	c Jones b Khan	20	not out	2
PS Jones	not out	53	c Stevens b Tredwell	0
Extras	b 4, lb 13, nb 2	19	b 3, lb 3, w 7, nb 4	17
	(all out 83.5 overs)	303	(all out 95 overs)	303

Bowling
Parnell 14-2-61-1. Khan 15.5-3-41-2. Cook 21-7-48-2. McLaren 11-2-44-1. Tredwell 22.5-92-4.
Khan 22-3-72-0. Parnell 15-0-44-1. Cook 13-2-38-1. McLaren 8-2-38-0. Tredwell 32.5-93-4. Kemp 5-1-12-3.
Fall of Wickets: 1-46, 2-68, 3-96, 4-126, 5-127, 6-172, 7-212, 8-221, 9-233
1-60, 2-179, 3-202, 4-202, 5-236, 6-250, 7-291, 8-296, 9-300

KENT	First Innings		Second Innings	
JL Denly	c Rogers b Groenewald	28	b Jones	3
RWT Key (capt)	c Klokker b Wagg	25	c Redfern b Wagg	110
*GO Jones	c Rogers b Groenewald	23	c Madsen b Groenewald	100
M van Jaarsveld	c Hinds b Wagg	12	c Smith b Wagg	51
DI Stevens	c Rogers b Groenewald	8	lbw b Groenewald	29
JM Kemp	b Wagg	8	c Klokker b Redfern	0
JC Tredwell	not out	86	not out	3
R McLaren	lbw b Wagg	29	c Madsen b Groenewald	5
WD Parnell	c Jones b Wagg	3	not out	0
SJ Cook	c Redfern b Groenewald	34		
A Khan	lbw b Smith	1		
Extras	b 1, lb 13, w 4, nb 14	32	b 6, lb 7, w 2, nb 2	17
	(all out 93 overs)	289	(7 wkts 70.5 overs)	318

Bowling
Wagg 36-7-96-5. Jones 21-6-57-0. Groenewald 18-3-69-4. Smith 10-1-23-1. Needham 4-0-30-0.
Wagg 15-0-87-2. Jones 13-1-56-1. Needham 13-1-54-0. Smith 8-1-24-0. Groenewald 12.5-1-52-3. Redfern 8-1-26-1. Park 1-0-6-0.
Fall of Wickets: 1-49, 2-67, 3-95, 4-106, 5-111, 6-135, 7-193, 8-201, 9-287
1-7, 2-182, 3-265, 4-279, 5-289, 6-307, 7-317

Kent won by 3 wickets – Kent (19pts), Derbyshire (6pts)

Round Thirteen: 31 July–3 August
Division Two

MIDDLESEX v. NORTHAMPTONSHIRE – at Lord's

NORTHANTS	First Innings		Second Innings	
SD Peters	lbw b Finn	13	lbw b Finn	25
BH Howgego	c Morgan b Finn	47	c Scott b Murtagh	6
RA White	c Malan b Finn	51	lbw b Murtagh	1
AG Wakely	lbw b Udal	61	c ℔ b Udal	24
*MH Wessels	c Kartik b Richardson	19	c Malan b Murtagh	57
N Boje (capt)	c Finn b Murtagh	55	c Robson b Udal	2
AJ Hall	c Shah b Murtagh	11	c Scott b Richardson	48
JJ van der Wath	c Shah b Richardson	7	c Shah b Kartik	85
MS Panesar	c Kartik b Richardson	2	c Kartik b Richardson	14
DS Lucas	b Murtagh	0	c Scott b Murtagh	14
DH Wigley	not out	6	not out	5
Extras	lb 8, nb 8	16	b 5, lb 10, w 1, nb 2	18
	(all out 96.5 overs)	288	(all out 103 overs)	293

Bowling
Murtagh 26.4-4-51-4. Finn 17-1-89-1. Kartik 23-8-38-1. Richardson 21-3-52-2. Udal 16-0-48-2.
Murtagh 26.4-4-51-4. Finn 17-1-89-1. Kartik 23-8-38-1. Richardson 21-3-52-2. Udal 16-0-48-2.
Fall of Wickets: 1-19, 2-106, 3-119, 4-157, 5-254, 6-262, 7-280, 8-280, 9-282
1-19, 2-25, 3-37, 4-75, 5-79, 6-161, 7-211, 8-273, 9-284

MIDDLESEX	First Innings		Second Innings	
SD Robson	c Wessels b van der Wath	75	lbw b Lucas	9
NRD Compton	c Boje b Wigley	82	c Wessels b Lucas	32
OA Shah	b Lucas	24	lbw b Lucas	4
EJG Morgan	lbw b Boje	71	lbw b Panesar	6
DJ Malan	c Howgego b Boje	10	lbw b Panesar	5
*BJM Scott	b van der Wath	20	lbw b Boje	23
SD Udal (capt)	b Hall	3	b van der Wath	55
M Kartik	not out	28	c Wessels b van der Wath	16
TJ Murtagh	lbw b van der Wath	9	c White b van der Wath	1
ST Finn	c Hall b van der Wath	3	not out	14
A Richardson	lbw b Hall	11	lbw b Lucas	4
Extras	b 2, lb 6, nb 16	24	b 2, lb 4, w 1, nb 10	17
	(all out 87.5 overs)	360	(all out 63 overs)	186

Bowling
van der Wath 22.1-1-107-4. Lucas 13-2-51-1. Panesar 9-1-31-0. Hall 13.5-2-44-2. Wigley 12-0-61-1. Boje 18-3-58-2.
Lucas 14-3-38-4. van der Wath 14-4-38-3. Panesar 10-2-34-2. Wigley 5-1-21-0. Hall 7-2-15-0. Boje 11-2-34-1.
Fall of Wickets: 1-167, 2-181, 3-200, 4-213, 5-298, 6-304, 7-316, 8-335, 9-345
1-25, 2-29, 3-52, 4-61, 5-66, 6-109, 7-150, 8-163, 9-164

Northamptonshire won by 35 runs – Middlesex (7pts), Northamptonshire (19pts)

GLOUCESTERSHIRE v. GLAMORGAN – at Bristol

GLOS	First Innings		Second Innings	
Kadeer Ali	c Bragg b Shantry	53	(2) not out	67
RJ Woodman	c Wallace b Shantry	15	(1) lbw b Harris	18
WTS Porterfield	c Dalrymple b Harris	22	c Wallace b Harrison	31
HJH Marshall	c Kruger	43	not out	27
APR Gidman (capt)	c Gibbs b Kruger	128		
CG Taylor	c Dalrymple b Croft	37		
JEC Franklin	c Bragg b Harrison	16		
*SJ Adshead	c Wallace b Kruger	1		
ID Saxelby	lbw b Harris	33		
J Lewis	not out	10		
SP Kirby	not out	0		
Extras	b 8, lb 6, w 6, nb 22	42	b 8, lb 9, nb 8	25
	(9 wkts dec 101.1 overs)	400	(2 wkts 68 overs)	168

Bowling
Harris 18-1-91-2. Harrison 20-4-88-1. Shantry 13-3-38-2. Kruger 23.1-7-77-3. Croft 22-3-68-1. Dalrymple 5-0-24-0.
Kruger 12-3-29-0. Harris 13-6-23-1. Croft 20-4-37-0. Harrison 12-1-34-1. Shantry 7-3-15-0. Dalrymple 4-0-13-0.
Fall of Wickets: 1-27, 2-86, 3-118, 4-195, 5-313, 6-337, 7-343, 8-347, 9-399
1-39, 2-114

GLAMORGAN	First Innings		
GP Rees	c Porterfield b Lewis	82	
WD Bragg	c Porterfield b Lewis	92	
HH Gibbs	c Adshead b Kirby	96	
MJ Powell	c Porterfield b Lewis	0	
JWM Dalrymple (capt)	lbw b Lewis	0	
*MA Wallace	c Gidman b Kirby	36	
JAR Harris	not out	5	
RDB Croft	c Adshead b Kirby	0	
AJ Shantry	c Adshead b Lewis	4	
DS Harrison	c Adshead b Lewis	6	
GJP Kruger			
Extras	b 2, lb 11, w 2, nb 14	29	
	(8 wkts dec 94.1 overs)	350	

Bowling
Kirby 20-3-58-3. Lewis 23-5-73-5. Franklin 15-0-94-0. Saxelby 14.1-5-50-0. Gidman 12-1-29-0. Taylor 7-2-22-0. Marshall 3-0-11-0.
Fall of Wickets: 1-218, 2-218, 3-224, 4-324, 5-337, 6-339, 7-344, 8-344

Match drawn – Gloucestershire (11pts), Glamorgan (11pts)

SURREY v. LEICESTERSHIRE – at The Oval

LEICESTERSHIRE	First Innings		Second Innings	
GP Smith	c Batty b Dernbach	46	not out	14
MAG Boyce	run out	0	not out	8
HH Dippenaar	c Walters b Dernbach	86		
HD Ackerman	c Walters b Schofield	75		
JWA Taylor	not out	207		
*TJ New	c Batty b Linley	53		
J du Toit	not out	100		
CW Henderson				
NL Buck				
AJ Harris				
HF Gurney				
Extras	b 4, lb 15, w 5, nb 2	26	w 1	1
	(5 wkts dec 157.2 overs)	593	(0 wkts 9 overs)	23

Bowling
Dernbach 30-9-92-2. Nel 30-6-113-0. Jordan 26.2-2-104-0. Linley 27-5-98-1. Schofield 36-2-123-1. Walters 4-0-14-0. Afzaal 4-0-30-0.
Dernbach 4-0-10-0. Schofield 4-1-5-0. Brown 1-0-8-0.
Fall of Wickets: 1-1, 2-140, 3-153, 4-258, 5-363

SURREY	First Innings		
*JN Batty	b Harris	0	
MJ Brown	c Ackerman b Henderson	46	
MR Ramprakash	b Buck	274	
SJ Walters (capt)	c Ackerman b Henderson	188	
U Afzaal	not out	70	
CP Murtagh	not out	14	
CP Schofield			
CJ Jordan			
A Nel			
JW Dernbach			
TE Linley			
Extras	b 4, lb 7, w 3, nb 2	16	
	(4 wkts dec 167 overs)	608	

Bowling
Harris 21-2-96-1. Buck 27-6-73-1. Gurney 26-6-99-0. Henderson 64-11-178-2. du Toit 19-1-89-0. Taylor 3-0-28-0. Dippenaar 7-0-34-0.
Fall of Wickets: 1-0, 2-75, 3-479, 4-565

Match drawn – Surrey (10pts), Leicestershire (8pts)

the second innings damage after Stephen Moore and Vikram Solanki had taken the total to 140 for 1.

Tom Smith's opening salvo of 6 for 46, as Yorkshire were bowled out for 181, looked likely to bring Lancashire victory in the Roses match at Old Trafford – especially when century-makers VVS Laxman and Mal Loye were adding 225 for the third wicket in reply. But Yorkshire, who began the final day at 71 for 2 and still 237 runs adrift, battled to a creditable draw thanks to the determined efforts of Jacques Rudolph and Andrew Gale, who both scored hundreds.

Derbyshire, beginning the last day at Canterbury on 236 for 4 in their second innings after edging the first three days against Kent, contrived to lose the match by three wickets with Rob Key and Geraint Jones easing to centuries to set up an impressively controlled chase to 318 at a required rate of around four and a half runs an over. James Tredwell also had a fine all-round game, with eight wickets and a vital unbeaten 86 in Kent's first innings.

Elsewhere in the second division there was an excellent win for Northamptonshire against Middlesex at Lord's, with the incisive swing bowling of David Lucas (4 for 38) and the all-round contribution of Johan van der Wath enabling Northants to overcome a 72-run first innings deficit, and high-scoring draws at Bristol and The Oval.

Rain delays were also a contributory factor to the deadlock between Gloucestershire and Glamorgan, but Surrey and Leicestershire could have played for a week without a positive result such was the trueness of the surface at Kennington. Only nine wickets fell overall as Leicestershire ran up 593 for 5 declared with 19-year-old James Taylor becoming the county's youngest double-century maker with 207 not out in seven hours, and then Mark Ramprakash leading Surrey's response with 274.

Ramprakash faced 380 balls, hitting a six and 39 fours, and his third wicket stand of 404 with Stewart Walters, who made a career-best 188, was just nine runs short of the county record for that wicket. Surrey finally declared at 608 for 4 but interest in the match had long since died.

Round Fourteen: 5–9 August

All three first division games were drawn, with an opening day washout at Edgbaston hardly helping the chances of a positive result there. Marcus Trescothick was able, however, to score a hundred in each innings for the second time in his career before Somerset and Warwickshire agreed on an early finish.

The matches at Horsham and the Rose Bowl followed an uncannily similar pattern with home sides Sussex and Hampshire, respectively, eventually both being forced to bat out 69 overs on the final day. Chris Nash's 87 and Michael Carberry's unbeaten 136 did those jobs quite comfortably, though.

Earlier, at Hove, Ed Joyce's first innings 183 from 300 balls, with 28 fours, was a brilliantly-played lone

Round Fourteen: 5–9 August Division One

WARWICKSHIRE v. SOMERSET – at Edgbaston

SOMERSET	First Innings		Second Innings	
ME Trescothick	lbw b Rankin	108	not out	107
AV Suppiah	c Ambrose b Rankin	7	c Clarke b Rankin	8
JL Langer (capt)	c Ambrose b Woakes	69		
JC Hildreth	not out	86	(3) c sub b Carter	11
Z de Bruyn	c Ambrose b Rankin	0	(4) lbw b Botha	9
*C Kieswetter	c Frost b Woakes	6	(5) b Trott	5
PD Trego	c Clarke b Woakes	1	(6) not out	4
BJ Phillips	c Clarke b Woakes	7		
AC Thomas	c Ambrose b Clarke	10		
AR Caddick				
CM Willoughby				
Extras	b 9, lb 10, w 2, nb 8	29	b 4, lb 1, w 1, nb 6	12
	(8 wkts dec 79.1 overs)	323	(4 wkts 37 overs)	156

Bowling
Rankin 17-2-71-3. Tahir 11-2-37-0. Carter 23-2-99-0. Woakes 25-6-89-4. Clarke 3.1-0-8-1.
Rankin 7-2-34-1. Tahir 7-2-18-0. Carter 3-0-21-1. Woakes 4-2-8-0. Clarke 6-0-26-0. Botha 7-0-34-1. Trott 3-1-10-1.
Fall of Wickets: 1-17, 2-192, 3-230, 4-234, 5-269, 6-279, 7-295, 8-323
1-23, 2-53, 3-125, 4-150

WARWICKSHIRE	First Innings	
IJ Westwood (capt)	b Willoughby	0
NM Carter	c Langer b Thomas	24
JO Troughton	c Trescothick b Willoughby	11
T Frost	c Trescothick b Thomas	94
IJL Trott	c Trescothick b Caddick	79
*TR Ambrose	c Langer b Thomas	0
R Clarke	c Kieswetter b Thomas	0
AG Botha	b Caddick	2
CR Woakes	c Kieswetter b Willoughby	13
N Tahir	c Suppiah b Willoughby	23
WB Rankin	not out	0
Extras	b 5, lb 6, w 2, nb 2	15
	(all out 66.2 overs)	261

Bowling
Willoughby 13.2-4-37-4. Caddick 18-4-67-2. Thomas 21-2-72-4. Phillips 8-1-42-0. Trego 4-0-22-0. de Bruyn 2-0-10-0.
Fall of Wickets: 1-0, 2-24, 3-61, 4-203, 5-207, 6-207, 7-210, 8-233, 9-252

Match drawn – Warwickshire (8pts), Somerset (10pts)

SUSSEX v. NOTTINGHAMSHIRE – at Horsham

SUSSEX	First Innings		Second Innings	
MH Yardy (capt)	b Adams	22	c Read b Shreck	24
CD Nash	b Shreck	4	lbw b Adams	87
EC Joyce	lbw b Voges	183	c Et b Patel	17
MW Goodwin	b Adams	11	b Patel	2
CD Hopkinson	c Read b Fletcher	15	not out	47
LJ Wright	c Read b Fletcher	4	not out	59
*AJ Hodd	lbw b Adams	0		
RSC Martin-Jenkins	c Brown b Fletcher	4		
OP Rayner	lbw b Patel	22		
CD Collymore	hit wkt b Shreck	23		
PS Sandri	not out	0		
Extras	b 4, lb 2, w 9, nb 6	21	b 2, lb 5, nb 6	13
	(all out 98.5 overs)	309	(4 wkts 69 overs)	249

Bowling
Shreck 22.5-1-92-2. Fletcher 19-5-58-3. Adams 26-10-64-3. Ealham 18-3-64-0. Patel 12-5-23-1. Voges 1-0-2-1.
Shreck 15-4-55-1. Adams 13-3-43-1. Patel 18-7-40-2. Ealham 9-3-31-0. Fletcher 8-1-50-0. Voges 5-1-11-0. Brown 1-0-12-0.
Fall of Wickets: 1-9, 2-43, 3-76, 4-120, 5-127, 6-128, 7-144, 8-204, 9-308
1-62, 2-128, 3-140, 4-140

NOTTS	First Innings	
SA Newman	b Rayner	25
MJ Wood	lbw b Wright	86
MA Wagh	b Martin-Jenkins	73
AC Voges	lbw b Rayner	139
SR Patel	c Goodwin b Martin-Jenkins	91
AD Brown	c Joyce b Rayner	42
*CMW Read (capt)	not out	25
MA Ealham	not out	9
AR Adams		
LJ Fletcher		
CE Shreck		
Extras	b 3, lb 10, w 10, nb 18	41
	(6 wkts dec 134 overs)	531

Bowling
Collymore 27-8-73-0. Sandri 14-2-80-0. Rayner 26-1-110-3. Wright 19-5-68-1. Martin-Jenkins 31-7-104-2. Yardy 13-0-61-0. Nash 4-0-22-0.
Fall of Wickets: 1-48, 2-180, 3-239, 4-407, 5-478, 6-501

Match drawn – Sussex (8pts), Nottinghamshire (12pts)

HAMPSHIRE v. LANCASHIRE – at the Rose Bowl

HAMPSHIRE	First Innings		Second Innings	
MA Carberry	c Chilton b Hogg	33	not out	136
JHK Adams	lbw b Newby	107	b Hogg	21
JP Crawley	c Laxman b Hogg	21	c Laxman b Parry	12
JM Vince	c Sutton b Newby	23	c Laxman b Keedy	9
LA Dawson	c Sutton b Newby	3	not out	5
SM Ervine	c Smith b Hogg	114		
AD Mascarenhas (capt)	c Sutton b Hogg	21		
*TG Burrows	c Laxman b Newby	0		
DA Griffiths	b Keedy	0		
Imran Tahir	b Smith	0		
JA Tomlinson	not out	6		
Extras	lb 3, w 2, nb 4	9	b 16, lb 4, nb 8	28
	(all out 105.2 overs)	337	(3 wkts 69 overs)	229

Bowling
Hogg 29.2-8-74-4. Newby 30-4-105-4. Smith 26-6-84-1. Keedy 11-0-49-1. Parry 9-2-22-0.
Hogg 11-3-39-1. Newby 12-2-30-0. Parry 13-3-38-1. Keedy 24-4-69-1. du Plessis 10-2-30-0.
Fall of Wickets: 1-65, 2-133, 3-183, 4-189, 5-194, 6-263, 7-274, 8-286, 9-287
1-75, 2-123, 3-142

LANCASHIRE	First Innings	
PJ Horton	c Imran Tahir b Griffiths	34
TC Smith	c Burrows b Griffiths	95
MB Loye	lbw b Mascarenhas	61
VVS Laxman	c Ervine b Griffiths	135
MJ Chilton	c Burrows b Griffiths	81
F du Plessis	not out	86
*LD Sutton (capt)	not out	30
KW Hogg		
SD Parry		
OJ Newby		
G Keedy		
Extras	b 2, lb 13, w 1, nb 30	46
	(5 wkts dec 144.1 overs)	568

Bowling
Tomlinson 24-4-80-0. Mascarenhas 24-8-59-1. Imran Tahir 28-3-112-0. Griffiths 30-5-103-4. Dawson 15-1-100-0. Ervine 11-0-51-0. Adams 1-0-5-0. Carberry 6-0-34-0. Vince 4-0-9-0.
Fall of Wickets: 1-62, 2-214, 3-214, 4-430, 5-487

Match drawn – Hampshire (8pts), Lancashire (12pts)

hand for Sussex until he was ninth out, while at the Rose Bowl it was Jimmy Adams's 107 and Sean Ervine's 114 which could not prevent Hampshire from shipping a sizeable first innings deficit. Nottinghamshire's Adam Voges, the Australian, led his team's march to a 500-plus total with 139, while for Lancashire it was the Indian Test star, VVS Laxman, whose 135 spearheaded their charge to 568 for 5 declared.

In Division Two there were three winning teams, with Gloucestershire getting their Championship season back on track with a deserved ten-wicket victory against Essex at Southend's Garon Park. The home side were always up against it once James Franklin and the outstanding Steve Adshead both scored hundreds and, after coming together at 170 for 6, added 169 for the seventh wicket.

Adshead went on to finish 156 not out, a career-best, and a Gloucestershire lead of 198 proved too much for Essex to handle on a wearing pitch. The other two victories in this division were welcome ones for Glamorgan, who crushed Leicestershire by an innings and 72 runs at Colwyn Bay, and Middlesex, who shocked leaders Kent by running out 47-run winners at Canterbury.

Robert Croft, with 121, and Adam Shantry, who made an unlikely hundred from No. 10 in the order, were just six runs short of Glamorgan's ninth wicket record when their stand of 197 finally came to an end but, by then, the Welsh county held a match-winning first innings lead on a surface which was now taking spin. Dean Cosker and Croft then shared six wickets in the Leicestershire second innings.

Gareth Berg was Middlesex's hero against Kent, hitting 57 not out and 98, although Chris Silverwood's belligerent 46, with ten fours, helped to push them just far enough ahead to withstand a dramatic late assault from Amjad Khan, the home No. 11, whose 62 not out took him a mere 43 balls.

Round Fourteen: 5–9 August Division Two

ESSEX v. GLOUCESTERSHIRE – at Southend

ESSEX	First Innings		Second Innings	
JK Maunders	lbw b Saxelby	28	c Dawson b Lewis	8
JER Gallian	c Taylor b Franklin	3	c Adshead b Lewis	6
T Westley	c Dawson b Kirby	7	c Gidman b Dawson	32
MJ Walker	c Kadeer Ali b Kirby	0	c Dawson b Kirby	7
ML Pettini (capt)	c Taylor b Lewis	91	lbw b Franklin	36
*JS Foster	c Adshead b Franklin	4	c Marshall b Saxelby	20
RN ten Doeschate	c Woodman b Dawson	43	lbw b Saxelby	33
GR Napier	c Adshead b Kirby	50	c Kadeer Ali b Saxelby	39
DD Masters	c Woodman b Franklin	55	c Dawson b Franklin	19
Danish Kaneria	c Taylor b Lewis	0	c Saxelby b Franklin	1
CJC Wright	not out	0	not out	15
Extras	b 2, lb 11, nb 6	19	b 8, lb 8, w 2, nb 2	20
	(all out 86.1 overs)	300	(all out 93.5 overs)	236

Bowling
Lewis 35-12-68-1. Wright 27-2-96-2. Danish Kaneria 44-9-158-3. Dawson 12-0-61-1. Marshall 7-1-20-0.
Kirby 18-4-36-1. Lewis 18-5-42-2. Franklin 16-5-51-3. Saxelby 16.5-4-31-3. Marshall 1-0-2-0. Dawson 24-2-86-1.
Fall of Wickets: 1-16, 2-26, 3-26, 4-42, 5-47, 6-138, 7-208, 8-296, 9-297 1-10, 2-17, 3-31, 4-87, 5-113, 6-148, 7-183, 8-215, 9-217

GLOS	First Innings		Second Innings	
Kadeer Ali	c Foster b Napier	76	(2) not out	13
RJ Woodman	c Maunders b Masters	1	(1) not out	23
SP Kirby	c Pettini b Napier	19		
HJH Marshall	c Napier b ten Doeschate	20		
APR Gidman (capt)	c Foster b Napier	14		
CG Taylor	b Wright	21		
JEC Franklin	lbw b Danish Kaneria	100		
*SJ Adshead	not out	156		
RKJ Dawson	b Wright	8		
ID Saxelby	lbw b Danish Kaneria	20		
J Lewis	c Foster b Napier	32		
Extras	b 3, lb 12, w 4, nb 12	31	lb 1, nb 2	3
	(all out 152.2 overs)	498	(0 wkts 10.2 overs)	39

Bowling
Masters 35-12-68-1. Wright 27-2-96-2. Danish Kaneria 44-9-158-3. Napier 28.2-5-99-3. ten Doeschate 16-2-48-1. Westley 2-0-14-0. Wright 5.2-0-19-0. Danish Kaneria 5-1-19-0.
Fall of Wickets: 1-11, 2-61, 3-94, 4-119, 5-163, 6-170, 7-339, 8-354, 9-428

Gloucestershire won by 10 wickets – Essex (5pts), Gloucestershire (21pts)

GLAMORGAN v. LEICESTERSHIRE – at Colwyn Bay

LEICESTERSHIRE	First Innings		Second Innings	
GP Smith	lbw b Harris	6	b Dalrymple	20
CEJ Thompson	c Wallace b Harrison	0	lbw b Cosker	16
HH Dippenaar (capt)	b Cosker	85	c Maynard b Croft	57
HD Ackerman	b Harris	92	lbw b Shantry	17
JWA Taylor	lbw b Harris	5	st Wallace b Shantry	1
*TJ New	c Maynard b Dalrymple	45	lbw b Croft	26
J du Toit	c Maynard b Dalrymple	42	c Dalrymple b Croft	0
CW Henderson	not out	10	run out	2
NL Buck	c Maynard b Dalrymple	0	lbw b Cosker	0
AJ Harris	not out	0	not out	3
HF Gurney			c Et b Cosker	12
Extras	b 3, lb 9, nb 8	26	lb 6, lb 6, nb 14	26
	(all out 84.3 overs)	313	(all out 70 overs)	181

Bowling
Harris 19-5-90-3. Harrison 14-3-54-1. Shantry 14-0-62-0. Croft 15-1-37-0. Cosker 15.3-4-47-2. Dalrymple 7-1-11-3.
Harris 16-3-62-0. Harrison 5-4-4-0. Dalrymple 16-0-52-1. Cosker 12-8-12-3. Shantry 6-1-9-2. Croft 9-1-2-4.
Fall of Wickets: 1-8, 2-8, 3-160, 4-174, 5-215, 6-274, 7-299, 8-299, 9-304 1-25, 2-57, 3-88, 4-96, 5-163, 6-163, 7-166, 8-166, 9-166

GLAMORGAN	First Innings	
GP Rees	c du Toit b Henderson	44
WD Bragg	c Gurney b Henderson	80
MJ Powell	b Henderson	40
JWM Dalrymple (capt)	b Gurney	40
TL Maynard	c Smith b Henderson	38
*MA Wallace	c Taylor b Henderson	19
JAR Harris	lbw b Henderson	0
RDB Croft	b Thompson	121
DA Cosker	c New b Buck	1
AJ Shantry	b Gurney	100
DS Harrison	not out	26
Extras	b 16, lb 21, w 5, nb 10, p 5	57
	(all out 176.2 overs)	566

Bowling
Harris 34-7-109-0. Buck 26-3-81-1. Gurney 31-0-119-2. Henderson 67-16-152-6. Thompson 15.2-2-45-1. Taylor 4-0-17-0. Dippenaar 1-0-1-0.
Fall of Wickets: 1-101, 2-157, 3-213, 4-252, 5-282, 6-282, 7-293, 8-296, 9-493

Glamorgan won by an innings and 72 runs – Glamorgan (21pts), Leicestershire (5pts)

KENT v. MIDDLESEX – at Canterbury

MIDDLESEX	First Innings		Second Innings	
SD Robson	run out	1	c Jones b Azhar Mahmood	3
NRD Compton	c Jones b Khan	7	c Jones b Tredwell	28
OA Shah	b Khan	16	c Kemp b Azhar Mahmood	16
EJG Morgan (capt)	c van Jaarsveld b A Mahmood	5	b Khan	30
DJ Malan	run out	0	c Jones b Tredwell	49
*BJM Scott	c Kemp b Cook	14	c van Jaarsveld b Khan	0
GK Berg	not out	57	c Kemp b Tredwell	98
M Kartik	c Kemp b Azhar Mahmood	28	c Khan b Tredwell	16
TJ Murtagh	c Northeast b A Mahmood	4	not out	11
CEW Silverwood	c Stevens b Khan	0	c Denly b Tredwell	46
ST Finn	run out	0	lbw b Azhar Mahmood	0
Extras	b 6, lb 3, nb 12	21	b 2, lb 11, w 4, nb 6	23
	(all out 36 overs)	155	(all out 93 overs)	320

Bowling
Khan 12-1-41-3. Azhar Mahmood 13-2-46-3. Kemp 6-0-36-0. Cook 4-0-17-1. Tredwell 1-0-6-0.
Khan 18-6-52-2. Azhar Mahmood 20-9-53-3. Cook 13-3-59-0. Tredwell 33-10-100-5. Stevens 1-1-0-0. Kemp 5-0-30-0. van Jaarsveld 3-0-13-0.
Fall of Wickets: 1-5, 2-30, 3-33, 4-39, 5-42, 6-70, 7-122, 8-138, 9-139 1-32, 2-50, 3-57, 4-117, 5-117, 6-209, 7-257, 8-258, 9-319

KENT	First Innings		Second Innings	
JL Denly	c Silverwood b Finn	3	c Kartik b Finn	25
RWT Key (capt)	run out	1	c Murtagh b Finn	0
*GO Jones	lbw b Murtagh	2	c Morgan b Silverwood	16
M van Jaarsveld	lbw b Murtagh	9	c Morgan b Berg	54
SA Northeast	c Scott b Silverwood	12	c Malan b Kartik	37
DI Stevens	c Robson b Kartik	67	lbw b Murtagh	4
JM Kemp	c Scott b Murtagh	3	lbw b Kartik	30
JC Tredwell	b Finn	9	(8) b Kartik	11
Azhar Mahmood	c Scott b Murtagh	0	(9) lbw b Kartik	0
SJ Cook	lbw b Kartik	17	c Morgan b Murtagh	27
A Khan	not out	1	not out	62
Extras	b 1, lb 5, w 1, nb 10	17	lb 19, nb 2	21
	(all out 37 overs)	141	(all out 91.4 overs)	287

Bowling
Murtagh 11-5-26-3. Finn 8-1-38-2. Silverwood 7-0-23-1. Berg 6-1-16-0. Kartik 5-0-32-3.
Murtagh 22.4-6-70-2. Finn 13-2-62-2. Silverwood 9-2-27-1. Kartik 35-19-53-4. Berg 9-2-36-1. Malan 3-0-20-0.
Fall of Wickets: 1-5, 2-8, 3-9, 4-22, 5-42, 6-52, 7-89, 8-90, 9-138 1-4, 2-42, 3-53, 4-128, 5-152, 6-162, 7-162, 8-178, 9-201

Middlesex won by 47 runs – Kent (3pts), Middlesex (17pts)

SURREY v. DERBYSHIRE – at Whitgift School

SURREY	First Innings		Second Innings	
*JN Batty	c Smith b Hayward	48	c Rogers b Jones	30
MJ Brown	c Madsen b Hayward	120	c Klokker b Wagg	56
MR Ramprakash	b Groenewald	80	not out	134
SJ Walters (capt)	lbw b Groenewald	28	c Rogers b Wagg	0
U Afzaal	c Hinds b Wagg	24	c Park b Wagg	85
MNW Spriegel	b Wagg	9		
CP Schofield	lbw b Groenewald	4	(6) not out	0
SJ King	b Groenewald	8		
JW Dernbach	c Rogers b Groenewald	2		
PT Collins	c Wagg b Groenewald	4		
A Nel	not out	1		
Extras	lb 12, nb 22	34	b 4, lb 7, w 2, nb 2	15
	(all out 108.1 overs)	362	(4 wkts dec 68 overs)	320

Bowling
Wagg 33.4-4-126-2. Hayward 18-5-44-2. Jones 17-2-73-0. Groenewald 24.1-5-50-6. Smith 8-0-27-0. Redfern 3-1-7-0. Hinds 4-0-18-0. Madsen 1-0-5-0.
Wagg 23-3-109-3. Groenewald 15-1-68-0. Hayward 9-0-51-0. Madsen 4-1-8-0. Jones 13-1-53-1. Smith 4-0-20-0.
Fall of Wickets: 1-113, 2-275, 3-275, 4-316, 5-336, 6-342, 7-342, 8-346, 9-350 1-63, 2-152, 3-152, 4-308

DERBYSHIRE	First Innings		Second Innings	
CJL Rogers (capt)	c Batty b Collins	80	c Batty b Nel	0
WL Madsen	lbw b Dernbach	1	not out	108
GT Park	c Walters b Collins	15	c Spriegel b King	5
GM Smith	c Batty b Nel	54	c Schofield b Collins	49
WW Hinds	c Schofield b Nel	5	c Brown b Afzaal	8
DJ Redfern	not out	55	lbw b Afzaal b Nel	13
*FA Klokker	b Dernbach	2	not out	32
GG Wagg	c Ramprakash b Collins	71		
TD Groenewald	b Nel	1		
PS Jones	c Batty b Nel	5		
M Hayward	b Dernbach	2		
Extras	b 4, lb 7, nb 32	43	b 2, lb 5, nb 10	17
	(all out 87.5 overs)	334	(5 wkts 78 overs)	232

Bowling
Nel 20.4-9-83-4. Dernbach 19.5-5-73-3. Collins 18-1-76-3. Walters 3-0-9-0. Schofield 15-2-50-0. Spriegel 8-0-32-0.
Nel 13-4-28-2. Collins 11-4-21-1. Schofield 22-4-80-0. King 17-2-61-1. Dernbach 11-4-25-0. Afzaal 2-0-9-1. Spriegel 2-1-1-0.
Fall of Wickets: 1-8, 2-47, 3-169, 4-178, 5-185, 6-209, 7-314, 8-315, 9-331 1-0, 2-30, 3-120, 4-153, 5-170

Match drawn – Surrey (11pts), Derbyshire (10pts)

At Whitgift School there was yet another masterclass from Mark Ramprakash, who scored 80 and 134 not out, from 150 balls and with three sixes and 11 fours, as Surrey had the best of their game with Derbyshire, for whom Wayne Madsen batted through 78 overs for his unbeaten 108 from 226 balls to ensure his side the draw.

Round Fifteen: 11–14 August

Lancashire held Durham to a draw at Old Trafford, where both Gary Keedy and Ian Blackwell impressed with their left-arm spin, and Nottinghamshire were also frustrated at Trent Bridge where Warwickshire were forced to follow on after Chris Read's 110 but survived as both Ian Bell and Jonathan Trott hit fine centuries.

But there were first division wins for Sussex and Yorkshire, with Chris Nash's 100 not out from 101 balls proving ultimately decisive at Hove where Matt Mason had earlier done an heroic job of single-handedly disguising Worcestershire's injury-ravaged fast bowling resources with a first innings haul of 7 for 60 from 30 overs.

The individual performance of this round, though, came at May's Bounty in Basingstoke where Adil Rashid underlined his immense all-round promise by first hitting an unbeaten 117, adding 192 for the eighth wicket with Ajmal Shahzad to earn Yorkshire a 274-run halfway lead, and then taking 5 for 41 with his leg-breaks as Hampshire were beaten by an innings and 22 runs. It was Yorkshire's first Championship win of the summer.

Essex, kept afloat earlier in the game by Matt Walker's

dedicated 150 from 340 balls, sped to a five-wicket victory on the last afternoon at Lord's when Middlesex gambled with an over-generous second innings declaration, and Kent were also second division winners when they overpowered Northamptonshire at Wantage Road.

Round Fifteen: 11–14 August Division One

LANCASHIRE v. DURHAM – at Old Trafford

DURHAM	First Innings		Second Innings	
MJ Di Venuto	c Hogg b Keedy	53	(2) c Horton b Keedy	84
MD Stoneman	lbw b Keedy	33	c du Plessis b Keedy	33
WR Smith (capt)	c Sutton b Parry	26	c Sutton b Laxman	1
GJ Muchall	lbw b Lungley	39	c Chilton b du Plessis	40
DM Benkenstein	c Horton b Keedy	16	run out	58
ID Blackwell	c Chilton b Parry	29	c Sutton b Parry	25
*P Mustard	c Chilton b Keedy	7	not out	50
LE Plunkett	c Parry b Keedy	28	not out	10
CD Thorp	c Chilton b Keedy	32		
G Onions	c Chilton b Lungley	0		
M Davies	not out	0		
Extras	b 2, lb 1, nb 4	7	b 9, lb 8, nb 2	19
	(all out 94.1 overs)	270	(6 wkts dec 104 overs)	320

Bowling
Hogg 14-5-40-0. Newby 13-0-55-0. Lungley 13-6-36-2. Keedy 36.1-8-85-6. Parry 18-1-51-2.
Hogg 3-2-4-0. Newby 5-0-23-0. Keedy 46-0-107-2. Parry 28-4-99-1. Laxman 7-3-13-1. Lungley 10-4-18-0. du Plessis 11-0-39-1.
Fall of Wickets: 1-87, 2-88, 3-149, 4-167, 5-187, 6-207, 7-213, 8-269, 9-270
1-60, 2-65, 3-153, 4-186, 5-235, 6-283

LANCASHIRE	First Innings		Second Innings	
PJ Horton	c Mustard b Thorp	0	c Benkenstein b Onions	3
SD Parry	lbw b Thorp	2	c Onions b Thorp	1
MB Loye	c Mustard b Blackwell	60	c Mustard b Onions	0
VVS Laxman	c Plunkett b Benkenstein	87	c Mustard b Onions	23
MJ Chilton	lbw b Blackwell	9	not out	79
F du Plessis	lbw b Blackwell	0	not out	54
*LD Sutton (capt)	lbw b Blackwell	0		
KW Hogg	lbw b Blackwell	42		
T Lungley	not out	27		
OJ Newby	lbw b Blackwell	0		
G Keedy	c Stoneman b Blackwell	17		
Extras	b 6, lb 12, nb 2	20	b 1, nb 2	3
	(all out 101.5 overs)	265	(4 wkts 59.1 overs)	163

Bowling
Onions 21-5-54-0. Thorp 17-2-40-2. Davies 6-2-21-0. Blackwell 38.5-10-85-7. Plunkett 9-1-30-0. Benkenstein 4-1-6-1. Smith 6-1-11-0.
Onions 10-4-39-3. Thorp 12-3-43-1. Blackwell 25-8-56-0. Plunkett 2.1-1-4-0. Davies 10-2-20-0.
Fall of Wickets: 1-1, 2-16, 3-101, 4-119, 5-119, 6-123, 7-207, 8-207, 9-213
1-4, 2-4, 3-4, 4-56

Match drawn – Lancashire (9pts), Durham (9pts)

SUSSEX v. WORCESTERSHIRE – at Hove

WORCS	First Innings		Second Innings	
DKH Mitchell	c Wright b Yasir Arafat	12	lbw b Martin-Jenkins	13
SC Moore	lbw b Martin-Jenkins	28	c Goodwin b Wright	18
VS Solanki (capt)	b Wright	19	lbw b Yasir Arafat	31
BF Smith	c Yardy b Yasir Arafat	32	lbw b Wright	5
MM Ali	b Collymore	22	b Yasir Arafat	3
*SM Davies	c Hodd b Wright	25	c Joyce b Rayner	67
GJ Batty	c Hodd b Wright	46	lbw b Collymore	22
GM Andrew	c Collymore b Wright	1		
MS Mason	c Hodd b Yasir Arafat	25	b Wright	28
Imran Arif	c Martin-Jenkins b Wright	27	b Rayner	35
M Ahmed	not out	0	not out	0
Extras	b 2, lb 10, nb 4	16	lb 4, nb 8	12
	(all out 82 overs)	256	(all out 57.2 overs)	235

Bowling
Yasir Arafat 22-4-83-3. Collymore 14-2-45-1. Martin-Jenkins 20-7-45-1. Wright 22-6-66-5. Rayner 4-2-5-0.
Yasir Arafat 19-1-98-3. Collymore 9-3-32-2. Martin-Jenkins 14-5-23-1. Wright 11-0-61-2. Rayner 4.2-0-17-2.
Fall of Wickets: 1-36, 2-50, 3-84, 4-121, 5-139, 6-154, 7-160, 8-204, 9-245
1-22, 2-48, 3-64, 4-71, 5-74, 6-108, 7-110, 8-155, 9-226

SUSSEX	First Innings		Second Innings	
MH Yardy (capt)	b Mason	29	c Solanki b Mason	6
CD Nash	c Davies b Mason	10	not out	100
EC Joyce	b Andrew	2	c Arif b Batty	53
OP Rayner	lbw b Mason	8		
MW Goodwin	c Smith b Mason	19	(4) not out	40
CD Hopkinson	c Solanki b Mason	19		
LJ Wright	c Mitchell b Mason	38		
*AJ Hodd	c Mitchell b Mason	73		
Yasir Arafat	c Davies b Batty	32		
RSC Martin-Jenkins	c Smith b Andrew	1		
CD Collymore	not out	4		
Extras	b 13, lb 10, w 2, nb 2	26	lb 5, w 2, nb 6	13
	(all out 85.1 overs)	280	(2 wkts 38.5 overs)	212

Bowling
Mason 30-9-60-7. Arif 12-1-60-0. Andrew 22.1-6-73-2. Ahmed 4-0-31-0. Batty 8-2-17-1. Mitchell 3-2-4-0.
Mason 4-1-17-1. Andrew 12.5-1-60-0. Arif 6-0-52-0. Batty 9-2-32-1. Ahmed 5-0-42-0. Ali 2-1-4-0.
Fall of Wickets: 1-17, 2-32, 3-51, 4-54, 5-91, 6-101, 7-170, 8-248, 9-266
1-10, 2-119

Sussex won by 8 wickets – Sussex (19pts), Worcestershire (5pts)

HAMPSHIRE v. YORKSHIRE – at Basingstoke

HAMPSHIRE	First Innings		Second Innings	
MA Carberry	c Bresnan b Shahzad	23	c Brophy b Shahzad	70
JHK Adams	b Kruis	79	b Bresnan	2
MJ Lumb	lbw b Bresnan	51	lbw b Bresnan	0
JM Vince	c Rudolph b Bresnan	18	lbw b Hoggard	43
LA Dawson	c Sayers b Kruis	1	c Sayers b Rashid	50
SM Ervine	c & b Hoggard	28	run out	48
AD Mascarenhas (capt)	c Brophy b Shahzad	14	c Brophy b Rashid	0
*TG Burrows	b Shahzad	16	not out	8
CT Tremlett	b Shahzad	0	c Brophy b Rashid	0
Imran Tahir	c Brophy b Bresnan	7	st Brophy b Rashid	0
DA Griffiths	not out	0	b Rashid	0
Extras	b 5, lb 2, w 2, nb 4	13	b 12, lb 8, w 1, nb 6	27
	(all out 90.1 overs)	250	(all out 79.5 overs)	252

Bowling
Bresnan 19.1-6-45-3. Hoggard 17-5-38-1. Shahzad 22-4-72-4. Kruis 19-4-51-2. McGrath 9-1-24-0. Rashid 4-1-13-0.
Hoggard 16-3-54-1. Bresnan 20-7-46-2. Shahzad 13-3-45-1. Kruis 10-1-39-0. Rashid 16.5-6-41-5. McGrath 4-2-7-0.
Fall of Wickets: 1-132, 2-119, 3-153, 4-154, 5-203, 6-220, 7-238, 8-238, 9-245
1-6, 2-10, 3-108, 4-137, 5-231, 6-231, 7-240, 8-240, 9-248

YORKSHIRE	First Innings	
JA Rudolph	c Ervine b Imran Tahir	90
JJ Sayers	c Dawson b Griffiths	50
A McGrath (capt)	c Burrows b Griffiths	0
AW Gale	c Dawson b Mascarenhas	13
JM Bairstow	lbw b Imran Tahir	13
*GL Brophy	c Carberry b Griffiths	53
TT Bresnan	run out	24
AU Rashid	not out	117
A Shahzad	c Adams b Tremlett	78
MJ Hoggard	c Mascarenhas b Tremlett	14
GJ Kruis	lbw b Imran Tahir	16
Extras	b 18, lb 16, w 3, nb 14	51
	(all out 165 overs)	524

Bowling
Mascarenhas 40-16-77-1. Tremlett 31-3-106-2. Ervine 27-10-67-0. Griffiths 32-5-117-3. Imran Tahir 33-7-116-3. Vince 2-0-7-0.
Fall of Wickets: 1-132, 2-134, 3-150, 4-173, 5-204, 6-262, 7-268, 8-460, 9-488

Yorkshire won by an innings and 22 runs –
Hampshire (4pts), Yorkshire (21pts)

NOTTINGHAMSHIRE v. WARWICKSHIRE – at Trent Bridge

NOTTS	First Innings		Second Innings	
SA Newman	lbw b Tahir	5	lbw b Rankin	0
MJ Wood	c Westwood b Tahir	14	not out	39
MA Wagh	b Tahir	10	not out	28
AC Voges	c Bell b Sreesanth	68		
SR Patel	lbw b Clarke	47		
AD Brown	c Clarke b Sreesanth	4		
*CMW Read (capt)	b Tahir	110		
MA Ealham	c Clarke b Sreesanth	37		
AR Adams	c Clarke b Rankin	32		
RJ Sidebottom	c Woakes b Clarke	4		
CE Shreck	not out	4		
Extras	b 4, lb 10, nb 35	49	nb 4	4
	(all out 84.1 overs)	388	(1 wkt dec 25 overs)	71

Bowling
Rankin 15-2-92-1. Tahir 20-1-89-4. Sreesanth 14-1-65-3. Woakes 16-0-76-0. Trott 4-0-7-0. Clarke 5.1-2-15-2. Botha 10-2-69-0.
Rankin 6-2-19-1. Tahir 5-2-16-0. Woakes 5-1-14-0. Sreesanth 4-1-7-0. Westwood 2-0-6-0. Botha 2-0-2-0. Clarke 1-0-7-0.
Fall of Wickets: 1-9, 2-32, 3-43, 4-141, 5-141, 6-224, 7-308, 8-366, 9-366
1-0

WARWICKSHIRE	First Innings		Second Innings	
IJ Westwood (capt)	c Adams b Shreck	12	c Voges b Ealham	11
AG Botha	c Adams b Shreck	19	c Patel b Adams	64
IR Bell	c Read b Sidebottom	9	lbw b Adams	126
IJ Trott	c Voges b Shreck	8	lbw b Sidebottom	121
JO Troughton	lbw b Sidebottom	9	(6) c Read b Adams	15
*TR Ambrose	c Read b Shreck	14	(7) not out	32
R Clarke	run out	67	(8) b Shreck	62
CR Woakes	b Adams	22	(9) not out	1
N Tahir	c Voges b Ealham	24	(5) c Read b Adams	22
S Sreesanth	not out	30		
WB Rankin	b Shreck	3		
Extras	lb 10, nb 6	16	b 4, lb 9, w 1, nb 2	16
	(all out 75.3 overs)	219	(7 wkts 144 overs)	470

Bowling
Sidebottom 20-7-37-3. Shreck 21.3-7-63-4. Adams 14-2-47-1. Ealham 13-3-41-1. Patel 6-0-19-0.
Sidebottom 28-6-97-1. Shreck 31-9-109-1. Adams 30-10-86-4. Ealham 26-16-46-1. Patel 23-3-97-0. Voges 6-0-22-0.
Fall of Wickets: 1-35, 2-36, 3-36, 4-48, 5-64, 6-66, 7-94, 8-163, 9-202
1-53, 2-101, 3-289, 4-334, 5-355, 6-370, 7-465

Match drawn – Nottinghamshire (11pts), Warwickshire (8pts)

The Warwickshire slip cordon waits expectantly for the next edge.

off spinner Jigar Naik dug Leicestershire out of a deep hole against Derbyshire and, eventually, enabled them to escape with a draw. Taylor scored 94 but Naik went on to complete a deserved maiden first-class hundred, following their 195-run stand for the eighth wicket. For Derbyshire, skipper Chris Rogers made 163 from 309 balls, with a six and 13 fours after Steffan Jones had fired the first significant shots of the game by picking up a first innings 4 for 43 as Leicestershire struggled to 177.

Round Sixteen: 19–23 August

A weakened Warwickshire were no match for Durham at the Riverside, with the champions recording their seventh win of the campaign to all but secure a successive Championship title. Callum Thorp's first day 5 for 49 undermined the Warwickshire first innings, while there was also a handy all-round contribution from Dale Benkenstein. Only Jim Troughton, with a second innings 111, threatened to deny Durham, although 17-year-old Birmingham schoolboy Ateeq Javid battled bravely for a two-hour 21.

Rob Key, Geraint Jones and Martin van Jaarsveld all made important runs for Kent, but it was the off spin of James Tredwell, who took five wickets in each innings and 10 for 100 in the match, which hastened Northants to a hefty 238-run loss as they subsided to 90 all out second time around.

At Grace Road, meanwhile, the sheer determination of 19-year-old James Taylor and 25-year-old Leicester-born

Round Fifteen: 11–14 August Division Two

MIDDLESEX v. ESSEX – at Lord's

MIDDLESEX	First Innings		Second Innings	
SD Robson	lbw b Palladino	110	c Cook b Danish Kaneria	12
NRD Compton	c Bopara b Napier	16	lbw b Danish Kaneria	13
OA Shah	lbw b Napier	8	lbw b Masters	10
EJG Morgan (capt)	c Foster b Napier	4	lbw b Danish Kaneria	8
DJ Malan	c Cook b Danish Kaneria	73	(6) not out	87
*BJM Scott	lbw b Danish Kaneria	0	(7) lbw b Danish Kaneria	44
GK Berg	lbw b ten Doeschate	66	(8) st Foster b Cook	29
M Kartik	c Foster b ten Doeschate	22	(9) not out	5
TJ Murtagh	lbw b Danish Kaneria	20		
ST Finn	st Foster b Danish Kaneria	7	(5) c Walker b Danish Kaneria	9
A Richardson	not out	3		
Extras	b 4, lb 17, w 2, nb 4	27	b 2, lb 4, nb 6	12
	(all out 118.5 overs)	356	(7 wkts dec 69.5 overs)	229

Bowling
Masters 27-9-61-0. Palladino 18-3-64-1. Napier 23-8-63-3. ten Doeschate 22-6-51-2. Danish Kaneria 23.5-2-74-4. Bopara 5-2-22-0.
Masters 16-4-39-1. Napier 11-3-26-0. Danish Kaneria 26-6-76-5. Palladino 8-2-28-0. ten Doeschate 6-1-21-0. Bopara 1-0-6-0. Cook 1-0-3-1. Pettini 0.5-0-24-0.
Fall of Wickets: 1-26, 2-44, 3-64, 4-207, 5-207, 6-262, 7-307, 8-340, 9-340 1-22, 2-31, 3-43, 4-55, 5-59, 6-157, 7-205

ESSEX	First Innings		Second Innings	
JK Maunders	c Morgan b Murtagh	23		
AN Cook	lbw b Murtagh	4	b Kartik	66
RS Bopara	c Kartik b Murtagh	1	not out	52
MJ Walker	c Compton b Kartik	150	c Compton b Kartik	12
ML Pettini (capt)	lbw b Murtagh	4	(1) c Scott b Murtagh	37
*JS Foster	run out	72	c Berg b Richardson	10
RN ten Doeschate	lbw b Murtagh	18	(5) b Kartik	40
GR Napier	lbw b Murtagh	3	(7) not out	13
DD Masters	not out	35		
AP Palladino	c Malan b Kartik	0		
Danish Kaneria	st Scott b Kartik	7		
Extras	b 10, lb 10, w 1, nb 10	31	lb 7, w 2, nb 2	11
	(all out 114.4 overs)	345	(5 wkts 43 overs)	241

Bowling
Murtagh 29-11-84-6. Finn 24-6-69-0. Richardson 19-2-71-0. Berg 16-4-46-0. Kartik 26.4-11-55-3.
Murtagh 14-0-71-1. Finn 4-0-31-0. Kartik 18-4-84-3. Richardson 7-0-48-1.
Fall of Wickets: 1-9, 2-15, 3-30, 4-32, 5-195, 6-244, 7-256, 8-333, 9-333 1-100, 2-108, 3-136, 4-212, 5-227

Essex won by 5 wickets – Middlesex (7pts), Essex (20pts)

NORTHAMPTONSHIRE v. KENT – at Northampton

KENT	First Innings		Second Innings	
JL Denly	c White b Lucas	15	c White b Boje	59
RWT Key (capt)	lbw b Hall	90	c Wessels b Lucas	15
*GO Jones	c Lucas b Wigley	11	b Boje	93
M van Jaarsveld	c Wakely b Panesar	19	not out	100
SA Northeast	lbw b van der Wath	35	c & b Boje	3
DI Stevens	b van der Wath	20	c Wigley b Boje	1
JM Kemp	lbw b Hall	12	not out	18
JC Tredwell	c Wakely b Boje	10		
SJ Cook	c Wessels b Panesar	6		
RS Ferley	c O'Brien b van der Wath	17		
P Edwards	not out	0		
Extras	b 4, w 1, nb 4	9	lb 5, w 2, nb 6	13
	(all out 80.4 overs)	244	(5 wkts dec 88.4 overs)	302

Bowling
van der Wath 12.4-2-32-3. Lucas 13-2-47-1. Wigley 10-3-31-1. Panesar 22-6-56-2. Boje 11-1-53-1. Hall 12-5-21-2.
van der Wath 16-5-43-0. Lucas 7-2-42-1. Panesar 21.4-1-71-0. Hall 12-5-24-0. Boje 20-2-59-4. Wigley 11-1-52-0. Wakely 1-0-6-0.
Fall of Wickets: 1-24, 2-63, 3-100, 4-170, 5-196, 6-197, 7-212, 8-219, 9-239 1-32, 2-117, 3-237, 4-251, 5-255

NORTHANTS	First Innings		Second Innings	
SD Peters	c Jones b Cook	8	lbw b Cook	1
*NJ O'Brien	c Kemp b Edwards	16	c & b Ferley	41
RA White	c Kemp b Edwards	21	c Tredwell b Cook	11
AG Wakely	c Key b Tredwell	33	lbw b Tredwell	4
MH Wessels	c Jones b Tredwell	74	c Stevens b Tredwell	4
N Boje (capt)	b Ferley	9	lbw b Ferley	6
AJ Hall	c Northeast b Tredwell	19	lbw b Tredwell	2
JJ van der Wath	c Northeast b Tredwell	2	c Jones b Tredwell	7
MS Panesar	lbw b Cook	2	c van Jaarsveld b Tredwell	7
DS Lucas	c Northeast b Tredwell	13	not out	2
DH Wigley	not out	8	c Jones b van Jaarsveld	0
Extras	b 4, lb 7, nb 2	13	b 2, lb 3	5
	(all out 73.4 overs)	218	(all out 46.1 overs)	90

Bowling
Cook 21-2-63-2. Edwards 12-3-26-2. Tredwell 24.4-3-68-5. Ferley 9-0-29-1. Kemp 7-0-21-0.
Cook 8-3-18-2. Edwards 2-0-6-0. Tredwell 20-10-32-5. Ferley 15-4-28-2. van Jaarsveld 1.1-0-1-1.
Fall of Wickets: 1-16, 2-53, 3-56, 4-115, 5-138, 6-169, 7-171, 8-180, 9-205 1-6, 2-38, 3-45, 4-51, 5-71, 6-74, 7-74, 8-87, 9-90

Kent won by 238 runs – Northamptonshire (4pts), Kent (18pts)

LEICESTERSHIRE v. DERBYSHIRE – at Grace Road

LEICESTERSHIRE	First Innings		Second Innings	
GP Smith	c Park b Groenewald	20	c sub b Jones	0
MAG Boyce	c Pipe b Jones	0	c Pipe b Jones	80
HH Dippenaar (capt)	c Pipe b Jones	0	c Park b Redfern	37
HD Ackerman	c Rogers b Smith	17	c Smith b Groenewald	29
JWA Taylor	lbw b Lawson	45	b Smith	94
*TJ New	c Park b Smith	17	c Pipe b Lawson	19
WA White	c sub b Smith	1	run out	4
CW Henderson	lbw b Lawson	16	c Pipe b Park	9
JHK Naik	b Jones	5	not out	109
NL Buck	not out	24	not out	5
AJ Harris	c Groenewald b Jones	7		
Extras	b 1, lb 10, w 4, nb 10	25	b 8, lb 13, w 1, nb 16, p 5	43
	(all out 68.1 overs)	177	(8 wkts 137 overs)	429

Bowling
Wagg 12.1-1-36-0. Jones 19.1-5-43-4. Smith 12-2-31-3. Groenewald 13.5-5-34-1. Lawson 10-4-20-2. Madsen 1-0-2-0.
Jones 34-8-92-2. Groenewald 30-6-97-1. Park 10-1-32-1. Smith 26-8-72-1. Lawson 28-5-78-1. Redfern 7-1-31-1. Madsen 2-1-1-0.
Fall of Wickets: 1-9, 2-9, 3-36, 4-63, 5-100, 6-107, 7-128, 8-145, 9-147 1-0, 2-107, 3-162, 4-162, 5-198, 6-209, 7-224, 8-419

DERBYSHIRE	First Innings	
CJL Rogers (capt)	c Taylor b White	163
WL Madsen	lbw b Henderson	19
GT Park	b Naik	41
GM Smith	b Harris	95
WW Hinds	c White b Naik	40
DJ Redfern	c New b White	19
*DJ Pipe	not out	32
TD Groenewald	lbw b Henderson	0
PS Jones	c Boyce b Henderson	19
MAK Lawson	not out	14
GG Wagg		
Extras	lb 5, w 9, nb 22	36
	(8 wkts dec 130 overs)	478

Bowling
Harris 24-4-78-1. Buck 21-4-87-0. White 20-2-89-2. Henderson 36-6-93-3. Naik 29-0-126-2.
Fall of Wickets: 1-49, 2-132, 3-321, 4-352, 5-399, 6-414, 7-414, 8-450

Match drawn – Leicestershire (6pts), Derbyshire (12pts)

The rest of the first division fixtures were all drawn, with Somerset's run glut with Sussex producing statistical interest if nothing else. On an even friendlier Taunton featherbed than usual, Sussex amassed 742 for 5 declared with Murray Goodwin beating his own record for the county's highest individual score with a career-best 344 not out from 351 balls, with six sixes and 43 fours.

Goodwin was joined by Carl Hopkinson in a county record fourth wicket stand of 363 and, like Hopkinson, Chris Nash also made a big hundred. It was Goodwin's seventh score of 200-plus for Sussex and the sixth highest in Championship history. Sussex's total, meanwhile, was their biggest in first-class cricket.

Somerset, in turn, then replied with 521 for 6, with centuries for Arul Suppiah and Craig Kieswetter, and three other half-centuries, but as a contest the game was meaningless.

At Trent Bridge there was another huge total put together, this time by Hampshire, with Michael Lumb hitting 37 fours in his 219 and Sean Ervine also reaching three figures as the visitors ran up 654 for 8 declared. Chris Read's 119 not out, and some stout lower-order resistance, hauled Nottinghamshire above 400 and, although they had to follow on, Mark Wagh guided them to safety with an unbeaten 136.

In the drawn Roses encounter at Headingley, meanwhile, 21-year-old Adil Rashid became the first Yorkshire player in history to score a hundred and take five wickets in consecutive first-class matches. Despite

Rashid's career-best 157 not out though, scored off 240 balls and including 12 fours, and his first innings 5 for 97, Lancashire survived for a draw thanks to the batting of Mark Chilton, Mal Loye and VVS Laxman and some helpful weather interruptions.

Round Sixteen: 19–23 August Division One

DURHAM v. WARWICKSHIRE – at the Riverside

WARWICKSHIRE	First Innings		Second Innings	
IJ Westwood (capt)	lbw b Thorp	5	c Plunkett b Claydon	2
AG Botha	c Stoneman b Benkenstein	23	c Mustard b Thorp	14
JO Troughton	lbw b Thorp	14	c Di Venuto b Blackwell	111
T Frost	c Mustard b Benkenstein	19	c Thorp b Claydon	4
*TR Ambrose	c Mustard b Benkenstein	0	c Di Venuto b Blackwell	39
R Clarke	lbw b Thorp	32	c Thorp b Blackwell	13
Ateeq Javid	lbw b Thorp	8	c Mustard b Davies	21
CR Woakes	c Mustard b Claydon	0	lbw b Davies	13
N Tahir	c Thorp b Plunkett	10	c Blackwell b Davies	1
S Sreesanth	c Blackwell b Thorp	5	c Chanderpaul b Claydon	4
WB Rankin	not out	2	not out	0
Extras	b 1, lb 5, w 1, nb 10	17	lb 2, w 4, nb 10	16
	(all out 55.1 overs)	135	(all out 93.4 overs)	238

Bowling
Claydon 15-8-25-1. Davies 2-1-1-0. Thorp 20.1-5-49-5. Plunkett 10-3-34-1. Benkenstein 8-2-20-3.
Claydon 21-4-75-3. Davies 14.4-6-19-3. Thorp 20-11-31-1. Plunkett 15-4-67-0. Blackwell 23-9-44-3.
Fall of Wickets: 1-11, 2-41, 3-70, 4-70, 5-71, 6-101, 7-103, 8-123, 9-127
1-4, 2-29, 3-34, 4-116, 5-150, 6-201, 7-228, 8-231, 9-238

DURHAM	First Innings		Second Innings	
MJ Di Venuto	c Ambrose b Tahir	40	(2) not out	41
MD Stoneman	c Ambrose b Woakes	3	(1) c Ambrose b Tahir	5
WR Smith (capt)	c Westwood b Rankin	16	c sub b Woakes	11
DM Benkenstein	c Clarke b Rankin	73		
S Chanderpaul	c Javid b Rankin	0	(4) not out	41
ID Blackwell	c Ambrose b Tahir	53		
*P Mustard	c Troughton b Rankin	25		
LE Plunkett	not out	31		
CD Thorp	b Rankin	0		
ME Claydon	c Sreesanth b Woakes	10		
M Davies	c Ambrose b Sreesanth	8		
Extras	b 6, lb 2, nb 6	14	nb 8	8
	(all out 72.1 overs)	273	(2 wkts 20.3 overs)	106

Bowling
Rankin 21-1-85-5. Tahir 21.5-7-2. Woakes 17-3-72-2. Sreesanth 10.1-1-35-1. Clarke 3-0-16-0.
Tahir 4-0-16-1. Sreesanth 6-0-27-0. Woakes 6-1-30-1. Clarke 2-0-21-0. Botha 2.3-0-12-0.
Fall of Wickets: 1-43, 2-43, 3-87, 4-97, 5-182, 6-202, 7-233, 8-233, 9-254
1-18, 2-38

Durham won by 8 wickets – Durham (19pts), Warwickshire (3pts)

SOMERSET v. SUSSEX – at Taunton

SUSSEX	First Innings	
MH Yardy (capt)	c Kieswetter b Willoughby	15
CD Nash	c Suppiah b Thomas	157
EC Joyce	lbw b Trego	37
MW Goodwin	not out	344
CD Hopkinson	b Suppiah	139
DR Smith	b Suppiah	4
*AJ Hodd	not out	18
RSC Martin-Jenkins		
OP Rayner		
Yasir Arafat		
CD Collymore		
Extras	b 12, lb 5, w 3, nb 8	28
	(5 wkts dec 164 overs)	742

Bowling
Willoughby 28-8-96-1. Thomas 27-4-97-1. Banks 21-3-114-0. Suppiah 19-1-117-2. Trego 18-3-71-1. de Bruyn 18-0-83-0. Waller 33-1-147-0.
Fall of Wickets: 1-44, 2-142, 3-313, 4-676, 5-680

SOMERSET	First Innings	
ME Trescothick	c Joyce b Smith	73
AV Suppiah	lbw b Rayner	133
JC Hildreth	c Hodd b Smith	11
Z de Bruyn	c Goodwin b Rayner	3
*C Kieswetter	not out	135
PD Trego	c Hopkinson b Rayner	67
OAC Banks	lbw b Rayner	53
MTC Waller	not out	3
JL Langer (capt)		
AC Thomas		
CM Willoughby		
Extras	b 12, lb 12, w 7, nb 12	43
	(6 wkts 133 overs)	521

Bowling
Yasir Arafat 22-4-98-0. Collymore 6-2-20-0. Rayner 52-7-186-4. Martin-Jenkins 6-2-19-0. Smith 36-15-91-2. Nash 3-0-6-0. Yardy 6-0-64-0. Goodwin 2-0-13-0.
Fall of Wickets: 1-169, 2-192, 3-203, 4-280, 5-411, 6-511

Match drawn – Somerset (10pts), Sussex (10pts)

NOTTINGHAMSHIRE v. HAMPSHIRE – at Trent Bridge

HAMPSHIRE	First Innings	
MA Carberry	retired hurt	86
JHK Adams	b Adams	55
MJ Lumb	c Read b Patel	219
JM Vince	c Newman b Patel	27
LA Dawson	lbw b Adams	43
*TG Burrows	c Shafayat b Shreck	20
SM Ervine	c Newman b Shafayat	104
AD Mascarenhas (capt)	not out	48
DG Cork	lbw b Patel	0
Imran Tahir	lbw b Patel	0
DA Griffiths	not out	20
Extras	b 7, lb 7, nb 18	32
	(8 wkts dec 161 overs)	654

Bowling
Shreck 27-5-115-1. Pattinson 22-1-144-0. Adams 35-7-108-2. Patel 48-6-199-4. Ealham 21-6-42-0. Shafayat 8-1-32-1.
Fall of Wickets: 1-146, 2-226, 3-331, 4-366, 5-574, 6-598, 7-599, 8-612

NOTTS	First Innings		Second Innings (following on)	
SA Newman	c Burrows b Cork	25	c Burrows b Griffiths	0
MJ Wood	c Adams b Griffiths	10	lbw b Mascarenhas	17
MA Wagh	lbw b Imran Tahir	8	not out	136
DJ Pattinson	lbw b Imran Tahir	0		
SR Patel	lbw b Ervine	35	(4) c Lumb b Imran Tahir	48
BM Shafayat	c Burrows b Griffiths	69	(5) b Imran Tahir	6
AD Brown	lbw b Imran Tahir	39	(6) not out	37
*CMW Read (capt)	not out	119		
MA Ealham	c Adams b Griffiths	32		
AR Adams	c Lumb b Imran Tahir	46		
CE Shreck	b Griffiths	2		
Extras	b 1, lb 10, w 1, nb 10	22	b 12, lb 6, nb 4, p 5	27
	(all out 114.1 overs)	407	(4 wkts 79 overs)	271

Bowling
Griffiths 28.1-4-144-4. Mascarenhas 18-6-42-0. Imran Tahir 36-7-106-4. Cork 17-3-48-1. Ervine 10-1-41-1. Dawson 5-0-15-0.
Griffiths 16-2-51-1. Mascarenhas 10-2-43-1. Cork 1-0-40-0. Imran Tahir 29-6-79-2. Ervine 14-5-35-0.
Fall of Wickets: 1-29, 2-46, 3-46, 4-48, 5-126, 6-183, 7-228, 8-297, 9-394
1-0, 2-48, 3-158, 4-183

Match drawn – Nottinghamshire (10pts), Hampshire (12pts)

YORKSHIRE v. LANCASHIRE – at Headingley

LANCASHIRE	First Innings		Second Innings	
PJ Horton	c Bairstow b Hoggard	2	(2) c Brophy b Rashid	28
SJ Croft	c Brophy b Bresnan	0	(1) c Brophy b Bresnan	15
MB Loye	c Bresnan b Rashid	24	not out	84
VVS Laxman	c Hoggard b Rashid	50	not out	65
MJ Chilton	not out	111		
F du Plessis	lbw b Wainwright	32		
*LD Sutton (capt)	c Brophy b Bresnan	4		
KW Hogg	c sub b Rashid	29		
T Lungley	c Bairstow b Bresnan	10		
OJ Newby	b Rashid	2		
G Keedy	c Sayers b Rashid	4		
Extras	b 3, lb 3, nb 2	8	lb 3, w 1	4
	(all out 122.2 overs)	276	(2 wkts 72 overs)	196

Bowling
Hoggard 18-7-40-1. Bresnan 31-13-46-3. Shahzad 18-7-48-0. Rashid 34.2-7-97-5. Wainwright 21-5-39-1.
Hoggard 10-2-24-0. Bresnan 11-2-30-1. Rashid 24-5-55-1. Wainwright 19-3-67-0. Shahzad 5-3-13-0. Sayers 3-0-4-0.
Fall of Wickets: 1-2, 2-3, 3-65, 4-92, 5-144, 6-159, 7-213, 8-241, 9-252
1-23, 2-65

YORKSHIRE	First Innings	
JA Rudolph	c du Plessis b Hogg	3
JJ Sayers	lbw b Lungley	17
A McGrath (capt)	c Croft b Lungley	17
AW Gale	c &t b Lungley	6
JM Bairstow	c &t b Newby	15
*GL Brophy	c Sutton b Keedy	99
TT Bresnan	c Lungley b Newby	46
AU Rashid	not out	157
A Shahzad	c Loye b du Plessis	32
DJ Wainwright	st Sutton b Keedy	1
MJ Hoggard	c Horton b Keedy	8
Extras	b 5, lb 6, nb 20	31
	(all out 141.2 overs)	429

Bowling
Hogg 33-10-75-1. Newby 24-4-102-2. Lungley 23-2-85-3. Keedy 46.2-11-104-3. Croft 2-0-12-0. du Plessis 11-1-33-1. Laxman 2-0-7-0.
Fall of Wickets: 1-0, 2-27, 3-35, 4-68, 5-72, 6-144, 7-312, 8-412, 9-413

Match drawn – Yorkshire (11pts), Lancashire (8pts)

All four Division Two matches produced positive results, with three exciting finishes to boot. Perhaps the best game was at Chesterfield where Northamptonshire finally emerged from a splendidly tight affair when, from 168 for 7 in their second innings, young David Willey made 42 to

give them hope of a victory against the odds and then the ninth wicket pair of Graeme White and David Lucas added an unbroken 37 to leave Derbyshire shattered.

Yet there was excitement aplenty at Swansea, too, with Glamorgan edging by 22 runs a low-scoring but totally absorbing match against Middlesex, for whom Shaun Udal took ten wickets in the game with his evergreen off spin, including a second innings 6 for 36 which left his team with a tantalising victory target of 190. But it was another veteran off spinner, Robert Croft, who had the last laugh with 5 for 65 and nine wickets of his own overall. Dean Cosker also enjoyed the conditions with six wickets in the match, while a third spinner, Jamie Dalrymple, took perhaps the most important scalp in the Middlesex second innings when he dismissed Owais Shah.

Leicestershire, meanwhile, hung on grimly in the field to grab the victory against Gloucestershire, by 44 runs, which James Taylor's first innings 83 not out, Josh Cobb's fluent 72 and superb swing bowling from Andrew Harris, who took 5 for 26 to wreck the visitors' first innings, had deserved. James Franklin, however, with an unbeaten five-hour 97, led a gallant Gloucestershire fourth innings chase that had the home side sweating.

Ravi Bopara, axed from England's Ashes squad, responded with a magnificent 201 – scored from 293 balls with two sixes and 20 fours – as Essex defeated Surrey by nine wickets at Colchester. Chris Schofield had rallied Surrey from 136 for 5 on the opening day, but Bopara's effort ultimately earned Essex a decisive 117-run lead and Danish Kaneria did the rest with 6 for 50 on a pitch now

Round Sixteen: 19–23 August Division Two

DERBYSHIRE v. NORTHAMPTONSHIRE – at Chesterfield

DERBYSHIRE	First Innings		Second Innings	
CJL Rogers (capt)	lbw b Brooks	27	b Lucas	14
WL Madsen	c White RA b van der Wath	4	c White RA b van der Wath	2
GT Park	c Peters b Brooks	55	c O'Brien b van der Wath	3
GM Smith	c Wessels b Hall	4	c O'Brien b Lucas	19
WW Hinds	b van der Wath	10	c Brooks b Hall	36
DJ Redfern	c O'Brien b van der Wath	4	c Hall b Willey	28
*DJ Pipe	b Lucas	58	c & b van der Wath	10
TD Groenewald	c O'Brien b Brooks	0	b van der Wath	50
PS Jones	b Brooks	22	c Hall b Brooks	27
MAK Lawson	c van der Wath b Lucas	16	b Lucas	21
M Hayward	not out	4	not out	2
Extras	b 1, lb 2, w 1, nb 12	14	b 4, lb 3, w 2, nb 12	21
	(all out 58.3 overs)	255	(all out 62.4 overs)	233

Bowling
van der Wath 19-3-92-3. Lucas 13.3-3-56-2. Brooks 16-1-76-4. Willey 2-0-17-0. Hall 8-2-11-1.
van der Wath 16.4-2-55-4. Lucas 17-3-65-3. Brooks 10-0-38-1. Hall 11-3-34-1. Willey 4-0-21-1. White GG 4-0-13-0.
Fall of Wickets: 1-47, 2-57, 3-108, 4-129, 5-133, 6-179, 7-193, 8-229, 9-233
1-6, 2-14, 3-36, 4-53, 5-84, 6-102, 7-140, 8-203, 9-227

NORTHANTS	First Innings		Second Innings	
SD Peters	lbw b Groenewald	39	c Pipe b Hinds	13
*NJ O'Brien	c Pipe b Groenewald	15	c Pipe b Jones	13
RA White	lbw b Hinds	62	c Pipe b Groenewald	37
DS Lucas	c Pipe b Smith	14	(10) not out	19
AG Wakely	c Pipe b Hinds	26	(4) b Jones	33
MH Wessels	c Rogers b Smith	3	(5) c Park b Jones	31
AJ Hall (capt)	c Rogers b Groenewald	36	(6) c Rogers b Hayward	20
DJ Willey	c Hinds b Groenewald	12	(7) c Rogers b Jones	42
JJ van der Wath	c Redfern b Groenewald	2	(8) c Rogers b Hayward	0
GG White	b Groenewald	0	(9) not out	29
JA Brooks	not out	0		
Extras	b 9, lb 12, nb 16	37	lb 5, w 1, nb 2	8
	(all out 67.1 overs)	246	(8 wkts 61.2 overs)	245

Bowling
Jones 15-4-51-0. Hayward 15-2-52-0. Groenewald 19.1-6-61-6. Smith 9-1-42-2. Hinds 9-2-19-2.
Jones 22-2-79-4. Hayward 9.2-0-66-2. Hinds 12-1-38-1. Groenewald 14-1-46-1. Smith 4-2-11-0.
Fall of Wickets: 1-42, 2-131, 3-135, 4-164, 5-170, 6-224, 7-232, 8-245, 9-245
1-21, 2-61, 3-83, 4-130, 5-137, 6-168, 7-168, 8-208

Northamptonshire won by 2 wickets –
Derbyshire (5pts), Northamptonshire (18pts)

GLAMORGAN v. MIDDLESEX – at Swansea

GLAMORGAN	First Innings		Second Innings	
GP Rees	c Scott b Finn	40	c Scott b Murtagh	26
WD Bragg	c Shah b Berg	28	c Robson b Finn	15
HH Gibbs	c Robson b Udal	8	c Robson b Kartik	20
MJ Powell	c Robson b Udal	29	c Morgan b Udal	8
JWM Dalrymple (capt)	c Malan b Kartik	40	lbw b Kartik	9
J Allenby	c Kartik b Finn	7	c Robson b Udal	1
*MA Wallace	c Finn b Berg	6	c Compton b Udal	4
JAR Harris	st Scott b Kartik	7	c Robson b Udal	4
RDB Croft	lbw b Udal	21	lbw b Udal	21
AJ Shantry	not out	1	c Berg b Udal	11
DA Cosker	c Robson b Udal	1	not out	0
Extras	b 10, lb 6, nb 10	26	b 3, lb 1	4
	(all out 86.5 overs)	224	(all out 42.2 overs)	135

Bowling
Murtagh 13-3-26-0. Finn 17-2-51-3. Berg 10-3-36-1. Udal 26.5-4-59-4. Kartik 20-9-36-2.
Murtagh 8-1-36-1. Finn 5-0-32-1. Kartik 16-8-27-2. Udal 13.2-2-36-6.
Fall of Wickets: 1-34, 2-45, 3-109, 4-113, 5-121, 6-139, 7-163, 8-194, 9-220
1-26, 2-58, 3-70, 4-71, 5-73, 6-73, 7-82, 8-82, 9-116

MIDDLESEX	First Innings		Second Innings	
SD Robson	c Gibbs b Cosker	49	(3) c Dalrymple b Cosker	3
NRD Compton	lbw b Shantry	7	(1) c Wallace b Croft	13
OA Shah	lbw b Allenby	11	(4) c Bragg b Dalrymple	18
EJG Morgan	c Wallace b Cosker	16	(5) lbw b Croft	17
DJ Malan	c Gibbs b Croft	11	(2) c Gibbs b Croft	47
*BJM Scott	b Croft	2	lbw b Cosker	18
GK Berg	lbw b Cosker	19	b Croft	6
M Kartik	run out	4	run out	13
SD Udal (capt)	not out	34	not out	4
TJ Murtagh	b Croft	14	c Wallace b Croft	7
ST Finn	lbw b Croft	1	lbw b Cosker	1
Extras	lb 2	2	b 4, lb 2	6
	(all out 82.4 overs)	170	(all out 54.2 overs)	167

Bowling
Harris 4-4-35-0. Shantry 8-1-22-1. Allenby 7-4-8-1. Croft 25.4-7-47-4. Cosker 21-1-54-3. Dalrymple 3-2-2-0.
Harris 8-1-26-0. Croft 22-3-65-5. Cosker 15.2-1-35-3. Dalrymple 9-0-35-1.
Fall of Wickets: 1-14, 2-49, 3-80, 4-89, 5-92, 6-109, 7-121, 8-123, 9-168
1-27, 2-38, 3-77, 4-98, 5-99, 6-125, 7-129, 8-149, 9-158

Glamorgan won by 22 runs – Glamorgan (18pts),
Middlesex (3pts)

LEICESTERSHIRE v. GLOUCESTERSHIRE – at Grace Road

LEICESTERSHIRE	First Innings		Second Innings	
PA Nixon	c Dawson b Franklin	57	b Kirby	0
GP Smith	lbw b Kirby	32	c Adshead b Kirby	1
HH Dippenaar (capt)	lbw b Lewis	7	b Saxelby	12
JJ Cobb	c Gidman b Dawson	72	b Marshall	11
JWA Taylor	not out	83	lbw b Saxelby	24
*TJ New	c Adshead b Dawson	0	lbw b Marshall	0
JGE Benning	b Kirby	37	c Taylor b Marshall	25
WA White	b Kirby	23	c Franklin b Saxelby	9
JHK Naik	lbw b Lewis	4	not out	21
CW Henderson	c Marshall b Kirby	34	c Woodman b Marshall	3
AJ Harris	b Lewis	2	lbw b Lewis	18
Extras	lb 2, w 6, nb 4	17	lb 10, lb 3, nb 2	15
	(all out 103.4 overs)	368	(all out 55.3 overs)	133

Bowling
Lewis 18.4-3-68-3. Franklin 19-7-62-1. Saxelby 16-1-41-0. Kirby 21-6-78-4. Gidman 1-0-9-0. Dawson 20-0-82-2. Taylor 7-1-21-0.
Kirby 14-4-48-2. Lewis 8.3-3-10-1. Saxelby 15-4-31-3. Dawson 1-0-7-0. Marshall 17-6-24-4.
Fall of Wickets: 1-51, 2-72, 3-175, 4-179, 5-182, 6-228, 7-281, 8-292, 9-366
1-1, 2-14, 3-14, 4-33, 5-33, 6-77, 7-82, 8-82, 9-95

GLOS	First Innings		Second Innings	
Kadeer Ali	b Harris	13	(2) b Henderson	48
RJ Woodman	c New b White	31	(1) lbw b Harris	5
HJH Marshall	lbw b Harris	0	lbw b Harris	36
APR Gidman (capt)	lbw b Harris	0	lbw b Harris	11
CG Taylor	b Naik	50	run out	19
JEC Franklin	lbw b Henderson	12	not out	97
*SJ Adshead	lbw b Harris	0	b White	18
RKJ Dawson	c & b White	14	lbw b Benning	49
ID Saxelby	b Harris	0	lbw b Henderson	17
J Lewis	run out	0	c Smith b Naik	1
SP Kirby	not out	13	b Naik	0
Extras	lb 2, w 1, nb 2	5	lb 8, lb 9, w 2	19
	(all out 50.1 overs)	138	(all out 134 overs)	319

Bowling
Harris 12-4-26-5. Henderson 19-4-48-1. White 8.1-0-28-2. Benning 9-2-26-0. Naik 9-0-30-1.
Harris 22-4-65-2. Benning 23-6-50-1. Henderson 43-6-106-2. White 22-4-49-2. Naik 24-10-32-2.
Fall of Wickets: 1-18, 2-26, 3-26, 4-77, 5-111, 6-111, 7-112, 8-112, 9-117
1-18, 2-76, 3-96, 4-122, 5-122, 6-169, 7-267, 8-301, 9-304

Leicestershire won by 44 runs –
Leicestershire (21pts), Gloucestershire (3pts)

ESSEX v. SURREY – at Colchester

SURREY	First Innings		Second Innings	
*JN Batty	c Pettini b Danish Kaneria	23	lbw b Danish Kaneria	0
MJ Brown	c Foster b Wright	0	c Westley b Wright	37
MR Ramprakash	c Foster b Masters	33	(4) c Foster b Danish Kaneria	62
SJ Walters (capt)	c Foster b Wright	41	(5) c Danish Kaneria b Phillips	6
U Afzaal	c Pettini b Danish Kaneria	17	(6) c ten Doeschate b Phillips	6
MNW Spiegel	c Westley b Phillips	61	(7) c Walker b Danish Kaneria	6
CP Schofield	c Foster b ten Doeschate	144	(8) lbw b Danish Kaneria	23
SC Meaker	c Pettini b Danish Kaneria	72	(9) c Maunders b Danish Kaneria	23
JW Dernbach	c Pettini b ten Doeschate	10	(10) c Bopara b Phillips	2
TE Linley	run out	4	(3) c Maunders b Danish Kaneria	0
PT Collins	not out	0	not out	1
Extras	b 4, lb 19	23	b 8, lb 1, nb 12	21
	(all out 128 overs)	428	(all out 69 overs)	190

Bowling
Masters 27-10-61-1. Wright 28-6-91-2. Danish Kaneria 38-7-120-3. ten Doeschate 18-4-71-2. Phillips 12-1-63-1. Bopara 2-1-2-0. Westley 3-0-5-0.
Danish Kaneria 27-13-50-6. Masters 7-3-16-0. Phillips 24-4-61-3. Wright 11-0-54-1.
Fall of Wickets: 1-2, 2-39, 3-104, 4-124, 5-136, 6-263, 7-388, 8-404, 9-428
1-0, 2-6, 3-88, 4-101, 5-115, 6-134, 7-135, 8-187, 9-190

ESSEX	First Innings		Second Innings	
JK Maunders	lbw b Schofield	39	c Walters b Dernbach	10
T Westley	c Batty b Collins	35	not out	45
RS Bopara	c Batty b Meaker	201	not out	15
MJ Walker	c Batty b Meaker	22		
ML Pettini (capt)	retired hurt	42		
*JS Foster	c Batty b Meaker	11		
RN ten Doeschate	not out	69		
TJ Phillips	c Linley b Schofield	69		
DD Masters	c Brown b Dernbach	43		
CJC Wright	b Collins	16		
Danish Kaneria	c Schofield b Collins	31		
Extras	b 8, lb 7, w 8, nb 6	29	lb 1, w 1, nb 2	4
	(all out 152.4 overs)	545	(1 wkt 12.4 overs)	74

Bowling
Dernbach 32-6-99-1. Collins 25.4-3-96-4. Linley 22-5-55-0. Schofield 27-1-117-2. Meaker 27-6-91-2. Spiegel 11-0-46-0. Afzaal 8-0-26-0.
Dernbach 6-0-31-1. Schofield 5-0-22-0. Afzaal 1-0-9-0. Spiegel 0.4-0-11-0.
Fall of Wickets: 1-77, 2-79, 3-137, 4-269, 5-412, 6-472, 7-487, 8-535, 9-545
1-20

Essex won by 9 wickets – Essex (21pts),
Surrey (6pts)

taking spin, and on which only Mark Ramprakash had the technique and the skill – before being seventh out for 62 – to counter the wiles of the Pakistan Test leg spinner.

Round Seventeen: 25–31 August

Nottinghamshire and Somerset, with draws at Worcester and the Rose Bowl respectively, could make no impression on Durham's big lead in Division One, and the champions – who sat out this round of games – were especially delighted when Notts failed by seven runs to pull off a remarkable run chase at New Road, after being set 358 in 74 overs to win.

It was Worcestershire, anchored to the bottom of the first division table, who had controlled the match with Gareth Andrew making an unbeaten 92 from No. 8 and then Imran Arif slicing through the Notts first innings with 5 for 93. Moeen Ali and Steven Davies then set up the declaration, only for Alistair Brown's 110-ball 84 and an unbeaten 70 from Chris Read, off 86 balls, to take Notts agonisingly close. The final over began with 21 runs still required but Read and Andre Adams, who hit two sixes in his late thrust, found that too much of an ask.

Somerset, meanwhile, suffered the indignity of following on against Hampshire, for whom Jimmy Adams had scored 147 and Imran Tahir a cavalier career-best 77 not out off 77 balls as the home side rattled up 548. Tahir then took 7 for 140 with his leg breaks and googlies but

Marcus Trescothick and Craig Kieswetter, with 118 and 73 and 94 and 70 respectively, at least ensured Somerset saved the game.

Yorkshire's rain-affected draw with Warwickshire at Scarborough featured a spirited 102 not out from No. 9 by David Wainwright, the left-arm spinner, and he and Gerard Brophy (85) hauled their side back to parity from the depths of 99 for 7. For Warwickshire there was an excellent 113 by Tim Ambrose and a violent 67 from 59 balls by Neil Carter, containing two sixes and ten fours.

In the second division, Kent moved 28 points clear at the top by overpowering Surrey by six wickets at Canterbury. Jon Batty and Michael Brown began the game by adding 171 for Surrey's first wicket, but things went downhill fast for them from there as Mark Ramprakash had his right thumb broken when gloving a vicious lifter from Simon Cook to second slip and Kent's batsmen – led by Geraint Jones's career-best 156, an attractive 112 from Darren Stevens and 92 off 79 balls by Justin Kemp, with three sixes and 11 fours – ensured a first innings lead. Stuart Meaker's four-hour unbeaten 64 was then not enough to stave off defeat, as Rob Key led a Kent charge to victory late on the fourth day.

A career-best 5 for 55 by Gareth Berg, and seven wickets in the match for the dependable Tim Murtagh, helped Middlesex to a 180-run win at Lord's against Gloucestershire, while a six-hour unbeaten 115 by Boeta

Round Seventeen: 25–31 August Division One

WORCESTERSHIRE v. NOTTINGHAMSHIRE – at New Road

WORCS	First Innings		Second Innings	
DKH Mitchell	c Read b Ealham	53	c Read b Adams	10
SC Moore	c Read b Adams	0	c Read b Adams	11
VS Solanki (capt)	c Brown b Adams	30	lbw b Adams	0
BF Smith	c Read b Shreck	52	b Shreck	10
MM Ali	b Adams	0	not out	84
*SM Davies	c Adams b Shreck	9	c Shafayat b Carter	76
AN Kervezee	lbw b Shreck	34	c Newman b Shreck	30
GM Andrew	not out	92	not out	5
RA Jones	b Ealham	31		
Imran Arif	b Adams	0		
JD Shantry	lbw b Ealham	0		
Extras	b 5, lb 14, nb 14	33	b 4, w 2, nb 10	16
	(all out 105.5 overs)	334	(6 wkts dec 52 overs)	242

Bowling
Shreck 23-2-102-3. Adams 29-9-81-4. Carter 18-5-68-0. Ealham 25.5-13-40-3. Patel 10-3-24-0.
Shreck 20-4-90-2. Adams 17-1-79-3. Ealham 7-1-31-0. Carter 6-0-28-1. Patel 2-0-10-0.
Fall of Wickets: 1-2, 2-51, 3-140, 4-141, 5-152, 6-181, 7-240, 8-324, 9-333
1-16, 2-16, 3-33, 4-34, 5-176, 6-229

NOTTS	First Innings		Second Innings	
SA Newman	c Mitchell b Arif	3	c Davies b Andrew	0
AD Hales	c Mitchell b Arif	12	c Davies b Jones	55
MA Wagh	c Davies b Arif	49	c Davies b Andrew	0
SR Patel	c Kervezee b Arif	46	c Davies b Jones	55
BM Shafayat	c Davies b Shantry	0	c Davies b Jones	30
AD Brown	not out	46	c Shantry b Andrew	84
*CMW Read (capt)	b Andrew	9	not out	70
MA Ealham	c Arif b Shantry	17	c Davies b Jones	10
AR Adams	c Moore b Jones	6	not out	29
CE Shreck	lbw b Jones	0		
A Carter	c & b Arif	4		
Extras	b 8, lb 11, w 2, nb 6	27	lb 10, w 6, nb 2	18
	(all out 54.5 overs)	219	(7 wkts 74 overs)	351

Bowling
Andrew 13-3-35-1. Arif 20.5-4-93-5. Shantry 14-2-53-2. Jones 7-3-19-2.
Arif 18-3-72-0. Andrew 21-3-97-3. Jones 18-2-105-4. Shantry 11-3-30-0.
Ali 6-1-37-0.
Fall of Wickets: 1-7, 2-22, 3-88, 4-105, 5-143, 6-158, 7-182, 8-200, 9-202
1-15, 2-15, 3-94, 4-144, 5-170, 6-285, 7-298

Match drawn – Worcestershire (10pts), Nottinghamshire (8pts)

HAMPSHIRE v. SOMERSET – at the Rose Bowl

HAMPSHIRE	First Innings		Second Innings	
JHK Adams	b Willoughby	147	not out	1
LA Dawson	lbw b Banks	55		
MJ Lumb	c Trescothick b Banks	68	(2) not out	3
JM Vince	c Langer b Willoughby	4		
SM Ervine	hit wkt b Banks	4		
*N Pothas	c Kieswetter b Willoughby	41		
AD Mascarenhas (capt)	lbw b Trego	31		
DG Cork	c Suppiah b Waller	52		
Imran Tahir	not out	77		
DA Griffiths	c Willoughby b Banks	5		
DR Briggs	c Banks b Suppiah	36		
Extras	b 10, lb 13, w 1, nb 4	28	lb 5	5
	(all out 163 overs)	548	(0 wkts 1.5 overs)	9

Bowling
Willoughby 35-12-117-3. Thomas 29-8-75-0. Banks 38-6-120-4. Waller 19-4-79-1.
Trego 28-12-68-1. Suppiah 6-0-24-1. de Bruyn 8-1-42-0.
Willoughby 1-0-1-0. Thomas 0.5-0-3-0.
Fall of Wickets: 1-104, 2-235, 3-240, 4-249, 5-326, 6-337, 7-422, 8-430, 9-468

SOMERSET	First Innings		Second Innings (following on)	
ME Trescothick	b Imran Tahir	118	c Cork b Briggs	73
AV Suppiah	c & b Imran Tahir	35	b Cork	21
JL Langer (capt)	c Cork b Imran Tahir	4	c Vince b Imran Tahir	0
JC Hildreth	c Mascarenhas b Imran Tahir	4	lbw b Cork	4
AC Thomas	c Pothas b Cork	15	(9) b Briggs	11
Z de Bruyn	c Adams b Cork	0	(5) c Pothas b Briggs	13
*C Kieswetter	c Pothas b Imran Tahir	94	(6) c Dawson b Griffiths	70
PD Trego	c Adams b Imran Tahir	20	(7) c Adams b Imran Tahir	27
OAC Banks	not out	45	(8) lbw b Ervine	6
MTC Waller	lbw b Imran Tahir	28	c Pothas b Griffiths	18
CM Willoughby	b Griffiths	4	(11) not out	5
Extras	b 6, lb 4, nb 24	34	b 1, lb 2, w 1, nb 10	14
	(all out 106 overs)	393	(all out 94 overs)	294

Bowling
Griffiths 19-2-74-1. Mascarenhas 10.5-2-31-0. Imran Tahir 35.1-6-140-7.
Cork 16-5-39-2. Briggs 13-2-70-0. Dawson 2-0-8-0. Ervine 10-2-21-0.
Ervine 11.1-2-39-1. Griffiths 12-2-25-2. Cork 16-2-48-2. Imran Tahir 35.5-21-117-2.
Briggs 19-3-62-3.
Fall of Wickets: 1-76, 2-78, 3-86, 4-129, 5-133, 6-280, 7-311, 8-322, 9-392
1-52, 2-117, 3-126, 4-149, 5-152, 6-210, 7-233, 8-261, 9-278

*Match drawn – Hampshire (11pts),
Somerset (10pts)*

YORKSHIRE v. WARWICKSHIRE – at Scarborough

WARWICKSHIRE	First Innings		Second Innings	
U Westwood (capt)	c Sayers b Shahzad	1	c Pyrah b Shahzad	58
AG Botha	b Kruis	13	c Pyrah b McGrath	33
IR Bell	b Shahzad	23	(4) lbw b Wainwright	35
JO Troughton	c Bairstow b Shahzad	9	(5) b Hoggard	40
T Frost	b Wainwright	35	(6) c Brophy b Pyrah	48
*TR Ambrose	c McGrath b Kruis	113	(7) lbw b Wainwright	33
R Clarke	c Brophy b Wainwright	22	(8) b Sayers	23
NM Carter	c McGrath b Pyrah	67	(9) c Rudolph b Sayers	11
CR Woakes	c Bairstow b Kruis	9	(10) not out	6
N Tahir	not out	3	(3) b Shahzad	0
S Sreesanth	b Shahzad	11	c Brophy b Sayers	1
Extras	b 4, lb 7, w 1	12	b 9, lb 15, w 1	25
	(all out 81.4 overs)	320	(all out 108.5 overs)	313

Bowling
Hoggard 18-3-51-0. Shahzad 17.4-3-78-4. Kruis 23-8-68-3. Wainwright 14-0-74-2. Pyrah 9-1-38-1.
Hoggard 20-9-42-1. Shahzad 19-3-57-2. Pyrah 17-2-64-1. Kruis 12-5-24-0.
Wainwright 30-8-71-2. McGrath 6-1-11-1. Sayers 4.5-0-20-3.
Fall of Wickets: 1-1, 2-28, 3-48, 4-53, 5-138, 6-178, 7-288, 8-300, 9-304
1-96, 2-97, 3-116, 4-159, 5-229, 6-256, 7-288, 8-304, 9-310

YORKSHIRE	First Innings		Second Innings	
JA Rudolph	c Troughton b Sreesanth	0	not out	21
JJ Sayers	c Bell b Tahir	21	not out	4
A McGrath (capt)	c Ambrose b Sreesanth	0		
AW Gale	c Woakes b Tahir	23		
JM Bairstow	c Frost b Carter	4		
*GL Brophy	c Clarke b Botha	85		
A Shahzad	c Westwood b Sreesanth	13		
RM Pyrah	c Frost b Sreesanth	0		
DJ Wainwright	not out	102		
MJ Hoggard	c Ambrose b Tahir	18		
GJ Kruis	c Ambrose b Sreesanth	30		
Extras	lb 5, w 3, nb 24	32	w 1, nb 4	5
	(all out 86.2 overs)	328	(0 wkts 8 overs)	30

Bowling
Sreesanth 15.2-3-93-5. Tahir 21-7-59-3. Carter 15-2-49-1. Woakes 19-5-63-0.
Clarke 4-0-20-0. Botha 12-2-39-1.
Sreesanth 4-1-17-0. Tahir 2-1-4-0. Bell 2-1-9-0.
Fall of Wickets: 1-0, 2-0, 3-47, 4-50, 5-67, 6-95, 7-99, 8-243, 9-291

*Match drawn – Yorkshire (10pts),
Warwickshire (10pts)*

Dippenaar enabled his Leicestershire side to earn themselves a creditable backs-to-the wall draw against Essex at Chelmsford.

The odds were firmly in Essex's favour after they had chalked up 517 for 9 declared, with centuries for John

Round Seventeen: 25–31 August Division Two

KENT v. SURREY – at Canterbury

SURREY	First Innings		Second Innings	
*JN Batty	c Jones b Edwards	96	lbw b Edwards	26
MJ Brown	c Jones b Khan	88	c Blake b Tredwell	5
SJ Walters (capt)	c Stevens b Khan	0	(4) c Northeast b Tredwell	6
MR Ramprakash	c van Jaarsveld b Cook	46	absent hurt	
U Afzaal	c Jones b Edwards	3	lbw b Tredwell	44
MNW Spriegel	lbw b Khan	49	(3) b Edwards	6
CP Schofield	c van Jaarsveld b Edwards	9	(6) b Khan	36
SC Meaker	c van Jaarsveld b Khan	23	(7) not out	64
JW Dernbach	c Northeast b Kemp	5	(8) c Stevens b Kemp	16
TE Linley	not out	35	(9) c Tredwell b Khan	36
PT Collins	b Khan	23	(10) c Key b Khan	12
Extras	b 4, lb 22, w 4, nb 16	46	b 6, lb 21, w 3, nb 12	42
	(all out 129.3 overs)	423	(all out 101.5 overs)	293

Bowling
Khan 31.3-4-113-5. Cook 23-7-54-1. Edwards 21-6-72-3. Tredwell 38-9-100-0. Kemp 15-4-58-1. Stevens 1-1-0-0.
Cook 19-5-62-0. Khan 17.5-5-49-3. Edwards 14-2-52-2. Tredwell 35-10-72-3. van Jaarsveld 6-1-11-0. Kemp 10-4-20-1.
Fall of Wickets: 1-171, 2-175, 3-235, 4-239, 5-275, 6-302, 7-340, 8-347, 9-365
1-38, 2-38, 3-55, 4-57, 5-135, 6-163, 7-208, 8-275, 9-293

KENT	First Innings		Second Innings	
SA Northeast	c & b Spriegel	48	c Walters b Meaker	28
RWT Key (capt)	lbw b Dernbach	13	lbw b Meaker	50
*GO Jones	b Meaker	156	st Batty b Afzaal	45
M van Jaarsveld	lbw b Schofield	28	c Collins b Spriegel	19
DI Stevens	c Walters b Schofield	112	not out	35
JM Kemp	run out	92	not out	9
AJ Blake	b Schofield	1		
JC Tredwell	c Spriegel b Linley	11		
SJ Cook	lbw b Meaker	2		
A Khan	lbw b Meaker	5		
P Edwards	not out	0		
Extras	b 6, lb 16, w 6, nb 16, p 5	49	lb 2, w 6, nb 6	14
	(all out 110.3 overs)	517	(4 wkts 35 overs)	200

Bowling
Dernbach 23-6-100-1. Collins 13-2-66-0. Linley 28-5-89-1. Meaker 22.3-2-114-3. Spriegel 5-0-31-1. Schofield 19-2-90-3.
Dernbach 9-0-35-0. Collins 3-0-16-0. Linley 7-0-43-0. Meaker 4-0-29-2. Schofield 5-0-39-0. Spriegel 5-0-22-1. Afzaal 2-0-14-1.
Fall of Wickets: 1-21, 2-112, 3-193, 4-376, 5-430, 6-440, 7-479, 8-485, 9-499
1-90, 2-91, 3-130, 4-185

Kent won by 6 wickets – Kent (22pts), Surrey (7pts)

MIDDLESEX v. GLOUCESTERSHIRE – at Lord's

MIDDLESEX	First Innings		Second Innings	
SD Robson	c Dawson b Kirby	83		
NRD Compton	c Taylor b Marshall	28	(1) c Saxelby b Marshall	83
AB London	b Marshall	68	run out	11
DJ Malan	c Marshall b Saxelby	38	b Taylor	20
NJ Dexter	c Adshead b Saxelby	51	not out	39
*BJM Scott	lbw b Saxelby	6	c Dawson b Saxelby	22
GK Berg	c Adshead b Kirby	5	c Adshead b Kirby	7
SD Udal (capt)	c Saxelby b Kirby	45	c Gidman b Kirby	26
M Kartik	c Kadeer Ali b Kirby	1	(2) st Adshead b Dawson	57
TJ Murtagh	not out	3		
ST Finn	run out	4		
Extras	lb 10	10	lb 6, nb 2	8
	(all out 104.4 overs)	342	(7 wkts dec 71.1 overs)	273

Bowling
Lewis 21-6-64-0. Franklin 18-6-44-0. Kirby 21-4-77-4. Saxelby 21.4-3-58-3. Marshall 17-5-52-2. Dawson 4-0-23-0. Taylor 2-0-14-0.
Saxelby 16-2-51-1. Kirby 14.1-3-41-2. Lewis 5-0-24-0. Dawson 13-0-60-1. Franklin 10-2-35-0. Marshall 8-1-32-1. Taylor 5-1-24-1.
Fall of Wickets: 1-46, 2-142, 3-226, 4-226, 5-244, 6-263, 7-321, 8-326, 9-335
1-128, 2-150, 3-155, 4-184, 5-226, 6-237, 7-273

GLOS	First Innings		Second Innings	
Kadeer Ali	c Scott b Murtagh	4	(2) c Compton b Berg	48
RJ Woodman	c Malan b Finn	9	(1) lbw b Murtagh	4
HJH Marshall	c Malan b Murtagh	17	c Scott b Murtagh	0
APR Gidman (capt)	lbw b Murtagh	0	lbw b Finn	4
CG Taylor	c Finn b Kartik	65	c Scott b Finn	25
JEC Franklin	b Finn	16	not out	80
*SJ Adshead	c Robson b Kartik	14	b Berg	0
RKJ Dawson	b Berg	0	c Malan b Berg	35
ID Saxelby	lbw b Kartik	17	c Scott b Berg	0
J Lewis	not out	20	c Scott b Berg	9
SP Kirby	c Dexter b Murtagh	18	c Dexter b Murtagh	7
Extras	b 4, lb 11, w 1, nb 14	30	b 1, lb 8, nb 4	13
	(all out 70.3 overs)	210	(all out 60.5 overs)	225

Bowling
Murtagh 16.3-3-61-4. Finn 17-4-47-2. Udal 6-2-10-0. Berg 12-5-28-1. Dexter 2-1-5-0. Kartik 17-4-44-3.
Murtagh 18.5-2-83-3. Finn 14-3-52-2. Berg 14-1-55-5. Kartik 1-0-4-0. Udal 9-4-12-0. Malan 2-0-7-0. London 2-0-3-0.
Fall of Wickets: 1-10, 2-28, 3-28, 4-77, 5-107, 6-148, 7-149, 8-149, 9-178
1-4, 2-4, 3-21, 4-73, 5-118, 6-118, 7-196, 8-196, 9-204

*Middlesex won by 180 runs –
Middlesex (20pts), Gloucestershire (4pts)*

ESSEX v. LEICESTERSHIRE – at Chelmsford

ESSEX	First Innings			
JK Maunders	c Nixon b Harris	150		
AN Cook	b White	31		
V Chopra	c New b White	13		
MJ Walker	lbw b Naik	31		
T Westley	lbw b Harris	71		
*JS Foster (capt)	not out	103		
TJ Phillips	st New b Henderson	22		
Danish Kaneria	c Benning b Henderson	0		
RN ten Doeschate	c & b Naik	1		
DD Masters	not out	67		
CJC Wright	not out	1		
Extras	b 8, lb 14, w 1, nb 4	27		
	(9 wkts dec 151.1 overs)	517		

Bowling
Harris 29-6-109-2. Benning 36-6-111-0. White 21-0-101-2. Naik 25-3-73-2. Henderson 40.1-6-101-2.
Fall of Wickets: 1-52, 2-80, 3-151, 4-310, 5-321, 6-392, 7-392, 8-399, 9-503

LEICESTERSHIRE	First Innings		Second Innings (following on)	
PA Nixon	c Foster b Danish Kaneria	40	c Foster b Wright	4
MAG Boyce	b Danish Kaneria	70	c Walker b Danish Kaneria	14
HH Dippenaar (capt)	c Phillips b Danish Kaneria	0	not out	115
JHK Naik	c Phillips b Danish Kaneria	10	c Danish Kaneria b Phillips	20
JWA Taylor	not out	112	lbw b Danish Kaneria	62
*TJ New	c Maunders b Danish Kaneria	14	lbw b Danish Kaneria	10
JGE Benning	retired hurt	36	not out	21
WA White	c Foster b ten Doeschate	11		
CW Henderson	lbw b Danish Kaneria	14		
AJ Harris	lbw b Danish Kaneria	7		
Extras	b 9, lb 10, w 1, nb 6	26	b 6, lb 1, nb 4	11
	(9 wkts 118.4 overs)	344	(6 wkts 101.5 overs)	258

Bowling
Masters 21-9-61-0. Wright 16-3-59-0. Danish Kaneria 49.4-16-116-8. ten Doeschate 14-2-55-1. Phillips 18-7-34-0.
Masters 14-4-27-0. Wright 15-0-48-1. Phillips 25-9-44-1. Danish Kaneria 36.5-12-87-4. ten Doeschate 4-1-18-0. Westley 4-0-18-0. Cook 1-0-3-0. Chopra 2-0-6-0.
Fall of Wickets: 1-83, 2-87, 3-111, 4-115, 5-152, 6-178, 7-277, 8-322, 9-344
1-9, 2-34, 3-88, 4-89, 5-218, 6-230

*Match drawn – Essex (11pts),
Leicestershire (9pts)*

NORTHAMPTONSHIRE v. GLAMORGAN – at Northampton

NORTHANTS	First Innings		Second Innings	
SD Peters	c Rees b Croft	163	st Wallace b Croft	86
RA White	c Rees b Harris	0	lbw b Harris	9
AG Wakely	b Kruger	5	c Rees b Croft	29
*MH Wessels	c Wallace b Allenby	39	b Dalrymple	92
N Boje (capt)	run out	5	lbw b Croft	4
AJ Hall	lbw b Allenby	89	c Powell b Harris	25
DJ Willey	c Rees b Croft	8	b Dalrymple	16
MS Panesar	lbw b Croft	0	lbw b Croft	14
DS Lucas	b Harris	16	not out	25
DH Wigley	c Gibbs b Harris	10	not out	3
JA Brooks	not out	10		
Extras	lb 3, w 2	5	lb 8, lb 7, nb 4	19
	(all out 88.2 overs)	350	(8 wkts 92 overs)	312

Bowling
Harris 17.2-2-92-3. Kruger 19-4-66-1. Shantry 11-0-68-0. Allenby 18-3-54-2. Croft 18-1-53-3. Dalrymple 5-0-14-0.
Harris 17-2-60-2. Kruger 12-0-51-0. Shantry 4-0-28-0. Allenby 7-2-18-0. Croft 32-4-71-4. Dalrymple 15-3-46-2. Bragg 5-0-23-0.
Fall of Wickets: 1-3, 2-16, 3-84, 4-98, 5-289, 6-312, 7-312, 8-313, 9-333
1-11, 2-116, 3-144, 4-152, 5-203, 6-240, 7-253, 8-309

GLAMORGAN	First Innings			
GP Rees	lbw b Hall	31		
WD Bragg	c Boje b Lucas	28		
HH Gibbs	st Wessels b Panesar	42		
MJ Powell	c Wessels b Brooks	55		
JWM Dalrymple (capt)	lbw b Boje	27		
J Allenby	b Wigley	55		
*MA Wallace	b Panesar	42		
JAR Harris	c Wessels b Hall	26		
RDB Croft	b Brooks	14		
AJ Shantry	lbw b Panesar	32		
GJP Kruger	not out	5		
Extras	b 8, lb 14, nb 4	26		
	(all out 122.3 overs)	383		

Bowling
Lucas 24-3-88-1. Brooks 24-4-70-2. Wigley 18-4-78-1. Panesar 33.3-12-55-3. Hall 14-5-33-2. Boje 9-0-37-1.
Fall of Wickets: 1-71, 2-77, 3-137, 4-196, 5-212, 6-299, 7-317, 8-338, 9-365

*Match drawn – Northamptonshire (11pts),
Glamorgan (11pts)*

Opposite Imran Arif, the Worcestershire fast bowler, is pictured in action during an extremely difficult season for the injury-ravaged club.

Maunders and James Foster, and then watched Danish Kaneria finish with 8 for 116 as Leicestershire were bowled out for 344 in reply despite a stubborn and skilful 112 not out from teenager James Taylor. But South African Dippenaar showed his Test class to lead the second innings resistance and, once again, Taylor impressed against Kaneria to score 62 and add 129 with his captain.

At Northampton, though, the draw was a less interesting affair, thanks in part to some bad weather, although home opener Stephen Peters will at least remember the game fondly after taking the Glamorgan bowlers for 163 and 86.

Round Eighteen: 1–6 September

A much-anticipated shoot-out between Durham and Somerset at Riverside was ruined when bad weather washed away both the third and fourth days, although in the playing time that was possible it was the champions who clearly held the upper hand.

Somerset were going along comfortably at 127 for 2 before collapsing in a heap to 174 all out, with Ian Blackwell enjoying the startling figures of 8.1-5-7-5 against his former county. Shivnarine Chanderpaul then earned Durham a first innings lead of 98 by grinding his way to a five and three-quarter hour 117 not out.

Rain similarly wrecked Lancashire's fixture against Sussex at Old Trafford, and the weather also intervened to a certain extent to help Yorkshire fight back and secure a creditable draw against Nottinghamshire at Trent Bridge, with Jacques Rudolph (149) and Joe

Round Eighteen: 1–6 September Division One

DURHAM v. SOMERSET – at the Riverside

SOMERSET	First Innings		Second Innings	
ME Trescothick	c Smith b Onions	31	not out	18
AV Suppiah	c Mustard b Plunkett	53	not out	21
JL Langer (capt)	b Onions	12		
JC Hildreth	c Thorp b Blackwell	27		
Z de Bruyn	lbw b Blackwell	16		
*C Kieswetter	c Di Venuto b Plunkett	0		
PD Trego	c Di Venuto b Plunkett	4		
OAC Banks	not out	16		
BJ Phillips	lbw b Blackwell	0		
AC Thomas	c Di Venuto b Blackwell	0		
CM Willoughby	b Blackwell	0		
Extras	lb 8, w 3, nb 4	15	b 1, lb 1	2
	(all out 59.1 overs)	174	(0 wkts 12.5 overs)	41

Bowling
Onions 17-2-49-2. Harrison 8-3-24-0. Thorp 5-0-21-0. Plunkett 21-6-65-3. Blackwell 8.1-5-7-5.
Onions 6-0-25-0. Harrison 6-2-14-0. Plunkett 0.5-0-0-0.
Fall of Wickets: 1-89, 2-89, 3-127, 4-147, 5-148, 6-152, 7-162, 8-162, 9-166

DURHAM	First Innings	
MJ Di Venuto	c Trescothick b Willoughby	22
KJ Coetzer	b Phillips	30
WR Smith (capt)	c Kieswetter b Willoughby	6
S Chanderpaul	not out	117
DM Benkenstein	c Suppiah b de Bruyn	30
ID Blackwell	c Kieswetter b Phillips	0
*P Mustard	c Langer b Phillips	2
LE Plunkett	b Willoughby	32
CD Thorp	c Hildreth b Willoughby	15
G Onions	c Kieswetter b Willoughby	0
SJ Harmison	c Kieswetter b Trego	0
Extras	b 9, lb 12, w 2	23
	(all out 89.5 overs)	272

Bowling
Willoughby 22-7-56-5. Thomas 20-4-54-0. Phillips 20-2-46-3. Trego 11.5-4-42-1. Banks 2-0-15-0. de Bruyn 11-3-31-1. Suppiah 3-1-7-0.
Fall of Wickets: 1-24, 2-24, 3-104, 4-161, 5-162, 6-166, 7-235, 8-267, 9-271

Match drawn – Durham (9pts), Somerset (7pts)

LANCASHIRE v. SUSSEX – at Old Trafford

LANCASHIRE	First Innings		Second Innings	
PJ Horton	c Yardy b Collymore	6	not out	0
*LD Sutton	c Rayner b Martin-Jenkins	17	not out	0
MB Loye	c Chawla b Rayner	58		
VVS Laxman	lbw b Smith	6		
MJ Chilton	c Yardy b Smith	26		
F du Plessis	c Joyce b Martin-Jenkins	54		
KW Hogg	run out	6		
G Chapple (capt)	c Rayner b Martin-Jenkins	39		
SI Mahmood	lbw b Martin-Jenkins	0		
OJ Newby	c Rayner b Martin-Jenkins	3		
G Keedy	not out	4		
Extras	b 1, lb 3, w 5, nb 8	17		0
	(all out 87.4 overs)	236	(0 wkts 0.2 overs)	0

Bowling
Collymore 16-5-44-1. Martin-Jenkins 14.4-4-43-5. Smith 21-8-47-2. Chawla 24-6-75-0. Rayner 12-1-23-1. Smith 0.2-0-0-0.
Fall of Wickets: 1-10, 2-50, 3-71, 4-105, 5-131, 6-141, 7-223, 8-223, 9-229

SUSSEX	First Innings	
MH Yardy (capt)	c Sutton b Newby	86
JS Gatting	b Mahmood	10
EC Joyce	lbw b Mahmood	40
MW Goodwin	c Sutton b Mahmood	29
CD Hopkinson	c Laxman b Hogg	19
*AJ Hodd	c Laxman b Hogg	0
DR Smith	lbw b Newby	8
RSC Martin-Jenkins	lbw b Hogg	0
P Chawla	not out	32
OP Rayner	c Laxman b Newby	3
CD Collymore	c Laxman b Mahmood	4
Extras	w 1, nb 8	9
	(all out 73.3 overs)	240

Bowling
Mahmood 24.3-4-87-4. Hogg 15-4-53-3. Chapple 15-5-38-0. Newby 15-1-49-3. Keedy 4-1-13-0.
Fall of Wickets: 1-27, 2-121, 3-163, 4-190, 5-191, 6-200, 7-200, 8-203, 9-209

Match drawn – Lancashire (8pts), Sussex (8pts)

NOTTINGHAMSHIRE v. YORKSHIRE – at Trent Bridge

YORKSHIRE	First Innings		Second Innings	
JA Rudolph	b Pattinson	42	c Ealham b Franks	149
JJ Sayers	b Franks	53	b Franks	86
A McGrath (capt)	c Ealham b Shreck	0	b Franks	40
AW Gale	c Read b Pattinson	5	b Pattinson	9
JM Bairstow	lbw b Ealham	49	c Brown b Hales	81
*GL Brophy	c Read b Franks	0	c Ê b Patel	29
A Shahzad	c Read b Shreck	19	b Hales	45
RM Pyrah	lbw b Shreck	9	not out	50
DJ Wainwright	c Brown b Franks	37	c Ê b Brown	6
MJ Hoggard	not out	12	not out	0
GJ Kruis	c Read b Ealham	1		
Extras	b 4, lb 16, w 5, nb 4	29	b 10, lb 6, w 5, nb 2	23
	(all out 111.3 overs)	256	(8 wkts 174 overs)	518

Bowling
Shreck 33-10-57-3. Pattinson 29-6-74-2. Franks 20-7-52-3. Ealham 22.3-11-38-2. Patel 7-1-15-0.
Shreck 27-7-88-0. Pattinson 25-6-69-1. Ealham 19-5-46-0. Franks 30-12-71-3. Patel 36-9-122-1. Hales 20-4-63-2. Newman 6-1-25-0. Read 1-0-2-0. Brown 10-2-16-1.
Fall of Wickets: 1-72, 2-73, 3-100, 4-132, 5-132, 6-174, 7-192, 8-199, 9-255
1-244, 2-254, 3-284, 4-304, 5-384, 6-426, 7-503, 8-514

NOTTS	First Innings	
SA Newman	c Gale b Hoggard	79
AD Hales	c Ê b Pyrah	35
MA Wagh	c Brophy b Pyrah	0
SR Patel	c Bairstow b Shahzad	7
BM Shafayat	b Hoggard	66
AD Brown	b Wainwright	0
*CMW Read (capt)	st Brophy b Wainwright	42
PJ Franks	c Ê b Shahzad	64
MA Ealham	lbw b Kruis	36
DJ Pattinson	b Shahzad	3
CE Shreck	not out	0
Extras	b 8, lb 8, w 2, nb 2	20
	(all out 85.2 overs)	352

Bowling
Hoggard 17-5-60-2. Shahzad 22.2-1-101-3. Kruis 11-0-73-1. Pyrah 17-3-53-2. Wainwright 12-4-49-2.
Fall of Wickets: 1-76, 2-78, 3-101, 4-152, 5-153, 6-231, 7-299, 8-345, 9-349

Match drawn – Nottinghamshire (11pts), Yorkshire (9pts)

WARWICKSHIRE v. WORCESTERSHIRE – at Edgbaston

WARWICKSHIRE	First Innings	
U Westwood (capt)	run out	133
AG Botha	b Jones	22
IR Bell	b Arif	36
IJL Trott	c Smith b Jones	93
JO Troughton	c Davies b Mason	22
T Frost	c Moore b Andrew	24
*TR Ambrose	c Mitchell b Jones	8
CR Woakes	c Solanki b Jones	21
N Tahir	c Mason b Jones	15
S Sreesanth	not out	23
WB Rankin	c Solanki b Jones	0
Extras	b 16, lb 16, nb 8	46
	(all out 117 overs)	443

Bowling
Mason 26-7-59-1. Arif 25-3-112-1. Andrew 23-1-104-1. Jones 29-6-100-6. Mitchell 10-2-16-0. Ali 4-1-17-0.
Fall of Wickets: 1-79, 2-188, 3-255, 4-301, 5-344, 6-361, 7-382, 8-399, 9-426

WORCS	First Innings		Second Innings (following on)	
DKH Mitchell	c Ambrose b Woakes	30	c Trott b Woakes	25
SC Moore	run out	5	c Bell b Rankin	63
VS Solanki (capt)	lbw b Woakes	27	b Woakes	10
BF Smith	b Woakes	4	c Troughton b Woakes	0
MM Ali	c Bell b Woakes	0	c Bell b Sreesanth	11
*SM Davies	c Bell b Woakes	8	b Sreesanth	62
AN Kervezee	c Botha b Tahir	33	c Westwood b Sreesanth	12
GM Andrew	c Ambrose b Sreesanth	0	c Trott b Botha	23
RA Jones	lbw b Tahir	24	c Sreesanth b Rankin	12
MS Mason	not out	8	not out	8
Imran Arif	b Rankin	1	b Woakes	6
Extras	lb 6, nb 8	14	b 9, lb 13, w 1, nb 16	39
	(all out 48.1 overs)	154	(all out 82.4 overs)	271

Bowling
Sreesanth 15-3-45-1. Tahir 12-3-25-2. Rankin 9.1-1-38-1. Woakes 12-5-40-5.
Tahir 16-4-33-0. Rankin 22-1-93-2. Sreesanth 16-3-56-3. Woakes 17.4-3-42-4. Trott 3-1-9-0. Botha 8-2-16-1.
Fall of Wickets: 1-29, 2-45, 3-63, 4-71, 5-83, 6-90, 7-97, 8-142, 9-153
1-91, 2-91, 3-95, 4-124, 5-124, 6-155, 7-226, 8-247, 9-264

Warwickshire won by an innings and 18 runs – Warwickshire (22pts), Worcestershire (3pts)

Sayers (86) leading the second innings resistance with a stand of 244 for the first wicket.

The elements could not prevent Worcestershire, however, from going down to an innings and 18-run defeat against close rivals Warwickshire at Edgbaston.

Round Eighteen: 1–6 September Division Two

GLOUCESTERSHIRE v. SURREY – at Bristol

SURREY	First Innings		Second Innings	
*JN Batty	c Adshead b Saxelby	43	c Adshead b Marshall	40
MJ Brown	lbw b Franklin	37	b Ireland	39
A Harinath	c Marshall b Kirby	18	c Adshead b Kirby	44
SJ Walters (capt)	c Adshead b Kirby	2	lbw b Saxelby	1
U Afzaal	c Adshead b Franklin	23	(6) c Gidman b Ireland	15
CP Schofield	b Saxelby	5	(7) c Taylor b Marshall	71
SC Meaker	b Franklin	3	(8) lbw b Marshall	2
AJ Tudor	not out	17	(9) c Ireland b Taylor	33
HMRKB Herath	c Kadeer Ali b Ireland	1	(10) not out	52
TE Linley	c Kirby b Ireland	6	(5) c Porterfield b Marshall	17
JW Dernbach	c Franklin b Kirby	18	b Kirby	6
Extras	b 1, lb 5, nb 4	10	lb 9, lb 10	19
	(all out 58 overs)	183	(all out 96.5 overs)	339

Bowling
Saxelby 12-1-64-2. Franklin 12-5-28-3. Kirby 17-7-32-3. Ireland 17-7-53-2. Kirby 18.5-5-48-2. Saxelby 13-1-59-1. Ireland 22-5-83-2. Franklin 13-4-36-0. Marshall 19-6-52-4. Taylor 10-2-32-1.
Fall of Wickets: 1-70, 2-102, 3-104, 4-112, 5-127, 6-136, 7-137, 8-138, 9-150
1-75, 2-93, 3-128, 4-143, 5-170, 6-170, 7-177, 8-249, 9-332

GLOS	First Innings	
Kadeer Ali	c Walters b Tudor	39
RJ Woodman	c Batty b Tudor	32
WTS Porterfield	b Linley	5
HJH Marshall	run out	84
APR Gidman (capt)	c Brown b Herath	176
CG Taylor	b Meaker	111
JEC Franklin	not out	25
*SJ Adshead	st Batty b Herath	16
ID Saxelby	not out	1
AJ Ireland		
SP Kirby		
Extras	b 2, lb 18, nb 14	34
	(7 wkts dec 116 overs)	523

Bowling
Dernbach 27-3-109-0. Linley 20-6-70-1. Tudor 26-3-109-2. Meaker 10-2-64-1. Herath 28-1-116-2. Schofield 1-0-6-0. Walters 4-0-29-0.
Fall of Wickets: 1-77, 2-84, 3-88, 4-261, 5-458, 6-492, 7-521

Gloucestershire won by an innings and 1 run – Gloucestershire (22pts), Surrey (2pts)

Ian Westwood, with 133, and Jonathan Trott (93) laid the foundations for Warwickshire before 20-year-old pace prospect Chris Woakes got among the visiting batsmen to take 5 for 40 and 4 for 42 in a sustained piece of seam and swing bowling.

In the second division the Gloucestershire seamers paved the way for the innings and one run win over Surrey at Bristol by dismissing the visitors for just 183 on the opening day. Then Alex Gidman, the captain, took over by compiling a superb 176 and being joined in a fifth wicket stand of 197 by Chris Taylor, who made 111. Hamish Marshall also stroked a stylish 84, as Gloucestershire topped 500, and later took vital wickets with his occasional medium pace as Surrey were bowled out again.

A closely fought affair at Northampton was decided, in the end, by some forthright strokeplay by Northants pair Rob White, who finished unbeaten on 85, and Stephen Peters, who opened up with 73. Middlesex all-rounder Gareth Berg could not have done much more for his side, however, scoring 94 not out to rally them from 47 for 6 in their second innings after taking 5 for 68 to earn a slender first innings advantage. John Simpson, a 21-year-old wicketkeeper, also distinguished himself on his first-class debut by top scoring with 87 from 141 balls, with a six and 11 fours, and then making an equally spirited 41 in Middlesex's second innings.

Leicestershire's game against Glamorgan at Grace Road, which featured another fine innings from James Taylor, was a rain-affected draw, while Kent successfully batted throughout the final day – with unbeaten

---

NORTHAMPTONSHIRE v. MIDDLESEX – at Northampton

MIDDLESEX	First Innings		Second Innings	
NRD Compton	c O'Brien b van der Wath	4	c O'Brien b Lucas	5
AB London	b Peters b Hall	31	c O'Brien b van der Wath	4
DM Housego	c Wessels b van der Wath	9	c O'Brien b Lucas	0
DJ Malan	c Wessels b Lucas	39	(5) lbw b Panesar	26
NJ Dexter	c Boje b Daggett	30	(6) c O'Brien b Lucas	1
*JA Simpson	b Daggett	87	(7) c O'Brien b Hall	41
GK Berg	run out	18	(8) not out	94
SD Udal (capt)	retired hurt	4	(11) absent hurt	
M Kartik	c Lucas b van der Wath	7	(3) b van der Wath	29
TJ Murtagh	c Wessels b Daggett	2	(4) b v der Wath	0
ST Finn	not out	1	(4) lbw b Murtagh	0
Extras	b 9, lb 6, w 2, nb 2	19	b 3, lb 4	7
	(all out 75 overs)	251	(all out 59 overs)	207

Bowling
van der Wath 23-7-75-3. Lucas 11-4-35-1. Daggett 16-3-47-3. Panesar 8-1-31-0. Hall 16-3-42-1. Boje 1-0-6-0.
Lucas 15-3-43-4. van der Wath 14-5-32-3. Panesar 7-0-26-1. Daggett 7-1-25-0. Hall 10-0-44-1. Boje 6-2-30-0.
Fall of Wickets: 1-4, 2-21, 3-97, 4-97, 5-148, 6-202, 7-230, 8-248, 9-251
1-6, 2-8, 3-9, 4-18, 5-29, 6-47, 7-147, 8-200, 9-207

NORTHANTS	First Innings		Second Innings	
SD Peters	c Compton b Murtagh	73	c Dexter b Murtagh	73
*NJ O'Brien	c Malan b Finn	1	c Simpson b Finn	0
AG Wakely	b Murtagh	9	lbw b Kartik	13
MH Wessels	c Compton b Finn	6	lbw b Kartik	0
RA White	b Berg	47	not out	85
N Boje (capt)	c Kartik b Berg	51	not out	30
AJ Hall	c Housego b Finn	38		
JJ van der Wath	b Berg	31		
DS Lucas	not out	25		
MS Panesar	c Dexter b Berg	7		
LM Daggett	c Simpson b Berg	1		
Extras	b 4, lb 6, w 1, nb 12	23	b 5, lb 2, w 2, nb 10	19
	(all out 58 overs)	239	(4 wkts 45.4 overs)	220

Bowling
Murtagh 13-4-35-2. Finn 13-2-82-3. Berg 16-1-68-5. Kartik 12-3-31-0. Dexter 4-2-5-0. Murtagh 12-1-47-1. Finn 8-1-62-1. Kartik 16-4-39-2. Berg 6-1-43-0. London 2-0-10-0. Malan 1.4-0-12-0.
Fall of Wickets: 1-2, 2-2, 3-14, 4-40, 5-88, 6-145, 7-194, 8-205, 9-231
1-4, 2-65, 3-65, 4-121

Northamptonshire won by 6 wickets – Northamptonshire (18pts), Middlesex (5pts)

LEICESTERSHIRE v. GLAMORGAN – at Grace Road

LEICESTERSHIRE	First Innings		Second Innings	
PA Nixon	b Kruger	32	st Wallace b Croft	29
MAG Boyce	b Kruger	0	run out	22
HH Dippenaar (capt)	c & b Kruger	24	c Dalrymple b Ashling	8
JJ Cobb	c Wallace b Harris	5	c & b Dalrymple	12
JWA Taylor	b Harris	19	not out	96
*TJ New	lbw b Harris	4	c Rees b Dalrymple	12
JGE Benning	lbw b Ashling	9	lbw b Cosgrove	6
WA White	lbw b Ashling	68	not out	38
CW Henderson	not out	79		
IE O'Brien	lbw b Ashling	28		
AJ Harris	lbw b Harris	4		
Extras	b 1, lb 7, nb 2	10	b 5, lb 9	14
	(all out 93 overs)	282	(6 wkts 92 overs)	259

Bowling
Harris 31-8-85-4. Kruger 27-8-66-3. Ashling 15-2-66-2. Croft 10-2-27-0. Cosgrove 5-2-16-0. Dalrymple 5-1-14-1.
Harris 12-3-17-0. Kruger 13-0-45-0. Croft 31-9-52-1. Ashling 11-1-50-1. Dalrymple 19-3-62-2. Cosgrove 4-0-19-1.
Fall of Wickets: 1-2, 2-57, 3-62, 4-64, 5-68, 6-87, 7-95, 8-215, 9-267
1-53, 2-56, 3-62, 4-160, 5-182, 6-201

GLAMORGAN	First Innings		Second Innings	
GP Rees	b O'Brien	2		
WD Bragg	c New b White	20		
MJ Cosgrove	lbw b Harris	12		
MJ Powell	lbw b Benning	61		
JWM Dalrymple (capt)	lbw b Benning	37		
TL Maynard	lbw b Henderson	2		
*MA Wallace	c Benning b Henderson	14		
JAR Harris	b Benning	0		
RDB Croft	not out	40		
GJP Kruger	c Boyce b O'Brien	0		
CP Ashling	b Benning	12		
Extras	b 4, lb 11, w 1, nb 2	18		
	(all out 75.5 overs)	218		

Bowling
O'Brien 20-2-52-2. Harris 11-1-53-1. White 9-2-24-1. Henderson 19.5-5-31-3. Benning 14-3-43-3.
Fall of Wickets: 1-2, 2-37, 3-64, 4-146, 5-147, 6-151, 7-154, 8-186, 9-187

Match drawn – Leicestershire (9pts), Glamorgan (8pts)

DERBYSHIRE v. KENT – at Derby

KENT	First Innings		Second Innings	
SA Northeast	c Hinds b Lungley	7	c Smith b Lungley	6
RWT Key (capt)	lbw b Jones	30	not out	141
*GO Jones	c Madsen b Lungley	108	c Madsen b Smith	60
M van Jaarsveld	c Hinds b Jones	4	not out	101
DI Stevens	c Sadler b Lungley	16		
JM Kemp	c Pipe b Jones	19		
AJ Blake	c Park b Jones	44		
JC Tredwell	not out	22		
SJ Cook	c & b Wagg	2		
A Khan	lbw b Groenewald	0		
P Edwards	c Pipe b Jones	5		
Extras	lb 6, lb 9, nb 9	24	b 9, lb 2, nb 14	25
	(all out 83.5 overs)	281	(2 wkts 88 overs)	333

Bowling
Lungley 17-1-56-3. Wagg 21-3-86-1. Jones 20.5-6-35-5. Groenewald 16-2-52-1. Smith 6-0-27-0. Park 3-0-10-0.
Lungley 11-1-55-1. Wagg 20-2-80-0. Jones 10-3-21-0. Groenewald 14-1-57-0. Smith 20-2-55-1. Park 6-0-27-0. Madsen 6-0-22-0. Pipe 1-0-5-0.
Fall of Wickets: 1-34, 2-46, 3-68, 4-121, 5-158, 6-234, 7-258, 8-263, 9-264
1-6, 2-139

DERBYSHIRE	First Innings	
CJL Rogers (capt)	c Hinds b Khan	208
WL Madsen	c Jones b Khan	75
GT Park	not out	178
GM Smith	c Stevens b Khan	59
WW Hinds	c Kemp b Khan	18
JL Sadler	not out	24
*DJ Pipe		
GG Wagg		
TD Groenewald		
T Lungley		
PS Jones		
Extras	b 7, lb 11, w 1, nb 2	21
	(4 wkts dec 132 overs)	583

Bowling
Khan 24-3-110-4. Cook 28-4-94-0. Edwards 16-4-84-0. Kemp 25-5-79-0. Tredwell 31-3-137-0. Stevens 4-0-35-0. van Jaarsveld 0-2-0-26-0.
Fall of Wickets: 1-216, 2-341, 3-459, 4-483

Match drawn – Derbyshire (12pts), Kent (7pts)

centuries from Rob Key and Martin van Jaarsveld leading the way – after Chris Rogers's 208 and a career-best 178 not out from Garry Park had spearheaded a Derbyshire run-glut at Derby.

Round Nineteen: 9–13 September

Durham won their second successive Championship title in real style at the Riverside, running up a mammoth first innings total of 648 for 5 declared against their nearest challengers, Nottinghamshire, and then bowling them out twice – despite some stubborn resistance from the likes of Alex Hales, Alistair Brown and Chris Read.

As in 2008, when they clinched their historic first Championship, Steve Harmison was the bowler to take the final wicket and he said afterwards, 'This is a wonderful achievement for the whole club. Indeed, there was more pressure on us to perform this year, as champions, so that makes it even better.'

Thousands gathered on the outfield at the end of the match to see Will Smith, the 26-year-old captain, receive the Championship trophy. He spoke afterwards of the togetherness of the squad, and the all-round strength in depth that had enabled Durham to be so far ahead of the pack – even with regular England call-ups for Graham Onions and Paul Collingwood, plus Harmison's absence towards the end of the Ashes series.

Durham's huge total in this match was based on a first wicket partnership of 314 between Michael Di Venuto, who made 219, and Kyle Coetzer, the Scotland batsman

who was one of three other top-order players to make a century. Shivnarine Chanderpaul and Dale Benkenstein, the other two, shared a fourth wicket stand worth 203.

Liam Plunkett's 6 for 85 and Mark Davies's 4 for 87 then enabled Durham to work their way steadily through

Round Nineteen: 9–13 September Division One

DURHAM v. NOTTINGHAMSHIRE – at the Riverside

DURHAM	First Innings	
MJ Di Venuto	c Shafayat b Fletcher	219
KJ Coetzer	run out	107
WR Smith (capt)	c Shafayat b Fletcher	27
S Chanderpaul	not out	109
DM Benkenstein	c Shafayat b Hales	105
ID Blackwell	c Hales b Patel	29
*P Mustard	not out	6
LE Plunkett		
ME Claydon		
SJ Harmison		
M Davies		
Extras	b 13, lb 20, w 1, nb 12	46
	(5 wkts dec 171 overs)	**648**

Bowling
Shreck 7-3-26-0. Pattinson 28-7-106-0. Fletcher 34-6-125-2. Ealham 16-0-49-0. Patel 60-7-206-1. Hales 14-4-59-1. Brown 7-0-29-0.
Fall of Wickets: 1-314, 2-377, 3-382, 4-585, 5-632

NOTTS	First Innings		Second Innings (following on)	
SA Newman	lbw b Davies	16	c Plunkett b Claydon	9
AD Hales	c Plunkett b Davies	62	c Coetzer b Blackwell	78
MA Wagh	c Plunkett b Davies	3	c Mustard b Davies	6
SR Patel	c Coetzer b Plunkett	44	(5) c Davies b Harmison	4
BM Shafayat	lbw b Plunkett	4	(6) run out	32
AD Brown	c Mustard b Davies	59	(7) b Plunkett	28
*CMW Read (capt)	c Benkenstein b Plunkett	65	(8) lbw b Plunkett	24
MA Ealham	c Benkenstein b Plunkett	49	(9) b Harmison	18
LJ Fletcher	b Davies	1	(10) c Coetzer b Harmison	1
DJ Pattinson	c Mustard b Plunkett	59	(4) b Plunkett	4
CE Shreck	not out	0	not out	0
Extras	b 6, lb 16	22	lb 8	8
	(all out 102 overs)	**384**	(all out 85.2 overs)	**212**

Bowling
Harmison 28-1-108-0. Davies 25-5-87-4. Blackwell 17-3-46-0. Claydon 11-1-36-0. Plunkett 21-4-85-6.
Plunkett 21-6-64-3. Claydon 11-3-31-1. Davies 14-4-29-1. Blackwell 19-11-27-1. Harmison 18.2-6-38-3. Benkenstein 2-0-15-0.
Fall of Wickets: 1-23, 2-33, 3-129, 4-133, 5-152, 6-247, 7-269, 8-270, 9-383
1-21, 2-48, 3-52, 4-61, 5-119, 6-163, 7-187, 8-204, 9-205
Durham won by an innings and 52 runs –
Durham (22pts), Nottinghamshire (5pts)

WORCESTERSHIRE v. HAMPSHIRE – at New Road

HAMPSHIRE	First Innings		Second Innings	
JHK Adams	lbw b Ali	91	not out	7
LA Dawson	c Davies b Jones	37	not out	0
MJ Lumb	c Smith b Shantry	11		
JM Vince	c Davies b Whelan	16		
SM Ervine	c Davies b Jones	14		
*N Pothas	c Solanki b Shantry	93		
AD Mascarenhas (capt) b Ali		2		
DG Cork	c Jones b Ali	43		
Imran Tahir	c Mitchell b Mason	28		
JA Tomlinson	b Ali	23		
DA Griffiths	not out	4		
Extras	b 6, lb 6, w 7, nb 2	21		0
	(all out 107.1 overs)	**383**	(0 wkts 1.3 overs)	**7**

Bowling
Mason 26-5-78-1. Jones 26-2-104-2. Shantry 25-7-68-2. Whelan 14-1-78-1. Mitchell 5-1-14-0. Ali 11.1-5-29-4.
Shantry 1-0-3-0. Jones 0.3-0-4-0.
Fall of Wickets: 1-50, 2-73, 3-95, 4-119, 5-280, 6-280, 7-283, 8-322, 9-378

WORCS	First Innings		Second Innings (following on)	
DKH Mitchell	c Cork b Tomlinson	37	lbw b Cork	0
SC Moore	b Tomlinson	35	c Lumb b Tomlinson	28
VS Solanki (capt)	c Cork b Griffiths	8	lbw b Cork	3
BF Smith	c Adams b Cork	9	c Adams b Cork	0
MM Ali	b Mascarenhas	12	c Dawson b Cork	37
*SM Davies	c Lumb b Imran Tahir	24	c Adams b Cork	31
AN Kervezee	lbw b Imran Tahir	5	c Mascarenhas b Imran Tahir	54
RA Jones	lbw b Imran Tahir	1	c Cork b Imran Tahir	36
CD Whelan	c Pothas b Griffiths	1	not out	21
MS Mason	lbw b Imran Tahir	0	c Pothas b Griffiths	4
JD Shantry	not out	5	c Lumb b Imran Tahir	0
Extras	b 1, lb 5, w 6, nb 10	22	lb 4, nb 4, p 5	13
	(all out 57 overs)	**159**	(all out 58.2 overs)	**227**

Bowling
Cork 12-4-30-1. Mascarenhas 12-5-21-1. Ervine 2-0-17-0. Tomlinson 11-4-28-2. Griffiths 14-4-39-2. Imran Tahir 6-0-18-4.
Cork 14-7-14-5. Mascarenhas 2-0-5-0. Griffiths 11-0-69-1. Tomlinson 15-2-55-1. Imran Tahir 12.2-5-44-3. Ervine 4-0-31-0.
Fall of Wickets: 1-70, 2-81, 3-89, 4-111, 5-111, 6-131, 7-135, 8-150, 9-150
1-0, 2-6, 3-6, 4-58, 5-103, 6-128, 7-198, 8-218, 9-223
Hampshire won by 10 wickets –
Worcestershire (3pts), Hampshire (21pts)

SUSSEX v. WARWICKSHIRE – at Hove

SUSSEX	First Innings		Second Innings	
MH Yardy (capt)	c Ambrose b Rankin	29	lbw b Tahir	27
CD Nash	b Tahir	16	lbw b Woakes	44
EC Joyce	lbw b Woakes	107	lbw b Botha	2
MW Goodwin	b Botha	32	c Ambrose b Rankin	16
CD Hopkinson	b Botha	8	(6) lbw b Botha	1
*AJ Hodd	c Westwood b Tahir	0	(3) c Trott b Rankin	33
DR Smith	c Sreesanth b Botha	5	c Ambrose b Rankin	8
RSC Martin-Jenkins	c Trott b Tahir	12	(9) not out	10
P Chawla	c Bell b Botha	6	(10) c Westwood b Botha	9
OP Rayner	lbw b Woakes	22	(11) c Westwood b Botha	2
RJ Kirtley	not out	2	(5) lbw b Botha	10
Extras	b 8, lb 6, w 2, nb 4	20	lb 4, w 2, nb 4	10
	(all out 89.2 overs)	**254**	(all out 82 overs)	**172**

Bowling
Sreesanth 15-4-41-0. Tahir 18-4-48-3. Rankin 14-2-54-1. Woakes 11.2-3-34-2. Botha 31-10-63-4.
Sreesanth 10-4-32-0. Tahir 11-4-28-1. Woakes 18-10-30-1. Botha 36-15-51-5. Rankin 7-1-27-3.
Fall of Wickets: 1-31, 2-84, 3-149, 4-185, 5-186, 6-187, 7-219, 8-226, 9-239
1-70, 2-79, 3-113, 4-133, 5-137, 6-139, 7-148, 8-150, 9-166

WARWICKSHIRE	First Innings	
IJ Westwood (capt)	lbw b Smith	57
AG Botha	lbw b Rayner	1
N Tahir	run out	0
IR Bell	c sub b Chawla	104
IJL Trott	c Chawla	56
JO Troughton	b Kirtley	85
*TR Ambrose	c sub b Nash	50
CR Woakes	lbw b Chawla	0
R Clarke	not out	52
S Sreesanth	lbw b Kirtley	0
WB Rankin	c Kirtley b Chawla	1
Extras	b 9, lb 7, w 2, nb 4	22
	(all out 140.5 overs)	**428**

Bowling
Chawla 57.5-12-151-4. Rayner 21-5-47-1. Kirtley 20-3-59-2.
Martin-Jenkins 11-0-33-0. Smith 24-7-81-1. Nash 5-1-28-1. Yardy 2-0-13-0.
Fall of Wickets: 1-8, 2-10, 3-120, 4-212, 5-239, 6-336, 7-337, 8-413, 9-413
Warwickshire won by an innings and 2 runs –
Sussex (4pts), Warwickshire (20pts)

SOMERSET v. LANCASHIRE – at Taunton

LANCASHIRE	First Innings		Second Innings	
PJ Horton	c Kieswetter b Willoughby	173	(2) c Kieswetter b Stiff	32
*LD Sutton	c Kieswetter b Phillips	26	(1) c Kieswetter b Thomas	16
MB Loye	lbw b Willoughby	14	not out	151
VVS Laxman	c Kieswetter b Willoughby	12	not out	113
MJ Chilton	c Kieswetter b Willoughby	2		
F du Plessis	c Kieswetter b Phillips	1		
KW Hogg	c Trescothick b Willoughby	69		
G Chapple (capt)	lbw b Willoughby	0		
SI Mahmood	c Suppiah b Thomas	9		
OJ Newby	c Kieswetter b Phillips	13		
G Keedy	not out	3		
Extras	b 10, lb 8, w 6	24	nb 2	2
	(all out 105.1 overs)	**344**	(2 wkts 111 overs)	**314**

Bowling
Willoughby 28-6-109-5. Thomas 22-2-58-1. Phillips 19-1-6-46-4. Stiff 15-2-47-0. Trego 9-1-34-0. Suppiah 4-0-7-0. de Bruyn 8-3-25-0.
Willoughby 23-5-64-0. Thomas 16-9-42-1. Stiff 18-1-70-1. Phillips 10-0-27-0. Suppiah 28-3-75-0. Trego 7-1-24-0. de Bruyn 6-2-12-0.
Fall of Wickets: 1-58, 2-99, 3-119, 4-128, 5-153, 6-303, 7-303, 8-318, 9-330
1-27, 2-67

SOMERSET	First Innings	
ME Trescothick (capt)	b Mahmood	102
AV Suppiah	b Chapple	95
Z de Bruyn	c Laxman b Hogg	71
JC Hildreth	b Mahmood	5
JC Buttler	c Sutton b Chapple	30
*C Kieswetter	c du Plessis b Newby	153
PD Trego	c Mahmood b Keedy	80
BJ Phillips	not out	1
DA Stiff	c Sutton b Keedy	0
AC Thomas		
CM Willoughby		
Extras	b 9, lb 5, nb 6	20
	(8 wkts dec 171 overs)	**557**

Bowling
Chapple 28-11-81-2. Mahmood 26-6-96-2. Keedy 36.1-3-143-2. Newby 17-4-88-1. Hogg 15-9-51-1. Laxman 2-0-5-0. du Plessis 7-0-39-0.
Fall of Wickets: 1-193, 2-221, 3-230, 4-299, 5-350, 6-533, 7-557, 8-557
Match drawn – Somerset (12pts),
Lancashire (8pts)

Liam Plunkett takes the wicket of Nottinghamshire's Samit Patel, and Durham can start to celebrate a second successive Championship title.

Nottinghamshire's first innings, and there were three more wickets for Plunkett, plus three for Harmison, after Notts followed on.

Elsewhere in Division One there were wins for Hampshire, who beat poor Worcestershire by ten wickets at New Road with Dominic Cork picking up remarkable figures of 5 for 14 from 14 overs in the home side's second innings, and Warwickshire. Their win at Hove, based on nine wickets from Ant Botha's left-arm spin and a solid batting display in which Ian Bell made 104, left Sussex staring at relegation. Only Ed Joyce, with a first innings century, performed with the bat for them.

Lancashire batted out the final day of a high-scoring draw at Taunton, where Craig Kieswetter

Round Nineteen: 9–13 September Division Two

MIDDLESEX v. KENT – at Uxbridge

KENT	First Innings		Second Innings	
SA Northeast	c Simpson b Murtagh	84	not out	19
RWT Key (capt)	c & b Silverwood	46	not out	17
*GO Jones	b Murtagh	20		
M van Jaarsveld	c London b Finn	86		
DI Stevens	b Malan	208		
JM Kemp		138		
JC Tredwell	c Dexter b Udal	19		
Azhar Mahmood	c Compton b Udal	29		
SJ Cook				
RS Ferley				
A Khan				
Extras	lb 9, nb 8, p 5	22		0
	(7 wkts dec 153 overs)	652	(0 wkts 5.1 overs)	36

Bowling
Murtagh 24-2-114-2. Finn 21-3-88-1. Berg 23-3-102-0. Udal 37-3-115-2.
Silverwood 22-2-73-1. Dexter 8-0-41-0. Malan 15-0-82-1. London 3-0-23-0.
Murtagh 2-0-16-0. Silverwood 2-0-11-0. London 1-0-3-0. Housego 0.1-0-6-0.
Fall of Wickets: 1-116, 2-145, 3-156, 4-349, 5-577, 6-608, 7-652

MIDDLESEX	First Innings		Second Innings (following on)	
AB London	lbw b Tredwell	7	lbw b Azhar Mahmood	0
NRD Compton	b Azhar Mahmood	30	b Cook	9
DM Housego	lbw b Azhar Mahmood	20	b Cook	19
DJ Malan	lbw b Tredwell	3	lbw b Ferley	80
NJ Dexter	c Key b Khan	146	c Kemp b Tredwell	118
*JA Simpson	c Northeast b Azhar Mahmood	18	st Jones b Ferley	14
GK Berg	b Ferley	67	c Khan b Ferley	3
SD Udal (capt)	c Northeast b Khan	1	c van Jaarsveld b Tredwell	14
TJ Murtagh	lbw b van Jaarsveld	22	not out	35
CEW Silverwood	st Jones b van Jaarsveld	10	lbw b Tredwell	14
ST Finn	not out	10	run out	0
Extras	b 8, lb 4, nb 10	22	b 10, lb 6, nb 4	20
	(all out 110 overs)	356	(all out 116 overs)	326

Bowling
Khan 13-0-64-2. Cook 6-0-19-0. Tredwell 44-7-127-2. Ferley 18-2-59-1.
Azhar Mahmood 22-5-60-3. van Jaarsveld 7-1-15-2.
Azhar Mahmood 14-5-37-1. Khan 12-0-43-0. Cook 13-1-42-2. van Jaarsveld 5-0-17-0.
Tredwell 34-11-82-3. Ferley 33-9-73-3. Stevens 1-1-0-0. Kemp 4-0-16-0.
Fall of Wickets: 1-29, 2-57, 3-68, 4-72, 5-128, 6-247, 7-257, 8-314, 9-328
1-0, 2-28, 3-33, 4-235, 5-243, 6-255, 7-264, 8-286, 9-313

Kent won by 10 wickets – Middlesex (5pts),
Kent (22pts)

GLAMORGAN v. ESSEX – at Cardiff

GLAMORGAN	First Innings		Second Innings	
GP Rees	b Napier	122	c Maunders b Westley	38
MJ Cosgrove	b Napier	53	c Foster b Napier	1
WD Bragg	lbw b Danish Kaneria	0	c Foster b Masters	47
MJ Powell	c Masters b Danish Kaneria	21	b Westley	0
JWM Dalrymple (capt)	b Danish Kaneria	44	not out	98
J Allenby	b Danish Kaneria	5	c Foster b Phillips	4
*MA Wallace	st Foster b Danish Kaneria	5	c Foster b Danish Kaneria	48
RDB Croft	c Foster b Masters	27	run out	0
AJ Shantry	not out	9	b Danish Kaneria	4
DA Cosker	lbw b Danish Kaneria	0	c Foster b Danish Kaneria	14
GJP Kruger	c Westley b Danish Kaneria	2	c Foster b Napier	7
Extras	b 8, lb 5, w 2, nb 8	23	b 7, lb 10, nb 10	27
	(all out 93.3 overs)	311	(all out 94 overs)	296

Bowling
Masters 21-5-50-1. Wright 10-2-45-0. Napier 17-3-54-2. Danish Kaneria 34.3-4-111-7.
Phillips 9-0-36-0. Westley 2-0-2-0.
Masters 18-2-48-1. Napier 8-1-35-2. Danish Kaneria 39-6-108-3. Phillips 17-2-41-1.
Westley 8-1-33-2. Wright 4-0-14-0.
Fall of Wickets: 1-98, 2-99, 3-151, 4-220, 5-228, 6-240, 7-292, 8-302, 9-303
1-20, 2-79, 3-81, 4-117, 5-146, 6-217, 7-221, 8-241, 9-273

ESSEX	First Innings		Second Innings	
JK Maunders	lbw b Croft	44	(2) c Allenby b Dalrymple	12
AN Cook	c Allenby b Croft	57	(6) c Rees b Shantry	17
T Westley	lbw b Croft	1	(1) b Cosker	2
MJ Walker	c Rees b Cosker	25	(3) c Cosgrove b Cosker	15
ML Pettini (capt)	b Cosker	90	(4) c Rees b Cosker	37
*JS Foster	lbw b Allenby	7	(5) lbw b Croft	73
GR Napier	c Dalrymple b Cosker	11	c Cosgrove b Cosker	2
TJ Phillips	lbw b Cosker	20	lbw b Croft	0
DD Masters	b Cosker	11	b Cosker	0
CJC Wright	not out	1	not out	1
Danish Kaneria	b Cosker	0	not out	0
Extras	b 3, lb 13, w 3, nb 2	21	b 6, lb 2, nb 14	22
	(all out 103.4 overs)	288	(9 wkts 101 overs)	181

Bowling
Shantry 11-2-30-0. Allenby 9-1-31-1. Kruger 9-1-18-0. Croft 34-8-78-3.
Cosker 31.4-6-91-6. Dalrymple 9-3-24-0.
Croft 32-9-50-2. Cosker 36-19-35-5. Dalrymple 17-4-34-1. Cosgrove 4-1-8-0.
Allenby 3-1-9-0. Kruger 6-0-28-0. Shantry 3-2-9-1.
Fall of Wickets: 1-98, 2-107, 3-107, 4-171, 5-194, 6-207, 7-253, 8-279, 9-288
1-9, 2-18, 3-38, 4-106, 5-164, 6-178, 7-178, 8-180, 9-180

Match drawn – Glamorgan (10pts), Essex (9pts)

SURREY v. NORTHAMPTONSHIRE – at The Oval

SURREY	First Innings		Second Innings	
*JN Batty	c Peters b van der Wath	110	c Hall b Boje	37
MJ Brown	c O'Brien b van der Wath	31	c Hall b Panesar	42
SJ Walters (capt)	c Lucas b Boje	20	c O'Brien b Daggett	14
U Afzaal	c Peters b van der Wath	62	lbw b Boje	4
MNW Spriegel	b Lucas	3	lbw b Boje	31
CP Schofield	b Hall	57	b Daggett	56
AJ Tudor	c Hall b Boje	13	not out	20
HMRKB Herath	c Hall b Boje	10	c Wessels b Boje	9
JW Dernbach	lbw b Hall	7	lbw b Panesar	4
JE Anyon	not out	0	not out	1
Extras	b 10, lb 4, w 8, nb 6	28	b 12, lb 14, w 2	28
	(all out 116.1 overs)	376	(9 wkts 136 overs)	282

Bowling
van der Wath 22-3-84-3. Lucas 22-2-75-1. Daggett 19-4-53-1. Panesar 20-3-56-0.
Boje 23-7-61-3. Hall 9.1-3-33-2.
Lucas 10-1-26-0. van der Wath 13-5-16-0. Boje 43-14-75-4. Panesar 51-14-85-2.
Hall 3-0-15-0. Daggett 15-1-39-3. Wessels 1-1-0-0.
Fall of Wickets: 1-50, 2-80, 3-153, 4-257, 5-274, 6-320, 7-353, 8-366, 9-375
1-80, 2-84, 3-98, 4-119, 5-171, 6-230, 7-247, 8-262, 9-269

NORTHANTS	First Innings	
SD Peters	c Spriegel b Dernbach	2
*NJ O'Brien	c Walters b Schofield	128
AG Wakely	b Dernbach	0
MH Wessels	run out	109
RA White	c Batty b Herath	66
N Boje (capt)	c Batty b Dernbach	49
AJ Hall	lbw b Schofield	59
JJ van der Wath	not out	50
DS Lucas	c Spriegel b Herath	7
MS Panesar	c Afzaal b Herath	1
LM Daggett	lbw b Herath	0
Extras	b 12, lb 3, w 2, nb 4	21
	(all out 126 overs)	492

Bowling
Dernbach 20-3-82-3. Tudor 13-1-85-0. Anyon 7-0-59-0. Herath 47-6-151-4.
Schofield 36-4-82-2. Spriegel 3-0-18-0.
Fall of Wickets: 1-28, 2-28, 3-187, 4-304, 5-342, 6-405, 7-467, 8-478, 9-488

Match drawn – Surrey (10pts),
Northamptonshire (12pts)

hit eight sixes in an explosive 153 and there were also centuries for Paul Horton, Marcus Trescothick, Mal Loye and VVS Laxman.

In the second division there was more heavy scoring by Kent at Uxbridge, where excellent centuries in both innings against his former club by Neil Dexter could not save Middlesex from a ten-wicket defeat. Darren Stevens hit a career-best 208, with 34 fours, in Kent's inexorable progress towards 652 for 7 declared, with Justin Kemp finishing 138 not out, and then it was just a matter of whether Middlesex could be winkled out twice in the time remaining, on a slow and lifeless surface.

Glamorgan were left frustrated at Cardiff, with Essex's last pair of Chris Wright – who batted 22 balls for his 0 not out – and Danish Kaneria holding out for the draw at 181 for 9. On a turning pitch there were creditable innings from Gareth Rees, Mark Pettini, Jamie Dalrymple and James Foster, but in the main it was the spinners who held sway with Kaneria taking ten wickets in the match and Dean Cosker's slow left-armers bringing him overall figures of 11 for 126.

Northamptonshire, meanwhile, had the better of a draw at The Oval, with Niall O'Brien and Riki Wessels both hitting centuries, but Surrey fought hard to bat through the final day, which they began level with Northants on 116 for 3, with Matt Spriegel resisting for almost three hours for 56.

Round Twenty: 15–19 September

Sussex were left facing almost certain relegation when they collapsed in spectacular fashion to 83 all out at Hove, with Matthew Hoggard taking a last afternoon hat-trick as Yorkshire won by 156 runs.

For much of the match it looked as if Sussex could achieve the victory they so badly needed, especially with Yorkshire also not safe from the drop, but initially they let their visitors off the hook when, from 209 for 7, Ajmal Shahzad and David Wainwright both hit 80s to add 157 for the eighth wicket.

Sussex, however, still earned a handy first innings lead – and maximum batting points, with Rory Hamilton-Brown scoring a magnificent unbeaten 171 from only 210 balls. Piyush Chawla's five wickets could not prevent Yorkshire from scrapping their way to 284, leaving Sussex 240 to win. They did not even come close.

The other two first division matches were drawn, with rain on days one and four at the Rose Bowl and, at Taunton, a resilient second innings batting performance by Somerset saving face after they had been forced to follow on by bottom club Worcestershire, for whom Daryl Mitchell scored a career-best 298 in eight and a quarter hours, with a six and a remarkable 54 fours.

AGGERS' VIEW

' Winning back-to-back County Championships is a superb achievement for a county that did not even play first-class cricket until 1992. But Durham are now the shining light as far as the modern county club is concerned. They produce their own players, both for the county stage and for England, and they have made some canny signings to help themselves develop and move forward as a team. Ian Blackwell's move from Somerset to the North East was the signing of the summer for Durham. When you compare what has happened in recent years at Durham with what has gone on at Surrey, for instance, it is clear that Durham's progress under the stewardship of Geoff Cook and other dedicated servants has made them a model of how a county club should be run. '

Essex's thrilling six-wicket win at Northampton, meanwhile, propelled them into the heart of the second division promotion race, at the expense of a Northants side who had looked big favourites to join Kent in the top two places. Kent secured their position as Division Two champions with maximum bonus points in a draw at Canterbury against Leicestershire, who saw Paul Nixon bat gallantly on the last day for a match-saving 173 not out against the county he represented for three seasons in the middle of his 20-year career.

Danish Kaneria's first innings 5 for 86 and Ryan ten Doeschate's 75 kept Essex in the game at Wantage Road but, from 90 for 7 in their second innings, Northants rallied through David Lucas's career-best unbeaten 55 and, with time running out in a match already badly-hit by the weather, they clawed their way to 195.

This left Essex to score 242 in 52 overs and, despite Johan van der Wath's five wickets, they got there with just one ball to spare with Alastair Cook providing the initial impetus with 87 and then Graham Napier and young Tom Westley keeping their heads to add an unbroken 37 in the last four overs.

Derbyshire and Glamorgan, meanwhile, the latter for the second week running, were left just one wicket away from completing the victories they required to keep their mathematical promotion hopes alive. At Uxbridge it seemed as if Derbyshire must win, as Middlesex slid to 149 for 7 on the final afternoon, but 20-year old Adam London batted courageously for two hours with a broken and dislocated finger to score 65 and some determined tail-end support ultimately meant that off spinner Greg Smith's career-best 5 for 65 was in vain.

At Cardiff a fascinating final day saw Gloucestershire finish just 15 runs short of their target of 296 after a difficult chase on a turning pitch, but with Glamorgan straining unsuccessfully to take their last remaining wicket after Jon Lewis fell for 28 with two overs left.

Round Twenty-One: 23–26 September

With just five overs of the 2009 Championship season left to be bowled, Essex completed a dramatic and controversial five-wicket victory against Derbyshire at Derby to pip Northamptonshire for the second promotion place alongside Kent.

Northants had thrashed Leicestershire by an innings and 196 runs at Grace Road, completing the win inside three days after brilliant batting from Rob White, who hit four sixes in his 193, Andrew Hall, who hit 159 in a sixth wicket stand of 268, and Nicky Boje (90 not out) had seen them recover from 44 for 4 to reach an eventual 600 for 8 declared. Leicestershire were then dismissed twice, with only James Benning and a dogged James Taylor resisting David Lucas's destructive 7 for 45.

For the next 24 hours Northants watched to see how events would unfold at Derby, where Derbyshire captain Chris Rogers's first innings 222, with a six and 31 fours, had put the home side in complete command. Essex struggled to stay in touch, despite Tom Westley's fine maiden first-class hundred, and it came as something of a surprise when Rogers declared his team's second innings to leave Essex to score 359 in 65 overs.

It was a tough target, of course, but the pitch remained good and Rogers knew he had an injury-weakened attack. He also knew that Essex would have to go for any target he set them, and many at Northampton certainly felt he could have batted on for at least another five overs.

As it was, Essex were 203 for 5 when James Foster was dismissed, leaving them needing another 156 from just 22 overs. Rogers's calculations seemed to be good especially, as he pointed out later, Derbyshire themselves wanted enough time to complete a win that would clinch third position.

What happened next left everyone associated with Northants distraught, as Ryan ten Doeschate emerged to join Mark Pettini and immediately began to set about the Derbyshire bowling. With eight sixes and nine fours, he careered to a 59-ball 108 not out, hitting his second fifty from just 22 balls, and such was the ferocity of his assault – with Pettini sensibly playing the support role with 85 not out from 94 balls – that, in the end, Essex had five overs in hand. Ten Doeschate and Pettini had secured promotion with a stand of 156 in just 17 overs.

Nineteen-year-old Sam Northeast carried his bat to score 128 at Bristol, his maiden first-class hundred, but it was not enough to prevent Kent from slipping to an innings defeat against Gloucestershire, for whom James Franklin was in sparkling all-round form with 5 for 30 and 104, while at The Oval there were seven individual century-makers on a pitch which made bowling a thankless task.

Round Twenty: 15–19 September Division One

SUSSEX v. YORKSHIRE – at Hove

YORKSHIRE	First Innings		Second Innings	
JA Rudolph	lbw b Lewry	0	b Chawla	70
JJ Sayers	st Hodd b Chawla	10	c Hodd b Collymore	31
A Lyth	lbw b Collymore	50	b Yardy	31
A McGrath (capt)	c Hodd b Chawla	37	c Hamilton-Brown b Chawla	37
AW Gale	c Gatting b Hamilton-Brown	60	c Hodd b Chawla	22
JM Bairstow	lbw b Chawla	0	lbw b Smith	2
*GL Brophy	b Chawla	34	c Gatting b Chawla	30
A Shahzad	lbw b Hamilton-Brown	88	c Yardy b Chawla	0
DJ Wainwright	not out	85	not out	14
Azeem Rafiq	lbw b Smith	0	b Smith	0
MJ Hoggard	b Nash	17	b Lewry	26
Extras	b 8, lb 11, w 1, nb 14	34	b 14, lb 5, nb 2	21
	(all out 136 overs)	403	(all out 98.1 overs)	284

Bowling
Lewry 23-6-51-1. Collymore 21-5-69-1. Smith 19-4-60-1. Chawla 46-9-115-4. Hamilton-Brown 15-2-49-2. Nash 9-2-29-1. Yardy 3-1-11-0.
Lewry 9.1-2-27-1. Collymore 10-2-31-1. Chawla 41-10-112-5. Smith 32-9-75-2. Yardy 6-1-20-1.
Fall of Wickets: 1-0, 2-41, 3-75, 4-96, 5-104, 6-164, 7-209, 8-366, 9-368
1-55, 2-106, 3-147, 4-185, 5-188, 6-220, 7-220, 8-245, 9-246

SUSSEX	First Innings		Second Innings	
MH Yardy (capt)	c Lyth b Shahzad	58	c Hall b Hoggard	13
CD Nash	c Sayers b Wainwright	42	c Brophy b Shahzad	26
JS Gatting	lbw b Hoggard	46	(1) c Sayers b Shahzad	20
MW Goodwin	b Wainwright	63	c Brophy b Wainwright	5
CD Hopkinson	lbw b Shahzad	0	(6) b Wainwright	6
RJ Hamilton-Brown	not out	171	(3) run out	2
*AJ Hodd	c Rudolph b Shahzad	22	c Brophy b Hoggard	2
DR Smith	c ? b Shahzad	11	b Hoggard	0
P Chawla	c Rudolph b Wainwright	6	c Bairstow b Hoggard	0
CD Collymore	lbw b Wainwright	6	lbw b Wainwright	0
JD Lewry	lbw b Wainwright	0	b Wainwright	0
Extras	b 4, lb 12, nb 2, p 5	23	b 4, lb 5	9
	(all out 119.5 overs)	448	(all out 25.3 overs)	83

Bowling
Shahzad 29-7-84-4. Hoggard 26-5-70-1. Wainwright 31.5-4-134-5. Rafiq 29-2-128-0. McGrath 4-11-10.
Shahzad 9-0-33-1. Hoggard 8-3-29-4. Wainwright 8.3-4-12-4.
Fall of Wickets: 1-68, 2-130, 3-165, 4-165, 5-293, 6-392, 7-408, 8-420, 9-448
1-37, 2-39, 3-46, 4-64, 5-71, 6-80, 7-80, 8-80, 9-81

Yorkshire won by 156 runs – Sussex (7pts), Yorkshire (20pts)

HAMPSHIRE v. DURHAM – at the Rose Bowl

DURHAM	First Innings		Second Innings	
MJ Di Venuto	lbw b Cork	62	not out	8
KJ Coetzer	b Briggs	20	not out	0
WR Smith (capt)	c Imran Tahir b Griffiths	150		
S Chanderpaul	b Briggs	4		
DM Benkenstein	c Dawson b Briggs	24		
ID Blackwell	c Adams b Imran Tahir	56		
*P Mustard	c Adams b Imran Tahir	35		
LE Plunkett	lbw b Imran Tahir	37		
SG Borthwick	not out	26		
M Davies	c Adams b Imran Tahir	1		
SJ Harmison	lbw b Griffiths	0		
Extras	b 3, lb 5, w 2, nb 14	24		0
	(all out 132.4 overs)	439	(0 wkts 3.5 overs)	8

Bowling
Cork 21-4-63-1. Griffiths 19.4-3-66-2. Briggs 38-5-126-3. Ervine 16-4-37-0.
Imran Tahir 35-3-133-4. Dawson 3-1-6-0.
Vince 2-0-8-0. Griffiths 1.5-1-0-0.
Fall of Wickets: 1-73, 2-99, 3-110, 4-152, 5-261, 6-313, 7-376, 8-435, 9-435

HAMPSHIRE	First Innings	
JHK Adams	c Harmison b Borthwick	57
LA Dawson	c Mustard b Blackwell	29
MJ Lumb	lbw b Blackwell	6
JM Vince	c Smith b Borthwick	8
CC Benham	c Di Venuto b Borthwick	100
*N Pothas (capt)	b Blackwell	78
DA Griffiths	b Plunkett	1
SM Ervine	c Mustard b Blackwell	67
DG Cork	c Mustard b Harmison	24
Imran Tahir	not out	0
DR Briggs	c Plunkett b Blackwell	0
Extras	b 7, lb 3, nb 4	14
	(all out 119.3 overs)	384

Bowling
Harmison 21-5-78-1. Davies 14-3-36-0. Blackwell 39.3-9-110-5. Borthwick 27-2-95-3.
Plunkett 14-4-49-1. Benkenstein 3-1-6-0. Smith 1-1-0-0.
Fall of Wickets: 1-52, 2-72, 3-87, 4-114, 5-266, 6-267, 7-345, 8-384, 9-384

*Match drawn – Hampshire (10pts),
Durham (11pts)*

SOMERSET v. WORCESTERSHIRE – at Taunton

WORCS	First Innings	
DKH Mitchell	b Trego	298
SC Moore	c Kieswetter b Stiff	32
VS Solanki (capt)	c Trescothick b Willoughby	15
MM Ali	c Kieswetter b Willoughby	1
AN Kervezee	c Suppiah b Stiff	19
DA Wheeldon	c Phillips b Thomas	87
GM Andrew	c de Bruyn b Thomas	0
*OB Cox	b Trego	61
RA Jones	not out	18
MS Mason	b Trego	4
JD Shantry	b Stiff	1
Extras	b 5, lb 14, nb 16	35
	(all out 141.2 overs)	571

Bowling
Willoughby 35-9-126-2. Thomas 23-5-104-2. Phillips 26-6-74-0. Stiff 17.2-0-102-3.
Trego 20-4-89-3. Suppiah 6-0-57-0.
Fall of Wickets: 1-73, 2-109, 3-111, 4-191, 5-409, 6-415, 7-539, 8-542, 9-548

SOMERSET	First Innings		Second Innings (following on)	
ME Trescothick	st Cox b Ali	72	c Mitchell b Mason	9
AV Suppiah	c Cox b Andrew	83		
JL Langer (capt)	c Wheeldon b Shantry	46	c Ali b Andrew	64
JC Hildreth	c Solanki b Mason	24	c Cox b Jones	18
Z de Bruyn	c Cox b Jones	15	c Solanki b Shantry	106
*C Kieswetter	lbw b Mason	1	c Kervezee b Andrew	90
PD Trego	c Ali b Mason	0	lbw b Andrew	9
BJ Phillips	c Jones b Shantry	18	c Solanki b Andrew	84
AC Thomas	c Cox b Andrew	38	not out	54
DA Stiff	not out	30	not out	1
CM Willoughby	c Shantry b Andrew	1		
Extras	lb 6, w 3, nb 4	13	b 5, lb 6, w 2, nb 2	15
	(all out 78.3 overs)	280	(8 wkts 133 overs)	523

Bowling
Mason 24-9-60-3. Jones 11-1-42-1. Andrew 17.3-3-75-3. Shantry 16-4-65-2. Ali 10-2-32-1.
Mason 14-5-28-1. Jones 29-3-142-1. Ali 26-3-136-0. Andrew 30-4-117-5. Shantry 21-6-61-1. Mitchell 6-1-11-0. Solanki 7-2-17-0.
Fall of Wickets: 1-45, 2-143, 3-161, 4-189, 5-189, 6-189, 7-190, 8-239, 9-247
1-0, 2-142, 3-163, 4-175, 5-342, 6-366, 7-398, 8-523

*Match drawn – Somerset (8pts),
Worcestershire (12pts)*

Glamorgan, however, could have forced victory on the back of Garnett Kruger's extra pace and bounce, but dropping Jon Batty on 13 and 96 ultimately proved crucial as the former Surrey captain ground out a match-saving 120 in the company of Stewart Walters (82).

In the first division, Sussex's relegation was confirmed when they gained just one batting point at Trent Bridge, despite a fine 135 from Chris Nash, but an excellent tussle then developed with Nottinghamshire owing much to the batting of their captain Chris Read, who made 88 and 83, and the slow left-arm spin of Samit Patel, who took a career-best 6 for 84, as they claimed victory by 35 runs to deny a brave Sussex chase and secure themselves a £225,000 cheque as Championship runners-up.

Durham, £500,000 richer as champions, piled up 634 for 8 declared at New Road, with Shivnarine Chanderpaul scoring 201 from 382 balls and adding 226 with Dale Benkenstein (109) after Michael Di Venuto had skipped to 113 from just 114 balls, but were denied victory when Steven Davies thumped an emotional 97 in his final innings for Worcestershire. Davies, bound for Surrey, faced only 75 balls but hit three sixes and 16 fours in a counter-attack from 169 for 5 which continued as both Gareth Andrew and Richard Jones completed unbeaten half-centuries to ensure the draw.

Poor weather contributed to the draw at Headingley, where Hampshire's Michael Lumb scored 81 and 64 against his former club, while across the Pennines at Old Trafford there was a ten-wicket victory inside three days for Lancashire against Warwickshire. Glen Chapple's

6 for 19 wrecked the visitors' first innings and Gary Keedy, with 6 for 50, finished the job after VVS Laxman's 113 had put Lancashire into an impregnable position.

Mark Baldwin has covered county cricket for The Times *since 1998.*

Round Twenty: 15–19 September Division Two

ESSEX v. NORTHAMPTONSHIRE – at Chelmsford

NORTHANTS	First Innings		Second Innings	
SD Peters	lbw b Danish Kaneria	37	lbw b Masters	2
*NJ O'Brien	c Napier b Wright	14	c Pettini b Napier	38
PW Harrison	c Cook b Masters	32	lbw b Masters	3
MH Wessels	st Foster b Danish Kaneria	10	c Pettini b Wright	8
RA White	c Maunders b Danish Kaneria	30	b Wright	8
N Boje (capt)	lbw b Danish Kaneria	8	c ten Doeschate b Wright	8
AJ Hall	c Foster b Masters	85	b Danish Kaneria	29
JJ van der Wath	c Foster b Napier	10	b Napier	0
DS Lucas	c Foster b Danish Kaneria	20	not out	55
MS Panesar	not out	32	c Walker b Wright	19
LM Daggett	b Masters	0	c Walker b Napier	2
Extras	b 6, lb 3, nb 12	21	b 1, lb 6, w 2, nb 14	23
	(all out 90.3 overs)	299	(all out 59.3 overs)	195

Bowling
Masters 19.3-7-57-3. Wright 15-1-61-1. Napier 18-4-74-1. Danish Kaneria 36-12-86-5. Westley 2-0-12-0.
Masters 19-5-35-2. Danish Kaneria 21-3-64-1. Napier 7.3-1-46-3. Wright 12-3-43-4.
Fall of Wickets: 1-40, 2-67, 3-79, 4-143, 5-143, 6-153, 7-180, 8-251, 9-297
1-8, 2-28, 3-55, 4-71, 5-85, 6-85, 7-90, 8-150, 9-183

ESSEX	First Innings		Second Innings	
JK Maunders	c White b van der Wath	10	c O'Brien b van der Wath	46
AN Cook	c Peters b Lucas	4	c O'Brien b van der Wath	87
T Westley	b Lucas	3	(8) not out	15
MJ Walker	c Hall b Panesar	40	(3) c O'Brien b van der Wath	39
ML Pettini (capt)	c Hall b Boje	47	b Hall	5
*JS Foster	c Peters b Hall	28	b van der Wath	4
RN ten Doeschate	c Daggett b Hall	75	(4) c O'Brien b van der Wath	7
GR Napier	not out	7	(7) not out	22
DD Masters	c Hall b Panesar	5		
Danish Kaneria	not out	15		
CJC Wright				
Extras	b 4, lb 11, nb 8	23	b 4, lb 11, w 1	16
	(8 wkts dec 78.4 overs)	253	(6 wkts 51.5 overs)	242

Bowling
van der Wath 14-4-37-1. Lucas 11-4-16-2. Daggett 8-4-23-0. Hall 12.4-3-38-2.
Panesar 25-6-71-2. Boje 8-0-53-1.
van der Wath 17.5-3-71-5. Lucas 5-1-30-0. Hall 14-0-51-1. Boje 5-0-29-0.
Panesar 8-0-29-0. Daggett 2-0-17-0.
Fall of Wickets: 1-14, 2-14, 3-21, 4-102, 5-128, 6-217, 7-226, 8-231
1-130, 2-159, 3-175, 4-192, 5-204, 6-205

Essex won by 4 wickets – Essex (19pts), Northamptonshire (4pts)

KENT v. LEICESTERSHIRE – at Canterbury

LEICESTERSHIRE	First Innings		Second Innings	
PA Nixon	c van Jaarsveld b Khan	5	not out	173
MAG Boyce	b Khan	8	c Kemp b van Jaarsveld	98
HH Dippenaar (capt)	b Cook	54	(4) not out	30
JJ Cobb	lbw b McLaren	8	(3) c £ b Tredwell	28
JWA Taylor	lbw b Cook	6		
*TJ New	c Jones b Cook	3		
JGE Benning	c van Jaarsveld b Khan	16		
JHK Naik	c Kemp b Khan	8		
WA White	c Tredwell b Cook	8		
IE O'Brien	c van Jaarsveld b Cook	0		
AJ Harris	not out	22		
Extras	lb 5, w 3, nb 2	10	b 5, lb 7, w 1, nb 8	21
	(all out 57 overs)	148	(2 wkts 122 overs)	350

Bowling
Cook 18-3-44-5. Khan 16-6-46-4. Stevens 2-1-3-0. McLaren 10-3-22-1.
Kemp 11-2-28-0.
Khan 20-2-74-0. Cook 22-8-41-0. Tredwell 34-11-80-1. McLaren 13-3-32-0.
Kemp 10-4-29-0. van Jaarsveld 9-2-33-1. Key 9-1-32-0. Blake 4-0-15-0.
Northeast 1-0-2-0.
Fall of Wickets: 1-14, 2-21, 3-35, 4-52, 5-70, 6-96, 7-118, 8-118, 9-119
1-204, 2-259

KENT	First Innings	
SA Northeast	b White	21
RWT Key (capt)	c Taylor b Harris	12
*GO Jones	c Nixon b Harris	89
M van Jaarsveld	c New b Benning	146
DI Stevens	b Naik	18
A Khan	c Cobb b White	16
JM Kemp	lbw b White	8
AJ Blake	c New b Harris	33
JC Tredwell	c New b Harris	30
R McLaren	c New b Harris	43
SJ Cook	not out	23
Extras	b 4, lb 6, nb 4	14
	(all out 100.4 overs)	453

Bowling
O'Brien 21-6-64-0. Harris 19.4-1-84-4. White 18-1-91-3. Benning 15-0-101-1.
Naik 24-3-95-1. Cobb 3-1-8-1.
Fall of Wickets: 1-32, 2-75, 3-153, 4-203, 5-249, 6-263, 7-344, 8-363, 9-426

Match drawn – Kent (12pts), Leicestershire (7pts)

MIDDLESEX v. DERBYSHIRE – at Uxbridge

DERBYSHIRE	First Innings		Second Innings	
CJL Rogers (capt)	c Simpson b Murtagh	25	not out	112
WL Madsen	c Housego b Burton	167	c Kartik b Udal	89
GT Park	b Burton	28	b Malan	3
GM Smith	b Kartik	62	not out	42
WW Hinds	c Simpson b Burton	28		
JL Sadler	not out	12		
*DJ Pipe	not out	38		
GG Wagg				
TD Groenewald				
MAK Lawson				
PS Jones				
Extras	b 5, lb 14, w 2, nb 20	41	b 20, lb 11, w 2, nb 2	35
	(5 wkts dec 90 overs)	401	(2 wkts dec 54.1 overs)	281

Bowling
Murtagh 22-2-83-1. Burton 22-1-121-3. Berg 13-2-45-0. Kartik 19-3-72-1.
Udal 14-1-61-0.
Murtagh 6-2-21-0. Burton 13-0-60-0. Berg 6-0-35-0. Kartik 5-0-25-0. Udal 6-0-27-1.
Malan 15-0-66-1. Dexter 2.1-0-5-0. Housego 1-0-11-0.
Fall of Wickets: 1-46, 2-142, 3-271, 4-350, 5-351
1-181, 2-193

MIDDLESEX	First Innings		Second Innings	
DM Housego	lbw b Jones	4	b Groenewald	34
NRD Compton	b Groenewald	178	lbw b Groenewald	8
DJ Malan	run out	21	c Pipe b Smith	52
NJ Dexter	c Rogers b Jones	13	b Park	34
*JA Simpson	c Pipe b Smith	9	lbw b Smith	1
GK Berg	c Madsen b Jones	70	b Smith	0
SD Udal (capt)	b Jones	20	(8) b Smith	0
M Kartik	c Jones b Smith	1	(9) c Rogers b Lawson	22
TJ Murtagh	c Jones b Wagg	14	(10) not out	18
DA Burton	not out	2	(11) not out	0
AB London	c Jones b Smith	4	b Smith	65
Extras	lb 5, nb 12	17	b 5, lb 10, nb 10	25
	(9 wkts dec 87 overs)	353	(9 wkts 85 overs)	259

Bowling
Wagg 26-3-97-1. Jones 19-4-69-4. Smith 11-1-73-2. Groenewald 12-3-60-1.
Lawson 10-1-41-0. Park 2-0-8-0.
Jones 14-3-36-0. Wagg 19-2-61-0. Lawson 12-3-32-1. Smith 23-7-65-5.
Groenewald 14-4-42-2. Park 3-0-8-1.
Fall of Wickets: 1-9, 2-75, 3-105, 4-122, 5-257, 6-280, 7-295, 8-341, 9-349
1-34, 2-59, 3-135, 4-136, 5-142, 6-143, 7-149, 8-206, 9-254

Match drawn – Middlesex (9pts), Derbyshire (12pts)

GLAMORGAN v. GLOUCESTERSHIRE – at Cardiff

GLAMORGAN	First Innings		Second Innings	
GP Rees	c Gidman b Franklin	88	lbw b Dawson	43
MJ Cosgrove	c Kirby b Lewis	80	c Porterfield b Kirby	1
WD Bragg	lbw b Dawson	1	c Adshead b Lewis	11
MJ Powell	b Kirby	84	c Porterfield b Lewis	41
*JWM Dalrymple (capt)	lbw b Banerjee	0	c Dawson b Kirby	6
J Allenby	lbw b Lewis	79	c Taylor b Lewis	3
*MA Wallace	c Adshead b Lewis	12	b Dawson	25
JAR Harris	c Marshall b Dawson	18	c Marshall b Kirby	10
RDB Croft	not out	22	not out	21
DA Cosker	lbw b Dawson	0	not out	2
GJP Kruger	c Franklin b Dawson	6		
Extras	b 5, lb 5, nb 10	20	b 3, lb 2, w 3	8
	(all out 109.4 overs)	410	(8 wkts dec 62.3 overs)	171

Bowling
Lewis 22.5-5-62-3. Franklin 15-3-58-1. Kirby 22-1-88-1. Marshall 5-2-30-0.
Banerjee 16-3-66-1. Dawson 24.4-5-76-4. Taylor 2-0-5-0.
Lewis 20-6-47-3. Kirby 16.3-1-44-3. Franklin 6-0-23-0. Dawson 18-0-47-2.
Taylor 2-0-5-0.
Fall of Wickets: 1-141, 2-148, 3-216, 4-225, 5-337, 6-353, 7-376, 8-390, 9-390
1-18, 2-49, 3-82, 4-93, 5-103, 6-138, 7-140, 8-156

GLOS	First Innings		Second Innings	
Kadeer Ali	c Allenby	42	(7) b Kruger	19
WTS Porterfield	c Cosgrove b Kruger	0	(1) c Allenby b Croft	81
HJH Marshall	b Harris	5	c Wallace b Harris	35
APR Gidman (capt)	c Wallace b Allenby	47	c Rees b Croft	52
CG Taylor	b Harris	0	c Allenby b Dalrymple	24
JEC Franklin	lbw b Dalrymple	66	lbw b Dalrymple	6
*SJ Adshead	lbw b Cosgrove	48	c Allenby b Harris	0
RKJ Dawson	c Wallace b Harris	50	c Bragg b Croft	15
J Lewis	b Kruger	5	c Wallace b Dalrymple	28
V Banerjee	not out	6	(11) not out	0
SP Kirby	b Harris	10	(10) not out	7
Extras	lb 12, nb 2	14	b 5, lb 2, w 1, nb 6	14
	(all out 92 overs)	286	(9 wkts 100 overs)	281

Bowling
Harris 24.2-1-69-4. Kruger 18-3-61-2. Allenby 15-3-34-2. Cosker 15-4-43-0.
Croft 13-2-32-0. Dalrymple 9-2-37-2.
Harris 12-1-56-2. Kruger 15-4-63-1. Allenby 3-1-8-0. Croft 38-8-67-3.
Cosker 18-3-57-0. Dalrymple 14-1-42-3.
Fall of Wickets: 1-4, 2-13, 3-94, 4-95, 5-111, 6-201, 7-242, 8-257, 9-278
1-4, 2-54, 3-126, 4-163, 5-177, 6-227, 7-243, 8-253, 9-281

Match drawn – Glamorgan (12pts), Gloucestershire (9pts)

Round Twenty-One: 23–26 September Division One

NOTTINGHAMSHIRE v. SUSSEX – at Trent Bridge

NOTTS	First Innings		Second Innings	
BM Shafayat	c Yardy b Smith	45	lbw b Collymore	4
AD Hales	lbw b Lewry	33	b Chawla	38
MA Wagh	b Chawla	67	(4) lbw b Smith	2
SR Patel	b Martin-Jenkins	21	(5) c Martin-Jenkins b Smith	54
A Patel	lbw b Smith	0	(6) c Hodd b Nash	37
AD Brown	c Hamilton-Brown b M-Jenkins	10	(7) lbw b Smith	1
*CMW Read (capt)	lbw b Collymore	88	(8) c Collymore b Smith	83
MA Ealham	lbw b Chawla	13	(9) lbw b Lewry	24
AR Adams	b Chawla	3	(10) c Yardy b Lewry	25
LJ Fletcher	not out	19	(3) lbw b Collymore	0
CE Shreck	b Smith	0	not out	0
Extras	b 9, lb 16, nb 4	29	b 13, lb 2, w 1, nb 2	18
	(all out 105 overs)	**328**	(all out 90.3 overs)	**286**

Bowling
Lewry 9-1-40-1. Collymore 24-5-59-1. Martin-Jenkins 19-3-69-2. Smith 27-7-73-3. Chawla 26-8-62-3.
Collymore 15-3-41-2. Lewry 12-3-53-2. Smith 25.3-7-58-4. Martin-Jenkins 9-2-32-0. Chawla 18-3-55-1. Hamilton-Brown 4-0-8-0. Nash 7-0-24-1.
Fall of Wickets: 1-70, 2-86, 3-137, 4-138, 5-163, 6-239, 7-277, 8-293, 9-319
1-4, 2-4, 3-15, 4-86, 5-106, 6-107, 7-187, 8-244, 9-286

SUSSEX	First Innings		Second Innings	
MH Yardy (capt)	c Read b Fletcher	21	b Ealham	48
CD Nash	c Brown b Patel SR	135	lbw b Fletcher	70
JS Gatting	c Adams b Fletcher	12	c Wagh b Fletcher	70
MW Goodwin	c Patel SR b Shreck	20	c Ealham b Patel SR	9
RJ Hamilton-Brown	lbw b Patel SR	1	c Read b Patel SR	4
*AJ Hodd	b Adams	12	lbw b Ealham	11
RSC Martin-Jenkins	c Read b Adams	1	c Brown b Patel SR	15
DR Smith	c Patel A b Adams	5	c Patel A b Patel SR	80
P Chawla	st Read b Patel SR	16	st Read b Patel SR	8
CD Collymore	b Adams	9	c Hales b Patel SR	3
JD Lewry	not out	0	not out	1
Extras	b 1, lb 8, w 2	11	b 5, lb 10, nb 2	17
	(all out 75.1 overs)	**243**	(all out 75.1 overs)	**336**

Bowling
Shreck 13-3-51-1. Fletcher 15-1-43-2. Adams 22-7-63-4. Ealham 11-3-37-0. Patel SR 14.1-3-40-3.
Shreck 5-1-26-0. Fletcher 21-3-93-2. Adams 11-1-59-0. Patel SR 24.1-1-84-6. Ealham 14-2-59-2.
Fall of Wickets: 1-74, 2-104, 3-156, 4-161, 5-202, 6-208, 7-218, 8-218, 9-243
1-114, 2-145, 3-170, 4-176, 5-199, 6-224, 7-278, 8-303, 9-309

Nottinghamshire won by 35 runs – Nottinghamshire (20pts), Sussex (4pts)

WORCESTERSHIRE v. DURHAM – at New Road

WORCS	First Innings		Second Innings	
DKH Mitchell	lbw b Benkenstein	67	c Mustard b Plunkett	26
SC Moore	c Chanderpaul b Davies	23	lbw b Blackwell	16
VS Solanki (capt)	b Plunkett	4	b Plunkett	31
MM Ali	c Benkenstein b Plunkett	19	lbw b Plunkett	25
AN Kervezee	c Di Venuto b Benkenstein	46	c Mustard b Claydon	48
*SM Davies	c Chanderpaul b Claydon	31	c sub b Plunkett	97
DA Wheeldon	c Claydon b Harmison	14	c Di Venuto b Blackwell	30
GM Andrew	b Plunkett	77	not out	59
RA Jones	lbw b Davies	27	not out	53
CD Whelan	not out	23		
JD Shantry	c Mustard b Plunkett	6		
Extras	b 3, lb 10, w 4, nb 2	19	b 14, lb 9, w 2	25
	(all out 98.5 overs)	**356**	(7 wkts 91 overs)	**410**

Bowling
Harmison 22-9-47-1. Davies 20-3-71-2. Plunkett 26.5-4-104-4. Claydon 14-2-57-1. Benkenstein 9-2-38-2. Blackwell 7-2-26-0.
Davies 19-3-64-0. Claydon 12-3-53-1. Plunkett 29-1-132-4. Blackwell 27-2-124-2. Benkenstein 2-1-5-0. Smith 2-0-9-0.
Fall of Wickets: 1-48, 2-54, 3-116, 4-120, 5-197, 6-197, 7-226, 8-304, 9-334
1-41, 2-55, 3-93, 4-128, 5-169, 6-286, 7-291

DURHAM	First Innings	
MJ Di Venuto	b Ali	113
KJ Coetzer	c Jones b Andrew	44
WR Smith (capt)	c Davies b Shantry	28
S Chanderpaul	not out	201
DM Benkenstein	c Davies b Andrew	109
ID Blackwell	lbw b Jones	9
*P Mustard	c Davies b Jones	25
LE Plunkett	c Wheeldon b Mitchell	52
ME Claydon	c Davies b Whelan	10
M Davies	not out	16
SJ Harmison		
Extras	b 3, lb 13, w 3, nb 8	27
	(8 wkts dec 172.1 overs)	**634**

Bowling
Andrew 41-11-121-2. Jones 28-4-129-2. Shantry 39.1-9-102-1. Whelan 28-2-94-1. Ali 21-1-104-1. Mitchell 11-1-52-1. Solanki 4-0-16-0.
Fall of Wickets: 1-124, 2-185, 3-207, 4-433, 5-444, 6-480, 7-583, 8-600

Match drawn – Worcestershire (9pts), Durham (12pts)

YORKSHIRE v. HAMPSHIRE – at Headingley

HAMPSHIRE	First Innings		Second Innings	
JHK Adams	b Kruis	51	b Wainwright	72
LA Dawson	c Gale b Wainwright	45	c Shahzad b Kruis	35
MJ Lumb	c McGrath b Shahzad	81	c Brophy b Lyth	64
CC Benham	c McGrath b Shahzad	16	not out	67
SM Ervine	c Brophy b McGrath	26	not out	18
*N Pothas	c Brophy b Kruis	38		
AD Mascarenhas (capt)	c McGrath b Hoggard	8		
DG Cork	not out	42		
JA Tomlinson	b Shahzad	14		
DA Griffiths	b Kruis	0		
DR Briggs	c Rudolph b Shahzad	1		
Extras	b 8, lb 13, w 2, nb 6	29	b 15, lb 3, w 2, nb 8	28
	(all out 115.3 overs)	**351**	(3 wkts 98 overs)	**284**

Bowling
Hoggard 27-6-115-1. Shahzad 29.3-9-75-4. Kruis 23-8-51-3. McGrath 20-4-46-1. Wainwright 16-6-43-1.
Hoggard 11-3-31-0. Shahzad 13-4-27-0. Kruis 14-5-50-1. McGrath 15-2-39-0. Wainwright 20-6-49-1. Lyth 19-9-38-1. Rudolph 5-0-32-0. Brophy 1-1-0-0.
Fall of Wickets: 1-95, 2-110, 3-152, 4-219, 5-260, 6-275, 7-311, 8-345, 9-346
1-105, 2-142, 3-262

YORKSHIRE	First Innings	
JA Rudolph	c Tomlinson b Briggs	68
JJ Sayers	c Tomlinson b Cork	95
DJ Wainwright	c Briggs b Mascarenhas	21
A Lyth	c Adams b Griffiths	26
A McGrath (capt)	c Dawson b Tomlinson	25
AW Gale	c Pothas b Tomlinson	1
JM Bairstow	not out	50
*GL Brophy	c Pothas b Griffiths	0
A Shahzad	c Pothas b Ervine	4
MJ Hoggard	c Benham b Ervine	0
GJ Kruis	c Cork b Briggs	20
Extras	lb 6, w 6, nb 26	38
	(all out 109.4 overs)	**348**

Bowling
Griffiths 23-7-73-2. Mascarenhas 22-8-44-1. Cork 19-7-44-1. Tomlinson 21-4-83-2. Briggs 15.4-3-37-2. Ervine 9-0-61-2.
Fall of Wickets: 1-162, 2-209, 3-231, 4-259, 5-273, 6-273, 7-277, 8-317, 9-319

Match drawn – Yorkshire (10pts), Hampshire (11pts)

Round Twenty-One: 23–26 September Division Two

DERBYSHIRE v. ESSEX – at Derby

DERBYSHIRE	First Innings		Second Innings	
CJL Rogers (capt)	c Masters b Napier	222	c Cook b Danish Kaneria	42
WL Madsen	lbw b Wright	16	c Walker b Wright	0
GT Park	c Walker b Wright	57	not out	103
DJ Redfern	c Maunders b Wright	48		
WW Hinds	b Masters	37	b Danish Kaneria	36
JL Sadler	c Walker b Masters	8	not out	27
GM Smith	b Danish Kaneria	6	(4) c & b Danish Kaneria	16
*DJ Pipe	c Walker b Wright	21		
GG Wagg	lbw b Danish Kaneria	0		
JL Clare	lbw b Danish Kaneria	0		
PS Jones	not out	19		
Extras	b 5, lb 24, w 1, nb 10	40	lb 8, nb 8	16
	(all out 128.4 overs)	**474**	(4 wkts dec 64 overs)	**240**

Bowling
Masters 33-10-72-2. Wright 27.4-5-97-4. Napier 34-7-111-1. Danish Kaneria 22-1-114-3. ten Doeschate 7-1-34-0. Westley 5-1-17-0.
Napier 10-2-30-0. Wright 16-2-59-1. ten Doeschate 5-0-26-0. Danish Kaneria 17-1-36-3. Westley 3-0-3-0. Cook 7-0-40-0. Pettini 6-0-38-0.
Fall of Wickets: 1-61, 2-182, 3-312, 4-400, 5-420, 6-429, 7-439, 8-439, 9-439
1-20, 2-63, 3-85, 4-143

ESSEX	First Innings		Second Innings	
JK Maunders	c Rogers b Wagg	5	c Wagg b Smith	55
AN Cook	c Pipe b Wagg	8	c Sadler b Clare	25
T Westley	c Pipe b Jones	132	c Jones b Wagg	40
MJ Walker	c Hinds b Clare	75	c Sadler b Smith	18
ML Pettini (capt)	c Madsen b Jones	14	not out	85
*JS Foster	c Redfern b Clare	15	c Park b Smith	13
RN ten Doeschate	run out	41	not out	108
GR Napier	c Pipe b Clare	0		
CJC Wright	not out	24		
Danish Kaneria	c Madsen b Wagg	10		
DD Masters				
Extras	b 11, lb 6, w 1, nb 14	32	b 5, lb 4, w 2, nb 4	15
	(9 wkts dec 107.5 overs)	**356**	(5 wkts 60 overs)	**359**

Bowling
Jones 28-3-87-2. Wagg 31.5-10-79-3. Smith 10-0-41-0. Clare 23-4-64-3. Park 9-0-43-0. Hinds 6-0-25-0.
Jones 11-0-68-0. Wagg 19-0-102-1. Clare 6-0-35-1. Smith 18-0-96-3. Park 1-0-12-0. Madsen 4-0-29-0. Redfern 1-0-8-0.
Fall of Wickets: 1-9, 2-14, 3-238, 4-244, 5-271, 6-299, 7-299, 8-346, 9-356
1-45, 2-114, 3-139, 4-160, 5-203

Essex won by 5 wickets – Derbyshire (8pts), Essex (20pts)

NORTHAMPTONSHIRE v. LEICESTERSHIRE – at Northampton

NORTHANTS	First Innings	
SD Peters	c New b Gurney	3
*NJ O'Brien	c Taylor b Harris	6
PW Harrison	c New b Benning	18
AG Wakely	c New b Benning	5
MH Wessels	lbw b Henderson	65
RA White	c White b Harris	193
AJ Hall	c & b White	159
N Boje (capt)	not out	90
JJ van der Wath	b Henderson	30
DS Lucas	not out	5
LM Daggett		
Extras	b 5, lb 9, w 1, nb 11	26
	(8 wkts dec 116.2 overs)	**600**

Bowling
Harris 23-1-150-2. Gurney 22-3-131-1. White 18.2-1-115-1. Benning 15-3-53-2. Henderson 33-6-116-2. Cobb 5-0-21-0.
Fall of Wickets: 1-9, 2-13, 3-33, 4-44, 5-153, 6-421, 7-562, 8-595

LEICESTERSHIRE	First Innings		Second Innings (following on)	
PA Nixon	c Wakely b Boje	52	c O'Brien b Lucas	8
MAG Boyce (capt)	c Peters b Daggett	20	c O'Brien b Lucas	12
GP Smith	c Wakely b Hall	26	(4) lbw b Lucas	9
JJ Cobb	c O'Brien b Hall	0	(5) b van der Wath	1
JWA Taylor	c Peters b Hall	0	(6) not out	30
*TJ New	not out	46	(7) b Lucas	0
JGE Benning	c Wakely b van der Wath	19	(8) c Lucas b Boje	72
WA White	lbw b Lucas	4	(10) c Wessels b Lucas	0
CW Henderson	c O'Brien b van der Wath	10	b Lucas	42
AJ Harris	st O'Brien b Boje	20	(3) c O'Brien b Lucas	4
HF Gurney	b Hall	0	b van der Wath	0
Extras	b 4, lb 9, w 4, nb 4	21	lb 6, nb 2	8
	(all out 60.4 overs)	**218**	(all out 56.4 overs)	**186**

Bowling
van der Wath 16-4-49-2. Lucas 12-1-50-1. Daggett 10-1-51-1. Hall 9.4-0-41-4. Boje 13-7-14-2.
van der Wath 17.4-2-78-2. Lucas 16-4-45-7. Hall 9-4-22-0. Boje 11-5-10-1. Daggett 3-0-25-0.
Fall of Wickets: 1-51, 2-106, 3-106, 4-106, 5-111, 6-151, 7-156, 8-169, 9-209
1-26, 2-30, 3-31, 4-40, 5-44, 6-45, 7-151, 8-183, 9-183

Northamptonshire won by an innings and 196 runs – Northamptonshire (22pts), Leicestershire (3pts)

GLOUCESTERSHIRE v. KENT – at Bristol

KENT	First Innings		Second Innings	
SA Northeast	c Porterfield b Lewis	7	not out	128
RWT Key (capt)	c Adshead b Lewis	50	b Kirby	46
*GO Jones	c Adshead b Franklin	44	(11) absent hurt	
DI Stevens	lbw b Franklin	0	c Adshead b Marshall	17
JB Hockley	lbw b Franklin	7	c Dawson b Lewis	10
JM Kemp	c Dawson b Saxelby	21	b Marshall	1
AJ Blake	c sub b Lewis	47	(3) c Lewis b Saxelby	0
JC Tredwell	c Kadeer Ali b Lewis	6	(7) c Saxelby b Ireland	8
SJ Cook	not out	60	(8) c Adshead b Ireland	0
MP Coles	b Franklin	14	(9) b Kirby	16
A Khan	lbw b Franklin	0	(10) c Franklin b Lewis	29
Extras	lb 2, nb 6	8	b 4, lb 2, nb 4	10
	(all out 62 overs)	**264**	(all out 56.3 overs)	**265**

Bowling
Lewis 21-9-50-4. Franklin 13-3-30-5. Kirby 12.1-1-73-0. Saxelby 10.5-0-73-1. Marshall 4-0-20-0. Dawson 1-0-16-0.
Lewis 12.3-2-45-2. Ireland 16-1-91-2. Kirby 12-1-54-2. Saxelby 5-1-16-1. Marshall 11-2-53-2.
Fall of Wickets: 1-20, 2-101, 3-106, 4-107, 5-122, 6-139, 7-181, 8-214, 9-248
1-101, 2-106, 3-140, 4-155, 5-158, 6-173, 7-179, 8-222, 9-265

GLOS	First Innings	
Kadeer Ali	lbw b Khan	25
WTS Porterfield	lbw b Tredwell	42
HJH Marshall	c Jones b Stevens	87
APR Gidman (capt)	c Tredwell b Cook	15
CG Taylor	c Jones b Coles	69
†JEC Franklin	retired not out	104
*SJ Adshead	c Key b Tredwell	114
RKJ Dawson	c Tredwell b Khan	18
ID Saxelby	c Tredwell b Khan	5
J Lewis	c Hockley b Tredwell	43
SP Kirby	not out	19
AJ Ireland	lbw b Coles	0
Extras	b 3, lb 1, w 1, nb 6	11
	(all out 123.4 overs)	**552**

Bowling
Khan 28-5-120-3. Cook 23-2-97-1. Stevens 10-2-55-1. Kemp 17-3-46-0. Coles 17.4-0-130-2. Tredwell 28-2-100-3.
Fall of Wickets: 1-52, 2-136, 3-161, 4-208, 5-295, 6-462, 7-468, 8-512, 9-543
† Replaced by AJ Ireland

Gloucestershire won by an innings and 23 runs – Gloucestershire (22pts), Kent (4pts)

LANCASHIRE v. WARWICKSHIRE – at Old Trafford

WARWICKSHIRE	First Innings		Second Innings	
IJ Westwood (capt)	c Sutton b Mahmood	11	c Smith b Mahmood	30
AG Botha	c Chilton b Chapple	5	c Chilton b Mahmood	8
IR Bell	c Smith b Hogg	5	lbw b Hogg	9
IJL Trott	c Sutton b Chapple	1	lbw b Keedy	44
JO Troughton	c Horton b Chapple	48	lbw b Keedy	27
*TR Ambrose	c Horton b Hogg	3	b Keedy	55
R Clarke	b Smith	1	c Horton b Keedy	40
NM Carter	c Laxman b Chapple	59	b Keedy	0
CR Woakes	c Sutton b Chapple	2	not out	15
AS Miller	c Horton b Chapple	0	run out	4
WB Rankin	not out	0	b Keedy	2
Extras	lb 3, nb 10	13	lb 6, lb 6, nb 2	14
	(all out 44.4 overs)	148	(all out 74.2 overs)	244

Bowling
Mahmood 12-1-61-1. Chapple 14.4-6-19-6. Hogg 8-3-29-2. Smith 10-1-36-1. Chapple 8-0-30-0. Mahmood 16-1-64-2. Hogg 12-2-56-1. Keedy 27.2-9-50-6. Smith 10-3-30-0. Croft 1-0-2-0.
Fall of Wickets: 1-16, 2-26, 3-29, 4-37, 5-41, 6-48, 7-121, 8-131, 9-131
1-30, 2-49, 3-53, 4-103, 5-162, 6-215, 7-215, 8-236, 9-242

LANCASHIRE	First Innings		Second Innings	
PJ Horton	lbw b Woakes	3	(2) not out	0
TC Smith	c Westwood b Rankin	45	(1) not out	4
MB Loye	run out	13		
VVS Laxman	b Miller	113		
MJ Chilton	lbw b Clarke	19		
SJ Croft	b Miller	79		
*LD Sutton	not out	45		
G Chapple (capt)	c Ambrose b Miller	14		
KW Hogg	st Ambrose b Botha	23		
SI Mahmood	lbw b Miller	1		
G Keedy	c Ambrose b Rankin	18		
Extras	b 10, lb 16, w 6, nb 6	38		
	(all out 126 overs)	389	(0 wkts 0.2 overs)	4

Bowling
Woakes 26-6-80-1. Rankin 20-4-57-2. Miller 25-7-76-4. Carter 18-5-37-0. Botha 27-6-85-1. Clarke 10-2-28-1. Trott 0.2-0-4-0.
Fall of Wickets: 1-6, 2-44, 3-45, 4-110, 5-264, 6-282, 7-296, 8-352, 9-353

Lancashire won by 10 wickets –
Lancashire (21pts), Warwickshire (3pts)

SURREY v. GLAMORGAN – at The Oval

SURREY	First Innings		Second Innings	
*JN Batty	c Wallace b Kruger	13	b Harris	120
MJ Brown	b Harris	9	b Kruger	17
A Harinath	c Allenby b Croft	57	(4) b Kruger	0
SJ Walters (capt)	lbw b Kruger	7	(5) c Dalrymple b Harris	82
U Afzaal	b Kruger	170	(9) not out	2
MNW Spriegel	c Cosker b Croft	100	c sub b Harris	0
CP Schofield	b Kruger	8	lbw b Croft	21
CJ Jordan	c Wallace b Kruger	42	not out	37
HMRKB Herath	c Wallace b Kruger	8		
RJ Logan	lbw b Cosker	0	(3) c Wallace b Kruger	6
JW Dernbach	not out	4		
Extras	b 2, lb 6, w 2, nb 2	12	b 4, lb 1, nb 2, p 5	12
	(all out 122.4 overs)	430	(7 wkts 104 overs)	309

Bowling
Harris 21-6-88-1. Kruger 26-5-93-6. Allenby 13-4-39-0. Cosgrove 8-1-31-0. Croft 34-4-107-2. Cosker 17.4-3-54-1. Dalrymple 1-0-10-0.
Harris 19-4-70-3. Kruger 12-2-28-3. Cosker 26-8-70-0. Croft 35-6-91-1. Allenby 3-0-8-0. Dalrymple 5-1-18-0. Cosgrove 4-0-14-0.
Fall of Wickets: 1-23, 2-23, 3-51, 4-154, 5-335, 6-349, 7-400, 8-425, 9-426
1-20, 2-41, 3-63, 4-237, 5-237, 6-256, 7-302

GLAMORGAN	First Innings			
GP Rees	c Batty b Logan	154		
MJ Cosgrove	run out	175		
WD Bragg	c Walters b Jordan	33		
MJ Powell	c Walters b Logan	12		
JWM Dalrymple (capt)	b Jordan	4		
J Allenby	b Herath	137		
*MA Wallace	lbw b Herath	139		
JAR Harris	c Batty b Schofield	15		
RDB Croft	not out	1		
DA Cosker				
GJP Kruger				
Extras	b 10, lb 17, w 3, nb 2	32		
	(8 wkts dec 145.2 overs)	702		

Bowling
Dernbach 26-2-106-0. Logan 30-6-101-2. Jordan 16-1-85-2. Herath 33.2-1-164-2. Schofield 31-1-176-1. Spriegel 9-1-43-0.
Fall of Wickets: 1-315, 2-368, 3-400, 4-400, 5-405, 6-645, 7-692, 8-702

Match drawn – Surrey (10pts), Glamorgan (11pts)

Division One – Final Table

	P	W	L	D	Bat	Bowl	Pens	Pts
Durham	16	8	0	8	49	48	1.00	240.00
Nottinghamshire	16	4	2	10	56	41	0.00	193.00
Somerset	16	3	1	12	50	43	1.00	182.00
Lancashire	16	4	2	10	35	44	0.00	175.00
Warwickshire	16	3	3	10	54	38	0.00	174.00
Hampshire	16	3	3	10	50	40	3.00	169.00
Yorkshire	16	2	2	12	46	44	0.00	166.00
Sussex	16	2	6	8	45	39	1.00	143.00
Worcestershire	16	0	10	6	30	40	0.00	94.00

Division Two – Final Table

	P	W	L	D	Bat	Bowl	Pens	Pts
Kent	16	8	3	5	43	44	0.00	219.00
Essex	16	6	3	7	40	43	1.00	194.00
Northamptonshire	16	6	4	6	40	45	0.00	193.00
Gloucestershire	16	6	6	4	39	46	0.00	185.00
Glamorgan	16	2	2	12	56	43	0.00	175.00
Derbyshire	16	2	3	11	55	45	0.00	172.00
Surrey	16	1	4	11	54	36	0.00	148.00
Middlesex	16	2	7	7	43	41	0.00	140.00
Leicestershire	16	2	3	11	31	35	0.00	138.00

Angus Fraser, Middlesex Director of Cricket

'Coming back into the game after my time in journalism, as cricket correspondent for *The Independent*, was a decision I made because I wanted to do something for a club that I hold very dear from my own playing days. I am not here to have a nice cosy time watching a bit of cricket, I want to get things right at Middlesex, I want to achieve things for the club as well as producing good players for England.

I knew the situation here was not something that could be changed overnight, but my first season as director of cricket has been a very disappointing one. People ask if I have enjoyed coming back into cricket, but that is not a word I would use to describe last summer! We have underachieved as a team, and it hurts. The only positive note is that I genuinely believe we have a number of exciting young players at Middlesex, and managing them and helping them to develop is something I am very much looking forward to doing.

I always expected us to be inconsistent in our cricket last season, as that is the nature of a largely inexperienced team, but we were more inconsistent than I foresaw and one of the challenges now is to improve that side of things significantly.

Perhaps the biggest change I have seen in the game, compared to when I last played seven or eight years ago, is that players – in general – have greater demands and expectations than they used to have.

On the good side, they want more from their clubs to help them become better cricketers, but in some cases they also have a slightly false impression of where they are as players. Not many seem to underestimate their standing in the game these days. Managing that sort of situation can be difficult, and everything seems more complicated now in relation to the management of players. But changing the culture in certain areas is all part of what needs to be done at Middlesex.'

COUNTY CHAMPIONSHIP FEATURES 2009

BEST INDIVIDUAL SCORES

MW Goodwin	344*	Sussex v. Somerset	at Taunton
JC Hildreth	303*	Somerset v. Warwickshire	at Taunton
DKH Mitchell	298	Worcestershire v. Somerset	at Taunton
MR Ramprakash	274	Surrey v. Leicestershire	at The Oval
RWT Key	270*	Kent v. Glamorgan	at Cardiff
MJ Di Venuto	254*	Durham v. Sussex	at the Riverside
JO Troughton	223	Warwickshire v. Hampshire	at Edgbaston
CJL Rogers	222	Derbyshire v. Essex	at Derby
MJ Lumb	219	Hampshire v. Nottinghamshire	at Trent Bridge
MJ Di Venuto	219	Durham v. Nottinghamshire	at the Riverside
A McGrath	211	Yorkshire v. Warwickshire	at Edgbaston
CJL Rogers	208	Derbyshire v. Kent	at Derby
DI Stevens	208	Kent v. Middlesex	at Uxbridge
JWA Taylor	207*	Leicestershire v. Surrey	at The Oval
VS Solanki	206*	Worcestershire v. Yorkshire	at Headingley
U Afzaal	204*	Surrey v. Northamptonshire	at Northampton
MA Carberry	204	Hampshire v. Warwickshire	at the Rose Bowl
S Chanderpaul	201*	Durham v. Worcestershire	at New Road
RS Bopara	201	Essex v. Surrey	at Colchester
JA Rudolph	198	Yorkshire v. Worcestershire	at Headingley

BEST INNINGS BOWLING (6 wickets or more)

JC Tredwell	8/66	Kent v. Glamorgan	at Canterbury
Danish Kaneria	8/116	Essex v. Leicestershire	at Chelmsford
DS Lucas	7/24	Northamptonshire v. Gloucestershire	at Cheltenham
G Onions	7/38	Durham v. Warwickshire	at Edgbaston
MS Mason	7/39	Worcestershire v. Lancashire	at Old Trafford
DS Lucas	7/45	Northamptonshire v. Leicestershire	at Northampton
MS Mason	7/60	Worcestershire v. Sussex	at Hove
TJ Murtagh	7/82	Middlesex v. Derbyshire	at Derby
ID Blackwell	7/85	Durham v. Lancashire	at Old Trafford
Danish Kaneria	7/111	Essex v. Glamorgan	at Cardiff
Imran Tahir	7/140	Hampshire v. Somerset	at the Rose Bowl
G Chapple	6/19	Lancashire v. Warwickshire	at Old Trafford
SJ Harmison	6/20	Durham v. Nottinghamshire	at Trent Bridge
SI Mahmood	6/30	Lancashire v. Durham	at the Riverside
G Onions	6/31	Durham v. Somerset	at Taunton
AJ Ireland	6/31	Gloucestershire v. Leicestershire	at Bristol
G Chapple	6/34	Lancashire v. Worcestershire	at New Road
GG Wagg	6/35	Derbyshire v. Surrey	at Derby
A Nel	6/36	Surrey v. Northamptonshire	at Northampton
SD Udal	6/36	Middlesex v. Glamorgan	at Swansea

BEST MATCH BOWLING

DS Lucas	12/73	Northamptonshire v. Gloucestershire	at Cheltenham
Danish Kaneria	12/203	Essex v. Leicestershire	at Chelmsford
JM Anderson	11/109	Lancashire v. Sussex	at Hove
LE Plunkett	11/119	Durham v. Worcestershire	at the Riverside
JC Tredwell	11/120	Kent v. Glamorgan	at Canterbury
DA Cosker	11/126	Glamorgan v. Essex	at Cardiff
P Chawla	11/170	Sussex v. Somerset	at Hove
SD Udal	10/95	Middlesex v. Glamorgan	at Swansea
JC Tredwell	10/100	Kent v. Northamptonshire	at Northampton
SI Mahmood	10/140	Lancashire v. Worcestershire	at New Road
Danish Kaneria	10/219	Essex v. Glamorgan	at Cardiff
IE O'Brien	9/68	Leicestershire v. Middlesex	at Grace Road
SJ Harmison	9/74	Durham v. Lancashire	at the Riverside
G Onions	9/80	Durham v. Hampshire	at the Riverside
CR Woakes	9/82	Warwickshire v. Worcestershire	at Edgbaston
RDB Croft	9/112	Glamorgan v. Middlesex	at Swansea

BEST MATCH BOWLING (continued)

AG Botha	9/114	Warwickshire v. Sussex	at Hove
GJP Kruger	9/121	Glamorgan v. Surrey	at The Oval
SR Patel	9/124	Nottinghamshire v. Sussex	at Trent Bridge
G Onions	9/127	Durham v. Warwickshire	at Edgbaston

HIGHEST TEAM TOTALS

742 for 5d	Sussex v. Somerset	at Taunton
702 for 8d	Glamorgan v. Surrey	at The Oval
672 for 4d	Somerset v. Warwickshire	at Taunton
654 for 8d	Hampshire v. Nottinghamshire	at Trent Bridge
652 for 7d	Kent v. Middlesex	at Uxbridge
648 for 5d	Durham v. Nottinghamshire	at the Riverside
634 for 8d	Durham v. Worcestershire	at New Road
630 for 8d	Warwickshire v. Hampshire	at Edgbaston
620 for 7d	Kent v. Surrey	at The Oval
620 for 8d	Sussex v. Worcestershire	at New Road
608 for 4d	Surrey v. Leicestershire	at The Oval
600 for 8d	Yorkshire v. Warwickshire	at Edgbaston
600 for 8d	Northamptonshire v. Leicestershire	at Northampton
593 for 5d	Leicestershire v. Surrey	at The Oval
583 for 4d	Derbyshire v. Kent	at Derby
571	Worcestershire v. Somerset	at Taunton
568 for 5d	Lancashire v. Hampshire	at the Rose Bowl
566	Glamorgan v. Leicestershire	at Colwyn Bay
557 for 5d	Kent v. Glamorgan	at Cardiff
557 for 8d	Somerset v. Lancashire	at Taunton

LOWEST TEAM TOTALS

69	Somerset v. Durham	at Taunton
83	Nottinghamshire v. Durham	at Trent Bridge
83	Sussex v. Yorkshire	at Hove
90	Northamptonshire v. Kent	at Northampton
91	Middlesex v. Leicestershire	at Grace Road
96	Hampshire v. Durham	at the Riverside
105	Hampshire v. Durham	at the Riverside
111	Worcestershire v. Warwickshire	at New Road
116	Lancashire v. Durham	at the Riverside
119	Gloucestershire v. Essex	at Bristol
123	Kent v. Essex	at Tunbridge Wells
131	Surrey v. Derbyshire	at Derby
132	Worcestershire v. Hampshire	at the Rose Bowl
133	Leicestershire v. Gloucestershire	at Bristol
133	Leicestershire v. Gloucestershire	at Grace Road
135	Lancashire v. Durham	at the Riverside
135	Warwickshire v. Durham	at the Riverside
135	Glamorgan v. Middlesex	at Swansea
138	Somerset v. Nottinghamshire	at Trent Bridge
138	Gloucestershire v. Leicestershire	at Grace Road

HUNDREDS IN EACH INNINGS

Name	For	Against	Venue	Date	1st	2nd
ME Trescothick	Somerset	Warwickshire	Edgbaston	5 August	108	107*
NJ Dexter	Middlesex	Kent	Uxbridge	9 September	146	118

FASTEST COUNTY CHAMPIONSHIP HUNDREDS

Name	No. of balls	Match	Venue	Date
PD Trego	54	Somerset v. Yorkshire	Taunton	3 July
RN ten Doeschate	57	Essex v. Derbyshire	Derby	26 September
R Clarke	78	Warwicks v. Hants	Edgbaston	24 April
PP Chawla	82	Sussex v. Worcs	New Road	13 June
GO Jones	84	Kent v. Surrey	Canterbury	29 August
Azeem Rafiq	92	Yorkshire v. Worcs	New Road	19 June
MH Wessels	94	Northants v. Surrey	The Oval	10 September
CG Taylor	97	Glos v. Surrey	Bristol	4 September
CD Nash	99	Sussex v. Worcs	Hove	13 August

MOST HUNDREDS

Player	100s	Matches
ME Trescothick (Somerset)	8	16
M van Jaarsveld (Kent)	7	15
CJL Rogers (Derbyshire)	6	13
MJ Di Venuto (Durham)	6	16
MR Ramprakash (Surrey)	5	11
DM Benkenstein (Durham)	5	16
GO Jones (Kent)	5	16
VVS Laxman (Lancashire)	4	11
MA Carberry (Hampshire)	4	12
IR Bell (Warwickshire)	4	13
RWT Key (Kent)	4	14
CD Nash (Sussex)	4	14
IJL Trott (Warwickshire)	4	14
APR Gidman (Gloucestershire)	4	15
CMW Read (Nottinghamshire)	4	16
JA Rudolph (Yorkshire)	4	16
C Kieswetter (Somerset)	4	16
PJ Hughes (Middlesex)	3	3
S Chanderpaul (Durham)	3	5
JL Denly (Kent)	3	9

MOST FIFTIES (including hundreds)

Player	50s	Matches
ME Trescothick (Somerset)	17	16
M van Jaarsveld (Kent)	14	15
MA Carberry (Hampshire)	12	12
JHK Adams (Hampshire)	12	16
MJ Di Venuto (Durham)	11	16
C Kieswetter (Somerset)	11	16
CJL Rogers (Derbyshire)	10	13
CD Nash (Sussex)	10	14
HH Dippenaar (Leicestershire)	10	15
U Afzaal (Surrey)	10	16
CMW Read (Nottinghamshire)	10	16
GO Jones (Kent)	10	16
GT Park (Derbyshire)	10	16
JA Rudolph (Yorkshire)	10	16
MR Ramprakash (Surrey)	9	11
IJL Trott (Warwickshire)	9	14
JWA Taylor (Leicestershire)	9	15
MJ Powell (Glamorgan)	9	16
DM Benkenstein (Durham)	9	16
AV Suppiah (Somerset)	9	16

LEADING DUCK-MAKERS

Player	Ducks	Matches
Imran Tahir (Hampshire)	6	12
SJ Harmison (Durham)	5	13
ST Finn (Middlesex)	5	14
SP Kirby (Gloucestershire)	5	16
JA Rudolph (Yorkshire)	5	16
CM Willoughby (Somerset)	5	16
HJH Marshall (Gloucestershire)	5	16
JD Lewry (Sussex)	4	6
CT Tremlett (Hampshire)	4	7
DR Smith (Sussex)	4	9
DA Griffiths (Hampshire)	4	9
ID Saxelby (Gloucestershire)	4	9
Danish Kaneria (Essex)	4	11
PS Jones (Kent)	4	12
SA Newman (Surrey)	4	12
SD Udal (Middlesex)	4	14
MAG Boyce (Leicestershire)	4	14
J Lewis (Gloucestershire)	4	15
MJ Lumb (Hampshire)	4	15
HH Dippenaar (Leicestershire)	4	15

LEADING RUN SCORERS

Player	Runs	Matches
ME Trescothick (Somerset)	1817	16
MJ Di Venuto (Durham)	1601	16
M van Jaarsveld (Kent)	1475	15
CJL Rogers (Derbyshire)	1461	13
MR Ramprakash (Surrey)	1350	11
JA Rudolph (Yorkshire)	1334	16
CD Nash (Sussex)	1298	14
GO Jones (Kent)	1291	16
JHK Adams (Hampshire)	1280	16
U Afzaal (Surrey)	1269	16
MA Carberry (Hampshire)	1251	12
C Kieswetter (Somerset)	1242	16
IJL Trott (Warwickshire)	1207	14
CMW Read (Nottinghamshire)	1203	16
AV Suppiah (Somerset)	1201	16
JWA Taylor (Leicestershire)	1184	15
AJ Hall (Northamptonshire)	1161	16
DM Benkenstein (Durham)	1155	16
RWT Key (Kent)	1145	14
JJ Sayers (Yorkshire)	1103	16

MOST SIXES

Player	Sixes	Matches
C Kieswetter (Somerset)	29	16
PD Trego (Somerset)	23	16
WW Hinds (Derbyshire)	21	16
AR Adams (Nottinghamshire)	16	11
JJ van der Wath (Northamptonshire)	16	13
CMW Read (Nottinghamshire)	14	16
M van Jaarsveld (Kent)	13	15
RA White (Northamptonshire)	13	16
SD Udal (Middlesex)	12	14
JM Kemp (Kent)	12	14
DJ Hussey (Nottinghamshire)	10	3
DR Smith (Sussex)	10	9
EJG Morgan (Middlesex)	10	10
RN ten Doeschate (Essex)	10	14
GT Park (Derbyshire)	10	16
P Chawla (Sussex)	9	6
NM Carter (Warwickshire)	9	9
RWT Key (Kent)	9	14
SM Ervine (Hampshire)	9	15
GO Jones (Kent)	9	16

MOST FOURS

Player	Fours	Matches
ME Trescothick (Somerset)	264	16
CD Nash (Sussex)	221	14
MJ Di Venuto (Durham)	220	16
CJL Rogers (Derbyshire)	196	13
M van Jaarsveld (Kent)	177	15
GO Jones (Kent)	176	16
MA Carberry (Hampshire)	171	12
U Afzaal (Surrey)	171	16
JHK Adams (Hampshire)	169	16
CMW Read (Nottinghamshire)	168	16
AJ Hall (Northamptonshire)	164	16
AV Suppiah (Somerset)	163	16
DKH Mitchell (Worcestershire)	154	16
C Kieswetter (Somerset)	152	16
MR Ramprakash (Surrey)	151	11
IJL Trott (Warwickshire)	143	14
JA Rudolph (Yorkshire)	143	16
DM Benkenstein (Durham)	142	16

LEADING WICKET-TAKERS

Player	Wickets	Matches
Danish Kaneria (Essex)	75	11
JC Tredwell (Kent)	69	16
SP Kirby (Gloucestershire)	64	16
TJ Murtagh (Middlesex)	60	13
DS Lucas (Northants)	58	15
J Lewis (Gloucestershire)	57	15
RDB Croft (Glamorgan)	56	16
CM Willoughby (Somerset)	54	16
ST Finn (Middlesex)	53	14
Imran Tahir (Hampshire)	52	12
SJ Harmison (Durham)	51	13
JJ van der Wath (Northamptonshire)	50	13
LE Plunkett (Durham)	49	12
GG Wagg (Derbyshire)	47	14
G Onions (Durham)	45	7
DD Masters (Essex)	45	15
AR Adams (Nottinghamshire)	43	11
MS Mason (Worcestershire)	43	14
MJ Hoggard (Yorkshire)	43	15
ID Blackwell (Durham)	43	16

MOST CATCHES (excluding wicketkeepers)

Player	Catches	Matches
JM Kemp (Kent)	30	14
M van Jaarsveld (Kent)	30	15
MJ Di Venuto (Durham)	23	16
R Clarke (Warwickshire)	22	13
CJL Rogers (Derbyshire)	21	13
ME Trescothick (Somerset)	21	16
DJ Malan (Middlesex)	19	15
DG Cork (Hampshire)	18	12
AD Brown (Nottinghamshire)	18	16
AV Suppiah (Somerset)	18	16
WTS Porterfield (Gloucestershire)	17	9
JL Langer (Somerset)	17	15
JHK Adams (Hampshire)	17	16
JWM Dalrymple (Glamorgan)	17	16
DKH Mitchell (Worcestershire)	17	16
AJ Hall (Northamptonshire)	16	16
PJ Horton (Lancashire)	16	16
NJ Dexter (Middlesex)	15	10
VVS Laxman (Lancashire)	15	11
SJ Walters (Surrey)	15	11

MOST DISMISSALS (wicketkeepers)

Player	Dismissals	Matches
P Mustard (Durham)	62	16
JS Foster (Essex)	61	15
LD Sutton (Lancashire)	56	16
JN Batty (Surrey)	50	16
CMW Read (Nottinghamshire)	50	16
C Kieswetter (Somerset)	48	16
GO Jones (Kent)	44	16
SM Davies (Worcestershire)	41	14
TR Ambrose (Warwickshire)	40	16
DJ Pipe (Derbyshire)	38	14
GL Brophy (Yorkshire)	37	13
MA Wallace (Glamorgan)	36	16
NJ O'Brien (Northamptonshire)	33	8
SD Snell (Gloucestershire)	30	9
TJ New (Leicestershire)	28	12
N Pothas (Hampshire)	24	11
AJ Hodd (Sussex)	24	13
SJ Adshead (Gloucestershire)	23	7
BJM Scott (Middlesex)	20	8
DC Nash (Middlesex)	16	5

DERBYSHIRE CCC

FIRST–CLASS MATCHES

BATTING

	GM Smith	GT Park	WW Hinds	DJ Pipe	DJ Redfern	GG Wagg	CJL Rogers	WL Madsen	PS Jones	TD Groenewald	ID Hunter	SD Stubbings	MAK Lawson	J Needham	M Hayward	JL Clare	T Lungley	JL Sadler	FA Klokker	SG Law	Extras	Total	Wickets	Result	Points
v. Essex (Chelmsford) 15–18 April	36	41	24	39	50	24*				2	28					2	0			29	51	326	10		
	59	7	8	64*	26						0									3	12	179	6	D	10
v. Surrey (Derby) 22–25 April	94*	4	26	6	28	35				47	7	0	0			0				0	27	274	10		
	27*	50	9	8*	17							83								7	19	220	5	W	19
v. Glamorgan (Cardiff) 28 April–1 May	19	64	12	44	13	1				8	4	24*	4		5						12	210	10		
	3*	6	1		3							15*			6						6	34	3	D	7
v. Gloucestershire (Chesterfield) 6–9 June	24	62	30	0	74	28	104			29*	6						29*				16	402	8		
																								D	10
v. Glamorgan (Derby) 11–14 June	12	76	30	22	11	0	27		24	33*	43					0					29	307	10		
	0	10	119*	10	1	4	21		27*		49						33				20	294	8	D	10
v. Leicestershire (Derby) 30 June–3 July	40	72	40	49	50	16	47			3*	19	6	0								23	365	10		
																								D	11
v. Northamptonshire (Northampton) 7–10 July	22	33	148	63	95		49			7	42		17*			6					20	502	9		
																								D	12
v. Gloucestershire (Cheltenham) 12–15 July	126	25	0	22	4	31	81	7	0	26			1*								3	326	10		
	34	9	54	0*	31		3	170*					5								17	323	6	W	20
v. Middlesex (Derby) 21–24 July	6	32	7	7	13	14	0	43	54*	48				6							17	247	10		
	4	16	25*		43	5	76	71		7											11	258	7	D	8
v. Kent (Canterbury) 31 July–3 August	0	11	74		29	21	53	3	53*	7				20					13		19	303	10		
	44	53	16		13	23	107	19	0	3				2*					6		17	303	10	L	4
v. Surrey (Whitgift School) 6–9 August	54	15	5		55*	71	80	1	5	1				2					2		43	334	10		
	49	5	8		13		0	108*											32*		17	232	5	D	10
v. Leicestershire (Grace Road) 11–14 August	95	41	40	32*	19		163	19	19	0			14*								36	478	8		
																								D	12
v. Northamptonshire (Chesterfield) 19–21 August	25	55	10	58	4		27	19	22	1			16	4*							14	255	10		
	19	3	36	10	28		14	2	27	50			21	2*							21	233	10	L	5
v. Kent (Derby) 2–5 September	59	178*	18				208	75										24*			21	583	4		
																								D	12
v. Middlesex (Uxbridge) 15–18 September	62	28	28	38*			25	167										12*			41	401	5		
	42*	3					112*	89													35	281	2	D	12
v. Essex (Derby) 23–26 September	6	57	37	21	48	0	222	16	19*								0	8			40	474	10		
	16	103*	36			42	0											27*			16	240	4	L	8
Matches	16	16	16	14	14	14	13	9	9	9	7	6	6	5	5	5	4	3	2	2					
Innings	27	27	26	18	23	14	21	16	9	11	7	11	5	7	5	5	4	4	4	4					
Not Out	4	2	2	5	1	1	1	2	3	1	3	1	2	3	2	0	1	3	1	0					
High Score	126	178*	148	64*	95	71	222	170*	54*	50	47	83	24*	20	6	6	33	27*	32*	29					
Runs	977	1059	841	493	668	273	1461	809	199	194	129	296	75	55	14	13	62	71	53	39					
Average	42.47	42.36	35.04	37.92	30.36	21.00	73.05	57.78	33.16	19.40	32.25	29.60	25.00	13.75	4.66	2.60	20.66	71.00	17.66	9.75					
100s	1	2	2	0	0	0	6	3	0	0	0	0	0	0	0	0	0	0	0	0					
50s	6	8	2	3	5	1	4	3	2	1	0	1	0	0	0	0	0	0	0	0					
Catches/Stumpings	5/0	14/0	7/0	36/2	8/0	4/0	21/0	8/0	4/0	2/0	2/0	4/0	3/0	3/0	1/0	1/0	2/0	3/0	3/0	2/0					

Home Ground: Derby
Address: County Ground, Nottingham Road, Derby, DE21 6DA
Tel: 01332 388101
Fax: 0844 586 0368
Email: info@derbyshireccc.com
Directions: *By road:* From the South & East, exit M1 junction 25, follow the A52 into Derby, take the fourth exit off the Pentagon Island. From the North, exit M1 junction 28, join the A38 into Derby, follow directional signs, the cricket ground is seen on the left approaching the city. From the West, on A50 follow signs for A52 Nottingham and on leaving the city centre inner ring road take the second exit off the Pentagon Island into the ground.

Capacity: 9,500
Other grounds used: Chesterfield
Year Formed: 1870

Chief Executive: Keith Loring
Head of Cricket: John Morris
Academy Director: Karl Krikken
Captain: Chris Rogers
County colours: Light and royal blue

Honours
County Championship
1936
Sunday League/NCL/Pro40
1990
Benson & Hedges Cup
1993
Gillette Cup/NatWest/C&G Trophy
1981

Website:
www.derbyshireccc.com

FIRST-CLASS MATCHES
BOWLING

	GG Wagg	TD Groenewald	GM Smith	PS Jones	ID Hunter	M Hayward	JL Clare	T Lungley	GT Park	J Needham	WW Hinds	MAK Lawson	DJ Redfern	DJ Pipe	WL Madsen	Overs	Total	Byes/Leg-byes	Wickets	Run outs
v. Essex (Chelmsford) 15-18 April			11-4-24-2 / 2-0-7-0		23-4-46-5 / 10-2-42-2		18-7-44-2 / 3-2-1-1	12-2-60-1 / 11-1-62-0	5-0-12-0 / 1-1-0-0				2-0-7-0			69 / 29	194 / 120	8 / 1	10 / 3	
v. Surrey (Derby) 22-25 April	15.4-5-35-6 / 29-6-94-1		11.2-7-18-3 / 14-5-35-1		12-3-27-0 / 26-2-88-3		14-5-31-1 / 17-3-53-2		9.3-1-25-3			12-1-39-0				53 / 107.3	131 / 360	20 / 26	10 / 10	
v. Glamorgan (Cardiff) 28 April-1 May	21-5-50-3		9-1-39-0		22-6-46-1		14-1-72-0		16-5-51-2	11-0-60-0		23-1-77-0				116 / –	403 / –	8 / –	6 / –	
v. Gloucestershire (Chesterfield) 6-9 June	24-5-71-1		17-2-64-0		15-3-65-2			20.5-0-88-1	10-0-30-0		11-1-28-1	10-0-46-0				107.5 / –	403 / –	11 / –	5 / –	
v. Glamorgan (Derby) 11-14 June	35-6-87-3 / 13-1-46-2	18-3-45-1 / 4-1-18-0	21-7-41-3 / 5-1-13-0		12-0-29-1 / 7-2-17-0			18-2-67-2 / 3-1-4-0	3-0-12-0 / 1-0-5-0	4-0-10-0		5-0-23-0				111 / 38	317 / 136	16 / 10	10 / 2	
v. Leicestershire (Derby) 30 June-3 July	22.1-6-72-2 / 15-3-70-3		19-5-64-1 / 3-0-9-0		26-6-82-5 / 7-2-34-1	25-6-68-1 / 10-0-36-1			7-0-18-0	12-0-51-0 / 11-3-29-1		7-1-24-0 / 5-0-15-0				118.1 / 51	412 / 209	33 / 16	10 / 7	1
v. Northamptonshire (Northampton) 7-10 July		20-3-81-1 / 9-1-32-1			15.4-2-90-1 / 6-1-17-0	22-2-99-4	18-3-92-0 / 6-2-15-0		3-0-12-0	16-2-47-3 / 14-2-25-0		2-1-4-0			6-0-15-0	96.4 / 41	433 / 104	8 / 0	9 / 1	
v. Gloucestershire (Cheltenham) 12-15 July	15.4-3-49-1 / 33-4-96-2	13.2-1-48-2 / 20-4-64-3	7-3-12-2 / 1-0-16-0	18.2-6-44-4 / 27-7-64-2					2-0-6-0 / 14.4-3-51-3							56.2 / 95.4	164 / 300	5 / 9	10 / 10	1
v. Middlesex (Derby) 21-24 July	30-4-88-5 / 12-0-56-0	13-2-41-2 / 2-0-17-0	2-0-17-0 / 3-0-19-0		12.4-3-30-1 / 3-1-12-0	11-3-43-1 / 4-1-13-0										68.4 / 24	226 / 121	7 / 4	9 / 1	1
v. Kent (Canterbury) 31 July-3 August	36-7-96-5 / 15-0-87-2	18-3-69-4 / 12.5-1-52-3	10-1-23-1 / 8-1-24-0	21-6-57-0 / 13-1-56-1					1-0-6-0	8-0-30-0 / 13-1-54-0		8-1-26-1				93 / 70.5	289 / 318	14 / 13	10 / 7	
v. Surrey (Whitgift School) 6-9 August	33-4-126-2 / 23-3-109-3	24.1-5-50-6 / 15-1-68-0	8-0-27-0 / 4-0-20-0	17-2-73-0 / 13-1-53-1			18-5-44-2 / 9-0-51-0			4-0-18-0		3-1-7-0			1-0-5-0 / 4-1-8-0	108.1 / 68	362 / 320	12 / 11	10 / 4	
v. Leicestershire (Grace Road) 11-14 August	12.1-3-36-0	13.5-5-34-1 / 30-6-97-1	12-2-31-3 / 26-8-72-1	11-1-5-43-4 / 34-8-92-2				10-1-32-1				10-4-20-2 / 28-5-78-1	7-1-31-1		1-0-2-0 / 2-1-1-0	68.1 / 137	177 / 429	11 / 21	10 / 8	1
v. Northamptonshire (Chesterfield) 19-21 August		19.1-6-61-6 / 14-1-46-1	9-1-42-2 / 4-2-11-0	15-4-51-0 / 22-2-79-4			15-2-52-0 / 9.2-0-66-2			9-2-19-2 / 12-1-38-1						67.1 / 61.2	246 / 245	21 / 5	10 / 8	
v. Kent (Derby) 2-5 September	21-3-86-1 / 20-2-80-0	16-2-52-1 / 14-1-57-0	6-0-27-0 / 20-2-55-1	20.5-6-35-5 / 10-3-21-0				17-1-56-3 / 11-1-55-1	3-0-10-0 / 6-0-27-0					1-0-5-0	6-0-22-0	83.5 / 88	281 / 333	15 / 11	10 / 2	
v. Middlesex (Uxbridge) 15-18 September	26-3-97-1 / 19-2-61-0	12-3-60-1 / 14-4-42-2	18-1-73-2 / 23-7-65-5	19-4-69-4 / 14-3-36-0					2-0-8-0 / 3-0-8-1			10-1-41-0 / 12-3-32-1				87 / 85	353 / 259	5 / 15	9 / 9	
v. Essex (Derby) 23-26 September	31.5-10-79-3 / 19-0-102-1		10-0-41-0 / 18-0-96-3	28-3-87-2 / 11-0-68-0			23-4-64-3 / 6-0-35-1	9-0-43-0 / 1-0-12-0			6-0-25-0		1-0-8-0		4-0-29-0	107.5 / 60	356 / 359	17 / 9	9 / 5	
Overs	521.3	273.2	330.2	318	181.4	123.2	119	92.5	90.3	101.4	60	105	32	1	18					
Maidens	85	49	64	65	33	19	27	8	8	11	6	15	3	0	2					
Runs	1773	921	1098	970	593	472	407	392	311	353	181	333	117	5	67					
Wickets	47	34	32	30	21	11	10	8	7	7	4	4	2	0	0					
Average	37.72	27.08	34.31	32.33	28.23	42.90	40.70	49.00	44.42	50.42	45.25	83.25	58.50							

FIELDING

38	DJ Pipe (36 ct, 2 st)
21	CJL Rogers
14	GT Park
8	DJ Redfern
8	WL Madsen
7	WW Hinds
5	GM Smith
4	PS Jones
4	SD Stubbings
4	GG Wagg
3	JL Sadler
3	FA Klokker
3	MAK Lawson
3	J Needham
2	SG Law
2	ID Hunter
2	T Lungley
2	TD Groenewald
1	M Hayward
1	JL Clare

Division Two – Final Table

	P	W	L	D	Bat	Bowl	Pens	Pts
Kent	16	8	3	5	43	44	0.00	219.00
Essex	16	6	3	7	40	43	1.00	194.00
Northamptonshire	16	6	4	6	40	45	0.00	193.00
Gloucestershire	16	6	6	4	39	46	0.00	185.00
Glamorgan	16	2	2	12	56	43	0.00	175.00
Derbyshire	16	2	3	11	55	45	0.00	172.00
Surrey	16	1	4	11	54	36	0.00	148.00
Middlesex	16	2	7	7	43	41	0.00	140.00
Leicestershire	16	2	3	11	31	35	0.00	138.00

FPT, T20 & Pro40

Derbyshire Phantoms

Limited overs nickname:
DERBYSHIRE PHANTOMS

DURHAM CCC

FIRST-CLASS MATCHES
BATTING

	DM Benkenstein	ID Blackwell	P Mustard	MJ Di Venuto	WR Smith	LE Plunkett	SJ Harmison	GJ Muchall	MD Stoneman	CD Thorp	ME Claydon	M Davies	G Onions	KJ Coetzer	S Chanderpaul	GR Breese	BW Harmison	SG Borthwick	Extras	Total	Wickets	Result	Points
v. MCC (Lord's) 9-12 April	12	102*		53	71*		5	49											19	311	4	D	
v. Durham UCCE (Durham) 15-17 April	1	46	12		63	8	25*	13	6		0				14	0			12	200	10	W	
			23*						35*										3	61	0		
v. Yorkshire (Riverside) 22-25 April	17	95	94*	36	21	10	3	13	2	42		4							25	362	10		11
	22	6	1*	143	67			51*	0										13	303	5	D	
v. Somerset (Taunton) 28 April-1 May	181	50	4	53	7		10*	68	38	32	38		0						62	543	10	D	12
v. Sussex (Hove) 6-9 May	136	2	32	20	12	94*	0	24	2	29	6								23	380	10		11
	7	39*		103	7			106*	24										13	299	4	D	
v. Hampshire (Riverside) 6-8 June	22	68	32	7	80		0	28	44	0	10		1*						19	311	10	W	20
v. Lancashire (Riverside) 11-13 June	26	20	51	16	11		0	18	45	4	6		12*						35	244	10		18
	1	74	7	0	1		0	18	2	24	0		7*		18				11	145	10	W	
v. Warwickshire (Edgbaston) 16-19 June	14	158	24	40	1		1	39	64	7			1*		48				36	433	10		22
				13*	9*														0	22	0	W	
v. Worcestershire (Riverside) 30 June-3 July	25	1	63*	0	0	29		0		17	6	6	30						17	194	10		
	17	3	2*	100*	16			14					15						12	179	5		
v. Yorkshire (Headingley) 10-13 July	62	12	7	29		3	0	0	22		20	0*	0						23	178	10		
	36	32	85	84		65		15	12		1*	6	38						47	421	9	D	7
v. Nottinghamshire (Trent Bridge) 15-18 July	105	38	40	22	87	9		10	24	5	3	1*							12	356	10	W	20
v. Sussex (Riverside) 31 July-3 August	69	2*		254*	101			14	5										28	473	4		
				39*	21*				18										2	80	1	W	21
v. Lancashire (Old Trafford) 11-14 August	16	29	7	53	26	28		39	33	32	0*	0							7	270	10		
	58	25	50*	84	1	10*		40	33										19	320	6	D	9
v. Warwickshire (Riverside) 19-21 August	73	53	25	40	16	31*			3	0	10	8			0				14	273	10		
				41*	11				5						41*				8	106	2	W	19
v. Somerset (Riverside) 1-4 September	30	0	2	22	0	32	1			15			0	30	117*				23	272	10	D	9
v. Nottinghamshire (Riverside) 9-12 September	105	29	6*	219	27									107	109*				46	648	5	W	22
v. Hampshire (Rose Bowl) 15-18 September	24	56	35	62	150	37	1						0	20	4		26*		24	439	10		
				8*									0*						0	8	0	D	11
v. Worcestershire (New Road) 23-26 September	109	9	25	113	28	52					10	16*		44	201*				27	634	8	D	12
Matches	18	18	18	17	17	14	14	13	13	13	12	9	8	6	5	2	1	1					
Innings	24	24	22	27	25	13	11	19	21	12	12	8	8	9	6	2	1	1					
Not Out	0	3	7	6	3	3	2	2	1	0	1	4	4	1	4	0	0	1					
High Score	181	158	94*	254*	150	94*	25*	106*	64	42	38	16*	12*	107	201*	48	0	26*					
Runs	1168	949	627	1654	834	408	41	515	466	207	110	37	25	284	472	62	0	26					
Average	48.66	45.19	41.80	78.76	37.90	40.80	4.55	30.29	23.30	17.25	10.00	9.25	6.25	35.50	236	31.00	0.00	-					
100s	5	2	0	6	2	0	0	1	0	0	0	0	0	1	3	0	0	0					
50s	4	6	5	6	5	3	0	2	1	0	0	0	0	0	0	0	0	0					
Catches/Stumpings	10/0	4/0	69/1	23/0	6/0	13/0	2/0	14/0	14/0	15/0	3/0	2/0	3/0	7/0	3/0	3/0	1/0	0/0					

Home Ground: Chester-le-Street
Address: County Ground, The Riverside, Chester-le-Street, County Durham, DH3 3QR
Tel: 0191 3871717
Fax: 01913 874698
Email: reception@durhamccc.co.uk
Directions: *By rail:* Chester-le-Street station (approx 5 minutes by taxi or a 10-minute walk). *By road:* Easily accessible from junction 63 of the A1(M).

Capacity: 15,000
Year formed: 1882

Chief Executive: David Harker
Head Coach: Geoff Cook
Captain: Will Smith
County colours: Yellow, blue and burgundy

Honours
County Championship
2008, 2009
Friends Provident Trophy
2007

Website:
www.durhamccc.co.uk

FIRST-CLASS MATCHES
BOWLING

	LE Plunkett	SJ Harmison	ID Blackwell	G Onions	CD Thorp	ME Claydon	M Davies	DM Benkenstein	GR Breese	SG Borthwick	WR Smith	BW Harmison	Overs	Total	Byes/Leg-byes	Wickets	Run outs
v. MCC (Lord's) 9-12 April	12-2-41-1			14-2-42-1	13-5-15-4	7-2-14-1		1-0-7-0					47	126	7	7	
													–	–	–	–	–
v. Durham UCCE (Durham) 15-17 April	17-5-42-3	11-3-40-0	9-6-10-1			12-8-11-1		7-3-16-0	9.1-5-10-4			6-1-19-0	71.1	154	6	10	1
	6-1-18-2	5-3-7-1	17.4-8-42-3			5-1-18-1			11-4-16-2				44.4	104	3	10	1
v. Yorkshire (Riverside) 22-25 April	13-3-38-1	23.1-3-76-4	10-5-19-1	19-4-49-3	18-2-57-1		2-0-15-0						85.1	272	18	10	
	17-3-55-1	23-8-32-1	11-2-21-0	28-9-56-5	11.4-5-18-0								90.4	193	11	7	
v. Somerset (Taunton) 28 April-1 May		8-2-29-1		14.2-4-31-6	6-2-5-3								28.2	69	4	10	
		27-7-100-0	21-2-81-1	29-5-110-1	29-9-80-1	23-3-95-2							129	485	19	5	
v. Sussex (Hove) 6-9 May	24-1-105-4	23-2-58-1	13-3-30-1		14-5-48-0	20-1-90-4		4-0-17-0			1-0-11-0		98	363	14	10	
	13-2-36-2	13-3-41-1	7-0-16-0		10-3-29-1	6-0-29-1							50	169	7	5	
v. Hampshire (Riverside) 6-8 June		17-4-53-4		19-7-22-3	9-4-16-1	5-0-20-2							50.4	105	4	10	
		8-4-15-2		14.2-2-58-6	12-4-21-2								34.2	96	2	10	
v. Lancashire (Riverside) 11-13 June		14.1-5-28-4		13-4-40-4	7-2-21-0	9-4-19-2							43.1	116	8	10	
		17-7-46-5	2-0-10-1	14-4-28-3	10-4-19-0	9-1-29-1							52	135	3	10	
v. Warwickshire (Edgbaston) 16-19 June		20-6-44-5	25-7-47-2	22.1-2-89-2	11-2-25-0				5-1-17-1	9-2-43-0			92.1	276	11	10	
		17-5-59-2	25-4-53-1	22-9-38-7	6-1-19-0					8-4-7-0			78	177	1	10	
v. Worcestershire (Riverside) 30 June-3 July	23.1-3-63-6		8-5-10-0		16-8-34-1	17-4-32-1	13-5-29-1	2-1-11-1					79.1	193	11	10	
	24-6-56-5		16-7-22-2		13-6-27-1	11-0-50-1	10-2-19-1						74	179	5	10	
v. Yorkshire (Headingley) 10-13 July	19-4-68-0	25-6-60-5	26-4-66-3			21-4-76-1	13-6-33-1						104	313	10	10	
	11-4-22-2	11-3-22-0	21-10-23-2			3-0-17-0	3.3-2-4-0	1-1-0-0					50.3	98	10	4	
v. Nottinghamshire (Trent Bridge) 15-18 July	13.2-1-56-4	16-7-45-1	8-3-6-3			11-4-30-2	2-2-0-0	12-5-31-0					62.2	171	3	10	
		13-5-20-6	3.4-0-16-1			9-2-33-1		7-2-13-2					32.4	83	1	10	
v. Sussex (Riverside) 31 July-3 August	11-2-34-2	20.2-5-58-1	4-0-15-0		25-5-86-5		16-4-41-1						76.2	245	11	10	1
	8-2-50-0	23-1-68-3	25-10-52-2		16-0-79-2		18-5-44-3						79.3	304	11	10	
v. Lancashire (Old Trafford) 11-14 August	9-1-30-0		38.5-10-85-7	21.5-4-54-0	17-2-40-2		6-2-21-0		4-1-6-1		6-1-11-0		101.5	265	18	10	
	2.1-1-4-0		25-8-56-0	10.4-0-39-3	12-3-43-1		10-2-20-0						59.1	163	1	4	
v. Warwickshire (Riverside) 19-21 August	10-3-34-1				20.1-5-49-5	15-8-25-1	2-1-1-0	8-2-20-3					55.1	135	6	10	
	15-4-67-0		23-9-44-3		20-11-31-1	21-4-75-3	14.4-6-19-3						93.4	238	2	10	
v. Somerset (Riverside) 1-4 September	21-6-65-3	8-3-24-0	8.1-5-7-5		17-2-49-2	5-0-21-0							59.1	174	8	10	
	0.5-0-0-0	6-2-14-0			6-2-5-0								12.5	41	2	0	
v. Nottinghamshire (Riverside) 9-12 September	21-4-85-6	28-1-108-0	17-3-46-0			11-1-36-0		25-5-87-4					102	384	22	10	
	21-6-64-3	18.2-6-38-3	19-11-27-1			11-3-31-1		14-4-29-1	2-0-15-0				85.2	212	8	10	1
v. Hampshire (Rose Bowl) 15-18 September	14-4-49-1	21-5-78-1	39.3-9-110-5					14-3-36-0	3-1-6-0	27-2-95-3	1-1-0-0		119.3	384	10	10	
													–	–	–	–	–
v. Worcestershire (New Road) 23-26 September	26.5-4-104-4	22-9-47-1	7-2-26-0			14-2-57-1	20-3-71-2	9-2-38-2					98.5	356	13	10	
	29-1-132-4		27-2-124-2			12-3-53-1	19-3-64-0	2-1-5-0			2-0-9-0		91	410	23	7	

	LE Plunkett	SJ Harmison	ID Blackwell	G Onions	CD Thorp	ME Claydon	M Davies	DM Benkenstein	GR Breese	SG Borthwick	WR Smith	BW Harmison
Overs	381.2	428.1	456.5	262.5	320.5	234	217.1	50	37.1	27	10	6
Maidens	73	116	135	63	94	51	60	13	15	2	2	1
Runs	1318	1201	1064	730	846	777	562	173	76	95	31	19
Wickets	55	52	47	46	34	25	19	8	6	3	0	0
Average	23.96	23.09	22.63	15.86	24.88	31.08	29.57	21.62	12.66	31.66		

FIELDING

70	P Mustard (69 ct, 1 st)
23	MJ Di Venuto
15	CD Thorp
14	GJ Muchall
14	MD Stoneman
13	LE Plunkett
10	DM Benkenstein
7	KJ Coetzer
6	WR Smith
4	ID Blackwell
3	S Chanderpaul
3	GR Breese
3	G Onions
3	ME Claydon
2	SJ Harmison
2	M Davies
1	BW Harmison
0	SG Borthwick

Division One – Final Table

	P	W	L	D	Bat	Bowl	Pens	Pts
Durham	16	8	0	8	49	48	1.00	240.00
Nottinghamshire	16	4	2	10	56	41	0.00	193.00
Somerset	16	3	1	12	50	43	1.00	182.00
Lancashire	16	4	2	10	35	44	0.00	175.00
Warwickshire	16	3	3	10	54	38	0.00	174.00
Hampshire	16	3	3	10	50	40	3.00	169.00
Yorkshire	16	2	2	12	46	44	0.00	166.00
Sussex	16	2	6	8	45	39	1.00	143.00
Worcestershire	16	0	10	6	30	40	0.00	94.00

FPT & Pro40

T20

Limited overs nickname:
DURHAM DYNAMOS

ESSEX CCC

FIRST-CLASS MATCHES
BATTING

	MJ Walker	JS Foster	ML Pettini	DD Masters	RN ten Doeschate	CJC Wright	V Chopra	JK Maunders	Danish Kaneria	GR Napier	AN Cook	JD Middlebrook	T Westley	JER Gallian	MA Chambers	JC Mickleburgh	TJ Phillips	AP Palladino	HM Amla	RS Bopara	AJ Wheater	MS Westfield	GW Flower	JS Ahmed	Extras	Total	Wickets	Result	Points
v. Derbyshire (Chelmsford) 15-18 April	17	40	28	20	1	8	39				0	11	2*	5											23	194	10		
	7		1*				56							44*	1										11	120	3	D	7
v. Gloucestershire (Bristol) 21-23 April	9	0	8	0	42	21	15						17	8	0*	32									25	177	10		
	48*		28*				1							11	0										13	101	3	W	17
v. West Indians (Chelmsford) 25-27 April		23					50			46	46	4		0*	58							1	9	5	21	263	10		
		48*					14			74*				0	23										16	175	3	D	
v. Kent (Chelmsford) 29 April-2 May	98	99	27	0	3	6	12	23		41				4*	7										50	370	10		
	16	13	0	20	36	0	10	4		4				0*	15										37	155	10	L	7
v. Northamptonshire (Northampton) 6-9 May	16	38	3		10	2	42	0	7				18	0*	62										23	221	10		
	35	84	29		45	16*	0		17	16			19	5	16										26	308	10	L	4
v. Middlesex (Chelmsford) 6-9 June	5		10	22	19		0			37	31	2		10	8*						0				13	157	10		
	19		21		0					84*	9*	12													14	159	4	D	
v. Cambridge UCCE (Fenner's) 11-13 June	21						88	61		9*				125		18	11								32	365	6		
	50*									45						48					36				9	188	3	D	
v. Kent (Tunbridge Wells) 16-19 June	41	36	55	2	40	0	3	12		64*	8			1											18	280	10		
	5	37	101*		0		63		48*	30				14											22	320	6	W	19
v. Glamorgan (Chelmsford) 7-10 July	4	0	10	33	26	1	31	35		13			15*						4						28	200	10		
	15	64	21		88*	8	8	10*											181						16	411	6	D	7
v. Surrey (Guildford) 15-18 July	27	48	10	9	159*	2	31	43		16								5	26						25	401	10		
	21		9*		85		0												81*						5	201	3	D	10
v. Leicestershire (Grace Road) 21-24 July	116*	85	24	0			5	56											118						23	427	6	D	12
v. Gloucestershire (Southend) 5-8 August	0	4	91	55	43	0*	28	0		50				7	3										19	300	10		
	7	20	36	19	33	15*	8	1		39				32	6										20	236	10	L	5
v. Middlesex (Lord's) 11-14 August	150	72	1	35*	18		23	7	3	4								0*		1					31	345	10		
	12	10	37		40					13*	66									52*					11	241	5	W	20
v. Surrey (Colchester) 19-22 August	22	11	42rh	43	7*	16	39	31							35		69			201					29	545	9		
	12						10								45*					15*					4	74	1	W	21
v. Leicestershire (Chelmsford) 26-29 August	31	103*		67	1	1*	13	150	0	31				71			22								27	517	9	D	11
v. Glamorgan (Cardiff) 10-13 September	25	7	90	11		1*	44	0	11	57			1				20								21	288	10		
	15	73	37	0		0*	12	1*	2	17			2				0								22	181	9	D	9
v. Northamptonshire (Chelmsford) 15-18 September	40	28	47	5	75		10	15*	7*	0			3												23	253	8		
	39	5	5	7			46		22*	87			15*												16	242	6	W	19
v. Derbyshire (Derby) 23-26 September	75	15	14		41	24*	5	10	0	8				132											32	356	9		
	18	13	85*		108*		55			25				40											15	359	5	W	20
Matches	17	16	15	15	14	14	12	11	11	10	9	8	7	7	7	6	4	4	3	2	2	2	1	1					
Innings	31	26	28	16	22	16	21	18	15	16	17	11	12	13	8	12	5	2	5	4	2	1	1	1					
Not Out	3	2	6	1	4	7	0	0	6	2	3	2	1	7	0	0	0	1	2	0	0	0	0	0					
High Score	150	103*	101*	67	159*	24*	88	150	37	64*	87	46	132	125	8*	62	69	5	181	201	36	1	9	5					
Runs	1004	976	870	341	823	130	537	621	158	348	613	196	387	245	19	285	122	5	410	269	36	1	9	5					
Average	35.85	40.66	39.54	22.73	45.72	14.44	25.57	34.50	12.15	34.80	40.86	24.50	38.70	20.41	19.00	23.75	24.40	2.50	102.50	134.50	18.00	1.00	9.00	5.00					
100s	2	1	1	0	2	0	0	1	0	0	0	0	1	1	0	0	0	0	2	1	0	0	0	0					
50s	3	6	4	2	2	0	5	3	0	2	5	0	1	0	0	2	1	0	1	1	0	0	0	0					
Catches/Stumpings	13/0	60/4	10/0	7/0	5/0	2/0	6/0	12/0	5/0	3/0	11/0	2/0	3/0	5/0	1/0	3/0	2/0	0/0	2/0	2/0	6/0	0/0	0/0	0/0					

Home Ground: Chelmsford
Address: Ford County Ground, New Writtle Street, Chelmsford, Essex, CM2 0PG
Tel: 01245 252420
Fax: 01245 254030
Email: administration.essex@ecb.co.uk
Directions: By rail: Chelmsford station (8 minutes' walk away). By road: M25 then A12 to Chelmsford. Exit Chelmsford and follow AA signs to Essex Cricket Club.
Capacity: 6,500
Other grounds used: Colchester, Southend-on-Sea
Year formed: 1876

Chief Executive: David East
First Team Coach: Paul Grayson
Captain: Mark Pettini
County colours: Royal and navy blue

Website:
www.essexcricket.org.uk

Honours
County Championship
1979, 1983, 1984, 1986, 1991, 1992
Sunday League/NCL/Pro40
1981, 1984, 1985, 2005, 2006
Refuge Assurance Cup
1989
Benson & Hedges Cup
1979, 1998
Gillette Cup/NatWest/C&G Trophy/
Friends Provident Trophy
1985, 1997, 2008

FIRST-CLASS MATCHES
BOWLING

	Danish Kaneria	DD Masters	CJC Wright	GR Napier	RN ten Doeschate	MA Chambers	JD Middlebrook	AP Palladino	TJ Phillips	MS Westfield	AN Cook	JS Ahmed	T Westley	MJ Walker	ML Pettini	RS Bopara	V Chopra	JC Mickleburgh	Overs	Total	Byes/Leg-byes	Wickets	Run outs
v. Derbyshire (Chelmsford) 15-18 April		28-11-40-2	29.4-7-86-4	19-1-95-2	17-3-63-1	12-5-23-1													105.4	326	19	10	
		9-5-6-1	10-2-17-1	11-1-57-1	10-0-53-1	15-3-43-2													55	179	3	6	
v. Gloucestershire (Bristol) 21-23 April		16-8-16-3	15.3-5-38-2	18-1-62-5		12-2-25-0	1-0-6-0										2-0-4-0		64.3	155	4	10	
		12-5-12-3	13-3-40-1	11.1-0-35-3		13-1-30-3													49.1	119	2	10	
v. West Indians (Chelmsford) 25-27 April				14-3-62-4	4-3-2-1				13.1-5-25-3		11-1-55-2						2-1-1-0		44.1	146	1	10	
																			-	-	-	-	
v. Kent (Chelmsford) 29 April-2 May	13-2-48-2	14-6-18-2	13-2-48-2	11-2-40-1	11-1-45-2												4.1-1-17-0	7.5-1-28-0	62	205	5	10	1
	46-7-172-4	31-9-82-1	32-5-98-2	16-3-51-0	12.4-1-58-2														149.4	512	6	9	
v. Northamptonshire (Northampton) 6-9 May		18-5-46-2	22-2-77-3	23.5-5-107-4	9-1-49-0	4-2-5-1							1.2-0-11-0						91.5	354	11	10	
		15-3-44-1	8-1-37-0	7-0-37-0	2-0-20-0	6-1-21-1													39.2	176	6	2	
v. Middlesex (Chelmsford) 6-9 June	12-0-52-1	20.4-4-65-5	21-5-71-4		14-0-50-0	4-0-21-0								1-0-7-0					72.4	274	8	10	
	28-6-85-4	20.1-3-39-2	16-1-60-0		11-1-35-1	13-1-63-0													88.1	297	15	7	
v. Cambridge UCCE (Fenner's) 11-13 June						10-3-26-1	24-5-80-3	11-5-36-1	17-2-72-1	18-8-35-1							5-1-11-0		80	262	13	7	
							11-5-22-1	6-2-8-1	5-1-6-1	4-0-22-0									31	71	2	3	
v. Kent (Tunbridge Wells) 16-19 June	4-0-19-0	19-8-34-4	10-2-34-0	15-4-32-4	2.3-0-4-2						1-0-5-1			1-0-4-0					50.3	123	0	10	
	42-8-92-6	34-14-78-2	11-2-36-0	15.2-4-54-1	16-2-62-0														120.2	355	24	10	
v. Glamorgan (Chelmsford) 7-10 July		34-7-79-1	26-2-119-1	27-5-112-3	24-0-110-1				21-3-87-3										132	515	8	9	
																			-	-	-	-	
v. Surrey (Guildford) 15-18 July		39-16-86-4		14.3-2-59-2	11-4-44-0				23-1-76-1	31-8-72-1									118.3	352	15	8	
v. Leicestershire (Grace Road) 21-24 July		18-6-49-2	16-3-52-3	9-1-53-0	1.2-0-4-1				18-3-68-4										62.2	238	12	10	
		5-2-13-1	7-1-38-1	3-1-13-0	4-0-33-0				7-3-26-1										26	123	0	3	
v. Gloucestershire (Southend) 5-8 August	44-9-158-3	35-12-68-1	27-2-96-2	28.2-5-99-3	16-2-48-1								2-0-14-0						152.2	498	15	10	
	5-1-19-0	5.2-0-19-0																	10.2	39	1	0	
v. Middlesex (Lord's) 11-14 August	23.5-2-74-4	27-9-61-0		23-8-63-3	22-6-51-2				18-3-64-1							5-2-22-0			118.5	356	21	10	
	26-6-76-5	16-4-39-1		31-3-26-0	6-1-21-0				8-2-28-0		1-0-3-1				0.5-0-24-0	1-0-6-0			69.5	229	6	7	
v. Surrey (Colchester) 19-22 August	38-7-120-3	27-10-61-1	28-6-91-2		18-4-71-2				12-1-63-1		3-0-5-0					2-1-2-0			128	428	15	10	
	27-13-50-6	7-3-16-0	11-0-54-1						24-4-61-3										69	190	9	10	
v. Leicestershire (Chelmsford) 26-29 August	49.4-16-116-8	21-9-61-0	16-3-59-0		14-2-55-1				18-7-34-0		1-0-3-0		4-0-18-0			2-0-6-0			118.4	344	19	10	
	36.5-12-87-4	14-4-27-0	15-0-48-1		4-1-18-0				25-9-44-1										101.5	258	7	6	
v. Glamorgan (Cardiff) 10-13 September	34.3-4-111-7	21-5-50-1	10-2-45-0	17-3-54-2					9-0-36-0				2-0-2-0						93.3	311	13	10	
	39-6-108-3	18-2-48-1	4-0-14-0	8-1-35-2					17-2-41-1				8-1-33-2						94	296	17	10	1
v. Northamptonshire (Chelmsford) 15-18 September	36-12-86-5	19.3-7-57-3	15-1-61-1	14-7-16-3									2-0-12-0						90.3	299	9	10	
	21-3-64-1	19.5-3-52-2	12-3-43-4	7.3-1-46-3															59.3	195	7	10	
v. Derbyshire (Derby) 23-26 September	22-1-114-3	33-10-72-2	27.4-5-97-4	34-6-111-1	7-1-34-0								5-1-17-0						128.4	474	29	10	
	17-1-36-3	16-2-59-1	10-2-30-0	5-0-26-0						7-0-40-0			3-0-3-0			6-0-38-0			64	240	8	4	

	Danish Kaneria	DD Masters	CJC Wright	GR Napier	RN ten Doeschate	MA Chambers	JD Middlebrook	AP Palladino	TJ Phillips	MS Westfield	AN Cook	JS Ahmed	T Westley	MJ Walker	ML Pettini	RS Bopara	V Chopra	JC Mickleburgh
Overs	597.5	557.2	437.1	271.3	246	141.4	138	99	127	35.1	10	11	29	3.2	6.5	8	15.1	7.5
Maidens	124	184	67	55	32	19	29	26	26	13	0	1	2	0	0	3	3	1
Runs	1777	1212	1538	1005	970	526	449	302	357	82	51	55	104	22	62	30	39	28
Wickets	75	45	40	29	22	15	14	9	8	4	2	2	2	0	0	0	0	0
Average	23.69	26.93	38.45	34.65	44.09	35.06	32.07	33.55	44.62	20.50	25.50	27.50	52.00	-	-	-	-	-

FIELDING

64	JS Foster (60 ct, 4 st)
13	MJ Walker
12	JK Maunders
11	AN Cook
10	ML Pettini
7	DD Masters
6	V Chopra
6	AJ Wheater
5	JER Gallian
5	Danish Kaneria
5	RN ten Doeschate
3	GR Napier
3	T Westley
3	JC Mickleburgh
2	JD Middlebrook
2	TJ Phillips
2	RS Bopara
2	CJC Wright
2	HM Amla
1	MA Chambers
0	GW Flower
0	AP Palladino
0	MS Westfield
0	JS Ahmed

Division Two – Final Table

	P	W	L	D	Bat	Bowl	Pens	Pts
Kent	16	8	3	5	43	44	0.00	219.00
Essex	16	6	3	7	40	43	1.00	194.00
Northamptonshire	16	6	4	6	40	45	0.00	193.00
Gloucestershire	16	6	6	4	39	46	0.00	185.00
Glamorgan	16	2	2	12	56	43	0.00	175.00
Derbyshire	16	2	3	11	55	45	0.00	172.00
Surrey	16	1	4	11	54	36	0.00	148.00
Middlesex	16	2	7	7	43	41	0.00	140.00
Leicestershire	16	2	3	11	31	35	0.00	138.00

FPT & Pro40

T20

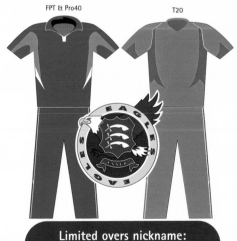

Limited overs nickname:
ESSEX EAGLES

GlamorganCricket
CricedMorgannwg

GLAMORGAN CCC

FIRST-CLASS MATCHES
BATTING

Match	JWM Dalrymple	GP Rees	MJ Powell	RDB Croft	MA Wallace	JAR Harris	AJ Shantry	GJP Kruger	MJ Cosgrove	WD Bragg	BJ Wright	DS Harrison	DA Cosker	TL Maynard	J Allenby	HH Gibbs	MP O'Shea	CP Ashling	Extras	Total	Wickets	Result	Points
v. Oxford UCCE (The Parks) 15-17 April		33*	0*						23	8									10	74	2	D	
v. Middlesex (Lord's) 22-25 April	28	6	51	42	128		1	4*	120	38		51		16					20	505	10		11
	112*	9	24	52	17		20		8	28				0					8	278	8	D	
v. Derbyshire (Cardiff) 28-1 May	102	11	108	40	17*				50	6				51*					18	403	6	D	12
v. Kent (Canterbury) 6-9 May	79	5	65	17	1		14	11*			41	0	4				50		20	307	10		6
	10	25	1	7	0		0	5*			81	1	4				25		21	180	10	L	
v. Surrey (Cardiff) 6-9 June	72	1	10	2	13	9	23*	15	59	12	27								28	271	10	D	9
v. Derbyshire (Derby) 11-14 June	128	42	0	28	0	20	13	0	0	14			46*						26	317	10		10
		0	42*						74*	4									16	136	2	D	
v. Northamptonshire (Cardiff) 16-19 June	1	4	88	43	32	17	1		102*	6	1		10						3	308	10		10
	70*	116*	2						22	15									7	232	3	D	
v. Essex (Chelmsford) 7-10 July	50	59	102	30	37	76*	38	28*		1	13					53			28	515	9	D	12
v. Kent (Cardiff) 15-18 July	35	80	30	36	23	4	17	4*		0			25			36			27	317	10		4
	24	0	60	28	4	28	6	4*		10			0			4			27	195	10	L	
v. Gloucestershire (Bristol) 31 July-3 August	0	82	0	0	36	5*	4			92	6*					96			29	350	8	D	11
v. Leicestershire (Colwyn Bay) 5-8 August	40	44	40	121	19	0	100		80		26*	1	38						57	566	10	W	21
v. Middlesex (Swansea) 20-22 August	40	40	29	21	6	7	11*		28				1		7	8			26	224	10		18
	2	26	8	22	4	4	21		15				8*		1	20			4	135	10	W	
v. Northamptonshire (Northampton) 26-29 August	27	31	55	14	42	26	32	5*	28						55	42			26	383	10	D	11
v. Leicestershire (Grace Road) 2-5 September	37	2	61	40*	14	0	0		12		20			2				12	18	218	10	D	8
v. Essex (Cardiff) 10-13 September	44	122	21	27	5		9*	2	53	0			0		5				23	311	10		10
	98*	38	0	0	48		4	7	1	47			14		12				27	296	10	D	
v. Gloucestershire (Cardiff) 16-19 September	0	88	84	22*	12	18		6	80	1			0		79				20	410	10		12
	6	43	41	21*	25	10			1	11			2*		3				8	171	8	D	
v. Surrey (The Oval) 23-26 September	4	154	12	1*	139	15			175	33				137					32	702	8	D	11
Matches	17	17	17	17	17	14	13	13	10	9	9	8	8	6	5	5	1	1					
Innings	23	25	25	21	22	16	17	13	15	12	14	7	11	7	8	7	2	1					
Not Out	3	2	2	4	0	3	3	7	2	0	0	2	3	1	0	0	0	0					
High Score	128	154	108	121	139	76*	100	28*	175	92	81	51	46*	51*	137	96	50	12					
Runs	1009	1061	934	574	645	256	314	91	780	367	279	98	107	115	299	259	75	12					
Average	50.45	46.13	40.60	33.76	29.31	19.69	22.42	15.16	60.00	30.58	19.92	19.60	13.37	19.16	37.37	37.00	37.50	12.00					
100s	3	3	2	1	2	0	1	0	3	0	0	0	0	0	1	0	0	0					
50s	5	4	7	1	0	1	0	0	5	2	1	1	0	1	2	2	1	0					
Catches/Stumpings	17/0	15/0	8/0	4/0	31/6	1/0	0/0	2/0	4/0	4/0	3/0	2/0	5/0	6/0	6/0	7/0	0/0	0/0					

Home Ground: Cardiff
Address: The SWALEC Stadium, Cardiff, CF11 9XR
Tel: 029 2040 9380
Fax: 029 2040 9390
Email: info@glamorgancricket.co.uk
Directions: *By rail:* Cardiff Central station.
By road: From the North, A470 and follow signs to Cardiff until junction with Cardiff bypass then A48 Port Talbot and City Centre. Cathedral Road is situated off A48 for Sophia Gardens.

Capacity: 4,000
Other grounds used: Swansea, Colwyn Bay, Abergavenny
Year formed: 1888

Executive Chairman: Paul Russell
Cricket Director: Matthew Maynard
First XI Coach: Adrian Shaw
Captain: Jamie Dalrymple
County colours: Navy blue and yellow/gold

Honours
County Championship
1948, 1969, 1997
Sunday League/NCL/Pro40
1993, 2002, 2004

Website:
www.glamorgancricket.com

FIRST-CLASS MATCHES
BOWLING

	RDB Croft	JAR Harris	GJP Kruger	AJ Shantry	DA Cosker	JWM Dalrymple	DS Harrison	MJ Cosgrove	J Allenby	CP Ashling	BJ Wright	WD Bragg	Overs	Total	Byes/Leg-byes	Wickets	Run outs
v. Oxford UCCE (The Parks) 15-17 April	17-2-46-2	14-3-57-2		12-1-31-2		7-3-2-17-2	13-3-38-1	7-1-14-1					70.3	208	5	10	
	-	-											-	-	-	-	
v. Middlesex (Lord's) 22-25 April	28-6-79-0		20-3-85-4	22-3-69-0		6-0-35-1	25-3-117-3	4-1-12-0					105	414	17	8	
	5-1-7-0		7-0-42-0	4-1-8-1			10-1-26-2	2-0-9-0					28	94	2	3	
v. Derbyshire (Cardiff) 28 April-1 May	21.5-5-45-3	14-2-54-3	7-0-28-0			4-0-15-0	18-3-60-4						64.5	210	8	10	
	8-5-6-3	3-0-7-0	3-0-8-0			7-1-10-0							21	34	3	3	
v. Kent (Canterbury) 6-9 May	17-2-66-2			15-4-42-2	20-3-54-3	10.3-1-35-1		15-0-66-0			2-0-8-0		79.3	282	11	10	2
	26-2-96-1			15-1-66-0	21-2-68-2	9-0-41-0		18-0-100-2			2-0-15-0		91	409	23	5	
v. Surrey (Cardiff) 6-9 June	18-4-41-0	28-2-113-2	16.3-2-77-4	25-7-73-4		3-0-13-0			9-1-36-0				99.3	368	15	10	
	8-1-23-1	7-2-19-0		4-2-3-1		4-0-15-0							30	82	6	3	
v. Derbyshire (Derby) 11-14 June	37.4-14-74-4	20-4-58-0	20-4-46-1	18-2-44-1	17-5-29-1			8-1-30-3					120.4	307	25	10	
	42-13-62-4	5-0-16-0	6-0-56-0	4-1-15-1	27-5-59-0		23-4-73-2						107	294	13	8	1
v. Northamptonshire (Cardiff) 16-19 June	24.5-4-43-1	24-7-59-2		11-4-25-1	9-2-15-1		23.1-6-71-3	12-2-39-0					91.1	215	2	8	
	22-14-16-1	9-3-37-2		7-2-22-2	23-10-46-1	2.5-0-5-0	3-0-9-0						66.5	140	5	6	
v. Essex (Chelmsford) 7-10 July	2.5-0-5-1	15-3-37-3	13-4-34-1	15-0-62-5				12-2-39-0					57.5	200	23	10	
	41-4-107-2	23-8-58-1	14-2-64-0	17-6-56-0			13-0-52-1	19-2-64-2					127	411	10	6	
v. Kent (Cardiff) 15-18 July	22-1-99-1	29.4-5-118-3	21-0-107-1	18-2-74-0	28-4-122-0		1-0-11-0				4-0-18-0		123.4	557	8	5	
	-												-	-	-	-	
v. Gloucestershire (Bristol) 31 July-3 August	22-3-68-1	18-1-91-2	23.1-7-77-3	13-3-38-2			5-0-24-0	20-4-88-1					101.1	400	14	9	
	20-4-37-0	13-6-23-1	12-3-29-0	7-3-15-0									68	168	17	2	
v. Leicestershire (Colwyn Bay) 5-8 August	15-1-37-0	19-5-90-3			14-0-62-0	15.3-4-47-2	7-1-11-3	14-3-54-1					84.3	313	12	10	1
	15-4-30-3	16-3-62-0			6-1-9-2	12-8-12-3	16-0-52-1	5-4-4-0					70	181	12	10	1
v. Middlesex (Swansea) 20-22 August	25.4-7-47-4		18-4-35-0	8-1-22-1		21-1-54-3	3-2-2-0		7-4-8-1				82.4	170	2	10	1
	22-3-65-5		8-1-26-0			15.2-1-35-3	9-0-35-1						54.2	167	6	10	1
v. Northamptonshire (Northampton) 26-29 August	18-1-53-3	17.2-2-92-3	19-4-66-1	11-0-68-0			5-0-14-0		18-3-54-2				88.2	350	3	10	1
	32-4-71-4	17-2-60-2	12-0-51-0	4-0-28-0			15-3-46-2		7-2-18-0			5-0-23-0	92	312	15	8	
v. Leicestershire (Grace Road) 2-5 September	10-2-27-0		31-8-85-4	27-8-66-3			5-1-14-1	5-2-16-0		15-2-66-2			93	282	10	10	
	31-9-52-1		12-3-17-0	13-0-45-0			19-3-62-2	4-0-19-1		13-1-50-1			92	259	14	6	1
v. Essex (Cardiff) 10-13 September	34-8-78-3		9-1-18-0	11-2-30-0	31.4-6-91-6		9-3-24-0		9-1-31-1				103.4	288	16	10	
	32-9-50-2		6-0-28-0	3-2-9-1	36-19-35-5		17-4-34-1	4-1-8-0	3-1-9-0				101	181	8	9	
v. Gloucestershire (Cardiff) 16-19 September	13-2-32-0	24.2-1-69-4	18-3-61-2		15-4-43-0		7-0-22-1		3-0-13-1		15-3-34-2		95.2	286	12	10	
	38-8-67-3	12-1-56-2	15-4-63-1		18-3-57-0		14-3-23-3				3-1-8-0		100	281	7	9	
v. Surrey (The Oval) 23-26 September	34-4-107-2	23-6-88-1	26-5-93-6		17.4-3-54-1		1-0-10-0	8-1-31-0	13-4-39-0				122.4	430	8	10	
	35-6-91-7	19-4-70-3	12-2-28-3		26-8-70-0		5-1-18-0	4-0-14-0	3-0-8-0				104	309	5	7	

	RDB Croft	JAR Harris	GJP Kruger	AJ Shantry	DA Cosker	JWM Dalrymple	DS Harrison	MJ Cosgrove	J Allenby	CP Ashling	BJ Wright	WD Bragg
Overs	737	439.2	353.4	278	312.1	231.5	207.1	58	78	28	8	5
Maidens	154	86	59	47	83	29	32	8	19	3	0	0
Runs	1727	1498	1283	898	769	726	770	202	209	116	41	23
Wickets	58	43	33	29	26	22	20	6	6	3	0	0
Average	**29.77**	**34.83**	**38.87**	**30.96**	**29.57**	**33.00**	**38.50**	**33.66**	**34.83**	**38.66**	**–**	**–**

FIELDING

37	MA Wallace (31 ct, 6 st)
17	JWM Dalrymple
15	GP Rees
8	MJ Powell
7	HH Gibbs
6	J Allenby
6	TL Maynard
5	DA Cosker
4	RDB Croft
4	WD Bragg
4	MJ Cosgrove
3	BJ Wright
2	DS Harrison
2	GJP Kruger
1	JAR Harris
0	AJ Shantry
0	MP O'Shea
0	CP Ashling

Division Two – Final Table

	P	W	L	D	Bat	Bowl	Pens	Pts
Kent	16	8	3	5	43	44	0.00	219.00
Essex	16	6	3	7	40	43	1.00	194.00
Northamptonshire	16	6	4	6	40	45	0.00	193.00
Gloucestershire	16	6	6	4	39	46	0.00	185.00
Glamorgan	16	2	2	12	56	43	0.00	175.00
Derbyshire	16	2	3	11	55	45	0.00	172.00
Surrey	16	1	4	11	54	36	0.00	148.00
Middlesex	16	2	7	7	43	41	0.00	140.00
Leicestershire	16	2	3	11	31	35	0.00	138.00

FPT & Pro40   T20

GLAMORGAN DRAGONS

Limited overs nickname:
GLAMORGAN DRAGONS

GLOUCESTERSHIRE CCC

FIRST-CLASS MATCHES
BATTING

	HJH Marshall	Kadeer Ali	SP Kirby	APR Gidman	CG Taylor	J Lewis	JEC Franklin	WTS Porterfield	ID Saxelby	SD Snell	SJ Adshead	RKJ Dawson	V Banerjee	AJ Ireland	CM Spearman	RJ Woodman	TP Stayt	GP Hodnett	GM Hussain	Extras	Total	Wickets	Result	Points
v. Surrey (The Oval) 15-18 April	76	90	0	69	9	39*	11		0	4		16			0					19	333	10	D	10
v. Essex (Bristol) 21-23 April	64	6	6*	1	10	2	21	10	18		0	11								6	155	10		
	3	27	2*	5	16	1	13	0	7		11	28								6	119	10	L	3
v. Northamptonshire (Northampton) 28 April-1 May	12	9	0	39	32	0	38	25	60*	47		6								26	294	10		
	69	45	3	1	55	0	11	0	5*	11		16								21	237	10	W	19
v. Leicestershire (Bristol) 6-9 May	0	3	27	159	18	3		12		85				0*		6	36			44	393	10		
		38*						32*												2	72	0	W	21
v. Derbyshire (Chesterfield) 6-9 June	158	0		135	38*			4*								16		31		21	403	5	D	11
v. Middlesex (Bristol) 18-20 June	18	21	2*		40	54	67	53		15			2	1	57					12	342	10		
	28*	8*						4												5	45	1	W	20
v. Kent (Beckenham) 30 June-3 July	4	27	0*		7	7	19		0				0		47				8	19	166	10		
	45	38	0			61*	41	11	8				1		13				8	17	255	10	L	3
v. Derbyshire (Cheltenham) 12-15 July	7	25	9	55	6	6	14			2			5*	16	7					12	164	10		
	0	44	16	60	9	0	109			13			8	2*	27					12	300	10	L	3
v. Northamptonshire (Cheltenham) 20-22 July	6	0		0	8	51	13*	24		0		21		2						22	147	10		
	0	6	4		7	0	29*	26	4		1	44			0					21	142	10	L	3
v. Glamorgan (Bristol) 31 July-3 August	43	53	0*	128	37	10*	16	22	33		1					15				42	400	10		
	27*	67*						31								18				25	168	2	D	11
v. Essex (Southend) 5-8 August	20	76	19	14	21	32	100	20			156*	8			1					31	498	10		
	3	13*													23*					3	39	1	W	21
v. Leicestershire (Grace Road) 19-22 August	0	13	13*	0	50	0	12		0		0	14				31				5	138	10		
	36	48	0	10	19	1	97*		17		18	49				5				19	319	10	L	3
v. Middlesex (Lord's) 27-30 August	17	4	18	7	65	20*	16		17		14	0				9				30	210	10		
	0	48	9	7	25	4	80*		0		0	35				4				13	225	10	L	4
v. Surrey (Bristol) 2-5 September	84	39		176	111		25*	5	1*		16					32				34	523	7	W	22
v. Glamorgan (Cardiff) 16-19 September	5	42	3	47	0	5	66	0			48	50	6*							14	286	10		
	35	19	7*	52	24	28	6	81			0	15	0*							14	281	9	D	9
v. Kent (Bristol) 23-25 September	87	25	19*	15	69	43	104ret*	42	5		114	18		0						11	552	10	W	22
Matches	16	16	16	15	15	15	14	9	9	9	7	7	7	7	6	6	1	1	1					
Innings	26	28	22	23	22	22	22	12	13	14	10	10	10	12	9	10	1	1	2					
Not Out	2	4	8	0	1	6	4	1	3	1	1	0	3	2	0	1	0	0	0					
High Score	158	90	27	176	111	61*	109	81	60*	85	156*	50	16	16	57	32	36	31	8					
Runs	844	834	157	1028	705	358	904	341	168	215	367	254	71	21	206	144	36	31	16					
Average	35.16	34.75	11.21	44.69	33.57	22.37	50.22	22.73	16.80	16.53	40.77	25.40	7.88	4.20	22.88	16.00	36.00	31.00	8.00					
100s	1			4	1	0	3	0	0	0	2	0	0	0	0	0	0	0	0					
50s	5	4	0	4	5	2	4	2	1	1	0	1	0	0	1	0	0	0	0					
Catches/Stumpings	13/0	10/0	2/0	9/0	11/0	5/0	6/0	17/0	5/0	28/2	22/1	12/0	2/0	2/0	9/0	3/0	0/0	0/0	1/0					

Home Ground: Bristol
Address: County Ground, Nevil Road, Bristol, BS7 9EJ
Tel: 0117 9108000
Fax: 0117 9241193
Email: reception@glosccc.co.uk
Directions: *By road:* M5, M4, M32 into Bristol, exit at second exit (Fishponds/Horfield), then third exit – Muller Road. Almost at end of Muller Road (bus station on right), turn left at Ralph Road. Go to the top, turn left and then right almost immediately into Kennington Avenue. Follow the signs for County Cricket.

Capacity: 8,000
Other grounds used: Gloucester, Cheltenham College
Year formed: 1870

Chief Executive: Tom Richardson
Director of Cricket: John Bracewell
Captain: Alex Gidman
County colours: Navy blue, light blue and yellow

Honours
Sunday League/NCL/Pro40
2000
Benson & Hedges Cup
1977, 1999, 2000
Gillette Cup/NatWest/C&G Trophy
1973, 1999, 2000, 2003, 2004

Website:
www.gloscricket.co.uk

FIRST-CLASS MATCHES
BOWLING

	SP Kirby	J Lewis	JEC Franklin	AJ Ireland	V Banerjee	ID Saxelby	HJH Marshall	RKJ Dawson	CG Taylor	APR Gidman	TP Stayt	GM Hussain	RJ Woodman	GP Hodnett	Kadeer Ali	Overs	Total	Byes/Leg-byes	Wickets	Run outs
v. Surrey (The Oval) 15-18 April	14-5-44-2	12-2-28-1	12-3-23-3		13-4-26-2	10.5-2-33-2			11-5-11-1							61.5	160	6	10	
		4-0-13-1	3-0-7-0		12-4-29-0											30	64	4	2	
v. Essex (Bristol) 21-23 April	18-4-49-0	23-7-39-2	6-3-7-2		1-0-7-0	12-2-34-1	2-1-1-1			15.1-6-23-3						77.1	177	17	10	1
	7-2-14-1	10-1-34-1				5-3-16-1	4-0-24-0		1-0-1-0							27	101	12	3	
v. Northamptonshire (Northampton) 28 April-1 May	14.1-2-41-4	12-5-24-2	8-2-23-0		21-5-62-4				5-2-8-0							60.1	161	3	10	
	20.5-3-76-3	2-0-14-0			32-6-90-2		2-0-19-1		2-0-7-0	4-0-11-1					4-0-15-0	89.5	326	9	10	
v. Leicestershire (Bristol) 6-9 May	13-3-39-1	17-7-22-1		14-4-31-6						7-1-14-0	12-4-19-1		2-1-4-1			65	133	4	10	
	23.5-5-70-2	23-8-39-4		21-3-78-2					12-4-44-1	8-2-21-0	22-3-58-1		3-2-4-0			112	331	17	10	
v. Derbyshire (Chesterfield) 6-9 June	22-8-51-1	17-3-71-2		14-2-77-2			1-0-4-0	25-3-118-1	5-3-7-1	5-1-23-0				6-0-41-1		95	402	10	8	
																-	-	-	-	
v. Middlesex (Bristol) 18-20 June	9-3-16-2	13-2-34-3	10-2-33-1	11-2-42-2	7.5-2-26-2											50.5	153	2	10	
	14-5-30-3	14-3-54-3	13-2-50-0	9-2-28-1	16.2-3-66-2											66.2	233	5	10	1
v. Kent (Beckenham) 30 June-3 July	13-2-25-2	13-2-27-1	14-2-38-2		19.2-4-58-3		1-0-5-0					14-1-73-2				74.2	231	5	10	
	26-9-44-5	20-6-57-1	17-4-57-0		25-4-58-4							8-0-34-0				96	266	16	10	
v. Derbyshire (Cheltenham) 12-15 July	14-3-50-2	17-4-40-3	18.4-3-59-3	14-2-79-1	19-0-84-1				6-1-11-0							88.4	326	3	10	
	19.5-5-58-2	11-3-24-1	14-4-28-1	16-3-51-1	18-3-95-0		2-0-11-1		2-0-9-0	7-2-32-0						89	323	15	6	
v. Northamptonshire (Cheltenham) 20-22 July	21-3-75-4	9.4-1-39-3	20-3-60-3	10-3-30-0				8-3-14-0								68.4	232	14	10	
	2-0-10-0		1-0-1-0	3-0-21-0				7-0-20-0	4.2-1-6-1							17.2	58	0	1	
v. Glamorgan (Bristol) 31 July-3 August	20-3-58-3	23-5-73-5	15-0-94-0				14.1-5-50-0	3-0-11-0	7-2-22-0	12-1-29-0						94.1	350	13	8	
																-	-	-	-	
v. Essex (Southend) 5-8 August	16-5-51-3	18.1-7-31-2	16-1-61-3				17-1-63-1	7-1-20-0	12-0-61-1							86.1	300	13	10	
	18-4-36-1	18-5-42-2	16-5-23-3				16.5-4-31-3	1-0-2-0	24-2-86-1							93.5	236	16	10	
v. Leicestershire (Grace Road) 19-22 August	21-6-78-4	18.4-3-68-3	19-7-62-1				16-1-41-0		21-0-82-2	7-1-21-0	1-0-9-0					103.4	368	7	10	
	14.4-4-48-2	8.3-3-10-1					15.4-3-31-3	17-6-24-4	1-0-7-0							55.3	133	13	10	
v. Middlesex (Lord's) 27-30 August	21-4-77-4	21-6-64-0	18-6-44-0				21.4-3-58-3	17-5-52-2	4-0-23-0	2-0-14-0						104.4	342	10	10	1
	14.1-3-41-2	5-0-24-0	10-2-35-0				16.2-5-51-1	8-1-32-1	13-0-60-1	5-1-24-1						71.1	273	6	7	1
v. Surrey (Bristol) 2-5 September	17-7-32-3		12-5-28-3	17-7-53-2			12-1-64-2									58	183	6	10	
	18.5-5-48-2		14-3-46-0	22-5-83-2			13-1-59-1	19-6-52-4		10-2-32-1						96.5	339	19	10	
v. Glamorgan (Cardiff) 16-19 September	22-1-88-1	22-5-62-3	15-3-58-1		16-3-66-1		5-2-30-0	24.4-5-76-4		5-0-20-0						109.4	410	10	10	
	16.3-1-44-3	20-6-47-3	6-0-23-0					18-0-47-2		2-0-5-0						62.3	171	5	8	
v. Kent (Bristol) 23-25 September	12.1-1-73-0	21-9-50-4	13-3-30-5			10.5-0-73-1	4-0-20-0		1-0-16-0							62	264	2	10	
	12-1-54-2	12.3-2-45-2		16-1-91-2		5-1-16-1	11-2-53-2									56.3	265	6	9	

	SP Kirby	J Lewis	JEC Franklin	AJ Ireland	V Banerjee	ID Saxelby	HJH Marshall	RKJ Dawson	CG Taylor	APR Gidman	TP Stayt	GM Hussain	RJ Woodman	GP Hodnett	Kadeer Ali
Overs	472.4	426.3	292.4	167	200.3	185.2	104	158.4	86.2	59.1	34	22	5	6	4
Maidens	107	110	63	34	38	30	24	13	22	13	7	1	3	0	0
Runs	1420	1146	904	664	667	620	360	610	242	162	77	107	8	41	15
Wickets	64	57	31	21	21	20	16	12	6	4	2	2	1	1	0
Average	22.18	20.10	29.16	31.61	31.76	31.00	22.50	50.83	40.33	40.50	38.50	53.50	8.00	41.00	-

FIELDING

30	SD Snell (28 ct, 2 st)
23	SJ Adshead (22 ct, 1 st)
17	WTS Porterfield
13	HJH Marshall
12	RKJ Dawson
11	CG Taylor
10	Kadeer Ali
9	APR Gidman
9	CM Spearman
6	JEC Franklin
5	J Lewis
5	ID Saxelby
3	RJ Woodman
2	SP Kirby
2	V Banerjee
2	AJ Ireland
1	GM Hussain
0	GP Hodnett
0	TP Stayt

Division Two – Final Table

	P	W	L	D	Bat	Bowl	Pens	Pts
Kent	16	8	3	5	43	44	0.00	219.00
Essex	16	6	3	7	40	43	1.00	194.00
Northamptonshire	16	6	4	6	40	45	0.00	193.00
Gloucestershire	16	6	6	4	39	46	0.00	185.00
Glamorgan	16	2	2	12	56	43	0.00	175.00
Derbyshire	16	2	3	11	55	45	0.00	172.00
Surrey	16	1	4	11	54	36	0.00	148.00
Middlesex	16	2	7	7	43	41	0.00	140.00
Leicestershire	16	2	3	11	31	35	0.00	138.00

FPT & Pro40

T20

GLADIATORS

Limited overs nickname:
GLOUCESTERSHIRE GLADIATORS

HAMPSHIRE CCC

FIRST-CLASS MATCHES
BATTING

	JHK Adams	MJ Lumb	SM Ervine	LA Dawson	MA Carberry	DG Cork	Imran Tahir	JA Tomlinson	N Pothas	AD Mascarenhas	DA Griffiths	JM Vince	JP Crawley	CT Tremlett	CC Benham	TG Burrows	DR Briggs	DJ Balcombe	MJ North	H Riazuddin	BV Taylor	TW Parsons	Extras	Total	Wickets	Result	Points
v. Worcestershire (Rose Bowl) 15–17 April	49	0	28	66	4	25		0*	13			2	0					10					19	216	10		
	8	0	8*		58								31*										2	107	3	W	18
v. Warwickshire (Edgbaston) 22–25 April	1		30	22	77	5		8	122*			30	36					0	15				33	379	10		
	39	84	21	2	65	7*			65*			6											12	301	6	D	9
v. Sussex (Rose Bowl) 29 April–2 May	61	30	109	27*	17	2		2*	74					4	1								23	350	8		
	55*	0		72											0*								0	127	2	D	11
v. Loughborough UCCE (Rose Bowl) 6–8 May	4	172		4						9*		13	14		111	32	0			3		0	16	378	10		
	67			31								6*	54*		0								2	160	2	D	
v. Durham (Riverside) 6–8 June	8	20	2	0	0	13	0	6*	35	0		10											11	105	10		
	11	32	22	6*	0	6	0	1	8	2		5											3	96	10	L	
v. Nottinghamshire (Rose Bowl) 11–14 June	112	43	1	27	26	0		3*	36	1		13			13								20	295	10		
	6	26	21	5	4	0		2	63*	3		75			7								8	220	10	L	5
v. Lancashire (Liverpool) 17–20 June	9	16		25	5	24*	6		86	108		46			0								19	345	10		
	46*			62*																			10	118	0	W	20
v. Somerset (Taunton) 10–13 July	33	11	10	0	123	33	14*		15	0		2	7										16	264	10		
	29	3	58	69	52				49*				81*										16	357	5	D	8
v. Sussex (Arundel Castle) 15–18 July	33	46	17	5	112	36	25*	0		22		26				2							22	346	10	D	10
v. Warwickshire (Rose Bowl) 21–24 July	90	20	82	18	204		8	7*	0rh			14	28		0								34	505	9	D	10
v. Lancashire (Rose Bowl) 6–9 August	107		114	3	33		0	6*	21	0		23	21		0								9	337	10		
	21			23*	136*							9	12										28	229	3	D	8
v. Yorkshire (Basingstoke) 11–14 August	79	51	28	1	23		7		14	0*		18		0	16								13	250	10		
	2	0	48	50	70		4		0	0		43		0	8*								27	252	10	L	
v. Nottinghamshire (Trent Bridge) 19–22 August	55	219	104	43	86rh	0	0			48*	20*	27			20								32	654	8	D	12
v. Somerset (Rose Bowl) 27–30 August	147	68	4	55			77*		41	31	5	4					36						28	548	10		
	1*	3*																					5	9	0	D	
v. Worcestershire (New Road) 9–11 September	91	11	14	37	43	28	23		93	2	4*	16											21	383	10		
	7*			0*																			0	7	0	W	21
v. Durham (Rose Bowl) 15–18 September	57	6	67	29	24		0*		78	1		8			100	0							14	384	10	D	10
v. Yorkshire (Headingley) 23–26 September	51	81	26	45	42*		14		38	8	0				16		1						29	351	10		
	72	64	18*	35											67*								28	284	3	D	10
Matches	17	16	15	15	12	12	12	12	11	10	10	9	8	7	6	6	3	3	1	1	1	1					
Innings	30	24	22	23	21	15	15	14	15	11	13	13	14	8	9	7	3	3	1	1	0	1					
Not Out	4	1	2	4	3	2	4	7	4	2	4	1	3	0	2	1	0	0	0	0	0	0					
High Score	147	219	114	69	204	52	77*	23	122*	108	20*	75	81*	36	111	32	36	10	15	3	0	0					
Runs	1351	1006	832	571	1251	290	206	92	816	254	45	301	308	75	316	78	37	10	15	3	0	0					
Average	51.96	43.73	41.60	30.05	69.50	22.30	18.72	13.14	74.18	28.22	5.00	25.08	28.00	9.37	45.14	13.00	12.33	3.33	15.00	3.00	–	0.00					
100s	3	2	3	0	4	0	0	0	1	1	0	0	0	0	2	0	0	0	0	0	0	0					
50s	10	5	3	4	8	1	1	0	1	5	0	0	1	2	0	1	0	0	0	0	0	0					
Catches/Stumpings	18/0	10/0	6/0	13/0	6/0	18/0	4/0	3/0	24/0	4/0	0/0	3/0	7/0	2/0	7/0	14/1	1/0	0/0	0/0	0/0	0/0	0/0					

Home Ground: Southampton
Address: The Rose Bowl, Botley Road, West End, Southampton, SO30 3XH
Tel: 02380 472002
Fax: 02380 472122
Email: enquiries@rosebowlplc.com
Directions: From the North: M3 Southbound to junction 14, follow signs for M27 Eastbound (Fareham and Portsmouth). At junction 7 of M27, filter left onto Charles Watts Way (A334) and from there follow the brown road signs to the Rose Bowl. From the South: M27 to junction 7 and follow the brown road signs to the Rose Bowl.

Capacity: 22,000
Year formed: 1863

Chairman and Chief Executive: Rod Bransgrove
Director of Cricket: Tim Tremlett
First Team Manager: Giles White
Captain: Dimitri Mascarenhas
County colours: Navy blue, old gold

Website:
www.rosebowlplc.com

Honours
County Championship
1961, 1973
Sunday League/NCL/Pro40
1975, 1978, 1986
Benson & Hedges Cup
1988, 1992
Gillette Cup/NatWest/C&G Trophy/
Friends Provident Trophy
1991, 2005, 2009

FIRST-CLASS MATCHES
BOWLING

	Imran Tahir	DA Griffiths	JA Tomlinson	DG Cork	CT Tremlett	AD Mascarenhas	SM Ervine	LA Dawson	DJ Balcombe	DR Briggs	TW Parsons	H Riazuddin	MA Carberry	BV Taylor	JHK Adams	JM Vince	Overs	Total	Byes/Leg-byes	Wickets	Run outs
v. Worcestershire (Rose Bowl) 15-17 April			13.1-2-47-1	8-2-10-4	13-4-18-1		8-4-13-1	2-0-11-1	8-3-21-2								52.1	132	12	10	
			15-5-53-3	16-4-27-2	16-8-24-2		3-1-9-1	4-0-18-0	14-3-56-2								68	189	2	10	
v. Warwickshire (Edgbaston) 22-25 April			29-3-104-1	19-4-55-1	24-5-87-1		17-3-50-0	8.5-0-75-2	22-1-97-0				17-1-105-1		12-0-49-1		148.5	630	8	8	1
v. Sussex (Rose Bowl) 29 April-2 May			25-3-96-3	22-4-83-3	10-2-33-0		18-5-47-0	2-1-3-2					4-0-12-0	21-4-52-1			102	336	10	10	1
v. Loughborough UCCE (Rose Bowl) 6-8 May		18.2-2-62-4					12-1-53-2	19-3-76-3		9-2-24-0	17-4-47-1				3-0-22-0		78.2	289	5	10	
		10-3-28-0					12-1-56-1	15-3-38-2		9-2-39-3	5-0-25-1						51	196	10	9	2
v. Durham (Riverside) 6-8 June	27-7-85-5	20-6-73-1	23-7-72-2	20-5-45-1			13-5-29-1										103	311	7	10	
v. Nottinghamshire (Rose Bowl) 11-14 June	34-5-130-2	16.2-4-48-4	21.1-6-73-1	15-5-36-0			13.5-7-22-3						2-0-7-0	1-0-7-0			103.2	326	3	10	
	29-8-103-1	15-2-67-1	15-4-60-3	14-1-56-0									10-0-64-1	1-0-5-0	2-0-13-0		86	380	12	6	
v. Lancashire (Liverpool) 17-20 June	7-2-14-0		9.5-0-54-1	16-4-43-3	13-3-49-4	15-4-46-2											60.5	208	2	10	
	32.5-4-108-6		9-2-32-0	8-1-17-0	11-3-35-2	16-2-43-1							3-1-10-0				79.5	254	9	10	1
v. Somerset (Taunton) 10-13 July	30-0-141-1		27-1-119-3		25-1-111-2	33-9-87-1	7.4-1-39-2	5-1-7-1									127.4	510	6	10	
v. Sussex (Arundel Castle) 15-18 July	36.2-4-140-5		27-6-108-3	21-6-54-0			20-6-57-2	12-1-68-0	1-0-8-0				1-1-0-0				117.2	441	6	10	
	6-0-29-1		6-0-27-1	3-0-15-0			0.1-0-0-0	7-2-22-0	9-0-41-0								32.1	138	4	2	
v. Warwickshire (Rose Bowl) 21-24 July	28-0-91-0		27-5-102-3		30-5-101-0		18-2-63-2	20-2-97-1	6-2-13-1				0.1-0-10-0				129	484	17	7	
	7-5-2-2								6-3-7-0								13.1	23	4	2	
v. Lancashire (Rose Bowl) 6-9 August	28-3-112-0	27-5-103-4	24-4-80-0				24-8-59-1	11-0-51-0	19.1-1-100-0				6-0-34-0	1-0-5-0	4-0-9-0		144.1	568	15	5	
v. Yorkshire (Basingstoke) 11-14 August	33-7-116-3	32-5-117-3			31-3-106-2	40-16-77-1	27-10-67-0								2-0-7-0		165	524	34	10	1
v. Nottinghamshire (Trent Bridge) 19-22 August	36-7-106-4	28.1-4-144-4	17-3-48-1				18-6-42-0	10-1-41-1	5-0-15-0								114.1	407	11	10	
	29-6-79-2	16-2-51-1	10-1-40-0				10-2-43-1	14-5-35-0									79	271	18	4	
v. Somerset (Rose Bowl) 27-30 August	35.1-6-140-7	19-2-74-1	16-5-39-2				10.5-2-31-0	2-0-8-0		13-2-70-0							106	393	10	10	
	36-9-120-2	12-2-25-2	16-2-48-2				11-2-36-1			19-3-62-3							94	294	3	10	
v. Worcestershire (New Road) 9-11 September	6-0-18-4	14-4-39-2	11-4-28-2	12-4-30-1			12-5-21-1	2-0-17-0									57	159	6	10	
	12.2-5-44-3	11-0-69-1	15-2-55-1	14-7-14-5			2-0-5-0	4-0-31-0									58.2	227	4	10	
v. Durham (Rose Bowl) 15-18 September	35-3-133-4	19.4-3-66-2	21-4-63-1				16-4-37-0	3-1-6-0		38-5-126-3						2-0-8-0	132.4	439	8	10	
		1.5-1-0-0															3.5	8	0	0	
v. Yorkshire (Headingley) 23-26 September			23-7-73-2	21-4-83-2	19-7-44-1		22-8-44-1	9-0-61-2		15.4-3-37-2							109.4	348	6	10	

	Imran Tahir	DA Griffiths	JA Tomlinson	DG Cork	CT Tremlett	AD Mascarenhas	SM Ervine	LA Dawson	DJ Balcombe	DR Briggs	TW Parsons	H Riazuddin	MA Carberry	BV Taylor	JHK Adams	JM Vince
Overs	487.4	283.2	318.1	287	173	241	233.3	97	78	85.4	18	22	43.1	21	18	10
Maidens	81	52	58	69	34	70	55	11	13	13	4	4	3	4	0	0
Runs	1711	1039	1193	767	564	618	793	421	288	295	63	72	242	52	88	37
Wickets	52	32	30	27	14	13	13	10	9	8	3	2	2	1	1	0
Average	32.90	32.46	39.76	28.40	40.28	47.53	61.00	42.10	32.00	36.87	21.00	36.00	121.00	52.00	88.00	-

FIELDING

24	N Pothas (24 ct)
18	DG Cork
18	JHK Adams
15	TG Burrows (14 ct, 1 st)
13	LA Dawson
10	MJ Lumb
7	JP Crawley
7	CC Benham
6	MA Carberry
6	SM Ervine
4	AD Mascarenhas
4	Imran Tahir
3	JA Tomlinson
3	JM Vince
2	CT Tremlett
1	DR Briggs
0	BV Taylor
0	MJ North
0	DA Griffiths
0	DJ Balcombe
0	TW Parsons
0	H Riazuddin

Division One – Final Table

	P	W	L	D	Bat	Bowl	Pens	Pts
Durham	16	8	0	8	49	48	1.00	240.00
Nottinghamshire	16	4	2	10	56	41	0.00	193.00
Somerset	16	3	1	12	50	43	1.00	182.00
Lancashire	16	4	2	10	35	44	0.00	175.00
Warwickshire	16	3	3	10	54	38	0.00	174.00
Hampshire	16	3	3	10	50	40	3.00	169.00
Yorkshire	16	2	2	12	46	44	0.00	166.00
Sussex	16	2	6	8	45	39	1.00	143.00
Worcestershire	16	0	10	6	30	40	0.00	94.00

FPT & Pro40   T20

HAMPSHIRE HAWKS

Limited overs nickname:
HAMPSHIRE HAWKS

KENT CCC

FIRST-CLASS MATCHES
BATTING

	GO Jones	DI Stevens	JC Tredwell	M van Jaarsveld	RWT Key	JM Kemp	SJ Cook	SA Northeast	A Khan	JL Denly	R McLaren	JB Hockley	WD Parnell	P Edwards	AJ Blake	Azhar Mahmood	RH Joseph	MJ Saggers	RS Ferley	PS Jones	MP Coles	Extras	Total	Wickets	Result	Points
v. Loughborough UCCE (Canterbury) 15-17 April	54	193*		34	26		64			36	55*											37	499	5	D	
v. Northamptonshire (Canterbury) 21-24 April	103	73	15*	107	2				27		27		0			35	0		10			18	417	10	D	11
v. Essex (Chelmsford) 29 April-2 May	1	15	10	35			3		0		46	69			1	5*		0				20	205	10		
	45	136*	79	102			22		19		72	3			0*	0*		16				18	512	9	W	20
v. Glamorgan (Canterbury) 6-9 May	0	3	59	0	25			87			4		90		0*	0		0				14	282	10		
	133		2*	182	13			15			19*		18									27	409	5	W	19
v. Leicestershire (Grace Road) 6-9 June	87		13*				26	116*														23	265	2	D	9
v. Essex (Tunbridge Wells) 16-19 June	9	6	28	13	0	36	1		18	0	1				9*							2	123	10		
	28	43	8	73	21	6	8*		16	123	2				1							26	355	10	L	3
v. Gloucestershire (Beckenham) 30 June-3 July	46	31	3	53	33	40	0	0*	0		10											5	231	10		
	4	3	6	62	12	41	40*	30	5		42					4						17	266	10	W	18
v. Surrey (The Oval) 10-13 July	0	0	60	110	123	183				123	4*											17	620	7	D	12
v. Glamorgan (Cardiff) 15-18 July	68	12		96	270*	90			1													20	557	5	W	22
v. Derbyshire (Canterbury) 31 July-3 August	23	8	86*	12	25	8	34	1		28	29	3										32	289	10		
	100	29	3*	51	110	0	3				5	0*										17	318	7	W	19
v. Middlesex (Canterbury) 5-7 August	2	67	9	9	1	3	17	12	1*	3				0								17	141	10		
	16	4	11	54	0	30	27	37	62*	25				0								21	287	10	L	3
v. Northamptonshire (Northampton) 11-14 August	11	20		19	90	12	6	35	15				0*						17			9	244	10		
	93	1		100*	15	18*	3	59														13	302	5	W	18
v. Surrey (Canterbury) 28-31 August	156	112	11	28	13	92	2	48	5				0*		1							49	517	10		
	45	35*		19	50	9*		28														14	200	4	W	22
v. Derbyshire (Derby) 2-5 September	108	16	22*	4	30	19	2	7	0					5	44							24	281	10		
	60			101*	141*			6														25	333	2	D	7
v. Middlesex (Uxbridge) 9-12 September	20	208	19	86	46	138*		84	0*							29						22	652	7		
					17*			19*														0	36	0	W	22
v. Leicestershire (Canterbury) 15-18 September	89	18	30	146	12	8	23*	21	16	43						33						14	453	10	D	12
v. Gloucestershire (Bristol) 23-25 September	44	0	6	50	21		60*	7	0	7					47						14	8	264	10		
	ah	17	8	46	1		0	128*	29	10					0						16	10	265	9	L	4

	GO Jones	DI Stevens	JC Tredwell	M van Jaarsveld	RWT Key	JM Kemp	SJ Cook	SA Northeast	A Khan	JL Denly	R McLaren	JB Hockley	WD Parnell	P Edwards	AJ Blake	Azhar Mahmood	RH Joseph	MJ Saggers	RS Ferley	PS Jones	MP Coles
Matches	17	17	17	16	15	14	13	11	11	10	7	5	5	5	4	4	4	4	3	3	2
Innings	26	24	21	25	25	21	13	19	12	15	8	8	6	4	5	6	5	4	1	4	2
Not Out	0	3	5	3	3	3	4	2	3	1	1	2	1	2	0	0	2	2	0	0	0
High Score	156	208	86*	182	270*	183	60*	128*	62*	123	43	72	90	5	47	35	9*	5*	17	16	16
Runs	1345	1050	485	1509	1171	780	220	667	153	578	126	240	183	5	125	78	11	5	17	26	30
Average	51.73	50.00	30.31	68.59	53.22	43.33	24.44	39.23	17.00	41.28	18.00	40.00	36.60	2.50	25.00	13.00	3.66	2.50	17.00	6.50	15.00
100s	5	4	0	7	4	2	0	1	0	3	0	0	0	0	0	0	0	0	0	0	0
50s	6	2	4	7	3	2	1	3	1	1	1	2	2	0	0	0	0	0	0	0	0
Catches/Stumpings	41/3	11/0	12/0	30/0	15/0	30/0	0/0	10/0	2/0	5/0	1/0	5/0	0/0	0/0	1/0	0/0	0/0	0/0	1/0	1/0	0/0

Home Ground: Canterbury
Address: St Lawrence Ground, Old Dover Road, Canterbury, CT1 3NZ
Tel: 01227 456886
Fax: 01227 762168
Email: jon.fordham.kent@ecb.co.uk
Directions: From the North, from M20 junction 7 turn left onto A249. At M2 junction 5 (Sittingbourne) bear right onto M2. At junction 7 (Boughton Street) turn right on to A2. Follow this to junction with A2050, turn left. Follow yellow signs to cricket ground. From the South, from M20 junction 13 bear right onto A20. Follow this road to junction with A260. Bear left and continue to junction with A2 (north). Continue to junction with A2050 and then proceed as north.

Capacity: 15,000
Other grounds used: Beckenham, Maidstone, Tunbridge Wells
Year formed: 1859

Chief Executive: Paul Millman
Director of Cricket: Graham Ford
Coaching Coordinator: Simon Willis
Captain: Robert Key
County colours: Navy blue, silver and yellow

Honours
County Championship
1906, 1909, 1910, 1913, 1970, 1978
Joint Champions 1977
Sunday League/NCL/Pro40
1972, 1973, 1976, 1995, 2001
Benson & Hedges Cup
1973, 1978
Gillette Cup/NatWest/C&G Trophy
1967, 1974
Twenty20 Cup
2007

Website:
ww.kentccc.com

FIRST-CLASS MATCHES
BOWLING

Match	JC Tredwell	A Khan	SJ Cook	Azhar Mahmood	R McLaren	WD Parnell	RH Joseph	MJ Saggers	JM Kemp	RS Ferley	P Edwards	PS Jones	M van Jaarsveld	MP Coles	DI Stevens	RWT Key	JL Denly	AJ Blake	SA Northeast	Overs	Total	Byes/Leg-byes	Wickets	Run outs
v. Loughborough UCCE (Canterbury) 15-17 April																				-	-	-	-	
																				-	-	-	-	
v. Northamptonshire (Canterbury) 21-24 April	30.2-9-84-2			23-6-73-4				23-8-48-2			14-1-31-0	25-8-68-1	1-0-5-0		12-2-42-1					128.2	355	4	10	
	37-16-67-3			10-3-39-0				20-7-42-2			16-2-54-0	20-2-64-0			2-1-4-0	9-3-14-1		21-7-51-0		135	348	13	7	1
v. Essex (Chelmsford) 29 April-2 May	2-0-13-0				27.5-7-78-4	20-2-104-2	22-8-45-3		9-2-35-0			17-3-61-1			7-1-15-0					104.5	370	19	10	
	8-5-9-1				19-3-56-3	13.2-0-55-6	8-3-17-0					9-5-9-0								57.2	155	9	10	
v. Glamorgan (Canterbury) 6-9 May	24-8-54-3				25.4-6-97-2	15-3-50-1			20-5-58-3			6-0-30-1			5-1-9-0					95.4	307	8	10	
	28-7-66-8				17-5-29-1	10-0-32-0						3-1-8-1			11-0-31-0					69	180	14	10	
v. Leicestershire (Grace Road) 6-9 June	2-0-20-0		26-8-78-5		16-3-62-2		25.3-2-89-1	15.5-3-53-0	13.1-3-49-1						12-0-35-0					110.3	403	17	9	
																				-	-	-	-	
v. Essex (Tunbridge Wells) 16-19 June	17-4-40-1	17-3-46-1	14-5-27-1		17.2-2-80-4		13.3-2-43-2		10-3-27-1						2-0-12-0					90.5	280	5	10	
	11-4-23-0	22-5-58-1	22-6-56-2		20-9-72-3				14.4-3-58-0						9-1-40-0		1-0-2-0			99.4	320	11	6	
v. Gloucestershire (Beckenham) 30 June-3 July	16-4-52-3	12-6-23-0	11.1-3-22-5	12-3-35-2	5-1-18-0									3-0-18-0						56.1	166	16	10	
	34-9-84-4	5-1-29-0	16.3-5-39-5		8-2-29-0															82.3	255	11	10	
v. Surrey (The Oval) 10-13 July	25-4-76-3	18-5-56-3	21-5-66-0		24-3-87-1	16-3-59-1			3-1-14-1			6-2-10-0			2-1-1-0					115	386	17	10	1
	23-7-42-2	7-3-14-0	7-1-12-0		6-1-26-1							12-3-52-0				4-1-13-0	3-0-7-0			62	170	4	3	
v. Glamorgan (Cardiff) 15-18 July	27-8-71-0	15-1-62-1	15-5-35-3		18.3-6-51-4	20-6-61-2			1-0-10-0						3-1-14-0					99.3	313	13	10	
	20.5-7-48-4	11-3-33-2	10-5-10-0		8-1-47-2	12-3-44-2														61.5	195	13	10	
v. Derbyshire (Canterbury) 31 July-3 August	22-5-92-4	15.5-3-41-2	21-7-48-2		11-2-44-1	14-2-61-1			5-1-12-3											83.5	303	17	10	
	32-5-93-4	22-3-72-0	13.2-2-38-1		8-2-38-0	15-0-44-1														95	303	6	10	1
v. Middlesex (Canterbury) 5-7 August	1-0-6-0	12-1-41-3	4-0-17-1	13-2-46-3					6-0-36-0						3-0-13-0					36	155	9	10	3
	33-10-100-5	18-6-52-2	13-3-59-0	20-9-53-3					5-0-30-0							1-1-0-0				93	320	13	10	
v. Northamptonshire (Northampton) 11-14 August	24.4-3-68-5		21-2-63-2						7-0-21-0	9-0-29-1	12-3-26-2	1.1-0-1-1								73.4	218	11	10	
	20-10-32-5		8-3-18-2							15-4-28-2	2-0-6-0									46.1	90	5	10	
v. Surrey (Canterbury) 28-31 August	38-9-100-0	31.3-4-113-5	23-7-54-1						15-4-58-1		21-6-72-3				1-1-0-0					129.3	423	26	10	
	35-10-72-3	17.5-5-49-3	19-5-62-0						10-4-20-1		14-2-52-2				6-1-11-0					101.5	293	27	10	
v. Derbyshire (Derby) 2-5 September	31-3-137-0		26-3-110-4	28-4-94-0					25-5-79-0		16-4-84-0				2-0-26-0	4-0-35-0				132	583	18	4	
v. Middlesex (Uxbridge) 9-12 September	44-7-127-2	13-0-64-2	6-0-19-0	22-5-60-3						18-2-59-1					7-1-15-2					110	356	12	10	
	34-11-82-3	12-0-43-0	13-1-42-2	14-5-37-1					4-0-16-0	33-9-73-3					5-0-17-0	1-1-0-0				116	326	16	10	
v. Leicestershire (Canterbury) 15-18 September		16-6-46-4	18-4-34-5	10-3-22-1					11-2-28-0						2-1-3-0					57	148	5	10	
		34-11-80-1	20-2-74-0	22-8-41-0	13-3-32-0				10-4-29-0				9-2-33-1				9-1-32-0	4-0-15-0	1-0-2-0	122	350	12	2	
v. Gloucestershire (Bristol) 23-25 September	28-2-100-3	28-5-120-3	23-2-97-1						17-3-46-0						17.4-0-130-2	10-2-55-1				123.4	552	4	10	

	JC Tredwell	A Khan	SJ Cook	Azhar Mahmood	R McLaren	WD Parnell	RH Joseph	MJ Saggers	JM Kemp	RS Ferley	P Edwards	PS Jones	M van Jaarsveld	MP Coles	DI Stevens	RWT Key	JL Denly	AJ Blake	SA Northeast
Overs	681.5	339.1	374.1	130.3	164.5	166.3	97.2	108.5	165.5	75	95	80	71.1	17.4	68	5	22	25	4 / 1
Maidens	178	65	88	38	38	35	9	34	35	15	18	19	10	0	13	5	7	0	0
Runs	1838	1146	1047	382	608	529	373	264	568	189	325	240	241	130	256	59	60	15	2
Wickets	69	36	34	21	19	17	12	10	8	7	7	4	4	2	2	1	0	0	0
Average	26.63	31.83	30.79	18.19	32.00	31.11	31.08	26.40	71.00	27.00	46.42	60.00	60.25	65.00	128.00	59.00	-	-	-

FIELDING

44	GO Jones (41 ct, 3 st)
30	JM Kemp
30	M van Jaarsveld
15	RWT Key
12	JC Tredwell
11	DI Stevens
10	SA Northeast
5	JB Hockley
5	JL Denly
2	A Khan
1	PS Jones
1	RS Ferley
1	R McLaren
1	AJ Blake
1	P Edwards
0	MJ Saggers
0	SJ Cook
0	Azhar Mahmood
0	RH Joseph
0	WD Parnell
0	MP Coles

Division Two – Final Table

	P	W	L	D	Bat	Bowl	Pens	Pts
Kent	16	8	3	5	43	44	0.00	219.00
Essex	16	6	3	7	40	43	1.00	194.00
Northamptonshire	16	6	4	6	40	45	0.00	193.00
Gloucestershire	16	6	6	4	39	46	0.00	185.00
Glamorgan	16	2	2	12	56	43	0.00	175.00
Derbyshire	16	2	3	11	55	45	0.00	172.00
Surrey	16	1	4	11	54	36	0.00	148.00
Middlesex	16	2	7	7	43	41	0.00	140.00
Leicestershire	16	2	3	11	31	35	0.00	138.00

FPT & Pro40

T20

Limited overs nickname:
KENT SPITFIRES

LANCASHIRE CCC

FIRST-CLASS MATCHES
BATTING

	PJ Horton	LD Sutton	G Keedy	MJ Chilton	MB Loye	KW Hogg	F du Plessis	OJ Newby	VVS Laxman	G Chapple	SI Mahmood	TC Smith	SJ Croft	AG Prince	T Lungley	A Flintoff	KR Brown	SD Parry	JM Anderson	Extras	Total	Wickets	Result	Points
v. Durham UCCE (Durham) 11-13 April	105	53*		114ret	13rh	25						51*	1	11			18			13	404	6		
		8				1*						104*	42	18			0			10	183	4	W	
v. Sussex (Hove) 21-24 April	1	20	7	89		6				4	26	0	59	56					9*	22	299	10		
	4					58*						5		91*						2	160	2	W	19
v. Nottinghamshire (Old Trafford) 29 April-2 May	6	12	3	7		0	24	5*		4		4	31	74						19	189	10		
	14			56*			4					7		135*						14	230	3	D	7
v. Worcestershire (New Road) 6-8 May	5	9	1*	55		60	10			89	0	22	43	18						35	347	10		
	24			11*			34					18	9*	21						5	122	4	W	20
v. Somerset (Old Trafford) 6-9 June	69	20	2*	2	31	0	15			55	1	12	48							31	286	10		
	68	6*		15	39	4				4*	0	0	34							21	191	6	D	9
v. Durham (Riverside) 11-13 June	0	21	0*	2	14	41	1			0	7		17	3						10	116	10		
	11	19*	0	22	30	5	0			21	16		3	0						8	135	10	L	3
v. Hampshire (Liverpool) 17-20 June	37	25	2		18	9	6			21	27	30*	7			12				14	208	10		
	39	17	0		55	16	15			1	34*	0	0			54				23	254	10	L	4
v. Nottinghamshire (Trent Bridge) 30 June-3 July	9	34	0	5	84	17*	4		30	55			25				3			19	285	10		
	0			7*	31*	34											19			6	97	3	D	9
v. Worcestershire (Old Trafford) 10-12 July	4	0	1*	13	24	1		14	19	44	3		9							13	145	10		
	77			45	17				64*				40*							21	264	3	W	17
v. Warwickshire (Edgbaston) 15-18 July	43	26	1*	85	29	1	79	6	9		7	5								26	317	10		
																							D	9
v. Yorkshire (Old Trafford) 31 July-3 August	84	30*		38*	146		18		109			40								24	489	5		
																							D	12
v. Hampshire (Rose Bowl) 6-9 August	34	30*		81	61		86*		135			95								46	568	5		
																							D	12
v. Durham (Old Trafford) 11-14 August	0	0	17	9	60	42	0	1	87						27*			2		20	265	10		
	3			79*	0	54*			23									1		3	163	4	D	9
v. Yorkshire (Headingley) 19-22 August	2	4	4	111*	24	29	32	2	50				0		10					8	276	10		
	28			84*					65*				15							4	196	2	D	8
v. Sussex (Old Trafford) 2-5 September	6	17	4*	26	58	6	54	3	6	39	0									17	236	10		
	0*	0*																		0	0	0	D	8
v. Somerset (Taunton) 9-12 September	173	26	3*	0	14	69	1	13	12	0	9									24	344	10		
	32	16			151*				113*											2	314	2	D	8
v. Warwickshire (Old Trafford) 23-25 September	3	45*	18	19	13	23			113	14	1	23	79							38	389	10		
	0*											4*								0	4	0	W	21
Matches	17	17	17	16	14	14	13	13	11	11	11	9	9	6	2	2	2	2	1					
Innings	30	23	16	23	22	15	20	11	16	14	12	15	14	12	2	4	4	4	1					
Not Out	2	7	7	6	4	2	3	1	3	2	1	3	2	2	1	0	0	0	1					
High Score	173	53*	18	114	151*	69	86*	15	135	89	30*	104*	79	135*	27*	54	19	2	9*					
Runs	881	438	63	891	996	333	531	64	857	390	100	390	360	526	37	69	40	3	9					
Average	31.46	27.37	7.00	52.41	55.33	25.61	31.23	6.40	65.92	32.50	9.09	32.50	30.00	52.60	37.00	17.25	10.00	1.50	-					
100s	2	0	0	2	2	0	0	0	4	0	0	1	0	1	0	0	0	0	0					
50s	4	1	0	6	6	2	5	0	4	3	0	2	2	3	0	1	0	0	0					
Catches/Stumpings	16/0	56/3	0/0	15/0	4/0	2/0	8/0	2/0	15/0	3/0	6/0	7/0	6/0	9/0	2/0	3/0	5/0	1/0	1/0					

Home Ground: Old Trafford
Address: Old Trafford Cricket Ground, Talbot Road, Manchester, M16 0PX
Tel: 0161 282 4000
Fax: 0161 282 4100
Email: enquiries@lccc.co.uk
Directions: *By rail:* Manchester Piccadilly or Victoria then Metro link to Old Trafford. *By road:* M63, Stretford slip-road (junction 7) on to A56; follow signs.
Capacity: 21,500
Other grounds used: Blackpool, Liverpool, Alderley Edge

Year formed: 1864
Chief Executive: Jim Cumbes
Director of Cricket: Mike Watkinson
Head Coach: Peter Moores
Captain: Glen Chapple
County colours: Red, white and navy blue

Website:
www.lccc.co.uk

Honours
County Championship
1881, 1897, 1904, 1926, 1927, 1928, 1930, 1934. Joint Champions 1879, 1882, 1889, 1950
Sunday League/NCL/Pro40 1970, 1989, 1998, 1999
Benson & Hedges Cup 1984, 1990, 1995, 1996
Gillette Cup/NatWest/C&GTrophy 1970, 1971, 1972, 1975, 1990, 1996, 1998

FIRST-CLASS MATCHES
BOWLING

Match	G Keedy	SI Mahmood	G Chapple	KW Hogg	OJ Newby	TC Smith	JM Anderson	A Flintoff	T Lungley	SJ Croft	F du Plessis	SD Parry	MJ Chilton	KR Brown	VVS Laxman	PJ Horton	Overs	Total	Byes/Leg-byes	Wickets	Run outs
v. Durham UCCE (Durham) 11-13 April	26-14-23-1			11-5-22-4	12-4-28-2	8.4-2-20-2				6-0-21-1							63.4	118	4	10	
	30-10-60-2			8-3-13-0	11-4-21-4	10-2-31-0				8-1-51-1			5.2-3-3-2				72.2	183	4	10	1
v. Sussex (Hove) 21-24 April	5-0-15-0	19-6-48-0	31-6-69-4			28-10-58-0	32-11-56-6			3-2-6-0	2-0-4-0						120	289	33	10	
	20.5-4-45-5	6-2-18-0	11-2-24-0			3-0-16-0	19-4-53-5				2-0-7-0						61.5	167	4	10	
v. Nottinghamshire (Old Trafford) 29 April-2 May	10-1-42-0		33-7-87-2	26-8-52-1	29-3-98-3	28-9-75-2											126	367	13	9	1
v. Worcestershire (New Road) 6-8 May	17-5-44-1	17.3-5-65-4		17-9-34-6	7-0-23-0	5-0-28-0				1-1-0-0							47.3	167	17	10	
		28.1-7-75-6		23-6-54-0	20-3-77-2	15-2-43-1											103.1	301	8	10	
v. Somerset (Old Trafford) 6-9 June	25.5-3-86-4	19-2-82-0		24-7-45-2		16-4-58-2	15-3-49-0				4-0-14-2						103.5	343	9	10	
v. Durham (Riverside) 11-13 June		14-4-62-2	25-5-58-3			15-2-65-1		15.5-3-47-4			1-0-1-0						69.5	244	12	10	
	5-0-19-0	14-7-30-6	9-2-33-1			6-0-26-1		15.4-9-30-2									50.4	145	6	10	
v. Hampshire (Liverpool) 17-20 June	19-5-59-2		18.1-0-98-1	23-6-77-3	9-0-48-2			17-2-60-2			4.1-0-18-0						86.1	345	3	10	
	10-1-52-0		1-0-7-0	5-1-19-0				3-1-12-0									23.1	118	10	0	
v. Nottinghamshire (Trent Bridge) 30 June-3 July	23-4-76-1		28-6-92-2	15-1-58-0	22.3-5-68-3					6-0-42-2				6-0-30-2		1-0-10-0	101.3	388	22	10	
	27-1-98-2		16.2-6-89-2	13-1-49-2	6-0-32-1					3-0-21-0				2-0-7-0			67	289	13	7	
v. Worcestershire (Old Trafford) 10-12 July	1-0-5-0	15.3-5-51-3	16-4-36-2		12-6-26-3	13-1-47-1											57.3	172	7	10	
	17.1-2-60-4	16-3-42-2	9-2-29-0		19-6-53-3	11-0-49-0											72.1	236	3	10	1
v. Warwickshire (Edgbaston) 15-18 July	36-6-104-1	26.1-4-104-1			27-4-80-3	17-4-62-3	10-1-45-0				1-0-5-0						117.1	403	3	8	
v. Yorkshire (Old Trafford) 31 July-3 August		14.3-3-57-3		14-7-23-1	11-1-44-0	13-3-46-6											52.3	181	11	10	
	40-5-132-1	17-1-71-1		13-5-15-0	11.4-0-57-0	18-3-62-2					4-0-7-0					1-1-0-0	104.4	354	10	4	
v. Hampshire (Rose Bowl) 6-9 August	11-0-48-1			29.2-8-74-4	30-4-105-4	26-6-84-1						9-2-22-0					105.2	337	3	10	
	24-4-69-1			11-3-39-1	12-2-30-0						7-0-32-0	13-3-38-1			2-1-1-0		69	229	20	3	
v. Durham (Old Trafford) 11-14 August	36.1-8-85-6			14-5-40-0	13-0-55-0				13-6-36-2			18-1-51-2			7-3-13-1		94.1	270	3	10	
	46-10-107-2			3-2-4-0	5-0-23-0				4-0-18-0		11-0-39-1	28-4-99-1					104	320	17	6	1
v. Yorkshire (Headingley) 19-22 August	46.2-11-104-3				33-10-75-1	24-4-102-2			23-2-85-3	2-0-12-0	11-1-33-1				2-0-7-0		141.2	429	11	10	
v. Sussex (Old Trafford) 2-5 September	4-1-13-0	24.3-4-87-4	15-5-38-0	15-4-53-3	15-1-49-3												73.3	240	0	10	
v. Somerset (Taunton) 9-12 September	36.1-3-143-2	28-6-96-2	28-11-81-2	19-5-91-1	17-4-88-1					7-0-39-0					2-0-5-0		137.1	557	14	10	
v. Warwickshire (Old Trafford) 23-25 September		12-1-61-1	14.4-6-19-6	8-3-29-2		10-1-36-1											44.4	148	3	10	
	27.2-9-50-6	16-1-64-2	8-0-30-0	12-2-56-1		10-3-30-0				1-0-2-0							74.2	244	12	10	1

	G Keedy	SI Mahmood	G Chapple	KW Hogg	OJ Newby	TC Smith	JM Anderson	A Flintoff	T Lungley	SJ Croft	F du Plessis	SD Parry	MJ Chilton	KR Brown	VVS Laxman	PJ Horton
Overs	543.5	306.3	335.4	338.2	297.1	199.4	51	51.3	40	30	54.1	68	5.2	8	13	2
Maidens	107	59	87	91	43	45	15	15	8	4	1	10	3	0	4	1
Runs	1540	1118	884	1000	1107	623	109	149	139	155	199	210	3	37	26	10
Wickets	45	38	35	34	31	15	11	8	5	4	4	4	2	2	1	0
Average	**34.22**	**29.42**	**25.25**	**29.41**	**35.70**	**41.53**	**9.90**	**18.62**	**27.80**	**38.75**	**49.75**	**52.50**	**1.50**	**18.50**	**26.00**	**–**

FIELDING

59	LD Sutton (56 ct, 3 st)
16	PJ Horton
15	MJ Chilton
15	VVS Laxman
9	AG Prince
8	F du Plessis
7	TC Smith
6	SI Mahmood
6	SJ Croft
5	KR Brown
4	MB Loye
3	G Chapple
3	A Flintoff
2	T Lungley
2	KW Hogg
2	OJ Newby
1	JM Anderson
1	SD Parry
0	G Keedy

Division One – Final Table

	P	W	L	D	Bat	Bowl	Pens	Pts
Durham	16	8	0	8	49	48	1.00	240.00
Nottinghamshire	16	4	2	10	56	41	0.00	193.00
Somerset	16	3	1	12	50	43	1.00	182.00
Lancashire	16	4	2	10	35	44	0.00	175.00
Warwickshire	16	3	3	10	54	38	0.00	174.00
Hampshire	16	3	3	10	50	40	3.00	169.00
Yorkshire	16	2	2	12	46	44	0.00	166.00
Sussex	16	2	6	8	45	39	1.00	143.00
Worcestershire	16	0	10	6	30	40	0.00	94.00

FPT & Pro40

T20

Limited overs nickname:
LANCASHIRE LIGHTNING

LEICESTERSHIRE CCC

FIRST-CLASS MATCHES
BATTING

	TJ New	JWA Taylor	HH Dippenaar	AJ Harris	MAG Boyce	JJ Cobb	HD Ackerman	WA White	CW Henderson	HF Gurney	PA Nixon	J Allenby	IE O'Brien	JHK Naik	JGE Benning	GP Smith	CD Crowe	NL Buck	GW Walker	ACF Wyatt	J du Toit	SJ Cliff	CEJ Thompson	Extras	Total	Wickets	Result	Points
v. Loughborough UCCE (Grace Road) 11-13 April	9	14	3		1	86	43		1*		7					1	0							18	183	9	D	
v. Northamptonshire (Grace Road) 15-18 April	0		12	17	4	1	0	6	10		31	62*										26		14	183	10		
	11		68*		25	4	20				39*													7	174	4	D	7
v. West Indians (Grace Road) 20-22 April	4	4	4		45	11	37*	0			28				0	21			3					25	182	10		
	0	5	40*		55	53	18							16*		16								35	238	6	D	
v. Middlesex (Southgate) 28 April-1 May	66	9	0	0*	27	60	29	32			8		2			10								15	258	10		
	43	122*	93		1	0	60	19			31					25*								6	400	7	D	8
v. Gloucestershire (Bristol) 6-9 May	54	8	0	0	23	2	14				0		23			0				1*				8	133	10		
	41	35	52	9	85		10				8		31			41*			0					19	331	10	L	
v. Kent (Grace Road) 6-9 June	85*	0	89		0	38	46	67	11	0	0*	14												53	403	9	D	9
v. Surrey (Grace Road) 16-19 June	44	16	39	13	5	1	21		12	0*		0		7										7	165	10		
	27*	23*	143		29	40	180					11												34	487	5	D	7
v. Derbyshire (Derby) 30 June-3 July	66	89	38	4	9	8	49			1*	96	5						3						44	412	10		
	63*	4	1								52	0*							13					34	209	7	D	12
v. Middlesex (Grace Road) 10-13 July	42	5	4	13	0	95	8		24*		2	20						5						26	244	10		
			4*		4	2	0*																	0	10	2	W	18
v. Essex (Grace Road) 21-24 July	9	88	4	0	4	14	15		8*		71	1							0					21	238	10		
			9		45*	6	19					34*												10	123	3	D	
v. Surrey (The Oval) 31 July-3 August	53	207*	86	0	75										46						100*			26	593	5		
				8*												14*								1	23	0	D	8
v. Glamorgan (Colwyn Bay) 5-8 August	45	5	85		92			10*	8						6	0					42		0	20	313	10		
	26	2	57	3*		17		2	12						20	0					0		16	26	181	10	L	5
v. Derbyshire (Grace Road) 11-14 August	17	45	0	7			17	1	16					5		20		24*						25	177	10		
	19	94	37		80		29	4	9					109*		0		5*						43	429	8	D	6
v. Gloucestershire (Grace Road) 19-22 August	0	83*	7	2		72		23	34			57			4	37	32							17	368	10		
	0	24	12	18		11		3	3			0				21*	25	1						15	133	10	W	21
v. Essex (Chelmsford) 26-29 August	14	112*	0	7	70	4		11	14			40			10	36rh								26	344	9		
	10	62	115*		14	1						4			20	21*								11	258	6	D	9
v. Glamorgan (Grace Road) 2-5 September	4	19	24	4	0	5		68	79*		32		28		9									10	282	10		
	12	96*	8		22	34		38*			29				6									14	259	6	D	
v. Kent (Canterbury) 15-18 September	3	6	54	22*	8	8		8			5		0	8		16								10	148	10		
			30*		98	28					173*													21	350	2	D	7
v. Northamptonshire (Northampton) 23-25 September	46*	0		20	20	0		4	10	0	52				19	26								21	218	10		
	0	30*		4	12	1		0	42	0	8				72	9								8	186	10	L	3
Matches	18	17	17	16	15	14	12	12	10	10	9	7	7	6	5	5	4	4	3	3	2	1	1					
Innings	30	28	31	19	29	26	21	19	13	11	17	10	9	10	9	10	7	5	4	3	3	1	2					
Not Out	4	7	5	3	2	0	1	2	2	6	2	2	1	3	2	1	2	2	0	1	1	0	0					
High Score	85*	207*	143	22*	98	95	180	68	79*	24*	173*	96	31	109*	72	46	41*	24*	13	3	100*	26	16					
Runs	813	1207	1121	143	738	510	827	340	241	54	531	363	110	200	241	174	114	29	21	4	142	26	16					
Average	31.26	57.47	43.11	8.93	27.33	19.61	41.35	20.00	21.90	10.80	35.40	45.37	13.75	28.57	34.42	19.33	22.80	9.66	5.25	2.00	71.00	26.00	8.00					
100s	0	3	2	0	0	0	1	0	0	0	1	0	0	1	0	0	0	0	0	0	1	0	0					
50s	6	6	8	0	5	4	5	1	1	0	2	4	0	0	1	0	0	0	0	0	1	0	0					
Catches/Stumpings	29/1	9/0	6/0	0/0	5/0	4/0	5/0	5/0	1/0	2/0	10/0	4/0	1/0	1/0	2/0	2/0	0/0	1/0	0/0	1/0	1/0	0/0	0/0					

Home Ground: Grace Road, Leicester
Address: County Ground, Grace Road, Leicester, LE2 8AD
Tel: 0871 2821879
Fax: 0871 2821873
Email: enquiries@leicestershireccc.co.uk
Directions: *By road:* Follow signs from city centre, or from southern ring road from M1 or A6.
Capacity: 12,000
Other ground used: Oakham School
Year formed: 1879

Chief Executive: David Smith
Senior Coach: Tim Boon
Club Captain: Paul Nixon
County colours: Dark green and yellow

Honours
County Championship
1975, 1996, 1998
Sunday League/NCL/Pro40
1974, 1977
Benson & Hedges Cup
1972, 1975, 1985
Twenty20 Cup
2004, 2006

Website:
www.leicestershireccc.co.uk

FIRST-CLASS MATCHES
BOWLING

	AJ Harris	CW Henderson	IE O'Brien	WA White	HF Gurney	J Allenby	JHK Naik	ACF Wyatt	JGE Benning	NL Buck	CD Crowe	SJ Cliff	GW Walker	HH Dippenaar	CEJ Thompson	JJ Cobb	PA Nixon	TJ New	J du Toit	JWA Taylor	Overs	Total	Byes/Leg-byes	Wickets	Run outs
v. Loughborough UCCE (Grace Road) 11-13 April				13-4-42-1	17-6-45-0	7-3-11-1		13-4-34-2		14-4-35-1	20-5-49-0			1-0-3-0		5-0-21-0					90	264	–	24	5
v. Northamptonshire (Grace Road) 15-18 April	29-6-106-4	22.5-5-49-1		17-5-54-2		20-6-47-1						23-2-92-2				1-0-1-0	3-1-10-0				115.5	387	–	28	10
v. West Indians (Grace Road) 20-22 April				14-1-82-0	22-6-58-1	4.1-1-13-0	16.5-6-33-1	21-7-42-3			17-3-48-0			0.5-0-6-1		4-0-19-0					99.5	320	–	14	6
v. Middlesex (Southgate) 28 April-1 May	23-4-105-3		24-2-116-1	20-1-94-3							42-6-158-0						3-0-8-0	1-0-5-0			113	493	–	6	7
v. Gloucestershire (Bristol) 6-9 May	30.3-8-85-3 / 5-1-15-0		32-8-78-2	10-2-31-0		20-6-44-2 / 7-0-39-0				22-5-84-3 / 2-0-7-0					1.1-0-9-0		2-0-17-0			7-1-20-0	123.3 / 15.1	393 / 72	–	34 / 2	10 / 0
v. Kent (Grace Road) 6-9 June	12-4-37-0	24-3-99-0		7-0-52-0	17.5-6-55-1													3-0-10-0			63.5	265	12	2	1
v. Surrey (Grace Road) 16-19 June	27-5-81-2	26-2-71-1		31-8-82-5	30-7-73-2													1-0-2-0			115	329	–	20	10
v. Derbyshire (Derby) 30 June-3 July	20-4-92-0		29.3-3-87-6	20-4-68-2	18-4-30-1								26-7-75-1								113.3	365	–	13	–
v. Middlesex (Grace Road) 10-13 July	15-5-49-1 / 13-6-24-4		15.3-6-39-6 / 15.2-5-29-3	11-0-46-2 / 9-2-30-1	4-0-17-1 / 3-2-1-2								1-1-0-0								52.3 / 40.2	159 / 91	–	8 / 7	10 / 10
v. Essex (Grace Road) 21-24 July	25-6-75-0		24-6-82-1		22-1-96-1	20.3-6-70-3								23-0-84-1		1-0-1-0					115.3	427	–	19	6
v. Surrey (The Oval) 31 July-3 August	21-2-96-1	64-11-178-2			26-6-99-0					27-6-73-1			7-0-34-0					19-1-89-0	3-0-28-0		167	608	–	11	4
v. Glamorgan (Colwyn Bay) 5-8 August	32-7-109-0	67-16-152-6			31-0-119-2					26-3-81-1				1-0-1-0	15.2-2-45-1					4-0-17-0	176.2	566	–	37	10
v. Derbyshire (Grace Road) 11-14 August	24-4-78-1	36-6-93-3		20-2-89-2				29-0-126-2		21-4-87-0											130	478	–	5	8
v. Gloucestershire (Grace Road) 19-22 August	12-4-26-5 / 22-4-65-2	19-4-48-1 / 43-6-106-2		8.1-0-28-2 / 22-4-49-2					2-0-8-1 / 24-10-32-2	9-2-26-0 / 23-6-50-1											50.1 / 134	138 / 319	2 / 17	10 / 17	1 / 1
v. Essex (Chelmsford) 26-29 August	29-6-109-2	40.1-6-101-2		21-0-101-2					25-3-73-2	36-6-111-0											151.1	517	22	9	1
v. Glamorgan (Grace Road) 2-5 September	13-1-53-1	19.5-5-31-3		20-2-52-2	9-2-24-1					14-3-43-3											75.5	218	–	15	10
v. Kent (Canterbury) 15-18 September	19.4-1-84-4		21-6-64-0	18-1-91-3				24-3-95-1		15-0-101-1						3-1-8-1					100.4	453	–	10	10
v. Northamptonshire (Northampton) 23-25 September	23-1-150-2	33-6-116-2		18.2-1-115-1	22-3-131-1					15-3-53-2						5-0-21-0					116.2	600	–	14	8

	AJ Harris	CW Henderson	IE O'Brien	WA White	HF Gurney	J Allenby	JHK Naik	ACF Wyatt	JGE Benning	NL Buck	CD Crowe	SJ Cliff	GW Walker	HH Dippenaar	CEJ Thompson	JJ Cobb	PA Nixon	TJ New	J du Toit	JWA Taylor
Overs	395.1	394.5	181.2	197.3	228.5	112.4	120.5	61	112	88	103	23	50	9.5	15.2	19	1.1	8	19	19
Maidens	79	70	38	23	42	33	22	17	20	17	19	2	8	0	2	1	0	1	1	1
Runs	1439	1044	547	852	829	262	367	159	384	276	346	92	159	44	45	71	9	36	89	82
Wickets	35	23	21	19	16	11	9	7	7	3	3	2	2	1	1	1	0	0	0	0
Average	41.11	45.39	26.04	44.84	51.81	23.81	40.77	22.71	54.85	92.00	115.33	46.00	79.50	44.00	45.00	71.00	-	-	-	-

FIELDING

- TJ New (29 ct, 1 st)
- PA Nixon
- JWA Taylor
- HH Dippenaar
- HD Ackerman
- MAG Boyce
- WA White
- J Allenby
- JJ Cobb
- JGE Benning
- HF Gurney
- GP Smith
- CW Henderson
- JHK Naik
- J du Toit
- IE O'Brien
- ACF Wyatt
- NL Buck
- AJ Harris
- CD Crowe
- GW Walker
- CEJ Thompson
- SJ Cliff

Division Two – Final Table

	P	W	L	D	Bat	Bowl	Pens	Pts
Kent	16	8	3	5	43	44	0.00	219.00
Essex	16	6	3	7	40	43	1.00	194.00
Northamptonshire	16	6	4	6	40	45	0.00	193.00
Gloucestershire	16	6	6	4	39	46	0.00	185.00
Glamorgan	16	2	2	12	56	43	0.00	175.00
Derbyshire	16	2	3	11	55	45	0.00	172.00
Surrey	16	1	4	11	54	36	0.00	148.00
Middlesex	16	2	7	7	43	41	0.00	140.00
Leicestershire	16	2	3	11	31	35	0.00	138.00

FPT & Pro40

T20

LEICESTERSHIRE FOXES

Limited overs nickname:
LEICESTERSHIRE FOXES

MIDDLESEX CCC

FIRST-CLASS MATCHES
BATTING

Match	DJ Malan	NRD Compton	SD Udal	ST Finn	GK Berg	TJ Murtagh	NJ Dexter	EJG Morgan	M Kartik	OA Shah	BJM Scott	SD Robson	A Richardson	DC Nash	BA Godleman	CEW Silverwood	AB London	PJ Hughes	AJ Strauss	JA Simpson	DM Housego	DA Burton	D Evans	Extras	Total	Wickets	Result	Points
v. Glamorgan (Lord's) 22-25 April	88		20	3	23*	72	26			14		3*		23				118						24	414	8		
	13*												3					65*						5	94	3	D	11
v. Leicestershire (Southgate) 28 April-1 May	0	0				51*	27	114*		3				1				139	150					8	493	7		
																											D	12
v. Surrey (The Oval) 6-9 May	86	23	36	1		5	8	13		0			0*	37				195						41	445	10		
	1	28	6	0			28	41		1*			1	1				57						20	184	9	D	11
v. Essex (Chelmsford) 6-9 June	1	24	7	12	56		29		62*		43		3	9					16					12	274	10		
	3	44	36*				42				23			26					97					17	297	7	D	9
v. Gloucestershire (Bristol) 18-20 June		7	8	24*	29	6	6			25			10	1					32	1				4	153	10		
		17	27	1	8	43	10			57		38			26*				0	0				6	233	10	L	3
v. Surrey (Lord's) 30 June-3 July	54	2	33	5	0		14	8*		159	43				48	7								12	385	10		
	30	100*	2				8*	4		61	21													20	246	5	D	10
v. Leicestershire (Grace Road) 10-13 July	67*	4	0	5	0	1	30	11		12			9	12										8	159	10		
	13	0	5	1	10	4	1	2*		18			14	14										9	91	10	L	3
v. Derbyshire (Derby) 21-24 July	11	6	0	8	12	5	7			129*	1		18*	9										20	226	9		
		62*								23*	29													7	121	1	D	8
v. Northamptonshire (Lord's) 31 July-3 August	10	82	3	3		9	71	28*		24	20	75	11											24	360	10		
	5	32	55	14*		1	6	16		4	23	9	4											17	186	10	L	3
v. Kent (Canterbury) 5-7 August	2	7		0	57*	4	5	28		16	14	1				0								21	155	10		
	49	28		0	46	11*	30	16		16	0	3				46								23	320	10	W	17
v. Essex (Lord's) 11-14 August	73	16		7	66	20	4	22		8	0	110	3*											27	356	10		
	87*	13		9	29		8	5*		10	44	12												12	229	7	L	7
v. Glamorgan (Swansea) 20-22 August	11	7	34*	1		19	14	16		4	11	2		49										2	170	10		
	47	13	16*	1		8	17	13		18	18	3												6	167	10	L	3
v. Gloucestershire (Lord's) 27-30 August	38	28	45	4	5	3*	51			1	6	83					68							10	342	10		
	20	83	26		7			39*		57		22					11							8	273	7	W	20
v. Northamptonshire (Northampton) 2-4 September	39	4	4rh	1*	18	2	30			7							31			87	9			19	251	9		
	26	5	absent	0	94*	0	1			29							4			41	0			7	207	9	L	5
v. Kent (Uxbridge) 9-12 September	3	30	1	10*	67	22	146										10	7		18	20			22	356	10		
	80	9	14	0	3	35*	118										14	0		14	19			20	326	10	L	5
v. Derbyshire (Uxbridge) 15-18 September	21	178	20		70	14	13	1									4*			9	4	2*		17	353	9		
	52	8	0		0	18*	34			22							65			1	34	0*		25	259	9	D	9
Matches	15	14	14	14	13	13	10	10	10	8	8	7	6	5	5	5	4	3	3	3	3	2	1					
Innings	28	28	24	22	23	20	19	18	19	16	14	13	7	8	9	8	8	5	5	6	6	4	0					
Not Out	3	2	4	4	2	6	2	1	5	2	1	0	4	0	0	1	1	1	0	0	0	2	0					
High Score	88	178	55	24*	98	51*	146	114*	62*	159	44	110	18*	43	48	46	68	195	150	87	34	2*	0					
Runs	930	860	398	107	668	249	709	413	336	591	167	441	40	152	160	113	190	574	295	170	86	3	0					
Average	37.20	33.07	19.90	5.94	31.80	17.78	41.70	24.29	24.00	42.21	12.84	33.92	13.33	19.00	17.77	16.14	27.14	143.50	59.00	28.33	14.33	1.50	–					
100s	0	2	0	0	0	0	2	1	0	2	0	1	0	0	0	0	0	3	1	0	0	0	0					
50s	8	3	1	0	7	1	2	1	2	2	0	2	0	0	0	0	2	2	1	1	0	0	0					
Catches/Stumpings	19/0	8/0	4/0	4/0	9/0	2/0	15/0	12/0	11/0	5/0	18/2	12/0	5/0	16/0	3/0	2/0	1/0	4/0	2/0	5/0	2/0	0/0	0/0					

Home Ground: Lord's
Address: Lord's Cricket Ground, London, NW8 8QN
Tel: 0207 289 1300
Fax: 0207 289 5831
Email: enquiries@middlesexccc.com
Directions: *By underground:* St John's Wood on Jubilee Line. *By bus:* 13, 82, 113 stop along east side of ground; 139 at south-west corner; 274 at top of Regent's Park.
Capacity: 30,000
Other grounds used: Southgate, Uxbridge, Richmond
Year formed: 1864

Chief Executive: Vinny Codrington
Head Coach: Toby Radford (left club during 2009 season)
Captain: Shaun Udal
County colours: Pink and navy blue

Website:
www.middlesexccc.com

Honours
County Championship
1903, 1920, 1921, 1947, 1976, 1980, 1982, 1985, 1990, 1993. Joint Champions 1949, 1977
Sunday League/NCL/Pro40 1992
Benson & Hedges Cup 1983, 1986
Gillette Cup/NatWest/C&G Trophy 1977, 1980, 1984, 1988, 1989
Twenty20 Cup 2008

FIRST-CLASS MATCHES
BOWLING

	TJ Murtagh	ST Finn	SD Udal	M Kartik	GK Berg	A Richardson	DA Burton	DJ Malan	NJ Dexter	CEW Silverwood	D Evans	OA Shah	AJ Strauss	NRD Compton	DM Housego	SD Robson	PJ Hughes	AB London	Overs	Total	Byes/Leg-byes	Wickets	Run outs
v. Glamorgan (Lord's) 22-25 April	30-3-103-2		22.3-0-87-3	20-3-65-1	30-8-54-0			5-0-19-1	11-4-37-2		22-1-121-1								140.3	505	19	10	
	12-2-38-2		14-2-28-1		15-4-46-1				4.5-0-23-1		20-2-69-2								89.5	278	2	8	
v. Leicestershire (Southgate) 28 April-1 May	15.1-4-60-1	14-1-56-3	20-4-54-1			22-11-42-2		7-2-21-2	6-1-21-1				2-1-10-0						84.1	258	4	10	
	32-9-83-5	21-1-107-0				22-5-58-0		14-2-28-1								2-0-3-0			135	400	6	7	
v. Surrey (The Oval) 6-9 May	31-5-97-3		26-2-111-3	29-8-47-2		35.2-6-64-2		9-0-20-0	15-6-26-0					2-0-5-0					131.2	388	12	10	
	10-0-45-2		22-4-58-2	33.1-12-74-6		6-2-20-0		10-5-24-0	5-1-20-0								1-0-6-0		86.1	242	1	10	
v. Essex (Chelmsford) 6-9 June			21.3-8-57-5				2-1-1-1	13-2-35-4	4-2-12-0	15-5-40-0									55.3	157	12	10	
			17-1-67-3	10-3-15-0			15.1-7-19-1	8-3-14-0		12-2-34-0									62.1	159	10	4	
v. Gloucestershire (Bristol) 18-20 June			21-2-69-1	10-4-26-2	17-3-65-1		18.2-2-68-5		14-5-39-1	20-3-68-0									100.2	342	7	10	
			4-1-16-0		3.5-2-20-1					1-0-3-0		1-0-1-0							9.5	45	5	1	
v. Surrey (Lord's) 30 June-3 July			26-5-120-2	26-1-72-0	39.2-12-65-5	15-0-42-1		2-0-10-0	4-2-10-1	22-6-61-1									134.2	392	12	10	
			12-5-29-2	7-0-24-1	14-5-26-2			2-0-4-0	5-1-15-0										40	99	1	5	
Leicestershire (Grace Road) 10-13 July	17-1-70-4	24-5-76-4		14-0-20-1		12-2-29-0		7.2-1-25-1											70.2	244	24	10	
	2-1-4-1	2-1-6-1																	4.1	10	0	2	
v. Derbyshire (Derby) 21-24 July	22-5-82-7		18.4-0-59-3	5-1-20-0	15.5-4-45-0	15-6-32-0													75.4	247	9	10	
	11-1-52-0		10.1-0-49-3	16-3-53-3		12-0-53-0		8-1-29-1											61.1	258	3	7	
v. Northamptonshire (Lord's) 31 July-3 August	22.5-5-63-3		18-3-41-3	11-3-28-1		19.5-5-32-3		3-0-16-0								2-0-5-0			96.5	288	8	10	
	26-4-51-4		17-1-89-1	10-0-48-2	23-8-38-1	21-3-52-2													103	293	15	10	
v. Kent (Canterbury) 5-7 August	11-5-26-3		8-1-38-2	5-0-32-3		6-1-16-0				7-0-23-1									37	141	6	10	1
	22.4-6-70-2		13-2-62-2	35-19-53-4		9-2-36-1		3-0-20-0		9-2-27-1									91.4	287	19	10	
v. Essex (Lord's) 11-14 August	29-11-84-6		24-6-69-0	26.4-11-55-3		16-4-46-0													114.4	345	20	10	1
	14-0-71-1		4-0-31-0	18-4-84-3		7-0-48-1													43	241	7	10	
v. Glamorgan (Swansea) 20-22 August	13-3-26-0		17-2-51-3	26.5-4-59-4	20-9-36-2	10-3-36-1													86.5	224	16	10	
	8-1-36-1		5-0-32-1	13.2-2-36-6	16-6-27-2														42.2	135	4	10	
v. Gloucestershire (Lord's) 27-30 August	16.3-3-61-4		17-4-47-2	6-2-10-0	17-4-44-3	12-5-28-1			2-1-5-0										70.3	210	15	10	
	18.5-2-83-3		13-3-52-2	9.4-1-2-0	1-0-4-0	14-1-55-5		2-0-7-0								2-0-3-0			60.5	225	9	10	
v. Northamptonshire (Northampton) 2-4 September	13-4-35-2		13-2-82-3	12-3-31-0		16-1-68-5			4-2-13-0										58	239	10	10	
	12-1-47-1		8-1-62-1	14-4-39-2		6-1-43-0		1.4-0-12-0								2-0-10-0			45.4	220	7	4	
v. Kent (Uxbridge) 9-12 September	24-2-114-2		21-3-88-1	37-3-115-2		23-3-102-0		15-0-82-1	8-0-41-0	22-2-73-1					0.1-0-6-0			3-0-23-0	153	652	9	7	
	2-0-16-0									2-0-11-0								1-0-3-0	5.1	36	0	0	
v. Derbyshire (Uxbridge) 15-18 September	22-2-83-1		14-1-61-0	19-3-72-1	13-2-45-0	22-1-121-3													90	401	19	5	
	6-2-21-0		6-0-27-1	5-0-25-0	6-0-35-0	13-0-60-0		15-0-66-1	2.1-0-5-0						1-0-11-0				54.1	281	31	2	

	TJ Murtagh	ST Finn	SD Udal	M Kartik	GK Berg	A Richardson	DA Burton	DJ Malan	NJ Dexter	CEW Silverwood	D Evans	OA Shah	AJ Strauss	NRD Compton	DM Housego	SD Robson	PJ Hughes	AB London
Overs	443	418.3	368.5	317.1	249.1	222.2	53.2	96.4	88	115	42	1	2	2	1.1	2	3	8
Maidens	81	64	67	103	46	53	3	10	25	21	3	0	1	0	0	0	0	0
Runs	1521	1624	1007	755	886	618	249	358	266	355	190	1	10	5	17	5	9	39
Wickets	60	53	37	33	23	11	8	7	6	4	3	0	0	0	0	0	0	0
Average	25.35	30.64	27.21	22.87	38.52	56.18	31.12	51.14	44.33	88.75	63.33	-	-	-	-	-	-	-

FIELDING

20	BJM Scott (18 ct, 2 st)
19	DJ Malan
16	DC Nash
15	NJ Dexter
12	EJG Morgan
12	SD Robson
11	M Kartik
9	GK Berg
8	NRD Compton
5	OA Shah
5	A Richardson
5	JA Simpson
4	SD Udal
4	ST Finn
4	PJ Hughes
3	BA Godleman
2	CEW Silverwood
2	AJ Strauss
2	TJ Murtagh
2	DM Housego
1	AB London
0	DA Burton
0	D Evans

Division Two – Final Table

	P	W	L	D	Bat	Bowl	Pens	Pts
Kent	16	8	3	5	43	44	0.00	219.00
Essex	16	6	3	7	40	43	1.00	194.00
Northamptonshire	16	6	4	6	40	45	0.00	193.00
Gloucestershire	16	6	6	4	39	46	0.00	185.00
Glamorgan	16	2	2	12	56	43	0.00	175.00
Derbyshire	16	2	3	11	55	45	0.00	172.00
Surrey	16	1	4	11	54	36	0.00	148.00
Middlesex	16	2	7	7	43	41	0.00	140.00
Leicestershire	16	2	3	11	31	35	0.00	138.00

FPT & Pro40

T20

Limited overs nickname:
MIDDLESEX PANTHERS

NORTHAMPTONSHIRE CCC

FIRST-CLASS MATCHES

BATTING

	RA White	AJ Hall	DS Lucas	N Boje	MH Wessels	SD Peters	JJ van der Wath	MS Panesar	AG Wakely	DH Wigley	DJ Willey	NJ O'Brien	BH Howgego	LM Daggett	MAG Nelson	JA Brooks	SP Crook	PW Harrison	GG White	D Murphy	Extras	Total	Wickets	Result	Points
v. Leicestershire (Grace Road) 15-18 April	7	124*	15	9	21	31	24	24		0	60		24								48	387	10		
																								D	11
v. Kent (Canterbury) 21-24 April	41	38	9	98	27	32	12	15		10*	31		18								24	355	10		
	70	3	13	70*	8	107		2*			47		5								23	348	7	D	10
v. Gloucestershire (Northampton) 28 April-1 May	26	5	2	58	23			0	4	0*	3	13					16				11	161	10		
	23	91	13	17	50			5*	1	0	47	9					55				15	326	10	L	3
v. Essex (Northampton) 6-9 May	70	58	13	0	84		4		4*		30	23			27		13				28	354	10		
	76*			34*	24						29										13	176	2	W	21
v. Surrey (Northampton) 11-14 June	6	23	0	4		59	28	38		2*	4		12							14	19	209	10		
	8	45	4	15		78	35	6*		1	1		1							14	18	226	10	L	3
v. Glamorgan (Cardiff) 16-19 June	2	44		10		6	26	0*	113*						10					2	2	215	8		
	12	17*		52		7	5		0		4*				38						5	140	6	D	8
v. Derbyshire (Northampton) 7-10 July	18	52	12*	30	27	175	82		4		5	0	28								28	433	9		
	1*					64*						36	3								3	104	1	D	11
v. Gloucestershire (Cheltenham) 20-22 July	0	41	0	87*	23	1		16		30	9	0	28*								25	232	10		
	5*					25															0	58	1	W	18
v. Australians (Northampton) 24-26 July	5			50					62		19	30	9		34				3*		14	226	7		
	1		22	33				16	1		2	58	46	9	10*				0		19	217	10	L	
v. Middlesex (Lord's) 31 July-3 August	51	11	0	55	19	13	7	2	61	6*			47								16	288	10		
	1	48	8	2	57	25	85	14	24	8*			6								18	293	10	W	19
v. Kent (Northampton) 11-14 August	21	19	13	9	74	8	2	2	33	8*	16										13	218	10		
	11	2	2*	6	4	8	7	7	4	0	41										5	90	10	L	4
v. Derbyshire (Chesterfield) 19-21 August	62	36	14		3	39	2		26			12	15			0*					37	246	10		
	37	20	19*		31	13	0		33			42	13						29*		8	245	8	W	18
v. Glamorgan (Northampton) 26-29 August	0	89	16	5	39	163		0	5	10	8					10*					5	350	10		
	9	25	25*	5	92	86		4	29	3*	16										19	312	8	D	11
v. Middlesex (Northampton) 2-4 September	47	38	25*	51	6	0	31	7	9			1		1							23	239	10		
	85*			30*	0	73					13	0									19	220	4	W	18
v. Surrey (The Oval) 9-12 September	66	59	7	49	109	2	50*	1	0			128		0							21	492	10		
																								D	12
v. Essex (Chelmsford) 15-18 September	30	85	20	8	10	37	10	32*			14		0					32			21	299	10		
	8	29	55*	8	8	2	0	19			38		2					3			23	195	10	L	4
v. Leicestershire (Northampton) 23-25 September	193	159	5*	90*	65	3	30		5		6							18			26	600	8		
																								W	22
Matches	17	16	16	15	15	14	13	13	12	12	10	9	6	5	4	3	2	2	2	2					
Innings	31	25	24	25	25	25	19	20	20	15	17	16	11	4	7	3	3	3	4	3					
Not Out	4	2	7	5	0	1	1	5	1	8	1	0	1	0	0	3	0	0	2	0					
High Score	193	159	55*	98	109	175	85	38	113*	16	60	128	47	2	38	10*	55	32	29*	14					
Runs	992	1161	312	801	887	1050	452	182	457	74	331	434	219	3	131	20	84	53	32	30					
Average	36.74	50.47	18.35	40.05	35.48	43.75	25.11	12.13	24.05	10.57	20.68	27.12	21.90	0.75	18.71	–	28.00	17.66	16.00	10.00					
100s	1	2	0	0	1	3	0	0	1	0	0	1	0	0	0	0	0	0	0	0					
50s	7	6	1	8	7	5	3	0	2	0	1	1	0	0	0	0	1	0	0	0					
Catches/Stumpings	11/0	16/0	5/0	7/0	27/1	12/0	4/0	0/0	10/0	5/0	3/0	34/1	3/0	1/0	3/0	1/0	2/0	0/0	0/0	7/0					

Home Ground: County Ground
Address: Abington Avenue, Northampton, NN1 4PR
Tel: 01604 514455/514444
Fax: 01604 609288
Email: commercial@nccc.co.uk
Directions: Junction 15 from M1 onto A508 (A45) towards Northampton. Follow the dual carriageway for approx. 3 miles. Keeping in left-hand lane, take next exit from dual carriageway marked A428 Bedford and Town Centre. Move into middle lane approaching the roundabout at bottom of slip road. Take second exit following signs for Abington/Kingsthorpe on to Rushmere Road. Follow Rushmere Road (A5095) across the junction with Billing Road and continue straight on through Abington Park to traffic lights at main junction with Wellingborough Road.

Capacity: 6,500
Other grounds used: Campbell Park, Milton Keynes
Year formed: 1878

Chief Executive: Mark Tagg
First XI Coach: David Capel
Captain: Nicky Boje
County colours: Claret and navy

Honours
Benson & Hedges Cup
1980
Gillette Cup/NatWest/C&G Trophy
1976, 1992

Website:
www.northantscricket.com

FIRST-CLASS MATCHES
BOWLING

Match	DS Lucas	JJ van der Wath	AJ Hall	DH Wigley	N Boje	MS Panesar	JA Brooks	LM Daggett	SP Crook	DJ Willey	GG White	MH Wessels	AG Wakely	Overs	Total	Byes/Leg-byes	Wickets	Run outs
v. Leicestershire (Grace Road) 15-18 April	19-5-46-4	14-3-40-4	6-1-20-1	14.1-5-32-1	2-0-3-0	16-6-30-0				5-0-22-0				71.1	183	12	10	
	10-1-26-0	10-3-19-1	7-5-5-2	10-3-35-1	3-1-6-0	18-3-57-0								63	174	4	4	
v. Kent (Canterbury) 21-24 April	26-6-68-2	6-0-26-0	20-2-89-3	19-0-96-1	8-2-35-0	22-2-75-2				6.4-1-21-2				107.4	417	7	10	
														–	–	–	–	
v. Gloucestershire (Northampton) 28 April-1 May	17-3-32-1		15-5-22-1	25-5-72-6	11-4-19-2	13-2-49-0			15-2-62-0	5-0-19-0				101	294	19	10	
	12.4-3-39-4		5-0-13-1	20-3-80-3	7-3-23-1	17-2-49-1			6-1-23-0					67.4	237	10	10	
v. Essex (Northampton) 6-9 May	13-4-27-0		13.1-4-29-5	17-4-61-2	9-2-14-2	4-0-9-0		8-1-31-0	12-2-37-1					76.1	221	13	10	
	21-8-59-1		15.4-4-42-1	22-7-66-1	9-2-20-1	27-11-33-1			13-3-71-5					108.4	308	17	10	
v. Surrey (Northampton) 11-14 June	26-5-83-3	22-5-76-2	22-6-55-0	35-4-134-4	26-8-66-1	28-9-69-0				5-2-19-0				164	530	23	10	
														–	–	–	–	
v. Glamorgan (Cardiff) 16-19 June		16-2-64-0	12.1-3-37-3	20-3-78-5	5-2-11-0	28-4-81-1				11-1-37-1				92.1	308	0	10	
		6-1-32-0	2-0-14-0	10-3-42-0	20-6-62-2	20-6-68-1							1-0-13-0	59	232	1	3	
v. Derbyshire (Northampton) 7-10 July	19.5-5-64-2	26-3-97-1	20-8-52-1	25-7-96-2	32-8-111-1					4-0-29-0			9-0-45-0	135.5	502	8	9	
														–	–	–	–	
v. Gloucestershire (Cheltenham) 20-22 July	15-4-49-5	14.4-4-47-3	5-1-20-2	5-1-16-0	1-0-2-0	2-0-5-0								42.4	147	8	10	
	10.3-1-24-7	11-4-27-1	6-0-45-1	6-0-39-1										33.3	142	7	10	
v. Australians (Northampton) 24-26 July	15-3-44-2					16-3-63-1	20-3-89-2			15-1-58-1	13-1-48-1			79	308	6	8	
	6-0-31-0					14-3-77-1	11-1-52-0			11-0-52-1	11-1-49-1			53	270	9	3	
v. Middlesex (Lord's) 31 July-3 August	13-2-51-1	22-1-107-4	13.5-2-44-2	12-0-61-1	18-3-58-2	9-1-31-0								87.5	360	8	10	
	14-3-38-4	14-4-38-3	7-2-15-0	5-1-21-0	11-2-34-1	12-0-34-2								63	186	6	10	
v. Kent (Northampton) 11-14 August	13-2-47-1	12.4-2-32-3	12-5-21-2	10-3-31-1	11-1-53-1	22-6-56-2								80.4	244	4	10	
	7-2-42-1	16-5-43-0	12-5-24-0	11-1-52-0	20-2-59-4	21.4-1-71-0							1-0-6-0	88.4	302	5	5	
v. Derbyshire (Chesterfield) 19-21 August	13.3-3-56-2	13-3-92-3	8-2-11-1							2-0-17-0				58.3	255	3	10	
	17-3-65-3	16.4-2-55-4	11-3-34-1							4-0-21-1	4-0-13-0			62.4	233	7	10	
v. Glamorgan (Northampton) 26-29 August	24-3-88-1		14-5-33-2	18-4-78-1	9-0-37-1	33.3-12-55-3		24-4-70-2						122.3	383	22	10	
														–	–	–	–	
v. Middlesex (Northampton) 2-4 September		11-4-35-1	23-7-75-3	16-3-42-1	1-0-6-0	8-1-31-0		16-3-47-3						75	251	15	9	1
		15-3-43-4	14-5-32-3	10-0-44-1	6-2-30-0	7-0-26-1		7-1-25-0						59	207	7	9	
v. Surrey (The Oval) 9-12 September	22-2-75-1	23-3-84-3	9.1-3-33-2		23-7-61-3	20-3-56-0	19-4-53-1							116.1	376	14	10	
	10-1-26-0	13-5-16-0	3-0-15-0		43-14-75-4	51-14-85-2	15-1-39-3					1-1-0-0		136	282	26	9	
v. Essex (Chelmsford) 15-18 September	11-4-16-2	14-4-37-1	12.4-3-38-2		8-0-53-1	25-6-71-2		8-4-23-0						78.4	253	15	8	
	5-1-30-0	17.5-3-71-5	14-0-51-1		5-0-29-0	8-0-29-0		2-0-17-0						51.5	242	15	6	
v. Leicestershire (Northampton) 23-25 September	12-1-50-1	16-4-49-2	9.4-0-41-4		13-7-14-2			10-1-51-1						60.4	218	13	10	
	16-4-45-7	17.4-2-78-2	9-4-22-0		11-5-10-1			3-0-25-0						56.4	186	6	10	
Overs	414.3	364.3	310.2	314.1	311	412.1	81	88	48	68.4	28	1	11					
Maidens	86	75	76	60	81	89	9	15	8	5	2	1	0					
Runs	1299	1237	911	1230	891	1070	325	311	193	295	110	0	64					
Wickets	60	50	40	32	30	18	9	8	6	6	2	0	0					
Average	21.65	24.74	22.77	38.43	29.70	59.44	36.11	38.87	32.16	49.16	55.00							

FIELDING

35	NJ O'Brien (34 ct, 1 st)
28	MH Wessels (27 ct, 1 st)
16	AJ Hall
12	SD Peters
11	RA White
10	AG Wakely
7	N Boje
7	D Murphy
5	DS Lucas
5	DH Wigley
4	JJ van der Wath
3	MAG Nelson
3	BH Howgego
3	DJ Willey
2	SP Crook
1	LM Daggett
1	JA Brooks
0	MS Panesar
0	PW Harrison
0	GG White

Division Two – Final Table

	P	W	L	D	Bat	Bowl	Pens	Pts
Kent	16	8	3	5	43	44	0.00	219.00
Essex	16	6	3	7	40	43	1.00	194.00
Northamptonshire	16	6	4	6	40	45	0.00	193.00
Gloucestershire	16	6	6	4	39	46	0.00	185.00
Glamorgan	16	2	2	12	56	43	0.00	175.00
Derbyshire	16	2	3	11	55	45	0.00	172.00
Surrey	16	1	4	11	54	36	0.00	148.00
Middlesex	16	2	7	7	43	41	0.00	140.00
Leicestershire	16	2	3	11	31	35	0.00	138.00

FPT, T20 & Pro40

STEELBACKS

Limited overs nickname:
STEELBACKS

NOTTINGHAMSHIRE CCC

FIRST–CLASS MATCHES
BATTING

	CMW Read	AD Brown	SR Patel	MA Wagh	MA Ealham	BM Shafayat	AR Adams	CE Shreck	AC Voges	LJ Fletcher	RJ Sidebottom	DJ Pattinson	AD Hales	MJ Wood	SA Newman	PJ Franks	WI Jefferson	DJ Hussey	A Patel	GP Swann	A Carter	SCJ Broad	KJ O'Brien	JF Brown	MHA Footitt	Extras	Total	Wickets	Result	Points
v. Worcestershire (Trent Bridge) 21–24 April	125	4	95	19	21*	14	4		99		19									26		60				19	505	10	W	21
v. Lancashire (Old Trafford) 29 April–2 May	63	21		17	34	33			95	8*	11*	17				51				0						17	367	9	D	11
v. Somerset (Trent Bridge) 6–9 May	41	63	11	10	5	19	24		63	0*	13	0														12	261	10		
		63*	35	14		32			73*			28														16	261	4	W	19
v. Warwickshire (Edgbaston) 6–9 June	15*	64	4	147	14*	20			76							21										15	376	6	D	11
v. Hampshire (Rose Bowl) 11–14 June	16	5	41	21	70*	20	5		25	92	12					12										7	326	10		
	116*	148	0	20	10*	11			49																	24	380	6	W	20
v. Oxford UCCE (The Parks) 18–20 June			45			15			53*					23	33		133		4				13		9*	18	346	7		
			37			90*								36	47	1			69*				5			8	293	5	D	
v. Lancashire (Trent Bridge) 30 June–3 July	1	54	25	40	18	14	12*		46	4						11		126								37	388	10		
	21*	7	1	131	5	30			0*							2		74								18	289	7	D	11
v. Durham (Trent Bridge) 15–18 July	48	36	7	1	24	16	6	1*	3				12						9							8	171	10		
	4	5	14	6	17*	12	2	4					9						9							1	83	10	L	2
v. Yorkshire (Scarborough) 21–24 July	20	5	8	6		7	84		0	10*					4		48	189								14	395	10	D	11
v. Somerset (Taunton) 31 July–3 August	98	28	19	64*		6			10	5	1			9	87	4										25	356	10	D	10
v. Sussex (Horsham) 5–8 August	25*	42	91	73	9*				139					86	25											41	531	6		12
v. Warwickshire (Trent Bridge) 11–14 August	110	0	47	10	37	32	4*		68	12				14	5											49	388	10		
			28*											39*	0											4	71	1	D	11
v. Hampshire (Trent Bridge) 19–22 August	119*	39	35	8	32	69	46	2	0					10	25											22	407	10		
		37*	48	136*	6									17	0											27	271	4	D	10
v. Worcestershire (New Road) 25–28 August	9	46*	46	49	17	0	6	0					12	3							4					27	219	10		
	70*	84	55	0	10	30	29*						55	0												18	351	7	D	11
v. Yorkshire (Trent Bridge) 3–6 September	42	0	7	0	36	66	0*		3					35	79	64										20	352	10	D	11
v. Durham (Riverside) 9–12 September	65	59	44	3	49	4	0*	1	59					62	16											22	384	10		
	24	28	4	6	18	32	0*	1	4					78	9											8	212	10	L	5
v. Sussex (Trent Bridge) 23–26 September	88	10	21	67	13	45	3	0	19*					33	0											29	328	10		
	83	1	54	2	24	4	25	0*	0					38	37											18	286	10	W	20

	CMW Read	AD Brown	SR Patel	MA Wagh	MA Ealham	BM Shafayat	AR Adams	CE Shreck	AC Voges	LJ Fletcher	RJ Sidebottom	DJ Pattinson	AD Hales	MJ Wood	SA Newman	PJ Franks	WI Jefferson	DJ Hussey	A Patel	GP Swann	A Carter	SCJ Broad	KJ O'Brien	JF Brown	MHA Footitt
Matches	16	16	16	15	14	14	11	11	8	8	8	8	7	7	7	5	4	3	2	2	2	1	1	1	1
Innings	22	24	25	24	20	23	13	12	10	8	9	8	12	11	11	6	6	5	4	2	1	1	2	0	1
Not Out	6	3	0	2	7	1	1	7	1	3	3	0	1	1	0	0	0	0	1	0	0	0	0	0	1
High Score	125	148	95	147	70*	90*	84	12*	139	92	46	59	78	86	87	64	133	189	69*	26	4	60	13	0	9*
Runs	1203	849	794	814	493	590	300	28	697	121	100	102	447	270	249	201	181	407	110	26	4	60	18	0	9
Average	75.18	40.42	31.76	37.00	37.92	26.81	25.00	5.60	77.44	24.20	16.66	12.75	40.63	27.00	22.63	33.50	30.16	81.40	36.66	13.00	4.00	60.00	9.00	–	–
100s	4	1	0	3	0	0	0	0	1	0	0	0	0	0	0	0	1	2	0	0	0	0	0	0	0
50s	6	6	4	2	2	3	1	0	6	1	0	0	4	1	2	2	0	1	1	0	0	1	0	0	0
Catches/Stumpings	46/4	18/0	9/0	4/0	6/0	13/0	13/0	1/0	8/0	0/0	1/0	1/0	3/0	0/0	3/0	1/0	7/0	5/0	2/0	1/0	0/0	2/0	1/0	0/0	0/0

Home Ground: Trent Bridge
Address: Trent Bridge, Nottingham, NG2 6AG
Tel: 0115 982 3000
Fax: 0115 945 5730
Email: administration@nottsccc.co.uk
Directions: *By road:* Follow signs from ring road towards city centre.
Capacity: 17,000
Year formed: 1841

Chief Executive: Derek Brewer
Director of Cricket: Mick Newell
Captain: Chris Read
County colours: Green and gold

Website:
www.nottsccc.co.uk

Honours
County Championship
1883, 1884, 1885, 1886, 1907, 1929, 1981, 1987, 2005
Sunday League/NCL/Pro40
1991
Benson & Hedges Cup
1976, 1989
Gillette Cup/NatWest/C&G Trophy
1987

FIRST-CLASS MATCHES

BOWLING

Opponent (Venue) Date	AR Adams	SR Patel	RJ Sidebottom	LJ Fletcher	MA Ealham	CE Shreck	PJ Franks	DJ Pattinson	SCJ Broad	GP Swann	MHA Footitt	AC Voges	AD Hales	A Carter	KJ O'Brien	A Patel	BM Shafayat	AD Brown	JF Brown	CMW Read	DJ Hussey	SA Newman	Overs	Total	Byes/Leg-byes	Wickets	Run outs
Worcestershire (Trent Bridge) 21-24 April	27-9-71-0	20-6-39-2			22-5-63-0		12-0-45-0		31-5-79-5	22.4-5-52-3													134.4	354	5	10	
	21-6-59-3	9-3-18-1			10-4-19-2				17-7-27-2	10.2-5-19-2													67.2	146	4	10	
Lancashire (Old Trafford) 29 April-2 May	19-4-49-4			18-9-48-2	15.3-6-30-2		13-3-41-1	7-2-10-1				4-0-18-0	1-0-3-0					2.1-0-8-0					72.3	189	11	10	
	12-3-30-0			18-5-54-1	15-5-33-2		11-3-30-0	15-2-46-0															78.1	230	8	3	
Somerset (Trent Bridge) 6-9 May	11-3-30-3		19-7-32-3		16.4-6-38-4	13-4-36-0																	59.4	138	2	10	
	23-3-70-2	12-1-59-1	21-3-86-1		22-3-71-3	21-4-74-3																	99	383	23	10	
Warwickshire (Edgbaston) 6-9 June			17-3-49-2		24.2-4-115-4	18-5-46-1	26-5-95-1	19-4-84-1															104.2	402	13	9	
Hampshire (Rose Bowl) 11-14 June		28-10-81-5	16-3-56-3		16.4-7-34-2	14-1-59-0		16-3-62-0				4-1-3-1											90.4	295	3	10	
		29-3-79-1	11-4-24-2		11-4-32-1	11-4-22-1		15.5-4-53-4															81.5	220		10	
Oxford UCCE (The Parks) 18-20 June		6-2-12-1				14-1-73-2				16-5-58-3				19-7-41-1	9-4-9-1	10.5-2-34-1			1-0-4-0				75.5	252	21	10	1
		5-1-15-0				11-3-32-0								10.3-2-27-1	5-0-24-1	4-1-12-0	3-0-31-0						38	151	10	2	
Lancashire (Trent Bridge) 30 June-3 July		18-4-46-1	26-8-59-2		18-6-31-5	27-5-87-1		18-7-55-1													2-2-0-0		107	285	7	10	
		3-0-3-0	8-1-23-1			9-0-32-0		8-1-25-1															33	97	4	3	1
Durham (Trent Bridge) 15-18 July	26-4-80-3		15-3-39-0		27.5-5-85-4		22-5-40-3	31-6-112-0													1-0-10-0		122.5	356	10	10	
Yorkshire (Scarborough) 21-24 July	20-9-39-4	7-0-27-0	21.5-7-59-5	19-8-44-0			11-1-50-1														2-0-8-0		80.5	231	4	10	
	21-7-58-1	13-1-46-0	18-4-66-3	9-3-20-0			13-2-35-1									1-0-6-0							75	232	1	5	
Somerset (Taunton) 31 July-3 August	21-3-86-1	15-3-52-0	28.4-6-106-5				23-5-62-2	3-0-7-0	11-0-82-0			1-0-1-0											100.4	401	5	8	
	11-2-22-0	27-1-113-1	8-2-28-0				7-0-12-0	5-0-37-0	16-1-73-0			11.3-0-41-1						2-0-12-0					97.3	344	6	2	
Sussex (Horsham) 5-8 August	26-10-64-3	12-5-23-1	19-5-58-3	18-3-64-0			22.5-1-92-2					1-0-2-1						1-0-12-0					98.5	309	6	10	
	13-3-43-1	18-7-40-2	8-1-50-0	9-3-31-0			15-4-55-1					5-1-11-0											69	249	7	4	
Warwickshire (Trent Bridge) 11-14 August	14-2-47-1	6-0-19-0	20-7-37-3				13-3-41-1	21.3-7-63-4				1-0-2-0											75.3	219	10	10	1
	30-10-86-4	23-3-97-0	28-6-87-1				26-16-46-1	31-9-109-1				6-0-22-0											144	470	13	7	
Hampshire (Trent Bridge) 19-22 August	35-7-108-2	48-6-199-4					21-6-42-0	27-5-115-1			22-1-144-0						8-1-32-1						161	654	14	8	
Worcestershire (New Road) 25-28 August	29-9-81-4	10-3-24-0			25.5-13-40-3	23-2-102-3						18-5-68-0											105.5	334	19	10	
	17-1-79-3	2-0-10-0			7-1-31-0	20-4-90-2						6-0-28-1											52	242	4	6	
Yorkshire (Trent Bridge) 3-6 September		7-1-15-0			22.3-11-38-2	33-10-57-3	20-7-52-3	29-6-74-2						20-4-63-2				10-2-16-1		1-0-2-0		6-1-25-0	111.3	256	20	10	
		36-9-123-1			19.5-5-46-0	30-12-71-3	25-6-69-1																174	519	16	8	
Durham (Riverside) 9-12 September		60-7-206-1	34-6-125-2		16-0-49-0	7-3-26-0		28-7-106-0						19-2-74-1				7-0-29-0					171	648	33	5	1
Sussex (Trent Bridge) 23-26 September	22-7-63-4	14.1-3-40-3	15-1-43-2	11-3-37-0		13-3-51-1																	75.1	243	9	10	
	11-1-59-0	24.1-1-84-6	21-3-83-2	14-2-59-2		5-1-26-0																	75.1	336	15	10	

	AR Adams	SR Patel	RJ Sidebottom	LJ Fletcher	MA Ealham	CE Shreck	PJ Franks	DJ Pattinson	SCJ Broad	GP Swann	MHA Footitt	AC Voges	AD Hales	A Carter	KJ O'Brien	A Patel	BM Shafayat	AD Brown	JF Brown	CMW Read	DJ Hussey	SA Newman
Overs	409	484.2	260.2	245.3	387	363.2	141	219.5	48	55	16	33.3	40	53	14	14.5	11	23.1	1	1	5	6
Maidens	103	86	70	62	117	77	37	40	12	14	5	2	6	15	4	3	1	2	0	0	2	1
Runs	1224	1558	760	800	983	1281	428	872	106	127	58	100	140	164	33	46	63	83	4	2	18	25
Wickets	43	33	31	29	28	21	11	10	7	6	3	3	3	3	2	1	1	1	0	0	0	0
Average	28.46	47.21	24.51	27.58	35.10	61.00	38.90	87.20	15.14	21.16	19.33	33.33	46.66	54.66	16.50	46.00	63.00	83.00				

FIELDING

- CMW Read (46 ct, 4 st)
- AD Brown
- BM Shafayat
- AR Adams
- SR Patel
- AC Voges
- WI Jefferson
- MA Ealham
- DJ Hussey
- MA Wagh
- SA Newman
- AD Hales
- A Patel
- SCJ Broad
- PJ Franks
- RJ Sidebottom
- GP Swann
- CE Shreck
- KJ O'Brien
- DJ Pattinson
- JF Brown
- MJ Wood
- MHA Footitt
- LJ Fletcher
- A Carter

Division One – Final Table

	P	W	L	D	Bat	Bowl	Pens	Pts
Durham	16	8	0	8	49	48	1.00	240.00
Nottinghamshire	16	4	2	10	56	41	0.00	193.00
Somerset	16	3	1	12	50	43	1.00	182.00
Lancashire	16	4	2	10	35	44	0.00	175.00
Warwickshire	16	3	3	10	54	38	0.00	174.00
Hampshire	16	3	3	10	50	40	3.00	169.00
Yorkshire	16	2	2	12	46	44	0.00	166.00
Sussex	16	2	6	8	45	39	1.00	143.00
Worcestershire	16	0	10	6	30	40	0.00	94.00

FPT & Pro40

T20

OUTLAWS

Limited overs nickname:
NOTTS OUTLAWS

SOMERSET CCC

FIRST-CLASS MATCHES
BATTING

	ME Trescothick	C Kieswetter	AV Suppiah	PD Trego	Z de Bruyn	CM Willoughby	JC Hildreth	JL Langer	AC Thomas	DA Stiff	BJ Phillips	OAC Banks	AR Caddick	MTC Waller	WJ Durston	JC Buttler	MK Munday	ML Turner	Extras	Total	Wickets	Result	P
v. Warwickshire (Taunton) 15-18 April	52	150*	38		4		303*	76											49	672	4	D	1
v. Durham (Taunton) 28 April-1 May	12	0	12	0	0	0	0	35*	2	0		4							4	69	10		
	105	106	29	21*	6		71	122*											25	485	5	D	6
v. Nottinghamshire (Trent Bridge) 6-9 May	13	5	0	4	64	0*	2	11		9	0	28							2	138	10		
	98	52	14	23	54	0*	18	35		21	39	4							25	383	10	L	3
v. Lancashire (Old Trafford) 6-9 June	95	45	47	0	7	5	60	2	17	7	41*								17	343	10	D	1
v. Yorkshire (Headingley) 11-14 June	0	83	20	3	0	0	20	0	64*	28						1			11	230	10		
	78	25	15	23	70*		5	46	12*										22	296	6	W	1
v. Sussex (Hove) 16-19 June	109	1	49	92*	50	23	2	4	4	4				15					14	367	10		
	11	7	50	5	5	0	23	33	22	14*				2					6	178	10	W	2
v. Yorkshire (Taunton) 30 June-3 July	146	28	17	7	31	6	51	4	13	6*				1					16	326	10		
	96	17	131	103*	27*		18	24		49									14	479	6	W	2
v. Hampshire (Taunton) 10-13 July	22	43	52	50	24	0*	155	30	70	25			3						36	510	10	D	
v. Worcestershire (New Road) 21-24 July	142	59*	47	1	9		16	107		0*									47	428	6	D	1
v. Nottinghamshire (Taunton) 31 July-3 August	37	67	51	66*	74		79	6						11*	1	0			9	401	8		
	99		151		28*										54*				12	344	2	D	2
v. Warwickshire (Edgbaston) 5-8 August	108	6	7	1	0		86*	69	10		7								29	323	8		
	107*	5	8	4*	9		11												12	156	4	D	1
v. Sussex (Taunton) 19-22 August	73	135*	133	67	3		11					53		3*					43	521	6	D	1
v. Hampshire (Rose Bowl) 27-30 August	118	94	35	20	0	0	4	0	15			45*		28					34	393	10		
	73	70	21	27	13	5*	4	32	11			6		18					14	294	10	D	1
v. Durham (Riverside) 1-4 September	31	0	53	4	16	0	27	12	0		0	16*							15	174	10		
	18*		21*																2	41	0	D	7
v. Lancashire (Taunton) 9-12 September	102	153	95	80	71		5			0	1*					30			20	557	8	D	1
v. Worcestershire (Taunton) 16-19 September	72	1	22	0	15	1	24	46	38	30*	18								13	280	10		
	0	90	83	9	106		18	64	54*	0*	84								15	523	8	D	8
Matches	16	16	16	16	16	16	15	15	14	10	7	6	5	4	1	1	1	1					
Innings	26	24	26	23	25	13	23	21	15	14	8	7	3	6	2	1	1	0					
Not Out	2	3	1	5	3	4	2	2	3	5	2	2	1	1	1	0	0	0					
High Score	146	153	151	103*	106	23	303*	122*	70	49	84	53	11*	28	54*	30	1	0					
Runs	1817	1242	1201	610	686	40	934	831	338	193	190	156	15	67	54	30	1	0					
Average	75.70	59.14	48.04	33.88	31.18	4.44	44.47	43.73	28.16	21.44	31.66	31.20	7.50	13.40	54.00	30.00	1.00	–					
100s	8	4	3	1	1	0	2	2	0	0	0	0	0	0	0	0	0	0					
50s	9	7	6	5	6	0	4	4	3	0	1	1	0	0	1	0	0	0					
Catches/Stumpings	21/0	48/0	18/0	5/0	3/0	4/0	10/0	17/0	2/0	0/0	4/0	1/0	1/0	1/0	0/0	0/0	0/0	1/0					

Home Ground: Taunton
Address: County Ground, St James Street, Taunton, Somerset, TA1 1JT
Tel: 0845 337 1875
Fax: 01823 332395
Email: info@somersetcountycc.co.uk
Directions: By road: M5 junction 25, follow A358 to town centre. Signposted from there.
Capacity: 6,500

Other grounds used: Bath
Year formed: 1875

Chief Executive: Richard Gould
Director of Cricket: Brian Rose
Head Coach: Andy Hurry
Captain: Justin Langer
County colours: Brown and red

Honours
Sunday League/NCL/Pro40
1979
Benson & Hedges Cup
1981, 1982
Gillette Cup/NatWest/C&G Trophy
1979, 1983, 2001
Twenty20 Cup
2005

Website:
www.somersetcountycc.co.uk

FIRST-CLASS MATCHES
BOWLING

	CM Willoughby	AC Thomas	DA Stiff	PD Trego	AV Suppiah	BJ Phillips	AR Caddick	OAC Banks	Z de Bruyn	MTC Waller	MK Munday	ML Turner	ME Trescothick	WJ Durston	Overs	Total	Byes/Leg-byes	Wickets	Run outs
v. Warwickshire	31.4-7-87-3			13-2-56-0	28-9-100-4				20-2-88-1	16-3-44-0		21-3-82-2			129.4	500	43	10	
(Taunton) 15-18 April	5-2-10-0			3-1-5-0		6-1-34-1	4-1-6-0		6-3-9-0			9-1-29-0	5-2-10-0		38	108	5	1	
v. Durham	31-10-75-1	21.5-5-86-2	25-4-134-2	26-6-73-2	7-1-23-0			15-0-75-2	9-0-53-0						134.5	543	24	10	1
(Taunton) 28 April-1 May																			
v. Nottinghamshire	28.5-7-81-5		20-3-63-1	12-3-53-3	2-0-6-0	15-6-30-1		3-0-13-0	2-0-13-0						82.5	261	2	10	
(Trent Bridge) 6-9 May	24-5-89-2		19-7-57-2		4-0-21-0	10-1-40-0		6.1-1-22-0	8-3-22-0						71.1	261	10	4	
v. Lancashire	11-3-30-0	17-4-80-2		20-4-72-4	14-3-34-2	9-2-25-2	11-2-34-0								82	286	11	10	
(Old Trafford) 6-9 June	13-4-38-1	7-1-11-0		6-2-21-1	13-3-45-1		7-3-11-0		9-1-47-3						61	191	6	6	
v. Yorkshire	23.3-11-30-3	20-1-48-3	17-2-47-1	13-4-31-1	3-1-9-0				7-2-27-0			16-0-68-2			99.3	277	17	10	
(Headingley) 11-14 June	24-9-46-3	21-4-78-2	12-1-49-2	12-3-24-1								9.1-0-46-2			78.1	248	5	10	
v. Sussex	20-9-43-1	18-6-53-5	11-1-43-2	2-0-8-0					4-0-19-0	10.4-2-27-2					65.4	197	4	10	
(Hove) 16-19 June	24.5-6-80-4	25-3-99-3	15-0-49-1	7-1-25-1					8-2-22-0	9-2-30-1					88.5	313	8	10	
v. Yorkshire	23-3-78-1	24-3-65-3	19-2-92-4	13-4-30-1	8-4-28-0		20-2-94-0		5-1-27-1						112	438	24	10	
(Taunton) 30 June-3 July	19-6-39-2	13-1-63-1	11-0-52-1	6-0-34-0	27.5-4-99-0		15-4-45-0		5-0-27-1						96.5	363	4	5	
v. Hampshire	14-5-48-1	10.3-4-22-2	15-1-91-5	1-0-12-0	10-5-27-2		11-1-60-0								61.3	264	4	10	
(Taunton) 10-13 July	25-6-86-0	22-8-59-0	13-3-46-0	11-2-33-1	24-7-58-3		22-6-68-1		4-1-6-0						121	357	1	5	
v. Worcestershire	16-5-45-2	11-3-34-1	5-0-38-1	5-0-25-1	11-3-28-2		14.1-3-53-3								62.1	225	2	10	
(New Road) 21-24 July	14-6-40-1	6-0-31-1	10-0-47-0	4-1-29-0	5-4-1-0		11-2-42-1		6-1-31-1						56	225	4	4	
v. Nottinghamshire	22.3-6-71-4	23-3-83-1		7-0-34-0	7-1-12-1		20-2-96-3			11-2-37-1				2-0-13-0	92.3	356	10	10	
(Taunton) 31 July-3 August																			
v. Warwickshire	13.2-4-37-4	21-2-72-4		4-0-22-0		8-1-42-0	18-4-67-2		2-0-10-0						66.2	261	11	10	
(Edgbaston) 5-8 August															-	-	-	-	
v. Sussex	28-8-96-1	27-4-97-1		18-3-71-1	19-1-117-2			21-3-114-0	18-0-83-0	33-1-147-0					164	742	17	5	
(Taunton) 19-22 August															-	-	-	-	
v. Hampshire	35-12-117-3	29-8-75-0		28-12-68-1	6-0-24-1			38-6-120-4	8-1-42-0	19-4-79-1					163	548	23	10	
(Rose Bowl) 27-30 August	1-0-1-0	0.5-0-3-0													1.5	9	5	0	
v. Durham	22-7-56-5	20-4-54-0		11.5-4-42-1	3-1-7-0	20-2-46-3		2-0-15-0	11-3-31-1						89.5	272	21	10	
(Riverside) 1-4 September															-	-	-	-	
v. Lancashire	28-6-109-5	22-2-58-1	15-2-47-0	9-1-34-0	4-0-7-0		19.1-6-46-4		8-3-25-0						105.1	344	18	10	
(Taunton) 9-12 September	23-5-64-0	19-6-42-1	18-1-70-1	7-1-24-0	28-3-75-0		10-0-27-0		6-2-12-0						111	314	0	2	
v. Worcestershire	35-9-126-2	23-5-104-2	17.2-0-102-3	20-4-89-3	20-6-57-0	26-6-74-0									141.2	571	19	10	
(Taunton) 16-19 September															-	-	-	-	

	CM Willoughby	AC Thomas	DA Stiff	PD Trego	AV Suppiah	BJ Phillips	AR Caddick	OAC Banks	Z de Bruyn	MTC Waller	MK Munday	ML Turner	ME Trescothick	WJ Durston
Overs	555.4	401.1	268.2	256.5	212.5	158.1	131.1	111.1	136	82.4	25.1	30	5	2
Maidens	161	77	33	57	47	37	24	15	23	11	0	4	2	0
Runs	1622	1317	1120	889	682	456	525	456	541	320	114	111	10	13
Wickets	54	35	31	19	15	12	10	7	7	5	4	2	0	0
Average	30.03	37.62	36.12	46.78	45.46	38.00	52.50	65.14	77.28	64.00	28.50	55.50	–	–

FIELDING

48	C Kieswetter (48 ct)
21	ME Trescothick
18	AV Suppiah
17	JL Langer
10	JC Hildreth
5	PD Trego
4	BJ Phillips
4	CM Willoughby
3	Z de Bruyn
2	AC Thomas
1	AR Caddick
1	OAC Banks
1	ML Turner
1	MTC Waller
0	WJ Durston
0	MK Munday
0	DA Stiff
0	JC Buttler

Division One – Final Table

	P	W	L	D	Bat	Bowl	Pens	Pts
Durham	16	8	0	8	49	48	1.00	240.00
Nottinghamshire	16	4	2	10	56	41	0.00	193.00
Somerset	16	3	1	12	50	43	1.00	182.00
Lancashire	16	4	2	10	35	44	0.00	175.00
Warwickshire	16	3	3	10	54	38	0.00	174.00
Hampshire	16	3	3	10	50	40	3.00	169.00
Yorkshire	16	2	2	12	46	44	0.00	166.00
Sussex	16	2	6	8	45	39	1.00	143.00
Worcestershire	16	0	10	6	30	40	0.00	94.00

FPT, T20 & Pro40

Limited overs nickname:
SOMERSET SABRES

SURREY CCC

FIRST–CLASS MATCHES
BATTING

	U Afzaal	MJ Brown	JN Batty	CP Schofield	JW Dernbach	MR Ramprakash	SJ Walters	A Nel	CJ Jordan	Murtaza Hussain	MNW Spiegel	MA Butcher	SA Newman	SC Meaker	TE Linley	PT Collins	AJ Tudor	A Harinath	HMRKB Herath	RJ Harris	CP Murtagh	JGE Benning	LJ Evans	SJ King	GD Elliott	RJ Logan	JE Anyon	Extras	Total	Wickets	Result	Pts
v. Gloucestershire (The Oval) 15-18 April	65	8	11	29	9*		9	7	8	0												0	1					13	160	10		
	10*	35*								4													9					6	64	2	D	7
v. Derbyshire (Derby) 22-25 April	3	1	36	10	4*		12	6					12		1							5	6					35	131	10		
	59	28	9	31*	6		15	3					124		8							36	7					34	360	10	L	3
v. Middlesex (The Oval) 6-9 May	82	7	29	47	16*	133	32		0		22	3													1			16	388	10		
	6	73	30	20	4	37	2		26*		2	15													22			5	242	10	D	10
v. Glamorgan (Cardiff) 6-9 June	13	40	42		10	138	2	31*	5			65	0					4										18	368	10		
	1*	6				35						27*	7															6	82	3	D	11
v. Northamptonshire (Northampton) 11-14 June	204*	12	48	15	19	17	6			34	32	10								94								39	530	10	W	21
v. Leicestershire (Grace Road) 16-19 June	29	101	0	16	1*	85			18	1	7	40	9															22	329	10	D	10
v. Middlesex (Lord's) 30 June-3 July	58	44	24			136	6	9	34*	13	49			0								0						19	392	10		
	1	13	0			49*	3		30*	2																		1	99	5	D	
v. Kent (The Oval) 10-13 July	46	55	44	54		86	12	28	24		9					1*	0											27	386	10		
	24*	25	48		5						60*																	8	170	3	D	
v. Essex (Guildford) 15-18 July	116	17	30	7*	0*	0	142	0	8										15									17	352	8	D	11
v. Leicestershire (The Oval) 31 July-3 August	70*	46	0			274	188												14*									16	608	4	D	10
v. Derbyshire (Whitgift School) 6-9 August	24	120	48	4	2	80	28	1*			9			4										8				34	362	10		
	85	56	30	0*		134*	0																	0				15	320	4	D	11
v. Essex (Colchester) 19-22 August	17	0	23	144	10	33	41				61			72	4	0*												23	428	10		
	6	37	0	24	2	62	9				6			23	0	0*												21	190	10	L	6
v. Kent (Canterbury) 28-31 August	3	88	96	9	5	46	0				49			23	35*	23												46	423	10		
	44	5	26	36	16	ah	6				6			64*	36	12												42	293	9	L	7
v. Gloucestershire (Bristol) 2-5 September	23	37	43	5	18	2					3	6					17*	18	1									10	183	10		
	15	39	40	71	6	1					2	17					33	44	52*									19	339	10	L	2
v. Northamptonshire (The Oval) 9-12 September	62	31	110	57	2	40					3						13	20	10								0*	28	376	10		
	31	42	37	36	4	4					56						20*	14	9								1*	28	282	9	L	10
v. Glamorgan (The Oval) 23-26 September	170	9	13	8	4*	7	42				100							57			8					0		12	430	10		
	2*	17	120	21			82				37*							0			12					6		12	309	7	D	10

	U Afzaal	MJ Brown	JN Batty	CP Schofield	JW Dernbach	MR Ramprakash	SJ Walters	A Nel	CJ Jordan	Murtaza Hussain	MNW Spiegel	MA Butcher	SA Newman	SC Meaker	TE Linley	PT Collins	AJ Tudor	A Harinath	HMRKB Herath	RJ Harris	CP Murtagh	JGE Benning	LJ Evans	SJ King	GD Elliott	RJ Logan	JE Anyon
Matches	16	16	16	14	14	11	11	9	8	7	6	5	5	5	5	5	4	3	3	2	2	2	2	1	1	1	1
Innings	28	28	26	21	19	17	18	10	10	8	11	8	8	9	6	8	6	6	5	2	2	3	4	2	2	2	2
Not Out	6	1	0	3	6	2	0	2	3	1	0	2	0	1	1	3	2	0	1	0	1	0	1	0	0	0	2
High Score	204*	120	120	144	19	274	188	32	42	34	100	65	124	72	36	23	33	57	52*	94	15	36	9	8	22	6	1*
Runs	1269	992	937	644	138	1350	573	117	213	111	294	251	217	214	98	49	83	165	80	98	29	41	23	8	23	6	1
Average	57.68	36.74	36.03	35.77	10.61	90.00	31.83	14.62	30.42	15.85	26.72	41.83	27.12	26.75	19.60	9.80	20.75	27.50	20.00	49.00	29.00	13.66	5.75	4.00	11.50	3.00	–
100s	3	2	2	1	0	5	2	0	0	0	1	0	1	0	0	0	0	0	0	0	0	0	0	0	0	0	0
50s	7	4	1	3	0	4	1	0	0	0	2	2	0	2	0	0	0	1	1	1	0	0	0	0	0	0	0
Catches/Stumpings	3/0	7/0	46/4	7/0	1/0	5/0	15/0	3/0	4/0	0/0	7/0	10/0	2/0	0/0	1/0	1/0	0/0	0/0	1/0	2/0	0/0	0/0	0/0	2/0	0/0	0/0	

Home Ground: The Oval
Address: The Oval, Kennington, London, SE11 5SS
Tel: 08712 461 100
Fax: 020 7820 5601
Email: enquiries@surreycricket.com
Directions: *By road:* The Oval is located south of the Thames in Kennington on the A202, near the junction with the A3 and A24, just south of Vauxhall Bridge and 10 minutes from Victoria and Waterloo stations. *By rail:* Take South West Trains to Vauxhall which is a short walk from the ground. The station is well served by trains from throughout Surrey and Hampshire as well as from the Greater London area. Connections include Clapham Junction and Waterloo.

Capacity: 23,000
Other grounds used: Guildford, Whitgift School
Year formed: 1845

Chief Executive: Paul Sheldon
Cricket Manager: Chris Adams
Captain: Mark Butcher (retired during 2009 season)
County colours: Gold and brown

Website:
www.surreycricket.com

Honours
County Championship
1890, 1891, 1892, 1894, 1895, 1899, 1914,
1952, 1953, 1954, 1955, 1956, 1957, 1958,
1971, 1999, 2000, 2002
Joint Champions 1950
Sunday League/NCL/Pro40
1996, 2003
Benson & Hedges Cup
1974, 1997, 2001
Gillette Cup/NatWest/C&G Trophy
1982, 1992
Twenty20 Cup
2003

FIRST-CLASS MATCHES
BOWLING

	JW Dernbach	A Nel	CP Schofield	Murtaza Hussain	PT Collins	CJ Jordan	SC Meaker	HMRKB Herath	TE Linley	U Afzaal	SJ King	AJ Tudor	RJ Harris	JGE Benning	RJ Logan	MNW Spriegel	MJ Brown	SA Newman	JE Anyon	SJ Walters	GD Elliott	Overs	Total	Byes/Leg-byes	Wickets	Run outs
Gloucestershire (The Oval) 15-18 Apil	18.3-1-79-4	22-6-52-4	18-1-60-0	23-7-61-0		12-3-46-0							7-1-25-2		1-0-1-0							101.3	333	9	10	
Derbyshire (Derby) 22-25 April	18.2-3-64-1	7.4-1-26-1	7-1-33-1		19.4-5-75-5	14-0-59-2			2-1-1-0						3-0-5-0							71.4	274	11	10	
	16-6-38-0	14-6-23-1	13.5-4-42-2		15-3-47-1	11-2-44-1			1-1-0-0						5-1-22-0							75.5	220	4	5	
Middlesex (The Oval) 6-9 May	17-2-52-2	20-3-78-2	19-0-85-0	44-11-101-4		20.1-1-86-2			2-0-8-0											2-0-15-0		124.1	445	20	10	
		4-0-45-0	6-0-49-4	13-0-70-4		2-0-11-0																25	184	9	9	1
Glamorgan (Cardiff) 6-9 June	23-4-82-6	17-5-50-1		26-10-56-1						1-0-1-0			17-5-66-2							1-0-4-0		85	271	12	10	
Northamptonshire (Northampton) 11-14 June	16.3-3-74-3	19-3-36-6	7-2-16-0											16.5-1-69-1								59.2	209	14	10	
	12-2-56-2	14-3-37-1	21-5-40-5	27.4-3-72-2						2-1-8-0												76.4	226	13	10	
Leicestershire (Grace Road) 16-19 June	14.1-3-47-6		5-1-25-0	2-1-1-1		16-3-54-3	7-0-32-0		18-1-51-3													44.1	165	6	10	
	19-1-83-0		31-5-66-0	34-6-96-2		22-5-80-0	18-0-71-0								2-0-12-0	3-0-10-0						147	487	18	5	
Middlesex (Lord's) 30 June-3 July		27-9-59-4		25-2-75-1	29-9-81-1					5-1-12-0	16.3-0-61-3	23-3-76-0				5-1-14-0						130.3	385	7	10	1
		11-6-15-0		15-1-69-2	11-5-24-0					13.5-0-60-2	6-0-34-0	11-6-37-1										67.5	246	7	5	
Kent (The Oval) 10-13 July			4-0-18-0	54.2-4-208-2	32-7-107-2	22-2-93-0			13-0-65-0				27-5-110-1							2-1-5-0		154.2	620	14	7	2
Essex (Guildford) 15-18 July	25-3-74-1	31-6-87-1	19-1-71-0			26-3-84-4				22.5-1-77-4												123.5	401	8	10	
	8-1-25-1	7-2-22-0	19-0-78-1			3-1-10-0				4.1-1-10-1	13-1-54-0											54.1	201	2	3	
Leicestershire (The Oval) 31 July-3 August	30-9-92-2	30-6-113-0	36-2-123-1			26.2-1-104-0				27-5-98-1	4-0-30-0									4-0-14-0		157.2	593	19	5	1
	4-0-10-0		4-1-5-0													1-0-8-0						9	23	0	0	
Derbyshire (Whitgift School) 6-9 August	19.5-5-73-3	24-9-83-4	15-2-50-0		18-1-76-3										8-0-32-0			3-0-9-0				87.5	334	11	10	
	11-4-25-0	13-4-28-2	2-4-80-0		11-4-21-1					2-0-9-1		17-2-61-1			2-1-1-0							78	232	7	5	
Essex (Colchester) 19-22 August	32-6-99-1			27-1-117-2	25.4-3-96-4	27-6-91-2				22-5-55-0					11-0-86-0	8-0-26-0						152.4	545	15	9	
	6-0-31-1			5-0-22-0						1-0-9-0						0.4-0-11-0						12.4	74	1	1	
Kent (Canterbury) 28-31 August	23-6-100-1			19-2-90-3	13-2-66-0	22.3-2-114-3			28-5-89-1							5-0-31-1						110.3	517	22	10	1
	9-0-35-0			5-0-39-0	3-0-16-0	4-0-29-2			7-0-43-0	2-0-14-1						5-0-22-1						35	200	2	4	
Gloucestershire (Bristol) 2-5 September	27-3-109-0		1-0-6-0			10-2-64-1			28-1-116-2	20-6-70-1			26-3-109-2							4-0-29-0		116	523	20	7	1
Northamptonshire (The Oval) 9-12 September	20-3-82-3	36-4-82-2							47-6-151-4				13-1-85-0			3-0-18-0			7-0-29-0			126	492	15	10	1
Glamorgan (The Oval) 23-26 September	26-2-106-0		31-1-176-1		16-1-85-2	33.2-1-164-2									30-6-101-2	9-1-43-0						145.2	702	27	8	1
Overs	395.2	260.4	363.5	271	137.2	208.2	110.4	108.2	131	87.5	39.3	100	33.5	15	30	44.4	3	3	7	19	2					
Maidens	67	69	35	47	25	36	11	8	23	6	2	18	6	2	6	2	0	0	2	0	0					
Runs	1436	754	1357	825	504	764	498	431	442	348	156	417	135	52	101	205	20	10	59	75	15					
Wickets	37	27	22	19	16	13	10	8	8	7	4	4	3	2	2	2	0	0	0	0	0					
Average	38.81	27.92	61.68	43.42	31.50	58.76	49.80	53.87	55.25	49.71	39.00	104.25	45.00	26.00	50.50	102.50	-	-	-	-	-					

FIELDING

0	JN Batty (46 ct, 4 st)
5	SJ Walters
0	MA Butcher
7	CP Schofield
7	MJ Brown
7	MNW Spriegel
5	MR Ramprakash
4	CJ Jordan
3	U Afzaal
3	A Nel
2	SA Newman
2	CP Murtagh
2	GD Elliott
1	AJ Tudor
1	TE Linley
1	JW Dernbach
1	PT Collins
1	RJ Harris
1	RJ Logan
0	JGE Benning
0	JE Anyon
0	A Harinath
0	LJ Evans
0	HMRKB Herath
0	Murtaza Hussain
0	SC Meaker
0	SJ King

Division Two – Final Table

	P	W	L	D	Bat	Bowl	Pens	Pts
Kent	16	8	3	5	43	44	0.00	219.00
Essex	16	6	3	7	40	43	1.00	194.00
Northamptonshire	16	6	4	6	40	45	0.00	193.00
Gloucestershire	16	6	6	4	39	46	0.00	185.00
Glamorgan	16	2	2	12	56	43	0.00	175.00
Derbyshire	16	2	3	11	55	45	0.00	172.00
Surrey	16	1	4	11	54	36	0.00	148.00
Middlesex	16	2	7	7	43	41	0.00	140.00
Leicestershire	16	2	3	11	31	35	0.00	138.00

FPT & Pro40   T20

SURREY CRICKET

Limited overs nickname:
SURREY BROWN CAPS

SUSSEX CCC

FIRST-CLASS MATCHES
BATTING

	MH Yardy	AJ Hodd	MW Goodwin	CD Nash	EC Joyce	CD Collymore	RSC Martin-Jenkins	OP Rayner	LJ Wright	CD Hopkinson	DR Smith	P Chawla	JD Lewry	RJ Hamilton-Brown	MJ Prior	Yasir Arafat	JS Gatting	RJ Kirtley	DG Wright	RG Aga	PS Sandri	TMJ Smith	MA Thornley	WAT Beer	Extras	Total	Wickets	Result
v. Cambridge UCCE (Fenner's) 15–17 April	50	10		23	9		40		106						106*		152								31	527	7	D
v. Lancashire (Hove) 21–24 April	35		11	22	90	0	67		6					4			4	1*				10			39	289	10	
	22		20	13	55	1*	13		35					0			1	2				1			4	167	10	L
v. Hampshire (Rose Bowl) 29 April–2 May	7	25	7	33	3	0*	16						15		140				42	24					24	336	10	D
v. Durham (Hove) 6–9 May	51	101	0	40	0	4	3	25	67				0				41*								31	363	10	
	12	21*	21	85*	3				4				12												11	169	5	D
v. Yorkshire (Headingley) 6–9 June	8	1	0	100*	11	33	4		0		12		20									8			20	217	10	
	110	7	19		24	2*	3	2*	14				46									19			11	257	8	D
v. Worcestershire (New Road) 11–14 June	152	43	16	52	21	1*	20				77	102*		82			33								21	620	9	W
	34*			25*																					2	61	0	
v. Somerset (Hove) 16–19 June	5	11	0	4	45		17*		10		30	0	0	59											16	197	10	
	6	2	5	134	30		27		11		24	27*	25	11											11	313	10	L
v. Australians (Hove) 24–27 June	5	40		45	15		35	25	22	8			37			11								28*	40	311	10	
	67	37*		34			17	4*	35	115			1												36	373	7	D
v. Warwickshire (Edgbaston) 7–10 July	57	59*	22	31	29				71	119	0		11												30	429	8	D
v. Hampshire (Arundel Castle) 15–18 July	5	11	65	57	2	0			60	104	49	9*					37								42	441	10	
	47*	3*	37	43																					8	138	2	D
v. Durham (Riverside) 31 July–3 August	97	4	6	19	36	11		24	0	14			4*			10									20	245	10	
	20	33	13	55	14	10		1	118*	7			0			18									15	304	10	L
v. Nottinghamshire (Horsham) 5–8 August	22	0	11	4	183	23	4	22	4	15											0*				21	309	10	
	24		2	87	17				59*	47*															13	249	4	D
v. Worcestershire (Hove) 11–13 August	29	73	12	10	2	4*	18	8	38	19							32								26	280	10	
	6		40*	100*	53																				13	212	2	W
v. Somerset (Taunton) 19–22 August	15	18*	344*	157	37					139	4														28	742	5	D
v. Lancashire (Old Trafford) 2–5 September	86	0	29		40	4	0	3		19	8	32*				10									9	240	10	D
v. Warwickshire (Hove) 9–12 September	29	0	32	16	107		12	22	8	0	6								2*						20	254	10	
	27	33	16	44	2		10*	2	1	8	9								10						10	172	10	L
v. Yorkshire (Hove) 16–19 September	58	22	63	42	6				0	11	6	0		171*	46										23	448	10	
	13*	2	5	26	0				6	0	0	0		2	20										9	83	10	L
v. Nottinghamshire (Trent Bridge) 23–26 September	21	12	20	135	9	1					5	16	0*	1	12										11	243	10	
	48	11	9	70	3	15					80	8	1*	4	70										17	336	10	L
Matches	18	17	16	16	16	14	14	12	10	10	9	6	6	6	5	5	4	4	3	3	2	1	1	1				
Innings	31	25	27	28	26	17	19	13	16	15	14	10	10	10	8	5	6	4	4	3	1	2	2	1				
Not Out	3	3	3	3	1	5	2	1	2	1	0	3	4	2	0	0	0	1	1	1	1	0	0	1				
High Score	152	101	344*	157	183	23	67	60	118*	139	80	102*	25	171*	140	37	152	33	42	24	0*	19	10	28*				
Runs	1168	576	800	1393	994	89	351	202	690	566	261	206	51	349	362	108	310	56	88	27	0	27	11	28				
Average	41.71	26.18	33.33	55.72	39.76	7.41	20.64	16.83	49.29	40.43	18.64	29.42	8.50	43.63	45.25	21.60	51.66	18.66	29.33	13.50	–	13.50	5.50	–				
100s	2	1	1	4	3	0	0	0	3	3	0	1	0	2	1	0	1	0	0	0	0	0	0	0				
50s	7	2	2	6	3	0	1	1	3	0	2	0	2	0	1	0	1	0	0	0	0	0	0	0				
Catches/Stumpings	14/0	27/3	6/0	3/0	12/0	2/0	5/0	16/0	3/0	2/0	1/0	2/0	0/0	6/0	12/0	0/0	2/0	2/0	0/0	0/0	1/0	1/0	0/0	2/0				

Home Ground: Hove
Address: County Ground, Eaton Road, Hove, BN3 3AN
Tel: 08712 461100
Fax: 01273 771549
Email: simon.dyke@sussexcricket.co.uk
Directions: *By rail:* Hove station is a 10-minute walk.
By road: Follow AA signs. Street parking at no cost.
Capacity: 5,500

Other grounds used: Arundel Castle, Horsham
Year formed: 1839

Chief Executive: David Brooks
Cricket Manager: Mark Robinson
Captain: Mike Yardy
County colours: Black and white

Honours
County Championship
2003, 2006, 2007
Sunday League/NCL/Pro40
1982, 2008, 2009
Gillette Cup/NatWest/C&G Trophy
1963, 1964, 1978, 1986, 2006
Twenty20 Cup
2009

Website:
www.sussexcricket.co.uk

FIRST-CLASS MATCHES
BOWLING

FIRST-CLASS MATCHES	P Chawla	CD Collymore	DR Smith	RSC Martin-Jenkins	LJ Wright	OP Rayner	Yasir Arafat	JD Lewry	CD Nash	RJ Kirtley	DG Wright	MH Yardy	RJ Hamilton-Brown	RG Aga	EC Joyce	MW Goodwin	AJ Hodd	TMJ Smith	PS Sandri	WAT Beer	Overs	Total	Byes/Leg-byes	Wickets	Run outs
v. Cambridge UCCE (Fenner's) 15-17 April			2-0-12-0	3-0-7-0					6-3-8-1				7-4-8-2								18	36	1	3	
																					–	–	–	–	
v. Lancashire (Hove) 21-24 April		27-7-73-2	25-10-50-3	27.5-8-80-5					2-1-1-0		21-10-43-0		7-0-28-0					4-1-11-0			113.5	299	13	10	
		7-3-11-2	8-4-23-0	5-0-27-0					4-0-19-0		9-3-19-0							8.4-0-59-0			41.4	160	2	2	
v. Hampshire (Rose Bowl) 29 April-2 May		26-8-64-2		22.5-5-69-2					9-0-38-0	21-7-54-2	4-0-15-0			17-1-82-1	2-0-9-1						101.5	350	19	8	
		6-0-20-0		8-2-27-0					2-1-3-1	6-3-7-0	5-0-11-0	10-2-12-1	13-1-37-0								50	127	0	2	
v. Durham (Hove) 6-9 May		18-4-74-1		18.1-5-65-2	26-3-82-2	18.5-1-51-2			6-0-27-0		26.5-10-64-3			2-1-2-0							115.5	380	15	10	
		16-4-52-0		22-7-52-1	14-4-38-1	27-2-83-1			8-1-31-0				2-0-8-0	6-1-28-0							95	299	7	4	1
v. Yorkshire (Headingley) 6-9 June		27-9-68-4	9.5-4-22-2	18-5-38-3					13-4-19-0		27-8-66-1										94.5	225	12	10	
		18-2-54-2	14-2-62-1						14-6-56-0		17-4-67-1	2-0-15-3									67	272	18	7	
v. Worcestershire (New Road) 11-14 June	21.3-2-89-2	6	17-5-42-3	20-8-44-2	12-3-41-1							17-2-57-1		2-0-8-0							89.3	288	7	10	1
	51-11-152-6		12-2-37-0	18.2-6-46-1	8-1-18-0				18-7-35-1	13.5-1-61-2				9-1-19-0							130.1	392	24	10	
v. Somerset (Hove) 16-19 June	35-7-118-5		13-1-31-0	9-2-30-0	15.2-2-54-0			20-7-82-2	14-5-39-1												106.2	367	13	10	2
	21.3-4-52-6		23-4-64-3		8-1-24-1			7-0-33-0													59.3	178	5	10	
v. Australians (Hove) 24-27 June					12-2-56-0	10-2-33-1	26-4-66-2						18-4-61-1						13-1-73-3	11-0-52-0	90	349	8	7	
					10-1-52-1	7-0-33-0	30-8-68-2						20-6-61-1						12-2-70-1	16.1-1-77-2	95.1	379	18	7	
v. Warwickshire (Edgbaston) 7-10 July		20-6-54-2	9-1-45-0	26-2-94-3	28.1-6-82-3	3-1-7-0	6-0-19-0										1.4-0-7-0				115.1	407	5	10	
		6-1-9-1	9-1-15-1		3-1-7-0	6-0-19-0	8-0-34-0														33.4	97	6	2	
v. Hampshire (Arundel Castle) 15-18 July		29-10-66-4			17-3-41-1	31.1-9-61-3	20-2-89-1	14-0-60-1	3-2-1-0			5-0-19-0									119.1	346	9	10	
																					–	–	–	–	
v. Durham (Riverside) 31 July-3 August		24-6-61-1			19-1-75-0	29-2-107-0	30-6-96-2	21-8-56-0	4-1-9-1			10-1-56-0									137	473	13	4	
		1-0-5-0				8-3-16-1	4-0-32-0	5.4-1-27-0													18.4	80	0	1	
v. Nottinghamshire (Horsham) 5-8 August		27-8-73-0		31-7-104-2	19-5-68-1	26-1-110-3			4-0-22-0			13-0-61-0							14-2-80-0		134	531	13	6	
																					–	–	–	–	
v. Worcestershire (Hove) 11-13 August		14-2-45-1		20-7-45-1	22-6-66-5	4-2-5-0	22-4-83-3														82	256	12	10	
		9-3-32-2		14-5-23-1	11-0-61-2	4.2-0-17-2	19-1-98-3														57.2	235	4	10	
v. Somerset (Taunton) 19-22 August		6-2-20-0		36-15-91-2	6-2-19-0			52-7-186-4	24-4-98-0					6-0-64-0		2-0-13-0					133	521	24	6	
																					–	–	–	–	
v. Lancashire (Old Trafford) 2-5 September	24-6-75-0	16-5-44-1	21-8-47-2	14.4-4-43-5	12-1-23-1																87.4	236	4	10	1
			0.2-0-0-0																		0.2	0	0	0	
v. Warwickshire (Hove) 9-12 September	57.5-12-151-4			24-7-81-1	11-0-33-0			21-5-47-1		5-1-28-1	20-3-59-2			2-0-13-0							140.5	428	16	10	1
																					–	–	–	–	
v. Yorkshire (Hove) 16-19 September	46-9-115-4	21-5-69-1		19-4-60-1				23-6-51-1	9-2-29-1		3-1-11-0			15-2-49-2							136	403	19	10	
	41-10-112-5	10-2-31-1		32-9-75-2				6-1-20-1													98.1	284	19	10	
v. Nottinghamshire (Trent Bridge) 23-26 September	26-8-82-3	24-5-59-1		27-7-73-3	19-3-69-2				9-1-40-1												105	328	25	10	
	18-3-55-1	15-3-41-2		25.3-7-58-4	9-2-32-0			7-0-24-1	12-3-53-2					4-0-8-0							90.3	286	15	10	
Overs	341.5	396	301	299.4	230.1	350.3	151	159.1	114.4	94.5	83.5	69	37	44	2	2	1.4	12.4	39	27.1					
Maidens	72	102	84	77	37	60	24	39	22	19	33	4	6	6	0	0	0	1	5	1					
Runs	981	1104	814	901	783	1004	621	535	394	307	187	320	109	155	9	13	7	70	223	129					
Wickets	36	33	26	24	22	24	12	10	7	8	5	4	3	3	1	0	0	0	4	2					
Average	27.25	33.45	32.56	37.54	35.59	41.83	51.75	53.50	56.28	38.38	37.40	80.00	36.33	51.66	9.00	–	–	–	55.75	64.5					

FIELDING

30	AJ Hodd (27 ct, 3 st)
16	OP Rayner
14	MH Yardy
12	EC Joyce
6	MJ Prior
6	MW Goodwin
6	RJ Hamilton-Brown
5	RSC Martin-Jenkins
3	CD Nash
3	LJ Wright
2	MAT Beer
2	CD Collymore
2	CD Hopkinson
2	P Chawla
2	JS Gatting
2	RJ Kirtley
1	PS Sandri
1	DR Smith
1	MA Thornley
0	Yasir Arafat
0	RG Aga
0	JD Lewry
0	TMJ Smith
0	DG Wright

Division One – Final Table

	P	W	L	D	Bat	Bowl	Pens	Pts
Durham	16	8	0	8	49	48	1.00	240.00
Nottinghamshire	16	4	2	10	56	41	0.00	193.00
Somerset	16	3	1	12	50	43	1.00	182.00
Lancashire	16	4	2	10	35	44	0.00	175.00
Warwickshire	16	3	3	10	54	38	0.00	174.00
Hampshire	16	3	3	10	50	40	3.00	169.00
Yorkshire	16	2	2	12	46	44	0.00	166.00
Sussex	16	2	6	8	45	39	1.00	143.00
Worcestershire	16	0	10	6	30	40	0.00	94.00

FPT & Pro40

T20

Limited overs nickname:
SUSSEX SHARKS

WARWICKSHIRE CCC

FIRST-CLASS MATCHES

BATTING

	JO Troughton	TR Ambrose	CR Woakes	IJL Trott	IJ Westwood	T Frost	R Clarke	AG Botha	IR Bell	WB Rankin	N Tahir	NM Carter	S Sreesanth	JS Patel	JE Anyon	Ateeq Javid	KHD Barker	AS Miller	DL Maddy	SH Choudhry	SA Piolet	CS MacLeod	RM Johnson	NS Poonia	Extras	Total	Wickets	Result	P
v. **Somerset**	77	57	63	0		7	0	15	172			21			15*				17						56	500	10		
(Taunton) 15-18 April						46*			13*										36						13	108	1	D	1
v. **Hampshire**	223	153	8*	22		4	112	51	29										8						20	630	8		
(Edgbaston) 22-25 April																												D	1
v. **Yorkshire**	0	0	30	161*	41	8	9		37	0		32		120											44	482	10		
(Edgbaston) 6-9 May					19*	5			30*																6	60	1	D	9
v. **Nottinghamshire**	73	0	33	37	73	37			60			47		3*	14*		0								25	402	9		
(Edgbaston) 6-9 June																												D	1
v. **Durham UCCE**						105					0				9	7	0	1*		75	5	26	22	6	9	265	10		
(Durham) 11-13 June						16										12	23				26*		11	0	6	94	5	W	
v. **Durham**	16	10	24	25	8	56		29*	79	7		0		6											16	276	10		
(Edgbaston) 16-19 June	5	9	1	32	8	3		34*	57	2		23		2											1	177	10	L	4
v. **England XI**	5	7	13	19	2	14	12			1	7*					4	5								13	102	10		
(Edgbaston) 1-3 July	0	4*		14*	5											3									1	27	3	D	
v. **Sussex**	18	28	49*	166	5	0	36	46	2		22	17													18	407	10		
(Edgbaston) 7-10 July				9*	4	17			55*																12	97	2	D	1
v. **Lancashire**	2	28	37*	79	60	1	54	7	106		18*														11	403	8		
(Edgbaston) 15-18 July																												D	1
v. **Hampshire**	12	4	131*	184*	13	15	46	40	7																32	484	7		
(Rose Bowl) 21-24 July				0*	14*	3			0																6	23	2	D	1
v. **Worcestershire**	6	63	2	67	22	37	50	18		1	5*	13													25	309	10		
(New Road) 31 July-3 August				16*	18*							4													9	47	1	W	2
v. **Somerset**	11	0	13	79	0	94	0	2		0*	23	24													15	261	10		
(Edgbaston) 5-8 August																												D	8
v. **Nottinghamshire**	9	1	22	15	12		67	19	1	3	24		30*												16	219	10		
(Trent Bridge) 11-14 August	15	32*	1*	121	11		62	64	126		22														16	470	7	D	8
v. **Durham**	14	0	0		5	19	32	23		2*	10		5			8									17	135	10		
(Riverside) 19-21 August	111	39	13		2	4	13	14		0*	1		4			21									16	238	10	L	3
v. **Yorkshire**	9	113	9		1	35	22	13	23		5*	67	11												12	320	10		
(Scarborough) 26-29 August	40	33	6*		58	48	23	33	35		0	11	1												25	313	10	D	1
v. **Worcestershire**	22	8	21	93	133	24		22	36	0	15		23*												46	443	10		
(Edgbaston) 2-5 September																												W	2
v. **Sussex**	85	50	0	56	57		52*	1	104	1	0		0												22	428	10		
(Hove) 9-12 September																												W	2
v. **Lancashire**	48	3	2	1	11		1	5	5	0*		59						0							13	148	10		
(Old Trafford) 23-25 September	27	55	15*	44	30		40	8	9	2		0						0							14	244	10	L	3

	JO Troughton	TR Ambrose	CR Woakes	IJL Trott	IJ Westwood	T Frost	R Clarke	AG Botha	IR Bell	WB Rankin	N Tahir	NM Carter	S Sreesanth	JS Patel	JE Anyon	Ateeq Javid	KHD Barker	AS Miller	DL Maddy	SH Choudhry	SA Piolet	CS MacLeod	RM Johnson	NS Poonia
Matches	17	17	17	15	15	15	14	14	13	13	12	9	5	3	3	3	3	3	2	1	1	1	1	1
Innings	23	23	22	22	25	23	18	19	21	13	14	13	7	4	3	6	4	3	3	1	2	1	2	2
Not Out	0	2	7	6	3	1	1	2	3	4	4	0	2	1	2	0	0	1	0	0	1	0	0	0
High Score	223	153	131*	184*	133	105	112	64	172	7	24	67	30*	120	15*	21	23	1*	36	75	26*	26	22	6
Runs	828	697	493	1240	612	598	631	444	986	19	152	318	74	131	38	55	28	1	61	75	31	26	33	6
Average	**36.00**	**33.19**	**32.86**	**77.50**	**27.81**	**27.18**	**37.11**	**26.11**	**54.77**	**2.11**	**15.20**	**24.46**	**14.80**	**43.66**	**38.00**	**9.16**	**7.00**	**0.50**	**20.33**	**75.00**	**31.00**	**26.00**	**16.50**	**3.00**
100s	2	2	1	4	1	1	1	0	4	0	0	0	0	1	0	0	0	0	0	0	0	0	0	0
50s	3	4	1	5	4	2	5	2	4	0	0	2	0	0	0	0	0	0	0	1	0	0	0	0
Catches/Stumpings	10/0	38/2	4/0	11/0	10/0	8/0	25/0	5/0	10/0	2/0	2/0	0/0	3/0	1/0	0/0	3/0	0/0	0/0	2/0	0/0	0/0	3/0	7/0	0/0

Home Ground: Edgbaston
Address: County Ground, Edgbaston, Birmingham, B5 7QU
Tel: 0870 0621902
Fax: 0121 4464544
Email: info@edgbaston.com
Directions: *By rail:* New Street station, Birmingham. *By road:* M6 to A38(M) to city centre, then follow signs to County Ground.
Capacity: 21,000

Other grounds used: Stratford upon Avon
Year formed: 1882

Chief Executive: Colin Povey
Director of Coaching: Ashley Giles
Captain: Ian Westwood
County colours: Blue and yellow

Honours

County Championship
1911, 1951, 1972, 1994, 1995, 2004
Sunday League/NCL/Pro40
1980, 1994, 1997
Benson & Hedges Cup
1994, 2002
Gillette Cup/NatWest/C&G Trophy
1989, 1993, 1995

Website:
www.thebears.co.uk

FIRST–CLASS MATCHES
BOWLING

	N Tahir	CR Woakes	WB Rankin	AG Botha	NM Carter	S Sreesanth	R Clarke	SA Piolet	AS Miller	JS Patel	IJL Trott	JE Anyon	IJ Westwood	T Frost	CS MacLeod	DL Maddy	KHD Barker	IR Bell	SH Choudhry	Ateeq Javid	Overs	Total	Byes/Leg-byes	Wickets	Run outs
v. Somerset (Taunton) 15-18 April		27-4-107-3		41-6-178-0	11-1-44-0		22-0-99-0				13-1-64-0	33-6-124-1				7.1-0-31-0					154.1	672	25	4	
																					-	-	-	-	
v. Hampshire (Edgbaston) 22-25 April		33-8-93-1	25-7-64-3	5-0-13-0			11.5-0-63-2		27-5-79-3							19-7-48-1	3-0-7-0				123.5	379	12	10	
		18-4-49-0	24-5-76-2	42-7-103-4			5-1-14-0		9-0-29-0							5-1-21-0					103	301	9	6	
v. Yorkshire (Edgbaston) 6-9 May		26-10-68-1	27-6-85-0		30.4-4-129-4		25-8-64-1				36-1-150-1	16-2-62-1					5-0-27-0				167.4	600	15	8	
		10-2-29-1	9-1-48-0		2-0-5-0		8-2-28-2				11-1-40-0	2-0-6-0									42	162	6	3	
v. Nottinghamshire (Edgbaston) 6-9 June		17-0-68-1			16-3-51-1						14-0-97-2	5-0-20-0	11.2-1-75-1			14-1-54-0					77.2	376	11	6	1
																					-	-	-	-	
v. Durham UCCE (Durham) 11-13 June	7-0-22-1						18-11-17-6	13-4-33-1				8-3-15-0		6-2-10-1		8-2-10-0		1-0-11-0			61	118	0	9	
	9.3-3-30-4						9-2-26-4	9-2-32-0				13-3-38-2		4-0-16-0		4-1-16-0					48.3	167	9	10	
v. Durham (Edgbaston) 16-19 June		32-7-105-4	24-5-68-1	12-2-34-0	23-5-90-2						33-2-112-3	1-1-0-0									125	433	24	10	
		2-0-6-0	2-0-16-0																		4	22	0	0	
v. England XI (Edgbaston) 1-3 July	15-2-54-3	16-1-50-0	11-0-60-1				13-2-46-2				7-1-21-1					15-2-51-1			1-0-3-0		78	290	5	8	
	10-2-26-0	14-4-32-1	13-0-55-1				5-0-27-0				10-0-44-0					12-2-44-0			12-0-75-0		76	319	16	3	1
v. Sussex (Edgbaston) 7-10 July	28-7-83-4	14-1-67-0		29-5-84-1	22.2-1-96-1		10-1-54-0				12-2-26-2		2-0-4-0								117.2	429	15	8	
v. Lancashire (Edgbaston) 15-18 July	17-5-55-4	15-3-51-1	13-4-33-1	17-2-86-4			10-1-36-0				9-1-37-0										81	317	19	10	
																					-	-	-	-	
v. Hampshire (Rose Bowl) 21-24 July	17-1-71-1	17-1-67-1	27-1-117-3	35-4-111-1			15-1-59-0				4-0-11-0		15-2-39-2	5.1-1-12-1							135.1	505	18	10	
v. Worcestershire (New Road) 31 July-3 August	5-3-6-0	13.5-4-30-4	7-0-31-1		12-2-37-5						5-0-25-0										37.5	111	7	10	
	19.5-5-67-5	10-1-35-0	20-7-56-4		14-5-46-1		5-3-9-0														73.5	244	6	10	
v. Somerset (Edgbaston) 5-8 August	11-2-37-0	25-6-89-4	17-2-71-3		23-2-99-0		3-1-0-8-1														79.1	323	19	8	
	7-2-18-0	4-2-8-0	7-2-34-1	7-0-34-1	3-0-21-1		6-0-26-0				3-1-10-1										37	156	5	4	
v. Nottinghamshire (Trent Bridge) 11-14 August	20-1-89-4	10-0-76-0	15-2-92-1	10-0-30-0		14-1-65-3	5.1-2-15-2				4-0-7-0										84.1	388	14	10	
	5-2-16-0	5-1-14-0	6-2-19-1	2-0-2-0		4-1-7-0	1-0-7-0						2-0-6-0								25	71	0	1	
v. Durham (Riverside) 19-21 August	21-5-57-2	17-3-72-2	21-1-85-5			10.1-1-35-1	3-0-7-0														72.1	273	8	10	
	4-0-16-1	6-1-30-1		2.3-0-12-0		6-0-27-0	2-0-21-0														20.3	106	0	2	
v. Yorkshire (Scarborough) 26-29 August	21-7-59-3	19-5-63-0		12-2-39-1	15-2-49-1		15.2-3-93-5	4-0-20-0											2-1-9-0		86.2	328	5	10	
	2-1-4-0						4-1-17-0														8	30	0	0	
v. Worcestershire (Edgbaston) 2-5 September	12-3-25-2	12-5-40-5	9.1-1-38-1				15-3-45-1														48.1	154	6	10	1
	14-3-32-0	19.4-4-43-4	22-1-93-2	8-2-16-1			16-3-56-3				3-1-9-0										82.4	271	22	10	
v. Sussex (Hove) 9-12 September	18-4-48-3	11.2-3-34-2	14-2-54-1			15.4-4-41-0															89.2	254	14	10	
	11-4-28-1	18-10-30-1	7-1-27-3			36-15-51-5	10-4-32-0														82	172	4	10	
v. Lancashire (Old Trafford) 23-25 September		26-6-80-1	20-4-57-2	27-6-85-1	18-5-37-0		10-2-28-1		25-7-76-4												126	389	26	10	1
													0.2-0-4-0								0.2	4	0	0	

	N Tahir	CR Woakes	WB Rankin	AG Botha	NM Carter	S Sreesanth	R Clarke	SA Piolet	AS Miller	JS Patel	IJL Trott	JE Anyon	IJ Westwood	T Frost	CS MacLeod	DL Maddy	KHD Barker	IR Bell	SH Choudhry	Ateeq Javid
Overs	274.2	445.5	340.1	316.3	190	109.3	164.1	27	83	94	94.2	65.2	19	5.1	10	31.1	53	10	1	13
Maidens	62	96	54	61	30	21	23	13	18	4	10	13	2	1	2	8	8	1	0	0
Runs	843	1436	1279	941	704	418	640	43	249	399	346	252	49	12	26	100	175	43	11	78
Wickets	38	38	37	23	16	13	11	10	8	6	5	4	2	1	1	1	1	0	0	0
Average	22.18	37.78	34.56	40.91	44.00	32.15	58.18	4.30	31.12	66.50	69.20	63.00	24.50	12.00	26.00	100.00	175.00			

FIELDING

40	TR Ambrose (38 ct, 2 st)
25	R Clarke
11	IJL Trott
10	IR Bell
10	JO Troughton
10	IJ Westwood
8	T Frost
7	RM Johnson
5	AG Botha
4	CR Woakes
3	S Sreesanth
3	CS MacLeod
3	Ateeq Javid
2	DL Maddy
2	N Tahir
2	WB Rankin
1	JS Patel
0	NM Carter
0	NS Poonia
0	JE Anyon
0	SH Choudhry
0	AS Miller
0	SA Piolet
0	KHD Barker

Division One – Final Table

	P	W	L	D	Bat	Bowl	Pens	Pts
Durham	16	8	0	8	49	48	1.00	240.00
Nottinghamshire	16	4	2	10	56	41	0.00	193.00
Somerset	16	3	1	12	50	43	1.00	182.00
Lancashire	16	4	2	10	35	44	0.00	175.00
Warwickshire	16	3	3	10	54	38	0.00	174.00
Hampshire	16	3	3	10	50	40	3.00	169.00
Yorkshire	16	2	2	12	46	44	0.00	166.00
Sussex	16	2	6	8	45	39	1.00	143.00
Worcestershire	16	0	10	6	30	40	0.00	94.00

FPT & Pro40

T20

Limited overs nickname:
THE BEARS

WORCESTERSHIRE CCC

FIRST-CLASS MATCHES
BATTING

	DKH Mitchell	MM Ali	VS Solanki	SM Davies	SC Moore	BF Smith	MS Mason	CD Whelan	GJ Batty	GM Andrew	Imran Arif	AN Kervezee	RA Jones	AA Noffke	DA Wheeldon	Kabir Ali	JD Shantry	JP Knappett	OB Cox	ID Fisher	M Ahmed	Extras	Total	Wickets	Result	Points
v. Oxford UCCE (The Parks) 11-13 April	140*		27			61*									22							48	298	2	D	
v. Hampshire (Rose Bowl) 15-17 April	31	12	6	4	25	21	7	0	5	0*						0						21	132	10		
	4	3	73	8	1	19	25	47	0	4*						1						4	189	10	L	3
v. Nottinghamshire (Trent Bridge) 21-24 April	80	3	50	126	8	0	4	2	22	1*				39								19	354	10		
	9	8	64	11	4	24	1*	0	3	3				13								6	146	10	L	5
v. Yorkshire (Headingley) 28 April-1 May	10	153	206*	20*							2											14	405	3	D	10
v. Lancashire (New Road) 6-8 May	9	35	22	48	0	1	9	7	0	14	4*											18	167	10		
	20	80	35	9	53	43	14	7	0	30	0*											10	301	10	L	3
v. Sussex (New Road) 11-14 June	19	5	15	15	0	80	7*	19	17					89		10						12	288	10		
	99	124	33	35	6	1	22*	24	3					0		9						36	392	10	L	4
v. Yorkshire (New Road) 16-19 June	68	55	1	112	60	15	11*	5	25					35		3						25	415	10		
	32	14*	48		52	48*																9	203	3	D	11
v. Durham (Riverside) 30 June-3 July	13	9				33	2	0	19			6		50	7	28		4*				22	193	10		
	15	10				3	5	21	4			66		11	0	30*		1				13	179	10	L	3
v. Lancashire (Old Trafford) 10-12 July	0	8	35	39	23	16	15	13*	1	9		5										8	172	10		
	12	3	9	25	107	28	2	3	4	19*		16										8	236	10	L	3
v. Somerset (New Road) 21-24 July	20	0	12	44		38	4	12	4	43*		0										41	225	10		
	4	16	93	7*	17	80*																8	225	4	D	
v. Warwickshire (New Road) 31 July-3 August	6	4	27	19	28	1	2			1	0*	0	4									19	111	10		
	0	47	46	0	88	2	0			14	0*	26	3									12	244	10	L	3
v. Sussex (Hove) 11-13 August	12	22	19	25	28	32	25		46	4	27										0*	16	256	10		
	13	3	31	67	28	5	28		22	1	35										0*	12	235	10	L	5
v. Nottinghamshire (New Road) 25-28 August	53	0	30	9	0	52			92*	0		34	31		0							33	334	10		
	10	84*	0	76	11	10			5*			30										16	242	6	D	10
v. Warwickshire (Edgbaston) 2-5 September	30	0	27	8	5	4	8*			0	1	33	24									14	154	10		
	25	11	10	62	63	0	8*			23	6	12	12									39	271	10	L	3
v. Hampshire (New Road) 9-11 September	37	12	8	24	35	9	0	1				5	1				5*					22	159	10		
	0	37	3	31	28	0	4	21*				54	36				0					13	227	10	L	3
v. Somerset (Taunton) 16-19 September	298	1	15		32		4		0			19	18*		87		1		61			35	571	10	D	12
v. Durham (New Road) 23-26 September	67	19	4	31	23		23*			77		46	27		14		6					19	356	10		
	26	25	31	97	16					59*		48	53*		30							25	410	7	D	9
Matches	17	17	16	14	14	14	14	12	11	10	9	8	7	6	5	4	4	2	1	1	1					
Innings	31	30	29	26	27	27	23	17	16	16	13	14	11	9	6	7	5	2	1	0	2					
Not Out	1	2	1	2	0	3	6	3	0	5	7	0	2	0	0	1	1	1	0	0	2					
High Score	298	153	206*	126	107	80*	28	47	46	92*	35	66	53*	89	87	30*	6	4*	61	0	0*					
Runs	1162	803	980	952	738	626	207	205	175	391	81	381	209	258	160	81	12	5	61	0	0					
Average	38.73	28.67	35.00	39.66	27.33	26.08	12.17	14.64	10.93	35.54	13.50	27.21	23.22	28.66	26.66	13.50	3.00	5.00	61.00	-	-					
100s	2	2	1	2	1	0	0	0	0	0	0	0	0	0	0	0	0	0	0	0	0					
50s	5	3	4	4	5	4	0	0	0	3	0	2	1	2	1	0	0	0	1	0	0					
Catches/Stumpings	18/0	4/0	13/0	39/2	5/0	9/0	6/0	2/0	9/0	0/0	4/0	2/0	3/0	0/0	3/0	2/0	2/0	5/0	4/1	0/0	0/0					

Home Ground: New Road, Worcester
Address: County Ground, New Road, Worcester, WR2 4QQ
Tel: 01905 748474
Fax: 01905 748005
Email: admin@wccc.co.uk
Directions: From the M5 junction 7, follow the brown 'broken stumps' logos to WCCC.
Capacity: 4,500

Other grounds used: Kidderminster, RGS Worcester
Year formed: 1865

Chief Executive: Mark Newton
Director of Cricket: Steve Rhodes
Captain: Vikram Solanki
County colours: Green, black and white

Honours
County Championship
1964, 1965, 1974, 1988, 1989
Sunday League/NCL/Pro40
1971, 1987, 1988, 2007
Benson & Hedges Cup
1991
Gillette Cup/NatWest/C&G Trophy
1994

Website:
www.wccc.co.uk

FIRST–CLASS MATCHES

BOWLING

	MS Mason	GM Andrew	RA Jones	CD Whelan	Imran Arif	Kabir Ali	AA Noffke	GJ Batty	DKH Mitchell	JD Shantry	MM Ali	VS Solanki	ID Fisher	M Ahmed	Overs	Total	Byes/Leg-byes	Wickets	Run outs
v. Oxford UCCE (The Parks) 11–13 April		8-1-27-1		9-4-27-0	12-3-44-2			9-4-17-1					3-0-15-0		41	143	13	4	
															–	–	–	–	
v. Hampshire (Rose Bowl) 15–17 April	17.4-6-47-2			10-2-34-1	11-1-42-4	18-3-74-3		7-1-17-0							63.4	216	2	10	
	5-1-13-0			7-1-30-0	5-0-18-0	5-0-23-0		10-3-23-1	1-1-0-2						33	107	0	3	
v. Nottinghamshire (Trent Bridge) 21–24 April	26-9-83-3			27-1-116-3	26-4-120-1		25-8-73-0	33.2-6-90-1			1-0-10-0				138.2	505	13	10	2
															–	–	–	–	
v. Yorkshire (Headingley) 28 April–1 May	31-8-75-0			21-1-105-1	12-0-75-0		29-6-77-1	26-2-78-0	17-3-49-4						136	460	1	6	
															–	–	–	–	
v. Lancashire (New Road) 6–8 May	24-8-76-3	5-0-32-0		25-2-95-5	10-0-65-2			20-3-48-0	6-1-15-0						90	347	15	10	
	6-3-16-0	8-1-35-1		6-2-11-1	8-0-40-1										33.5	122	5	4	
v. Sussex (New Road) 11–14 June	27-2-112-0			26-1-151-3		22-1-79-1	27-3-92-4	29-5-123-0	7-0-19-0		3-0-30-0				141	620	14	9	1
	2-0-14-0			2-0-10-0		3-0-22-0		2-0-9-0	1-0-4-0						10	61	2	0	
v. Yorkshire (New Road) 16–19 June	22-8-67-1			25-4-130-4		25-2-127-1	28-8-71-1	25-5-79-2	4-1-11-0		2-0-9-1				131	516	16	10	
															–	–	–	–	
v. Durham (Riverside) 30 June–3 July	21-8-55-3			6.5-1-34-1		18-4-68-6	10-4-28-0	10-1-48-0							55.5	194	9	10	
	11-2-35-3			5-0-37-1		6-0-23-0	7-2-11-1				2-0-17-0				41	179	8	5	
v. Lancashire (Old Trafford) 10–12 July	17-11-39-7	5-0-21-0		6-1-31-0			16-3-48-3								44	145	6	10	
	32-13-77-1	11-0-26-0		4.1-1-17-0			16-4-46-0		21-1-71-2		4-1-12-0				88.1	264	15	3	
v. Somerset (New Road) 21–24 July	28-6-111-3	26-2-111-1	4.3-0-29-0	10-0-67-0				12-1-56-0		7-0-25-2					87.3	428	29	6	
															–	–	–	–	
v. Warwickshire (New Road) 31 July–3 August	21-4-51-2	14-2-57-3	20.1-4-66-4		15-1-78-1				6-0-19-0		2-0-24-0	1-0-3-0			79.1	309	11	10	
	4-0-13-1		0.5-0-5-0		4-1-28-0										8.5	47	1	1	
v. Sussex (Hove) 11–13 August	30-9-60-7	22.1-6-73-2			12-1-60-0			8-2-17-1	9-2-17-0				4-0-31-0		85.1	280	22	10	
	4-1-17-1	12.5-1-60-0			6-0-52-0			9-2-32-1			2-1-4-0		5-0-42-0		38.5	212	5	2	
v. Nottinghamshire (New Road) 25–28 August		13-3-35-1	7-3-19-2		20.5-4-93-5					14-2-53-2					54.5	219	19	10	
		21-3-97-3	18-2-105-4		18-3-72-0					11-3-30-0	6-1-37-0				74	351	10	7	
v. Warwickshire (Edgbaston) 2–5 September	26-7-59-1	23-1-104-1	29-6-100-6		25-3-112-1					10-2-16-0	4-1-17-0				117	443	35	10	1
															–	–	–	–	
v. Hampshire (New Road) 9–11 September	26-5-78-1		26-2-104-2		14-1-78-1					5-1-14-0	25-7-68-2	11.1-5-29-4			107.1	383	12	10	
			0.3-0-4-0								1-0-3-0				1.3	7	0	0	
v. Somerset (Taunton) 16–19 September	24-9-60-3	17.3-3-75-3	11-1-42-1							16-4-65-2	10-2-32-1				78.3	280	6	10	
	14-5-28-1	30-4-117-5	29-3-142-1						6-1-11-0	21-6-61-1	26-3-136-0	7-2-17-0			133	523	11	8	
v. Durham (New Road) 23–26 September		41-11-121-2		28-4-129-2	28-2-94-1					11-1-52-1	39.1-9-102-1	21-1-104-1	4-0-16-0		172.1	634	16	8	
															–	–	–	–	

	MS Mason	GM Andrew	RA Jones	CD Whelan	Imran Arif	Kabir Ali	AA Noffke	GJ Batty	DKH Mitchell	JD Shantry	MM Ali	VS Solanki	ID Fisher	M Ahmed
Overs	418.4	257.3	174	232	184.5	97	158	227.1	90	127.1	94.1	12	3	9
Maidens	125	38	25	24	21	10	38	37	13	31	15	2	0	0
Runs	1186	991	745	1067	899	416	452	724	252	382	461	36	15	73
Wickets	43	23	22	22	17	11	10	10	9	8	7	0	0	0
Average	27.58	43.08	33.86	48.50	52.88	37.81	45.20	72.40	28.00	47.75	65.85	–	–	–

FIELDING

41	SM Davies (39 ct, 2 st)
18	DKH Mitchell
13	VS Solanki
9	BF Smith
9	GJ Batty
6	MS Mason
5	SC Moore
5	JP Knappett
5	OB Cox (4 ct, 1 st)
4	MM Ali
4	Imran Arif
3	RA Jones
3	DA Wheeldon
2	Kabir Ali
2	CD Whelan
2	AN Kervezee
2	JD Shantry
0	ID Fisher
0	GM Andrew
0	AA Noffke
0	M Ahmed

Division One – Final Table

	P	W	L	D	Bat	Bowl	Pens	Pts
Durham	16	8	0	8	49	48	1.00	240.00
Nottinghamshire	16	4	2	10	56	41	0.00	193.00
Somerset	16	3	1	12	50	43	1.00	182.00
Lancashire	16	4	2	10	35	44	0.00	175.00
Warwickshire	16	3	3	10	54	38	0.00	174.00
Hampshire	16	3	3	10	50	40	3.00	169.00
Yorkshire	16	2	2	12	46	44	0.00	166.00
Sussex	16	2	6	8	45	39	1.00	143.00
Worcestershire	16	0	10	6	30	40	0.00	94.00

FPT & Pro40 T20

WORCESTERSHIRE ROYALS

Limited overs nickname:
WORCESTERSHIRE ROYALS

YORKSHIRE CCC

FIRST–CLASS MATCHES
BATTING

	JA Rudolph	JJ Sayers	AW Gale	A McGrath	MJ Hoggard	GL Brophy	A Shahzad	JM Bairstow	DJ Wainwright	TT Bresnan	GJ Kruis	AU Rashid	A Lyth	MP Vaughan	Azeem Rafiq	SA Patterson	Naved-ul-Hasan	RM Pyrah	LJ Hodgson	JE Lee	Extras	Total	Wickets	Result	Points
v. Cambridge UCCE	1	22	93	46	0*	39	6		22			20				30*			32		35	346	9		
(Fenner's) 11-13 April	31	25*																			8	64	1	D	
v. Durham	51	5	11	27	1	75				40	0*	11	24			3					24	272	10		
(Riverside) 22-25 April	16	30	27	26	27					20	6*	20	4*								17	193	7	D	9
v. Worcestershire	198	49	21	120		16	20*			17*			5								14	460	6	D	9
(Headingley) 28 April-1 May																									
v. Warwickshire	62	173	12	211		40*	5				1*	0		16			32				48	600	8		
(Edgbaston) 6-9 May	30	14	53*	0								58*									7	162	3	D	11
v. Sussex	15	29	11	24		75*		36	7	0		0		13		1					14	225	10		
(Headingley) 6-9 June	89	15	25	58		7*			1*	7				39		6					25	272	10	D	7
v. Somerset	14	60	35	16	1	33	8*	28	1	48							10				23	277	10		
(Headingley) 11-14 June	22	18	30	9	4	14	4	82*	23	7							22				13	248	10	L	5
v. Worcestershire	9	44	101	6	56*		19	0		97	16			43	100						25	516	10	D	12
(New Road) 16-19 June																									
v. Somerset	191	8	17	40	26		27*	39				36			4	8				2	40	438	10		
(Taunton) 30 June-3 July	0	152	16	25		16*	66*						71								17	363	5	L	8
v. Durham	5	37	84	19	0		41*	8		36		32	4				22				25	313	10		
(Headingley) 10-13 July	39	14	24*	0			9*					2									10	98	4	D	10
v. Nottinghamshire	0	17	6	15	11	5		84*	29	7	37	4									16	231	10		
(Scarborough) 21-24 July	12	36	99	9		51*		4		16*											5	232	5	D	8
v. Lancashire	14	34	54	9	1	15	26*	5		0		2				0					21	181	10		
(Old Trafford) 31 July-3 August	127	1	121	14		21*		52*													18	354	4	D	5
v. Hampshire	90	50	8	0	14	53	78	13		24	26	117*									51	524		W	21
(Basingstoke) 11-14 August																									
v. Lancashire	0	17	6	17	8	99	32	15	1	46		157*									31	429	10	D	11
(Headingley) 19-22 August																									
v. Warwickshire	0	21	23	0	18	85	13	4	102*		30						0				32	328	10		
(Scarborough) 26-29 August	21*	4*																			5	30		D	10
v. Nottinghamshire	42	53	5	0	12*	0	19	49	37			1						9			29	256	10		
(Trent Bridge) 3-6 September	149	86	9	40	0*	29	45	82	6									50*			23	519	8	D	9
v. Sussex	0	10	60	25	17	34	88	0	85*			50				0					34	403	10		
(Hove) 16-19 September	70	31	22	37	26	30	0	2	14*			31				0					21	284	10	W	20
v. Hampshire	68	95	1	25	0	0	4	50*	21		20	26									38	348	10	D	10
(Headingley) 23-26 September																									
Matches	17	17	17	17	16	14	14	12	10	10	9	7	5	5	4	4	4	3	1	1					
Innings	29	29	26	27	17	22	18	19	13	14	9	9	8	7	5	4	6	4	1	1					
Not Out	1	2	1	1	4	5	6	6	4	2	2	4	0	0	0	2	0	1	0	0					
High Score	198	173	121	211	56*	99	88	84*	102*	97	37	157*	71	43	100	30*	32	50*	32	2					
Runs	1366	1150	921	871	195	748	451	592	378	372	131	387	240	147	117	45	93	59	32	2					
Average	48.78	42.59	36.84	33.50	15.00	44.00	37.58	45.53	42.00	31.00	18.71	77.40	30.00	21.00	23.40	22.50	15.50	19.66	32.00	2.00					
100s	4	2	2	2	0	0	0	0	1	0	0	2	0	0	1	0	0	0	0	0					
50s	6	5	5	2	1	6	2	6	1	1	0	1	2	0	0	0	0	1	0	0					
Catches/Stumpings	14/0	16/0	6/0	11/0	5/0	37/2	4/0	21/0	0/0	5/0	1/0	4/0	1/0	0/0	1/0	0/0	0/0	3/0	0/0	1/0					

Home Ground: Headingley
Address: Headingley Carnegie Cricket Ground, Leeds, LS6 3BU
Tel: 0871 971 1222
Fax: 0113 2784099
Email: cricket@yorkshireccc.com
Directions: From M1 South leave at junction 43 to M621 as far as junction 2. From M62 West leave at junction 27 to take M621 as far as junction 2. From M62 East leave at junction 29 to join M1 northbound to junction 2 of M621. At junction 2 of the M621 follow the signs for Headingley stadium along A643. Follow Leeds Inner Ring Road (A58(M)) to A660 which is signposted to Headingley stadium. Signs along this route will indicate when you have reached the Headingley area and on Test match days additional temporary signing will direct you to the free Park & Ride car park to the north of Headingley at Beckett Park.
Capacity: 20,000
Other grounds used: Scarborough
Year formed: 1863

Chief Executive: Stewart Regan
Operations Director: Ian Dews
Director of Cricket: Martyn Moxon
Captain: Anthony McGrath
County colours: Gold and black

Website:
www.yorkshireccc.com

Honours
County Championship
1867, 1869, 1870, 1893, 1896, 1898, 1901, 1902, 1905, 1908, 1912, 1919, 1922, 1923, 1924, 1925, 1931, 1932, 1933, 1935, 1937, 1938, 1939, 1946, 1959, 1960, 1962, 1963, 1966, 1967, 1968, 2001
Joint Champions 1949
Sunday League/NCL/Pro40
1983
Benson & Hedges Cup
1987
Gillette Cup/NatWest/C&G Trophy
1965, 1969, 2002

FIRST-CLASS MATCHES
BOWLING

	MJ Hoggard	A Shahzad	AU Rashid	DJ Wainwright	TT Bresnan	GJ Kruis	Naved-ul-Hasan	Azeem Rafiq	SA Patterson	A McGrath	RM Pyrah	JJ Sayers	JE Lee	A Lyth	GL Brophy	AW Gale	JA Rudolph	LJ Hodgson	Overs	Total	Byes/Leg-byes	Wickets	Run outs
v. Cambridge UCCE (Fenner's) 11-13 April	13-7-19-3	13-5-29-1		6-0-27-0				14.1-4-41-4	3-2-1-2									10-3-30-0	59.1	155	8	10	
v. Durham (Riverside) 22-25 April	24-5-82-4		8.3-0-37-1		27-7-63-3	22-2-80-1			22-6-61-1	9-5-19-0									112.3	362	20	10	
	15-1-57-2		26-1-88-3		9-2-40-0	9-1-31-0			17-2-62-0	3-0-15-0									79	303	10	5	
v. Worcestershire (Headingley) 28 April-1 May	21-4-60-1	22-8-64-2		13-2-52-0	28-6-94-0				22-6-92-0	8-1-31-0							2-0-5-0		116	405	7	3	
v. Warwickshire (Edgbaston) 6-9 May	16.1-2-67-1	21-2-72-2	22-6-89-2			22-3-89-2		27-5-102-3		14-4-31-0									122.1	482	32	10	
	3-1-5-0	2-0-8-0	5-0-19-0			6-1-25-1													16	60	3	1	
v. Sussex (Headingley) 6-9 June			2-0-4-0			24-9-44-2	17-7-36-2	19.3-3-59-2	11-0-34-3	9-3-26-1									82.3	217	14	10	
			10-1-46-3			18-4-44-0	12-2-40-0	9.5-1-45-2	16-2-55-2	5-0-19-0									70.5	257	8	8	1
v. Somerset (Headingley) 11-14 June	16-3-56-5	14.5-3-41-2			17-4-49-3	12-3-26-0	15-1-47-0										1-0-1-0		74.5	230	11	10	
	14-1-52-0	15.3-3-45-2			18-0-66-2	20-4-55-1	17-3-57-1												85.3	296	20	6	
v. Worcestershire (New Road) 16-19 June		29-3-88-2	25-3-93-2		23.3-8-58-2	20-5-65-3		19-5-62-1			2-0-3-0						5-0-27-0	8-0-24-0	121.3	415	22	10	
		13-2-43-0			4-0-19-0	7-1-15-1		22-0-82-2						1-0-11-0					57	203	6	3	
v. Somerset (Taunton) 30 June-3 July	19.4-2-82-5	20-3-57-2						13-0-54-0	14-2-55-1			13-1-63-2							79.4	326	15	10	
	24-0-118-3	19-1-119-0						14.3-0-72-2	21-2-98-1			6-0-50-0					1-0-14-0		85.3	479	8	6	
v. Durham (Headingley) 10-13 July	17.2-6-36-2	12-3-39-3	18-4-32-3		13-3-24-0		10-1-38-1												70.2	178	9	10	1
	29-9-67-3	18-3-55-1	43-7-124-2		29-1-69-2		25.4-9-64-1										3-0-8-0		147.4	421	34	9	
v. Nottinghamshire (Scarborough) 21-24 July	21-5-57-2		14-0-97-2		12-3-42-0	30-5-116-4	19.1-3-79-2												96.1	395	4	10	
v. Lancashire (Old Trafford) 31 July-3 August	29-7-86-1	30-6-107-1	27-0-126-2		34-11-90-1						17-1-58-0	1-0-5-0							138	489	17	5	
v. Hampshire (Basingstoke) 11-14 August	17-5-38-1	22-4-72-4	4-1-13-0		19.1-6-45-3		19-4-51-2			9-1-24-0									90.1	250	7	10	
	16-3-54-1	13-3-45-1	16.5-6-41-5		20-7-46-2		10-1-39-0			4-2-7-0									79.5	252	20	10	1
v. Lancashire (Headingley) 19-22 August	18-7-40-1	18-7-48-0	34.2-7-97-5		21-5-39-1	31-13-46-3							3-0-4-0						122.2	276	6	10	
	10-2-24-0	5-3-13-0	24-5-55-1		19-3-67-0	11-2-30-1													72	196	3	2	
v. Warwickshire (Scarborough) 26-29 August	18-3-51-0	17.4-3-78-4			14-0-74-2	23-8-68-3					9-1-38-1								81.4	320	11	10	
	20-9-42-1	19-3-57-2			30-8-71-2	12-5-24-0				6-1-11-1	17-2-64-1	4.5-0-20-3							108.5	313	24	10	
v. Nottinghamshire (Trent Bridge) 3-6 September	17-5-60-2	22.2-1-101-3			12-4-49-2	17-0-73-1					17-3-53-2								85.2	352	16	10	
v. Sussex (Hove) 16-19 September	26-5-70-1	29-7-84-4			31.5-4-134-5			29-2-128-0		4-1-11-0									119.5	448	16	10	
	8-3-29-4	9-0-33-1			8.3-4-12-4														25.3	83	9	10	1
v. Hampshire (Headingley) 23-26 September	27-6-115-1	29.3-9-75-4			16-6-43-1		23-8-51-3			20-4-46-1						19-9-38-1	5-0-32-0		115.3	351	21	10	
	11-3-31-0	13-4-27-0			20-6-49-1		14-5-50-1			15-2-39-0						1-1-0-0			98	284	18	3	

	MJ Hoggard	A Shahzad	AU Rashid	DJ Wainwright	TT Bresnan	GJ Kruis	Naved-ul-Hasan	Azeem Rafiq	SA Patterson	A McGrath	RM Pyrah	JJ Sayers	JE Lee	A Lyth	GL Brophy	AW Gale	JA Rudolph	LJ Hodgson
Overs	479.1	422.5	242.4	250.2	352.4	252.1	124	124.3	110.1	109	60	10.5	19	19	1	1	25	10
Maidens	107	86	37	50	91	56	23	9	22	26	7	0	1	9	1	0	0	3
Runs	1486	1405	818	824	909	816	412	487	409	280	213	32	113	38	0	11	111	30
Wickets	46	41	26	26	24	22	10	10	7	5	4	3	2	1	0	0	0	0
Average	32.30	34.26	31.46	31.69	37.87	37.09	41.20	48.70	58.42	56.00	53.25	10.66	56.50	38.00	-	-	-	-

FIELDING

39	GL Brophy (37 ct, 2 st)
21	JM Bairstow
16	JJ Sayers
14	JA Rudolph
11	A McGrath
6	AW Gale
5	MJ Hoggard
5	TT Bresnan
4	A Shahzad
4	AU Rashid
3	RM Pyrah
1	GJ Kruis
1	A Lyth
1	Azeem Rafiq
1	JE Lee
0	MP Vaughan
0	SA Patterson
0	Naved-ul-Hasan
0	DJ Wainwright
0	LJ Hodgson

Division One – Final Table

	P	W	L	D	Bat	Bowl	Pens	Pts
Durham	16	8	0	8	49	48	1.00	240.00
Nottinghamshire	16	4	2	10	56	41	0.00	193.00
Somerset	16	3	1	12	50	43	1.00	182.00
Lancashire	16	4	2	10	35	44	0.00	175.00
Warwickshire	16	3	3	10	54	38	0.00	174.00
Hampshire	16	3	3	10	50	40	3.00	169.00
Yorkshire	16	2	2	12	46	44	0.00	166.00
Sussex	16	2	6	8	45	39	1.00	143.00
Worcestershire	16	0	10	6	30	40	0.00	94.00

FPT & Pro40

T20

Limited overs nickname:
YORKSHIRE CARNEGIE

COUNTY REVIEW *South Coast*

BRUCE TALBOT, of the *Brighton Evening Argus*, reviews a season of one-day triumphs and relegation despair for Sussex, and a summer of solid achievement for local rivals Hampshire...

When you win two of the four trophies available and reach the final of another competition it can only be judged a successful season. But Sussex's failure to hang on to their first division status in the County Championship cast a big shadow over a remarkable transformation which saw them become unquestionably the best one-day side in the country.

A year after winning just twice in the Twenty20 Cup they became champions of the shortest format for the first time. They also won the last ever NatWest Pro40 League, thus retaining their title with more victories than any other side, and also reached their tenth Lord's final where fierce rivals Hampshire beat them to the Friends Provident Trophy.

Sussex's squad seemed to cover most bases with power-hitters Dwayne Smith, Luke Wright, Rory Hamilton-Brown and Chris Nash providing the momentum while the more prosaic Ed Joyce, Murray Goodwin and Mike Yardy kept the scoreboard and the strike ticking over. James Kirtley demonstrated there was no substitute for experience with 44 wickets in all one-day formats while Yardy made good use of his spinners, particularly at Hove where Sussex didn't lose a limited-overs game all season.

Somerset beat them in the Pro40 but, more importantly, Sussex had won at Taunton in the quarter-final of the FPT, never looking back after Marcus Trescothick was caught off the first ball of the day. Joyce scored his fourth competition hundred of the season in the semi-final win over Gloucestershire but Sussex saved arguably their worst limited-overs performance of the summer for the final

where Smith's 59 off 26 balls, Kirtley's 3 for 9 and a stunning catch by Yardy which clinched victory were all memorable highlights.

Yet while Sussex swept nearly all before them in one-day cricket their form in the Championship rarely hit those heights. They had stayed up by a handful of points in 2008 despite winning just twice and that was never likely to be enough in 2009, especially with Worcestershire – against whom they recorded their two wins of last summer – quickly marooned at the bottom.

On 13 occasions Sussex squandered strong positions or simply fell apart, most spectacularly in the home games against Warwickshire and Yorkshire at the end of the season when a win in either might have kept them up. While their last five wickets averaged 81, the opposition's put on 121, highlighting the lack of penetration in their attack. Leg-spinner Piyush Chawla was leading-wicket taker with 36 despite only playing six games while, of the seamers, only Corey Collymore (33) took more than 30 wickets. Life after Mushtaq Ahmed proved tougher than Sussex had anticipated.

Chris Nash scored nearly 1,300 runs and Rory Hamilton-Brown put down a marker for the future when he scored 171 against Yorkshire, easily the best individual batting performance of a dispiriting four-day campaign.

New blood will be needed at Hove in 2010, too, especially with Jason Lewry and Carl Hopkinson retiring at the end of the season and Tom Smith, the young left-arm spinner, leaving for Middlesex. Lewry, 38, took 621 first-class wickets in 16 years, making him the most prolific wicket-taker among Sussex seamers in the last four decades, while Hopkinson hung up his playing boots at the age of just 28 to concentrate on his new job as Sussex fielding coach.

Winning the Friends Provident Trophy, meanwhile, and staying in Division One of the Championship, constituted a good first full season as Hampshire manager for Giles White.

Above Corey Collymore, the Sussex and former West Indies fast bowler, is pictured in action at Hove.

Left Ed Joyce swings to leg during his prolific season for Sussex, the club he joined from Middlesex the previous winter.

against Hampshire at Lord's when they never recovered from Dominic Cork's new-ball burst.

Coach Mark Robinson had begun formulating his plans for Twenty20 while watching enviously as an unheralded Middlesex team, ironically led by Joyce, won the 2008 competition. Sussex lost just twice in the group stage, eased to victory over Warwickshire and Northamptonshire in the knockout rounds, before outplaying Somerset in the final

Hampshire also reached their first Twenty20 Cup quarter-final for five years and the county's outstanding crop of teenagers added more experience to their blossoming talent during an inconsistent NatWest Pro40 campaign.

There were some outstanding individual performers throughout the summer. James Vince and Danny Briggs, 18-year-olds produced by Hampshire's academy, both made their debuts, but 2009 will be remembered for the six-wicket FPT final win against Sussex, inspired by the evergreen Cork. Cork is older than Vince and Briggs combined but was at his Lord's best while inspiring Hampshire to a first trophy in four years. He may have turned 38 in August but Cork proved one of the shrewdest signings of the season, providing energy and experience as well as excellence with the ball in a summer when Hampshire's pace attack was not helped by the slowness of the Rose Bowl wickets.

Cork's former England team-mate John Crawley called time on an outstanding career – he played 37 Tests for England and scored 24,361 first-class runs in 351 matches at an average of 46.49 – but, for Jimmy Adams, 2009 was a breakthrough season and he deservedly won the county's Player of the Year award.

Another of Hampshire's homegrown products, Adams finally established himself as a one-day regular seven years after making his debut. Adams also scored more Championship runs than any Hampshire player (1,279 at 53.29), while the prolific Michael Carberry (1,251 at 69.50) was being touted for an England debut ahead of the Ashes decider following a prolific run in mid-summer before injury cruelly ruled him out of the season's final month.

Michael Lumb scored Hampshire's first Twenty20 hundred but the low point of the Hawks' season came in the shortest format, just a few days after their FPT win, when Northamptonshire Steelbacks denied them a first finals day appearance.

Jimmy Adams, the Hampshire opener, was a deserved winner of the club's Player of the Year award.

FRIENDS PROVIDENT TROPHY

by Mark Baldwin

Dimitri Mascarenhas's Hampshire were only troubled by one other county during an otherwise all-conquering march to Lord's and their second Friends Provident Trophy triumph in five seasons.

Their road to the summer's showpiece cup final, and an impressive win against Sussex, featured two defeats to Worcestershire, but Hampshire did not lose any other game while adding to their 2005 success – and in Michael Lumb and Jimmy Adams they found the most destructive opening pair in the competition.

The two left-handed batsmen wrought havoc in Hampshire's last three matches before Lord's. After adding an unbroken 149 to spearhead a ten-wicket canter against Nottinghamshire in the last group match, Lumb and Adams just seemed to get better and better. In the quarter-final, against Middlesex at the Rose Bowl, they put on an opening stand of 156 to set up a forbidding 50-over total of 310 for 4, with Lumb's 100 taking him just 98 balls, with ten fours, and Adams's 76 from 77 balls including eight boundaries.

Then, as Lancashire were brushed aside at Old Trafford in the semi-final, it was again Lumb with 76 from 79 balls and Adams with a 71-ball 78 who provided the firmest of foundations with a first wicket partnership of 159. This time Adams struck two sixes and six fours, and Lumb one six and six fours.

And, just as their quarter-final total had proved too much for Middlesex, a semi-final total of 271 – despite a Lancashire fightback in the field – was enough to earn Hampshire a Lord's day out. Imran Tahir took 3 for 38 with his leg breaks and googlies, and Lancashire's challenge was all but over when Indian Test batsman VVS Laxman was fifth out for 54, to a second brilliant diving catch by Adams, with their score at 123.

The campaign, however, had got off to an unpromising start against Worcestershire, for whom Moeen Ali hit 125 from just 109 balls and added 164 for the fourth

wicket with Ben Smith. A 50-over total of 320 for 8 was too steep for Hampshire to chase down, although John Crawley did make 100 and Lumb 61.

But Leicestershire were beaten in home and away fixtures on successive Sundays, with Chris Benham the batting star in both games. One further point was gained from the abandoned match in Ireland, and then a double over Nottinghamshire and a 77-run win in the return match with the Irish, at the Rose Bowl, saw Hampshire cruise into the last eight.

Dominic Cork was another Hampshire hero as positive momentum built up. Cork hit eye-catching form with the ball in those three games, returning figures of 3 for 13,

Dominic Cork at 38 – still with a spring in his step.

4 for 20 and 4 for 18 respectively. Sean Ervine and Michael Carberry put Ireland's bowlers to the sword at the Rose Bowl, meanwhile, as Hampshire totalled a ground one-day record 316 for 2. Ervine's unbeaten 167, from 140 balls, contained four sixes and 20 fours and Carberry's 121 not out included three sixes and 11 fours. Their unbroken third wicket stand of 260 was also a record.

It was the perfect way to bounce back from the second loss to Worcestershire, four days earlier, in which the batting failed for the only time in the competition and Hampshire were bowled out for just 138.

In the final itself, on 25 July, openers Adams and Lumb had to be content with a mere 93 for the first wicket, but that was easily enough to set up a straightforward chase to overhaul Sussex's inadequate 219 for 9. Only Luke Wright, with three wickets with his energetic fast-medium, then threatened to make life evenly mildly difficult for Hampshire as Carberry, Benham and Pothas all added solid contributions to those of Adams and Lumb at the top of the order.

Victory arrived, in the end, by six wickets and with more than nine overs to spare and – despite the unbeaten 92 with which the resilient Mike Yardy had earlier tried to hold the crumbling Sussex innings together – there was only ever going to be one Man of the Match award recipient.

After his three-wicket new-ball spell, followed up by the late wicket of Robin Martin-Jenkins, it was the irrepressible Cork – for his 4 for 41 and, at 37, his ageless enthusiasm – who went up to receive the award and milk the applause of his new Hampshire fan club.

The winter move to the South Coast had indeed reinvigorated Cork, who now proudly clutched his match award fully 16 years after he had also been declared Man of the Match when his 92 not out helped Derbyshire to beat Lancashire in the 1993 Benson and Hedges Cup final at Lord's.

Group A

19 April
at Trent Bridge
Leicestershire 155 all out (45.4 overs) (GP Swann 3 for 24)
Nottinghamshire 159 for 2 (30 overs) (MA Wagh 68*,
AD Hales 52)
Nottinghamshire (2pts) won by 8 wickets

at the Rose Bowl
Worcestershire 320 for 8 (50 overs) (MM Ali 125,
BF Smith 70, SM Davies 50, CT Tremlett 3 for 76)
Hampshire 267 all out (48.1 overs) (JP Crawley 100,
MJ Lumb 61, GJ Batty 5 for 35)
Worcestershire (2pts) won by 53 runs

26 April
at Belfast
Worcestershire 180 for 8 (33 overs) (WK McCallan 3 for 26)
Ireland 128 for 9 (33 overs) (PR Stirling 51)
Worcestershire (2pts) won by 52 runs

at Grace Road
Leicestershire 238 for 6 (50 overs) (MAG Boyce 80,
HH Dippenaar 65, LA Dawson 4 for 48)
Hampshire 242 for 6 (48.1 overs) (CC Benham 79)
Hampshire (2pts) won by 4 wickets

3 May
at the Rose Bowl
Hampshire 300 for 5 (50 overs) (CC Benham 108*, N Pothas 57*)
Leicestershire 254 all out (49.2 overs) (PA Nixon 50,
BV Taylor 3 for 46, SM Ervine 3 for 50)
Hampshire (2pts) won by 46 runs

at Trent Bridge
Nottinghamshire 346 for 9 (50 overs) (AD Hales 106,
AD Brown 89, WI Jefferson 57*, P Connell 4 for 71)
Ireland 212 for 9 (50 overs) (AR White 51*, MA Ealham 4 for 40,
SR Patel 3 for 30)
Nottinghamshire (2pts) won by 134 runs

Opposite Worcestershire's Moeen Ali celebrates after catching Hampshire's Liam Dawson during Worcestershire's victory at the Rose Bowl.

4 May
at Grace Road
Ireland 197 for 5 (31 overs) (PR Stirling 80, KJ O'Brien 67*)
Leicestershire 201 for 3 (29 overs) (HD Ackerman 118*)
Leicestershire (2pts) won by 7 wickets

at New Road
Nottinghamshire 188 for 8 (40 overs) (MA Wagh 85, AA Noffke 3 for 37)
Worcestershire 138 for 0 (23.1 overs) (SM Davies 82*)
Worcestershire (2pts) won by 10 wickets – DL Method: target 138 from 26 overs

10 May
at Eglinton
Ireland v. **Hampshire**
Match abandoned (1pt each)

at Trent Bridge
Worcestershire 209 for 8 (50 overs) (DKH Mitchell 59, MM Ali 58)
Nottinghamshire 211 for 6 (44.3 overs) (MA Wagh 52)
Nottinghamshire (2pts) won by 4 wickets

12 May
at New Road
Leicestershire 282 for 3 (50 overs) (JWA Taylor 101, HD Ackerman 63, HH Dippenaar 63*)
Worcestershire 264 all out (48.2 overs) (SM Davies 62, BF Smith 54, SC Moore 51, CW Henderson 3 for 44)
Leicestershire (2pts) won by 18 runs

at the Rose Bowl
Nottinghamshire 202 all out (49.1 overs) (WI Jefferson 93, PJ Franks 50, AD Mascarenhas 4 for 39, DG Cork 3 for 13, BV Taylor 3 for 40)
Hampshire 203 for 4 (43.2 overs) (MJ Lumb 57)
Hampshire (2pts) won by 6 wickets

14 May
at Dublin
Ireland v. **Leicestershire**
Match abandoned (1pt each)

at New Road
Worcestershire 246 for 8 (50 overs) (BV Taylor 3 for 37)
Hampshire 138 all out (38.5 overs) (CD Whelan 4 for 27)
Worcestershire (2pts) won by 108 runs

16 May
at Grace Road
Worcestershire 67 for 1 (8 overs)
Leicestershire
Match abandoned (1pt each)

at Dublin
Ireland 140 for 8 (34 overs) (SR Patel 6 for 13)
Nottinghamshire 141 for 8 (33.5 overs)
Nottinghamshire (2pts) won by 2 wickets

18 May
at the Rose Bowl
Hampshire 316 for 2 (50 overs) (SM Ervine 167*, MA Carberry 121*)
Ireland 239 for 9 (50 overs) (KJ O'Brien 94, DG Cork 4 for 20)
Hampshire (2pts) won by 77 runs

19 May
at Grace Road
Nottinghamshire 149 for 3 (35.3 overs)
Leicestershire 67 for 5 (10 overs)
Nottinghamshire (2pts) won by 9 runs – DL Method: target 77 from 10 overs

20 May
at Trent Bridge
Nottinghamshire 145 all out (46.1 overs) (DG Cork 4 for 18)
Hampshire 149 for 0 (29.1 overs) (JHK Adams 73*, MJ Lumb 72*)
Hampshire (2pts) won by 10 wickets

at New Road
Ireland 152 all out (48.5 overs) (CD Whelan 3 for 22)
Worcestershire 58 all out (20.3 overs) (P Connell 5 for 19)
Ireland (2pts) won by 94 runs

Group A – Final Table

	P	W	L	T	NR	RR	Pts
Hampshire	8	5	2	0	1	0.33	11
Nottinghamshire	8	5	3	0	0	0.42	10
Worcestershire	8	4	3	0	1	0.28	9
Leicestershire	8	2	4	0	2	-0.64	6
Ireland	8	1	5	0	2	-0.74	4

Top two teams qualify for Quarter-finals

Group B

19 April
at Edgbaston
Warwickshire 271 for 9 (50 overs) (IR Bell 108, JO Troughton 53, Z de Bruyn 3 for 30, AC Thomas 3 for 65)
Somerset 272 for 2 (46 overs) (C Kieswetter 138*, Z de Bruyn 73*)
Somerset (2pts) won by 8 wickets

26 April
at Lord's
Middlesex 302 for 7 (50 overs) (BA Godleman 82,
PJ Hughes 74, JD Nel 3 for 62)
Scotland 140 all out (37.1 overs)
Middlesex (2pts) won by 162 runs

at Taunton
Somerset 291 for 3 (38 overs) (PD Trego 73*, Z de Bruyn 71*,
ME Trescothick 70, JC Hildreth 67)
Kent 181 all out (33.1 overs) (AC Thomas 3 for 38,
OAC Banks 3 for 40)
Somerset (2pts) won by 110 runs

3 May
at Southgate
Middlesex 133 all out (36.4 overs) (JC Tredwell 6 for 27)
Kent 137 for 4 (37.2 overs)
Kent (2pts) won by 6 wickets

at Edgbaston
Scotland 182 all out (48.3 overs) (CJ Borgas 59, GM Hamilton 51)
Warwickshire 183 for 3 (30.4 overs) (NM Carter 65, IR Bell 51*)
Warwickshire (2pts) won by 7 wickets

4 May
at Bath
Middlesex 65 all out (24.1 overs) (PD Trego 4 for 17,
BJ Phillips 3 for 23)
Somerset 66 for 2 (8.3 overs)
Somerset (2pts) won by 8 wickets

at Canterbury
Scotland 227 for 7 (50 overs) (GM Hamilton 75, CJ Borgas 65,
RH Joseph 3 for 55)
Kent 206 for 6 (42.2 overs) (JL Denly 97*)
*Kent (2pts) won by 4 wickets – DL Method: target 206 from
44 overs*

10 May
at Canterbury
Warwickshire 218 all out (49.2 overs) (JO Troughton 62,
IJL Trott 53, WD Parnell 3 for 27, RS Ferley 3 for 34)
Kent 219 for 6 (41.5 overs)
Kent (2pts) won by 4 wickets

11 May
at Canterbury
Middlesex 322 for 5 (50 overs) (EJG Morgan 161,
NRD Compton 131)
Kent 242 all out (45.4 overs) (JM Kemp 69, GO Jones 57,
CEW Silverwood 3 for 26)
Middlesex (2pts) won by 80 runs

at Taunton
Somerset 403 for 3 (50 overs) (JC Hildreth 151,
ME Trescothick 144, PD Trego 74*)
Scotland 252 for 9 (50 overs) (RR Watson 67, GM Hamilton 62,
NFI McCallum 50, PD Trego 3 for 43, AC Thomas 3 for 46)
Somerset (2pts) won by 151 runs

12 May
at Edgbaston
Middlesex 165 all out (47.3 overs) (EJG Morgan 62,
NM Carter 3 for 40)
Warwickshire 166 for 4 (35.4 overs) (IR Bell 60*,
NM Carter 56)
Warwickshire (2pts) won by 6 wickets

14 May
at Taunton
Somerset 135 for 2 (22 overs) (ME Trescothick 84*)
Warwickshire
Match abandoned (1pt each)

at Edinburgh
Middlesex 280 for 4 (50 overs) (SD Udal 79*, EJG Morgan 55)
Scotland 142 all out (34.3 overs) (SD Udal 3 for 32)
Middlesex (2pts) won by 138 runs

16 May
at Canterbury
Somerset 296 all out (50 overs) (JL Langer 77, Z de Bruyn 72,
ME Trescothick 56, SJ Cook 3 for 29, WD Parnell 3 for 43)
Kent 251 for 9 (50 overs) (M van Jaarsveld 132*,
PD Trego 4 for 56, AC Thomas 3 for 48)
Somerset (2pts) won by 45 runs

at Edinburgh
Warwickshire 242 for 6 (50 overs) (JO Troughton 77)
Scotland 187 all out (43.4 overs) (AG Botha 3 for 27)
*Warwickshire (2pts) won by 50 runs – DL Method: target 238
from 48 overs*

17 May
at Lord's
Middlesex 341 for 7 (50 overs) (PJ Hughes 119, OA Shah 82,
NJ Dexter 65*, PD Trego 4 for 65)
Somerset 293 for 5 (39.1 overs) (JL Langer 78*, Z de Bruyn 70,
ME Trescothick 62, ST Finn 3 for 67)
*Somerset (2pts) won by 5 wickets – DL Method: target 290 from
41 overs*

18 May
at Lord's
Warwickshire 276 for 7 (50 overs) (IJL Trott 120,
NM Carter 68)

Middlesex 278 for 6 (49.3 overs) (NJ Dexter 69*, OA Shah 63, PJ Hughes 57, AG Botha 3 for 47)
Middlesex (2pts) won by 4 wickets

at Edinburgh
Kent 65 for 4 (19.5 overs)
Scotland 80 for 1 (14.5 overs)
Scotland (2pts) won by 9 wickets – DL Method: target 77 from 18 overs

20 May
at Edinburgh
Somerset 220 for 8 (50 overs) (JH Stander 3 for 45)
Scotland 183 all out (46.2 overs) (CJ Borgas 78*, AC Thomas 4 for 22, Z de Bruyn 3 for 24)
Somerset (2pts) won by 37 runs

at Edgbaston
Kent 265 all out (49.2 overs) (JL Denly 115, JB Hockley 50, SA Piolet 3 for 53)
Warwickshire 241 for 6 (46.5 overs) (JO Troughton 67, SJ Cook 4 for 37)
Match tied (1pt each) – DL Method: target 242 from 46.5 overs

Group B – Final Table

	P	W	L	T	NR	RR	Pts
Somerset	8	7	0	0	1	2.00	15
Middlesex	8	4	4	0	0	0.14	8
Warwickshire	8	3	3	1	1	0.46	8
Kent	8	3	4	1	0	-0.40	7
Scotland	8	1	7	0	0	-1.78	2

Top two teams qualify for Quarter-finals

Mike Yardy's Sussex endured a slow start to their Friends Provident Trophy campaign, but then went up through the gears until running out of inspiration on the big day itself at Lord's.

Ironically, too, given that it was Gloucestershire who were overpowered at the semi-final stage, Sussex's journey to their 25 July showdown with South Coast rivals Hampshire began with a crushing defeat against the same opposition, at Bristol. Worse, the second group game up at Headingley against Yorkshire was also lost, by the smaller margin of 14 runs, and it is a measure of Sussex's improvement after that unencouraging beginning that they made their way to Lord's at all.

Mike Yardy, here in action with the ball, made a huge impact in his first season as Sussex captain.

The rot was stopped when Durham were beaten by eight wickets at Chester-le-Street, Ed Joyce scoring the first of three glittering hundreds that lit up Sussex's progress to their own second final in four seasons.

Then, back at Hove for four successive group games in mid-May, only a no-result in the return fixture against Gloucestershire interrupted a run of victories in which Surrey, Durham again and Yorkshire were beaten by the similar method of batting first, running up a sizeable score and restricting the opponent's reply.

It was a close-run thing against Surrey, for whom Scott Newman's 126-ball 130, with three sixes and ten fours, threatened to trump Murray Goodwin's earlier tour de force. Goodwin's 144 came off only 119 balls and featured two sixes and 16 fours, and Yardy's 59 and a quickfire 43 from 30 balls by Rory Hamilton-Brown ensured a challenging 313 for 7. Newman, however, was joined by Michael Brown in an opening stand worth 154 and it took all Sussex's resilience to survive that onslaught. In the end, 15 were needed off the final over, and five from the last ball, as Sussex squeezed home by two runs.

Joyce's 127 from 125 balls, on the following day, was ultimately enough to see off Durham, despite Phil Mustard's run-a-ball 92. James Kirtley recorded his competition-best figures, 6 for 50, as Durham's chase fell away. And, after Yorkshire were beaten by 60 runs, with Chris Nash picking up four wickets and Yasir Arafat 3 for 44, Sussex could afford a defeat at The Oval, in their final group game, as they had already qualified for the quarter-finals. In a match against Surrey reduced to 39 overs per side, Mark Ramprakash's 102 with five sixes and five fours proved too much to handle for a side missing several rested regulars.

Sussex were saving their best for the knockout stages, though, and brilliant batting from Goodwin, Joyce and skipper Yardy, whose cool unbeaten 57 took him only 43 balls, enabled them to overhaul Somerset's 285 for 8 in the quarter-final at Taunton. Kirtley had dismissed Marcus Trescothick with the very first ball of the match, but Craig Kieswetter struck 106 from 112 balls and put on 167 with Zander de Bruyn, who hit 96, to rally Somerset from 39 for 3.

Joyce was also the hero of the semi-final, at a packed Hove, and his 146 from 139 balls with three sixes and 13 fours – and an excellent 60 from Goodwin – enabled Sussex to reach a daunting 326 for 7 from their 50 overs. Gloucestershire, led by their captain Alex Gidman's brave 117-ball 116, fought hard to chase down the target, but Yardy's low-trajectory left-arm spinners brought him crucial wickets, and confirmed his side's place in the Lord's final.

Sadly for Yardy, his players, and the county's supporters, however, they performed nowhere near their best against a pumped-up Hampshire in what was – from Sussex's perspective – a bitterly disappointing and one-sided final.

Dominic Cork's new ball burst, plus the wasteful run out of Goodwin for 1, reduced Sussex to 43 for 4 after Yardy had chosen to bat, and when Wright was bowled by Chris Tremlett for seven to leave the scoreboard showing 77 for 5 it was left to the captain's brave 92 not out to engineer some damage limitation in the company of Dwayne Smith and Hamilton-Brown. Sussex's eventual total of 219 for 9 was never likely to be anywhere near enough, however, and that is how it proved as their South Coast rivals eased to a six-wicket win.

Group C

19 April
at the Riverside
Yorkshire 268 for 7 (50 overs) (JA Rudolph 73, GL Brophy 66*)
Durham 188 all out (41 overs) (DM Benkenstein 68, TT Bresnan 3 for 28, GJ Kruis 3 for 28)
Yorkshire (2pts) won by 80 runs

at Bristol
Sussex 227 all out (49.5 overs) (MH Yardy 58, MJ Prior 50, V Banerjee 3 for 47)
Gloucestershire 228 for 3 (46.2 overs) (CM Spearman 69*, CG Taylor 68*)
Gloucestershire (2pts) won by 7 wickets

26 April
at Headingley
Yorkshire 227 for 5 (50 overs) (MP Vaughan 82, GL Brophy 68*, RSC Martin-Jenkins 3 for 49)
Sussex 213 all out (48.4 overs) (TT Bresnan 4 for 35)
Yorkshire (2pts) won by 14 runs

at Bristol
Gloucestershire 268 for 9 (50 overs) (WTS Porterfield 74, CG Taylor 63, A Nel 3 for 39)
Surrey 140 all out (38.2 overs) (ID Saxelby 4 for 31)
Gloucestershire (2pts) won by 128 runs

3 May
at Headingley
Gloucestershire 269 all out (49 overs) (CM Spearman 92, Kadeer Ali 63, RM Pyrah 4 for 54)
Yorkshire 241 for 8 (50 overs) (JA Rudolph 118, J Lewis 3 for 46)
Gloucestershire (2pts) won by 28 runs

at the Riverside
Durham 266 for 7 (50 overs) (DM Benkenstein 77*, P Mustard 61)
Surrey 265 for 6 (50 overs) (MR Ramprakash 109*, SA Newman 70, ID Blackwell 3 for 43)
Durham (2pts) won by 1 run

4 May

at the Riverside

Durham 192 all out (48.2 overs) (WR Smith 65,
RJ Hamilton-Brown 3 for 37)
Sussex 193 for 2 (43.2 overs) (EC Joyce 103*)
Sussex (2pts) won by 8 wickets

at Headingley

Surrey 184 for 7 (47 overs) (MNW Spriegel 56*)
Yorkshire 104 all out (30.2 overs) (GD Elliott 4 for 14,
CP Schofield 3 for 16, JW Dernbach 3 for 23)
*Surrey (2pts) won by 63 runs – DL Method: target 168 from
33 overs*

10 May

at Bristol

Gloucestershire 301 for 8 (50 overs) (CG Taylor 71,
WTS Porterfield 68, HJH Marshall 56)
Durham 153 all out (40.3 overs) (AJ Ireland 3 for 12,
JEC Franklin 3 for 18)
Gloucestershire (2pts) won by 148 runs

at Hove

Sussex 313 for 7 (50 overs) (MW Goodwin 144, MH Yardy 59,
PT Collins 3 for 56)
Surrey 311 for 6 (50 overs) (SA Newman 130, MJ Brown 66)
Sussex (2pts) won by 2 runs

11 May

at Bristol

Yorkshire 217 for 9 (50 overs) (A McGrath 67, RM Pyrah 67,
J Lewis 4 for 43, JEC Franklin 3 for 38)
Gloucestershire 221 for 7 (49.2 overs) (SJ Adshead 56,
JEC Franklin 51*, DJ Wainwright 3 for 33, GJ Kruis 3 for 45)
Gloucestershire (2pts) won by 3 wickets

at Hove

Sussex 313 for 6 (50 overs) (EC Joyce 127, JS Gatting 50)
Durham 257 all out (46.5 overs) (P Mustard 92, RJ Kirtley 6 for 50)
Sussex (2pts) won by 56 runs

13 May

at The Oval

Surrey 306 for 6 (50 overs) (MR Ramprakash 121,
MNW Spriegel 64)
Gloucestershire 142 all out (33.3 overs)
Surrey (2pts) won by 164 runs

at Headingley

Durham 166 all out (49.3 overs) (RM Pyrah 3 for 23)
Yorkshire 167 for 8 (49.2 overs) (JJ Sayers 51,
ID Blackwell 3 for 26)
Yorkshire (2pts) won by 2 wickets

15 May

at Hove

Gloucestershire 306 for 9 (50 overs) (CM Spearman 67,
SJ Adshead 66*)
Sussex
Match abandoned (1pt each)

at The Oval

Durham 287 for 4 (50 overs) (WR Smith 77, KJ Coetzer 61,
ID Blackwell 57)
Surrey 227 all out (47.2 overs) (U Afzaal 58, SA Newman 53,
GR Breese 3 for 42)
Durham (2pts) won by 60 runs

18 May

at Hove

Sussex 269 for 7 (50 overs) (MH Yardy 68,
RM Pyrah 3 for 65)
Yorkshire 209 all out (47.3 overs) (MP Vaughan 66,
A McGrath 53, CD Nash 4 for 40,
Yasir Arafat 3 for 44)
Sussex (2pts) won by 60 runs

19 May

at The Oval

Surrey 241 for 7 (39 overs) (MR Ramprakash 102)
Sussex 162 all out (30 overs) (CP Schofield 5 for 32)
*Surrey (2pts) won by 79 runs – DL Method: target 242 from
39 overs*

20 May

at the Riverside

Gloucestershire 254 for 8 (50 overs) (SJ Adshead 87,
JEC Franklin 85, N Killeen 5 for 48)
Durham 255 for 6 (48.1 overs) (ID Blackwell 64, P Mustard 57,
V Banerjee 3 for 60)
Durham (2pts) won by 4 wickets

at The Oval

Surrey 329 for 8 (50 overs) (SA Newman 177, SJ Walters 85,
GJ Kruis 3 for 24, Naved-ul-Hasan 3 for 75)
Yorkshire 330 for 6 (49.4 overs) (A Lyth 83, MP Vaughan 74,
Naved-ul-Hasan 53*)
Yorkshire (2pts) won by 4 wickets

Group C – Final Table

	P	W	L	T	NR	RR	Pts
Gloucestershire	8	5	2	0	1	0.45	11
Sussex	8	4	3	0	1	1.52	9
Yorkshire	8	4	4	0	0	-0.15	8
Durham	8	3	5	0	0	-0.63	6
Surrey	8	3	5	0	0	0.30	6

Top two teams qualify for Quarter-finals

Group D

19 April
at Chelmsford
Northamptonshire 281 all out (50 overs) (SP Crook 72,
MH Wessels 57, N Boje 56)
Essex 282 for 3 (48.2 overs) (V Chopra 76,
MJ Walker 69*, ML Pettini 57)
Essex (2pts) won by 7 wickets

at Old Trafford
Lancashire 241 for 6 (50 overs) (TC Smith 66,
F du Plessis 66, DS Harrison 3 for 44)
Glamorgan 161 all out (40.2 overs) (MA Wallace 60,
SI Mahmood 3 for 17, KW Hogg 3 for 21)
Lancashire (2pts) won by 80 runs

26 April
at Northampton
Northamptonshire 240 all out (47.3 overs)
(AJ Hall 81, SI Mahmood 3 for 38, TC Smith 3 for 52)
Lancashire 241 for 4 (44.5 overs)
(PJ Horton 100)
Lancashire (2pts) won by 6 wickets

at Derby
Glamorgan 205 for 9 (50 overs) (JWM Dalrymple 75*,
TD Groenewald 3 for 33)
Derbyshire 206 for 6 (46 overs) (DJ Redfern 53)
Derbyshire (2pts) won by 4 wickets

3 May
at Old Trafford
Derbyshire 240 for 6 (50 overs) (WW Hinds 95,
SD Stubbings 50)
Lancashire 241 for 2 (46.3 overs) (PJ Horton 111*,
MJ Chilton 101*)
Lancashire (2pts) won by 8 wickets

at Chelmsford
Essex 297 for 6 (50 overs) (V Chopra 99,
GW Flower 54)
Glamorgan 299 for 2 (46.1 overs) (GP Rees 123*,
MJ Cosgrove 72, TL Maynard 59*)
Glamorgan (2pts) won by 8 wickets

4 May
at Derby
Derbyshire 192 for 7 (43.1 overs)
(WW Hinds 81, GR Napier 3 for 35)
Essex 194 for 4 (40.1 overs)
(V Chopra 69)
Essex (2pts) won by 6 wickets

at Northampton
Northamptonshire 200 for 9 (39 overs) (DA Cosker 3 for 26,
DS Harrison 3 for 31)
Glamorgan 165 for 8 (39 overs) (DA Cosker 50*,
AJ Hall 4 for 14)
Northamptonshire (2pts) won by 35 runs

10 May
at Chelmsford
Lancashire 157 all out (44.4 overs) (DD Masters 3 for 19)
Essex 160 for 4 (44.1 overs) (V Chopra 72)
Essex (2pts) won by 6 wickets

at Northampton
Derbyshire 286 for 9 (50 overs) (SG Law 95, WW Hinds 57,
LM Daggett 4 for 51)
Northamptonshire 265 all out (49.2 overs)
(MAG Nelson 74)
Derbyshire (2pts) won by 21 runs

12 May
at Cardiff
Glamorgan 124 all out (46.2 overs) (Danish Kaneria 4 for 16,
DD Masters 3 for 21)
Essex 127 for 3 (25.5 overs)
Essex (2pts) won by 7 wickets

at Old Trafford
Northamptonshire 211 for 9 (50 overs) (N Boje 50)
Lancashire 213 for 4 (47.3 overs) (AG Prince 78)
Lancashire (2pts) won by 6 wickets

13 May
at Derby
Lancashire 296 for 8 (50 overs) (F du Plessis 112, TC Smith 59,
GM Smith 4 for 53)
Derbyshire 175 all out (38.4 overs) (CJL Rogers 68,
G Keedy 4 for 43)
*Lancashire (2pts) won by 114 runs – DL Method: target 290 from
48 overs*

15 May
at Cardiff
Glamorgan 172 for 8 (31 overs) (MJ Cosgrove 68,
OJ Newby 4 for 41)
Lancashire 208 for 2 (28 overs) (TC Smith 87*,
MJ Chilton 58*)
*Lancashire (2pts) won by 8 wickets – DL Method: target 208
from 31 overs*

at Derby
Derbyshire v. **Northamptonshire**
Match abandoned (1pt each)

Michael Lumb, of Hampshire, was one of the standout players in the 2009 Friends Provident Trophy.

17 May
at Northampton
Northamptonshire 124 for 4 (18 overs) (RA White 51, CJC Wright 3 for 22)
Essex
Match abandoned (1pt each)

18 May
at Chelmsford
Essex 192 all out (44.3 overs) (JS Foster 71, GM Smith 3 for 50)
Derbyshire 195 for 7 (46.2 overs) (SG Law 62*, Danish Kaneria 5 for 32)
Derbyshire (2pts) won by 3 wickets

19 May
At Swansea
Glamorgan v. **Northamptonshire**
Match abandoned (1pt each)

20 May
at Old Trafford
Lancashire 214 for 7 (50 overs) (F du Plessis 51)
Essex 207 for 5 (45.3 overs) (AN Cook 65, V Chopra 65)
Essex (2pts) won by 5 wickets – DL Method: target 207 from 46 overs

at Cardiff
Derbyshire 211 all out (49.1 overs) (CJL Rogers 59)
Glamorgan 212 for 5 (47.2 overs) (JWM Dalrymple 78*, BJ Wright 65)
Glamorgan (2pts) won by 5 wickets

Group D – Final Table

	P	W	L	T	NR	RR	Pts
Lancashire	8	6	2	0	0	0.63	12
Essex	8	5	2	0	1	0.41	11
Derbyshire	8	3	4	0	1	-0.29	7
Glamorgan	8	2	5	0	1	-0.77	5
Northamptonshire	8	1	4	0	3	-0.16	5

Top two teams qualify for Quarter-finals

Quarter-finals

23 May
at Old Trafford
Lancashire 262 for 6 (50 overs) (F du Plessis 113*)
Essex 195 all out (44 overs) (G Keedy 4 for 45)
Lancashire won by 67 runs

at the Rose Bowl
Hampshire 310 for 4 (50 overs) (MJ Lumb 100, JHK Adams 76, LA Dawson 51*)
Middlesex 266 all out (49.2 overs) (NJ Dexter 79, BV Taylor 3 for 44)
Hampshire won by 44 runs

at Taunton
Somerset 285 for 8 (50 overs) (C Kieswetter 106, Z de Bruyn 96, Yasir Arafat 3 for 52)
Sussex 288 for 4 (49.1 overs) (MW Goodwin 93, EC Joyce 74, MH Yardy 57*)
Sussex won by 6 wickets

16 June
at Bristol
Nottinghamshire 189 all out (44.2 overs) (CMW Read 57, J Lewis 4 for 34, SP Kirby 3 for 33)
Gloucestershire 190 for 4 (37.3 overs) (CM Spearman 50*)
Gloucestershire won by 6 wickets

Semi-finals

5 July
at Hove
Sussex 326 for 7 (50 overs) (EC Joyce 146,
MW Goodwin 60)
Gloucestershire 292 all out (47.4 overs)
(APR Gidman 116, HJH Marshall 57, MH Yardy 4 for 54)
Sussex won by 34 runs

at Old Trafford
Hampshire 271 all out (48.4 overs) (JHK Adams 78,
MJ Lumb 76, G Chapple 3 for 46, G Keedy 3 for 49,
SI Mahmood 3 for 56)
Lancashire 207 all out (45.4 overs) (VVS Laxman 54,
Imran Tahir 3 for 38)
Hampshire won by 64 runs

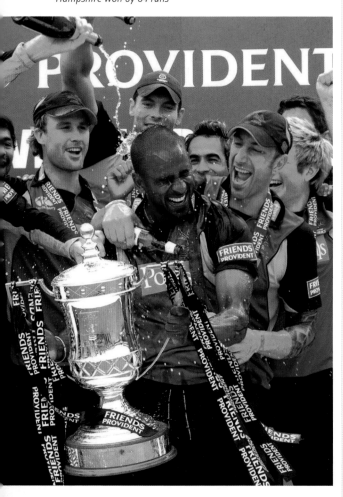

Hampshire captain Dimitri Mascarenhas is showered with champagne as he clutches the Friends Provident Trophy at the after-match presentation ceremony.

FINAL – HAMPSHIRE v. SUSSEX
25 July 2009 at Lord's

SUSSEX

EC Joyce	b Cork	15
CD Nash	lbw b Cork	21
*MJ Prior	c Pothas b Cork	0
MW Goodwin	run out	1
MH Yardy (capt)	not out	92
LJ Wright	b Tremlett	7
DR Smith	c Carberry b Imran Tahir	20
RJ Hamilton-Brown	c Mascarenhas b Imran Tahir	32
Yasir Arafat	c Pothas b Mascarenhas	9
RSC Martin-Jenkins	c Benham b Cork	4
RJ Kirtley	not out	3
Extras	lb 9, w 4, nb 2	15
	(9 wkts 50 overs)	**219**

	O	M	R	W
Cork	10	1	41	4
Mascarenhas	9	0	27	1
Imran Tahir	10	0	50	2
Tremlett	10	0	40	1
Ervine	6	0	31	0
Dawson	5	0	21	0

Fall of Wickets
1-30, 2-30, 3-39, 4-43, 5-77, 6-111, 7-171, 8-186, 9-203

HAMPSHIRE

MJ Lumb	c Prior b Wright	38
JHK Adams	lbw b Wright	55
MA Carberry	c & b Yasir Arafat	30
SM Ervine	c Nash b Wright	15
CC Benham	not out	37
*N Pothas	not out	35
LA Dawson		
AD Mascarenhas (capt)		
DG Cork		
CT Tremlett		
Imran Tahir		
Extras	lb 2, w 5, nb 4	11
	(4 wkts 40.3 overs)	**221**

	O	M	R	W
Kirtley	5	0	26	0
Yasir Arafat	10	0	54	1
Martin-Jenkins	4	0	21	0
Wright	9	1	50	3
Nash	3	0	15	0
Hamilton-Brown	3.3	0	27	0
Yardy	6	1	26	0

Fall of Wickets
1-93, 2-110, 3-137, 4-154

Umpires: NJ Llong & NA Mallender
Toss: Sussex
Man of the Match: DG Cork

Hampshire won by 6 wickets

COUNTY REVIEW *South East*

MARK PENNELL, who covers county cricket in the South East for local and national media, looks at the contrasting fortunes of Kent, Essex, Middlesex and Surrey...

For county supporters across the Home Counties it was either a matter for champagne celebrations or a desire to drown the sorrows with flat beer come the season's end. While Essex and Kent toasted LV County Championship promotion, so neighbours Middlesex and Surrey suffered miserably, with both only narrowly avoiding the wooden spoon.

Before a ball had been bowled, Surrey's new cricket manager Chris Adams told supporters that a side in transition would struggle to be competitive. How right he was. Under three different captains – Mark Butcher, Michael Brown and Stewart Walters – the Brown Caps had to wait until 14 June for their first Championship win, against Northamptonshire at Wantage Road. Sadly it also proved to be their last.

Surrey drew 11 of their second division starts, including all six games at The Oval, where taking 20 opposition wickets proved nigh-on impossible for a rookie attack shorn for much of the time of the injured Andre Nel and lacking the wiles of Harbhajan Singh, who had been expected to

join as overseas player during the second half of the season, but didn't due to international commitments.

Again Mark Ramprakash excelled with the bat, scoring 1,350 Championship runs at an average of 90 (the best in the country), but only Usman Afzaal joined him in the 1,000-run club. Adams cleared out his perceived dead wood by axing Jimmy Ormond and loaning out Scott Newman and James Benning, only to lose veteran skipper Butcher to injury and ultimately retirement.

Surrey wins were just as scarce in the one-day format. Two successes in both the NatWest Pro40 and Twenty20 Cup were barely eclipsed by three victories in the Friends Provident Trophy.

There were glimpses of quality from bowling all-rounders Stuart Meaker, Chris Jordan and Jade Dernbach, who also topped the four-day wicket-taking tally with 37 victims, albeit for almost 39 runs each.

The signings of Steven Davies and Gareth Batty from Worcestershire marked the start of Adams' team-rebuilding plans, but many more new faces need to follow if Surrey are to strut once more in 2010.

At the fading grandeur of the St Lawrence Ground in Canterbury, Kent accomplished their main task for 2009 by winning Championship promotion at their first attempt. Though a 25-point wining margin over second-placed Essex suggests a runaway title success, Rob Key's side still discovered ways of making life difficult. Most of their eight wins saw Kent rally from poor starts and come from behind during a campaign where consistency in both form and fitness once again proved irritatingly elusive.

Four batsmen topped 1,000 first-class runs for the season: Key and Darren Stevens did so with late a flurry, both having suffered disappointing starts. Geraint Jones and Martin van Jaarsveld proved the class acts and leading scorers with 1,475 and 1,291 runs respectively – both career-best tallies. Whether Jones can sustain such form when batting at No. 3 in Division One will be a key to Kent's survival in 2010.

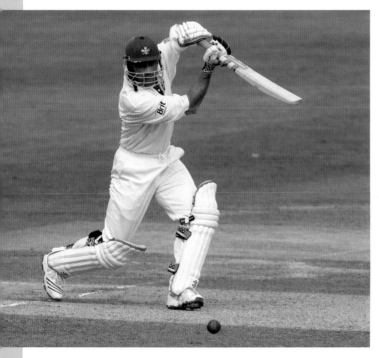

Mark Ramprakash was in peerless form again in 2009, his 1,350 runs at 90 in the County Championship provoking calls for a Test return a fortnight before his 40th birthday.

James Tredwell, the Kent off spinner, enjoyed the best season of his career.

Off spinner James Tredwell was crowned bowler of the season for his 69 wickets at an average of 26.63, comfortably his top season's return for Kent. Simon Cook was easily the most consistent seam bowler on show, meanwhile. A willing workhorse with a shrewd mind, he took 34 Championship wickets costing 30 runs apiece. Amjad Khan finished with 36 at 31.83, but too often struggled for consistent lines, particularly in the limited-overs format.

Kent qualified for Twenty20 Cup finals day for a third straight season, but the Spitfires then misfired woefully to lose their semi-final against Somerset. In addition, they generally underachieved in the other two one-day competitions. A young, experimental side did wonders to win four NatWest Pro40 Division Two games, however, but went on to lose their last three to finish third, while a decent start with three Friends Provident Trophy victories tailed off into a fourth-placed finish.

Without their limited overs' guru Graham Ford, who has returned to his coaching role with the Natal Dolphins, Kent will do well to compete on a level playing field in 2010.

Close-season recruitment on a shoestring budget will be the first of many tests facing new head coach Paul Farbrace.

Mark Pettini's Essex left it until the 11th hour to seal their Championship elevation courtesy of a successful last-day run chase against Derbyshire inspired by Ryan ten Doeschate's unbeaten 108 from 59 balls.

Next-to-bottom by mid-June, Essex rallied sublimely to win six and draw seven in their rise to the first division. Tireless wrist-spinner Danish Kaneria did most to promote the cause with 75 wickets, including a hat-trick at Derby, at a meagre average of 23.69, while South Africa's Hashim Amla harvested 410 runs at an average of 102.50 during his brief three-match, mid-season visit. Winter recruit Matthew Walker, an ever-present in the four-day side, just edged past 1,000 first-class runs, while James Foster made it into the 900s as did ten Doeschate, but at a much superior average of almost 46.

Promotion would surely have been secured sooner had the England management allowed Ravi Bopara to make more than his two Championship appearances. Even so, the all-rounder hit a season's best double-hundred and averaged 134.50. Bopara's absence was more keenly felt in one-day cricket where the Eagles struggled to spread their wings. After qualifying as runners-up in the Friends Provident Trophy with five victories, they crashed out by 65 runs to Lancashire in a one-sided Old Trafford quarter-final and never quite rediscovered their self-belief.

They finished fourth in a tough Twenty20 Cup group with a 50 per cent win ratio and notched five wins from eight starts to come fourth in the NatWest Pro40 Division One and end the summer with no silverware to show for their undoubted hard work.

Thirty-odd miles along the A12 in NW8, early season enthusiasm quickly waned at Lord's as Middlesex, despite a glut of runs from overseas prodigy Phillip Hughes, slumped to their worst ever Championship finish. The Australian left-hander plundered three centuries in each of his three Championship appearances, amassing 574 runs at an average of 143.50. Fortunately for England, it was form Hughes failed to transfer to the Ashes series.

Backroom manoeuvres, meanwhile, left coach Toby Radford in an untenable position yet things failed to improve after his mid-season departure. At least an inexperienced Middlesex batting order dug in to secure two wins that helped them to avoid taking the Championship wooden spoon for the first time in club history.

Qualification from their Friends Provident Trophy group as runners-up hinted at shoots of recovery, only for Shaun Udal's side to suffer quarter-final defeat to his former club Hampshire, at the Rose Bowl. The defence of their Twenty20 Cup title fell at the first hurdle, with Middlesex recording only two wins in their ten qualifiers, but at least the Panthers picked up a £25,000 end-of-season bonus for finishing second in NatWest Pro40 Division Two.

Incredibly, Tim Murtagh shook off a serious, mid-season leg injury to top the Championship bowling with 60 scalps, ably supported by the slippery Steve Finn who, with 53 wickets, should now feature on the radar of England's selectors as 'one to watch'. Indian spinner Murali Kartik's return of 33 wickets disappointed, as did his decision to join Somerset, leaving Middlesex with a major gap to plug in time for next summer.

Above Tim Murtagh, of Middlesex, was one of the season's most consistent performers with the ball.

Below Mark Pettini, the Essex captain, could celebrate promotion to the first division after a thrilling final-day win at Derby.

TWENTY20 CUP

by Mark Baldwin

Mike Yardy underlined his emergence as one of the best new captains on the county circuit by leading Sussex to Twenty20 Cup triumph at Edgbaston on 15 August.

Sussex were unquestionably the best limited-overs side in the county game in 2009, also reaching the final of the Friends Provident Trophy – where they were beaten by Hampshire – and then being crowned NatWest Pro40 champions, for the second year running, on the very last day of the season.

But it was their Twenty20 Cup finals day wins against Northamptonshire, in the semi-final, and then the emphatic 63-run victory against Somerset in the final itself, which gave Yardy the chance to lift his first silverware in his first season as the successor to Chris Adams, the most successful captain in Sussex's history.

'We were so focused, and we wanted to win the final,' said Yardy. 'I don't think the qualification for the Champions League tournament in India really mattered to the players. We genuinely didn't feel it would be enough just to qualify for the Champions League by reaching the final against Somerset.'

Dwayne Smith, the former West Indies all-rounder, was the star of Sussex's charge to 172 for 7 from their 20 overs in the final, hitting three sixes and seven fours in a violent 26-ball 59, and then James Kirtley's dismissal of Marcus Trescothick fatally undermined Somerset's chase.

Trescothick, who had almost single-handedly destroyed Kent in the other semi-final with 56 off just 32 balls with two sixes and eight fours, had reached 33 from only 15 balls against Sussex when Kirtley had him caught from a skied swipe. 'It was great to get Trescothick out,' said Kirtley. 'We talked to the Sky Sports commentators about what our options were against him and I decided to take the pace off the ball and thankfully it worked.'

Sussex coach Mark Robinson spoke afterwards about his pride in the overall performance on the day of Yardy and his team. He said, 'That was as good as it gets. I knew in the warm-ups that they were ready and so focused. Dwayne Smith gave us the impetus in the

final and we continued it when we bowled. It was an outstanding team performance – absolutely fantastic.'

The big-hitting Barbadian Smith added, 'I'm really pleased to have batted like that on such a big occasion. It was a shame to get out when I did but I was so pumped up that I was trying to hit the ball too hard! We played superbly as a team though – it was outstanding.'

However, Smith was only equal fourth in the list of Twenty20 Cup six-hitters in 2009, with 12. Above him

Dwayne Smith's powerful hitting was a big factor in Sussex's Twenty20 Cup success.

were Jim Allenby, who struck 20 sixes for Leicestershire before his mid-season move to Glamorgan, Darren Stevens of Kent with 15 and Hampshire's Michael Lumb, with 13.

Lumb, who scored 442, and Allenby, with 432, were also second and third respectively on the run-scorers' list, although way out in front with 525 from 11 innings at an average of 65.62, with five half-centuries, was Warwickshire's Jonathan Trott – the man who went on to score an Ashes century on his Test debut at The Oval in late August.

In all there were four centuries: by Lumb (124 not out from 69 balls, with 14 fours and four sixes, against Essex at the Rose Bowl), Allenby (110 from 58 balls, with seven fours and eight sixes, against Nottinghamshire at Grace Road), Alastair Cook and Vikram Solanki.

Cook's unbeaten 100, for Essex against Surrey at The Oval, took him just 57 balls and with 11 fours and four sixes the 24-year-old England Test opener showed that he might yet develop his game to the extent that he would be a one-day certainty for his country as much as an automatic choice in the five-day arena. Solanki's 48-ball 100, with 14 fours and two sixes, helped his Worcestershire side to the highest total in the competition in 2009, an intimidating 222 for 4 against Glamorgan at New Road on 24 June. It was one of six 20-over totals above 200.

Perhaps the most violent Twenty20 Cup innings of the season, though, came from Andrew Flintoff. Playing for Lancashire as part of his bid to regain full fitness ahead of the Ashes, against Derbyshire at Derby on 25 June, he struck 93 from only 41 balls, hitting nine fours and six sixes.

Alfonso Thomas, of Somerset, was the competition's leading wicket-taker, with 18, and of bowlers who took ten or more wickets, the most economical were Northamptonshire youngster David Willey (ten wickets at an economy rate of 5.13 runs per over), Yardy (13 at 5.38), Rana Naved of Yorkshire (11 at 5.85) and Nicky Boje, the Northants captain, with 12 wickets at 5.88.

As ever in 20-over cricket, there were numerous thrilling finishes and crowd numbers – especially in the second half of the group stage when the weather was warmer – were again high. The competition began in late May, much earlier than usual so as not to clash with the ICC World Twenty20 at the beginning on June, and crowds were, unsurprisingly, significantly smaller. Overall, however, the Twenty20 Cup maintained its huge popularity with the paying public. Surrey, for instance, attracted a total of around 40,000 spectators for the games against Kent, Essex and Middlesex in late June, despite the fact that they were all played in the space of four days.

One of those matches, indeed, featured one of the exciting finishes which makes Twenty20 so appealing to young and old alike, with Justin Kemp running out Jade Dernbach, the Surrey No. 11, from the fourth ball of the final over to clinch victory for Kent by a single run. A month earlier, Surrey had themselves pipped Hampshire by one run at The Oval.

There were other highlights too. On the very first day of competition Durham had squeezed past Nottinghamshire by one wicket in a remarkable finish at Trent Bridge. With scores level at the start of the last over, bowled by Mark Ealham, Durham had looked in danger of messing up spectacularly as Gordon Muchall was bowled by the wily Notts veteran and then Graham Onions run out desperately attempting the winning run.

Finally, from the last ball of the match, Mitchell Claydon managed to hit the ball to the mid-wicket boundary and Notts were denied what would have been a barely-believable tie.

Yet the strangest outcome to any match in the 2009 Twenty20 Cup came in the quarter-finals. Kent, Sussex and Northants had overcome, respectively, Durham, Warwickshire and Hampshire by batting first and then defending strongly in the field, but at Old Trafford there was just frustration as neither Lancashire nor Somerset could get out into the middle.

The England and Wales Cricket Board even extended the amount of reserve time available to a second day, in the hope that the Manchester rain would relent, but after three rain-sodden days it was decided that a bowl-out in the indoor school was the only answer, albeit a highly unsatisfactory one.

Lancashire, having practised, decided to overlook their specialist bowlers and go with the part-timers who had impressed the most at hitting a set of unguarded stumps. In the event, though, only Steven Cheetham could hit when it really mattered, and Somerset went through to finals day by a 5-1 margin.

North Division

25 May
at Trent Bridge
Nottinghamshire 163 for 6 (20 overs) (WI Jefferson 75, N Killeen 3 for 21)
Durham 167 for 9 (20 overs) (ID Blackwell 59, DM Benkenstein 53, DJ Pattinson 3 for 34)
Durham (2pts) won by 1 wicket

at Headingley
Leicestershire 148 for 3 (20 overs) (HD Ackerman 66*)
Yorkshire 149 for 7 (19.5 overs)
Yorkshire (2pts) won by 3 wickets

26 May
at Old Trafford
Yorkshire 105 for 8 (20 overs) (SD Parry 3 for 20)
Lancashire 107 for 4 (15.3 overs)
Lancashire (2pts) won by 6 wickets

at the Riverside
Derbyshire 175 for 6 (20 overs) (CJL Rogers 50, GT Park 50)
Durham 116 (15.3 overs) (T Lungley 3 for 16)
Derbyshire (2pts) won by 59 runs

28 May
at Old Trafford
Lancashire 151 for 6 (20 overs)
Nottinghamshire 140 for 7 (20 overs) (CMW Read 58*,
TC Smith 3 for 20)
Lancashire (2pts) won by 11 runs

at Grace Road
Leicestershire 127 for 9 (20 overs) (T Lungley 5 for 27)
Derbyshire 129 for 2 (19 overs) (CJL Rogers 58)
Derbyshire (2pts) won by 8 wickets

29 May
at the Riverside
Durham 144 for 8 (20 overs) (ACF Wyatt 3 for 14)
Leicestershire 148 for 3 (20 overs) (J Allenby 53,
PA Nixon 53*)
Leicestershire (2pts) won by 7 wickets

at Headingley
Yorkshire 111 for 8 (20 overs)
Lancashire 112 for 5 (19.1 overs)
Lancashire (2pts) won by 5 wickets

at Derby
Derbyshire 158 for 5 (20 overs) (WW Hinds 66, GM Smith 52)
Nottinghamshire 159 for 2 (15.1 overs) (GP Swann 90*)
Nottinghamshire (2pts) won by 8 wickets

31 May
at Chesterfield
Derbyshire 131 for 6 (20 overs)
Yorkshire 134 for 2 (16.1 overs) (AW Gale 79*)
Yorkshire (2pts) won by 8 wickets

at Grace Road
Leicestershire 147 for 3 (20 overs) (J Allenby 71*)
Lancashire 151 for 3 (16.3 overs) (F du Plessis 78*)
Lancashire (2pts) won by 7 wickets

at the Riverside
Durham 177 for 4 (20 overs) (MJ Di Venuto 55)

Nottinghamshire 169 all out (19.4 overs)
(ME Claydon 5 for 26)
Durham (2pts) won by 8 runs

2 June
at Old Trafford
Lancashire 165 for 7 (20 overs) (GT Park 3 for 23)
Derbyshire 127 for 9 (20 overs) (SI Mahmood 4 for 29)
Lancashire (2pts) won by 38 runs

at Headingley
Durham 116 for 8 (20 overs)
Yorkshire 117 for 8 (20 overs)
Yorkshire (2pts) won by 2 wickets

3 June
at Grace Road
Leicestershire 205 for 2 (20 overs) (J Allenby 110)
Nottinghamshire 135 all out (18.3 overs) (HF Gurney 3 for 21,
J Allenby 3 for 25, WA White 3 for 27)
Leicestershire (2pts) won by 70 runs

4 June
at Headingley
Nottinghamshire 155 for 6 (20 overs) (AC Voges 82*,
Naved-ul-Hasan 4 for 23)
Yorkshire 156 for 2 (18 overs) (AW Gale 91)
Yorkshire (2pts) won by 8 wickets

at Old Trafford
Durham 123 for 6 (20 overs) (GJ Muchall 50*)
Lancashire 124 for 4 (19.1 overs) (TC Smith 57*)
Lancashire (2pts) won by 6 wickets

at Derby
Leicestershire 144 for 6 (20 overs) (GT Park 3 for 29)
Derbyshire 130 for 5 (20 overs)
Leicestershire (2pts) won by 14 runs

22 June
at Liverpool
Leicestershire 146 for 5 (20 overs) (J Allenby 69)
Lancashire 138 (19.5 overs) (IE O'Brien 5 for 23)
Leicestershire (2pts) won by 8 runs

at Trent Bridge
Nottinghamshire 165 for 4 (20 overs) (AD Brown 66)
Yorkshire 154 for 8 (20 overs) (AW Gale 76)
Nottinghamshire (2pts) won by 11 runs

23 June
at Derby
Derbyshire 153 for 6 (20 overs) (SG Law 59)

Durham 154 for 4 (18 overs) (P Mustard 52, DA Warner 50)
Durham (2pts) won by 6 wickets

24 June
at Trent Bridge
Leicestershire 123 for 7 (20 overs) (RJ Sidebottom 3 for 16)
Nottinghamshire 124 for 1 (14.3 overs) (AD Brown 72)
Nottinghamshire (2pts) won by 9 wickets

at the Riverside
Durham 131 for 7 (20 overs) (TT Bresnan 3 for 26)
Yorkshire 90 for 9 (20 overs) (BW Harmison 3 for 20)
Durham (2pts) won by 41 runs

25 June
at Derby
Lancashire 220 for 5 (20 overs) (A Flintoff 93, VVS Laxman 63)
Derbyshire 164 for 7 (20 overs) (GM Smith 56, CJL Rogers 52)
Lancashire (2pts) won by 56 runs

26 June
at the Riverside
Durham v. **Lancashire**
Match abandoned (1pt each)

at Trent Bridge
Derbyshire 165 for 6 (20 overs) (GG Wagg 62,
MA Ealham 3 for 20)
Nottinghamshire 166 for 2 (16.4 overs) (AD Brown 65)
Nottinghamshire (2pts) won by 8 wickets

at Grace Road
Leicestershire 164 for 6 (20 overs)
Yorkshire 153 for 6 (20 overs) (JA Rudolph 61)
Leicestershire (2pts) won by 11 runs

28 June
at Grace Road
Leicestershire 133 for 8 (20 overs) (HH Dippenaar 63,
ME Claydon 3 for 14, BW Harmison 3 for 28)
Durham 137 for 4 (16.2 overs) (CW Henderson 3 for 32)
Durham (2pts) won by 6 wickets

at Trent Bridge
Nottinghamshire 173 for 7 (20 overs) (DJ Hussey 55)
Lancashire 175 for 1 (18 overs) (SJ Croft 83*, VVS Laxman 78*)
Lancashire (2pts) won by 9 wickets

at Headingley
Derbyshire 164 for 5 (20 overs)
Yorkshire 127 for 9 (19.5 overs) (J Needham 4 for 21)
Derbyshire (2pts) won by 37 runs

North Division – Final Table

	P	W	L	T	NR	RR	Pts
Lancashire	10	8	1	0	1	1.112	17
Durham	10	5	5	0	1	0.16	11
Leicestershire	10	5	5	0	0	-0.04	10
Nottinghamshire	10	4	6	0	0	-0.01	8
Yorkshire	10	4	6	0	0	-0.48	8
Derbyshire	10	3	7	0	0	-0.61	6

Top two teams qualify for Quarter-finals

Midlands/Wales/West Division

25 May
at Northampton
Northamptonshire 176 for 6 (20 overs)
Warwickshire 159 for 8 (20 overs) (JO Troughton 53,
IJ Harvey 4 for 18)
Northamptonshire (2pts) won by 17 runs

at New Road
Worcestershire 145 for 7 (20 overs) (SP Kirby 3 for 41)
Gloucestershire 122 all out (17.4 overs) (ID Fisher 3 for 16)
Worcestershire (2pts) won by 23 runs

Andrew Flintoff, in a rare outing for Lancashire, scored a brutal 93
against Derbyshire during his side's 56-run victory at Derby.

at Cardiff
Somerset 113 for 6 (20 overs) (Z de Bruyn 70*)
Glamorgan 112 for 9 (20 overs) (MTC Waller 3 for 17)
Somerset (2pts) won by 1 run

27 May
at Taunton
Warwickshire 187 for 5 (20 overs) (JO Troughton 50)
Somerset 190 for 5 (19.4 overs) (Z de Bruyn 72)
Somerset (2pts) won by 5 wickets

at Cardiff
Glamorgan 166 for 6 (20 overs) (MJ Cosgrove 52)
Gloucestershire 127 all out (19 overs) (RE Watkins 5 for 16)
Glamorgan (2pts) won by 39 runs

29 May
at Edgbaston
Worcestershire 148 for 8 (20 overs) (SM Davies 73,
KHD Barker 4 for 19)
Warwickshire 149 for 3 (18.2 overs) (JO Troughton 58,
IJL Trott 53*)
Warwickshire (2pts) won by 7 wickets

at Bristol
Gloucestershire 162 for 8 (20 overs) (CM Spearman 51,
AC Thomas 3 for 31)
Somerset 141 for 5 (20 overs)
Gloucestershire (2pts) won by 21 runs

at Northampton
Northamptonshire 195 for 3 (20 overs) (IJ Harvey 64,
MH Wessels 55*)
Glamorgan 155 for 9 (20 overs) (JJ van der Wath 3 for 23,
IJ Harvey 3 for 24)
Northamptonshire (2pts) won by 40 runs

30 May
at Cardiff
Glamorgan 129 for 8 (20 overs) (JWM Dalrymple 50,
NM Carter 3 for 16)
Warwickshire 133 for 4 (19.1 overs) (IJL Trott 55)
Warwickshire (2pts) won by 6 wickets

at New Road
Worcestershire 140 for 5 (20 overs) (SC Moore 62*,
DJ Willey 3 for 9)
Northamptonshire 142 for 4 (19 overs)
Northamptonshire (2pts) won by 6 wickets

1 June
at Taunton
Glamorgan 128 for 7 (20 overs) (JWM Dalrymple 56)

Somerset 132 for 0 (14.4 overs) (ME Trescothick 69*,
C Kieswetter 57*)
Somerset (2pts) won by 10 wickets

at Edgbaston
Northamptonshire 155 for 7 (20 overs) (RA White 59)
Warwickshire 131 for 6 (20 overs)
Northamptonshire (2pts) won by 24 runs

at Bristol
Worcestershire 188 for 5 (20 overs) (VS Solanki 51, SM Davies 50)
Gloucestershire 175 for 8 (20 overs) (APR Gidman 64)
Worcestershire (2pts) won by 13 runs

4 June
at Cardiff
Worcestershire 164 for 6 (20 overs)
Glamorgan 135 all out (20 overs) (GM Andrew 3 for 19)
Worcestershire (2pts) won by 29 runs

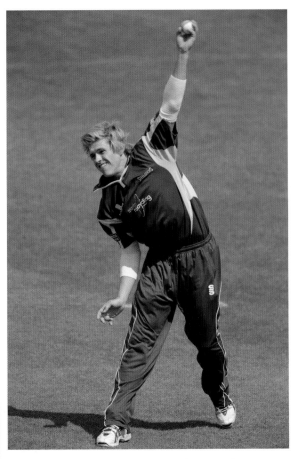

David Willey, the young Northamptonshire all-rounder, emerged as the most economical bowler in the 2009 Twenty20 Cup.

at Edgbaston
Gloucestershire 135 for 7 (20 overs)
Warwickshire 139 for 6 (19 overs)
Warwickshire (2pts) won by 4 wickets

at Northampton
Somerset 163 for 3 (20 overs) (Z de Bruyn 83*)
Northamptonshire 133 for 9 (20 overs) (CM Willoughby 4 for 29)
Somerset (2pts) won by 30 runs

22 June
at Bristol
Gloucestershire 141 all out (19.4 overs) (JS Patel 3 for 15,
R Clarke 3 for 20, AG Botha 3 for 31)
Warwickshire 144 for 3 (16.1 overs) (IJL Trott 73*)
Warwickshire (2pts) won by 7 wickets

23 June
at Taunton
Worcestershire 176 for 8 (20 overs)
Somerset 177 for 3 (19 overs)
Somerset (2pts) won by 7 wickets

at Edgbaston
Glamorgan 148 for 7 (20 overs) (JWM Dalrymple 63)
Warwickshire 149 for 6 (18.5 overs)
Warwickshire (2pts) won by 4 wickets

at Northampton
Northamptonshire 133 (20 overs) (GM Hussain 3 for 22)
Gloucestershire 134 for 8 (19.5 overs) (GP Hodnett 60, N Boje 3 for 23)
Gloucestershire (2pts) won by 2 wickets

24 June
at New Road
Worcestershire 222 for 4 (20 overs) (VS Solanki 100)
Glamorgan 121 for 6 (20 overs) (RDB Croft 52*)
Worcestershire (2pts) won by 101 runs

25 June
at Taunton
Northamptonshire 49 for 0 (5 overs)
Somerset
Match abandoned (1pt each)

26 June
at New Road
Worcestershire 162 for 6 (20 overs)
Warwickshire 166 for 3 (19.1 overs) (IJL Trott 86*)
Warwickshire (2pts) won by 7 wickets

at Taunton
Gloucestershire 173 all out (19.3 overs) (AC Thomas 3 for 31)

Somerset 175 for 7 (19 overs) (C Kieswetter 84)
Somerset (2pts) won by 3 wickets

at Cardiff
Northamptonshire 157 for 7 (20 overs) (MH Wessels 66*,
JAR Harris 4 for 23)
Glamorgan 137 for 9 (20 overs) (N Boje 3 for 14)
Northamptonshire (2pts) won by 20 runs

28 June
at Northampton
Worcestershire 109 for 9 (20 overs) (AJ Hall 4 for 19)
Northamptonshire 110 for 3 (18 overs) (SD Peters 61*)
Northamptonshire (2pts) won by 7 wickets

at Edgbaston
Warwickshire 193 for 6 (20 overs) (JO Troughton 62, R Clarke 51*)
Somerset 192 for 7 (20 overs) (JS Patel 3 for 23)
Warwickshire (2pts) won by 1 run

at Bristol
Gloucestershire 148 for 7 (20 overs) (DO Brown 56,
RE Watkins 3 for 23)
Glamorgan 151 for 4 (18.3 overs) (BJ Wright 55*)
Glamorgan (2pts) won by 6 wickets

Midlands/Wales/West Division – Final Table

	P	W	L	T	NR	RR	Pts
Northamptonshire	10	7	2	0	1	0.58	15
Warwickshire	10	7	3	0	0	0.24	14
Somerset	10	6	3	0	1	0.42	13
Worcestershire	10	5	5	0	0	0.58	10
Glamorgan	10	2	8	0	0	-1.03	4
Gloucestershire	10	2	8	0	0	-0.66	4

Top two teams qualify for Quarter-final plus Somerset with best 3rd-place points total

South Division

25 May
at Canterbury
Essex 187 for 7 (20 overs) (AN Cook 80)
Kent 16 for 0 (3.2 overs)
Match abandoned (1pt each)

at Lord's
Surrey 186 for 1 (20 overs) (U Afzaal 98*, MR Ramprakash 61*)
Middlesex 129 for 7 (20 overs) (CP Schofield 3 for 21)
Surrey (2pts) won by 57 runs

at the Rose Bowl
Sussex 133 for 8 (20 overs) (DR Smith 63,
H Riazuddin 3 for 15, DG Cork 3 for 30)
Hampshire 137 for 1 (16.1 overs) (JHK Adams 68*)
Hampshire (2pts) won by 9 wickets

26 May
at The Oval
Sussex 184 for 9 (20 overs) (LJ Wright 58)
Surrey 163 for 9 (20 overs) (MH Yardy 3 for 21)
Sussex (2pts) won by 21 runs

27 May
at The Oval
Surrey 125 for 8 (20 overs)
Hampshire 124 for 9 (20 overs)
Surrey (2pts) won by 1 run

at Lord's
Kent 191 for 3 (20 overs) (M van Jaarsveld 75*, DI Stevens 59*)
Middlesex 129 for 8 (20 overs)
Kent (2pts) won by 62 runs

28 May
at Hove
Essex 148 all out (19.4 overs)
Sussex 131 all out (19.1 overs) (CJC Wright 4 for 24, GR Napier 3 for 21)
Essex (2pts) won by 17 runs

29 May
at Hove
Hampshire 122 for 7 (20 overs)
Sussex 128 for 2 (17.1 overs) (CD Nash 56*)
Sussex (2pts) won by 8 wickets

at Chelmsford
Surrey 165 for 5 (20 overs) (SA Newman 81*)
Essex 169 for 6 (19.5 overs) (RS Bopara 53)
Essex (2pts) won by 4 wickets

at Canterbury
Middlesex 104 for 6 (20 overs)
Kent 107 for 6 (18.2 overs) (A Richardson 3 for 29)
Kent (2pts) won by 4 wickets

31 May
at Canterbury
Sussex 132 for 7 (20 overs) (Azhar Mahmood 3 for 16)
Kent 133 for 5 (17 overs) (GO Jones 56)
Kent (2pts) won by 5 wickets

at the Rose Bowl
Hampshire 191 for 6 (20 overs) (MJ Lumb 54)
Surrey 173 for 8 (20 overs) (MR Ramprakash 73)
Hampshire (2pts) won by 18 runs

1 June
at Chelmsford
Essex 205 for 4 (20 overs) (AN Cook 77, GW Flower 61)

Kent 169 for 7 (20 overs) (GW Flower 3 for 26)
Essex (2pts) won by 36 runs

at Hove
Middlesex 116 all out (19.3 overs) (RJ Hamilton-Brown 3 for 15, MH Yardy 3 for 22)
Sussex 120 for 3 (16.3 overs) (RJ Hamilton-Brown 69*)
Sussex (2pts) won by 7 wickets

2 June
at Uxbridge
Hampshire 181 for 6 (20 overs) (MA Carberry 56, SM Ervine 53)
Middlesex 125 all out (19 overs) (SM Ervine 4 for 16, LA Dawson 3 for 25)
Hampshire (2pts) won by 56 runs

3 June
at Chelmsford
Essex 126 for 7 (20 overs) (DR Smith 3 for 19)
Sussex 130 for 2 (18.2 overs) (MW Goodwin 64*)
Sussex (2pts) won by 8 wickets

4 June
at Hove
Sussex 131 for 3 (20 overs) (DR Smith 69*)
Kent 61 for 0 (11 overs)
Sussex (2pts) won by 2 runs – DL Method: target 64 from 11 overs

at the Rose Bowl
Hampshire 219 for 2 (20 overs) (MJ Lumb 124*, MA Carberry 62)
Essex 144 all out (18.4 overs) (MJ Walker 50, SM Ervine 3 for 19)
Hampshire (2pts) won by 75 runs

22 June
at Tunbridge Wells
Kent 182 for 4 (20 overs) (RWT Key 58*, DI Stevens 56)
Hampshire 174 for 7 (20 overs) (MJ Lumb 59)
Kent (2pts) won by 8 runs

at Chelmsford
Middlesex 148 all out (19.2 overs) (Danish Kaneria 3 for 21)
Essex 151 for 2 (19 overs) (ML Pettini 80*)
Essex (2pts) won by 8 wickets

at Hove
Surrey 123 all out (20 overs) (RSC Martin-Jenkins 3 for 17)
Sussex 125 for 4 (16.5 overs)
Sussex (2pts) won by 6 wickets

23 June
at the Rose Bowl
Hampshire 183 for 6 (20 overs) (MJ Lumb 93)
Middlesex 155 for 5 (20 overs) (BA Godleman 57)
Hampshire (2pts) won by 28 runs

24 June
at The Oval
Kent 168 for 6 (20 overs) (M van Jaarsveld 54)
Surrey 167 all out (19.4 overs) (U Afzaal 62)
Kent (2pts) won by 1 run

25 June
at The Oval
Essex 210 for 3 (20 overs) (AN Cook 100*, ML Pettini 87)
Surrey 126 all out (15.2 overs)
Essex (2pts) won by 84 runs

26 June
at Lord's
Middlesex 166 for 5 (20 overs) (NJ Dexter 73)
Essex 143 all out (19.2 overs) (V Chopra 51, T Henderson 3 for 34)
Middlesex (2pts) won by 23 runs

at the Rose Bowl
Hampshire 131 for 7 (20 overs)
Kent 132 for 3 (17.5 overs) (DI Stevens 62*)
Kent (2pts) won by 7 wickets

27 June
at The Oval
Surrey 160 for 5 (20 overs) (MJ Brown 77)
Middlesex 162 for 3 (18.2 overs) (OA Shah 61*)
Middlesex (2pts) won by 7 wickets

28 June
at Chelmsford
Essex 149 for 6 (20 overs) (SM Ervine 3 for 26)
Hampshire 153 for 4 (19.1 overs) (GW Flower 3 for 25)
Hampshire (2pts) won by 6 wickets

at Beckenham
Kent 184 for 7 (20 overs) (M van Jaarsveld 64, MNW Spriegel 4 for 33)
Surrey 168 for 9 (20 overs) (R McLaren 4 for 37)
Kent (2pts) won by 16 runs

at Lord's
Middlesex 127 for 8 (20 overs)
Sussex 130 for 4 (19 overs)
Sussex (2pts) won by 6 wickets

South Division – Final Table

	P	W	L	T	NR	RR	Pts
Kent	10	7	2	0	1	0.64	15
Sussex	10	7	3	0	0	0.32	14
Hampshire	10	6	4	0	0	0.85	12
Essex	10	5	4	0	1	0.15	11
Surrey	10	2	8	0	0	-0.66	4
Middlesex	10	2	8	0	0	-1.19	4

Top two teams qualify for Quarter-final plus Hampshire with 2nd best 3rd-place points total

Quarter-finals

27 July
at Canterbury
Kent 149 for 7 (20 overs) (BW Harmison 3 for 24)
Durham 93 all out (17.2 overs) (JC Tredwell 3 for 18)
Kent won by 56 runs

at Hove
Sussex 152 for 9 (20 overs)
Warwickshire 114 all out (19 overs) (IJL Trott 56, RJ Hamilton-Brown 4 for 15)
Sussex won by 38 runs

30 July
at Old Trafford
Lancashire v. **Somerset**
Match abandoned – Somerset won on a bowl-out

Somerset's Alfonso Thomas looks as if he is going to be bang on target during the quarter-final bowl-out against Lancashire at Old Trafford's indoor school.

at Northampton
Northamptonshire 134 for 6 (20 overs)
Hampshire 121 all out (19.4 overs) (AJ Hall 3 for 25)
Northamptonshire won by 13 runs

Semi-finals

15 August
at Edgbaston
Northamptonshire 136 for 6 (20 overs)
Sussex 137 for 3 (19.4 overs) (MW Goodwin 80*)
Sussex won by 7 wickets

Kent 145 for 5 (20 overs) (DI Stevens 77)
Somerset 146 for 3 (18.5 overs) (ME Trescothick 56)
Somerset won by 7 wickets

Amid the spray of champagne, Sussex captain Mike Yardy
brandishes the Twenty20 Cup at Edgbaston.

FINAL – SUSSEX v. SOMERSET
15 August 2009 at Edgbaston

SUSSEX

MW Goodwin	c Kieswetter b Willoughby	7
LJ Wright	run out	20
RJ Hamilton-Brown	lbw b Waller	25
DR Smith	st Kieswetter b Waller	59
EC Joyce	b Trego	4
MH Yardy (capt)	b Suppiah	4
CD Nash	b Thomas	28
Yasir Arafat	not out	20
*AJ Hodd		
WAT Beer		
RJ Kirtley		
Extras	b 1, lb 1, w 3	5
	(7 wkts 20 overs)	**172**

	O	M	R	W
Thomas	4	0	37	1
Willoughby	4	0	27	1
Phillips	3	0	36	0
Trego	4	0	26	1
Waller	3	0	33	2
Suppiah	2	0	11	1

Fall of Wickets

1-16, 2-48, 3-67, 4-80, 5-122, 6-126, 7-172

SOMERSET

ME Trescothick	c Hamilton-Brown b Kirtley	33
JL Langer (capt)	b Yasir Arafat	15
Z de Bruyn	c Yardy b Wright	22
JC Hildreth	c Hamilton-Brown b Beer	1
*C Kieswetter	st Hodd b Beer	1
PD Trego	c Smith b Hamilton-Brown	27
AV Suppiah	c Goodwin b Kirtley	2
BJ Phillips	c Hamilton-Brown b Kirtley	1
AC Thomas	c Yardy b Yasir Arafat	0
MTC Waller	run out	0
CM Willoughby	not out	0
Extras	lb 5, w 2	7
	(all out 17.2 overs)	**109**

	O	M	R	W
Wright	3	0	25	1
Yasir Arafat	2.2	0	14	2
Kirtley	2	1	9	3
Smith	1	0	3	0
Yardy	4	0	17	0
Beer	4	0	29	2
Hamilton-Brown	1	0	7	1

Fall of Wickets

1-43, 2-51, 3-57, 4-63, 5-104, 6-108, 7-109, 8-109, 9-109

Umpires: RK Illingworth & RA Kettleborough
Toss: Somerset
Man of the Match: DR Smith

Sussex won by 63 runs

NATWEST PRO40 LEAGUE

by Mark Baldwin

Sussex led from gun to tape to win back-to-back NatWest Pro40 League titles, but they needed a big assist from Durham on the final day of the season to flop over the finishing line just ahead of Somerset.

Indeed, if Durham had not won by two wickets at Taunton, less than an hour after Sussex had messed up in their last game at Worcestershire, then it would have been Justin Langer's Somerset who would have pipped them at the last.

There was as much relief as joy in the Sussex dressing room at New Road when the big screen at the ground – carrying Sky Sports' coverage from Taunton – showed Scott Borthwick hitting Alfonso Thomas through the legside for Durham's winning runs against Somerset. Zander de Bruyn, with 55 from 66 balls, and Arul Suppiah, who provided a burst of real acceleration with 52 from 29 balls, had given Somerset hope of setting Durham a target that might prove just beyond them.

Ed Joyce, of Sussex, gets in a bit of a tangle.

NatWest Pro40 Division One

13 July
at Chelmsford
Essex 263 for 8 (40 overs) (HM Amla 111, JS Foster 65)
Sussex 267 for 6 (38.2 overs) (EC Joyce 91,
DR Smith 60*)
Sussex (2pts) won by 4 wickets

15 July
at New Road
Worcestershire 190 for 9 (40 overs)
Yorkshire 178 all out (40 overs) (JA Rudolph 68,
GM Andrew 5 for 31, MM Ali 3 for 32)
Worcestershire (2pts) won by 12 runs

17 July
at Cheltenham
Gloucestershire 217 for 3 (32.4 overs) (Kadeer Ali 100*)
Worcestershire
Match abandoned (1pt each)

19 July
at Arundel Castle
Sussex 224 for 9 (40 overs)
Hampshire 220 for 8 (40 overs) (AD Mascarenhas 76,
MA Carberry 55, RJ Kirtley 4 for 38)
Sussex (2pts) won by 4 runs

at Cheltenham
Essex 191 for 5 (18 overs) (RN ten Doeschate 88)
Gloucestershire 193 for 4 (17.3 overs) (WTS Porterfield 97*,
JEC Franklin 60)
*Gloucestershire (2pts) won by 6 wickets – DL Method: target 193
from 18 overs*

at Trent Bridge
Nottinghamshire 247 for 5 (26 overs) (DJ Hussey 120*,
MJ Wood 91, AC Thomas 3 for 48)
Somerset
Match abandoned (1pt each)

NatWest Pro40 Division Two

14 July
at Edgbaston
Middlesex 10 for 0 (2 overs)
Warwickshire
Match abandoned (1pt each)

17 July
at Derby
Derbyshire v. **Northamptonshire**
Match abandoned (1pt each)

19 July
at Old Trafford
Lancashire v. **Derbyshire**
Match abandoned (1pt each)

at Edgbaston
Glamorgan 90 for 2 (18.3 overs)
Warwickshire
Match abandoned (1pt each)

at Guildford
Surrey 213 for 7 (40 overs) (MJ Brown 57,
TJ Murtagh 3 for 43)
Middlesex 217 for 1 (35.1 overs) (NRD Compton 87*,
DJ Malan 60, OA Shah 57*)
Middlesex (2pts) won by 9 wickets

at Northampton
Leicestershire 175 for 5 (30 overs)
Northamptonshire 37 for 1 (4.2 overs)
Match abandoned (1pt each)

21 July
at Cardiff
Glamorgan v. **Kent**
Match abandoned (1pt each)

22 July
at Old Trafford
Lancashire 221 for 7 (40 overs) (PJ Horton 84, TC Smith 54)
Surrey 213 for 6 (40 overs) (MJ Brown 87, SJ Walters 63)
Lancashire (2pts) won by 8 runs

4 August
at Northampton
Northamptonshire 102 for 7 (21 overs) (KW Hogg 3 for 18)
Lancashire 91 for 2 (11.5 overs)
Lancashire (2pts) won by 8 wickets – DL Method: target 88 from 18 overs

5 August
at Whitgift School
Surrey 282 for 5 (40 overs) (CP Schofield 66, MJ Brown 51)
Derbyshire 286 for 6 (39.1 overs) (GM Smith 77, GT Park 64)
Derbyshire (2pts) won by 4 wickets

Opposite Surrey batsman Michael Brown is struck in the face as he tries to pull during an innings of 57 against Middlesex at Guildford.

As news of Sussex's demise at Worcester began to circulate around the packed stands at Taunton, however, Durham's Gordon Muchall and Gareth Breese began to build sensibly on the whirlwind start that Phil Mustard and Ian Blackwell had given their side with an opening partnership of 79 in seven overs. Muchall's 61 was a cool innings in the circumstances, while Breese also batted superbly as the pressure grew, and Somerset could not prevent Durham from dashing the cup from their lips. It was Sussex's players, indeed, who were soon tasting the trophy-winning champagne.

Mark Robinson, the Sussex coach, admitted his players had felt tired in the last weeks of a season which – with Twenty20 Cup success and an appearance too in the Friends Provident Trophy final at Lord's – had confirmed their status as the domestic game's foremost limited-overs side. Relegation from the first division of the Championship had not helped their mood, either.

Yet, from the moment they began the defence of their 2008 title on 13 July, with an impressive run chase against Essex at Chelmsford, Sussex were the team to catch in the Pro40 League's first division. That opening victory owed much to Ed Joyce's 78-ball 91, as they chased down an Essex total of 263 for 8 based on a sublime 111 from Hashim Amla plus a 45-ball 65 from James Foster, and also to an explosive 60 not out from only 34 balls by Dwayne Smith, containing two sixes and seven fours.

Sussex then beat Hampshire by just four runs in an exciting finish at Arundel, where a late surge by Dimitri Mascarenhas, who struck 76, and Dominic Cork was in vain. An equation of 16 needed from the final over became five from two balls but Yasir Arafat then held his nerve to deny Cork.

Essex were on the wrong end of another inspired run chase at Cheltenham, meanwhile, where Ryan ten Doeschate's 88 from 43 balls proved insufficient to prevent Will Porterfield, with 97 not out from just 53 balls, and James Franklin (60 off 30 balls) from propelling Gloucestershire to a wonderful victory in a rain-shortened contest that packed in a whole afternoon's worth of entertainment.

Bad weather also affected a number of early matches in both the first and second divisions; at Trent Bridge a breathtaking 120 from 60 balls against Somerset by Nottinghamshire's Australian David Hussey, in which his century took a mere 50 balls, came in a rain-ruined game

NatWest Pro40 Division One

19 July (continued)
at Scarborough
Yorkshire 199 for 7 (37 overs) (AW Gale 83, GR Breese 3 for 34)
Durham 154 all out (29.4 overs) (P Mustard 55, Naved-ul-Hasan 3 for 44)
Yorkshire (2pts) won by 13 runs – DL Method: target 168 from 30 overs

24 July
at Cheltenham
Durham 206 all out (39.4 overs) (KJ Coetzer 63, SP Kirby 4 for 32)
Gloucestershire 205 all out (39.1 overs) (WTS Porterfield 62, J Lewis 54, ID Blackwell 4 for 36)
Durham (2pts) won by 1 run

5 August
at the Rose Bowl
Yorkshire 232 for 6 (40 overs) (JA Rudolph 79, AW Gale 54)
Hampshire 233 for 5 (40 overs) (MJ Lumb 53)
Hampshire (2pts) won by 5 wickets

6 August
at the Riverside
Durham 274 for 4 (40 overs) (P Mustard 92, DM Benkenstein 51*)

Worcestershire 129 all out (30.1 overs)
(ID Blackwell 3 for 11)
Durham (2pts) won by 145 runs

9 August
at Horsham
Gloucestershire 189 all out (39.5 overs) (HJH Marshall 50, RJ Kirtley 3 for 29, Yasir Arafat 3 for 30)
Sussex 192 for 1 (26.1 overs) (LJ Wright 95*, EC Joyce 66*)
Sussex (2pts) won by 9 wickets

at Southend
Essex 224 for 8 (40 overs) (RN ten Doeschate 64*, V Chopra 51, A Carter 3 for 32)
Nottinghamshire 190 all out (36.4 overs) (SR Patel 58, Danish Kaneria 3 for 28)
Essex (2pts) won by 34 runs

at Taunton
Yorkshire 208 all out (39.4 overs) (JA Rudolph 95, Z de Bruyn 4 for 20)
Somerset 211 for 5 (36.5 overs) (JC Hildreth 62*)
Somerset (2pts) won by 5 wickets

and in Division Two there were no results in both their first two matches for Warwickshire, Derbyshire and Northamptonshire.

Tom Maynard hit Glamorgan's fastest one-day century, on 9 August at Colwyn Bay, by reaching three figures from 57 balls and going on to score a 62-ball 108 with four sixes and 13 fours, but it was not enough to stop Northants winning the match by six runs. There was a similar story in another second division match on the same day at Canterbury, where Owais Shah compiled a magnificent 130 off 94 balls but Middlesex still lost by 12 runs to Kent, for whom Darren Stevens hit a 50-ball unbeaten 75.

Kent, like many counties in the second tier, used the competition to blood a clutch of youngsters. On 18

August, at Leicester, young wicketkeeper Paul Dixey won a closely fought contest with a six in the final over and, five days later, 20-year-old Alex Blake struck 80 from 70 balls as Kent kept up their own Division Two title challenge by beating Derbyshire at Chesterfield. Stevens's 52 from 30 balls and a 25-ball 51 by Azhar Mahmood were significant contributions, too, from the more experienced members of their predominantly youthful line-up.

The Leicestershire side which was heavily beaten by Warwickshire, at Edgbaston on 9 August, however, not only contained five England Under-19 players but also, in seamer Charlie Dagnall, a player attempting a mini-comeback to the professional game after taking time off from his job as a local radio presenter.

NatWest Pro40 Division Two

9 August
at Edgbaston
Leicestershire 158 for 8 (40 overs)
(NM Carter 3 for 22)
Warwickshire 161 for 1 (22.4 overs) (IJL Trott 73*,
NM Carter 63)
Warwickshire (2pts) won by 9 wickets

at Colwyn Bay
Northamptonshire 268 for 7 (40 overs) (NJ O'Brien 82,
SD Peters 69, RDB Croft 4 for 43)
Glamorgan 262 for 8 (40 overs) (TL Maynard 108, GP Rees 73,
N Boje 3 for 49, JJ van der Wath 3 for 55)
Northamptonshire (2pts) won by 6 runs

at Canterbury
Kent 258 for 4 (40 overs) (DI Stevens 75*, GO Jones 73,
JL Denly 66)
Middlesex 246 all out (38.3 overs) (OA Shah 130,
W Lee 3 for 39, MP Coles 3 for 50)
Kent (2pts) won by 12 runs

12 August
at The Oval
Glamorgan 192 for 5 (37 overs)
Surrey 156 for 2 (20.4 overs) (SJ Walters 67*)
*Surrey (2pts) won by 8 wickets – DL Method: target 153 from
24 overs*

16 August
at Lord's
Middlesex 201 for 7 (40 overs)
Leicestershire 174 all out (37.2 overs) (JWA Taylor 50,
OA Shah 4 for 11)
Middlesex (2pts) won by 27 runs

18 August
at Grace Road
Leicestershire 209 for 8 (40 overs) (JWA Taylor 95,
Azhar Mahmood 4 for 41)
Kent 211 for 7 (39.4 overs)
Kent (2pts) won by 3 wickets

19 August
at Cardiff
Middlesex 254 for 3 (40 overs) (NRD Compton 121,
DJ Malan 53)
Glamorgan 191 all out (35.2 overs) (TL Maynard 69,
GP Rees 58)
Middlesex (2pts) won by 63 runs

23 August
at Chesterfield
Derbyshire 259 for 8 (40 overs) (CJL Rogers 88,
P Edwards 3 for 57)
Kent 260 for 6 (38.2 overs) (AJ Blake 80, DI Stevens 52,
Azhar Mahmood 51)
Kent (2pts) won by 4 wickets

at Grace Road
Leicestershire 222 for 6 (40 overs) (JGE Benning 89,
TJ New 50)
Lancashire 146 all out (27.2 overs) (JHK Naik 3 for 21,
CW Henderson 3 for 30)
Leicestershire (2pts) won by 76 runs

26 August
at Lord's
Middlesex 112 for 3 (26.1 overs) (NRD Compton 52*)
Lancashire
Match abandoned (1pt each)

After three games in Division Two, it was Lancashire who led the way, but Middlesex's campaign had featured an early nine-wicket win over their London rivals Surrey at Guildford, in which Nick Compton hit an unbeaten 87, and by the time Compton's 107 had helped them to a 50-run win against Derbyshire at Uxbridge on 13 September they had taken over at the top of the table.

It was a creditable performance by a Middlesex team who had suffered a difficult season overall, but Warwickshire ultimately emerged as the top team in the second division with a fine win over Kent at Canterbury and then a thrilling last-ball victory by three wickets against Lancashire in the final round of matches on 27 September.

Neil Carter's 64-ball 100 had been enough to see off Kent, although such was the violence of his hitting as he swung six sixes and 13 fours that he slipped a disc in his back and ruled himself out for the rest of the season.

Even without Carter, though, Warwickshire managed to chase down Lancashire's 166 at Old Trafford with Jonathan Trott leading the way with 86 from 122 balls before being caught at mid-wicket at the start of the last over. Ant Botha was then run out, but Rikki Clarke stayed calm enough to claim the winning single from the final ball.

Back in Division One, meanwhile, Sussex had made it three wins out of three matches when Luke Wright's

Nick Compton, of Middlesex, hits out on his way to 52 against Lancashire before rain arrived at Lord's.

NatWest Pro40 Division One

13 August
at Bristol
Gloucestershire 116 all out (28.2 overs) (AC Thomas 4 for 18, BJ Phillips 3 for 24, ML Turner 3 for 27)
Somerset 119 for 2 (18.4 overs)
(ME Trescothick 80*)
Somerset (2pts) won by 8 wickets

17 August
at Taunton
Somerset 238 for 5 (40 overs) (Z de Bruyn 73)
Sussex 189 all out (36.4 overs) (EC Joyce 94, BJ Phillips 3 for 34)
Somerset (2pts) won by 49 runs

23 August
at the Riverside
Durham 207 for 5 (36 overs) (S Chanderpaul 54, P Mustard 50)

Hampshire 87 for 1 (11 overs) (MJ Lumb 57*)
Hampshire (2pts) won by 23 runs – DL Method: target 65 from 11 overs

At Colchester
Essex 247 for 5 (40 overs) (V Chopra 62, JS Foster 52*)
Worcestershire 248 for 7 (40 overs)
(VS Solanki 62, SM Davies 61, DKH Mitchell 50*, TJ Phillips 3 for 49)
Worcestershire (2pts) won by 3 wickets

25 August
at the Rose Bowl
Gloucestershire 184 for 8 (40 overs)
(DA Griffiths 4 for 29)
Hampshire 185 for 7 (37.1 overs) (JHK Adams 79, ID Saxelby 3 for 20)
Hampshire (2pts) won by 3 wickets

NatWest Pro40 Division One

28 August
at Hove
Sussex 277 for 6 (40 overs) (MW Goodwin 77, DR Smith 54)
Durham 84 all out (24.1 overs) (RJ Kirtley 5 for 26)
Sussex (2pts) won by 193 runs

29 August
at Trent Bridge
Nottinghamshire 282 for 7 (40 overs) (AD Hales 150*)
Worcestershire 286 for 3 (37.5 overs) (SM Davies 106, SC Moore 87*)
Worcestershire (2pts) won by 7 wickets

30 August
at Scarborough
Yorkshire 254 for 2 (40 overs) (A Lyth 109*, JA Rudolph 68)
Sussex 231 for 5 (31.3 overs) (JS Gatting 99*, DR Smith 58)
Sussex (2pts) won by 38 runs – DL Method: target 194 from 31.3 overs

31 August
at New Road
Hampshire 220 for 6 (40 overs) (SM Ervine 60*)
Worcestershire 222 for 3 (29.3 overs) (SM Davies 100, VS Solanki 82*)
Worcestershire (2pts) won by 7 wickets

Opposite Sussex's James Kirtley, one of the best limited-day bowlers in English cricket for a decade or more, celebrates taking the prized wicket of Shivnarine Chanderpaul during the 5 for 26 that helped to destroy Durham at Hove.

68-ball 95 not out – including a first 50 all in boundaries – plus an unbeaten 66 by Ed Joyce, a superb new-ball spell from James Kirtley and Yasir Arafat's hat-trick had proved too much for Gloucestershire at Horsham. They then continued to put in a string of excellent one-day displays to stay in charge at the head of the table.

Daryl Mitchell and Ian Fisher took 12 from the last over to guide Worcestershire to a three-wicket last-ball win against Essex, who then at last enjoyed some success when Alastair Cook made his second century in consecutive matches and James Foster finished off a tremendous pursuit of Durham's 276 for 6 by hitting

leg spinner Scott Borthwick for five successive sixes to end up on 83 not out.

Somerset stepped up their challenge by impressively outplaying Hampshire at the Rose Bowl by six wickets, where Craig Kieswetter made 81 from 87 balls, and then ending Worcestershire's own title hopes on 15 September by trouncing them by 84 runs at New Road. Zander de Bruyn scored an unbeaten 109 despite needing a runner for most of his innings.

In the end, though, Somerset could not quite do enough to deny Sussex on a dramatic last day of the 2009 domestic season which also saw Nottinghamshire skittled for just 57 by Gloucestershire at Trent Bridge – their lowest one-day total – and 40-year-old Mark Ealham finish his distinguished career with a second-ball duck.

County cricket, however, has always been a vehicle for youngsters trying to make their name as much as for

NatWest Pro40 Division Two

27 August
at Canterbury
Kent 167 for 6 (27 overs) (SA Northeast 69)
Surrey 110 for 5 (19.4 overs)
Kent (2pts) won by 8 runs – DL Method: target 119 runs from 19.4 overs

31 August
at Northampton
Northamptonshire 212 for 6 (40 overs) (AJ Hall 104*, SA Piolet 3 for 34)
Warwickshire 212 for 9 (40 overs) (IR Bell 65, LM Daggett 3 for 44)
Match tied (1pt each)

6 September
at Grace Road
Leicestershire 217 for 8 (40 overs)
Glamorgan 194 all out (39.5 overs) (WD Bragg 78, WA White 4 for 36)
Leicestershire (2pts) won by 23 runs

at Edgbaston
Warwickshire 246 for 6 (40 overs) (IR Bell 105)
Derbyshire 136 all out (29.3 overs) (NM Carter 3 for 18, S Sreesanth 3 for 36)
Warwickshire (2pts) won by 110 runs

at Old Trafford
Kent 162 all out (40 overs) (SJ Mullaney 3 for 36)
Lancashire 80 for 1 (17.4 overs) (PJ Horton 51)
Lancashire (2pts) won by 25 runs – DL Method: target 56 from 17.4 overs

11 September
at Derby
Leicestershire 194 for 8 (40 overs) (JGE Benning 61, TD Groenewald 3 for 33)
Derbyshire 198 for 1 (34.4 overs) (CJL Rogers 111*)
Derbyshire (2pts) won by 9 wickets

13 September
at Canterbury
Warwickshire 283 for 6 (40 overs) (NM Carter 103*, JO Troughton 53)
Kent 224 all out (35.2 overs) (GO Jones 63, AG Botha 3 for 72)
Warwickshire (2pts) won by 59 runs

at Uxbridge
Middlesex 242 for 6 (40 overs) (NRD Compton 107)
Derbyshire 192 all out (37.4 overs)
Middlesex (2pts) won by 50 runs

at Northampton
Surrey 134 all out (35.2 overs) (DS Lucas 3 for 32)
Northamptonshire 135 for 2 (15.3 overs) (NJ O'Brien 81*)
Northamptonshire (2pts) won by 8 wickets

14 September
at Cardiff
Glamorgan 219 all out (39.1 overs) (MJ Cosgrove 73)
Lancashire 192 all out (37.4 overs) (SJ Croft 50)
Glamorgan (2pts) won by 27 runs

veterans attempting to make the most of their autumn years in the game. And, although Mark Pettini's 101 not out won the day for Essex at Headingley, many Yorkshire eyes were on the performance of 18-year-old batsman Joe Root, who scored a fine 63 on his county debut.

The 40-over format, too, was not as dead as had first been thought when the final Pro40 League got under way in mid-July. The ECB's decision to replace the Friends Provident Trophy in 2010 with a new, 40-over league between all 18 counties plus Netherlands, Scotland and an ECB recreational team, split initially into three groups of seven and culminating in a Lord's final in mid-September, caught many in the game by surprise.

NatWest Pro40 Division One

2 September
at Trent Bridge
Yorkshire 63 for 2 (13.1 overs)
Nottinghamshire
Match abandoned (1pt each)

3 September
at Chelmsford
Hampshire 246 for 5 (40 overs) (JM Vince 93, LA Dawson 69*)
Essex 249 for 3 (38.5 overs) (AN Cook 104, V Chopra 101*)
Essex (2pts) won by 7 wickets

5 September
at the Riverside
Durham 276 for 6 (40 overs) (P Mustard 102, ID Blackwell 59)
Essex 279 for 3 (36.5 overs) (AN Cook 104*, JS Foster 83*, GR Napier 63)
Essex (2pts) won by 7 wickets

7 September
at Hove
Sussex 254 (40 overs) (AC Voges 3 for 25)
Nottinghamshire 102 all out (21.3 overs) (DR Smith 6 for 29)
Sussex (2pts) won by 152 runs

8 September
at Taunton
Somerset 205 all out (39.2 overs) (TJ Phillips 5 for 38)
Essex 206 for 8 (39.1 overs) (JK Maunders 78)
Essex (2pts) won by 2 wickets

10 September
at Headingley
Gloucestershire 172 all out (39.4 overs) (JEC Franklin 55, SA Patterson 3 for 35, JE Lee 3 for 43)
Yorkshire 173 for 2 (31.1 overs) (JA Rudolph 72*, JJ Sayers 55)
Yorkshire (2pts) won by 8 wickets

13 September
at the Riverside
Durham 224 for 6 (35 overs) (BW Harmison 67, P Mustard 61)
Nottinghamshire 220 for 9 (35 overs) (MA Wagh 56)
Durham (2pts) won by 4 runs

at the Rose Bowl
Hampshire 205 for 7 (40 overs) (CM Willoughby 3 for 36)
Somerset 207 for 4 (33 overs) (C Kieswetter 81)
Somerset (2pts) won by 6 wickets

14 September
at New Road
Somerset 236 for 5 (40 overs) (Z de Bruyn 109*, GM Andrew 3 for 49)
Worcestershire 152 all out (36.2 overs)
Somerset (2pts) won by 84 runs

19 September
at the Rose Bowl
Hampshire 281 for 6 (40 overs) (JHK Adams 73, MJ Lumb 61, JM Vince 55)
Nottinghamshire 139 all out (32.4 overs) (SM Ervine 3 for 23, Imran Tahir 3 for 30)
Hampshire (2pts) won by 142 runs

27 September
at Trent Bridge
Nottinghamshire 57 all out (18.5 overs) (AJ Ireland 3 for 10, DA Payne 3 for 10)
Gloucestershire 58 for 1 (7.3 overs)
Gloucestershire (2pts) won by 9 wickets

at Headingley
Yorkshire 187 for 7 (40 overs) (JE Root 63, GR Napier 4 for 33)
Essex 189 for 3 (33.3 overs) (ML Pettini 101*)
Essex (2pts) won by 7 wickets

at New Road
Worcestershire 214 for 6 (40 overs) (MM Ali 51)
Sussex 165 all out (34.5 overs) (ID Fisher 3 for 18, GJ Batty 3 for 45)
Worcestershire (2pts) won by 49 runs

at Taunton
Somerset 242 for 7 (40 overs) (Z de Bruyn 55, AV Suppiah 52*)
Durham 243 for 8 (39.4 overs) (GJ Muchall 61, BJ Phillips 3 for 34)
Durham (2pts) won by 2 wickets

NatWest Pro40 Division Two

16 September
at The Oval
Surrey 200 for 8 (40 overs) (MJ Brown 56, IJL Trott 3 for 36)
Warwickshire 204 for 1 (35 overs) (IR Bell 93*, IJL Trott 79*)
Warwickshire (2pts) won by 9 wickets

19 September
at Uxbridge
Middlesex 220 for 8 (40 overs) (T Henderson 55, GG White 3 for 30)
Northamptonshire 142 (36.2 overs) (GK Berg 3 for 18)
Middlesex (2pts) won by 78 runs

27 September
at Canterbury
Northamptonshire 244 for 6 (40 overs) (NJ O'Brien 72, RA White 70*)
Kent 145 all out (31.5 overs) (JB Hockley 55, DS Lucas 4 for 28, GG White 3 for 42)
Northamptonshire (2pts) won by 99 runs

at Derby
Derbyshire 214 for 9 (40 overs) (DS Harrison 3 for 55)
Glamorgan 215 for 5 (38.5 overs) (TL Maynard 69*, J Allenby 60)
Glamorgan (2pts) won by 5 wickets

at Grace Road
Leicestershire 225 for 4 (40 overs) (JWA Taylor 83*)
Surrey 228 for 6 (39.1 overs) (MNW Spriegel 81*, TMJ Smith 65)
Surrey (2pts) won by 4 wickets

at Old Trafford
Lancashire 166 all out (39.5 overs) (SJ Croft 70, KHD Barker 3 for 23)
Warwickshire 167 for 7 (40 overs) (IJL Trott 86)
Warwickshire (2pts) won by 3 wickets

Ian Bell was in prime form for Warwickshire in September's Pro40 games, hitting 105 against Derbyshire at Edgbaston and 93 not out against Surrey at The Oval.

Division One – Final Table

	P	W	L	T	NR	RR	Pts
Sussex	8	6	2	0	0	1.25	12
Somerset	8	5	2	0	1	1.14	11
Worcestershire	8	5	2	0	1	-0.33	11
Essex	8	5	3	0	0	0.33	10
Hampshire	8	4	4	0	0	0.23	8
Durham	8	4	4	0	0	-0.35	8
Yorkshire	8	2	5	0	1	-0.18	5
Gloucestershire	8	2	5	0	1	-0.35	5
Nottinghamshire	8	0	6	0	2	-2.41	2

No promotion or relegation

Division Two – Final Table

	P	W	L	T	NR	RR	Pts
Warwickshire	8	5	0	1	2	1.28	13
Middlesex	8	5	1	0	2	0.99	12
Kent	8	4	3	0	1	-0.63	9
Northamptonshire	8	3	2	1	2	0.60	9
Lancashire	8	3	3	0	2	-0.19	8
Glamorgan	8	2	4	0	2	-0.36	6
Derbyshire	8	2	4	0	2	-0.57	6
Leicestershire	8	2	5	0	1	-0.23	5
Surrey	8	2	6	0	0	-0.77	4

COUNTY REVIEW *North West*

ANDY WILSON, of *The Guardian*, considers how the summer of 2009 will be remembered by the players and supporters of Lancashire, Nottinghamshire and Derbyshire…

County cricket can be a strange business. Nottinghamshire finished second in the County Championship's first division table – 'the best of the rest', as their long-serving director of cricket Mick Newell described it, summarising the general consensus that Durham were in a league of their own – and Lancashire fourth, and they were the only two counties other than the champions to manage four wins in the elite competition.

Yet for large chunks of July and August, and even into early September, there was a more tangible feelgood factor at Derby, even though the Peakites were to finish sixth in Division Two.

That reflected a gulf in expectations at least as wide as that in resources between John Morris's lower league battlers and two traditional Test-staging counties, a status that Lancashire will be relieved to regain in 2010 after a damaging two-year hiatus.

There were reminders at either end of the summer that the club retains a pull despite the lack of recent success. Peter Moores grabbed the chance to make a quicker-than-planned return to the game following his Pietersen-driven England exit – partly for geographical reasons, as he had grown up 20 miles away from Old Trafford in Macclesfield – and Lancashire also proved an attractive option for Stephen Moore following a second relegation season in three years with Worcestershire.

But the flying start that Lancashire enjoyed under the new coach-captain combination of Moores and Glen Chapple – two wins out of three in the Championship, and impressive qualification for the quarter-finals of both the Friends Provident Trophy and the Twenty20 Cup – turned out to be flattering, raising expectations to an unrealistic level.

James Anderson played a crucial role in the first Championship win – an immediate and very satisfying return to Sussex for Moores - but he then disappeared with England for the rest of the season.

Lancashire had released their most experienced batsman and bowler, Stuart Law and Dominic Cork, at the end of 2008, and injuries to Chapple, Sajid Mahmood and Tom Smith were to leave them so short of seamers that they had to sign Tom Lungley on a month's loan from Derbyshire – and went into the Roses Match at Headingley with an attack of Lungley, Oliver Newby and Kyle Hogg.

So there were good reasons for the run of seven consecutive draws that sucked them into the relegation battle, before Chapple returned to inspire a victory over Warwickshire that lifted them to fourth.

The one-day knockout failures, both at Old Trafford against Hampshire in the FPT and Somerset in Twenty20, were harder to justify – a poor all-round performance in the former, and a left-field selection including Mark Chilton and VVS Laxman when the latter went to a bowl-out in the indoor school, which could only have been justified by success.

Lancashire fast bowler and captain Glen Chapple successfully appeals for an lbw decision against Sussex tail-ender Corey Collymore at Hove.

Nottinghamshire captain Chris Read was again in prolific form with the bat throughout the 2009 summer, but his days as an England wicketkeeper still seem to be over.

Nottinghamshire's second consecutive second-placed finish perhaps reflected the dearth of a credible challenge to Durham, as it came despite on-going problems at the top of their batting order, and serious disruption to their seam attack. That left an onerous burden on the shoulders of their captain Chris Read and the two Australians who shared overseas duties, Adam Voges and David Hussey.

Read responded magnificently with 1,203 Championship runs at 75, making him one of the four most consistent and prolific England-qualified batsmen in the competition – such an irony, given the previous criticisms of a former England coach – and the only problem with Hussey and Voges was that they could not be around more often (and ideally both at the same time).

Newell hopes that Hussey will be able to play virtually the full 2010 season, and has signed Neil Edwards from Somerset in the latest attempt to find a reliable opening pair, Will Jefferson having been released after failing to hit any heights (with the bat) in three years at Trent Bridge.

Any future appearances by Stuart Broad, meanwhile, must be regarded as a bonus but Notts will hope for better from Darren Pattinson and Charlie Shreck who struggled badly for form and fitness respectively, often leaving the underrated Andre Adams and promising Luke Fletcher to lead the attack.

Newell and Moores will have noted with some satisfaction that their counties were discovered to be the least reliant on imported labour in 2009, employing fewer players who had learned their cricket abroad than any of their rivals. Here again the contrast with Derbyshire is stark, as they were the worst offenders – a pejorative term which nevertheless seems suitable – in fielding nine 'foreigners' in addition to Chris Rogers, the official overseas player, who again provided outstanding value as opener and captain.

But the policy seemed to be working in mid-season as a victory over Gloucestershire at Cheltenham fired them into promotion contention. It was set up by a debut century from Wayne Madsen, a former South Africa hockey international who had been playing for Unsworth in the Central Lancashire League, and qualified for a European passport through his Italian grandmother. Tim Groenewald - another Kolpak recruit, from Warwickshire - also played a key role in that performance, as did Greg Smith, who had his best season for the county.

So it was hard to have too much sympathy when Derbyshire's promotion challenge petered out with their failure to convert potential winning positions at Leicester, Uxbridge or against Northamptonshire at Chesterfield – a defeat for which they gained pyrrhic revenge when Rogers's desperate declaration allowed Essex to claim a victory that denied Northants promotion on the last day of the season.

Other than Rogers's consistency at the top of the order, a couple of promising cameos by Dan Redfern, and Graham Wagg's increasingly regular willingness to switch from left arm seam to spin in the course of a match, innings – or, occasionally, over - the highlight of Derbyshire's season was the sight of Steffan Jones, shirt unbuttoned to the navel, swaggering in once again from the Pavilion End.

His recruitment in mid-season, on loan from Somerset, proved an inspired move by Morris, who juggled his limited resources shrewdly enough to earn a two-year extension to his contract - even if by the end of the season he, too, was suffering from the inability to fulfil raised expectations.

COUNTY REVIEW *Midlands*

PAUL BOLTON studies the impact, or otherwise, that four Midlands counties had in the domestic summer of 2009…

The solid progress made by Warwickshire and Northamptonshire was counter-balanced by the wretched campaigns endured by Worcestershire and Leicestershire in a season of contrasting fortunes for this quartet of Midlands' counties.

Warwickshire collected minor silverware for the second successive season though few at Edgbaston got too excited about winning the obsolescent NatWest Pro40 League Division Two. With no promotion at the end of the season the majority of the Pro40 second division counties used the competition to blood youngsters, but Warwickshire made it clear from the outset that they were out to win it. They recovered from having their first two home games washed out to clinch the title with an unbeaten record.

Warwickshire were inconsistent in the Friends Provident Trophy and Twenty20 Cup – where they missed out on an Edgbaston finals day for a third time – but their major achievement was to retain their place in the top flight of the County Championship.

They were candidates to finish as distant runners-up to Durham until they were trounced by Lancashire in the final round of matches, but such a high finish would have distorted their season. Their only Championship wins came against the relegated counties and they were themselves battling relegation until they completed their first double over Worcestershire since 1933 on the first weekend of September.

Warwickshire again struggled to force wins on the lifeless pitches at Edgbaston where six games were drawn and they managed only one win. It was a tough season for a young seam attack but the progress made by Boyd Rankin, Chris Woakes, Naqaash Tahir and, briefly, Andy Miller might encourage them to play on less batsmen-friendly surfaces next season.

Jonathan Trott's remarkable consistency – 1,400 first-class runs and a Twenty20 Cup record of 525 runs – was rewarded with Test selection and a match-winning role on his debut at The Oval. Trott's success also helped Warwickshire to absorb some collective batting failures, notably by the openers. Darren Maddy missed most of the season with a knee ligament injury, Tony Frost struggled for runs and returned to his 'proper' job as a trainee groundsman at the end of the season and new skipper Ian Westwood struggled to juggle the twin demands of captaincy and opening the batting.

Warwickshire tried and failed to sign Gareth Batty and Stephen Moore, who opted to join Surrey and Lancashire respectively, from neighbours Worcestershire who failed to win a Championship game for only the second time in their history and first since 1928.

For the third time Worcestershire were relegated after just one season in the top flight and just about everything that could go wrong, did so. Their survival hopes were pinned firmly to their four senior seamers staying fit for most of the summer but only the estimable Matt Mason did so. Former England paceman Simon Jones broke down in pre-season, did not bowl a ball and was released in mid-season. Kabir Ali played little because of back and hamstring

Johan van der Wath, Northamptonshire's South African fast bowler, is pictured in his delivery stride.

James Taylor of Leicestershire may be small in stature but, in 2009, he was big on runs and won the awards to prove it.

problems and Ashley Noffke made little impression before his early return to Australia.

There were few excuses for the regular batting collapses, however. There were individual highlights, including Daryl Mitchell's 298 at Taunton, Vikram Solanki's double-hundred at Headingley and Moeen Ali's maiden century, but far too many collective failures. Steven Davies's consistency with the bat and behind the stumps secured him a place in England's Test squad for the winter tour to South Africa, but by that time he had signed for Surrey.

Embarrassment by Ireland in the Friends Provident Trophy completed a depressing season at New Road, one that ended with dire warnings of financial cutbacks, which in turn means departing senior players are unlikely to be replaced with similar quality.

Leicestershire collected the Championship wooden spoon for the first time since 1962 but the gloom at Grace Road was lifted by the outstanding form of James Taylor. The diminutive 19-year-old right-hander scored almost 2,000 runs in all cricket, including 1,207 in the first-class game. Taylor also became the youngest Leicestershire batsman to make 1,000 Championship runs, a double-century and one-day century and was voted both Cricket Writers' Club and Professional Cricketers' Association Young Cricketer of the Year.

Taylor benefited from Leicestershire's policy of blooding home-grown youngsters, a policy that meant reduced opportunities for HD Ackerman, who returned to South Africa at the end of the season, and Paul Nixon, who lost his place as wicketkeeper to Tom New but later in the summer successfully re-invented himself as an opening batsman.

Boeta Dippenaar, who replaced Nixon as captain, will not be returning next season but the arrival of Will Jefferson from Nottinghamshire should help fill that gap. Nothing, meanwhile, was seen of Nadeem Malik, the leading wicket-taker in 2008, because of a mystery injury although AJ Harris led the attack well in his absence.

Northamptonshire expected to benefit from Monty Panesar's lengthy absences from England's Test squad, but the slow left-armer took only 18 Championship wickets. Despite his poor form Northamptonshire came within a whisker of winning Championship promotion – only Essex's last-day run chase at Derby denied them – and they also reached Twenty20 Cup finals day for the first time.

South African all-rounder Andrew Hall and Johan van der Wath contributed significantly to the success with Hall making most Championship runs – 1,161 – to go with his 40 wickets and van der Wath taking 50 wickets. But left-arm swing bowler David Lucas enjoyed an Indian summer with his third county, taking 58 Championship wickets including a career-best 7 for 24 and a match return of 12 for 73 against Gloucestershire. David Sales missed the entire season because of a knee injury but the consistency of Stephen Peters, Rob White, Nicky Boje and Hall helped to compensate for his absence.

Panesar, who lost his central contract as well as his England place, looked a forlorn figure when he was left out of Northamptonshire's side for their final match against Leicestershire.

COUNTY REVIEW *South West*

RICHARD LATHAM, who has reported on both Somerset and Gloucestershire cricket for more than 20 years, reports on a season of progress in the South West…

Somerset were the nearly men of the 2009 county cricket season, finishing third in the County Championship and runners-up in the Twenty20 Cup and Pro40 League. The Cidermen also reached the quarter-finals of the Friends Provident Trophy after a powerful group campaign, which saw them unbeaten in eight matches, before losing to Sussex, who were to pip them in the other two one-day competitions as well.

So Justin Langer's third season as captain ended without a trophy. He left at the end of it, having led the club from the second division of both the Championship and Pro40 League to be major contenders for both first division titles. Somerset's rise also coincided with Marcus Trescothick's retirement from international cricket. In 2009 he enjoyed his most prolific season ever at county level with 1,817 first-class runs at an average of 75.7 and 2,934 in all competitions, statistics that earned him the PCA award as Most Valuable Player.

Again problems bowling opponents out twice on their plum batting wickets at Taunton proved Somerset's undoing in their efforts to secure a first Championship title. They won only one four-day game at the County Ground and that with an extraordinary last-day batting effort to reach a target of 476 to beat Yorkshire.

Arul Suppiah and wicketkeeper Craig Kieswetter each passed 1,000 first class runs for the first time, while Charl Willoughby took 54 first-class wickets, having also taken 50-plus in his previous three seasons with the club. Alfonso Thomas proved himself among the most effective one-day bowlers in the country.

Peter Trego advanced his international claims and earned selection for England in the Hong Kong six-a-side tournament and, while Andy Caddick's illustrious career came to an end, youngsters Max Waller and Jos Buttler enjoyed promising introductions into the first team.

Six County Championship wins were not enough to secure Gloucestershire promotion from Division Two, but represented major progress after a disastrous 2008 campaign.

John Bracewell's return as director of cricket and Alex Gidman's appointment as captain had positive effects, with Gidman rising to his new responsibility by scoring 1,028 first class runs at an average of 44.69. No other Gloucestershire batsman reached 1,000 and some poor first-innings batting efforts meant the consistently good form of pace bowlers Steve Kirby, who took 64 first-class wickets, and Jon Lewis (57) did not bring the ultimate reward of a place in Division One.

James Franklin was a success as overseas player, scoring 904 first-class runs at an average of over 50 and claiming 31 wickets. The Kiwi all-rounder agreed a contract for 2010 before retiring from the final Championship match against Kent at Bristol to act as a replacement for the injured Jacob Oram in New Zealand's ICC Champions Trophy squad.

Gloucestershire missed out on promotion by nine points, finishing fourth, and also went close in the Friends Provident Trophy, reaching the semi-finals before losing a high-scoring game against Sussex at Hove by 34 runs. Form in the other two one-day competitions was less impressive. The Gladiators won only two of their ten Twenty20 Cup group matches and in the Pro40 League had just one victory from the first seven fixtures when winning their final game in spectacular fashion at Trent Bridge, bowling out Nottinghamshire for 57.

Craig Spearman's fine career with the county came to an end, while Academy products David Payne and Chris Dent provided a glimpse of the future.

Arul Suppiah enjoyed a successful season at the top of the Somerset batting order.

Glamorgan went into their final County Championship game of 2009 still in with a chance of promotion, but a draw against Surrey at The Oval saw them finish fifth in Division Two, 19 points behind runners-up Essex.

Only two four-day games were lost, but 12 draws meant another season of frustration. As a batting unit, the Welsh county prospered, their 56 bonus points being the highest in the division, but the bowling relied too heavily on spinners Robert Croft and Dean Cosker, who shared 84 first-class wickets, the evergreen Croft taking 58 of them, as well as averaging 33 with the bat.

Jamie Dalrymple enjoyed an excellent first year as captain, passing 1,000 runs at an average of over 50 and taking 22 wickets. Opener Gareth Rees also reached the 1,000 landmark, scoring three of the 16 first-class centuries the team recorded. Mike Powell averaged 40.46, while Australian Mark Cosgrove smacked 780 runs in just ten matches at an average of 60, also with three hundreds, and was quickly re-signed for 2010.

James Harris was the pick of the seam bowlers. The 19-year-old claimed 43 first-class victims and was rewarded with a call-up to the England Lions squad.

Progress in the Championship was not matched in one-day cricket which saw Glamorgan win only twice in each of the three competitions.

The signing in August of all-rounder Jim Allenby from Leicestershire to bat in the middle order and bowl first or second change gave the side a better balance. Alex Wharf announced his retirement at the end of the season.

Above Glamorgan's Gareth Rees pulls to the boundary off Jade Dernbach, the Surrey fast bowler.

Below Gloucestershire's players celebrate a wicket, but overall the county fell short of tangible success in 2009.

THE GREAT DEBATE: 40 or 50?

VIKRAM SOLANKI, the Worcestershire and former England batsman, gives the players' views on the ongoing debate about whether there should be a 40-over or 50-over domestic cup competition...

The decision of the England and Wales Cricket Board to make the third domestic competition next season a 40-overs competition is a disappointment to the Professional Cricketers' Association.

If a similar change was proposed at international level I would one hundred per cent endorse the move to 40-overs because it would support everything the players have said about the structure of domestic cricket mirroring international cricket.

The players' views have been consistent for a good number of years: we should have three competitions replicating international cricket and for county cricket to operate as something that will benefit the England cricket team.

It seems that the decision, which was taken after a 13 to 5 vote of the counties, reflects a split between commercial motives and cricketing arguments. It's my view that the decision to go to 40-overs cricket is based on short-term commercial gain to the possible detriment of improving the England ODI team and, therefore, long-term commercial gain.

If England are successful, long-term commercial gain is inevitable. The model is sound. Winning the Ashes in 2005 proved it and we hope for more of the same as a result of the recent Ashes success.

What we have at the moment is an England Test team that is the product of county cricket, and you cannot argue with that. Jonathan Trott's huge success on debut in the last Ashes Test speaks volumes for the product of county cricket.

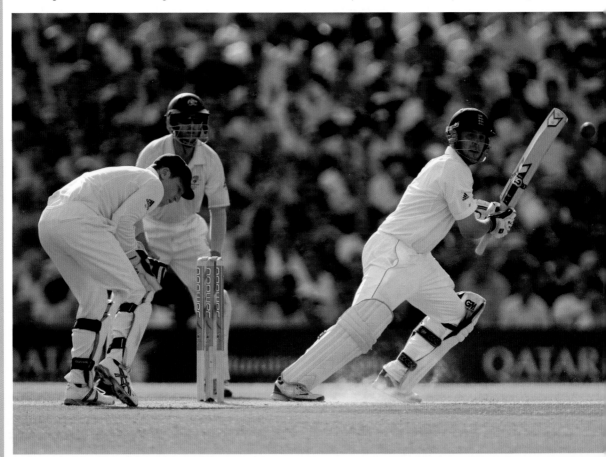

If that model is successful in Test cricket why is it that we are not replicating a similar sort of progression in one-day international cricket?

The playing format of County Championship cricket has been changed in the recent past so that it is similar to Test matches; attempts to improve the quality of pitches around the country have been made with the appointment of Pitch Liaison Officers. Everything is geared towards producing good Test match-type cricket in county cricket. Why would you want to set aside that model in one-day cricket? If it's worked in Test cricket then surely we should try to replicate the playing conditions in a similar manner in 50-overs cricket.

I am basing my opinion on the fact that we are aware that the 2011 World Cup will be a 50-overs competition and that the commercial rights to the 2015 World Cup have also been sold on the same basis.

I think it's probably too late to reverse the decision now because it has already been ratified by the ECB board. But it does ask questions about the structure of domestic cricket from next season to which the counties have agreed. There have also been changes to a number of other issues such as the non-appearance of a suggested P20 competition. In the light of such changes, perhaps the ECB would also re-address the subject of age-related payments that were to be enforced in the previously planned 50-overs competition.

It has been suggested that 40-overs cricket is more popular with spectators than 50-overs but I haven't seen any compelling evidence or research to support that. How can you possibly compare statistics for competitions that are played at two very different times of the year?

The 40-overs competition is played during the summer holiday period when the weather is usually better and people are available to watch cricket. The 50-overs competition has been played in the opening weeks of the season when the weather and conditions are not particularly conducive to either watching or playing good one-day cricket.

It must be said that players do enjoy playing 40-overs cricket. I think it's great and I enjoyed playing in front of a large Bank Holiday crowd during Worcestershire's Pro40

Jonathan Trott's Test debut hundred in the Ashes series decider at The Oval was also a massive plus mark for county cricket as a nursery for international-class players.

match against Hampshire at New Road. But I cannot accept that if it had been a 50-overs game that it would not have been an equally compelling game of cricket. There might have been more to it, actually, because those middle overs would have required some tactical manoeuvring.

A few seasons ago I would have agreed entirely that 50-overs cricket had become too uniform. But the addition of powerplays has brought a whole new tactical element to the game. During these powerplays, which make up 20 overs of each innings, certain fielding restrictions are imposed to prevent the game being too predictable. These fielding restrictions have developed over the last few years and although they may seem a bit complicated I think they are now about right.

There are two circles marked on the pitch for the powerplay: one is 15 yards from the wicket and the other is 30 yards. During a powerplay the fielding team is allowed only two or three fielders outside the 30-yard circle and has to have at least two fielders in close catching positions inside or near the 15-yard mark. Although the first ten overs of each innings are automatic powerplays, the other ten overs are taken in two blocks of five, one chosen by the fielding team and the other by the batting side.

What is so good about it is that there is no set way to go about your innings. Players have become adept at innovating ways of exploiting the new rules. There is no doubt that powerplays have enhanced the appeal of 50-overs cricket. There is talk of having similar fielding restrictions in the 40-overs competition but this will not cater for a phase of middle overs. That middle period is important in helping batsmen to work out ways of manoeuvring the ball about and hitting unprotected areas.

The ECB obviously realise the importance of 50-overs cricket because it is to continue at Under-19 and England Lions level. However, if a player comes out of the England Under-19s and does not go straight into the Lions squad he may not play any 50-overs cricket for three or four years.

As a result, youngsters are going to have to learn specific skills of the 50-overs game at the highest level should they make the grade, when ideally they should have gone through the finishing school of county cricket and therefore be prepared for what is required at the very top level.

Vikram Solanki is chairman of the Professional Cricketers' Association. This article first appeared on the TestMatchExtra.com cricket website.

OVERSEAS TEST MATCHES

by Mark Baldwin

Test cricket in this past year will be chiefly remembered, sadly, as much for what happened off the field as on it. With South Africa and Australia contesting two high-octane back-to-back series either side of the New Year, let alone the latest exciting Ashes chapter and many other performances of note, it is a situation of deep regret.

In the aftermath of the Mumbai attacks in late 2008, the world game – especially in the subcontinent – could ill afford further intrusions into its structure and viability. In the event, on 3 March, cricket was fortunate indeed not to have a major tragedy on its hands. The Lahore terrorist attack on the Sri Lankan team bus, as it travelled towards the Gaddafi Stadium for what should have been the resumption of the Second Test against Pakistan, injured five players and several officials, and left eight security personnel dead.

Indeed, only the bravery of Meher Mohammad Khalil, the Pakistani employed to drive the Sri Lankan squad from their Lahore hotel to the ground, saved players and

the team's support staff from far more serious consequences. As bullets riddled his bus, and players and officials hit the floor, Khalil stayed calm amid the sudden chaos and pressed down his accelerator hard in order to get the vehicle away from the scene as quickly as possible. His action almost certainly saved the lives of some high-profile cricketers, and also saved the game from the sort of terrorist atrocity against leading athletes that would have had the impact and ramifications of the assault on the Israeli team at the 1972 Munich Olympics.

As it was, then Sri Lankan captain Mahela Jayawardene was one of the players who suffered bullet or shrapnel wounds. Thilan Samaraweera needed surgery on a leg wound, and Ajantha Mendis was admitted to hospital for an operation to remove shrapnel from his head and back. In a separate, smaller vehicle, the ICC match officials – including former England batsman Chris Broad, the match referee – were even more fortunate to escape with their lives, although a Pakistani reserve umpire was badly wounded by a gunshot in his back and required lengthy treatment in hospital to survive.

Pakistani commandos and police, who formed the security escort, did lose their lives however, and no one can now give a time when international cricket can be played again in Pakistan. The ICC has ruled that in 2010 Pakistan will play its 'home' Test series against Australia in England, and that no matches in the 2011 World Cup will be staged there as originally intended.

Sri Lanka's cricketers, meanwhile, have shown admirable courage and statesmanship in the months since as they have determined to get back to playing cricket. The

Sri Lankan cricketer Thilan Samaraweera greets Mohammad Khalil, the Pakistani bus driver who drove the team to safety during the Lahore terrorist attack, at a special ceremony in Colombo.

AB de Villiers goes up on his toes to pull to leg during his unbeaten 106 on the last day of the epic opening Test between South Africa and Australia in Perth.

country's administrators, too, have displayed great fortitude. Kumar Sangakkara, the highly impressive captain who took over the job from his great friend Jayawardene immediately after the aborted Pakistan tour – as planned – said in the run-up to the ICC World Twenty20 in June, 'The guys have moved on very well. Playing cricket again is a sign of normality for us, and we are very well prepared mentally for it.'

Sangakkara himself ended the year as the number one ranked batsman in Tests and Jayawardene, who has stayed on in a senior batting role, has pledged to push himself 'to the limit' with the bat in the time left to him on the international stage. Two scores in the 90s against New Zealand during the SSC ground's Test, in Colombo, not only made him just the fourth player in history to do that but also took his run tally at his favourite venue to 2,467 from 22 Tests, at an average of 79.58.

Sri Lanka moved up to second place in the ICC Test rankings on the back of 2-0 series wins against Bangladesh away, Pakistan at home and New Zealand at home. Samaraweera came of age as a Test batsman, too, topping 1,000 runs in the calendar year with a startling surge of form that brought him successive double-hundreds against Pakistan and two other centuries against the New Zealanders.

The continued emergence of Mendis, as a mystery spinner to support the ageing but still effective Muttiah Muralitharan, plus the excellent performance of slow left-armer Rangana Herath as deputy for the injured Mendis against the Black Caps, maintained the potency of the Sri Lankan attack, although July saw the Test retirement of one of their most respected bowlers. Chaminda Vaas, the left-arm fast-medium purveyor of canny swing and seam, chose the end of the three-Test series against Pakistan to announce his decision. He took 355 wickets at 29.58 from 111 Tests, after debuting in August 1994, and wants to continue to challenge for a place in Sri Lanka's one-day side.

After an ovation from the crowd at the SSC ground, and a presentation from Sri Lanka Cricket, Vaas said, 'This is an emotional time for me. I have played international cricket for 16 years with pride and have performed to the best of my ability. In return, cricket has made me what I am today and I am grateful for all that I have received from the game.

'In my time Sri Lanka has made giant strides and is now able to rub shoulders with the best. While many people have contributed to this transformation, I am proud to have played my own little part in this process.' He mentioned Arjuna Ranatunga, the former captain, as the greatest influence on his career and said that Sangakkara could quickly become one of Sri Lanka's greatest captains.

South Africa, who ended this cricket year on top of the ICC Test rankings, were more than displeased that this achievement did not bring with it any individual nominations for the ICC's annual awards bash, especially as it was held in South Africa during the Champions Trophy tournament in October. Dale Steyn, the fast bowler, was at the time ranked as the number one bowler in Tests and Jacques Kallis had become only the eighth batsman to reach 10,000 Test runs when he passed the milestone during the first Test of South Africa's return series with Australia, at Johannesburg.

Winning a Test series for the first time in Australia, however, remained the defining and overwhelmingly pleasurable moment in South Africa's year – despite the deflating disappointment of losing the return rubber at home and the limited-overs tournament failures in the World Twenty20 and Champions Trophy.

It was beating Australia on their home soil which elevated Graeme Smith's team to pole position in the rankings in the first place (a position which they later regained thanks to England's Ashes success against the Australians), and in chasing down 414 to win the opening Test at Perth the South Africans made a statement of intent which reverberated around the world.

Hashim Amla, JP Duminy, AB de Villiers and Ashwell Prince all enhanced their reputations during the epic battles with Australia, while Steyn's match figures of 10 for 154 in Melbourne took his career wicket tally whistling past 150 in just 29 Tests, and at an average then of 22.66. Moreover, his strike rate of a wicket every 37.6 balls put him second only to George Lohmann among Test bowlers who had sent down at least 2,000 deliveries.

The partnership of captain Smith and head coach Mickey Arthur gained huge credit for the historic Test series win in Australia, but the lack of preparation for the home return series was a black mark. Smith himself, though, was extremely unlucky when he suffered broken bones in his hand in both the Sydney and Durban Tests, with his second injury clearly having a big impact on that series in particular.

ICC TEST RANKINGS		
1	South Africa	122
2	Sri Lanka	120
3	India	119
4	Australia	116
5	England	105
6	Pakistan	84
7	New Zealand	80
8	West Indies	76
9	Bangladesh	13

As at 24 October 2009

For New Zealand, meanwhile, there were struggles at Test level despite their familiar combativeness and success in the one-day international arena. A 2-0 defeat in Australia marked the end of John Bracewell's five years as head coach, but his successor Andy Moles, the former Warwickshire batsman, did not have much to shout about either in Test cricket.

New Zealand had slipped into eighth place in the Test rankings when Bracewell stood down, lamenting that 'in Tests, we lose the critical moments too often', but although Moles began with a 0-0 home draw with the West Indies he then oversaw a 1-0 home loss to India and a 2-0 beating in Sri Lanka in August, and by October had left his post by mutual consent

Daniel Vettori, the impressive captain of New Zealand, spins down another one.

Daniel Vettori, however, went past 300 Test wickets and remains one of the most respected international captains in the game. He and Moles, in the latter case only briefly, were also elevated on to the national selection panel, while New Zealand Cricket enjoyed a lucrative year financially mainly as a result of a television cash bonanza from coverage of the India visit.

The return to mainstream cricket of fast bowlers Shane Bond and Daryl Tuffey, following the amnesty granted to former Indian Cricket League players, was another boost to New Zealand, while the development of young talents like Daniel Flynn and Jesse Ryder offset the continuing injury problems that caused giant all-rounder Jacob Oram to retire from Test cricket in a bid to lengthen his one-day career.

Bangladesh, in theory, can also benefit from the return of 13 rebel players from the ICL, and the country was celebrating a first overseas Test series victory when West Indies – severely weakened by the absence of its leading players due to a pay dispute – were beaten 2-0 in the Caribbean. Shakib Al-Hasan, the highly promising all-rounder and stand-in captain in the injury absence of Mashrafe bin Mortaza, said the wins in St Vincent and Grenada represented Bangladesh's greatest cricketing achievement since being granted Test status in 2000.

But two-match Test series were lost in South Africa and Sri Lanka, both by 2-0 margins, even though Bangladesh distinguished themselves by totalling 413 in their second innings before going down in the First Test against the Sri Lankans by 107 runs, with Mohammad Ashraful hitting 101 and Shakib 96. Mortaza replaced Ashraful as captain following the World Twenty20.

Pakistan's proposed tour of Bangladesh in March was called off, by the Bangladesh government, in the wake of the Lahore terrorist attack and the only Test cricket played by Younis Khan's side – Younis took over from Shoaib Malik as captain in January – was home and away to Sri Lanka.

Younis himself scored 313 in the high-scoring stalemate Test in Karachi that preceded the Lahore outrage, and Pakistan were outplayed 2-0 in a three-match series four months later. In the First Test, in Galle, Pakistan also suffered the dismay of losing their last eight wickets for a mere 46 runs as they were bowled out for 117 to go down by 50 runs when, at the start of the final day, they looked certain to win. They did, however, get the better of the drawn Third Test and Younis said, 'We have played very little cricket in the past 18 months and we went a full year in 2008 without playing any Tests at all. Don't write this team off in Test cricket. When we start playing regularly again we will learn to adapt to the demands of the five-day game.'

It would never be wise, of course, to dismiss any Pakistan team at all as the country – even one currently ravaged by internal lawlessness, especially on its eastern borders – continues to produce cricketers of almost wondrous natural talent. Batsman Umar Akmal, brother of wicketkeeper Kamran Akmal, is one clear find of the past year, but the latest potential superstar is 17-year-old left-arm fast bowler Mohammad Aamer, who took 56 wickets in ten matches for Rawalpindi in his debut first-class season and underlined his emergence as an embryonic world-class talent by dismissing the prolific Tillakeratne Dilshan in the first over of the ICC World Twenty20 final at Lord's in June.

Pakistan's victory in that tournament, against a Sri Lanka team who after Lahore were the romantic choice of most neutrals, was a truly massive fillip for cricket there while the return from ICL exile of Mohammad Yousuf, Abdul Razzaq, Rana Naved and Imran Nazir – plus the comeback of paceman Mohammad Asif following a drugs ban – provided further timely boosts to Pakistani morale.

Above The Bangladesh team celebrate with the trophy after completing a historic 2-0 win in their short Test series against West Indies in the Caribbean.

Below Younis Khan, the captain of Pakistan, is pictured during his mammoth 313 against Sri Lanka in Karachi.

FIRST TEST – SOUTH AFRICA v. BANGLADESH
19–22 November 2008 at Bloemfontein

SOUTH AFRICA

	First Innings	
GC Smith (capt)	b Mahbubul Alam	157
ND McKenzie	c Mehrab Hossain b S Hossain	42
HM Amla	b Mashrafe bin Mortaza	112
JH Kallis	c M Ashraful b S Al Hasan	16
AG Prince	not out	59
AB de Villiers	c Mushfiqur Rahim b S Al Hasan	3
*MV Boucher	b Shakib Al Hasan	15
M Morkel	c M Ashraful b S Al Hasan	1
DW Steyn	c Tamim Iqbal b Shakib Al Hasan	1
M Ntini	c Mushfiqur Rahim b M Alam	5
PL Harris	absent hurt	
Extras	b 2, lb 10, nb 11	23
	(all out 122.5 overs)	**441**

	First Innings			
	O	M	R	W
Mashrafe bin Mortaza	22	4	69	1
Mahbubul Alam	24.5	8	62	2
Shahadat Hossain	25	1	125	1
Shakib Al Hasan	38	4	130	5
Naeem Islam	5	0	19	0
Mehrab Hossain	8	0	24	0

Fall of Wickets
1-102, 2-327, 3-327, 4-352, 5-365, 6-404, 7-420, 8-427, 9-441

BANGLADESH

	First Innings		Second Innings (following on)	
Tamim Iqbal	b Steyn	7	c Boucher b Ntini	20
Imrul Kayes	c Amla b Harris	10	b Steyn	4
Junaid Siddique	c Prince b Morkel	8	c Boucher b Kallis	27
M Ashraful (capt)	c McKenzie b Steyn	1	c McKenzie b Ntini	13
Mehrab Hossain	c Boucher b Ntini	12	not out	43
Shakib Al Hasan	c de Villiers b Ntini	14	c Boucher b Steyn	0
*Mushfiqur Rahim	lbw b Kallis	48	run out	0
Naeem Islam	c Harris b Ntini	8	c Boucher b Steyn	3
Mashrafe bin Mortaza	c & b Morkel	5	b Steyn	6
Shahadat Hossain	b Kallis	23	b Steyn	16
Mahbubul Alam	not out	1	c Prince b Kallis	0
Extras	b 4, lb 2, w 4, nb 6	16	b 7, lb 17, nb 3	27
	(all out 36.4 overs)	153	(all out 51.5 overs)	159

	First Innings				Second Innings			
	O	M	R	W	O	M	R	W
Steyn	9	2	36	2	18	4	63	5
Ntini	8	2	20	3	16	8	19	2
Morkel	8	0	55	2	13	6	36	0
Harris	7	1	26	1	-	-	-	-
Kallis	4.4	1	10	2	4.5	0	17	2

Fall of Wickets
1-8, 2-26, 3-33, 4-33, 5-50, 6-59, 7-71, 8-88, 9-148
1-13, 2-45, 3-67, 4-80, 5-81, 6-81, 7-92, 8-108, 9-152

Umpires: SJ Davis (Australia) & IJ Gould (England)
Toss: Bangladesh
Test debut: Imrul Kayes
Man of the Match: GC Smith

SECOND TEST – SOUTH AFRICA v. BANGLADESH
26–28 November 2008 at Centurion

BANGLADESH

	First Innings		Second Innings	
Tamim Iqbal	c Boucher b Morkel	31	c McKenzie b Morkel	20
Imrul Kayes	c Smith b Ntini	6	c Smith b Ntini	5
Junaid Siddique	c McKenzie b Ntini	67	c Amla b Kallis	16
M Ashraful (capt)	c & b Morkel	1	run out	21
Mehrab Hossain	c Kallis b Ntini	3	run out	0
Raqibul Hasan	c Smith b Morkel	15	run out	28
Shakib Al Hasan	b Morkel	30	c Ntini b Morkel	2
*Mushfiqur Rahim	c de Villiers b Zondeki	65	b Ntini	4
Mashrafe bin Mortaza	c Kallis b Ntini	12	not out	23
Shahadat Hossain	c Boucher b Steyn	4	c de Villiers b Zondeki	0
Mahbubul Alam	not out	1	c Boucher b Zondeki	1
Extras	lb 3, nb 12	15	b 5, lb 3, w 1, nb 2	11
	(all out 76.2 overs)	250	(all out 36.4 overs)	131

	First Innings				Second Innings			
	O	M	R	W	O	M	R	W
Steyn	17	4	80	1	8	2	23	0
Ntini	19.2	8	32	4	11	2	44	2
Kallis	12	4	30	0	6	1	24	1
Zondeki	10	3	32	1	4.4	2	10	2
Morkel	18	0	73	4	6	1	21	2
McKenzie	-	-	-	-	1	0	1	0

Fall of Wickets
1-25, 2-54, 3-57, 4-71, 5-122, 6-159, 7-166, 8-186, 9-194
1-8, 2-37, 3-47, 4-57, 5-68, 6-77, 7-95, 8-126, 9-127

SOUTH AFRICA

	First Innings	
GC Smith (capt)	lbw b Mahbubul Alam	27
ND McKenzie	c Hasan b Mashrafe bin Mortaza	0
HM Amla	c & b Shakib Al Hasan	71
JH Kallis	b Shakib Al Hasan	24
AG Prince	not out	162
AB de Villiers	st Mushfiqur Rahim b S Al Hasan	0
*MV Boucher	c Imrul Kayes b Shakib Al Hasan	117
M Morkel	b Shakib Al Hasan	0
M Zondeki	st Mushfiqur Rahim b S Al Hasan	0
M Ntini	c M Ashraful b Shahadat Hossain	0
DW Steyn	b Shahadat Hossain	1
Extras	lb 17, w 2, nb 8	27
	(all out 115.2 overs)	**429**

	First Innings			
	O	M	R	W
Mashrafe bin Mortaza	26	2	74	1
Mahbubul Alam	26	5	85	1
Shakib Al Hasan	28	3	99	6
Shahadat Hossain	22.2	2	89	2
Mehrab Hossain	11	1	50	0
Mohammad Ashraful	2	0	15	0

Fall of Wickets
1-3, 2-47, 3-112, 4-134, 5-134, 6-405, 7-405, 8-405, 9-412

Umpires: SJ Davis (Australia) & IJ Gould (England)
Toss: Bangladesh
Test debut: Raqibul Hasan
Man of the Match: AG Prince
Man of the Series: AG Prince

South Africa won by an innings and 129 runs

South Africa won by an innings and 48 runs

South Africa won series 2–0

SERIES AVERAGES
South Africa v. Bangladesh

SOUTH AFRICA

Batting	M	Inns	NO	Runs	HS	Av	100	50	c/st
GC Smith	2	2	0	184	157	92.00	1	–	3/-
HM Amla	2	2	0	183	112	91.50	1	1	2/-
MV Boucher	2	2	0	132	117	66.00	1	–	8/-
ND McKenzie	2	2	0	42	42	21.00	–	–	4/-
JH Kallis	2	2	0	40	24	20.00	–	–	2/-
M Morkel	2	2	0	8	8	4.00	–	–	2/-
M Ntini	2	2	0	5	5	2.50	–	–	1/-
AB de Villiers	2	2	0	3	3	1.50	–	–	3/-
DW Steyn	2	2	0	2	1	1.00	–	–	-/-
M Zondeki	1	1	0	0	0	0.00	–	–	-/-
AG Prince	2	2	2	221	162*	–	–	1	1	2/-
PL Harris	1	0	0	0	0	–	–	–	1/-

Bowling	Overs	Mds	Runs	Wkts	Av	Best	5/inn	10m
M Ntini	54.2	20	115	11	10.45	4-32	–	–
M Zondeki	14.4	5	42	3	14.00	2-10	–	–
JH Kallis	27.3	6	81	5	16.20	2-10	–	–
M Morkel	45	7	185	8	23.12	4-73	–	–
DW Steyn	52	12	202	8	25.25	5-63	1	–
PL Harris	7	1	26	1	26.00	1-26	–	–

Also bowled: ND McKenzie 1-0-1-0.

BANGLADESH

Batting	M	Inns	NO	Runs	HS	Av	100	50	c/st
Junaid Siddique	2	4	0	118	67	29.50	–	1	-/-
Mushfiqur Rahim	2	4	0	117	65	29.25	–	1	2/2
Raqibul Hasan	1	2	0	43	28	21.50	–	–	1/-
Tamim Iqbal	2	4	0	78	31	19.50	–	–	1/-
Mehrab Hossain	2	4	1	58	43*	19.33	–	–	1/-
Mashrafe bin Mortaza	2	4	1	46	23*	15.33	–	–	-/-
Shakib Al Hasan	2	4	0	46	30	11.50	–	–	1/-
Shahadat Hossain	2	4	0	43	23	10.75	–	–	1/-
Mohammad Ashraful	2	4	0	36	21	9.00	–	–	3/-
Imrul Kayes	2	4	0	25	10	6.25	–	–	1/-
Naeem Islam	1	2	0	11	8	5.50	–	–	-/-
Mahbubul Alam	2	4	2	3	1*	1.50	–	–	-/-

Bowling	Overs	Mds	Runs	Wkts	Av	Best	5/inn	10m
Shakib Al Hasan	66	7	229	11	20.81	6-99	2	–
Mahbubul Alam	50.5	13	147	3	49.00	2-62	–	–
Shahadat Hossain	47.2	3	214	3	71.33	2-89	–	–
Mashrafe bin Mortaza	48	6	143	2	71.50	1-69	–	–

Also bowled: Mohammad Ashraful 2-0-15-0, Naeem Islam 5-0-19-0, Mehrab Hossain 19-1-74-0.

FIRST TEST – SOUTH AFRICA v. AUSTRALIA
26 February–2 March 2009 at Johannesburg

AUSTRALIA

	First Innings		Second Innings	
PJ Hughes	c Boucher b Steyn	0	c de Villiers b Harris	75
SM Katich	c McKenzie b Steyn	3	c Boucher b Morkel	10
RT Ponting (capt)	b Ntini	83	c Amla b Kallis	25
MEK Hussey	c Kallis b Morkel	4	c Ntini b Kallis	0
MJ Clarke	c Boucher b Steyn	68	c Kallis b Harris	0
MJ North	st Boucher b Harris	117	b Kallis	5
*BJ Haddin	c Harris b Ntini	63	c Boucher b Ntini	37
AB McDonald	c Kallis b Steyn	0	c Boucher b Ntini	7
MG Johnson	not out	96	c Kallis b Ntini	1
PM Siddle	c Kallis b Morkel	9	not out	22
BW Hilfenhaus	c de Villiers b Morkel	0	b Steyn	16
Extras	b 6, lb 8, w 2, nb 7	23	lb 5, w 1, nb 3	9
	(all out 125.4 overs)	466	(all out 53.4 overs)	207

	First Innings				Second Innings			
	O	M	R	W	O	M	R	W
Steyn	30	4	113	4	16.4	5	51	1
Ntini	27	6	71	2	11	3	52	3
Morkel	28.4	3	117	3	10	1	41	1
Kallis	8	0	33	0	5	0	22	3
Harris	18	2	64	1	11	0	36	2
Duminy	14	2	54	0	–	–	–	–

Fall of Wickets
1-0, 2-18, 3-38, 4-151, 5-182, 6-295, 7-296, 8-413, 9-466
1-38, 2-99, 3-99, 4-99, 5-104, 6-138, 7-145, 8-147, 9-174

SOUTH AFRICA

	First Innings		Second Innings	
ND McKenzie	lbw b Siddle	36	c Haddin b Johnson	35
GC Smith (capt)	c Haddin b Johnson	0	c Johnson b Hilfenhaus	69
HM Amla	c Ponting b Hilfenhaus	1	c Hughes b Siddle	57
JH Kallis	c Hussey b Siddle	27	b Johnson	45
AB de Villiers	not out	104	lbw b McDonald	3
JP Duminy	c Haddin b Johnson	17	c Ponting b Siddle	29
*MV Boucher	c Haddin b Johnson	0	b Hilfenhaus	26
M Morkel	c & b Siddle	2	c Hughes b Johnson	2
PL Harris	lbw b North	1	c Katich b Siddle	8
DW Steyn	c North b McDonald	17	b Johnson	6
M Ntini	b Johnson	1	not out	0
Extras	b 4, lb 6, nb 4	14	b 1, lb 4, w 2, nb 4	11
	(all out 81.1 overs)	220	(all out 119.2 overs)	291

	First Innings				Second Innings			
	O	M	R	W	O	M	R	W
Johnson	18.1	7	25	4	34.2	2	114	4
Hilfenhaus	25	9	58	1	31	7	68	2
Siddle	21	1	76	3	25	8	46	3
McDonald	10	4	22	1	22	8	31	1
North	7	0	29	1	7	0	27	0

Fall of Wickets
1-1, 2-2, 3-49, 4-93, 5-138, 6-138, 7-154, 8-156, 9-208
1-76, 2-130, 3-206, 4-211, 5-229, 6-268, 7-272, 8-284, 9-289

Umpires: BF Bowden (New Zealand) & SA Bucknor (West Indies)
Toss: Australia
Test debuts: BW Hilfenhaus, PJ Hughes & MJ North
Man of the Match: MG Johnson

Australia won by 162 runs

SECOND TEST – SOUTH AFRICA v. AUSTRALIA
6–10 March 2009 at Durban

AUSTRALIA

	First Innings		Second Innings	
PJ Hughes	c McKenzie b Kallis	115	c Morkel b Ntini	160
SM Katich	c Smith b Steyn	108	c Harris b Kallis	30
RT Ponting (capt)	c McKenzie b Harris	9	c McKenzie b Morkel	81
MEK Hussey	b Morkel	50	c Kallis b Duminy	19
MJ Clarke	b Harris	3	not out	23
MJ North	c Steyn b Kallis	38	c de Villiers b Steyn	0
*BJ Haddin	c Amla b Ntini	5		
AB McDonald	not out	4		
MG Johnson	lbw b Ntini	0		
PM Siddle	c Boucher b Steyn	0		
BW Hilfenhaus	c Smith b Steyn	0		
Extras	b 6, lb 4, w 2, nb 8	20	b 12, lb 2, nb 4	18
	(all out 107.4 overs)	352	(5 wkts dec 94.4 overs)	331

	First Innings				Second Innings			
	O	M	R	W	O	M	R	W
Steyn	25.4	3	83	3	15.4	1	75	1
Ntini	19	4	58	2	15	2	55	1
Morkel	24	4	81	1	14	1	60	1
Kallis	15	4	49	2	8	0	21	1
Harris	21	5	66	2	31	8	68	0
Duminy	3	1	5	0	11	1	38	1

Fall of Wickets
1–184, 2–208, 3–259, 4–266, 5–329, 6–348, 7–348, 8–348, 9–352
1–55, 2–219, 3–260, 4–330, 5–331

SOUTH AFRICA

	First Innings		Second Innings	
ND McKenzie	c Haddin b Johnson	0	(2) c Haddin b Siddle	31
GC Smith (capt)	retired hurt	2	absent hurt	
HM Amla	lbw b Johnson	0	(1) c Ponting b Siddle	43
JH Kallis	c Ponting b McDonald	22	(3) c Ponting b Johnson	93
AB de Villiers	lbw b Hilfenhaus	3	(4) c Haddin b Siddle	84
JP Duminy	not out	73	(5) c Haddin b Hilfenhaus	17
*MV Boucher	b Johnson	1	(6) c & b North	25
PL Harris	b McDonald	4	(7) c Siddle b Katich	5
M Morkel	b McDonald	2	(8) c Haddin b Katich	24
DW Steyn	c Haddin b Siddle	8	(9) st Haddin b Katich	11
M Ntini	lbw b Siddle	0	(10) not out	4
Extras	b 10, lb 12, nb 1	23	b 9, lb 11, w 3, nb 10	33
	(all out 57.3 overs)	138	(all out 132.2 overs)	370

	First Innings				Second Innings			
	O	M	R	W	O	M	R	W
Johnson	16	5	37	3	33	9	78	1
Hilfenhaus	11	2	28	1	24	4	79	1
McDonald	12	4	25	3	16	3	47	0
Siddle	13.3	6	20	2	28	12	61	3
North	4	3	6	0	20	6	40	1
Clarke	1	1	0	0	-	-	-	-
Katich	-	-	-	-	11.2	1	45	3

Fall of Wickets
1–0, 2–0, 3–6, 4–62, 5–104, 6–104, 7–106, 8–138, 9–138
1–63, 2–80, 3–267, 4–279, 5–299, 6–307, 7–345, 8–363, 9–370

Umpires: Asad Rauf (Pakistan) & BF Bowden (New Zealand)
Toss: Australia
Man of the Match: PJ Hughes

Australia won by 175 runs

THIRD TEST – SOUTH AFRICA v. AUSTRALIA
19–23 March 2009 at Cape Town

AUSTRALIA

	First Innings		Second Innings	
PJ Hughes	lbw b Harris	33	c Kallis b Harris	32
SM Katich	c Khan b Harris	55	c Duminy b Harris	54
RT Ponting (capt)	c Boucher b Morkel	0	c Boucher b Steyn	12
MEK Hussey	b Steyn	20	c Duminy b Steyn	39
MJ Clarke	b Steyn	0	b Steyn	47
*BJ Haddin	lbw b Harris	42	c Duminy b Harris	18
AB McDonald	c Kallis b Ntini	13	c de Villiers b Harris	68
MG Johnson	c Prince b Steyn	35	not out	123
PM Siddle	c de Villiers b Ntini	0	c de Villiers b Harris	0
BE McGain	c de Villiers b Steyn	2	run out	0
BW Hilfenhaus	not out	0	c Prince b Harris	12
Extras	lb 6, w 1, nb 2	9	b 8, lb 2, w 2, nb 5	17
	(all out 72 overs)	209	(all out 121.5 overs)	422

	First Innings				Second Innings			
	O	M	R	W	O	M	R	W
Steyn	16	5	56	4	27	5	96	3
Ntini	17	7	38	2	19	6	66	0
Kallis	10	2	31	0	10	4	21	0
Morkel	12	3	44	1	20	1	88	0
Harris	17	5	34	3	42.5	9	127	6
Duminy	-	-	-	-	3	1	14	0

Fall of Wickets
1–58, 2–59, 3–81, 4–81, 5–152, 6–158, 7–190, 8–190, 9–209
1–57, 2–76, 3–138, 4–146, 5–191, 6–218, 7–381, 8–381, 9–388

SOUTH AFRICA

	First Innings	
I Khan	c & b Siddle	20
AG Prince	c Haddin b Hilfenhaus	150
HM Amla	c Haddin b Johnson	46
JH Kallis (capt)	c & b Hilfenhaus	102
AB de Villiers	c McDonald b Katich	163
JP Duminy	b Johnson	7
*MV Boucher	c Ponting b Johnson	12
JA Morkel	b McDonald	58
PL Harris	c Haddin b Johnson	27
DW Steyn	c Clarke b Katich	0
M Ntini	not out	4
Extras	b 19, lb 24, w 9, nb 10	62
	(all out 154.3 overs)	651

	First Innings			
	O	M	R	W
Johnson	37.3	5	148	4
Hilfenhaus	34	4	133	2
Siddle	35	15	67	1
McGain	18	2	149	0
McDonald	27	7	102	1
Katich	3	1	9	2

Fall of Wickets
1–65, 2–162, 3–322, 4–415, 5–443, 6–467, 7–591, 8–637, 9–637

Umpires: Asad Rauf (Pakistan) & SA Bucknor (West Indies)
Toss: Australia
Test debuts: BE McGain, I Khan & JA Morkel
Man of the Match: PL Harris
Man of the Series: MG Johnson

South Africa won by an innings and 20 runs

Australia won series 2–1

SERIES AVERAGES
South Africa v. Australia

SOUTH AFRICA

Batting	M	Inns	NO	Runs	HS	Av	100	50	c/st
AG Prince	1	1	0	150	150	150.00	1	–	2/-
AB de Villiers	3	5	1	357	163	89.25	2	1	7/-
JA Morkel	1	1	0	58	58	58.00	–	1	-/-
JH Kallis	3	5	0	289	102	57.80	1	1	8/-
JP Duminy	3	5	1	143	73*	35.75	–	1	3/-
GC Smith	2	3	1	71	69	35.50	–	1	2/-
HM Amla	3	5	0	147	57	29.40	–	1	2/-
ND McKenzie	2	4	0	102	36	25.50	–	–	4/-
I Khan	1	1	0	20	20	20.00	–	–	1/-
MV Boucher	3	5	0	64	26	12.80	–	–	8/1
PL Harris	3	5	0	45	27	9.00	–	–	2/-
DW Steyn	3	5	0	42	17	8.40	–	–	1/-
M Morkel	2	4	0	30	24	7.50	–	–	1/-
M Ntini	3	5	3	9	4*	4.50	–	–	1/-

Bowling	Overs	Mds	Runs	Wkts	Av	Best	5/inn	10m
PL Harris	140.5	29	395	14	28.21	6-127	1	–
JH Kallis	56	10	177	6	29.50	3-22	–	–
DW Steyn	131	23	474	16	29.62	4-56	–	–
M Ntini	108	28	340	10	34.00	3-52	–	–
M Morkel	76.4	9	299	6	49.83	3-117	–	–
JP Duminy	31	5	111	1	111.00	1-38	–	–
JA Morkel	32	4	132	1	132.00	1-44	–	–

AUSTRALIA

Batting	M	Inns	NO	Runs	HS	Av	100	50	c/st
MG Johnson	3	5	2	255	123*	85.00	1	1	1/-
PJ Hughes	3	6	0	415	160	69.16	2	1	2/-
SM Katich	3	6	0	260	108	43.33	1	2	1/-
MJ North	2	4	0	160	117	40.00	1	–	2/-
RT Ponting	3	6	0	210	83	35.00	–	2	6/-
BJ Haddin	3	5	0	165	63	33.00	–	1	13/1
MJ Clarke	3	6	1	141	68	28.20	–	1	1/-
AB McDonald	3	5	1	92	68	23.00	–	1	1/-
MEK Hussey	3	6	0	132	50	22.00	–	1	1/-
PM Siddle	3	5	1	31	22*	7.75	–	–	3/-
BW Hilfenhaus	3	5	1	28	16	7.00	–	–	1/-
BE McGain	1	2	0	2	2	1.00	–	–	-/-

Bowling	Overs	Mds	Runs	Wkts	Av	Best	5/inn	10m
SM Katich	14.2	2	54	5	10.80	3-45	–	–
PM Siddle	122.3	42	270	12	22.50	3-46	–	–
MG Johnson	139	28	402	16	25.12	4-25	–	–
AB McDonald	87	26	227	6	37.83	3-25	–	–
MJ North	38	9	102	2	51.00	1-29	–	–
BW Hilfenhaus	125	26	366	7	52.28	2-68	–	–

Also bowled: MJ Clarke 1-1-0-0, BE McGain 18-2-149-0.

FIRST TEST – SRI LANKA v. NEW ZEALAND
18-22 August 2009 at Galle

SRI LANKA

	First Innings		Second Innings	
NT Paranavitana	c McCullum b Martin	0	c Taylor b O'Brien	5
TM Dilshan	b O'Brien	92	not out	123
KC Sangakkara (capt)	c Flynn b Martin	8	run out	46
DPMD Jayawardene	c Taylor b O'Brien	114	c & b Patel	27
TT Samaraweera	c Patel b Vettori	159	c Taylor b Vettori	20
AD Mathews	c McCullum b Vettori	39		
*HAPW Jayawardene	c Flynn b Vettori	7	(6) not out	30
KMDN Kulasekara	c McCullum b Martin	18		
T Thushara	c O'Brien b Vettori	0		
M Muralitharan	c McCullum b Martin	8		
BAW Mendis	not out	0		
Extras	b 1, lb 2, w 2, nb 2	7	b 5, lb 3	8
	(all out 117.4 overs)	452	(4 wkts dec 49 overs)	259

	First Innings			Second Innings		
	O	M	R	W	O	M	R	W
Martin	23	5	77	4	5	1	25	0
O'Brien	21	1	125	2	8	1	45	1
Oram	7	1	25	0	5	0	31	0
Vettori	37.4	9	78	4	19	3	81	1
Patel	24	3	120	0	12	0	69	1
Ryder	5	1	24	0	–	–	–	–

Fall of Wickets
1-0, 2-16, 3-134, 4-300, 5-386, 6-408, 7-444, 8-444, 9-452
1-19, 2-120, 3-174, 4-205

NEW ZEALAND

	First Innings		Second Innings	
TG McIntosh	lbw b Muralitharan	69	(4) c Samaraweera b Thushara	0
MJ Guptill	b Thushara	24	(1) b Thushara	18
DR Flynn	b Mendis	14	(2) c Jayawardene DPMD b Kulasekara	0
JS Patel	lbw b Muralitharan	26	(9) st Jayawardene HAPW b Murali	22
LRPL Taylor	c Jayawardene HAPW b Thushara	35	(3) c J'wardene HAPW b J'wardene DPMD	16
JD Ryder	b Kulasekara	42	(7) c J'wardene HAPW b Murali	24
*BB McCullum	b Thushara	1	(8) run out	29
JDP Oram	c sub b Muralitharan	12	(5) lbw b Mendis	21
DL Vettori (capt)	b Thushara	42	(6) c J'wardene HAPW b Mendis	67
IE O'Brien	c Jayawardene HAPW b Murali	9	c Paranavitana b Muralitharan	5
CS Martin	not out	2	not out	0
Extras	b 6, lb 5, w 1, nb 11	23	b 4, lb 1, nb 3	8
	(all out 116 overs)	299	(all out 71.5 overs)	210

	First Innings			Second Innings		
	O	M	R	W	O	M	R	W
Kulasekara	10	2	41	1	8	2	20	1
Thushara	23	2	81	4	14	3	37	2
Mendis	39	8	85	1	18.5	4	50	2
Muralitharan	42	10	73	4	27	4	88	3
Paranavitana	2	0	8	0	–	–	–	–
Jayawardene DPMD	–	–	–	–	4	1	10	1

Fall of Wickets
1-45, 2-80, 3-129, 4-180, 5-188, 6-195, 7-223, 8-259, 9-290
1-1, 2-37, 3-39, 4-45, 5-86, 6-134, 7-167, 8-204, 9-210

Umpires: DJ Harper (Australia) & NJ Llong (England)
Toss: New Zealand
Man of the Match: DPMD Jayawardene

Sri Lanka won by 202 runs

SECOND TEST – SRI LANKA v. NEW ZEALAND
26-30 August 2009 at Colombo (SSC)

SRI LANKA

	First Innings		Second Innings	
NT Paranavitana	c Taylor b Vettori	19	(2) c McCullum b Vettori	34
TM Dilshan	c & b O'Brien	29	(1) c Guptill b Patel	33
KC Sangakkara (capt)	c Oram b Vettori	50	c Taylor b Patel	109
DPMD Jayawardene	c McCullum b O'Brien	92	c Taylor b O'Brien	96
TT Samaraweera	c McCullum b Patel	143	lbw b Vettori	25
CK Kapugedera	c Vettori b Patel	35	not out	7
*HAPW Jayawardene	c O'Brien b Martin	17		
KTGD Prasad	c Taylor b Patel	6		
HMRKB Herath	lbw b Patel	0		
M Muralitharan	not out	17		
T Thushara	c Patel b Vettori	0		
Extras	b 2, lb 5, nb 1	8	lb 1, w 2, nb 4	7
	(all out 130.3 overs)	416	(5 wkts dec 85.2 overs)	311

	First Innings				Second Innings			
	O	M	R	W	O	M	R	W
Martin	24	3	81	1	9	0	34	0
O'Brien	22	3	73	2	15.2	1	77	1
Vettori	40.3	12	104	3	24	4	62	2
Oram	21	7	56	0	-	-	-	-
Patel	20	3	78	4	34	2	122	2
Ryder	3	1	17	0	3	0	15	0

Fall of Wickets
1-34, 2-75, 3-115, 4-295, 5-367, 6-389, 7-396, 8-396, 9-415
1-56, 2-89, 3-262, 4-301, 5-311

NEW ZEALAND

	First Innings		Second Innings	
TG McIntosh	lbw b Prasad	5	b Prasad	7
MJ Guptill	c Muralitharan b Thushara	35	c Jayawardene HAPW b Herath	28
DR Flynn	c Jayawardene HAPW b Thushara	13	lbw b Herath	50
LRPL Taylor	c Jayawardene HAPW b Herath	81	c Jayawardene DPMD b Herath	27
JD Ryder	c Paranavitana b Herath	23	lbw b Herath	38
JS Patel	c Jayawardene DPMD b Murali	1	(9) c Kapugedera b Muralitharan	12
*BB McCullum	c Jayawardene DPMD b Murali	18	(6) b Muralitharan	13
JDP Oram	c Kapugedera b Herath	24	(7) c Sangakkara b Dilshan	56
DL Vettori (capt)	c Kapugedera b Dilshan	23	(8) c Herath b Muralitharan	140
IE O'Brien	lbw b Muralitharan	4	c Jayawardene HAPW b Herath	12
CS Martin	not out	0	not out	0
Extras	lb 3, w 2, nb 2	7	lb 13, nb 1	14
	(all out 77.4 overs)	234	(all out 123.5 overs)	397

	First Innings				Second Innings			
	O	M	R	W	O	M	R	W
Dilshan	3	0	12	1	6	0	15	1
Thushara	9	2	37	2	23.3	1	78	0
Prasad	6	0	41	1	15	1	56	1
Herath	34	11	70	3	48	9	139	5
Muralitharan	25.4	2	71	3	28.2	3	85	3
Paranavitana	-	-	-	-	1	0	2	0
Kapugedera	-	-	-	-	2	0	9	0

Fall of Wickets
1-14, 2-49, 3-63, 4-148, 5-149, 6-183, 7-183, 8-226, 9-234
1-36, 2-41, 3-97, 4-131, 5-158, 6-176, 7-300, 8-318, 9-387

Umpires: DJ Harper (Australia) & NJ Llong (England)
Toss: Sri Lanka
Man of the Match: TM Dilshan
Man of the Series: TT Samaraweera

SERIES AVERAGES
Sri Lanka v. New Zealand

SRI LANKA

Batting	M	Inns	NO	Runs	HS	Av	100	50	c/st
TM Dilshan	2	4	1	277	123*	92.33	1	1	-/-
TT Samaraweera	2	4	0	347	159	86.75	2	-	1/-
DPMD Jayawardene	2	4	0	329	114	82.25	1	2	4/-
KC Sangakkara	2	4	0	213	109	53.25	1	1	1/-
CK Kapugedera	1	2	1	42	35	42.00	-	-	3/-
AD Mathews	1	1	0	39	39	39.00	-	-	-/-
HAPW Jayawardene	2	3	1	54	30*	27.00	-	-	9/1
M Muralitharan	2	2	1	25	17*	25.00	-	-	1/-
KMDN Kulasekara	1	1	0	18	18	18.00	-	-	-/-
NT Paranavitana	2	4	0	58	34	14.50	-	-	2/-
KTGD Prasad	1	1	0	6	6	6.00	-	-	-/-
HMRKB Herath	1	1	0	0	0	0.00	-	-	1/-
T Thushara	2	2	0	0	0	0.00	-	-	-/-
BAW Mendis	1	1	1	0	0*	-	-	-	-/-

Bowling	Overs	Mds	Runs	Wkts	Av	Best	5/inn	10m
DPMD Jayawardene	4	1	10	1	10.00	1-10	-	-
TM Dilshan	9	0	27	2	13.50	1-12	-	-
M Muralitharan	123	19	317	13	24.38	4-73	-	-
HMRKB Herath	82	20	209	8	26.12	5-139	-	-
T Thushara	69.3	8	233	8	29.12	4-81	-	-
KMDN Kulasekara	18	4	61	2	30.50	1-20	-	-
BAW Mendis	57.5	12	135	3	45.00	2-50	-	-
KTGD Prasad	21	1	97	2	48.50	1-41	-	-

Also bowled: CK Kapugedera 2-0-9-0, NT Paranavitana 3-0-10-0.

NEW ZEALAND

Batting	M	Inns	NO	Runs	HS	Av	100	50	c/st
DL Vettori	2	4	0	272	140	68.00	1	1	1/-
LRPL Taylor	2	4	0	159	81	39.75	-	1	7/-
JD Ryder	2	4	0	127	42	31.75	-	-	-/-
JDP Oram	2	4	0	113	56	28.25	-	1	1/-
MJ Guptill	2	4	0	105	35	26.25	-	-	1/-
TG McIntosh	2	4	0	81	69	20.25	-	1	-/-
DR Flynn	2	4	0	77	50	19.25	-	1	2/-
BB McCullum	2	4	0	61	29	15.25	-	-	7/-
JS Patel	2	4	0	61	26	15.25	-	-	3/-
IE O'Brien	2	4	0	30	12	7.50	-	-	3/-
CS Martin	2	4	4	2	2*	-	-	-	-/-

Bowling	Overs	Mds	Runs	Wkts	Av	Best	5/inn	10m
DL Vettori	121.1	28	325	10	32.50	4-78	-	-
CS Martin	61	9	217	5	43.40	4-77	-	-
IE O'Brien	66.2	6	320	6	53.33	2-73	-	-
JS Patel	90	8	389	7	55.57	4-78	-	-

Also bowled: JD Ryder 11-2-56-0, JDP Oram 33-8-112-0.

Sri Lanka won by 96 runs

Sri Lanka won series 2-0

FIRST TEST – INDIA v. AUSTRALIA
9–13 October 2008 at Bangalore

AUSTRALIA

	First Innings		Second Innings	
ML Hayden	c Dhoni b Zaheer Khan	0	lbw b Zaheer Khan	13
SM Katich	c Dhoni b Sharma	66	c Laxman b Harbhajan Singh	34
RT Ponting (capt)	lbw b Harbhajan Singh	123	c Laxman b Sharma	17
MEK Hussey	b Zaheer Khan	146	b Harbhajan Singh	31
MJ Clarke	lbw b Zaheer Khan	11	c Sehwag b Sharma	6
SR Watson	b Sharma	2	b Sharma	41
*BJ Haddin	c Laxman b Sharma	33	not out	35
CL White	c Harbhajan Singh b Sharma	6	not out	18
B Lee	b Zaheer Khan	27		
MG Johnson	b Zaheer Khan	1		
SR Clark	not out	0		
Extras	lb 11, w 1, nb 3	15	b 13, lb 10, w 6, nb 4	33
	(all out 149.5 overs)	430	(6 wkts dec 73 overs)	228

	First Innings				Second Innings			
	O	M	R	W	O	M	R	W
Zaheer Khan	29.5	4	91	5	17	4	46	1
Sharma	30	7	77	4	14	3	40	3
Harbhajan Singh	41	8	103	1	27	5	76	2
Kumble	43	6	129	0	8	0	31	0
Sehwag	6	0	19	0	7	1	12	0

Fall of Wickets
1-0, 2-166, 3-226, 4-254, 5-259, 6-350, 7-362, 8-421, 9-429
1-21, 2-49, 3-99, 4-115, 5-128, 6-203

INDIA

	First Innings		Second Innings	
G Gambhir	lbw b Lee	21	b Johnson	29
V Sehwag	c Hayden b Johnson	45	c Hayden b Clark	6
R Dravid	lbw b Watson	51	c Ponting b Lee	5
SR Tendulkar	c White b Johnson	13	c Clarke b White	49
VVS Laxman	c Haddin b Johnson	0	not out	42
SC Ganguly	lbw b Johnson	47	not out	26
*MS Dhoni	b Clarke	9		
Harbhajan Singh	c Haddin b Watson	54		
Zaheer Khan	not out	57		
A Kumble (capt)	lbw b Watson	5		
I Sharma	b Clarke	6		
Extras	b 23, lb 23, nb 6	52	b 16, lb 3, nb 1	20
	(all out 119 overs)	360	(4 wkts 73 overs)	177

	First Innings				Second Innings			
	O	M	R	W	O	M	R	W
Lee	26	6	64	1	11	3	26	1
Clark	17	3	58	0	11	6	12	1
Johnson	27	4	70	4	8	3	23	1
Watson	19	4	45	3	5	2	8	0
White	13	2	39	0	18	4	49	1
Clarke	17	3	38	2	20	7	40	0

Fall of Wickets
1-70, 2-76, 3-94, 4-106, 5-155, 6-195, 7-232, 8-312, 9-343
1-16, 2-24, 3-77, 4-138

Umpires: Asad Rauf (Pakistan) & RE Koertzen (South Africa)
Toss: Australia
Test debut: CL White
Man of the Match: Z Khan

Match drawn

SECOND TEST – INDIA v. AUSTRALIA
17–21 October 2008 at Mohali

INDIA

	First Innings		Second Innings	
G Gambhir	c Haddin b Johnson	67	c Hussey b White	104
V Sehwag	c Haddin b Johnson	35	c Haddin b Siddle	90
R Dravid	b Lee	39		
SR Tendulkar	c Hayden b Siddle	88	(5) not out	10
VVS Laxman	c Haddin b Johnson	12		
SC Ganguly	c Lee b White	102	(4) c Clarke b Lee	27
I Sharma	c Katich b Siddle	9		
*MS Dhoni (capt)	lbw b Siddle	92	(3) not out	68
Harbhajan Singh	b White	1		
Zaheer Khan	run out	2		
A Mishra	not out	0		
Extras	b 4, lb 10, w 5, nb 3	22	lb 7, w 5, nb 3	15
	(all out 129 overs)	469	(3 wkts 65 overs)	314

	First Innings				Second Innings			
	O	M	R	W	O	M	R	W
Lee	24	5	86	1	14	0	61	1
Siddle	28	5	114	3	15	1	62	1
Johnson	27	4	85	3	14	0	72	0
Watson	24	3	71	0	5	0	20	0
Clarke	7	0	28	0	1	0	6	0
White	19	0	71	2	8	0	48	1
Hussey	-	-	-	-	8	0	38	0

Fall of Wickets
1-70, 2-146, 3-146, 4-163, 5-305, 6-326, 7-435, 8-442, 9-469
1-182, 2-224, 3-290

AUSTRALIA

	First Innings		Second Innings	
ML Hayden	b Zaheer Khan	0	lbw b Harbhajan Singh	29
SM Katich	b Mishra	33	c Tendulkar b Harbhajan Singh	20
RT Ponting (capt)	lbw b Sharma	5	b Sharma	2
MEK Hussey	c Dhoni b Sharma	54	lbw b Harbhajan Singh	1
MJ Clarke	lbw b Mishra	23	c Sehwag b Mishra	69
SR Watson	lbw b Mishra	78	lbw b Sharma	2
*BJ Haddin	b Harbhajan Singh	9	b Zaheer Khan	37
CL White	b Mishra	5	c Dhoni b Zaheer Khan	1
B Lee	c Dravid b Harbhajan Singh	35	b Zaheer Khan	0
MG Johnson	not out	0	c & b Mishra	26
PM Siddle	st Dhoni b Mishra	0	not out	0
Extras	lb 13, nb 4	17	lb 4, nb 4	8
	(all out 101.4 overs)	268	(all out 64.4 overs)	195

	First Innings				Second Innings			
	O	M	R	W	O	M	R	W
Zaheer Khan	25	7	56	1	15	3	71	3
Sharma	21	4	68	2	13	4	42	2
Harbhajan Singh	29	9	60	2	20	3	36	3
Mishra	26.4	8	71	5	11.4	2	35	2
Sehwag	-	-	-	-	5	2	7	0

Fall of Wickets
1-0, 2-17, 3-62, 4-102, 5-130, 6-146, 7-167, 8-240, 9-262
1-49, 2-50, 3-52, 4-52, 5-58, 6-142, 7-144, 8-144, 9-194

Umpires: Asad Rauf (Pakistan) & RE Koertzen (South Africa)
Toss: India
Test debuts: PM Siddle & A Mishra
Man of the Match: MS Dhoni

India won by 320 runs

INDIA

by Gulu Ezekiel

In a year marked by the retirements of some old hands, it was another golden oldie who made the last 12 months his own with a string of masterly match-winning centuries and a world record to boot.

India said goodbye to leg spinning maestro and captain Anil Kumble – only the second man to take ten wickets in a Test innings – midway through a successful home series against Australia. Another former captain, the always controversial and colourful Sourav Ganguly, also finally decided he had had enough of his numerous comebacks and bowed out in style in the same series. But Sachin Tendulkar continued to confound his critics, who had been busy writing him off over the last five years, even as he completed 20 years of international cricket, a remarkable achievement by any yardstick.

The Second Test at Mohali in October 2008 marked the moment when Tendulkar went past his great friend and rival Brian Lara to establish the world record for most Test runs. Three years earlier he had eclipsed compatriot Sunil Gavaskar to claim the record for most Test centuries. With the maximum runs and centuries in ODIs as well, Tendulkar now holds all major batting records and sits virtually unchallenged as the game's ultimate batsman.

Kumble quit international cricket at the end of the Third Test at New Delhi and Mahendra Singh Dhoni was handed the Test captaincy, having already tasted success as captain in the ODI and Twenty20 formats. He won his first Test as captain too, at Nagpur, and Ricky Ponting's Australians left India smarting from their 2-0 reverse.

After that it was time for Kevin Pietersen to lead England on his first overseas tour in November for seven ODIs and two Test matches. England had been totally outplayed and were heading for the first-ever 7-0 whitewash, after being trounced in the first five games, when the teams returned to their hotel rooms at the end of the Cuttack ODI on 26 November.

Tuning into the news, what unfolded before them was to transfix the nation for the next three days and have a deep, lasting and traumatic effect. Pakistan-based terrorists had attacked Mumbai and held the city hostage before being killed. But not before they had left almost 150 dead and the world in shock.

The English team left immediately and camped out in Dubai while a decision was taken on whether or not to resume the tour and play the Test matches. Finally, after much suspense and tension, Pietersen and his men did return to a grateful nation who received the

The extraordinary Virender Sehwag launches Monty Panesar for six during India's Chennai Test victory against England.

decision with tremendous goodwill. Even Sunil Gavaskar, a perennial opponent of English cricket, welcomed the team back with open arms.

The First Test match was shifted from Mumbai to Chennai and what unfolded did much to lift the morale of a shattered nation. England dominated until midway through the fourth day and Pietersen's declaration at 311 for 9 left India with the formidable task of scoring 387 in a day and a bit. That 'bit' proved sensational as Virender Sehwag cut loose and plundered 83 from 68 balls at the same ground where he had scored his second Test triple-century nine months earlier against South Africa.

The second season of the IPL ends with fireworks and celebrations by the Deccan Chargers, following their victory over the Royal Challengers Bangalore in the final held at the Wanderers Stadium in Johannesburg.

India went into the final day at 131 for 1 and the improbable – no side had ever gone beyond 300 to win a Test on Indian soil – suddenly looked possible. England hit back with three quick wickets, but then the sorcerer and his apprentice – Tendulkar and Yuvraj Singh – took control and the bowlers were made to look helpless. When victory came with the same boundary that brought up Tendulkar's 41st Test century, Indians reacted with a mixture of relief and elation.

Yes, it was just a cricket match. But what it meant to a still grieving country was immeasurable. And the grace with which Pietersen and his team-mates accepted the verdict won them more fans than all previous English teams put together.

After that, the rest of the season appeared anti-climatic. But there was more drama in store when the Indian government and the BCCI were locked in a confrontation over the staging of the second season of the IPL in April 2009 at a time when India was staging its general election, a massive exercise involving 700 million eligible voters.

With nerves still fraught, security became a concern and Lalit Modi and his associates shifted their annual jamboree to South Africa. Already the inaugural

Champions League, scheduled for November 2008, had been cancelled and another setback could have dealt a death blow to the IPL. There was a topsy-turvy ending to the IPL's 'Season Two' with 2008's last-placed Deccan Chargers beating the second last-placed Royal Challengers Bangalore in the final.

Before that India, under Dhoni, won a Test series in New Zealand for the first time since 1967-68 and their maiden ODI series there as well with Tendulkar once again the star of the show in both formats. The new captain, it appeared, had acquired the Midas touch.

India registered rare successes in ODI tours to both the West Indies and Sri Lanka. But the touch appeared to desert Dhoni when it came to the crunch in ICC tournaments. As reigning champions, India were a disappointment in the ICC World Twenty20 in England and then crashed out early in the Champions Trophy too. In both events the team badly missed key players who had picked up injuries in the IPL.

The question Indian cricket fans were left pondering at the end of the season was a disturbing one – had the priority of the Indian board shifted from the national team to the money-spinning IPL? It is an ongoing debate, and one that will continue to stir passions in the years ahead.

THIRD TEST – INDIA v. AUSTRALIA
29 October–2 November 2008 at Delhi

INDIA

	First Innings		Second Innings	
G Gambhir	b Watson	206	lbw b Johnson	36
V Sehwag	lbw b Lee	1	b Lee	16
R Dravid	c Hayden b Johnson	11	(4) b Lee	11
SR Tendulkar	c Haddin b Johnson	68	(5) c Hayden b White	47
VVS Laxman	not out	200	(6) not out	59
SC Ganguly	c Ponting b Katich	5	(7) not out	32
*MS Dhoni	c Haddin b Watson	27		
A Kumble (capt)	lbw b Johnson	45		
Zaheer Khan	not out	28		
I Sharma			(3) c Ponting b Clark	1
A Mishra				
Extras	b 6, lb 8, w 2, nb 6	22	lb 4, w 1, nb 1	6
	(7 wkts dec 161 overs)	613	(5 wkts dec 77.3 overs)	208

	First Innings				Second Innings			
	O	M	R	W	O	M	R	W
Lee	30	2	119	1	17	3	48	2
Clark	33	9	69	0	12	6	22	1
Johnson	32	4	142	3	12	0	23	1
Watson	20	4	66	2	7	0	27	0
White	15	1	73	0	8	0	23	1
Clarke	14	0	59	0	20.3	7	56	0
Katich	15	3	60	1	1	0	5	0
Ponting	2	0	11	0	–	–	–	–

Fall of Wickets
1-5, 2-27, 3-157, 4-435, 5-444, 6-481, 7-579
1-29, 2-34, 3-53, 4-93, 5-145

AUSTRALIA

	First Innings		Second Innings	
ML Hayden	lbw b Sehwag	83	not out	16
SM Katich	b Mishra	64	not out	14
RT Ponting (capt)	b Sehwag	87		
MEK Hussey	b Sehwag	53		
MJ Clarke	c Zaheer Khan b Mishra	112		
SR Watson	b Sehwag	36		
*BJ Haddin	st Dhoni b Kumble	17		
CL White	b Sehwag	44		
B Lee	lbw b Kumble	8		
MG Johnson	c & b Kumble	15		
SR Clark	not out	1		
Extras	b 28, lb 17, w 2, nb 10	57	lb 1	1
	(all out 179.3 overs)	577	(0 wkts 8 overs)	31

	First Innings				Second Innings			
	O	M	R	W	O	M	R	W
Zaheer Khan	23	5	86	0	–	–	–	–
Sharma	25	5	84	0	–	–	–	–
Kumble	43.3	9	112	3	4	0	14	0
Mishra	47	12	144	2	2	0	2	0
Sehwag	40	9	104	5	2	0	14	0
Tendulkar	1	0	2	0	–	–	–	–

Fall of Wickets
1-123, 2-202, 3-284, 4-326, 5-399, 6-426, 7-532, 8-555, 9-567

Umpires: Aleem Dar (Pakistan) & BF Bowden (New Zealand)
Toss: India
Man of the Match: VVS Laxman

Match drawn

FOURTH TEST – INDIA v. AUSTRALIA
6–10 November 2008 at Nagpur

INDIA

	First Innings		Second Innings	
V Sehwag	b Krejza	66	c Haddin b Lee	92
MK Vijay	c Haddin b Watson	33	lbw b Watson	41
R Dravid	c Katich b Krejza	0	c Haddin b Watson	3
SR Tendulkar	lbw b Johnson	109	run out	12
VVS Laxman	c Haddin b Krejza	64	b Krejza	4
SC Ganguly	c Clarke b Krejza	85	c & b Krejza	0
*MS Dhoni (capt)	b Krejza	56	c Hussey b Krejza	55
Harbhajan Singh	not out	18	b Watson	52
Zaheer Khan	b Krejza	1	c Haddin b Krejza	6
A Mishra	b Krejza	0	b Watson	7
I Sharma	c Katich b Krejza	0	not out	1
Extras	b 4, lb 2, w 1, nb 2	9	b 6, lb 3, w 6, nb 2, p 5	22
	(all out 124.5 overs)	441	(all out 82.4 overs)	295

	First Innings				Second Innings			
	O	M	R	W	O	M	R	W
Lee	16	2	62	0	10	3	27	1
Johnson	32	11	84	1	14	4	22	0
Watson	20	5	42	1	15.4	2	42	4
Krejza	43.5	1	215	8	31	3	143	4
White	10	1	24	0	2	0	15	0
Katich	3	0	8	0	–	–	–	–
Hussey	–	–	–	–	4	2	3	0
Clarke	–	–	–	–	6	1	29	0

Fall of Wickets
1-98, 2-99, 3-116, 4-262, 5-303, 6-422, 7-423, 8-437, 9-437
1-116, 2-132, 3-142, 4-163, 5-163, 6-166, 7-274, 8-286, 9-288

AUSTRALIA

	First Innings		Second Innings	
ML Hayden	run out	16	lbw b Harbhajan Singh	77
SM Katich	lbw b Zaheer Khan	102	c Dhoni b Sharma	16
RT Ponting (capt)	b Harbhajan Singh	24	run out	8
MEK Hussey	run out	90	(5) c Dravid b Mishra	19
MJ Clarke	c Dhoni b Sharma	8	(4) c Dhoni b Sharma	22
SR Watson	b Harbhajan Singh	2	c Dhoni b Harbhajan Singh	9
*BJ Haddin	c Dravid b Mishra	28	c Tendulkar b Mishra	4
CL White	c Sehwag b Harbhajan Singh	46	not out	26
JJ Krejza	lbw b Sharma	5	st Dhoni b Mishra	4
MG Johnson	c Zaheer Khan b Mishra	5	(11) lbw b Harbhajan Singh	11
B Lee	not out	1	(10) c Vijay b Harbhajan Singh	17
Extras	b 12, lb 3, w 2, nb 6, p 5	28	b 6, lb 1, w 4, nb 2	13
	(all out 134.4 overs)	355	(all out 50.2 overs)	209

	First Innings				Second Innings			
	O	M	R	W	O	M	R	W
Zaheer Khan	28	8	68	1	8	0	57	0
Harbhajan Singh	37	7	94	3	18.2	2	64	4
Sharma	26	8	64	2	9	0	31	2
Mishra	23.4	5	58	2	11	2	27	3
Sehwag	18	2	38	0	4	0	23	0
Tendulkar	2	0	13	0	–	–	–	–

Fall of Wickets
1-32, 2-74, 3-229, 4-255, 5-265, 6-266, 7-318, 8-333, 9-352
1-29, 2-37, 3-82, 4-150, 5-154, 6-161, 7-178, 8-190, 9-191

Umpires: Aleem Dar (Pakistan) & BF Bowden (New Zealand)
Toss: India
Test debuts: JJ Krejza & M Vijay
Man of the Match: JJ Krejza
Man of the Series: I Sharma

India won by 172 runs

India won series 2–0

SERIES AVERAGES
India v. Australia

FIRST TEST – AUSTRALIA v. NEW ZEALAND
20–23 November 2008 at Brisbane

INDIA

Batting	M	Inns	NO	Runs	HS	Av	100	50	c/st
VVS Laxman	4	7	3	381	200*	95.25	1	2	3/-
G Gambhir	3	6	0	463	206	77.16	2	1	-/-
MS Dhoni	4	6	1	307	92	61.40	-	4	8/3
SR Tendulkar	4	8	1	396	109	56.57	1	2	2/-
SC Ganguly	4	8	2	324	102	54.00	1	1	-/-
V Sehwag	4	8	0	351	92	43.87	-	3	3/-
Harbhajan Singh	3	4	1	125	54	41.66	-	2	1/-
MK Vijay	1	2	0	74	41	37.00	-	-	1/-
Zaheer Khan	4	5	2	94	57*	31.33	-	1	2/-
A Kumble	2	2	0	50	45	25.00	-	-	1/-
R Dravid	4	7	0	120	51	17.14	-	1	3/-
I Sharma	4	5	1	17	9	4.25	-	-	-/-
A Mishra	3	3	1	7	7	3.50	-	-	1/-

Bowling	Overs	Mds	Runs	Wkts	Av	Best	5/inn	10m
A Mishra	122	29	337	14	24.07	5-71	1	-
I Sharma	138	31	406	15	27.06	4-77	-	-
Harbhajan Singh	172.2	34	433	15	28.86	4-64	-	-
Zaheer Khan	145.5	31	475	11	43.18	5-91	1	-
V Sehwag	82	14	217	5	43.40	5-104	1	-
A Kumble	98.3	15	286	3	95.33	3-112	-	-

Also bowled: SR Tendulkar 3-0-15-0.

AUSTRALIA

Batting	M	Inns	NO	Runs	HS	Av	100	50	c/st
MEK Hussey	4	7	0	394	146	56.28	1	3	2/-
SM Katich	4	8	1	349	102	49.85	1	2	3/-
RT Ponting	4	7	0	266	123	38.00	1	1	3/-
MJ Clarke	4	7	0	251	112	35.85	1	1	3/-
ML Hayden	4	8	1	234	83	33.42	-	2	5/-
CL White	4	7	2	146	46	29.20	-	-	1/-
BJ Haddin	4	7	1	163	37	27.16	-	-	13/-
SR Watson	4	7	0	170	78	24.28	-	1	-/-
B Lee	4	6	1	71	35	14.20	-	-	1/-
MG Johnson	4	6	1	67	26	13.40	-	-	-/-
JJ Krejza	1	2	0	9	5	4.50	-	-	1/-
PM Siddle	1	2	1	0	0*	0.00	-	-	-/-
SR Clark	2	2	2	1	1*	-	-	-	-/-

Bowling	Overs	Mds	Runs	Wkts	Av	Best	5/inn	10m
JJ Krejza	74.5	4	358	12	29.83	8-215	1	1
SR Watson	115.4	20	321	10	32.10	4-42	-	-
MG Johnson	166	30	521	13	40.07	4-70	-	-
PM Siddle	43	6	176	4	44.00	3-114	-	-
B Lee	148	24	493	8	61.62	2-48	-	-
CL White	93	8	342	5	68.40	2-71	-	-
SM Katich	19	3	73	1	73.00	1-60	-	-
SR Clark	73	24	161	2	80.50	1-12	-	-
MJ Clarke	85.3	18	256	2	128.00	2-38	-	-

Also bowled: RT Ponting 2-0-11-0, MEK Hussey 12-2-41-0.

AUSTRALIA

	First Innings		Second Innings	
ML Hayden	c Taylor b Southee	8	c McCullum b Martin	0
SM Katich	c McCullum b Southee	10	not out	131
RT Ponting (capt)	c How b Southee	4	c Redmond b O'Brien	17
MEK Hussey	lbw b Martin	35	c McCullum b O'Brien	0
MJ Clarke	b Ryder	98	run out	9
A Symonds	c McCullum b O'Brien	26	c McCullum b Martin	20
SR Watson	c McCullum b O'Brien	1	lbw b Martin	5
*BJ Haddin	c How b Ryder	6	b Vettori	19
B Lee	c McCullum b Southee	4	b Vettori	7
MG Johnson	c Taylor b Vettori	5	c Vettori b Elliott	31
SR Clark	not out	13	c Vettori b Southee	18
Extras	lb 2, w 1, nb 1	4	lb 10, nb 1	11
	(all out 77 overs)	214	(all out 81.2 overs)	268

	First Innings				Second Innings			
	O	M	R	W	O	M	R	W
Martin	18	4	42	1	21	5	69	3
Southee	18	3	63	4	16.2	5	62	1
O'Brien	19	6	44	2	17	1	58	2
Elliott	10	4	29	0	6	1	15	1
Vettori	8	0	27	1	19	4	46	2
Ryder	4	1	7	2	2	0	8	0

Fall of Wickets
1-13, 2-22, 3-23, 4-96, 5-132, 6-139, 7-152, 8-160, 9-183
1-0, 2-40, 3-40, 4-53, 5-109, 6-115, 7-156, 8-186, 9-239

NEW ZEALAND

	First Innings		Second Innings	
AJ Redmond	c Ponting b Clark	3	c & b Clark	10
JM How	b Lee	14	c Ponting b Lee	0
JD Ryder	c Haddin b Watson	30	lbw b Johnson	24
LRPL Taylor	lbw b Lee	40	c Haddin b Johnson	75
*BB McCullum	c Ponting b Johnson	8	lbw b Clark	3
DR Flynn	not out	39	b Johnson	29
GD Elliott	b Watson	6	b Clark	4
DL Vettori (capt)	c Symonds b Johnson	2	c Symonds b Johnson	10
TG Southee	c Symonds b Johnson	0	not out	12
IE O'Brien	c Clarke b Johnson	1	c Clarke b Clark	3
CS Martin	b Clark	1	b Johnson	1
Extras	lb 3, nb 6	9	lb 5, w 2, nb 3	10
	(all out 50 overs)	156	(all out 54.3 overs)	177

	First Innings				Second Innings			
	O	M	R	W	O	M	R	W
Lee	16	5	38	2	9	0	53	1
Clark	15	2	46	2	17	5	43	4
Watson	10	2	35	2	5	1	19	0
Johnson	8	3	30	4	17.3	6	39	5
Symonds	1	0	4	0	4	0	12	0
Clarke	-	-	-	-	2	0	6	0

Fall of Wickets
1-7, 2-44, 3-64, 4-73, 5-108, 6-127, 7-143, 8-143, 9-149
1-1, 2-30, 3-40, 4-49, 5-133, 6-143, 7-160, 8-161, 9-164

Umpires: BR Doctrove (West Indies) & RE Koertzen (South Africa)
Toss: New Zealand
Man of the Match: MG Johnson

Australia won by 149 runs

SECOND TEST – AUSTRALIA v. NEW ZEALAND
28 November–2 December 2008 at Adelaide

SERIES AVERAGES
Australia v. New Zealand

AUSTRALIA

	First Innings		
ML Hayden	run out		24
SM Katich	c Ryder b Vettori		23
RT Ponting (capt)	c Fulton b O'Brien		79
MEK Hussey	c Redmond b Martin		70
MJ Clarke	c Ryder b O'Brien		110
A Symonds	c McCullum b Martin		0
*BJ Haddin	c Fulton b Redmond		169
B Lee	c Taylor b O'Brien		19
MG Johnson	c McCullum b Redmond		23
NM Hauritz	b Vettori		1
SR Clark	not out		1
Extras	b 2, lb 8, w 1, nb 5		16
	(all out 157.4 overs)		**535**

	First Innings			
	O	M	R	W
Martin	27	4	110	2
Southee	27	1	100	0
Vettori	59.4	20	124	2
O'Brien	31	6	111	3
Ryder	7	1	33	0
Redmond	6	0	47	2

Fall of Wickets
1-38, 2-49, 3-155, 4-244, 5-247, 6-428, 7-470, 8-526, 9-532

NEW ZEALAND

	First Innings		Second Innings (following on)	
AJ Redmond	c Symonds b Hauritz	83	c Clarke b Lee	19
JM How	c Haddin b Johnson	16	c Ponting b Lee	28
JD Ryder	c Clarke b Hauritz	13	c Symonds b Lee	3
LRPL Taylor	lbw b Clark	44	c & b Lee	1
PG Fulton	c Katich b Symonds	29	b Johnson	7
DR Flynn	b Lee	11	lbw b Johnson	9
*BB McCullum	c Haddin b Lee	30	not out	84
DL Vettori (capt)	not out	18	c Hayden b Hauritz	13
TG Southee	c Katich b Johnson	2	c Ponting b Hauritz	11
IEO'Brien	c Haddin b Lee	0	lbw b Lee	0
CS Martin	b Lee	0	b Johnson	0
Extras	b 4, lb 8, w 1, nb 11	24	b 7, lb 8, nb 13	28
	(all out 98.3 overs)	**270**	(all out 74.1 overs)	**203**

	First Innings				Second Innings			
	O	M	R	W	O	M	R	W
Lee	25.3	8	66	4	25	5	105	5
Clark	20	6	56	1	10	5	22	0
Johnson	25	4	56	2	15.1	7	29	3
Hauritz	16	2	63	2	24	11	32	2
Symonds	12	2	17	1	–	–	–	–

Fall of Wickets
1-46, 2-101, 3-130, 4-194, 5-200, 6-228, 7-266, 8-270, 9-270
1-39, 2-55, 3-58, 4-63, 5-76, 6-84, 7-105, 8-131, 9-181

Umpires: BR Doctrove (West Indies) & RE Koertzen (South Africa)
Toss: New Zealand
Man of the Match: BJ Haddin
Man of the Series: MJ Clarke

AUSTRALIA

Batting	M	Inns	NO	Runs	HS	Av	100	50	c/st
SM Katich	2	3	1	164	131*	82.00	1	–	2/-
MJ Clarke	2	3	0	217	110	72.33	1	1	4/-
BJ Haddin	2	3	0	194	169	64.66	1	–	5/-
MEK Hussey	2	3	0	105	70	35.00	–	1	-/-
RT Ponting	2	3	0	100	79	33.33	–	1	5/-
SR Clark	2	3	2	32	18	32.00	–	–	1/-
MG Johnson	2	3	0	59	31	19.66	–	–	-/-
A Symonds	2	3	0	46	26	15.33	–	–	5/-
ML Hayden	2	3	0	32	24	10.66	–	–	1/-
B Lee	2	3	0	30	19	10.00	–	–	1/-
SR Watson	1	2	0	6	5	3.00	–	–	-/-
NM Hauritz	1	1	0	1	1	1.00	–	–	-/-

Bowling	Overs	Mds	Runs	Wkts	Av	Best	5/inn	10m
MG Johnson	65.4	20	154	14	11.00	5-39	1	–
B Lee	75.3	18	262	12	21.83	5-105	1	–
NM Hauritz	40	13	95	4	23.75	2-32	–	–
SR Clark	62	18	167	7	23.85	4-43	–	–
SR Watson	15	3	54	2	27.00	2-35	–	–
A Symonds	17	2	33	1	33.00	1-17	–	–

Also bowled: MJ Clarke 2-0-6-0.

NEW ZEALAND

Batting	M	Inns	NO	Runs	HS	Av	100	50	c/st
BB McCullum	2	4	1	125	84*	41.66	–	1	9/-
LRPL Taylor	2	4	0	160	75	40.00	–	1	3/-
DR Flynn	2	4	1	88	39*	29.33	–	–	-/-
AJ Redmond	2	4	0	115	83	28.75	–	1	2/-
PG Fulton	1	2	0	36	29	18.00	–	–	2/-
JD Ryder	2	4	0	70	30	17.50	–	–	2/-
JM How	2	4	0	58	28	14.50	–	–	2/-
DL Vettori	2	4	1	43	18*	14.33	–	–	2/-
TG Southee	2	4	1	25	12*	8.33	–	–	-/-
GD Elliott	1	2	0	9	9	4.50	–	–	-/-
IE O'Brien	2	4	0	4	3	1.00	–	–	-/-
CS Martin	2	4	0	2	1	0.50	–	–	-/-

Bowling	Overs	Mds	Runs	Wkts	Av	Best	5/inn	10m
AJ Redmond	6	0	47	2	23.50	2-47	–	–
JD Ryder	13	2	48	2	24.00	2-7	–	–
IE O'Brien	67	13	213	7	30.42	3-111	–	–
CS Martin	66	13	221	6	36.83	3-69	–	–
DL Vettori	86.4	24	197	5	39.40	2-46	–	–
GD Elliott	16	5	44	1	44.00	1-15	–	–
TG Southee	61.2	9	225	5	45.00	4-63	–	–

Australia won by an innings and 62 runs

Australia won series 2–0

FIRST TEST – AUSTRALIA v. SOUTH AFRICA
17–21 December 2008 at Perth

AUSTRALIA

	First Innings		Second Innings	
ML Hayden	c Smith b Ntini	12	c & b Steyn	4
SM Katich	lbw b Morkel	83	c Boucher b Kallis	37
RT Ponting (capt)	c de Villiers b Ntini	0	c Boucher b Harris	32
MEK Hussey	c de Villiers b Steyn	0	b Ntini	8
MJ Clarke	c Smith b Harris	62	c Kallis b Steyn	25
A Symonds	c McKenzie b Harris	57	c Smith b Harris	37
*BJ Haddin	c Duminy b Ntini	46	st Boucher b Harris	94
B Lee	c Duminy b Steyn	29	c de Villiers b Kallis	5
JJ Krejza	not out	30	c de Villiers b Kallis	32
MG Johnson	lbw b Morkel	18	c Kallis b Morkel	21
PM Siddle	c Boucher b Ntini	23	not out	4
Extras	lb 7, w 3, nb 5	15	b 4, lb 7, w 2, nb 7	20
	(all out 98.5 overs)	375	(all out 97 overs)	319

	First Innings				Second Innings			
	O	M	R	W	O	M	R	W
Ntini	19.5	1	72	4	21	2	76	1
Steyn	23	4	81	2	19	3	81	2
Kallis	15	2	65	0	14	4	24	3
Morkel	20	1	80	2	16	4	42	1
Harris	21	2	70	2	27	3	85	3

Fall of Wickets
1-14, 2-14, 3-15, 4-164, 5-166, 6-259, 7-298, 8-303, 9-341
1-25, 2-59, 3-88, 4-88, 5-148, 6-157, 7-162, 8-241, 9-278

SOUTH AFRICA

	First Innings		Second Innings	
ND McKenzie	c Krejza b Johnson	2	(2) c Haddin b Johnson	10
GC Smith (capt)	b Johnson	48	(1) lbw b Johnson	108
HM Amla	b Krejza	47	c Haddin b Lee	53
JH Kallis	c Haddin b Johnson	63	c Hussey b Johnson	57
AB de Villiers	c Haddin b Johnson	63	not out	106
JP Duminy	c Haddin b Johnson	1	not out	50
*MV Boucher	c Katich b Siddle	26		
M Morkel	c Krejza b Johnson	1		
PL Harris	c Krejza b Johnson	0		
DW Steyn	c Haddin b Johnson	8		
M Ntini	not out	5		
Extras	lb 5, w 5, nb 7	17	b 13, lb 9, w 2, nb 6	30
	(all out 89.5 overs)	281	(4 wkts 119.2 overs)	414

	First Innings				Second Innings			
	O	M	R	W	O	M	R	W
Lee	21	3	59	0	27	4	73	1
Johnson	24	4	61	8	34.2	5	98	3
Krejza	25	2	102	1	24	2	102	0
Siddle	16.5	5	44	1	26	2	84	0
Symonds	3	1	10	0	-	-	-	-
Clarke	-	-	-	-	8	0	35	0

Fall of Wickets
1-16, 2-106, 3-110, 4-234, 5-237, 6-238, 7-241, 8-241, 9-256
1-19, 2-172, 3-179, 4-303

Umpires: Aleem Dar (Pakistan) & EAR de Silva (Sri Lanka)
Toss: Australia
Test debut: JP Duminy
Man of the Match: AB de Villiers

South Africa won by 6 wickets

SECOND TEST – AUSTRALIA v. SOUTH AFRICA
26–30 December 2008 at Melbourne

AUSTRALIA

	First Innings		Second Innings	
ML Hayden	c Duminy b Ntini	8	c Duminy b Steyn	23
SM Katich	b Steyn	54	c Boucher b Steyn	15
RT Ponting (capt)	c Amla b Harris	101	c Smith b Morkel	99
MEK Hussey	c Boucher b Steyn	0	c Amla b Morkel	2
MJ Clarke	not out	88	c McKenzie b Steyn	29
A Symonds	c Kallis b Morkel	27	c Kallis b Steyn	0
*BJ Haddin	c Smith b Ntini	40	c Kallis b Ntini	10
B Lee	c Kallis b Steyn	21	b Kallis	8
MG Johnson	b Steyn	0	not out	43
NM Hauritz	c Smith b Steyn	12	b Kallis	3
PM Siddle	c de Villiers b Kallis	19	c Boucher b Steyn	6
Extras	b 5, lb 12, nb 7	24	b 1, lb 3, nb 5	9
	(all out 113.4 overs)	394	(all out 84.2 overs)	247

	First Innings				Second Innings			
	O	M	R	W	O	M	R	W
Steyn	29	6	87	5	20.2	3	67	5
Ntini	27	7	108	2	14	1	26	1
Kallis	18.4	4	55	1	14	1	57	2
Morkel	22	3	89	1	15	2	46	2
Harris	17	3	38	1	21	1	47	0

Fall of Wickets
1-21, 2-128, 3-143, 4-184, 5-223, 6-277, 7-322, 8-326, 9-352
1-37, 2-40, 3-49, 4-145, 5-145, 6-165, 7-180, 8-212, 9-231

SOUTH AFRICA

	First Innings		Second Innings	
GC Smith (capt)	c Haddin b Siddle	62	lbw b Hauritz	75
ND McKenzie	b Siddle	0	not out	59
HM Amla	c Symonds b Johnson	19	not out	30
JH Kallis	c Haddin b Hauritz	26		
AB de Villiers	b Siddle	7		
JP Duminy	c Siddle b Hauritz	166		
*MV Boucher	c Hussey b Hauritz	3		
M Morkel	b Johnson	21		
PL Harris	c Johnson b Hussey	39		
DW Steyn	b Siddle	76		
M Ntini	not out	2		
Extras	b 5, lb 13, nb 15, p 5	38	lb 9, w 2, nb 8	19
	(all out 153 overs)	459	(1 wkt 48 overs)	183

	First Innings				Second Innings			
	O	M	R	W	O	M	R	W
Lee	13	2	68	0	10	0	49	0
Siddle	34	9	81	4	14	5	34	0
Johnson	39	6	127	2	11	1	36	0
Hauritz	43	13	98	3	10	0	41	1
Clarke	8	0	26	0	3	0	14	0
Hussey	5	0	22	1	-	-	-	-
Symonds	11	3	14	0	-	-	-	-

Fall of Wickets
1-1, 2-39, 3-102, 4-126, 5-132, 6-141, 7-184, 8-251, 9-431
1-121

Umpires: Aleem Dar (Pakistan) & BR Doctrove (West Indies)
Toss: Australia
Man of the Match: DW Steyn

South Africa won by 9 wickets

AUSTRALIA

by Jim Maxwell

Australia became mortal again in the past 12 months, losing three out of five Test series and their number one ICC ranking. The decline from the golden years of match-winning influences from Shane Warne and Glenn McGrath in particular was confirmed by Matthew Hayden's demise and subsequent retirement, placing even more reliance on the captain, Ricky Ponting, to score substantially.

Ponting contributed strongly, but his consistency faltered a touch as he scored 1,246 runs at 41.53 in 17 matches with four centuries. Australia won six and lost seven of those matches. Significantly, they also lost a Test series at home for the first time in 16 years.

Their 50-over form wavered too, with losing series at home and away to South Africa, and they nursed a distinctly moderate record of nine wins and 11 losses prior to the 6-1 win over England, which in turn, led into the revitalizing victory in the Champions Trophy.

But, overall, Australia's resilience and capacity to grab the key moments has waned. In the opening Tests of three series, Australia failed to convert a dominant position into a victory. They were results, indeed, which had a significant bearing on the outcomes of those series, as they lost 2-0 in India, 2-1 to South Africa at home, and then the Ashes by a 2-1 margin.

Ponting's captaincy skills, meanwhile, were challenged by injuries to his strike bowlers and a lack of quality spin support. In India, Brett Lee was underdone on his return from injury and struggled for form. Lee then asserted himself against New Zealand, but succumbed to another foot injury against South Africa and on the eve of the Ashes series was forced out with an abdominal injury. Stuart Clark's elbow injury and subsequent surgery undermined his effectiveness, despite his encouraging return in Australia's win against England at Headingley.

Opener Phil Jaques and leg spinner Bryce McGain sustained injuries prior to the start of the Indian series, and the selectors boldly opted for Cameron White, a part time spinner at best, to replace McGain. White struggled, while Jason Krezja, the off spinner originally selected for the tour, ended up watching most of the action before eventually making his debut in the Fourth Test.

Krezja's spectacular match figures, 12 for 248, suggested that he was a long-term proposition, but following injury and another expensive performance against South Africa in Perth, Krezja lost out to Nathan Hauritz, who had been recalled against New Zealand. Hauritz's selection underscored Australia's dearth of spin bowling talent since the retirements of Warne and

Matthew Hayden, here in Test action against India at the MCG, retired from international cricket in 2009 after being dropped by Australia's selectors.

Stuart MacGill. Hauritz was a marginal player at New South Wales whose first-class numbers were uninspiring. In fact, and to his enormous credit, he bowled above expectations on the Ashes tour and was a surprise omission from the deciding Test at The Oval.

The selectors initially showed faith in Hayden's fading powers at the top of the Aussie order after he had recovered from an Achilles injury to play in India. In 17 subsequent innings he was unconvincing, however, scoring a meagre 383 runs at an average of 23.93. Yet selection convener Andrew Hilditch was still talking about Hayden's longer-term value prior to dropping him from the limited-overs side, a decision that prompted Hayden to announce his retirement. Hayden's prodigious record included 30 Test centuries, proof of his own belief that if you reached fifty you should stroll to a century. He was a surprise replacement for Allan Border as a Cricket Australia director when Border stepped down during the Ashes series.

Freshened by the comfortable victory over New Zealand in the Trans-Tasman Trophy, Australia exuded confidence when South Africa arrived in Perth in late 2008. On a pitch that became progressively easier to bat on, South Africa chased down 414 to win, a remarkable achievement with 6 wickets in hand. Australia's batting was often careless, gifting wickets to the unheralded left-arm slow bowling of Paul Harris.

Ponting was left to rely on his young fast bowlers for wickets, and Mitchell Johnson produced the first of several distinguished performances in taking 8 for 61.

Johnson's pace, and low arm slinging style, surprised batsmen but at times his action betrayed him, as he lost control and gave away easy runs. Following a strong series in South Africa, abetted by some spectacular batting, Johnson then struggled for rhythm and confidence in England until Australia hit back in the Fourth Test. His 2008-09 figures were impressive, nevertheless, and his 80 wickets in 17 Tests enabled him to claim the ICC Test Player of the Year award.

Hayden's departure prompted the elevation of 20-year-old Phillip Hughes, the New South Wales prodigy with a unique, slashing technique. In his second Test, at Durban, Hughes became the youngest batsmen to score Test hundreds in each innings, blasting South Africa's errant attack mainly to the

Mitchell Johnson, the Australia fast bowler and dangerous lower–middle order hitter, emerged in late 2008 as one of the world's most exciting newcomers on the international stage.

offside boundary. Three matches later Hughes was dropped, a decision vindicated by Shane Watson's success, and made because the selectors felt the England bowlers, principally Andrew Flintoff, had stifled the talented youngster.

Ponting's plans, meanwhile, were also undermined by Andrew Symonds's indiscipline, and after another aberration prior to the ICC World Twenty20 tournament Symonds was sent home. He lost his Cricket Australia contract, too, and headed for the IPL retirement park alongside Hayden, Gilchrist and Warne.

Domestically, Victoria won the Sheffield Shield after overcoming the disappointments of losing to NSW by one run in the Twenty20 Big Bash final and their collapse against Queensland in the limited-overs final.

THIRD TEST – AUSTRALIA v. SOUTH AFRICA
3–7 January 2009 at Sydney

AUSTRALIA

	First Innings		Second Innings	
ML Hayden	b Steyn	31	b Morkel	39
SM Katich	c de Villiers b Kallis	47	lbw b Steyn	61
RT Ponting (capt)	c Boucher b Morkel	0	b Morkel	53
MEK Hussey	c Kallis b Harris	30	not out	45
MJ Clarke	c & b Duminy	138	c Amla b Harris	41
AB McDonald	c Boucher b Ntini	15		
*BJ Haddin	b Steyn	38		
MG Johnson	c Smith b Steyn	64		
NM Hauritz	c Duminy b Harris	41		
PM Siddle	lbw b Harris	23		
DE Bollinger	not out	0		
Extras	lb 7, w 3, nb 8	18	b 8, lb 9, nb 1	18
	(all out 136.2 overs)	445	(4 wkts dec 67.3 overs)	257

	First Innings				Second Innings			
	O	M	R	W	O	M	R	W
Steyn	27	5	95	3	13	1	60	1
Ntini	29	5	102	1	12	1	66	0
Morkel	27	3	89	1	12	2	38	2
Kallis	20	6	54	1	10	5	13	0
Harris	29.2	6	84	3	20.3	1	63	1
Duminy	4	0	14	1	–	–	–	–

Fall of Wickets
1-62, 2-63, 3-109, 4-130, 5-162, 6-237, 7-379, 8-381, 9-440
1-62, 2-134, 3-181, 4-257

SOUTH AFRICA

	First Innings		Second Innings	
ND McKenzie	lbw b Siddle	23	c Hussey b Bollinger	27
GC Smith (capt)	retired hurt	30	(11) b Johnson	3
HM Amla	lbw b McDonald	51	c Katich b Hauritz	59
JH Kallis	c Hayden b Johnson	37	c & b McDonald	4
AB de Villiers	run out	11	b Siddle	56
JP Duminy	lbw b Johnson	13	lbw b Johnson	16
*MV Boucher	b Siddle	89	lbw b Siddle	4
M Morkel	b Siddle	40	(2) c Johnson b Bollinger	0
PL Harris	lbw b Siddle	2	(8) lbw b Siddle	6
DW Steyn	b Siddle	6	(9) lbw b McDonald	28
M Ntini	not out	0	(10) not out	28
Extras	lb 12, w 9, nb 4	25	b 12, lb 18, w 4, nb 2, p 5	41
	(all out 120.5 overs)	327	(all out 114.2 overs)	272

	First Innings				Second Innings			
	O	M	R	W	O	M	R	W
Siddle	27.5	11	59	5	27	12	54	3
Bollinger	23	4	78	0	21	5	53	2
Johnson	28	6	69	2	23.2	7	49	2
McDonald	22	8	41	1	13	6	32	2
Hauritz	20	4	68	0	28	10	47	1
Clarke	–	–	–	–	2	1	2	0

Fall of Wickets
1-76, 2-131, 3-161, 4-166, 5-193, 6-308, 7-310, 8-316, 9-327
1-2, 2-68, 3-91, 4-110, 5-166, 6-172, 7-190, 8-202, 9-257

Umpires: BF Bowden (New Zealand) & EAR de Silva (Sri Lanka)
Toss: Australia
Test debuts: DE Bollinger & AB McDonald
Man of the Match: PM Siddle
Man of the Series: GC Smith

SERIES AVERAGES
Australia v. South Africa

AUSTRALIA

Batting	M	Inns	NO	Runs	HS	Av	100	50	c/st
MJ Clarke	3	6	1	383	138	76.60	1	2	-/-
JJ Krejza	1	2	1	62	32	62.00	-	-	3/-
SM Katich	3	6	0	297	83	49.50	-	3	2/-
RT Ponting	3	6	0	285	101	47.50	1	2	-/-
BJ Haddin	3	5	0	228	94	45.60	-	1	8/-
MG Johnson	3	5	1	146	64	36.50	-	1	2/-
A Symonds	2	4	0	121	57	30.25	-	1	1/-
ML Hayden	3	6	0	117	39	19.50	-	-	1/-
PM Siddle	3	5	1	75	23	18.75	-	-	1/-
NM Hauritz	2	3	0	56	41	18.66	-	-	-/-
MEK Hussey	3	6	1	85	45*	17.00	-	-	3/-
B Lee	2	4	0	63	29	15.75	-	-	-/-
AB McDonald	1	1	0	15	15	15.00	-	-	1/-
DE Bollinger	1	1	1	0	0*	-	-	-	-/-

Bowling	Overs	Mds	Runs	Wkts	Av	Best	5/inn	10m
MEK Hussey	5	0	22	1	22.00	1-22	-	-
AB McDonald	35	14	73	3	24.33	2-32	-	-
MG Johnson	159.4	29	440	17	25.88	8-61	1	1
PM Siddle	145.4	44	356	13	27.38	5-59	1	-
NM Hauritz	101	27	254	5	50.80	3-98	-	-
DE Bollinger	44	9	131	2	65.50	2-53	-	-
JJ Krejza	49	4	204	1	204.00	1-102	-	-
B Lee	71	9	249	1	249.00	1-73	-	-

Also bowled: A Symonds 14-4-24-0, MJ Clarke 21-1-77-0.

SOUTH AFRICA

Batting	M	Inns	NO	Runs	HS	Av	100	50	c/st
GC Smith	3	6	1	326	108	65.20	1	2	7/-
JP Duminy	3	5	1	246	166	61.50	1	1	6/-
AB de Villiers	3	5	1	243	106*	60.75	1	2	6/-
HM Amla	3	6	1	259	59	51.80	-	3	3/-
JH Kallis	3	5	0	187	63	37.40	-	2	7/-
MV Boucher	3	4	0	122	89	30.50	-	1	8/1
DW Steyn	3	4	0	118	76	29.50	-	1	1/-
ND McKenzie	3	6	1	121	59*	24.20	-	1	2/-
M Morkel	3	4	0	62	40	15.50	-	-	-/-
PL Harris	3	4	0	47	39	11.75	-	-	-/-
M Ntini	3	4	4	35	28*	-	-	-	-/-

Bowling	Overs	Mds	Runs	Wkts	Av	Best	5/inn	10m
JP Duminy	4	0	14	1	14.00	1-14	-	-
DW Steyn	131.2	22	471	18	26.16	5-67	2	1
JH Kallis	91.4	22	268	7	38.28	3-24	-	-
PL Harris	135.5	16	387	10	38.70	3-84	-	-
M Morkel	112	15	384	9	42.66	2-38	-	-
M Ntini	122.5	17	450	9	50.00	4-72	-	-

Australia won by 103 runs

South Africa won series 2–1

FIRST TEST – PAKISTAN v. SRI LANKA
21–25 February 2009 at Karachi

SRI LANKA

	First Innings		Second Innings	
BSM Warnapura	c Misbah-ul-Haq b Yasir Arafat	59	c Kamran Akmal b Umar Gul	2
NT Paranavitana	c Misbah-ul-Haq b Umar Gul	0	run out	9
KC Sangakkara	c Misbah-ul-Haq b Danish Kaneria	70	lbw b Danish Kaneria	65
DPMD J'wardene (capt)	c Kamran Akmal b Shoaib Malik	240	(5) c Faisal Iqbal b Danish Kaneria	22
TT Samaraweera	b Danish Kaneria	231	(6) not out	24
TM Dilshan	c Kamran Akmal b Shoaib Malik	0	(4) c Faisal Iqbal b Umar Gul	8
*HAPW Jayawardene	b Danish Kaneria	18	not out	7
WPUJC Vaas	not out	12		
CRD Fernando				
BAW Mendis				
M Muralitharan				
Extras	lb 4, w 1, nb 9	14	nb 7	7
	(7 wkts dec 155.2 overs)	644	(5 wkts 31 overs)	144

	First Innings				Second Innings			
	O	M	R	W	O	M	R	W
Umar Gul	24	2	92	1	9	1	41	2
Sohail Khan	21	2	131	0	6	0	33	0
Yasir Arafat	26	2	90	1	6	0	32	0
Shoaib Malik	36	3	140	2	1	0	3	0
Danish Kaneria	46.2	5	170	3	9	1	35	2
Younis Khan	1	0	6	0	-	-	-	-
Salman Butt	1	0	11	0	-	-	-	-

Fall of Wickets
1-3, 2-93, 3-177, 4-614, 5-614, 6-614, 7-644
1-2, 2-32, 3-45, 4-103, 5-120

PAKISTAN

	First Innings	
Khurram Manzoor	c Jayawardene HAPW b Mendis	27
Salman Butt	c J'wardene DPMD b Muralitharan	23
Younis Khan (capt)	b Fernando	313
Shoaib Malik	run out	56
Misbah-ul-Haq	lbw b Fernando	42
Faisal Iqbal	lbw b Jayawardene DPMD	57
*Kamran Akmal	not out	158
Yasir Arafat	not out	50
Sohail Khan		
Umar Gul		
Danish Kaneria		
Extras	b 4, lb 12, w 5, nb 18	39
	(6 wkts dec 248.5 overs)	765

	First Innings			
	O	M	R	W
Vaas	36	10	66	0
Fernando	39	2	124	2
Mendis	59	14	157	1
Muralitharan	65	14	172	1
Dilshan	19	3	82	0
Paranavitana	5	0	33	0
Sangakkara	10	0	34	0
Jayawardene DPMD	6.5	0	41	1
Warnapura	9	0	40	0

Fall of Wickets
1-44, 2-78, 3-227, 4-357, 5-531, 6-596

Umpires: SJ Davis (Australia) & SJA Taufel (Australia)
Toss: Sri Lanka
Test debuts: Khurram Manzoor, Sohail Khan & NT Paranavitana
Man of the Match: Younis Khan

Match drawn

SECOND TEST – PAKISTAN v. SRI LANKA
1–3 March 2009 at Lahore

SRI LANKA

	First Innings	
BSM Warnapura	c Misbah-ul-Haq b Umar Gul	8
NT Paranavitana	c Shoaib Malik b Umar Gul	21
KC Sangakkara	c Kamran Akmal b Yasir Arafat	104
DPMD J'wardene (capt)	c Kamran Akmal b Umar Gul	30
TT Samaraweera	run out	214
TM Dilshan	run out	145
*HAPW Jayawardene	c Kamran Akmal b Umar Gul	15
T Thushara	b Umar Gul	10
M Muralitharan	b Mohammad Talha	22
BAW Mendis	b Umar Gul	0
CRD Fernando	not out	14
Extras	b 4, lb 1, w 5, nb 13	23
	(all out 151 overs)	606

	First Innings			
	O	M	R	W
Umar Gul	37	2	135	6
Mohammad Talha	17	0	88	1
Yasir Arafat	20	2	106	1
Danish Kaneria	47	5	183	0
Shoaib Malik	28	3	80	0
Younis Khan	2	0	9	0

Fall of Wickets
1-16, 2-35, 3-96, 4-300, 5-507, 6-542, 7-566, 8-572, 9-572

PAKISTAN

	First Innings	
Khurram Manzoor	not out	59
Salman Butt	run out	48
Younis Khan (capt)		
Shoaib Malik		
Misbah-ul-Haq		
Faisal Iqbal		
*Kamran Akmal		
Yasir Arafat		
Mohammad Talha		
Umar Gul		
Danish Kaneria		
Extras	nb 3	3
	(1 wkt 23.4 overs)	110

	First Innings			
	O	M	R	W
Thushara	8	0	46	0
Fernando	2	0	20	0
Mendis	8	2	21	0
Muralitharan	4.4	0	23	0
Dilshan	1	1	0	0

Fall of Wickets
1-110

Umpires: SJ Davis (Australia) & SJA Taufel (Australia)
Toss: Pakistan
Test debut: Mohammad Talha

Match drawn

Series drawn

SERIES AVERAGES
Pakistan v. Sri Lanka

PAKISTAN

Batting	M	Inns	NO	Runs	HS	Av	100	50	c/st
Younis Khan	2	1	0	313	313	313.00	1	-	-/-
Khurram Manzoor	2	2	1	86	59*	86.00	-	1	-/-
Faisal Iqbal	2	1	0	57	57	57.00	-	1	2/-
Shoaib Malik	2	1	0	56	56	56.00	-	1	1/-
Misbah-ul-Haq	2	1	0	42	42	42.00	-	-	4/-
Salman Butt	2	2	0	71	48	35.50	-	-	-/-
Kamran Akmal	2	1	1	158	158*	-	1	-	6/-
Yasir Arafat	2	1	1	50	50*	-	-	1	-/-
Danish Kaneria	2	0	0	0	0	-	-	-	-/-
Umar Gul	2	0	0	0	0	-	-	-	-/-
Sohail Khan	1	0	0	0	0	-	-	-	-/-
Mohammad Talha	1	0	0	0	0	-	-	-	-/-

Bowling	Overs	Mds	Runs	Wkts	Av	Best	5/inn	10m
Umar Gul	70	5	268	9	29.77	6-135	1	-
Danish Kaneria	102.2	11	388	5	77.60	3-170	-	-
Mohammad Talha	17	0	88	1	88.00	1-88	-	-
Shoaib Malik	65	6	223	2	111.50	2-140	-	-
Yasir Arafat	52	4	228	2	114.00	1-90	-	-

Also bowled: Salman Butt-1-0-11-0, Younis Khan 3-0-15-0, Sohail Khan 27-2-164-0.

SRI LANKA

Batting	M	Inns	NO	Runs	HS	Av	100	50	c/st
TT Samaraweera	2	3	1	469	231	234.50	2	-	-/-
DPMD Jayawardene	2	3	0	292	240	97.33	1	-	1/-
KC Sangakkara	2	3	0	239	104	79.66	1	2	-/-
TM Dilshan	2	3	0	153	145	51.00	1	-	-/-
BSM Warnapura	2	3	0	69	59	23.00	-	1	-/-
M Muralitharan	2	1	0	22	22	22.00	-	-	-/-
HAPW Jayawardene	2	3	1	40	18	20.00	-	-	1/-
T Thushara	1	1	0	10	10	10.00	-	-	-/-
NT Paranavitana	2	3	0	30	21	10.00	-	-	-/-
BAW Mendis	2	1	0	0	0	0.00	-	-	-/-
CRD Fernando	2	1	1	14	14*	-	-	-	-/-
WPUJC Vaas	1	1	1	12	12*	-	-	-	-/-

Bowling	Overs	Mds	Runs	Wkts	Av	Best	5/inn	10m
DPMD Jayawardene	6.5	0	41	1	41.00	1-41	-	-
CRD Fernando	41	2	144	2	72.00	2-124	-	-
BAW Mendis	67	16	178	1	178.00	1-157	-	-
M Muralitharan	69.4	14	195	1	195.00	1-172	-	-

Also bowled: NT Paranavitana 5-0-33-0, KC Sangakkara 10-0-34-0, BSM Warnapura 9-0-40-0, T Thushara 8-0-46-0, WPUJC Vaas 36-10-66-0, TM Dilshan 20-4-82-0.

FIRST TEST – NEW ZEALAND v. WEST INDIES
11–15 December 2008 at Dunedin

NEW ZEALAND

	First Innings			Second Innings		
TG McIntosh	c Baker b Gayle		34	not out		24
JM How	c Chanderpaul b Powell		10	b Powell		10
DR Flynn	lbw b Gayle		95	(4) not out		4
LRPL Taylor	c Marshall b Gayle		15			
JD Ryder	c Chanderpaul b Powell		89			
*BB McCullum	c Ramdin b Taylor		25			
JEC Franklin	hit wkt b Edwards		7			
DL Vettori (capt)	c Marshall b Powell		30			
KD Mills	lbw b Edwards		12	(3) b Powell		0
MR Gillespie	not out		16			
IE O'Brien	c & b Edwards		4			
Extras	lb 16, w 9, nb 3		28	b 4, lb 1, nb 1		6
	(all out 116 overs)		365	(2 wkts 10 overs)		44

	First Innings			Second Innings		
	O	M	R	W	O	M	R	W
Taylor	23	7	61	1				
Powell	24	7	68	3	5	0	17	2
Edwards	22	4	91	3	5	0	22	0
Baker	25	3	85	0	-	-	-	-
Gayle	21	2	42	3	-	-	-	-
Nash	1	0	2	0	-	-	-	-

Fall of Wickets
1-10, 2-97, 3-128, 4-189, 5-278, 6-289, 7-310, 8-327, 9-347
1-33, 2-33

WEST INDIES

	First Innings		
CH Gayle (capt)	c Franklin b O'Brien		74
S Chattergoon	c O'Brien b Mills		13
RR Sarwan	c McCullum b Mills		8
XM Marshall	c Ryder b Vettori		20
S Chanderpaul	b Vettori		76
BP Nash	c Ryder b Mills		23
*D Ramdin	lbw b Vettori		5
JE Taylor	c McCullum b Vettori		106
DB Powell	lbw b Vettori		0
FH Edwards	c sub b Vettori		0
LS Baker	not out		0
Extras	b 1, lb 10, nb 4		15
	(all out 100 overs)		340

	First Innings			
	O	M	R	W
Gillespie	21	5	102	0
Mills	24	6	64	3
O'Brien	15	4	46	1
Vettori	25	7	56	6
Franklin	15	2	61	0

Fall of Wickets
1-66, 2-87, 3-114, 4-134, 5-162, 6-173, 7-326, 8-326, 9-334

Umpires: MR Benson (England) & AM Saheba (India)
Toss: New Zealand
Test debuts: TG McIntosh, LS Baker, BP Nash
Man of the Match: JE Taylor

Match drawn

SECOND TEST – NEW ZEALAND v. WEST INDIES
19–23 December 2008 at Napier

SERIES AVERAGES
New Zealand v. West Indies

WEST INDIES

	First Innings		Second Innings	
CH Gayle (capt)	c McCullum b O'Brien	34	c McCullum b Patel	197
S Chattergoon	c How b Vettori	13	c Taylor b Patel	25
RR Sarwan	c McCullum b Patel	11	lbw b Vettori	1
XM Marshall	c Ryder b O'Brien	6	c Taylor b Patel	18
S Chanderpaul	not out	126	c & b Patel	0
BP Nash	c Flynn b Franklin	74	c How b Franklin	65
*D Ramdin	b Vettori	6	c Flynn b Franklin	6
JE Taylor	c McCullum b O'Brien	17	lbw b O'Brien	8
SJ Benn	c McCullum b O'Brien	0	(11) not out	4
DB Powell	c McCullum b O'Brien	6	lbw b Vettori	22
FH Edwards	lbw b O'Brien	0	(9) c Taylor b Patel	20
Extras	lb 6, w 1, nb 7	14	lb 2, w 1, nb 6	9
	(all out 107 overs)	307	(all out 145 overs)	375

	First Innings				Second Innings			
	O	M	R	W	O	M	R	W
Franklin	16	2	57	1	17	3	61	2
Mills	15	4	48	0	6	1	21	0
Patel	25	12	41	1	46	16	110	5
O'Brien	26	6	75	6	24	3	90	1
Vettori	22	4	71	2	52	21	91	2
Ryder	3	0	9	0	–	–	–	–

Fall of Wickets
1-43, 2-54, 3-63, 4-74, 5-237, 6-257, 7-279, 8-279, 9-299
1-58, 2-61, 3-106, 4-106, 5-230, 6-252, 7-272, 8-342, 9-363

NEW ZEALAND

	First Innings		Second Innings	
TG McIntosh	b Taylor	136	lbw b Taylor	3
JM How	c Chattergoon b Edwards	12	c Gayle b Edwards	54
DR Flynn	c & b Edwards	57	run out	33
LRPL Taylor	c Ramdin b Edwards	4	lbw b Benn	46
JD Ryder	c Ramdin b Edwards	57	not out	59
*BB McCullum	c Ramdin b Taylor	31	c Ramdin b Taylor	19
JEC Franklin	c Gayle b Powell	0	not out	2
DL Vettori (capt)	c Ramdin b Edwards	29		
KD Mills	lbw b Edwards	18		
JS Patel	c Marshall b Edwards	2		
IE O'Brien	not out	0		
Extras	lb 19, nb 6	25	w 2, nb 2	4
	(all out 126.4 overs)	371	(5 wkts 51 overs)	220

	First Innings				Second Innings			
	O	M	R	W	O	M	R	W
Taylor	23	6	76	2	13	2	67	2
Powell	26	7	85	1	5	0	30	0
Edwards	29.4	6	87	7	11	0	46	1
Gayle	18	6	33	0	5	0	23	0
Nash	6	2	22	0	–	–	–	–
Benn	24	5	49	0	17	2	54	1

Fall of Wickets
1-19, 2-137, 3-145, 4-245, 5-316, 6-317, 7-319, 8-367, 9-368
1-8, 2-62, 3-96, 4-170, 5-203

Umpires: RE Koertzen (South Africa) & AM Saheba (India)
Toss: West Indies
Man of the Match: CH Gayle

NEW ZEALAND

Batting	M	Inns	NO	Runs	HS	Av	100	50	c/st
JD Ryder	2	3	1	205	89	102.50	–	3	3/-
TG McIntosh	2	4	1	197	136	65.66	1	–	-/-
DR Flynn	2	4	1	189	95	63.00	–	2	2/-
DL Vettori	2	2	0	59	30	29.50	–	–	-/-
BB McCullum	2	3	0	75	31	25.00	–	–	8/-
LRPL Taylor	2	3	0	65	46	21.66	–	–	3/-
JM How	2	4	0	86	54	21.50	–	1	2/-
KD Mills	2	3	0	30	18	10.00	–	–	-/-
JEC Franklin	2	3	1	9	7	4.50	–	–	1/-
IE O'Brien	2	2	1	4	4	4.00	–	–	1/-
JS Patel	1	1	0	2	2	2.00	–	–	1/-
MR Gillespie	1	1	1	16	16*	–	–	–	-/-

Bowling	Overs	Mds	Runs	Wkts	Av	Best	5/inn	10m
DL Vettori	99	32	218	10	21.80	6-56	1	–
JS Patel	71	28	151	6	25.16	5-110	1	–
IE O'Brien	65	13	211	8	26.37	6-75	1	–
KD Mills	45	11	133	3	44.33	3-64	–	–
JEC Franklin	48	7	179	3	59.66	2-61	–	–

Also bowled: JD Ryder 3-0-9-0, MR Gillespie 21-5-102-0.

WEST INDIES

Batting	M	Inns	NO	Runs	HS	Av	100	50	c/st
CH Gayle	2	3	0	305	197	101.66	1	1	2/-
S Chanderpaul	2	3	1	202	126*	101.00	1	1	-/-
BP Nash	2	3	0	162	74	54.00	–	2	-/-
JE Taylor	2	3	0	131	106	43.66	1	–	-/-
S Chattergoon	2	3	0	51	25	17.00	–	–	1/-
XM Marshall	2	3	0	44	20	14.66	–	–	3/-
DB Powell	2	3	0	28	22	9.33	–	–	-/-
RR Sarwan	2	3	0	20	11	6.66	–	–	-/-
FH Edwards	2	3	0	20	20	6.66	–	–	2/-
D Ramdin	2	3	0	17	6	5.66	–	–	6/-
SJ Benn	1	2	1	4	4*	4.00	–	–	-/-
LS Baker	1	1	1	0	0*	–	–	–	1/-

Bowling	Overs	Mds	Runs	Wkts	Av	Best	5/inn	10m
FH Edwards	67.4	10	246	11	22.36	7-87	1	–
CH Gayle	44	8	98	3	32.66	3-42	–	–
DB Powell	60	14	200	6	33.33	3-68	–	–
JE Taylor	59	15	204	5	40.80	2-67	–	–
SJ Benn	41	7	103	1	103.00	1-54	–	–

Also bowled: BP Nash 7-2-24-0, LS Baker 25-3-85-0.

Match drawn

Series drawn

FIRST TEST – NEW ZEALAND v. INDIA
18–21 March 2009 at Hamilton

NEW ZEALAND

	First Innings		Second Innings	
TG McIntosh	c Sehwag b Sharma	12	c Tendulkar b Zaheer Khan	0
MJ Guptill	c Dravid b Zaheer Khan	14	c Sehwag b Harbhajan Singh	48
DR Flynn	c Dhoni b Zaheer Khan	0	c Gambhir b Harbhajan Singh	67
LRPL Taylor	b Sharma	18	(5) c Sehwag b Patel	4
JD Ryder	c Laxman b Sharma	102	(6) lbw b Harbhajan Singh	21
JEC Franklin	c Dhoni b Sharma	0	(7) c Patel b Harbhajan Singh	14
*BB McCullum	c Laxman b Patel	3	(8) c Laxman b Yuvraj Singh	84
DL Vettori (capt)	c Dhoni b Patel	118	(9) c Dhoni b Harbhajan Singh	21
KD Mills	b Patel	0	(4) lbw b Patel	2
IE O'Brien	st Dhoni b Harbhajan Singh	8	c Laxman b Harbhajan Singh	14
CS Martin	not out		not out	0
Extras	lb 1, nb 3	4	b 1, lb 3	4
	(all out 78.2 overs)	279	(all out 102.3 overs)	279

	First Innings				Second Innings			
	O	M	R	W	O	M	R	W
Zaheer Khan	16	3	70	2	28	7	79	1
Sharma	19.2	4	73	4	22	7	62	0
Patel	18	4	60	3	17	2	60	2
Harbhajan Singh	22	7	57	1	28	2	63	6
Sehwag	3	0	18	0	-	-	-	-
Yuvraj Singh	-	-	-	-	7.3	2	11	1

Fall of Wickets
1-17, 2-17, 3-40, 4-51, 5-51, 6-60, 7-246, 8-246, 9-275
1-0, 2-68, 3-75, 4-110, 5-132, 6-154, 7-161, 8-199, 9-275

INDIA

	First Innings		Second Innings	
G Gambhir	c McCullum b Martin	72	not out	30
V Sehwag	run out	24		
R Dravid	b O'Brien	66	(2) not out	8
SR Tendulkar	c Taylor b O'Brien	160		
VVS Laxman	c Taylor b Martin	30		
Yuvraj Singh	b Martin	22		
*MS Dhoni (capt)	c McCullum b O'Brien	47		
Harbhajan Singh	c Vettori b Mills	16		
Zaheer Khan	not out	51		
I Sharma	c McCullum b Vettori	6		
MM Patel	c Martin b Vettori	9		
Extras	b 6, lb 3, nb 8	17	b 1	1
	(all out 152.4 overs)	520	(0 wkts 5.2 overs)	39

	First Innings				Second Innings			
	O	M	R	W	O	M	R	W
Martin	30	9	98	3	3	0	17	0
Mills	22	4	98	1	2.2	0	21	0
O'Brien	33	7	103	3	-	-	-	-
Franklin	23	1	98	0	-	-	-	-
Vettori	35.4	8	90	2	-	-	-	-
Ryder	9	5	24	0	-	-	-	-

Fall of Wickets
1-37, 2-142, 3-177, 4-238, 5-314, 6-429, 7-443, 8-457, 9-492

Umpires: SJA Taufel (Australia) & IJ Gould (England)
Toss: India
Test debut: MJ Guptill
Man of the Match: SR Tendulkar

India won by 10 wickets

SECOND TEST – NEW ZEALAND v. INDIA
26–30 March 2009 at Napier

NEW ZEALAND

	First Innings	
TG McIntosh	c Karthik b Sharma	12
MJ Guptill	c Sehwag b Zaheer Khan	8
JM How	b Zaheer Khan	1
LRPL Taylor	c Yuvraj Singh b Harbhajan Singh	151
JD Ryder	b Zaheer Khan	201
JEC Franklin	run out	52
*BB McCullum	c Tendulkar b Sharma	115
DL Vettori (capt)	b Sharma	55
JS Patel	c Sharma b Harbhajan Singh	1
IE O'Brien	not out	1
CS Martin		
Extras	b 7, lb 8, nb 7	22
	(9 wkts dec 154.4 overs)	619

	First Innings			
	O	M	R	W
Zaheer Khan	34	6	129	3
Sharma	27	5	95	3
Patel	28	3	128	0
Harbhajan Singh	41.4	7	120	2
Sehwag	12	0	73	0
Yuvraj Singh	12	0	59	0

Fall of Wickets
1-21, 2-22, 3-23, 4-294, 5-415, 6-477, 7-605, 8-618, 9-619

INDIA

	First Innings		Second Innings (following on)	
G Gambhir	c Vettori b Patel	16	lbw b Patel	137
V Sehwag (capt)	c McCullum b Vettori	34	lbw b Patel	22
R Dravid	c McCullum b Ryder	83	c How b Vettori	62
I Sharma	lbw b Vettori	0		
SR Tendulkar	c Taylor b Patel	49	(4) c McCullum b Martin	64
VVS Laxman	c McIntosh b Martin	76	(5) not out	124
Yuvraj Singh	c McIntosh b Martin	0	(6) not out	54
*KKD Karthik	c Ryder b Martin	6		
Harbhajan Singh	c Martin b O'Brien	18		
Zaheer Khan	c Ryder b O'Brien	8		
MM Patel	not out	0		
Extras	b 1, lb 7, nb 7	15	b 9, lb 1, nb 3	13
	(all out 93.5 overs)	305	(4 wkts 180 overs)	476

	First Innings				Second Innings			
	O	M	R	W	O	M	R	W
Martin	24	5	89	3	30	8	86	1
Franklin	15	4	34	0	21	5	48	0
Vettori	19	5	45	2	38	13	76	1
O'Brien	13.5	4	66	2	32	9	94	0
Patel	19	2	60	2	45	10	120	2
Ryder	3	1	3	1	11	5	38	0
Taylor	-	-	-	-	2	1	4	0
How	-	-	-	-	1	1	0	0

Fall of Wickets
1-48, 2-73, 3-78, 4-165, 5-246, 6-253, 7-270, 8-291, 9-305
1-30, 2-163, 3-260, 4-356

Umpires: IJ Gould (England) & BR Doctrove (West Indies)
Toss: New Zealand
Man of the Match: JD Ryder

Match drawn

THIRD TEST – NEW ZEALAND v. INDIA
3–7 April 2009 at Wellington

INDIA

	First Innings		Second Innings	
G Gambhir	lbw b Franklin	23	lbw b O'Brien	167
V Sehwag	c McCullum b O'Brien	48	c Taylor b Martin	12
R Dravid	c Franklin b Martin	35	c McCullum b Vettori	60
SR Tendulkar	c McCullum b Martin	62	c Taylor b Vettori	9
VVS Laxman	c McIntosh b Southee	4	b O'Brien	61
Yuvraj Singh	lbw b Ryder	9	c Taylor b Martin	40
*MS Dhoni (capt)	c O'Brien b Southee	52	not out	56
Harbhajan Singh	c Vettori b Martin	60	c Southee b Martin	0
Zaheer Khan	c McCullum b O'Brien	33	not out	18
I Sharma	c McCullum b Martin	18		
MM Patel	not out	15		
Extras	b 2, lb 8, w 3, nb 7	20	lb 5, w 1, nb 5	11
	(all out 92.1 overs)	379	(7 wkts dec 116 overs)	434

	First Innings				Second Innings			
	O	M	R	W	O	M	R	W
Martin	25.1	3	98	4	22	7	70	3
Southee	18	1	94	2	12	2	58	0
O'Brien	22	3	89	2	25	6	100	2
Franklin	14	4	38	1	16	3	72	0
Vettori	9	1	47	0	35	5	108	2
Ryder	4	2	3	1	6	1	21	0

Fall of Wickets
1-73, 2-75, 3-165, 4-173, 5-182, 6-204, 7-283, 8-315, 9-347
1-14, 2-184, 3-208, 4-314, 5-319, 6-397, 7-397

NEW ZEALAND

	First Innings		Second Innings	
TG McIntosh	c Yuvraj Singh b Zaheer Khan	32	c Dravid b Zaheer Khan	4
MJ Guptill	b Zaheer Khan	17	lbw b Harbhajan Singh	49
DR Flynn	c Dhoni b Zaheer Khan	2	b Zaheer Khan	10
LRPL Taylor	c Dhoni b Harbhajan Singh	42	b Harbhajan Singh	107
JD Ryder	c Dhoni b Zaheer Khan	3	c Dravid b Harbhajan Singh	0
JEC Franklin	c Sehwag b Harbhajan Singh	15	lbw b Tendulkar	49
*BB McCullum	c Dhoni b Harbhajan Singh	24	c Dravid b Tendulkar	6
DL Vettori (capt)	c Dhoni b Sharma	11	not out	15
TG Southee	c & b Zaheer Khan	16	c Dhoni b Harbhajan Singh	3
IE O'Brien	c Dhoni b Patel	19	not out	19
CS Martin	not out	4		
Extras	b 9, lb 3	12	b 10, lb 2, w 1, nb 6	19
	(all out 65 overs)	197	(8 wkts 94.3 overs)	281

	First Innings				Second Innings			
	O	M	R	W	O	M	R	W
Zaheer Khan	18	2	65	5	19.3	6	57	2
Sharma	14	3	47	1	12	2	57	0
Patel	8	2	20	1	13	4	22	0
Harbhajan Singh	23	4	43	3	33	8	59	4
Yuvraj Singh	2	0	10	0	1	0	4	0
Sehwag	–	–	–	–	7	0	25	0
Tendulkar	–	–	–	–	9	0	45	2

Fall of Wickets
1-21, 2-31, 3-80, 4-98, 5-120, 6-125, 7-138, 8-160, 9-181
1-30, 2-54, 3-84, 4-84, 5-226, 6-244, 7-253, 8-258

Umpires: DJ Harper (Australia) & SJA Taufel (Australia)
Toss: New Zealand
Man of the Match: G Gambhir

SERIES AVERAGES
New Zealand v. India

NEW ZEALAND

Batting	M	Inns	NO	Runs	HS	Av	100	50	c/st
JD Ryder	3	5	0	327	201	65.40	2	–	2/-
LRPL Taylor	3	5	0	322	151	64.40	2	–	6/-
DL Vettori	3	5	1	220	118	55.00	1	1	3/-
BB McCullum	3	5	0	232	115	46.40	1	1	11/-
MJ Guptill	3	5	0	136	49	27.20	–	–	-/-
JEC Franklin	3	5	0	130	52	26.00	–	1	1/-
IE O'Brien	3	5	2	61	19*	20.33	–	–	1/-
DR Flynn	2	4	0	79	67	19.75	–	1	-/-
TG McIntosh	3	5	0	60	32	12.00	–	–	3/-
TG Southee	1	2	0	19	16	9.50	–	–	1/-
KD Mills	1	2	0	2	2	1.00	–	–	-/-
JM How	1	1	0	1	1	1.00	–	–	1/-
JS Patel	1	1	0	1	1	1.00	–	–	-/-
CS Martin	3	3	3	4	4*	–	–	–	2/-

Bowling	Overs	Mds	Runs	Wkts	Av	Best	5/inn	10m
CS Martin	134.1	32	458	14	32.71	4-98	–	–
JD Ryder	33	14	89	2	44.50	1-3	–	–
JS Patel	64	12	180	4	45.00	2-60	–	–
IE O'Brien	125.5	29	452	9	50.22	3-103	–	–
DL Vettori	136.4	32	366	7	52.28	2-45	–	–
TG Southee	30	3	152	2	76.00	2-94	–	–
KD Mills	24.2	4	119	1	119.00	1-98	–	–
JEC Franklin	89	17	290	1	290.00	1-38	–	–

Also bowled: JM How 1-1-0-0, LRPL Taylor 2-1-4-0.

INDIA

Batting	M	Inns	NO	Runs	HS	Av	100	50	c/st
G Gambhir	3	6	1	445	167	89.00	2	1	1/-
MS Dhoni	2	3	1	155	56*	77.50	–	2	11/1
VVS Laxman	3	5	1	295	124*	73.75	1	2	4/-
SR Tendulkar	3	5	0	344	160	68.80	1	2	2/-
R Dravid	3	6	1	314	83	62.80	–	4	4/-
Zaheer Khan	3	4	2	110	51*	55.00	–	1	1/-
Yuvraj Singh	3	5	1	125	54*	31.25	–	1	2/-
V Sehwag	3	5	0	140	48	28.00	–	–	5/-
MM Patel	3	3	2	24	15*	24.00	–	–	1/-
Harbhajan Singh	3	4	0	94	60	23.50	–	1	-/-
I Sharma	3	3	0	24	18	8.00	–	–	1/-
KKD Karthik	1	1	0	6	6	6.00	–	–	1/-

Bowling	Overs	Mds	Runs	Wkts	Av	Best	5/inn	10m
Harbhajan Singh	147.4	28	342	16	21.37	6-63	1	–
SR Tendulkar	9	0	45	2	22.50	2-45	–	–
Zaheer Khan	115.3	24	400	13	30.76	5-65	1	–
I Sharma	94.2	21	334	8	41.75	4-73	–	–
MM Patel	84	15	290	6	48.33	3-60	–	–
Yuvraj Singh	22.3	2	84	1	84.00	1-11	–	–

Also bowled: V Sehwag 22-0-116-0.

Match drawn

India won series 1–0

WEST INDIES

by Tony Cozier

The demise of West Indies cricket, such a vital part of the world game for almost a century, drew ever closer in 2009. The perennial bickering between the West Indies Cricket Board (WICB) and the West Indies Players Association (WIPA) worsened to the extent that a second players' strike in four years caused a severely depleted team to take the field in the home series against Bangladesh and in the ICC Champions Trophy in South Africa.

If the status quo remained for the scheduled three Tests in Australia in November and December, Cricket Australia was known to have an alternative plan in place. It was that serious. At the same time, the Trinidad and Tobago Board's boycott of the WICB annual general meeting in August was the first inkling of the possible disintegration of an entity that had survived and flourished since 1900 when a combined West Indies team first toured England.

Under 37-year-old Floyd Reifer and carrying only four players with previous Test experience, the makeshift team hastily assembled to take on Bangladesh after the leading players, already selected, withdrew three days before the First Test, was beaten in both Tests and all three one-day internationals. The team was further undermined by slow, turning pitches that ideally suited Bangladesh's spin-based attack and by the all-round performance of the left-hander Shakib Al Hasan who took over the captaincy after Mashrafe bin Mortaza was injured on the second day of the series.

The Australian John Dyson was the only casualty of the debacle, however, dismissed without explanation halfway through his three-year contract, the ninth coach in 17 years. Otherwise, the same inexperienced second and third stringers were dispatched to the subsequent Champions Trophy with the same outcome: losses to Australia, India and Pakistan and elimination after the first round. Such developments further undermined the interest of a once passionate public. Numbers at the Bangladesh matches were often in three figures, seldom in four, never in five.

Outside the Caribbean, others were simply fed up with the recurring problems. The ICC made its displeasure plain, stating that it would extend the deadline for team disclosure for the Champions Trophy to the last moment to allow West Indies to be at their strongest. It was an unrealistic, but significant, gesture. Cricket Australia's stance carried more weight.

Unable to settle their disagreement themselves, the WICB and the WIPA turned to the relevant governments of the Caribbean Community (Caricom), a position always packed with potential political pitfalls. Shridath Ramphal, a former Guyana foreign minister and Commonwealth secretary general, was given the job of mediator. When he failed in the mission – he was, he claimed, close to settlement before the WICB changed its mind – the future seemed dire.

Finally, the warring parties appeared to comprehend the consequences of a continuing standoff. WICB president Julian Hunte and WIPA head, Dinanath Ramnarine, the former Test leg spinner, signed a peace pact in mid-October that cleared the way for Chris Gayle, Shivnarine Chanderpaul, Ramnaresh Sarwan, Dwayne Bravo and the other disgruntled players to sign retainer contracts and return for the tour of Australia and beyond. The two also agreed to send two outstanding issues for binding arbitration to judges from the Caribbean Court of Justice (CCJ).

Cynics waited to see if the deal would hold good.

Human nature being what it is, there were bound to be misgivings between those players who heeded WIPA's strike call and those who didn't. In the latter category, Kemar Roach, a bowler of genuine pace (he was timed as delivering the fastest ball in the Champions Trophy), middle-order batsman Travis Dowlin and all-rounders Darren Sammy and Dave Bernard made realistic cases for retention while the others were away. And there was doubt over whether Gayle should retain the leadership following his controversial comments in a British newspaper interview in May that he was tired of Test cricket and was likely to quit the captaincy 'soon'.

A hint that the same fragmentation that broke up the West Indies Federation in 1962 after four years emerged within the administration through the Trinidad and Tobago Board's decision to stay away from the WICB's AGM, the first time any affiliate had taken such action in the organisation's 82 years. Headed by the former West

Indies wicketkeeper Deryck Murray, it charged that the WICB had 'not functioned effectively and demonstrated little inclination to change, to meet the requirements of the modern cricket environment in which we operate'.

Murray claimed that his board had no intention of breaking away from West Indies cricket, simply to make a necessary point. His chief executive officer, Forbes Persaud, had the different, if personal, view that 'if something is not done to have cricket administration at the West Indies level properly restructured, we will have no choice but to think about playing as an individual territory on the international scene'.

Although it is, as yet, not a serious prospect, there are others in high places with the same opinion.

It is ironic that such upheavals followed some encouraging results on the field. After an evenly balanced series of two draws in New Zealand, the Wisden Trophy was regained for the first time in nine years with a narrow 1-0 triumph in the Caribbean, victory gained with the sensational dismantling of England for 51 in the First Test and then doggedly defended.

The Trophy remained in West Indies' grasp for less than two months, though. The players displayed their opposition to the immediate, hurriedly organised, unscheduled return mini-series of two Tests in England in May with the equivalent of a union go-slow. The predictable upshot was heavy defeats in both Tests and one-day internationals. Even so, they received five times their normal tour fees as an enticement to undertake a tour not on the ICC's programme.

The issues that boiled over into the strike back home were simmering even when Gayle's stated preference for the shortest form of the game was evident in the team's advance to the semi-final of the second ICC World Twenty20 tournament in England in June. West Indies players were introduced to the newest and shortest format by two seasons of the lucrative regional Stanford Twenty20 tournament and the much-hyped Twenty20 for $20 million match against England.

It was all heavily financed by the Antigua-based Texan Allen Stanford but, as it turned out, with other people's money. When he was arrested by U.S. government agencies in January and imprisoned for an alleged 'fraud of shocking magnitude', it ended the exercise.

Whatever Stanford's ways and means of pumping millions into West Indies cricket, Gayle's endorsement of his involvement echoed that of most of the players. 'Whichever way you look at it, Stanford has done a lot for the Caribbean,' he said.

He, indeed, did a lot for the bank accounts of Gayle and those in Stanford's so-called Super Stars who pocketed US$1 million each for their victory over England in the Super Series match before the Texan's assets were frozen.

But, as Stanford's 2008 champions Trinidad and Tobago's perky performance in the Champions League in India in October 2009 showed, his tournaments were also a helpful initiation into the ways of Twenty20.

Kemar Roach, the young Barbados fast bowler, appeals for a catch at the wicket during his impressive performances for a weakened West Indies team in their Test series at home to Bangladesh.

Chris Gayle, the West Indies captain, hits out during the ICC World Twenty20 tournament in England.

While he awaited his fate behind bars in Houston, though, there was nothing from the WICB about how it intended to fill the vacuum. For only the second time since it was inaugurated in 1966 as the Shell Shield, the first-class season was played on a home-and-way basis. It meant an increase from six to 12 matches for each team but no corresponding rise in standards.

Justifiably concerned over the continuing chaos in administration and the standoff between board and players, Carib Beer (first-class) and Kentucky Fried Chicken (one-day) withdrew their sponsorship of the major tournaments and no replacements were found. It was a heavy financial blow for the WICB.

Jamaica comfortably retained the four-day title, 27 points clear of the Windward Islands whose second place was their highest ever. Trinidad and Tobago defeated Barbados by seven wickets in the limited-overs final.

FIRST TEST – WEST INDIES v. BANGLADESH
9–13 July 2009 at Arnos Vale

BANGLADESH

	First Innings		Second Innings	
Tamim Iqbal	c Reifer b Best	14	c Dowlin b Bernard	128
Imrul Kayes	lbw b Sammy	33	c Roach b Austin	24
Junaid Siddique	c Dowlin b Bernard	27	c Richards b Sammy	78
Raqibul Hasan	c Sammy b Bernard	14	b Sammy	18
Mohammad Ashraful	c Walton b Best	6	lbw b Roach	3
Shakib Al Hasan	c Richards b Roach	17	c Austin b Sammy	30
*Mushfiqur Rahim	run out	36	b Roach	37
Mahmudullah	c Phillips b Roach	9	lbw b Roach	8
M bin Mortaza (capt)	c Walton b Roach	39	c Roach b Sammy	0
Shahadat Hossain	c Walton b Austin	33	not out	0
Rubel Hossain	not out	3	lbw b Sammy	1
Extras	b 2, lb 2, w 1, nb 2	7	lb 9, w 2, nb 7	18
	(all out 88.2 overs)	238	(all out 120.1 overs)	345

	First Innings				Second Innings			
	O	M	R	W	O	M	R	W
Best	17	4	58	2	13	3	49	0
Roach	23	11	46	3	26	4	67	3
Sammy	19	7	38	1	30.1	6	70	5
Bernard	11	2	30	2	4	0	32	1
Austin	13.2	5	35	1	30	4	78	1
Miller	5	1	27	0	17	4	40	0

Fall of Wickets
1-45, 2-49, 3-79, 4-98, 5-100, 6-121, 7-149, 8-172, 9-207
1-82, 2-228, 3-258, 4-261, 5-267, 6-327, 7-342, 8-344, 9-344

WEST INDIES

	First Innings		Second Innings	
DM Richards	lbw b Shakib Al Hasan	13	run out	14
OJ Phillips	c Raqibul Hasan b Rubel Hossain	94	lbw b Shakib Al Hasan	14
RA Austin	c Imrul Kayes b Rubel Hossain	17	(9) lbw b Mahmudullah	0
TM Dowlin	lbw b Shakib Al Hasan	22	(3) c Imrul Kayes b Mahmudullah	19
FL Reifer (capt)	c Shakib Al Hasan b Mahmudullah	25	(4) lbw b Mahmudullah	19
DE Bernard	c sub b Shahadat Hossain	53	(5) not out	52
*CAK Walton	c Shakib Al Hasan b Mahmudullah	0	(6) lbw b Mahmudullah	10
DJG Sammy	b Mahmudullah	48	(7) c S Hossain b Shakib Al Hasan	19
NO Miller	c Mushfiqur Rahim b R Hossain	0	(8) c Mushfiqur Rahim b M Ashraful	5
KAJ Roach	c sub b Mohammad Ashraful	6	c Mushfiqur Rahim b Mahmudullah	3
TL Best	not out	1	lbw b Shakib Al Hasan	9
Extras	b 4, lb 3, w 2, nb 19	28	b 5, lb 5, w 2, nb 5	17
	(all out 95.1 overs)	307	(all out 70.1 overs)	181

	First Innings				Second Innings			
	O	M	R	W	O	M	R	W
Mashrafe bin Mortaza	6.3	0	26	0	-	-	-	-
Shahadat Hossain	13	2	48	1	12	2	32	0
Shakib Al Hasan	35	10	76	2	28.1	11	39	3
Rubel Hossain	15	1	76	3	10	1	45	0
Mahmudullah	19.4	3	59	3	15	4	51	5
Mohammad Ashraful	6	0	15	1	5	1	4	1

Fall of Wickets
1-15, 2-94, 3-142, 4-176, 5-227, 6-227, 7-267, 8-267, 9-306
1-20, 2-33, 3-69, 4-72, 5-82, 6-119, 7-151, 8-164, 9-172

Umpires: EAR de Silva (Sri Lanka) & AL Hill (New Zealand)
Toss: Bangladesh
Test debuts: Mahmudullah, Rubel Hossain, RA Austin, TM Dowlin, NO Miller, OJ Phillips, DM Richards, KAJ Roach and CAK Walton
Man of the Match: Tamim Iqbal

Bangladesh won by 95 runs

SECOND TEST – WEST INDIES v. BANGLADESH
17-20 July 2009 at St George's

SERIES AVERAGES
West Indies v. Bangladesh

WEST INDIES

	First Innings			Second Innings	
DM Richards	c & b Mahmudullah	69	lbw b Shakib Al Hasan	12
OJ Phillips	c Iqbal b Shakib Al Hasan	23	c M Ashraful b Shakib Al Hasan	29
TM Dowlin	c Iqbal b Shakib Al Hasan	95	lbw b Enamul Haque jnr	49
RO Hinds	c & b Mahmudullah	2	c Mahmudullah b S Al Hasan	2
FL Reifer (capt)	lbw b Mahmudullah	1	lbw b Mahmudullah	3
DE Bernard	c M Ashraful b Shakib Al Hasan	17	st M Rahim b Enamul Haque jnr	69
DJG Sammy	lbw b Enamul Haque jnr	1	c Raqibul Hasan b Enamul Haque jnr	22
*CAK Walton	c M Ashraful b Enamul Haque jnr	2	c Mahmudullah b S Al Hasan	1
RA Austin	hit wkt b Shahadat Hossain	19	c Iqbal b Shahadat Hossain	3
TL Best	b Enamul Haque jnr	0	c M Rahim b Shakib Al Hasan	12
KAJ Roach	not out	4	not out	1
Extras	lb 1, nb 3	4	lb 2, nb 4	6
	(all out 76.1 overs)	**237**	(all out 70.5 overs)	**209**

	First Innings				Second Innings			
	O	M	R	W	O	M	R	W
Shahadat Hossain	9	2	30	1	4	0	18	1
Rubel Hossain	6	0	27	0	9	1	34	0
Enamul Haque jnr	24	2	62	3	17	3	48	3
Shakib Al Hasan	21.1	7	59	3	24.5	3	70	5
Mahmudullah	13	2	44	3	15	1	37	1
Mohammad Ashraful	3	0	14	0	1	1	0	0

Fall of Wickets
1-60, 2-104, 3-106, 4-114, 5-157, 6-158, 7-160, 8-219, 9-220
1-20, 2-72, 3-84, 4-95, 5-110, 6-166, 7-167, 8-187, 9-201

BANGLADESH

	First Innings			Second Innings	
Tamim Iqbal	c Walton b Bernard	37	c Walton b Sammy	18
Imrul Kayes	c Walton b Sammy	14	c Sammy b Roach	8
Enamul Haque jnr	c Walton b Roach	13		
Junaid Siddique	b Austin	7	(3) c Reifer b Sammy	5
Raqibul Hasan	c Walton b Roach	44	(4) c & b Sammy	65
Mohammad Ashraful	c Sammy b Hinds	12	(5) c Walton b Sammy	3
Shakib Al Hasan (capt)	c Austin b Roach	16	(6) not out	96
*Mushfiqur Rahim	c Walton b Roach	48	(7) c & b Sammy	12
Mahmudullah	c Austin b Roach	28	(8) not out	0
Shahadat Hossain	c Richards b Roach	0		
Rubel Hossain	not out	1		
Extras	lb 2, w 3, nb 7	12	b 1, lb 3, w 2, nb 4	10
	(all out 79.5 overs)	**232**	(6 wkts 54.4 overs)	**217**

	First Innings				Second Innings			
	O	M	R	W	O	M	R	W
Roach	23.5	8	48	6	13.4	4	68	1
Best	17	3	47	1	9	0	38	0
Sammy	15	3	45	1	16	1	55	5
Bernard	8	0	29	1	9	1	33	0
Austin	8	0	29	1	3	0	13	0
Hinds	8	1	32	1	4	0	6	0

Fall of Wickets
1-26, 2-51, 3-75, 4-77, 5-106, 6-150, 7-157, 8-219, 9-223
1-27, 2-29, 3-49, 4-67, 5-173, 6-201

Umpires: EAR de Silva (Sri Lanka) & AL Hill (New Zealand)
Toss: Bangladesh
Man of the Match: Shakib Al Hasan
Man of the Series: Shakib Al Hasan

WEST INDIES

Batting	M	Inns	NO	Runs	HS	Av	100	50	c/st
DE Bernard	2	4	1	191	69	63.66	–	3	-/-
TM Dowlin	2	4	0	185	95	46.25	–	1	2/-
OJ Phillips	2	4	0	160	94	40.00	–	1	1/-
DM Richards	2	4	0	108	69	27.00	–	1	3/-
DJG Sammy	2	4	0	90	48	22.50	–	–	5/-
FL Reifer	2	4	0	48	25	12.00	–	–	2/-
RA Austin	2	4	0	39	19	9.75	–	–	3/-
TL Best	2	4	1	22	12	7.33	–	–	-/-
KAJ Roach	2	4	2	14	6	7.00	–	–	2/-
CAK Walton	2	4	0	13	10	3.25	–	–	10/-
NO Miller	1	2	0	5	5	2.50	–	–	-/-
RO Hinds	1	2	0	4	2	2.00	–	–	-/-

Bowling	Overs	Mds	Runs	Wkts	Av	Best	5/inn	10m
DJG Sammy	80.1	17	208	12	17.33	5-55	2	–
KAJ Roach	86.3	27	229	13	17.61	6-48	1	–
DE Bernard	32	3	124	4	2-30	–	–
RO Hinds	12	1	38	1	38.00	1-32	–	–
RA Austin	54.2	9	155	3	51.66	1-29	–	–
TL Best	56	10	192	2	96.00	2-58	–	–

Also bowled: NO Miller 22-5-67-0.

BANGLADESH

Batting	M	Inns	NO	Runs	HS	Av	100	50	c/st
Shakib Al Hasan	2	4	1	159	96*	53.00	–	1	2/-
Tamim Iqbal	2	4	0	197	128	49.25	1	–	2/-
Raqibul Hasan	2	4	0	141	65	35.25	–	1	2/-
Mushfiqur Rahim	2	4	0	133	48	33.25	–	–	4/1
Junaid Siddique	2	4	0	117	78	29.25	–	1	-/-
Imrul Kayes	2	4	0	79	33	19.75	–	–	2/-
Mashrafe bin Mortaza	1	2	0	39	39	19.50	–	–	-/-
Shahadat Hossain	2	3	1	33	33	16.50	–	–	1/-
Mahmudullah	2	4	1	45	28	15.00	–	–	4/-
Enamul Haque jnr	1	1	0	13	13	13.00	–	–	-/-
Mohammad Ashraful	2	4	0	24	12	6.00	–	–	3/-
Rubel Hossain	2	3	2	5	3*	5.00	–	–	-/-

Bowling	Overs	Mds	Runs	Wkts	Av	Best	5/inn	10m
Mahmudullah	62.4	10	191	12	15.91	5-51	1	–
Mohammad Ashraful	15	2	33	2	16.50	1-4	–	–
Enamul Haque jnr	41	5	110	6	18.33	3-48	–	–
Shakib Al Hasan	109.1	31	244	13	18.76	5-70	1	–
Shahadat Hossain	38	6	128	3	42.66	1-18	–	–
Rubel Hossain	40	3	182	3	60.66	3-76	–	–

Also bowled: Mashrafe bin Mortaza 6.3-0-26-0.

Bangladesh won by 4 wickets

Bangladesh won series 2–0

FIRST TEST – BANGLADESH v. NEW ZEALAND
17–21 October 2008 at Chittagong

BANGLADESH

	First Innings		Second Innings	
Tamim Iqbal	c McCullum b Vettori	18	c & b Vettori	33
Junaid Siddique	lbw b O'Brien	0	c Redmond b Mills	6
Rajin Saleh	b O'Brien	20	lbw b Patel	6
M Ashraful (capt)	lbw b Vettori	2	c Redmond b Vettori	0
Mehrab Hossain	c Redmond b O'Brien	83	c Mills b Patel	6
*Mushfiqur Rahim	c How b Vettori	79	b O'Brien	32
Naeem Islam	st McCullum b Patel	14	(8) lbw b Vettori	19
Shakib Al Hasan	c Vettori b Patel	5	(7) c Taylor b Vettori	71
Mashrafe bin Mortaza	c Ryder b Vettori	0	st McCullum b Redmond	44
Abdur Razzak	c McCullum b Vettori	11	c Taylor b O'Brien	18
Shahadat Hossain	not out	0	not out	0
Extras	b 12, lb 1	13	b 4, lb 1, nb 2	7
	(all out 122.1 overs)	**245**	(all out 107.3 overs)	**242**

	First Innings				Second Innings			
	O	M	R	W	O	M	R	W
Mills	19	7	46	0	18	2	55	1
O'Brien	23	11	36	3	17	7	28	2
Oram	20	14	14	0	8	2	19	0
Ryder	3	1	10	0	-	-	-	-
Patel	21.1	7	67	2	20	7	53	2
Vettori	36	15	59	5	42	13	74	4
Redmond	-	-	-	-	2.3	1	8	1

Fall of Wickets
1-0, 2-34, 3-40, 4-44, 5-188, 6-229, 7-229, 8-229, 9-245
1-24, 2-36, 3-37, 4-49, 5-71, 6-127, 7-175, 8-180, 9-220

NEW ZEALAND

	First Innings		Second Innings	
AJ Redmond	lbw b Shakib Al Hasan	19	(2) c Junaid Siddique b S Al Hasan	79
JM How	c Rajin Saleh b Shakib Al Hasan	16	(1) b Abdur Razzak	36
JD Ryder	c Rajin Saleh b Shakib Al Hasan	1	run out	38
LRPL Taylor	lbw b Abdur Razzak	12	(5) c sub b Mashrafe bin Mortaza	9
*BB McCullum	c Abdur Razzak b S Al Hasan	25	(6) lbw b Abdur Razzak	2
DR Flynn	c Mushfiqur Rahim b Naeem Islam	19	(7) b Shakib Al Hasan	49
JDP Oram	c Mashrafe bin Mortaza b S Al Hasan	0	(8) not out	8
DL Vettori (capt)	not out	55	(4) b Abdur Razzak	76
KD Mills	c Mushfiqur Rahim b S Al Hasan	4	not out	1
JS Patel	c Shakib Al Hasan b M Ashraful	0		
IE O'Brien	b Shakib Al Hasan	5		
Extras	b 8, lb 6, nb 1	15	b 13, lb 3, w 3	19
	(all out 64.5 overs)	**171**	(7 wkts 137.5 overs)	**317**

	First Innings				Second Innings			
	O	M	R	W	O	M	R	W
Mashrafe bin Mortaza	7	4	13	0	14	4	37	1
Shahadat Hossain	11	0	35	0	11	1	46	0
Shakib Al Hasan	25.5	7	36	7	44.5	16	80	2
Abdur Razzak	16	3	51	1	50	15	93	3
Mehrab Hossain	1	0	8	0	2	0	6	0
Naeem Islam	3	0	11	1	12	3	15	0
Mohammad Ashraful	1	0	3	1	4	0	24	0

Fall of Wickets
1-27, 2-29, 3-46, 4-52, 5-99, 6-99, 7-100, 8-125, 9-154
1-55, 2-145, 3-185, 4-209, 5-216, 6-298, 7-316

Umpires: EAR de Silva (Sri Lanka) & DJ Harper (Australia)
Toss: Bangladesh
Test debuts: Naeem Islam & JD Ryder
Man of the Match: DL Vettori

New Zealand won by 3 wickets

SECOND TEST – BANGLADESH v. NEW ZEALAND
25–29 October 2008 at Mirpur

NEW ZEALAND

	First Innings		Second Innings	
AJ Redmond	lbw b Mashrafe bin Mortaza	2	(2) not out	30
JM How	b Mahbubul Alam	8	(1) c Abdur Razzak b M bin Mortaza	8
JD Ryder	c Mehrab Hossain b Abdur Razzak	91	not out	39
LRPL Taylor	b Shahadat Hossain	19		
*BB McCullum	c M Ashraful b Shakib Al Hasan	66		
DR Flynn	not out	35		
DL Vettori (capt)	b Mohammad Ashraful	22		
GD Elliott	not out	8		
KD Mills				
JS Patel				
IE O'Brien				
Extras	b 6, lb 3, nb 2	11	b 1, nb 1	2
	(6 wkts dec 75 overs)	**262**	(1 wkt dec 31 overs)	**79**

	First Innings				Second Innings			
	O	M	R	W	O	M	R	W
Mashrafe bin Mortaza	6	1	21	1	5	1	14	1
Mahbubul Alam	8	0	37	1	3	1	12	0
Abdur Razzak	25	2	72	1	7	1	12	0
Shahadat Hossain	8	0	39	1	6	0	20	0
Shakib Al Hasan	22	6	57	1	2	0	2	0
Mehrab Hossain	3	0	20	0	4	0	11	0
Mohammad Ashraful	3	0	7	1	1	0	4	0
Junaid Siddique	-	-	-	-	2	0	2	0
Tamim Iqbal	-	-	-	-	1	0	1	0

Fall of Wickets
1-10, 2-10, 3-49, 4-186, 5-201, 6-233
1-8

BANGLADESH

	First Innings	
Tamim Iqbal	c Taylor b Vettori	24
Junaid Siddique	st McCullum b Vettori	4
M Ashraful (capt)	lbw b Vettori	0
Rajin Saleh	lbw b Vettori	0
Mehrab Hossain	lbw b Patel	7
*Mushfiqur Rahim	c McCullum b O'Brien	7
Shakib Al Hasan	lbw b Vettori	49
Mashrafe bin Mortaza	c Flynn b O'Brien	48
Abdur Razzak	not out	16
Shahadat Hossain	c Vettori b O'Brien	4
Mahbubul Alam	not out	0
Extras	lb 2, w 6, nb 2	10
	(9 wkts dec 58.1 overs)	**169**

	First Innings			
	O	M	R	W
Mills	9	4	22	0
O'Brien	13.1	3	31	3
Patel	15	6	45	1
Vettori	19	6	66	5
Redmond	2	0	3	0

Fall of Wickets
1-13, 2-13, 3-13, 4-26, 5-44, 6-44, 7-122, 8-155, 9-169

Umpires: EAR de Silva (Sri Lanka) & DJ Harper (Australia)
Toss: Bangladesh
Test debut: Mahbubul Alam
Man of the Match: DL Vettori
Man of the Series: DL Vettori

Match drawn

New Zealand won series 1–0

SERIES AVERAGES
Bangladesh v. New Zealand

FIRST TEST – BANGLADESH v. SRI LANKA
26–31 December 2008 at Mirpur

BANGLADESH

Batting	M	Inns	NO	Runs	HS	Av	100	50	c/st
Shakib Al Hasan	2	3	0	125	71	41.66	-	1	1/-
Mushfiqur Rahim	2	3	0	118	79	39.33	-	1	2/-
Mehrab Hossain	2	3	0	96	83	32.00	-	1	1/-
Mashrafe bin Mortaza	2	3	0	92	48	30.66	-	-	1/-
Tamim Iqbal	2	3	0	75	33	25.00	-	-	-/-
Abdur Razzak	2	3	1	45	18	22.50	-	-	2/-
Naeem Islam	1	2	0	33	19	16.50	-	-	-/-
Rajin Saleh	2	3	0	26	20	8.66	-	-	2/-
Shahadat Hossain	2	3	2	4	4	4.00	-	-	-/-
Junaid Siddique	2	3	0	10	6	3.33	-	-	1/-
Mohammad Ashraful	2	3	0	2	2	0.66	-	-	1/-
Mahbubul Alam	1	1	1	0	0*	-	-	-	-/-

Bowling	Overs	Mds	Runs	Wkts	Av	Best	5/inn	10m
Shakib Al Hasan	94.4	29	175	10	17.50	7-36	1	-
Mohammad Ashraful	9	0	38	2	19.00	1-3	-	-
Naeem Islam	15	3	26	1	26.00	1-11	-	-
Mashrafe bin Mortaza	32	10	85	3	28.33	1-14	-	-
Abdur Razzak	98	21	228	5	45.60	3-93	-	-
Mahbubul Alam	11	1	49	1	49.00	1-37	-	-
Shahadat Hossain	36	1	140	1	140.00	1-39	-	-

Also bowled: Tamim Iqbal 1-0-1-0, Junaid Siddique 2-0-2-0, Mehrab Hossain 10-0-45-0.

NEW ZEALAND

Batting	M	Inns	NO	Runs	HS	Av	100	50	c/st
DL Vettori	2	3	1	153	76	76.50	-	2	3/-
JD Ryder	2	4	1	169	91	56.33	-	1	1/-
DR Flynn	2	3	1	103	49	51.50	-	-	1/-
AJ Redmond	2	4	1	130	79	43.33	-	1	3/-
BB McCullum	2	3	0	93	66	31.00	-	1	3/3
JM How	2	4	0	68	36	17.00	-	-	1/-
LRPL Taylor	2	3	0	40	19	13.33	-	-	3/-
JDP Oram	1	2	1	8	8*	8.00	-	-	-/-
KD Mills	2	2	1	5	4	5.00	-	-	1/-
IE O'Brien	2	1	0	5	5	5.00	-	-	-/-
JS Patel	2	1	0	0	0	0.00	-	-	-/-
GD Elliott	1	1	1	8	8*	-	-	-	-/-

Bowling	Overs	Mds	Runs	Wkts	Av	Best	5/inn	10m
AJ Redmond	4.3	1	11	1	11.00	1-8	-	-
IE O'Brien	53.1	21	95	8	11.87	3-31	-	-
DL Vettori	97	34	199	14	14.21	5-59	2	-
JS Patel	56.1	20	165	5	33.00	2-53	-	-
KD Mills	46	13	123	1	123.00	1-55	-	-

Also bowled: JD Ryder 3-1-10-0, JDP Oram 28-16-33-0.

SRI LANKA

	First Innings		Second Innings	
MG Vandort	c Shakib Al Hasan b S Hossain	44	b Mashrafe bin Mortaza	6
BSM Warnapura	lbw b Mashrafe bin Mortaza	14	lbw b Mahbubul Alam	9
KC Sangakkara	c M Ashraful b S Al Hasan	43	c Mushfiqur Rahim b M Hossain	67
DPMD J'wardene (capt)	b Shakib Al Hasan	3	c Junaid Siddique b M Hossain	166
TT Samaraweera	c Junaid Siddique b S Al Hasan	91	b Mashrafe bin Mortaza	62
TM Dilshan	b Shakib Al Hasan	14	c Mushfiqur Rahim b S Al Hasan	47
*HAPW Jayawardene	c Iqbal b Shahadat Hossain	6	not out	3
WPUJC Vaas	c Mushfiqur Rahim b M bin Mortaza	37	not out	15
KTGD Prasad	lbw b Shakib Al Hasan	3		
HMRKB Herath	run out	1		
M Muralitharan	not out	0		
Extras	b 4, lb 12, w 12, nb 9	37	b 16, lb 4, w 2, nb 8	30
	(all out 89.4 overs)	293	(6 wkts dec 108 overs)	405

	First Innings				Second Innings			
	O	M	R	W	O	M	R	W
Mashrafe bin Mortaza	18	2	68	2	21	3	60	2
Mahbubul Alam	19	4	56	0	17	1	62	1
Shahadat Hossain	16	2	55	2	14	1	66	0
Shakib Al Hasan	28.4	4	70	5	40	10	134	1
Mehrab Hossain	6	1	22	0	10	0	37	2
Mohammad Ashraful	2	0	6	0	5	0	24	0
Raqibul Hasan	-	-	-	-	1	0	2	0

Fall of Wickets
1-24, 2-119, 3-121, 4-135, 5-155, 6-171, 7-270, 8-285, 9-291
1-16, 2-18, 3-153, 4-291, 5-386, 6-388

BANGLADESH

	First Innings		Second Innings	
Tamim Iqbal	c Warnapura b Muralitharan	17	c Jayawardene HAPW b Prasad	47
Imrul Kayes	c Jayawardene HAPW b Vaas	33	run out	13
Junaid Siddique	b Muralitharan	29	c Jayawardene DPMD b Muralitharan	37
Mohammad Ashraful (capt)	c Dilshan b Vaas	12	(5) lbw b Vaas	101
Raqibul Hasan	b Prasad	11	(4) b Muralitharan	24
Mehrab Hossain	c Jayawardene DPMD b Herath	28	c sub b Muralitharan	23
Shakib Al Hasan	c J'wardene DPMD b Muralitharan	27	b Prasad	96
*Mushfiqur Rahim	not out	12	c Dilshan b Muralitharan	61
Mashrafe bin Mortaza	lbw b Muralitharan	5	c Jayawardene HAPW b Prasad	2
Shahadat Hossain	st J'wardene HAPW b Muralitharan	5	(11) not out	0
Mahbubul Alam	c Warnapura b Muralitharan	0	(10) run out	2
Extras	b 4	4	lb 3, nb 4	7
	(all out 60 overs)	178	(all out 126.2 overs)	413

	First Innings				Second Innings			
	O	M	R	W	O	M	R	W
Vaas	11	4	33	2	25	5	74	1
Prasad	13	0	61	1	25.2	5	105	3
Dilshan	2	0	2	0	2	0	4	0
Muralitharan	22	8	49	6	48	9	141	4
Herath	12	1	29	1	26	4	86	0

Fall of Wickets
1-44, 2-68, 3-90, 4-95, 5-117, 6-158, 7-162, 8-162, 9-176
1-40, 2-72, 3-124, 4-144, 5-180, 6-292, 7-403, 8-409, 9-411

Umpires: SA Bucknor (West Indies) & NJ Llong (England)
Toss: Sri Lanka
Man of the Match: Shakib Al Hasan

Sri Lanka won by 107 runs

SECOND TEST – BANGLADESH v. SRI LANKA
3–6 January 2009 at Chittagong

SRI LANKA

	First Innings		Second Innings	
BSM Warnapura	lbw b Mohammad Ashraful	63	lbw b Shahadat Hossain	27
*HAPW Jayawardene	lbw b Mashrafe bin Mortaza	0	c Shakib Al Hasan b M Ashraful	28
KC Sangakkara	b Mashrafe bin Mortaza	5	b Mohammad Ashraful	54
DPMD J'wardene (capt)	c Mushfiqur Rahim b S Al Hasan	11	c Imrul Kayes b E Haque jnr	22
TT Samaraweera	b Shahadat Hossain	19	lbw b Shakib Al Hasan	77
TM Dilshan	b Enamul Haque jnr	162	b Enamul Haque jnr	143
CK Kapugedera	lbw b Shakib Al Hasan	96	not out	60
WPUJC Vaas	lbw b Mashrafe bin Mortaza	3	not out	20
M Muralitharan	lbw b Shakib Al Hasan	0		
BAW Mendis	not out	6		
CRD Fernando	lbw b Shakib Al Hasan	0		
Extras	b 4, lb 8, w 1, nb 6	19	b 3, lb 3, w 4, nb 6	16
	(all out 94 overs)	384	(6 wkts dec 127 overs)	447

	First Innings				Second Innings			
	O	M	R	W	O	M	R	W
Mashrafe bin Mortaza	22	7	58	3	15	3	53	0
Shahadat Hossain	14	0	80	1	28	3	92	1
Shakib Al Hasan	30	6	109	4	20	2	79	1
Enamul Haque jnr	19	3	70	1	36	2	109	2
Mehrab Hossain	7	1	36	0	8	0	38	0
Mohammad Ashraful	2	0	19	1	17	1	57	2
Raqibul Hasan	–	–	–	–	1	0	3	0
Imrul Kayes	–	–	–	–	1	0	7	0
Tamim Iqbal	–	–	–	–	1	0	3	0

Fall of Wickets
1-1, 2-7, 3-39, 4-75, 5-194, 6-367, 7-376, 8-376, 9-384
1-55, 2-55, 3-123, 4-165, 5-310, 6-396

BANGLADESH

	First Innings		Second Innings	
Tamim Iqbal	c Jayawardene HAPW b Vaas	0	c Jayawardene HAPW b Vaas	17
Imrul Kayes	lbw b Vaas	6	c Jayawardene DPMD b Mendis	5
Junaide Siddique	b Fernando	28	lbw b Mendis	4
Raqibul Hasan	lbw b Mendis	0	b Fernando	10
M Ashraful (capt)	c J'wardene HAPW b Muralitharan	45	c Jayawardene HAPW b Mendis	7
Mehrab Hossain	lbw b Mendis	18	(8) lbw b Dilshan	5
Shakib Al Hasan	lbw b Mendis	0	st Jayawardene HAPW b Dilshan	46
*Mushfiqur Rahim	st Jayawardene HAPW b Mendis	21	(6) run out	43
Mashrafe bin Mortaza	c Dilshan b Muralitharan	63	c Jayawardene DPMD b Dilshan	0
Enamul Haque jnr	c J'wardene HAPW b Muralitharan	4	(11) not out	0
Shahadat Hossain	not out	5	(10) b Dilshan	1
Extras	b 5, lb 5, nb 8	18	b 4, lb 5, nb 11	20
	(all out 76.2 overs)	208	(all out 49.2 overs)	158

	First Innings				Second Innings			
	O	M	R	W	O	M	R	W
Vaas	10	5	21	2	8	3	16	1
Fernando	18	4	44	1	12	4	36	1
Mendis	28	5	71	4	15	4	57	3
Muralitharan	20.2	6	62	3	10	0	30	0
Dilshan	–	–	–	–	4.2	1	10	4

Fall of Wickets
1-0, 2-26, 3-33, 4-65, 5-90, 6-90, 7-122, 8-136, 9-145
1-18, 2-22, 3-32, 4-42, 5-52, 6-144, 7-154, 8-154, 9-156

Umpires: SA Buchnor (West Indies) & NJ Llong (England)
Toss: Sri Lanka
Man of the Match: TM Dilshan
Man of the Series: TM Dilshan

Sri Lanka won by 465 runs

Sri Lanka won series 2–0

SERIES AVERAGES
Bangladesh v. Sri Lanka

BANGLADESH

Batting	M	Inns	NO	Runs	HS	Av	100	50	c/st
Mushfiqur Rahim	2	4	1	137	61	45.66	–	1	4/-
Shakib Al Hasan	2	4	0	169	96	42.25	–	1	2/-
Mohammad Ashraful	2	4	0	165	101	41.25	1	–	1/-
Junaid Siddique	2	4	0	98	37	24.50	–	–	2/-
Tamim Iqbal	2	4	0	81	47	20.25	–	–	1/-
Mehrab Hossain	2	4	0	74	28	18.50	–	–	-/-
Mashrafe bin Mortaza	2	4	0	65	63	16.25	–	1	-/-
Imrul Kayes	2	4	0	57	33	14.25	–	–	1/-
Raqibul Hasan	2	4	0	45	24	11.25	–	–	-/-
Shahadat Hossain	2	4	2	11	5*	5.50	–	–	-/-
Enamul Haque jnr	1	2	1	4	4	4.00	–	–	-/-
Mahbubul Alam	1	2	0	2	2	1.00	–	–	-/-

Bowling	Overs	Mds	Runs	Wkts	Av	Best	5/inn	10m
Mashrafe bin Mortaza	76	15	239	7	34.14	3-58	–	–
Mohammad Ashraful	26	1	106	3	35.33	2-57	–	–
Shakib Al Hasan	118.4	22	392	11	35.63	5-70	1	–
Enamul Haque jnr	55	5	179	3	59.66	2-109	–	–
Mehrab Hossain	31	2	133	2	66.50	2-37	–	–
Shahadat Hossain	72	6	293	4	73.25	2-55	–	–
Mahbubul Alam	36	5	118	1	118.00	1-62	–	–

Also bowled: Tamim Iqbal 1-0-3-0, Raqibul Hasan 2-0-5-0, Imrul Kayes 1-0-7-0.

SRI LANKA

Batting	M	Inns	NO	Runs	HS	Av	100	50	c/st
CK Kapugedera	1	2	1	156	96	156.00	–	2	-/-
TM Dilshan	2	4	0	366	162	91.50	2	–	3/-
TT Samaraweera	2	4	0	249	91	62.25	–	3	-/-
DPMD Jayawardene	2	4	0	202	166	50.50	1	–	5/-
KC Sangakkara	2	4	0	169	67	42.25	–	2	-/-
WPUJC Vaas	2	4	2	75	37	37.50	–	–	-/-
BSM Warnapura	2	4	0	113	63	28.25	–	1	2/-
MG Vandort	1	2	0	50	44	25.00	–	–	-/-
HAPW Jayawardene	2	4	1	37	28	12.33	–	–	8/3
KTGD Prasad	1	1	0	3	3	3.00	–	–	-/-
HMRKB Herath	1	1	0	1	1	1.00	–	–	-/-
M Muralitharan	2	2	1	0	0*	0.00	–	–	-/-
CRD Fernando	1	1	0	0	0	0.00	–	–	-/-
BAW Mendis	1	1	1	6	6*	–	–	–	-/-

Bowling	Overs	Mds	Runs	Wkts	Av	Best	5/inn	10m
TM Dilshan	8.2	1	16	4	4.00	4-10	–	–
BAW Mendis	43	9	128	7	18.28	4-71	–	–
M Muralitharan	100.2	23	282	13	21.69	6-49	1	1
WPUJC Vaas	54	17	144	6	24.00	2-21	–	–
CRD Fernando	30	8	80	2	40.00	1-36	–	–
KTGD Prasad	38.2	5	166	4	41.50	3-105	–	–
HMRKB Herath	38	5	115	1	115.00	1-29	–	–

OVERSEAS ODIs

by Mark Baldwin

Australia re-established themselves at the top of the ICC ODI rankings by winning the Champions Trophy tournament in October, at the end of a year in which their mastery of the 50-overs format was challenged by both India and, in particular, South Africa.

The South Africans, indeed, took by a 7-3 margin the ten one-day internationals that they contested with Australia, home and away. Yet, for fast bowler Dale Steyn, the fact that South Africa crashed out of the Champions Trophy at the first round stage – having also disappointed in the ICC World Twenty20 three months earlier – was not merely a source of dismay. 'We were the number one ranked team going into the Champions Trophy, and it was a position we had held for some time,' he said. 'But until we actually win an ICC one-day

ICC ODI RANKINGS		
1	Australia	128
2	India	124
3	South Africa	121
4	New Zealand	110
5	Pakistan	109
6	England	106
7	Sri Lanka	106
8	West Indies	76
9	Bangladesh	55
10	Zimbabwe	27
11	Ireland	25
12	Kenya	0

As at 24 October 2009

tournament we cannot say we are the best limited-overs side in the world. Rankings don't mean anything when you are out there on the field.'

The emerging talents of left-arm spinner Roelof van der Merwe and teenage left-arm fast bowler Wayne Parnell just served to reinforce the strength in depth of South Africa's one-day armoury. That 'chokers' tag,

Marcus North, of Australia, has his stumps shattered by South Africa fast bowler Dale Steyn.

though, won't go away when the big games in the important tournaments continue to slip through South African fingers.

New Zealand won 61 of their 106 ODIs during the five-year tenure of former coach John Bracewell (but only 13 of their 41 Tests, with 20 defeats), and the reign of his successor Andy Moles began with a 2-1 victory in a rain-ravaged five-match series at home to the West Indies and a hard-fought 2-2 draw in Australia. But the Black Caps then slipped to a 3-1 loss at home to India and, before their tenacious progress into the Champions Trophy final, they also found both the Indians and Sri Lanka too hot to handle in the Compaq Cup event in September.

The absence of injured captain Daniel Vettori was a major blow to New Zealand in the Champions Trophy final, in which they were beaten by Australia, because the left-arm spinner is established as perhaps the most consistently outstanding limited-overs bowler in the world game. Moreover, in the likes of Brendon McCullum, Jesse Ryder, Ross Taylor and the batting newcomer, Martin Guptill, plus all-rounders such as

Zimbabwe's Charles Coventry forces one away during his record 194 not out against Bangladesh at Bulawayo. Wicketkeeper Mushfiqur Rahim looks on.

Vettori, James Franklin, Jacob Oram, Neil McCullum and Ian Butler, the Kiwis possess an array of effective one-day performers. As so often the case in the past, however, their relatively small pool of proven talent can seldom afford to be anything other than at full strength.

Pakistan, the World Twenty20 victors, did not enjoy similar success in 50-over cricket. In January they were tumbled out for just 75 in a Lahore decider, in reply to Sri Lanka's 309 for 5 in which Tillakeratne Dilshan struck a brilliant unbeaten 137, to lose that series 2-1. And, after a 3-2 defeat against Australia in neutral Abu Dhabi, Pakistan also lost a return series in Sri Lanka by the same margin. A semi-final defeat to New Zealand in the Champions Trophy confirmed that Pakistan still have much to do to improve their standing on the one-day international stage.

Bangladesh, meanwhile, improved their ranking mark by beating a second string West Indies in the Caribbean by a still impressive 3-0 scoreline, and beating Zimbabwe 2-1 at home and 4-1 away.

For Zimbabwe, though, the year at least saw some tangible progress on the cricket field to match the hope brought by the formation of a new government of national unity. South Africa resumed bilateral ties with its neighbour in May, having suspended contact the previous year at the destructive height of the Mugabe regime, and a stream of former players began to return

to Zimbabwean cricket – either in coaching or administrative roles, or in a playing capacity.

Brendan Taylor, Sean Williams, Mark Vermuelen, Charles Coventry and Graeme Cremer were all back in the Zimbabwe side by the final months of 2009, with Coventry playing one momentous innings against Bangladesh, but perhaps the most significant returns were those of Dave Houghton and Heath Streak.

With the ICC announcing a timescale for Zimbabwe's suspension from Test cricket, invoked in 2005, to end by March 2011, it was heartening to witness the arrival from exile of former Test captain and coach Houghton as the new director of national coaching – with an express brief to help the team prepare for its return to Tests. Streak, another former Zimbabwe captain and the best fast bowler the country has produced, was appointed first as bowling coach and then as head coach of the national side, with Walter Chawaguta, his predecessor in the job, retained as his assistant.

A revamped domestic structure featured five new franchises, which in turn attracted more formerly self-exiled players such as Dion Ebrahim, Greg Lamb and Barney Rogers, and Ozias Bute, the chief executive of Zimbabwe Cricket, said, 'A lot has been said and done in the past but we have collectively agreed to draw a line in the sand and allow for cricket to be the winner'.

AUSTRALIA v. SOUTH AFRICA

Match One
16 January 2009 Day/Night at Melbourne (MCG)
Australia 271 for 8 (50 overs) (SE Marsh 79, DJ Hussey 52)
South Africa 272 for 7 (49.3 overs) (JP Duminy 71,
ND McKenzie 63)
South Africa won by 3 wickets

Match Two
18 January 2009 at Hobart
Australia 249 for 9 (50 overs) (SE Marsh 78, RT Ponting 64,
M Ntini 3 for 39)
South Africa 244 for 6 (50 overs) (JH Kallis 72)
Australia won by 5 runs

Match Three
23 January 2009 Day/Night at Sydney
Australia 269 all out (49.2 overs) (DA Warner 69, J Botha 3 for 32)
South Africa 270 for 7 (46.3 overs) (HH Gibbs 64, JH Kallis 60)
South Africa won by 3 wickets

Match Four
26 January 2009 Day/Night at Adelaide
Australia 222 all out (48 overs) (RT Ponting 63,
DW Steyn 3 for 49, M Ntini 3 for 52)
South Africa 223 for 2 (38.1 overs) (AB de Villiers 82*,
HM Amla 80*)
South Africa won by 8 wickets

Match Five
30 January 2009 Day/Night at Perth
South Africa 288 for 6 (50 overs) (HM Amla 97,
AB de Villiers 60, JP Duminy 60*, JR Hopes 3 for 44)
Australia 249 all out (49 overs) (MEK Hussey 78, BJ Haddin 63,
LL Tsotsobe 4 for 50)
South Africa won by 39 runs
South Africa won the series 4–1

AUSTRALIA v. NEW ZEALAND

Match One
1 February 2009 Day/Night at Perth
Australia 181 all out (48.4 overs) (KD Mills 4 for 35)
New Zealand 182 for 8 (50 overs) (LRPL Taylor 64,
NW Bracken 3 for 35)
New Zealand won by 2 wickets

Match Two
6 February 2009 Day/Night at Melbourne (MCG)
Australia 225 for 5 (50 overs) (MJ Clarke 98, MEK Hussey 75)
New Zealand 226 for 4 (48.5 overs) (GD Elliott 61*)
New Zealand won by 6 wickets

Match Three
8 February 2009 Day/Night at Sydney
Australia 301 for 9 (50 overs) (BJ Haddin 109,
MJ Clarke 64, MEK Hussey 51, IE O'Brien 3 for 68)
New Zealand 269 all out (47.3 overs)
(GD Elliott 115)
Australia won by 32 runs

Match Four
10 February 2009 Day/Night at Adelaide
New Zealand 244 for 8 (50 overs) (LRPL Taylor 76,
MG Johnson 3 for 51)
Australia 247 for 4 (48.2 overs) (DJ Hussey 79,
MEK Hussey 75*)
Australia won by 6 wickets

Match Five
13 February 2009 Day/Night at Brisbane
Australia 168 for 4 (22 overs) (BJ Haddin 88*,
CJ Ferguson 55*)
New Zealand 123 for 6 (14 overs) (MJ Guptill 64*)
No result
Series drawn

SOUTH AFRICA v. KENYA

Match One
31 October 2008 Day/Night at Bloemfontein
South Africa 336 for 7 (50 overs) (JP Duminy 90,
JH Kallis 71, MV Boucher 57*, NO Odhiambo 3 for 59)
Kenya 177 all out (49.1 overs) (J Botha 4 for 19,
JP Duminy 3 for 31)
South Africa won by 159 runs

Match Two
2 November 2008 at Kimberley
Kenya 222 for 9 (50 overs) (S Waters 74,
JA Morkel 3 for 47)
South Africa 224 for 3 (35.3 overs) (JH Kallis 92*,
HM Amla 78)
South Africa won by 7 wickets
South Africa won the series 2–0

SOUTH AFRICA v. BANGLADESH

Match One
7 November 2008 Day/Night at Potchefstroom
South Africa 283 for 8 (50 overs) (JH Kallis 50,
Naeem Islam 3 for 60)
Bangladesh 222 all out (44.2 overs)
(Mohammad Ashraful 73, Shakib Al Hasan 51,
DW Steyn 4 for 16, JA Morkel 3 for 40)
South Africa won by 61 runs

Match Two
9 November 2008 at Benoni
South Africa 358 for 4 (50 overs) (HM Amla 140, GC Smith 65,
AB de Villiers 54*)
Bangladesh 230 all out (49.2 overs) (J Botha 3 for 27,
DW Steyn 3 for 48)
South Africa won by 128 runs

Match Three
12 November 2008 Day/Night at East London
South Africa v. **Bangladesh**
Match abandoned
South Africa won the series 2–0

SOUTH AFRICA v. AUSTRALIA

Match One
3 April 2009 Day/Night at Durban
Australia 286 for 7 (50 overs) (MEK Hussey 83*, BJ Haddin 53)
South Africa 145 all out (33.1 overs) (GC Smith 52,
NM Hauritz 4 for 29)
Australia won by 141 runs

Match Two
5 April 2009 at Centurion
Australia 131 all out (40.2 overs) (CJ Ferguson 50,
WD Parnell 4 for 25, DW Steyn 4 for 27)
South Africa 132 for 3 (26.2 overs)
South Africa won by 7 wickets

Match Three
9 April 2009 Day/Night at Cape Town
South Africa 289 for 6 (50 overs) (AB de Villiers 80,
JH Kallis 70, MG Johnson 4 for 34)
Australia 264 for 7 (50 overs) (CJ Ferguson 63, JR Hopes 63*,
R van der Merwe 3 for 37)
South Africa won by 25 runs

Match Four
13 April 2009 at Port Elizabeth
South Africa 317 for 6 (50 overs) (HH Gibbs 110, AB de Villiers 84)
Australia 256 all out (45.5 overs) (BJ Haddin 78, RT Ponting 53,
MJ Clarke 50, DW Steyn 4 for 44, R van der Merwe 3 for 46)
South Africa won by 61 runs

Match Five
17 April 2009 Day/Night at Johannesburg
Australia 303 for 7 (50 overs) (MJ Clarke 66, BJ Haddin 62,
JP Duminy 3 for 48)
South Africa 256 all out (45.5 overs) (HH Gibbs 82,
JH Kallis 64, MG Johnson 3 for 58)
Australia won by 47 runs
South Africa won the series 3–2

NEW ZEALAND v. WEST INDIES

Match One
31 December 2008 at Queenstown
West Indies 129 for 5 (35.4 overs)
New Zealand
No result

Match Two
3 January 2009 Day/Night at Christchurch
New Zealand 152 for 8 (28 overs) (FH Edwards 3 for 26)
West Indies 158 for 5 (27.5 overs) (RR Sarwan 67*)
*West Indies won by 5 wickets – DL Method: target 158 from
28 overs*

Match Three
7 January 2009 Day/Night at Wellington
West Indies 128 all out (41.4 overs) (DL Vettori 4 for 20)
New Zealand 129 for 3 (20.3 overs) (LRPL Taylor 51*,
DB Powell 3 for 25)
New Zealand won by 7 wickets

Match Four
10 January 2009 at Auckland
New Zealand 275 for 4 (50 overs) (MJ Guptill 122*,
LRPL Taylor 75)
West Indies 64 for 0 (10.3 overs)
No result

Match Five
13 January 2009 at Napier
West Indies 293 for 9 (50 overs) (CH Gayle 135, S Chanderpaul 94,
MR Gillespie 4 for 58, KD Mills 3 for 57)
New Zealand 211 for 5 (35 overs) (DB Powell 3 for 66)
*New Zealand won by 9 runs – DL Method: target 202 from
35 overs*
New Zealand won the series 2–1

NEW ZEALAND v. INDIA

Match One
3 March 2009 Day/Night at Napier
India 273 for 4 (38 overs) (MS Dhoni 84*, V Sehwag 77,
SK Raina 66)
New Zealand 162 for 9 (28 overs) (MJ Guptill 64,
Harbhajan Singh 3 for 27)
India won by 53 runs – DL Method: target 216 from 28 overs

Match Two
6 March 2009 Day/Night at Wellington
India 188 for 4 (28.4 overs) (SR Tendulkar 61, V Sehwag 54)
New Zealand
No result

Match Three

8 March 2009 Day/Night at Christchurch
India 392 for 4 (50 overs) (SR Tendulkar 163*, Yuvraj Singh 87, MS Dhoni 68)
New Zealand 334 all out (45.1 overs) (JD Ryder 105, BB McCullum 71, KD Mills 54)
India won by 58 runs

Match Four

11 March 2009 Day/Night at Hamilton
New Zealand 270 for 5 (47 overs) (BB McCullum 77, PD McGlashan 56*)
India 201 for 0 (23.3 overs) (V Sehwag 125*, G Gambhir 63*)
India won by 84 runs – DL Method: target 118 from 23.3 overs

Match Five

14 March 2009 Day/Night at Auckland
India 149 all out (36.3 overs) (JD Ryder 3 for 29)
New Zealand 151 for 2 (23.2 overs) (JD Ryder 63, MJ Guptill 57*)
New Zealand won by 8 wickets
India won the series 3–1

PAKISTAN v. WEST INDIES

Match One

12 November 2008 Day/Night at Abu Dhabi
West Indies 294 for 9 (50 overs) (CH Gayle 113, RR Sarwan 55, Sohail Tanvir 3 for 42, Umar Gul 3 for 66)
Pakistan 295 for 6 (49.5 overs) (Khurram Manzoor 69, Shoaib Malik 66, Younis Khan 56, LS Baker 3 for 47)
Pakistan won by 4 wickets

Match Two

14 November 2008 Day/Night at Abu Dhabi
Pakistan 232 all out (49 overs) (Misbah-ul-Haq 52, JE Taylor 3 for 38, DB Powell 3 for 50)
West Indies 208 (48.5 overs) (S Chanderpaul 107*, Umar Gul 3 for 44)
Pakistan won by 24 runs

Match Three

16 November 2008 Day/Night at Abu Dhabi
Pakistan 273 for 6 (50 overs) (Younis Khan 101, Misbah-ul-Haq 79*)
West Indies 242 all out (46.3 overs) (CH Gayle 122, RR Sarwan 62, Iftikhar Anjum 4 for 59, Umar Gul 3 for 31)
Pakistan won by 31 runs
Pakistan won the series 3–0

PAKISTAN v. SRI LANKA

Match One

20 January 2009 Day/Night at Karachi
Sri Lanka 219 all out (45.2 overs) (Iftikhar Anjum 4 for 42, Umar Gul 3 for 30)
Pakistan 220 for 2 (45.5 overs) (Salman Butt 100*, Khurram Manzoor 83)
Pakistan won by 8 wickets

Match Two

21 January 2009 Day/Night at Karachi
Sri Lanka 290 for 8 (50 overs) (TM Dilshan 76, SHT Kandamby 59, Umar Gul 4 for 58)
Pakistan 161 all out (34.5 overs) (Salman Butt 62, Shoaib Malik 54, M Muralitharan 3 for 19, BAW Mendis 3 for 29)
Sri Lanka won by 129 runs

Match Three

24 January 2009 Day/Night at Lahore
Sri Lanka 309 for 5 (50 overs) (TM Dilshan 137*, KC Sangakkara 50, Umar Gul 3 for 45)
Pakistan 75 all out (22.5 overs) (KMDN Kulasekara 3 for 17, T Thushara 3 for 33)
Sri Lanka won by 234 runs
Sri Lanka won the series 2–1

Tillakeratne Dilshan (right) and Kumar Sangakkara run hard in Sri Lanka's cause against Pakistan in Lahore.

PAKISTAN v. AUSTRALIA

Match One
22 April 2009 Day/Night at Dubai
Australia 168 all out (38.5 overs) (Shahid Afridi 6 for 38)
Pakistan 171 for 6 (44.1 overs)
Pakistan won by 4 wickets

Match Two
24 April 2009 Day/Night at Dubai
Pakistan 207 all out (46.2 overs) (Salman Butt 57,
NM Hauritz 3 for 41)
Australia 208 for 4 (45.1 overs) (A Symonds 58)
Australia won by 6 wickets

Match Three
27 April 2009 Day/Night at Abu Dhabi
Australia 198 for 7 (50 overs) (MJ Clarke 66,
Umar Gul 3 for 38)
Pakistan 171 all out (47.1 overs) (MJ Clarke 3 for 15)
Australia won by 27 runs

Match Four
1 May 2009 Day/Night at Abu Dhabi
Pakistan 197 all out (48.4 overs) (DE Bollinger 5 for 35)
Australia 200 for 2 (44.2 overs) (MJ Clarke 100*,
SR Watson 85*)
Australia won by 8 wickets

Match Five
3 May 2009 Day/Night at Abu Dhabi
Australia 250 for 4 (50 overs) (SR Watson 116*)
Pakistan 254 for 3 (47 overs) (Kamran Akmal 116*,
Misbah-ul-Haq 76*)
Pakistan won by 7 wickets
Australia won the series 3–2

SRI LANKA v. INDIA

Match One
28 January 2009 at Dambulla
Sri Lanka 246 for 7 (50 overs) (ST Jayasuriya 107,
I Sharma 3 for 52)
India 247 for 4 (48.1 overs) (G Gambhir 62, MS Dhoni 61*,
SK Raina 54)
India won by 6 wickets

Match Two
31 January 2009 Day/Night at Colombo (RPS)
India 256 for 9 (50 overs) (Yuvraj Singh 66)
Sri Lanka 241 all out (49.2 overs) (SHT Kandamby 93*,
DPMD Jayawardene 52, I Sharma 4 for 57)
India won by 15 runs

Match Three
3 February 2009 Day/Night at Colombo (RPS)
India 363 for 5 (50 overs) (Yuvraj Singh 117, V Sehwag 116,
YK Pathan 59*)
Sri Lanka 216 all out (41.4 overs) (KC Sangakkara 83,
PP Ojha 4 for 38)
India won by 147 runs

Match Four
5 February 2009 Day/Night at Colombo (RPS)
India 332 for 5 (50 overs) (G Gambhir 150, MS Dhoni 94,
KMDN Kulasekara 3 for 63)
Sri Lanka 265 all out (48 overs) (KC Sangakkara 56,
IK Pathan 3 for 58)
India won by 67 runs

Match Five
8 February 2009 at Colombo (SSC)
Sri Lanka 320 for 8 (50 overs) (TM Dilshan 97,
KC Sangakkara 84, I Sharma 3 for 60)
India 252 all out (48.5 overs) (Yuvraj Singh 73, RA Jadeja 60*,
MS Dhoni 53)
Sri Lanka won by 68 runs
India won the series 4–1

SRI LANKA v. PAKISTAN

Match One
30 July 2009 at Dambulla
Sri Lanka 232 for 9 (50 overs) (Mohammad Aamer 3 for 45)
Pakistan 196 all out (44.4 overs) (T Thushara 3 for 29)
Sri Lanka won by 36 runs

Match Two
1 August 2009 at Dambulla
Pakistan 168 all out (47 overs) (T Thushara 3 for 33)
Sri Lanka 169 for 4 (43.4 overs) (CK Kapugedera 67*)
Sri Lanka won by 6 wickets

Match Three
3 August 2009 at Dambulla
Pakistan 288 for 8 (50 overs) (Umar Akmal 66)
Sri Lanka 289 for 4 (46.3 overs) (DPMD Jayawardene 123,
WU Tharanga 76)
Sri Lanka won by 6 wickets

Match Four
7 August 2009 Day/Night at Colombo (RPS)
Pakistan 321 for 5 (50 overs) (Umar Akmal 102*,
Younis Khan 89, Kamran Akmal 57)
Sri Lanka 175 all out (36.1 overs) (WU Tharanga 80,
Iftikhar Anjum 5 for 30)
Pakistan won by 146 runs

Match Five
9 August 2009 Day/Night at Colombo (RPS)
Pakistan 279 for 8 (50 overs) (Younis Khan 76,
Misbah-ul-Haq 73*, KMDN Kulasekara 3 for 46)
Sri Lanka 147 all out (34.2 overs) (Mohammad Aamer 4 for 28,
Naved-ul-Hasan 4 for 44)
Pakistan won by 132 runs
Sri Lanka won the series 3–2

WEST INDIES v. INDIA

Match One
26 June 2009 at Kingston
India 339 for 6 (50 overs) (Yuvraj Singh 131, KKD Karthik 67)
West Indies 319 all out (48.1 overs) (S Chanderpaul 63,
A Nehra 3 for 49, YK Pathan 3 for 56)
India won by 20 runs

Match Two
28 June 2009 at Kingston
India 188 all out (48.2 overs) (MS Dhoni 95, R Rampaul 4 for 37,
DJ Bravo 3 for 26, JE Taylor 3 for 35)
West Indies 192 for 2 (34.1 overs) (RS Morton 85*, CH Gayle 64)
West Indies won by 8 wickets

Match Three
3 July 2009 at Gros Islet
West Indies 186 for 7 (27 overs) (RR Sarwan 62, A Nehra 3 for 21)
India 159 for 4 (21.5 overs)
India won by 6 wickets – DL Method: target 159 from 22 overs

Match Four
5 July 2009 at Gros Islet
West Indies 27 for 1 (7.3 overs)
India
No result
India won the series 2–1

WEST INDIES v. BANGLADESH

Match One
26 July 2009 at Roseau
Bangladesh 246 for 9 (50 overs) (Mohammad Ashraful 57,
Shakib Al Hasan 54, KAJ Roach 5 for 44)
West Indies 194 all out (43.4 overs) (DS Smith 65, Abdur Razzak 4 for 39)
Bangladesh won by 52 runs

Match Two
28 July 2009 at Roseau
West Indies 274 for 6 (50 overs) (TM Dowlin 100*)
Bangladesh 276 for 7 (49 overs) (Shakib Al Hasan 65,
Mohammad Ashraful 64)
Bangladesh won by 3 wickets

Match Three
31 July 2009 at St Kitts
West Indies 248 all out (47.4 overs) (ADS Fletcher 52)
Bangladesh 249 for 7 (48.5 overs) (Junaid Siddique 55,
Mahmudallah 51*, KAJ Roach 4 for 63)
Bangladesh won by 3 wickets
Bangladesh won the series 3–0

BANGLADESH v. NEW ZEALAND

Match One
9 October 2008 at Mirpur
New Zealand 201 for 9 (50 overs) (JDP Oram 57,
Mashrafe bin Mortaza 4 for 44, Abdur Razzak 3 for 32)
Bangladesh 202 for 3 (45.3 overs) (Junaid Siddique 85,
Mohammad Ashraful 60*)
Bangladesh won by 7 wickets

Match Two
11 October 2008 at Mirpur
New Zealand 212 for 9 (50 overs) (JDP Oram 75*, Syed Rasel 3 for 23)
Bangladesh 137 all out (42.4 overs) (KD Mills 3 for 13)
New Zealand won by 75 runs

Match Three
14 October 2008 at Chittagong
New Zealand 249 for 7 (50 overs) (LRPL Taylor 103, JM How 73)
Bangladesh 170 for 8 (50 overs)
New Zealand won by 79 runs
New Zealand won the series 2–1

BANGLADESH v. ZIMBABWE

Match One
19 January 2009 at Mirpur
Bangladesh 124 all out (48.1 overs) (RW Price 4 for 22, KM Dabengwa 3 for 15)
Zimbabwe 127 for 8 (49.2 overs) (Shakib Al Hasan 3 for 11,
Mashrafe bin Mortaza 3 for 21)
Zimbabwe won by 2 wickets

Match Two
21 January 2009 at Mirpur
Zimbabwe 160 for 9 (50 overs) (SC Williams 59, Nazmul Hossain 3 for 28)
Bangladesh 164 for 4 (44.5 overs) (Raqibul Hasan 52*)
Bangladesh won by 6 wickets

Match Three
23 January 2009 at Mirpur
Zimbabwe 119 for 9 (37 overs) (Shakib Al Hasan 3 for 15,
Mashrafe bin Mortaza 3 for 26)
Bangladesh 121 for 4 (32.3 overs)
Bangladesh won by 6 wickets
Bangladesh won the series 2–1

ZIMBABWE v. SRI LANKA

Match One
20 November 2008 at Harare
Zimbabwe 127 all out (31 overs) (M Muralitharan 4 for 14,
BAW Mendis 3 for 26)
Sri Lanka 130 for 4 (33.2 overs)
Sri Lanka won by 6 wickets

Match Two
22 November 2008 at Kanpur
Zimbabwe 67 all out (31 overs) (BAW Mendis 4 for 15,
MF Maharoof 3 for 26)
Sri Lanka 68 for 1 (17.4 overs)
Sri Lanka won by 9 wickets

Match Three
24 November 2008 at Harare
Sri Lanka 171 for 7 (28 overs) (KC Sangakkara 57,
T Mupariwa 4 for 39, E Chigumbura 3 for 37)
Zimbabwe 166 for 7 (28 overs) (H Masakadza 77)
Sri Lanka won by 5 runs

Match Four
30 November 2008 at Harare
Sri Lanka 152 all out (48.5 overs) (EC Rainsford 3 for 22)
Zimbabwe 133 all out (44 overs) (M Muralitharan 5 for 29,
KMDN Kulasekara 3 for 14)
Sri Lanka won by 19 runs

Match Five
28 November 2008 at Harare
Zimbabwe 146 all out (46.3 overs)
(BAW Mendis 6 for 29)
Sri Lanka 150 for 8 (47.3 overs) (J Mubarak 60*,
T Mupariwa 3 for 34, E Chigumbura 3 for 35)
Sri Lanka won by 2 wickets
Sri Lanka won the series 5–0

ZIMBABWE v. BANGLADESH

Match One
9 August 2009 at Bulawayo
Zimbabwe 207 all out (47.5 overs) (MA Vermeulen 92,
Nazmul Hossain 3 for 29)
Bangladesh 211 for 2 (34.3 overs) (Mohammad Ashraful 103*,
Tamim Iqbal 63)
Bangladesh won by 8 wickets

Match Two
11 August 2009 at Bulawayo
Bangladesh 320 for 8 (50 overs) (Shakib Al Hasan 104,
Tamim Iqbal 79, E Chigumbura 3 for 59)

Zimbabwe 271 all out (46.1 overs) (SC Williams 75,
CK Coventry 61)
Bangladesh won by 49 runs

Match Three
14 August 2009 at Bulawayo
Zimbabwe 323 for 7 (50 overs) (H Masakadza 102,
BRM Taylor 94, E Chigumbura 61*)
Bangladesh 254 all out (44.2 overs) (Raqibul Hasan 78,
Mahbubul Alam 59, T Mupariwa 3 for 32, RW Price 3 for 34)
Zimbabwe won by 69 runs

Match Four
16 August 2009 at Bulawayo
Zimbabwe 312 for 8 (50 overs) (CK Coventry 194*)
Bangladesh 313 for 6 (47.5 overs) (Tamim Iqbal 154,
RW Price 3 for 60)
Bangladesh won by 4 wickets

Match Five
18 August 2009 at Bulawayo
Zimbabwe 209 all out (46.4 overs) (BRM Taylor 61,
Dolar Mahmud 4 for 28)
Bangladesh 212 for 5 (47.5 overs) (Mushfiqur Rahim 98)
Bangladesh won by 5 wickets
Bangladesh won the series 4–1

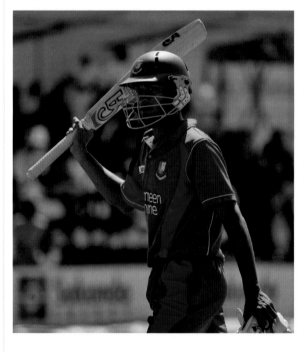

Bangladesh captain Shakib Al Hasan acknowledges the crowd's
applause after scoring 104 in the second one-day international
against Zimbabwe at Bulawayo.

TWENTY20 INTERNATIONALS

SOUTH AFRICA v. BANGLADESH

5 November 2008 Day/Night at Johannesburg
South Africa 118 for 7 (14 overs) (Abdur Razzak 4 for 16)
Bangladesh 109 for 8 (14 overs)
South Africa won by 12 runs – DL Method: target 122 from 14 overs

NEW ZEALAND v. WEST INDIES

Match One
26 December 2008 Day/Night at Auckland
New Zealand 155 for 7 (20 overs) (RL Taylor 63)
West Indies 155 for 8 (20 overs) (CH Gayle 67, DL Vettori 3 for 16)
West Indies won via a Super-Over

Match Two
28 December 2008 Day/Night at Hamilton
New Zealand 191 for 9 (20 overs) (JD Ryder 62, BB McCullum 59)
West Indies 155 for 7 (20 overs) (RR Sarwan 53)
New Zealand won by 36 runs
Series drawn

AUSTRALIA v. SOUTH AFRICA

Match One
11 January 2009 Day/Night at Melbourne (MCG)
Australia 182 for 9 (20 overs) (DA Warner 89, DW Steyn 3 for 38)
South Africa 130 all out (18 overs) (JP Duminy 78, DJ Hussey 3 for 25)
Australia won by 52 runs

Match Two
13 January 2009 Day/Night at Brisbane
South Africa 157 for 5 (20 overs) (JP Duminy 69*)
Australia 161 for 4 (18.5 overs) (MEK Hussey 53*)
Australia won by 6 wickets
Australia won the series 2–0

SRI LANKA v. INDIA

10 February 2009 Day/Night at Colombo (RPS)
Sri Lanka 171 for 4 (20 overs) (TM Dilshan 61)
India 174 for 7 (19.2 overs) (CM Bandara 3 for 32)
India won by 3 wickets

AUSTRALIA v. NEW ZEALAND

15 February 2009 at Sydney
Australia 150 for 7 (20 overs)
New Zealand 149 for 5 (20 overs) (BB McCullum 61)
Australia won by 1 run

NEW ZEALAND v. INDIA

Match One
25 February 2009 Day/Night at Christchurch
India 162 for 8 (20 overs) (S Raina 61*)
New Zealand 166 for 3 (18.5 overs) (BB McCullum 56*)
New Zealand won by 7 wickets

Match Two
27 February 2009 Day/Night at Wellington
India 149 for 6 (20 overs) (Yuvraj Singh 50)
New Zealand 150 for 5 (20 overs) (BB McCullum 69*)
New Zealand won by 5 wickets
New Zealand won the series 2–0

SOUTH AFRICA v. AUSTRALIA

Match One
27 March 2009 Day/Night at Johannesburg
Australia 166 for 7 (20 overs) (DJ Hussey 88*, RJ Peterson 3 for 30)
South Africa 168 for 6 (19.2 overs)
South Africa won by 4 wickets

Match Two
29 March 2009 Day/Night at Centurion
South Africa 156 for 5 (20 overs)
Australia 139 for 8 (20 overs)
South Africa won by 17 runs
South Africa won the series 2–0

PAKISTAN v. AUSTRALIA

7 May 2009 at Dubai
Australia 108 all out (19.5 overs) (Umar Gul 4 for 8, Shahid Afridi 3 for 14)
Pakistan 109 for 3 (16.2 overs) (Kamran Akmal 59*)
Pakistan won by 7 wickets

OTHER INTERNATIONAL MATCHES

T20 Canada 2008

10 October 2008 at King City
Match One
Zimbabwe 106 for 8 (18 overs) (BAW Mendis 4 for 15)
Sri Lanka 107 for 5 (16 overs)
Sri Lanka won by 5 wickets

Match Two
Pakistan 137 for 7 (20 overs) (Salman Butt 74,
HS Baidwan 3 for 15, U Bhatti 3 for 23)
Canada 102 for 9 (20 overs)
Pakistan won by 35 runs

11 October 2008 at King City
Match Three
Canada 135 for 7 (20 overs)
Zimbabwe 135 for 9 (20 overs)
(HS Baidwan 3 for 27)
Zimbabwe won via a bowl-out

Match Four
Sri Lanka 137 for 9 (20 overs) (Umar Gul 4 for 13)
Pakistan 141 for 7 (19.5 overs)
(K Weeraratne 4 for 19)
Pakistan won by 3 wickets

12 October 2008 at King City
Match Five
Zimbabwe 107 for 8 (20 overs) (H Masakadza 53,
Fawad Alam 3 for 7)
Pakistan 110 for 3 (19 overs) (Shoaib Khan 50,
CB Mpofu 3 for 16)
Pakistan won by 7 wickets

Match Six
Sri Lanka 153 for 7 (20 overs)
(WD Balaji Rao 3 for 21)
Canada 138 all out (20 overs) (R Cheema 68,
BAW Mendis 4 for 17, CRD Fernando 3 for 24)
Sri Lanka won by 15 runs

13 October 2008 at King City
Third Place Play-off
Zimbabwe 184 for 5 (20 overs) (H Masakadza 79)
Canada 75 all out (19.2 overs) (P Utseya 3 for 26)
Zimbabwe won by 109 runs

Final
Pakistan 132 for 7 (20 overs)
(BAW Mendis 3 for 23)
Sri Lanka 133 for 5 (19 overs)
Sri Lanka won by 5 wickets
Sri Lanka won the tournament

TRIANGULAR ONE-DAY SERIES in Kenya

Match One
17 October 2008 at Nairobi
Zimbabwe 303 for 8 (50 overs) (T Taibu 74, H Masakadza 72,
CJ Chibhabha 51, P Connell 3 for 68)
Ireland 147 all out (46.1 overs) (KM Dabengwa 3 for 17)
Zimbabwe won by 156 runs

Match Two
18 October 2008 at Nairobi
Ireland 285 for 6 (47 overs) (KJ O'Brien 83)
Kenya 199 all out (44 overs) (AR Cusack 3 for 29)
Ireland won by 86 runs

Match Three
19 October 2008 at Nairobi
Kenya 285 for 9 (50 overs) (SO Tikolo 102, A Obanda 71, CB Mpofu 6 for 52)
Zimbabwe 190 all out (38.1 overs) (S Matsikenyeri 56, HA Varaiya 3 for 53)
Kenya won by 95 runs

Match Four
21 October 2008 at Nairobi
Ireland v. **Zimbabwe**
Match abandoned

Match Five
22 October 2008 at Nairobi
Kenya v. **Ireland**
Match abandoned

Match Six
23 October 2008 at Nairobi
Kenya v. **Zimbabwe**
Match abandoned

Match Seven
25 October 2008 at Nairobi
Kenya v. **Zimbabwe**
Match abandoned
Teams shared the trophy

TRIANGULAR ONE-DAY SERIES in Bangladesh

Match One
10 **January** 2009 at Mirpur
Zimbabwe 205 for 9 (50 overs) (E Chigumbura 64,
Shakib Al Hasan 3 for 23, Naeem Islam 3 for 32)
Bangladesh 167 all out (46.2 overs) (Shakib Al Hasan 52)
Zimbabwe won by 38 runs

Match Two
12 January 2009 at Mirpur
Sri Lanka 210 for 6 (50 overs) (AD Mathews 52*, EC Rainsford 3 for 41)

Zimbabwe 80 all out (28.2 overs) (KMDN Kulasekara 3 for 13, BAW Mendis 3 for 15)
Sri Lanka won by 130 runs

Match Three
14 January 2009 at Mirpur
Sri Lanka 147 all out (30.3 overs) (ST Jayasuriya 54, Rubel Hossain 4 for 33, Mashrafe bin Mortaza 3 for 25)
Bangladesh 151 for 5 (23.5 overs) (Shakib Al Hasan 92*)
Bangladesh won by 5 wickets

Match Four – Final
16 January 2009 at Mirpur
Bangladesh 152 all out (49.4 overs) (KMDN Kulasekara 3 for 19, BAW Mendis 3 for 24)
Sri Lanka 153 for 8 (48.1 overs) (KC Sangakkara 59, Nazmul Hossain 3 for 30)
Sri Lanka won by 2 wickets
Sri Lanka won the tournament

ONE-DAY INTERNATIONALS Kenya v. Zimbabwe

Match One
27 January 2009 at Mombasa
Zimbabwe 306 for 7 (50 overs) (E Chigumbura 79, V Sibanda 77, H Masakadza 71)
Kenya 197 all out (46.2 overs) (JK Kamande 74)
Zimbabwe won by 109 runs

Match Two
29 January 2009 at Mombasa
Zimbabwe 351 for 7 (50 overs) (S Matsikenyeri 90, E Chigumbura 68, MN Waller 63)
Kenya 200 for 9 (45.1 overs) (SO Tikolo 56)
Zimbabwe won by 151 runs

Match Three
31 January 2009 at Nairobi
Kenya 234 all out (49.3 overs) (CO Obuya 55, AG Cremer 4 for 39)
Zimbabwe 236 for 6 (48.2 overs) (P Utseya 68*)
Zimbabwe won by 4 wickets

Match Four
1 February 2009 at Nairobi
Zimbabwe 285 for 8 (50 overs) (F Mutizwa 61, H Masakadza 58, P Utseya 51*, NO Odhiambo 3 for 56)
Kenya 219 all out (49 overs) (A Obanda 96*, E Chigumbura 4 for 28, AG Cremer 3 for 34)
Zimbabwe won by 66 runs

Match Five
4 February 2009 at Nairobi
Kenya 199 all out (48.5 overs) (CO Obuya 75, AG Cremer 4 for 31)
Zimbabwe 203 for 3 (35 overs) (H Masakadza 84*, SC Williams 63*, S Matsikenyeri 50)
Zimbabwe won by 7 wickets
Zimbabwe won the series 5–0

ICC WORLD CUP QUALIFIERS 2009 in South Africa

Tournament comprising 12 teams playing Group Phase, Super Eights and Finals.
Participants: Afghanistan, Bermuda, Canada, Denmark, Ireland, Kenya, Namibia, Netherlands, Oman, Scotland, Uganda and United Arab Emirates. Top four teams qualify for the 2011 World Cup.

7th Place Play-off
19 April 2009 at Krugersdorp
Namibia 267 for 9 (50 overs) (N Scholtz 54, F Ahmed 3 for 49)
United Arab Emirates 269 for 6 (41.3 overs) (K Khan 124, S Nayak 60)
United Arab Emirates won by 4 wickets

5th Place Play-off
19 April 2009 at Benoni
Afghanistan 295 for 8 (50 overs) (M Nabi 58, S Shenwari 52, J Blain 3 for 62)
Scotland 206 all out (40 overs) (K Hassan 3 for 33)
Afghanistan won by 89 runs

3rd Place Play-off
19 April 2009 at Potchesfstroom
Kenya 179 all out (43.1 overs) (E Schiferli 4 for 23, R Nijman 3 for 31)
Netherlands 184 for 4 (32.1 overs) (D van Bunge 80, B Zuiderent 57)
Netherlands won by 6 wickets

Final
19 April 2009 at Centurion
Canada 185 all out (48 overs) (D Johnston 5 for 14)
Ireland 188 for 1 (42.3 overs) (W Porterfield 104*)
Ireland won by 9 wickets
Ireland won the tournament

Teams qualifying for 2011 World Cup: Canada, Ireland, Kenya, Netherlands.
Teams granted One-Day International status (for four years): Afghanistan, Canada, Ireland, Kenya, Netherlands, Scotland.

ONE-DAY INTERNATIONALS Scotland v. Canada

Match One
7 July 2009 at Aberdeen
Scotland 286 for 4 (50 overs) (GM Hamilton 119, DF Watts 101)
Canada 287 for 4 (48.4 overs) (S Jyoti 117, A Bagai 92*)
Canada won by 6 wickets

Match Two
8 July 2009 at Aberdeen
Canada 250 for 9 (50 overs) (S Dhaniram 92, GD Drummond 4 for 41)
Scotland 253 for 5 (47.2 overs) (NFI McCallum 79*, RR Watson 74, GM Hamilton 59)
Scotland won by 5 wickets
Series drawn

ONE-DAY INTERNATIONALS Ireland v. Kenya

Match One
9 July 2009 at Dublin
Kenya 214 for 9 (50 overs) (KO Otieno 78, WK McCallan 4 for 30, AR Cusack 3 for 37)
Ireland 215 for 7 (48.5 overs) (WTS Porterfield 81, TM Odoyo 4 for 33)
Ireland won by 3 wickets

Match Two
11 July 2009 at Dublin
Kenya 175 all out (45.1 overs) (A Obanda 59, WB Rankin 3 for 40)
Ireland 104 for 1 (21 overs) (GC Wilson 51*)
Ireland won by 52 runs – DL Method: target 53 from 21 overs

Match Three
12 July 2009 at Dublin
Ireland 256 for 7 (50 overs) (PR Stirling 84)
Kenya 240 for 6 (46 overs) (CO Obuya 78*, MA Ouma 61)
Ireland won by 4 runs – DL Method: target 245 from 46 overs
Ireland won the series 3–0

ONE-DAY INTERNATIONALS Netherlands v. Canada

Match One
11 July 2009 at Amstelveen
Netherlands 237 for 7 (50 overs) (AN Kervezee 75, PW Borren 50)
Canada 187 all out (39 overs) (R Cheema 94, E Schiferli 4 for 44)
Netherlands won by 50 runs

Match Two
12 July 2009 at Amstelveen
Netherlands v. **Canada**
Match abandoned
Netherlands won the series 1–0

ONE-DAY INTERNATIONALS Canada v. Kenya

Match One
19 August 2009 at King City
Kenya 113 all out (33.1 overs) (K Chauhan 4 for 26)
Canada 117 for 1 (16.2 overs) (R Cheema 76*)
Canada won by 9 wickets

Match Two
22 August 2009 at King City
Canada 63 for 3 (17.1 overs) (TM Odoyo 3 for 11)
Kenya
No result

Match Three
23 August 2009 at King City
Canada v. **Kenya**
Match abandoned
Canada won the series 1–0

ONE-DAY INTERNATIONALS Scotland v. Ireland

Match One
22 August 2009 at Aberdeen
Ireland 205 for 9 (50 overs) (WTS Porterfield 50)
Scotland 109 all out (40.3 overs) (RM West 4 for 26)
Ireland won by 96 runs

Match Two
23 August 2009 at Aberdeen
Scotland v. **Ireland**
Match abandoned
Ireland won the series 1–0

ONE-DAY INTERNATIONAL Ireland v. England

27 August 2009 at Belfast
England 203 for 9 (50 overs) (JL Denly 67, DT Johnston 4 for 26)
Ireland 112 for 9 (20 overs) (OA Shah 3 for 15)
England won by 3 runs – DL Method: target 116 from 20 overs

ONE-DAY INTERNATIONAL Scotland v. Australia

28 August 2009 at Edinburgh
Australia 345 all out (50 overs) (DJ Hussey 111, AC Voges 72, SR Watson 68, G Goudie 5 for 73)
Scotland 156 all out (39.3 overs) (SR Watson 3 for 29)
Australia won by 189 runs

COMPAQ CUP

Match One
8 September 2009 Day/Night at Colombo (RPS)
Sri Lanka 216 for 7 (50 overs) (TT Samaraweera 104, AD Mathews 51, SE Bond 3 for 43)
New Zealand 119 all out (36.1 overs) (SL Malinga 4 for 28)
Sri Lanka won by 97 runs

Match Two
11 September 2009 Day/Night at Colombo (RPS)
New Zealand 155 all out (46.3 overs) (A Nehra 3 for 24, Yuvraj Singh 3 for 31)
India 156 for 4 (40.3 overs)
India won by 6 wickets

Match Three
12 September 2009 Day/Night at Colombo (RPS)
Sri Lanka 307 for 6 (50 overs) (ST Jayasuriya 98, SHT Kandamby 91*)
India 168 all out (37.2 overs) (AD Mathews 6 for 20)
Sri Lanka won by 139 runs

Final
14 September 2009 Day/Night at Colombo (RPS)
India 319 for 5 (50 overs) (SR Tendulkar 138, MS Dhoni 56, Yuvraj Singh 56*)
Sri Lanka 273 all out (46.4 overs) (SHT Kandamby 66, Harbhajan Singh 5 for 56)
India won by 46 runs
Compaq Cup champions India